Social Media Marketing

ALL-IN-ONE

Social Media Marketing

ALL-IN-ONE

4th Edition

by Jan Zimmerman and Deborah Ng

Social Media Marketing All-in-One For Dummies®, 4th Edition

Published by: **John Wiley & Sons, Inc.**, 111 River Street, Hoboken, NJ 07030-5774, www.wiley.com

Published simultaneously in Canada

For general information on our other products and services, please contact our Customer Care Department within the U.S. at 877-762-2974, outside the U.S. at 317-572-3993, or fax 317-572-4002. For technical support, please visit https://hub.wiley.com/community/support/dummies.

Wiley publishes in a variety of print and electronic formats and by print-on-demand. Some material included with standard print versions of this book may not be included in e-books or in print-on-demand. If this book refers to media such as a CD or DVD that is not included in the version you purchased, you may download this material at http://booksupport.wiley.com. For more information about Wiley products, visit www.wiley.com.

Library of Congress Control Number: 2017935000

ISBN 978-1-119-33039-4 (pbk); ISBN 978-1-119-33042-4 (ebk); ISBN 978-1-119-32992-3 (ebk)

Manufactured in the United States of America

10 9 8 7 6 5

Contents at a Glance

Introduction 1

Book 1: The Social Media Mix 5

CHAPTER 1: Making the Business Case for Social Media. 7
CHAPTER 2: Tallying the Bottom Line 33
CHAPTER 3: Plotting Your Social Media Marketing Strategy. 53
CHAPTER 4: Managing Your Cybersocial Campaign. 77

Book 2: Cybersocial Tools 99

CHAPTER 1: Discovering Helpful Tech Tools 101
CHAPTER 2: Leveraging SEO for Improved Visibility. 127
CHAPTER 3: Optimizing Social Media for Internal and External Searches 159
CHAPTER 4: Using Social Bookmarks, News, and Share Buttons. 181
CHAPTER 5: Making Social Media Mobile. 207

Book 3: Content Marketing 225

CHAPTER 1: Growing Your Brand with Content 227
CHAPTER 2: Exploring Content-Marketing Platforms. 237
CHAPTER 3: Developing a Content-Marketing Strategy. 263
CHAPTER 4: Getting Your Content to the Masses. 275

Book 4: Twitter 285

CHAPTER 1: Using Twitter as a Marketing Tool. 287
CHAPTER 2: Using Twitter as a Networking Tool. 299
CHAPTER 3: Finding the Right Twitter Tools. 313
CHAPTER 4: Social Listening with Twitter. 321
CHAPTER 5: Hosting Twitter Chats 327

Book 5: Facebook 337

CHAPTER 1: Using Facebook as a Marketing Tool 339
CHAPTER 2: Creating and Sharing Content on Facebook 357
CHAPTER 3: Advertising on Facebook. 373
CHAPTER 4: Streaming Live Video on Facebook 381

Book 6: LinkedIn 391
CHAPTER 1: Promoting Yourself with LinkedIn 393
CHAPTER 2: Promoting Your Business with LinkedIn 409
CHAPTER 3: Starting a LinkedIn Group 417
CHAPTER 4: Using LinkedIn as a Content Platform 429

Book 7: Getting Visual 435
CHAPTER 1: Pinning Down Pinterest 437
CHAPTER 2: Snapchatting It Up! 463
CHAPTER 3: Getting Started with Instagram 477

Book 8: Other Social Media Marketing Sites 489
CHAPTER 1: Weighing the Business Benefits of Minor Social Sites 491
CHAPTER 2: Maximizing Stratified Social Communities 503
CHAPTER 3: Profiting from Mid-Size Social Media Channels 535
CHAPTER 4: Integrating Social Media 545
CHAPTER 5: Advertising on Social Media 561

Book 9: Measuring Results and Building on Success 581
CHAPTER 1: Delving into Data 583
CHAPTER 2: Analyzing Content-Sharing Metrics 599
CHAPTER 3: Analyzing Twitter Metrics 617
CHAPTER 4: Analyzing Facebook Metrics 627
CHAPTER 5: Measuring Other Social Media Networks 635
CHAPTER 6: Comparing Metrics from Different Marketing Techniques 643
CHAPTER 7: Making Decisions by the Numbers 663

Index 677

Table of Contents

INTRODUCTION 1
About This Book 2
Foolish Assumptions 2
Icons Used in This Book 3
Beyond the Book 4
Where to Go from Here 4

BOOK 1: THE SOCIAL MEDIA MIX 5

CHAPTER 1: Making the Business Case for Social Media 7
Making Your Social Debut 8
Defining Social Media Marketing 9
Understanding the Benefits of Social Media 13
Casting a wide net to catch your target market 14
Branding 15
Building relationships 16
Improving business processes 16
Improving search engine rankings 17
Selling in the social media marketplace 17
Finding alternative advertising opportunities 19
Understanding the Cons of Social Media 19
Integrating Social Media into Your Overall Marketing Effort 20
Developing a Strategic Social Media Marketing Plan 22
Establishing goals 25
Setting quantifiable objectives 26
Identifying your target markets 26
Estimating costs 26
Valuing social media ROI 27

CHAPTER 2: Tallying the Bottom Line 33
Preparing to Calculate Return on Investment 34
Accounting for Customers Acquired Online 35
Comparing the costs of customer acquisition 36
One is silver and the other gold 38
Establishing Key Performance Indicators for Sales 39
Tracking Leads 43
Understanding Other Common Business Metrics 44
Break-even point 44
Profit margin 45
Revenue versus profit 45
Determining Return on Investment 45

CHAPTER 3: **Plotting Your Social Media Marketing Strategy** 53
Locating Your Target Market Online 54
Segmenting Your B2C Market 54
Demographics 56
Geographic location 58
Purchasing behavior in different life stages 60
Psychographics or lifestyle 61
Affinity groups 62
Researching B2B Markets 64
Conducting Other Types of Market Research Online 65
Identifying influencers 66
Understanding why people use social media services 66
Setting Up Your Social Media Marketing Plan 67

CHAPTER 4: **Managing Your Cybersocial Campaign** 77
Managing Your Social Media Schedule 78
Controlling the time commitment 78
Developing your social date book 79
Creating a social media dashboard 81
Building Your Social Media Marketing Dream Team 85
Seeking a skilled social media director 85
Looking inside 86
Hiring experts 87
Creating a Social Media Marketing Policy 87
Staying on the Right Side of the Law 90
Obtaining permission to avoid infringement 91
Respecting privacy 93
Revealing product endorsement relationships 93
Protecting Your Brand Reputation 95

BOOK 2: CYBERSOCIAL TOOLS 99

CHAPTER 1: **Discovering Helpful Tech Tools** 101
Keeping Track of the Social Media Scene 102
Saving Time with Content-Distribution Tools 104
Alternative content distribution services 104
Snipping Ugly URLs 106
Using E-Commerce Tools for Social Sites 108
Selling through links 108
Displaying products on social media channels 108
Selling directly on social media 110
Reviewing third-party products for selling through social media 115

Keeping Your Ear to the Social Ground 118
Deciding what to monitor and why. 118
Deciding which tools to use 119
Using free or inexpensive social monitoring tools 120
Measuring the Buzz by Type of Service 124

CHAPTER 2: **Leveraging SEO for Improved Visibility** 127
Making the Statistical Case for SEO 128
Thinking Tactically and Practically. 130
Focusing on the Top Search Engines 131
Knowing the Importance of Search Phrases 132
Choosing the right search terms. 133
Where to place search terms on your site. 136
Understanding tags and tag clouds 137
Maximizing Metatag Muscle 138
Tipping the scales with the page title metatag 139
Pumping up page description metatags 141
Optimizing Your Site and Content for Search Engines. 142
Writing an optimized first paragraph 143
Updating often. 145
Making your site search engine friendly 147
Optimizing for local search 153
Getting inbound links from social sharing, social bookmarks, and social news services. 155
Reaping other links from social media. 157

CHAPTER 3: **Optimizing Social Media for Internal and External Searches** 159
Placing Search Terms on Social Media. 160
Optimizing Blogs 161
Optimizing WordPress 164
Optimizing Blogger 164
Assigning permalinks 165
Optimizing Images, Video, and Podcasts. 166
Optimizing Specific Social Media Platforms. 167
Optimizing Twitter. 167
Optimizing Facebook 169
Optimizing Google+. 170
Optimizing Pinterest 171
Optimizing LinkedIn 172
Optimizing for Mobile Search 173
Gaining Visibility in Real-Time Search. 175
Gaining Traction on Google with Social Media 177
Monitoring Your Search Engine Ranking 178

CHAPTER 4: **Using Social Bookmarks, News, and Share Buttons** 181
Bookmarking Your Way to Traffic 182
Sharing the News 185
Benefiting from Social Bookmarks and News Services 186
Researching a Social Bookmark and Social News Campaign 187
Executing your plan 188
Monitoring results 189
Submitting to Bookmarking Services 190
Submitting to Social News Services 192
Selecting content for social news services 192
Preparing social news stories for success 193
Using Application-Specific Bookmarks 194
Timing Your Submissions 195
Encouraging Others to Bookmark or Rate Your Site 201
Using Social Media Buttons 202
Follow Us buttons 202
Share buttons 203

CHAPTER 5: **Making Social Media Mobile** 207
Understanding the Statistics of Mobile Device Usage 208
Exploring mobile use of social media 208
Demographics of mobile users 210
Reaching People on the Move with Social Media 212
Harvesting Leads and Sales from Social Mobile 216
Measuring Your Mobile Marketing Success 220
Counting on Tablets 221
Using Mobile Social Media for Advertising 222

BOOK 3: CONTENT MARKETING 225

CHAPTER 1: **Growing Your Brand with Content** 227
Introducing Content Marketing 228
Defining content marketing 228
Examining how content marketing can help your business 228
Determining the Best Content Platform for Your Needs 231
Selling Your Brand through Content Marketing 232
Making Your Content Stand Out 233

CHAPTER 2: **Exploring Content-Marketing Platforms** 237
Building a Blog 238
Understanding how blogging can benefit your business 238
Deciding if blogging is right for you 241
Setting up your blog 241

Using Podcasts and Video on Your Blog or Website 243
Deciding if podcasting is right for you 244
Using podcasts to drive traffic and land sales. 246
Creating viral videos 246
Interviewing experts on camera 248
Sharing Images 249
Using images for your online content 249
Legalities: What you need to know about sharing images 250
Finding images online. 251
Sharing images on photo-sharing sites 253
Using Social Media Platforms for Online Content 254
Deciding which social media platforms to use 255
Creating and sharing content with social media. 256
Understanding the importance of community 258
Guest Blogging to Grow Awareness and Expertise 258
Understanding guest blogging 259
Finding relevant blogs and pitching your content 260
Promoting your guest blog posts 261

CHAPTER 3: **Developing a Content-Marketing Strategy** 263
Determining Content Goals 263
Driving traffic 265
Making sales. 266
Establishing expertise. 268
Growing your online community 268
Collecting leads with your content 269
Putting a Strategy on Paper. 270
Understanding the elements of a content-marketing strategy 270
Doing a content inventory 271
Taking steps to achieve your goals 272
Delegating tasks. 273

CHAPTER 4: **Getting Your Content to the Masses** 275
Creating an Editorial Calendar to Keep Content Flowing 276
Exploring the benefits of an editorial calendar. 276
Deciding what to include on your calendar. 277
Finding the Right Mix between Evergreen and Timely Content 278
Executing Your Content Strategy 279
Sharing Your Content with the Public. 280
Measuring the Success of Your Content Strategy. 281

BOOK 4: TWITTER 285

CHAPTER 1: Using Twitter as a Marketing Tool.................. 287
Deciding Whether Twitter Is Right for You........................ 288
Communicating in 140 Characters.................................. 290
Promoting without Seeming like You're Promoting.................. 291
Researching Other Brands on Twitter.............................. 296
Knowing Quality Is More Important than Quantity.................. 297

CHAPTER 2: Using Twitter as a Networking Tool................. 299
Finding the Right People to Follow............................... 300
Finding Out Who Is Talking about You on Twitter.................. 301
Responding to Tweets... 302
Searching on Twitter... 303
Tweeting like a Pro.. 304
Articulating in 140 characters................................... 304
Using the hashtag.. 304
Sharing on Twitter... 305
Knowing when to @reply and direct message....................... 306
Retweeting and being retweeted................................... 306
Blocking people.. 307
Creating a successful Twitter campaign........................... 308
Using keywords in your tweets.................................... 310
Following the Twitter Rules of Etiquette......................... 310
Hosting a Tweet-Up... 311

CHAPTER 3: Finding the Right Twitter Tools..................... 313
Customizing Your Twitter Profile Page............................ 314
Creating a header photo.. 315
Creating a custom Twitter avatar................................. 316
Pinning Tweets... 317
Using a Twitter Application...................................... 318
Exploring Twitter desktop applications........................... 318
Tweeting from a gadget... 319

CHAPTER 4: Social Listening with Twitter....................... 321
Using Twitter to Listen to Your Customers........................ 321
Responding to questions and complaints........................... 324
Gaining new customers by being helpful........................... 326

CHAPTER 5: Hosting Twitter Chats............................... 327
Benefiting from Twitter Chats.................................... 327
Finding a Hashtag for Your Chat.................................. 328
Keeping Track of Who Says What................................... 329

Finding Guests for Your Twitter Chat 331
Promoting Your Twitter Chat 332
Hosting Your Twitter Chat 333

BOOK 5: FACEBOOK 337

CHAPTER 1: **Using Facebook as a Marketing Tool** 339
Understanding the Appeal of Brands on Facebook 340
Branding with Facebook Pages 341
Examining the Components of a Facebook Page 342
Making the Most of Your Facebook Page 345
Adding a profile picture 346
Adding a cover photo 346
Adding finishing touches 347
Understanding Your Facebook Administrative Functions 348
Filling Out What You're About 349
Using a Custom URL for Your Page 350
Inviting People to Join Your Community 351
Inviting friends to like your page 351
Getting likes from others 352
Liking Other Brands 353
Creating Facebook Events 354

CHAPTER 2: **Creating and Sharing Content on Facebook** 357
Creating a Facebook Content Strategy 358
Sharing Your Brand's Story 359
Creating Content That Sings 361
Sharing and Being Shared 362
Posting content that followers will want to share 363
Using hashtags in your posts 364
Bringing Your Community into the Mix 365
Selling on Facebook 365
Creating polls, quizzes, and contests 366
Offering discounts to your community 367
Using Closed or Secret Groups 368
Closed versus secret groups 368
Creating a Facebook group 369
Learning through Insights 370
Getting the scoop on your fans through Insights 370
Putting Insights data to good use 371

CHAPTER 3: **Advertising on Facebook** 373
Reaching More Fans with Ads 374
Deciding whether you want to invest in an ad 375
Choosing the right Facebook ad for you 375

Creating an ad with Ads Manager 377
Targeting your fans 378
Measuring Your Ad's ROI 379

CHAPTER 4: **Streaming Live Video on Facebook** 381
Understanding the Benefits of Live Streaming 382
Setting Up Your Live Stream 384
Engaging with Your Community via Facebook Live 388
Brainstorming Ideas for Live Videos 389

BOOK 6: LINKEDIN 391

CHAPTER 1: **Promoting Yourself with LinkedIn** 393
Exploring the Benefits of Using LinkedIn 394
Creating an Online Resume 395
Projecting a professional image on LinkedIn 396
Choosing and uploading a profile photo 398
Filling out your profile 400
Understanding Recommendations and Endorsements 402
Receiving recommendations 402
Giving recommendations 403
Asking for endorsements 405
Using LinkedIn Messages 407

CHAPTER 2: **Promoting Your Business with LinkedIn** 409
Exploring the Benefits of a Company Page 410
Creating a LinkedIn Company Page 410
Setting up your brand's profile 411
Adding and removing administrators 412
Sharing your brand's content 413
Selling and Promoting with LinkedIn Showcase Pages 414
Highlighting your products and services 414
Showcase pages 415

CHAPTER 3: **Starting a LinkedIn Group** 417
Exploring the Benefits of LinkedIn Groups 417
Growing a Community with a LinkedIn Group 418
Setting up a LinkedIn group 419
Choosing a standard or unlisted group 420
Establishing group guidelines 421
Growing Your Group 422
Inviting others to join your group 422
Approving or preapproving group members 423

Moderating Your LinkedIn Group .424
Appointing a manager or moderator .424
Managing a moderation queue .425
Featuring posts from community members .426
Adding a Jobs tab to your group .426
Sending a weekly email to your group .427

CHAPTER 4: **Using LinkedIn as a Content Platform** 429
Blogging on LinkedIn .430
Creating your first post .431
Writing in a professional voice .432
Promoting Your LinkedIn Posts on Other Social Channels .433

BOOK 7: GETTING VISUAL 435

CHAPTER 1: **Pinning Down Pinterest** 437
Understanding Pinterest .438
Getting Started .439
Joining Pinterest .441
Navigating Pinterest .442
Setting up your Pinterest profile .442
Getting on Board .445
Planning your initial boards .446
Creating your first board .447
Pinning on Pinterest .448
Pinning an image .448
Tagging .451
Following on Pinterest .452
Following friends .452
Following folks you don't know .452
Sharing on Pinterest .453
Sharing other people's pins .453
Using share buttons .454
Driving Traffic with Pinterest .455
Being descriptive but brief .456
Using keywords .458
Building Your Pinterest Community .459
Collaborating with group boards .459
Liking pins .460
Commenting on pins .461
Playing nice .461

CHAPTER 2: **Snapchatting It Up!** 463
Getting Started with Snapchat 463
Setting up an account 464
Understanding the lingo 467
Touring the Snapchat screens 467
Tips for adding followers 469
Taking Your First Snap 470
Telling Your Snapchat Story 471
Knowing who is viewing your stories 472
Engaging with Snapchat 473
Using lenses, filters, and geofilters 474

CHAPTER 3: **Getting Started with Instagram** 477
Promoting Your Brand on Instagram 478
Creating and Using Your Instagram Account 479
Setting up your account 479
Sharing photos 481
Controlling notifications 483
Determining What Is Photo-Worthy for Your Brand 484
Using Hashtags in Your Instagram Posts 485
Finding Friends and Fans on Instagram 487
Using Instagram Stories 488

BOOK 8: OTHER SOCIAL MEDIA MARKETING SITES 489

CHAPTER 1: **Weighing the Business Benefits of Minor Social Sites** 491
Reviewing Your Goals 492
Researching Minor Social Networks 493
Assessing the Involvement of Your Target Audience 496
Lurking 497
Responding 497
Quantifying market presence 498
Choosing Social Sites Strategically 498

CHAPTER 2: **Maximizing Stratified Social Communities** 503
Making a Bigger Splash on a Smaller Site 504
Taking Networking to the Next Level 504
Selecting Social Networks by Vertical Industry Sector 506
Selecting Social Networks by Demographics 510
Selecting Social Networks by Activity Type 512
Finding Yourself in the Real World with Geomarketing 515
Going geo for good reason 515
Deciding whether geomarketing is right for you 516

Spacing Out with Twitter 517
Checking in on Twitter 517
Searching real space with Twitter 518
Finding Your Business on Facebook 518
Geotagging on Facebook 518
Getting close with places nearby 518
Checking in on Facebook 518
Making a Facebook offer they can't refuse 519
Making Real Connections in Virtual Spaces 521
Meeting through Meetup 521
Tweeting for meeting in real space 522
Marketing with meet-ups and tweet-ups 522
Making Deals on Social Media 523
Offering savings, gaining customers 524
Making an attractive offer 525
Setting Terms for Your Coupon Campaign 526
The depth of the discount 526
The scope of the deal 526
Grappling with the gotchas 527
Measuring success 528
Further leveraging your deal 529
More upsides and downsides 530
Comparing LivingSocial and Groupon 531
Digging into Groupon 532
LivingSocial 532
Diversifying Your Daily Deals 533

CHAPTER 3: **Profiting from Mid-Size Social Media Channels** 535
Deciding Whether to Invest Your Time 535
Spotting Your Audience with Spotify 536
Turning Up New Prospects with Tumblr 538
Setting up an account 538
Advertising on Tumblr 539
Analyzing Tumblr results 540
Promoting Video with Vimeo 540
Signing up for a Vimeo business account 541
Advertising on Vimeo 541
Live Streaming with Periscope 542

CHAPTER 4: **Integrating Social Media** 545
Thinking Strategically about Social Media Integration 546
Integrating Social Media with E-Newsletters 547
Gaining more subscribers 549
Finding more followers and connections 549
Finding and sharing content 550

Integrating Social Media with Press Releases 551
Setting up an online newsroom 552
Cultivating influencers 552
Distributing your news 553
Emphasizing content 555
Pressing for attention 556
Measuring results 556
Integrating Social Media with Your Website 557
Coupons, discounts, and freebies 558
Contests and games 559
Microsites 560
Private membership sites 560

CHAPTER 5: **Advertising on Social Media** 561
Integrating Social Media with Paid Advertising 561
Advertising on social media sites 562
Exploring the growth in social advertising 563
Maximizing your advertising dollars 563
Advertising on Facebook and Instagram 564
Getting started 565
Boosting or promoting a post 567
Paying for your Facebook ads 568
Advertising on Twitter 568
Promoting your tweets 569
Promoting your account 569
Promoting a trend 570
Remarketing with Twitter 570
Engaging your Twitter audience 570
Pricing and bidding on Twitter 571
Dealing with Twitter cards 572
Advertising on LinkedIn 573
Targeting your LinkedIn ads 574
Pricing and bidding 575
Advertising on Pinterest 576
Pricing and bidding 576
Engagement ads 576

BOOK 9: MEASURING RESULTS AND BUILDING ON SUCCESS 581

CHAPTER 1: **Delving into Data** 583
Planning a Measurement Strategy 584
Monitoring versus measuring 585
Deciding what to measure 586
Establishing responsibility for analytics 587

Selecting Analytics Packages 589
Reviewing analytical options for social media. 592
Selecting a URL-shortening tool for statistics 593
Getting Started with Google Analytics 594
Integrating Google's Social Media Analytics 596

CHAPTER 2: **Analyzing Content-Sharing Metrics** 599
Measuring the Effectiveness of Content Sharing with Standard Analytics 599
Maximizing website stats 600
Tracking comments. 602
Evaluating Blog-Specific Metrics 603
Visualizing Video Success 605
Understanding Podcast Metrics 606
Measuring Your Results from Pinterest 609
Discovering details about your Pinterest profile 610
Finding out about your Pinterest audience. 611
Analyzing interactions between your website and Pinterest 612
Third-party Pinterest analytics. 614
Comparing Hard and Soft Costs versus Income. 614

CHAPTER 3: **Analyzing Twitter Metrics**. 617
Tracking Website Referrals with Google Analytics 618
Tracking Shortened Links. 618
Using Twitter Analytics 619
Using TweetDeck. 622
Using Third-Party Twitter Analytics Applications 622
Tracking Account Activity with the Notifications Tab 623
Checking your retweet ranking 624
Monitoring the Mentions tab. 624
Gleaning meaning from direct messages 625
Using the Hashtag as a Measurement Mechanism 625
Calculating the Twitter Follower-to-Following Ratio. 626

CHAPTER 4: **Analyzing Facebook Metrics**. 627
Monitoring Facebook Interaction with Insights 627
Using Page Insights. 628
Accessing Insights 628
Exporting Insights 629
Exploring the Insights Overview and Detail Pages. 630
Likes detail page 631
Reach detail page 632
Page Views detail page 633

CHAPTER 5: **Measuring Other Social Media Networks** 635
Plugging into Social Media 635
Measuring LinkedIn Success 636
Updates 637
Reach & Engagement 638
Followers 638
Monitoring Social Mobile Impact 640

CHAPTER 6: **Comparing Metrics from Different Marketing Techniques** 643
Establishing Key Performance Indicators 644
Overcoming measurement challenges 644
Using A/B testing 644
Comparing Metrics across Social Media 646
Tagging links 649
Analyzing the clickstream 651
Tracking your own outbound links 652
Integrating Social Media with Web Metrics 653
Using Advertising Metrics to Compare Social Media with Other Types of Marketing 655
Obtaining metrics for paid advertising 655
Applying advertising metrics to social media 658
Juxtaposing Social Media Metrics with Other Online Marketing 658
Contrasting Word-of-Web with Word-of-Mouth 660

CHAPTER 7: **Making Decisions by the Numbers** 663
Using Metrics to Make Decisions 663
Knowing When to Hold and When to Fold 664
Diagnosing Problems with Social Media Campaigns 669
Fixing Problems 670
Your social presence can't be found 671
Inappropriate match between channel and audience 671
Poor content 671
Lack of audience engagement 672
The four Ps of marketing 673
Adjusting to Reality 675

INDEX 677

Introduction

You sat back, sighing with relief that your website was running faultlessly, optimized for search engines, and producing traffic, leads, and sales. Maybe you ventured into email marketing or pay-per-click advertising to generate new customers. Then you thought with satisfaction, "I'll just let the money roll in."

Instead, you were inundated with stories about Facebook pages, Twitter and tweets, blogs and podcasts, Pinterest, Instagram, and all other manner of social media buzz. By now you've probably tried more than one of these social media platforms. Perhaps you haven't seen much in the way of results, or you're ready to explore ways to expand your reach, increase customer loyalty, and grow your sales with social media.

Much as you might wish it were otherwise, you must now stay up to date with rapidly changing options in the social media universe. As a marketer, you have no choice when more than 75 percent of Internet users visit blogs and social media and when your position in search engine results may depend on the recency and frequency of social media updates. Social media marketing is an essential component of online marketing.

The statistics are astounding: Facebook has more than 1.18 billion daily active users as of the third quarter of 2016; more than 2.7 million blog posts are published every day; more than 300 million tweets were sent per day on average in 2016; and nearly 5 billion hours of video are viewed each month on YouTube. New company names and bewildering new vocabulary terms continue to flood the online world: Periscope, Snapchat, pinning, location tagging, and sentiment monitoring, for example.

Should your new business get involved in social media marketing? Is it all more trouble than it's worth? Will you be hopelessly left behind if you don't participate? If you jump in, or if you've already waded into the social media waters, how do you keep it all under control and who does the work? Which platforms are the best for your business? Should you take advantage of new channels or stick with the comfortable ones you've already mastered? This book helps you answer both sets of questions: Should your business undertake social media marketing? If so, how? (Quick answer: If your customers use a social media service, use it. If not, skip it.)

About This Book

The philosophy behind this book is simple: Social media marketing is a means, not an end in itself. Social media services are tools, not new worlds. In the best of all worlds, you see results that improve customer acquisition, retention, and buying behavior — in other words, your bottom line. If this sounds familiar, that's because everything you already know about marketing is correct.

Having the most likes on Facebook or more retweets of your posts than your competitors doesn't mean much if these achievements don't have a positive effect on your business. Throughout this book, you'll find concrete suggestions for applying social media tactics to achieve those goals.

If you undertake a social media marketing campaign, we urge you to keep your plans simple, take things slowly, and always stay focused on your customers. Most of all, follow the precepts of guerrilla marketing: Target one niche market at a time, grow that market, and then reinvest your profits in the next niche.

Foolish Assumptions

We visualize our readers as savvy small-business owners, marketers in companies of any size, and people who work in any of the multiple services that support social media efforts, such as advertising agencies, web developers, graphic design firms, copywriting, or public relations. We assume that you

- Already have or will soon have a website or blog that can serve as the hub for your online marketing program
- Are curious about ubiquitous social media
- Are comfortable using search terms on search engines to find information online
- Know the realities of your industry, though you may not have a clue whether your competitors use social media
- Can describe your target markets, though you may not be sure whether your audience is using social media
- Are trying to decide whether using social media makes sense for your company (or your boss has asked you to find out)
- May already use social media personally and are interested in applying your knowledge and experience to business

» May already have tried using social media for your company but want to improve results or measure return on your investment

» Have a passion for your business, appreciate your customers, and enjoy finding new ways to improve your bottom line

If our assumptions are correct, this book will help you organize a social marketing presence without going crazy or spending all your waking hours online. It will help you figure out whether a particular technique makes sense, how to get the most out of it, and how to measure your results.

Icons Used in This Book

To make your experience easier, we use various icons in the margins to identify special categories of information.

TIP

These hints help you save time, energy, or aggravation. Sharing them is our way of sharing what we've figured out the hard way — so that you don't have to. Of course, if you prefer to get your education through the school of hard knocks, be our guest.

REMEMBER

This book has more details in it than any normal person can remember. This icon reminds you of points made elsewhere in the book or perhaps helps you recall business best practices that you know from your own experience.

WARNING

Heed these warnings to avoid potential pitfalls. Nothing we suggest will crash your computer beyond repair or send your marketing campaign into oblivion. But we tell you about business and legal pitfalls to avoid, plus a few traps that catch the unprepared during the process of configuring social media services. Not all those services create perfect user interfaces with clear directions!

TECHNICAL STUFF

The geeky-looking Dummies Man marks information to share with your developer or programmer — unless you are one. In that case, have at it. On the other hand, you can skip any of the technical-oriented information without damaging your marketing plans or harming a living being.

Beyond the Book

You can find an online cheat sheet on the book's companion website. Go to www.dummies.com and type *Social Media Marketing All-in-One For Dummies* in the Search box. The cheat sheet contains secrets for social media marketing success, online resources, and more.

The website also has a Downloads tab you can open to download copies of the Social Media Marketing Goals and Social Media Marketing Plan forms, which you can use to develop your own marketing plans. In addition, the website is the place to find any significant updates or changes that occur between editions of this book.

Where to Go from Here

As always with *All-in-One Dummies* books, the minibooks are self-contained. If there's a topic you want to explore immediately, start with the detailed Table of Contents or index.

If you're just starting out with social media, we recommend reading minibooks 1 and 2. The chapters in Book 1 act as an overview of social media and will help you figure out how to integrate social media into your online marketing plan, which in turn is part of your overall marketing plan. Remember, social media is the tail — your business is the dog! Book 1 will help you establish reasonable expectations for a return on investment and structure an appropriate allocation of time, personnel, and funds to achieve success.

Book 2 offers an overview of tools to manage your social media marketing efforts. You'll also learn how to leverage your existing search engine optimization approach to maximize the value of social media postings to earn better ranking on search results pages.

The six minibooks that follow focus on popular and niche social media services, with detailed how-to descriptions for putting together a content marketing strategy, marketing with social media, and advertising on social networks. The final minibook is a deep dive into social media analytics, so you can gather the information you need to make data-driven marketing decisions.

If you find errors in this book, or have suggestions for future editions, please email us at books@watermelonweb.com. We wish you a fun and profitable experience going social!

1 The Social Media Mix

Contents at a Glance

CHAPTER 1: Making the Business Case for Social Media 7
Making Your Social Debut 8
Defining Social Media Marketing. 9
Understanding the Benefits of Social Media 13
Understanding the Cons of Social Media. 19
Integrating Social Media into Your Overall Marketing Effort 20
Developing a Strategic Social Media Marketing Plan 22

CHAPTER 2: Tallying the Bottom Line 33
Preparing to Calculate Return on Investment. 34
Accounting for Customers Acquired Online 35
Establishing Key Performance Indicators for Sales 39
Tracking Leads 43
Understanding Other Common Business Metrics 44
Determining Return on Investment 45

CHAPTER 3: Plotting Your Social Media Marketing Strategy 53
Locating Your Target Market Online. 54
Segmenting Your B2C Market 54
Researching B2B Markets 64
Conducting Other Types of Market Research Online. 65
Setting Up Your Social Media Marketing Plan. 67

CHAPTER 4: Managing Your Cybersocial Campaign 77
Managing Your Social Media Schedule 78
Building Your Social Media Marketing Dream Team 85
Creating a Social Media Marketing Policy 87
Staying on the Right Side of the Law 90
Protecting Your Brand Reputation 95

IN THIS CHAPTER

» Accentuating the positives and eliminating the negatives

» Latching on to the affirmatives

» Integrating social media into your marketing plan

» Evaluating the worth of social media

Chapter 1 Making the Business Case for Social Media

In the best of all worlds, *social media* — a suite of online services that facilitates two-way communication and content sharing — can become a productive component of your overall marketing strategy. These services can enhance your company's online visibility, strengthen relationships with your clients, and expand word-of-mouth advertising, which is the best type.

Given its rapid rise in popularity and its hundreds of millions of worldwide users, social media marketing sounds quite tempting. These tools require minimal upfront cash and, theoretically, you'll find customers flooding through your cyberdoors, ready to buy. It sounds like a no-brainer — but it isn't, especially now that so many social media channels have matured into a pay-to-play environment with paid advertising.

Has someone finally invented a perfect marketing method that puts you directly in touch with your customers and prospects, costs nothing, and generates profits faster than a perpetual motion machine produces energy? The hype says "yes"; the real answer, unfortunately, is "no." Although marketing nirvana may not yet be at hand, the expanding importance of social media in the online environment means that your business needs to participate.

This chapter provides an overview of the pros and cons of social media to help you decide how to join the social whirl, and it gives a framework for approaching a strategic choice of which social media to use.

Making Your Social Debut

Like any form of marketing, social media takes some thought. It can become an enormous siphon of your time, and short-term profits are rare. Social media marketing is a long-term commitment.

So, should you or shouldn't you invest time and effort in this marketing avenue? If you answer in the affirmative, you immediately confront another decision: What form should that investment take? The number of options is overwhelming; you can never use every technique and certainly can't do them all at once.

Figure 1-1 shows that most small businesses involved in social media use Facebook, with Twitter and LinkedIn closely tied for second and third place. However, as the survey from Clutch notes, only 44 percent of all small businesses do any form of digital marketing. Of that number, nearly 60 percent used social media in 2016, but 75 percent planned to incorporate some form of social media in their marketing plans by 2017. For more details, see the survey at `https://clutch.co/agencies/resources/small-business-digital-marketing-and-social-media-habits-survey-2016`.

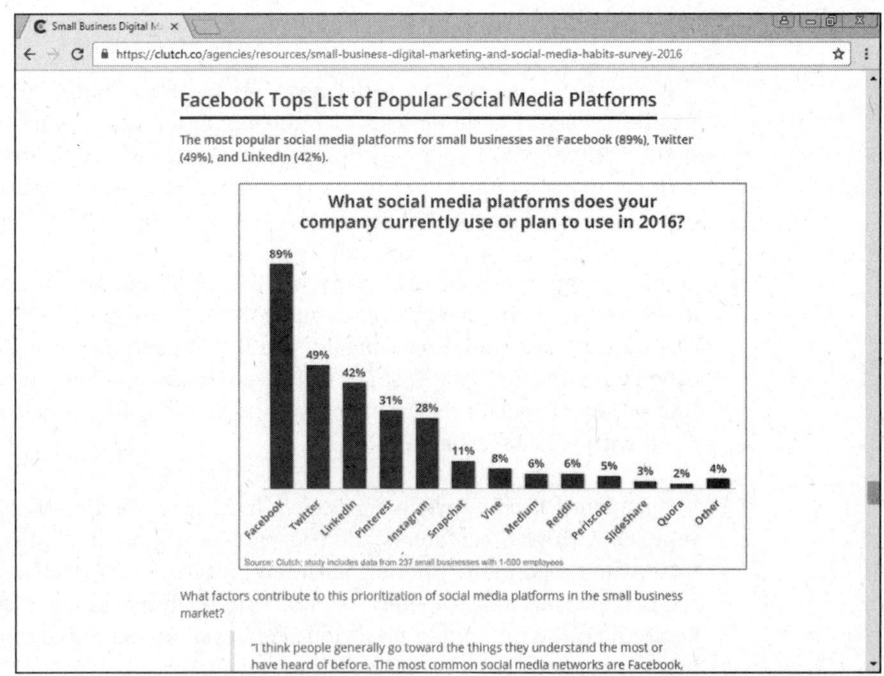

FIGURE 1-1: Most small companies using social media focus on Facebook.

Clutch.co report authored by Sarah Patrick

Defining Social Media Marketing

The bewildering array of social media (which seem to breed new services faster than rabbits can reproduce) makes it hard to discern what they have in common: shared information, often on a peer-to-peer basis. Although many social media messages look like traditional broadcasts from one business to many consumers, their interactive component offers an enticing illusion of one-to-one communication that invites individual readers to respond.

The phrase *social media marketing* generally refers to using these online services for *relationship selling* — selling based on developing rapport with customers. Social media services make innovative use of new online technologies to accomplish the familiar communication and marketing goals of this form of selling.

TIP

The tried-and-true strategies of marketing (such as solving customers' problems and answering the question, "What's in it for me?") are still valid. Social media marketing is a new technique, not a new world.

This book covers a variety of social media services (sometimes called social media *channels*). We use the phrase *social media site* to refer to a specific named online service or product.

You can categorize social media services, but they have fuzzy boundaries that can overlap. Some social media sites fall into multiple categories. For instance, some social networks and online communities allow participants to share photos and include a blog.

Here are the different types of social media services:

- **Social content-sharing services:** These services facilitate posting and commenting on text, videos, photos, and podcasts (audio).
  - *Blogs and content-posting sites:* Websites designed to let you easily update or change content and to allow readers to post their own opinions or reactions.

    Examples of blog tools are WordPress, Typepad, Blogger, Medium, and Tumblr. Blogs may be hosted on third-party sites (apps) or integrated into your own website using software.
  - *Video:* Examples are YouTube, Vimeo, Vine.co, Periscope.tv, Musical.ly, and Ustream.
  - *Images:* Flickr, Photobucket, Instagram, Snapchat, SlideShare, Pinterest, and Picasa. Figure 1-2 shows how Blue Rain Gallery attracts followers on Instagram by highlighting some of the beautiful works of art it sells.
  - *Audio:* Podbean or BlogTalkRadio.

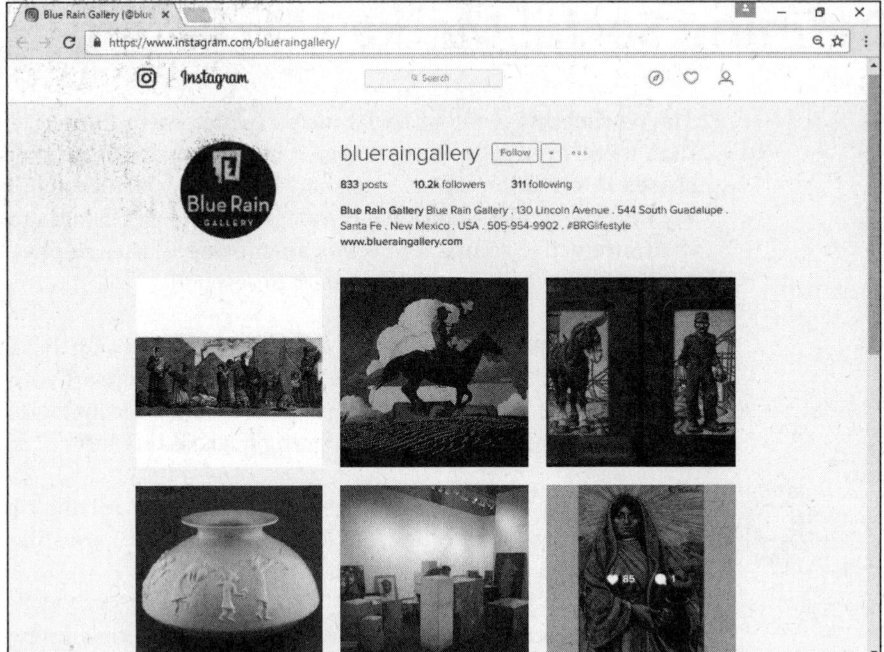

FIGURE 1-2: The Instagram page for Blue Rain Gallery uses strong images to grab viewers' attention.

Courtesy of Blue Rain Gallery

- **Social-networking services:** Originally developed to facilitate the exchange of personal information (messages, photos, video, and audio) to groups of friends and family, these full-featured services offer multiple functions. From a business point of view, many social-networking services support subgroups that offer the potential for more targeted marketing. Common types of social-networking services include
  - *Full networks,* such as Facebook, Google+, and MeetMe. Figure 1-3 shows how SVN/Walt Arnold Commercial Brokerage, Inc. uses its Facebook page to build its brand and enhance community relations.
  - *Short message networks* such as Twitter are often used for news, announcements, events, sales notices, and promotions. In Figure 1-4, Albuquerque Economic Development uses its Twitter account at `https://twitter.com/abqecondev` to assist new and expanding businesses in the Albuquerque, NM area.
  - *Professional networks,* such as LinkedIn and small profession-specific networks. Figure 1-5 shows how Array Technologies uses its LinkedIn page to make announcements, impart company news, and attract employees.
  - *Specialty networks* with unique content, such as the Q&A network Quora, or that operate within a vertical industry, demographic, or activity segment, as opposed to by profession or job title.

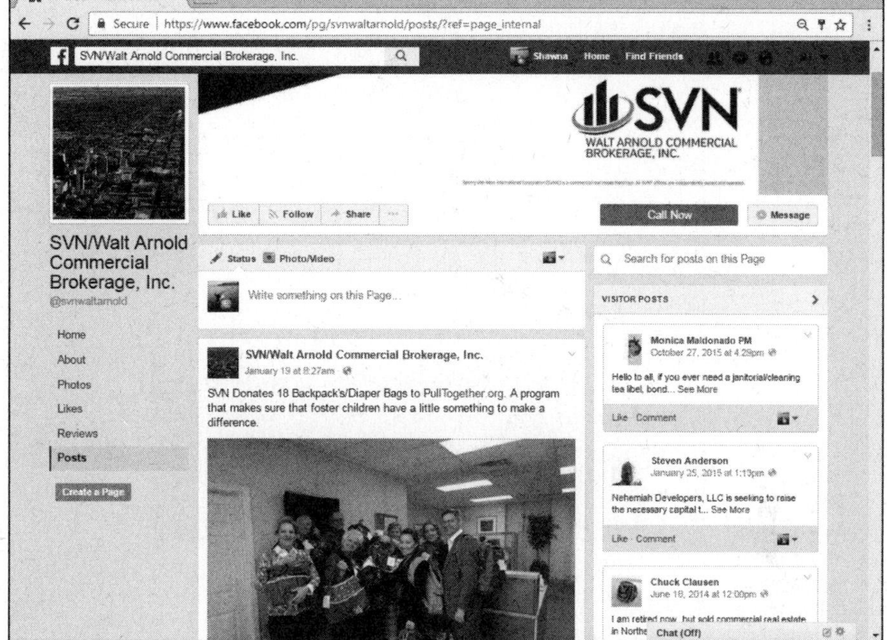

FIGURE 1-3: As part of its community-branding activities, Walt Arnold Commercial Brokerage describes its donation of filled backpacks and diaper bags to foster children.

Courtesy of SVN/Walt Arnold Commercial Brokerage, Inc.

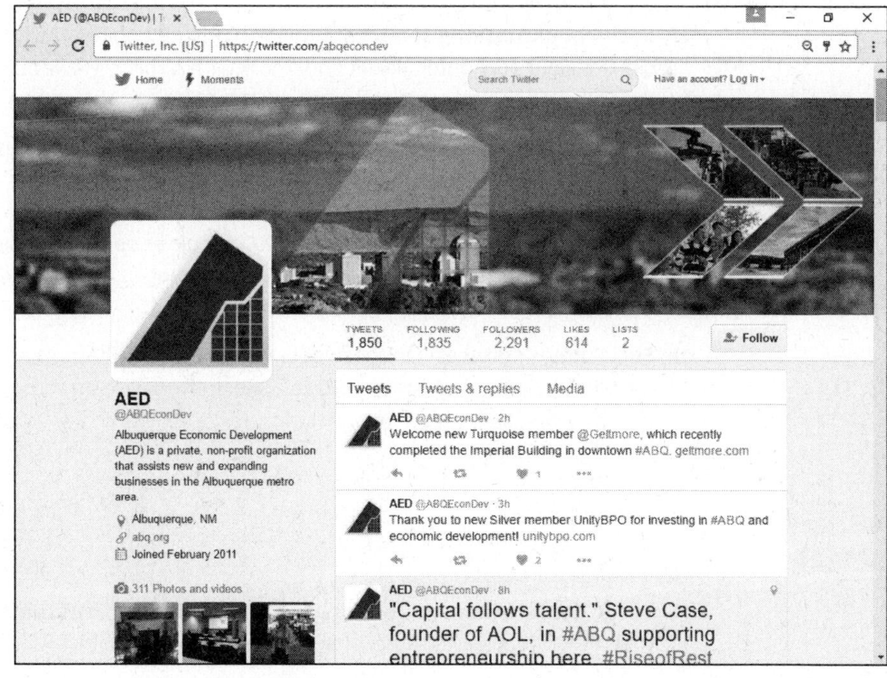

FIGURE 1-4: Twitter is an excellent way for Albuquerque Economic Development to announce news about local industry.

Courtesy of Albuquerque Economic Development

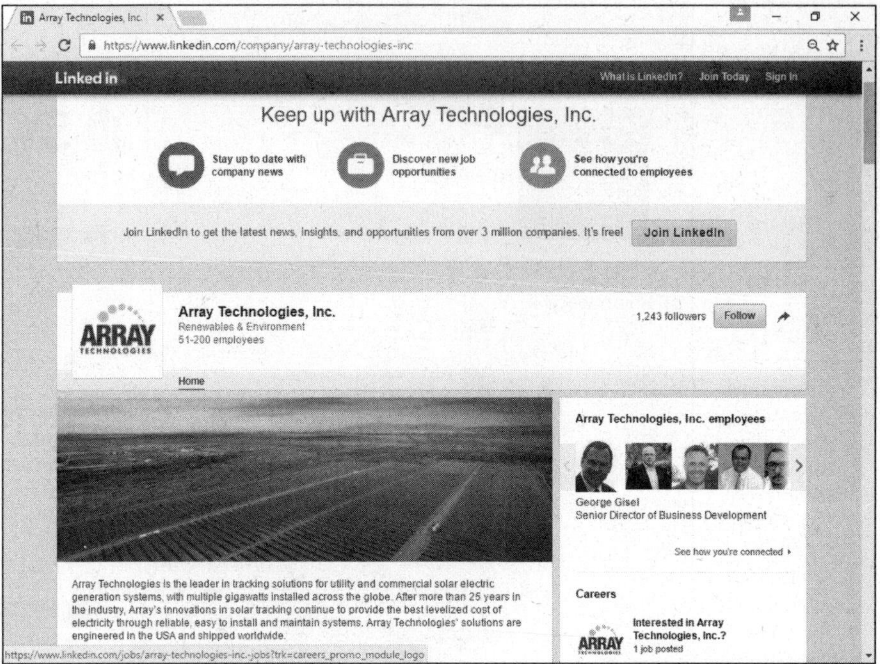

FIGURE 1-5: Array Technologies uses its LinkedIn presence to provide company updates.

Courtesy of Array Technologies, Inc.

- **Social-bookmarking services:** Similar to private bookmarks for your favorite sites on your computer, social bookmarks are publicly viewable lists of sites that others have recommended. Some are
  - *Recommendation services,* such as StumbleUpon and Delicious
  - *Social-shopping services,* such as Wanelo and ThisNext
  - *Other bookmarking services organized by topic or application,* such as sites where readers recommend books to others using bookmarking techniques
- **Social news services:** On these peer-based lists of recommended articles from news sites, blogs, or web pages, users often vote on the value of the postings. Social news services include
  - Digg
  - Reddit
  - Other news sites
- **Social geolocation and meeting services:** These services bring people together in real space rather than in cyberspace:

- Foursquare
- Meetup
- Other GPS (Global Positioning System) applications, many of which operate on mobile phones
- Other sites for organizing meet-ups and *tweet-ups* (gatherings organized by using Twitter)

» **Community-building services:** Many comment- and content-sharing sites have been around for a long time, such as forums, message boards, and Yahoo! and Google groups.

Other examples are

- *Community-building sites* with multiple sharing features, such as Ning
- *Wikis,* such as Wikipedia, for group-sourced content
- *Review sites,* such as TripAdvisor, Yelp, and Epinions, to solicit consumer views

As you surf the web, you can find dozens, if not hundreds, of social tools, *apps* (freestanding online applications), and *widgets* (small applications placed on other sites, services, or desktops). These features monitor, distribute, search, analyze, and rank content. Many are specific to a particular social network, especially Twitter. Others are designed to aggregate information across the social media landscape, including such monitoring tools as Google Alerts, Mention.net, or Social Mention, or such distribution tools as RSS (really simple syndication), which allows frequently updated data to be posted automatically to locations requested by subscribers

Book 2 offers a survey of many more of these tools; specific social media services are covered in their respective books.

Understanding the Benefits of Social Media

Social media marketing carries many benefits. One of the most important is that you don't have to front any cash for most social media services. Of course, there's a downside: Most services require a significant time investment to initiate and maintain a social media marketing campaign, and many limit distribution of unpaid posts, charging for advertising and distributing posts to your desired markets.

As you read the following sections, think about whether each benefit applies to your needs. How important is it to your business? How much time are you willing to allocate to it? What kind of payoff would you expect? Figure 1-6 shows how small retail businesses rate the relative effectiveness of social media in meeting their goals for acquiring and retaining customers.

Digital Tactics that Drive Customer Acquisition vs. Retention According to US SMB Retail Professionals, March 2016
% of respondents

	Acquisition	Retention
Email marketing	81%	80%
Organic search	62%	36%
Paid search	59%	43%
Social media	51%	44%
Retargeting	49%	37%
Affiliates	31%	21%
Referral marketing	21%	18%
Mobile marketing	16%	8%
Marketplaces	15%	11%
Comparison shopping engines	8%	3%
Other	2%	5%

Note: for their organization
Source: WBR Digital and emarsys, "Adapting to the pace of omnichannel commerce," June 7, 2016

Courtesy of WBR Digital

FIGURE 1-6: The effectiveness of social media compared to other digital-marketing tactics for small retail businesses.

Casting a wide net to catch your target market

The audience for social media is huge. By the second quarter of 2016, Facebook claimed 1.79 billion monthly active users worldwide, of which 1.66 billion were mobile users. Slightly less than 85 percent of Facebook's traffic comes from outside the US and Canada.

When compared to Google, this social media behemoth is in tight competition for the US audience. In October 2016, Facebook tallied about 207 million unique US visitors/viewers, while Google Sites surpassed it with more than 246 million. Keep in mind, of course, that visitors are conducting different activities on the two sites.

Twitter tallied more than 109 million US visitors/viewers in October 2016 and toted up about 500 million *tweets* (short messages) daily worldwide. A relatively small number of power users are responsible for the majority of tweets posted daily. In fact, about 44 percent of users create Twitter accounts without ever posting. More people read tweets than are accounted for, however, because tweets can be read on other websites.

Even narrowly focused networking sites claim hundreds of thousands of visitors. Surely, some of the people using these sites must be your customers or prospects. In fact, one popular use of social media is to cast a wide net to capture more potential visitors to your website. Figure 1-7 shows a classic conversion funnel, which demonstrates the value of bringing new traffic to the top of the funnel to produce more *conversions* (actions taken) at the bottom.

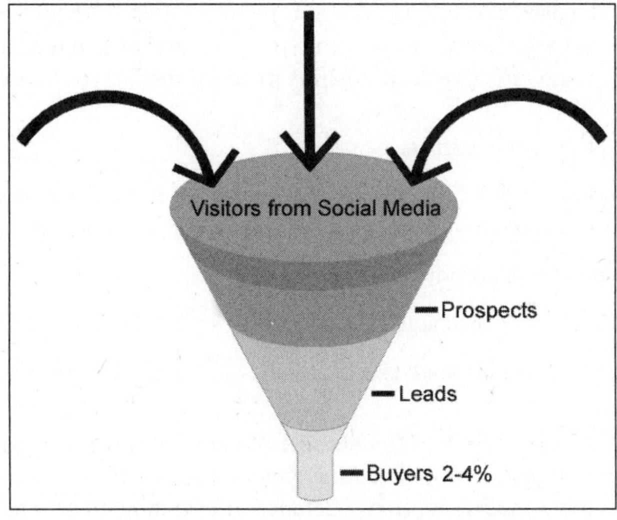

FIGURE 1-7: The classic conversion funnel shows that only 2 to 4 percent of funnel entries yield desired results.

Courtesy of Watermelon Mountain Web Marketing: `www.watermelonweb.com`

The conversion funnel works like this: If more people arrive at the top of the funnel, theoretically more will progress through the steps of prospect and qualified lead to become a customer. Only 2 to 4 percent, on average, make it through a funnel regardless of what action the funnel conversion depicts.

TIP

In Book 1, Chapter 3, we discuss how you can assess traffic on social media sites using Quantcast, Alexa, or other tools, and match their visitors to the profiles of your customers. Generally, these tools offer some information free, although several are freemium sites, with additional data available only with a paid plan.

Branding

Basic marketing focuses on the need for branding, name recognition, visibility, presence, or top-of-mind awareness. Call it what you will — you want people to remember your company name when they're in need of your product or service. Social media services, of almost every type, are excellent ways to build your brand.

REMEMBER

Social media works for branding as long as you get your name in front of the right people. Plan to segment the audience on the large social media services. You can look for more targeted groups within them or search for specialty services that may reach fewer people overall but more of the ones who are right for your business.

Building relationships

If you're focused on only short-term benefits, you'd better shake that thought loose and get your head into the long-term game that's played in the social media world. To build effective relationships in social media, you're expected to

- Establish your expertise.
- Participate regularly as a good citizen of whichever social media world you inhabit; follow site rules and abide by whatever conventions have been established.
- Avoid overt self-promotion.
- Resist hard-sell techniques except in paid advertising.
- Provide value with links, resources, and unbiased information.

Watch for steady growth in the number of your followers on a particular service or the number of people who recommend your site to others; increased downloads of articles or other tools that provide detailed information on a topic; or repeat visits to your site. All these signs indicate you're building relationships that may later lead to if not a direct sale then a word-of-web recommendation to someone who does buy.

In the world of social media, the term *engagement* refers to the length of time and quality of interaction between your company and your followers.

REMEMBER

Social media is a long-term commitment. Other than little experiments or pilot projects, don't bother starting a social media commitment if you don't plan to keep it going. Any short-term benefits you see aren't worth the effort you have to make.

Improving business processes

Already, many clever businesses have found ways to use social media to improve business processes. Though individual applications depend on the nature of your business, consider leveraging social media to

- Promptly detect and correct customer problems or complaints.
- Obtain customer feedback and input on new product designs or changes.

- Provide tech support to many people at one time; if one person has a question, chances are good that others do, too.
- Improve service delivery, such as cafes that accept to-go orders on Twitter or Facebook, or food carts that notify customers where and when their carts will arrive.
- Locate qualified new vendors, service providers, and employees by using professional networks such as LinkedIn.
- Collect critical market intelligence on your industry and competitors by watching content on appropriate social media.
- Use geolocation, tweets, and mobile search services to drive neighborhood traffic to brick-and-mortar stores during slow times and to acquire new customers.

REMEMBER

Marketing is only part of your company, but all of your company is marketing. Social media is a ripe environment for this hypothesis, where every part of a company, from human resources to tech support, and from engineering to sales, can be involved.

Improving search engine rankings

Just as you optimize your website, you should optimize your social media outlets for search engine ranking. Now that search engines are cataloging Twitter and Facebook and other appearances on social media, you can gain additional front-page real estate for your company on Google and Yahoo!/Bing (which now share the same search algorithms and usually produce similar results).

Search engines recognize most appearances on social media as inbound links, which also improve where your site will appear in natural search results.

TIP

Use a core set of search terms and keywords across as many sites as possible. Book 2, Chapters 2 and 3 deal with search engine optimization, including tactics to avoid because they could get you in trouble for spamming.

Optimization pays off in other ways: in results on real-time searches, which are now available on primary search engines; on external search engines that focus on blogs or other social media services; and on internal, site-specific search engines.

Selling in the social media marketplace

Conventional thinking several years ago suggested that social media was designed for long-term engagement, for marketing and branding rather than for sales.

However, more and more social media channels now offer the opportunity for direct sales from their sites. In addition to selling on major social media channels such as Facebook, Pinterest, Twitter (using the Buy Now feature), and Instagram (using third-party add-ons such as Olapic), you will also find selling opportunities on smaller, niche social media:

- **Sell music and event tickets.** SoundCloud and ReverbNation, which cater to music and entertainment, are appropriate social media sites for these products.
- **Include a link to your online store on social-shopping services.** Recommend products — particularly apparel, jewelry, beauty, and decor — as Stylehive does.
- **Offer promotional codes or special deals to followers.** Offering codes or deals on particular networks encourages your followers to visit your site to make a purchase. You can also announce sales or events.
- **Place links to online or third-party stores such as Etsy (see Book 2, Chapter 1) on your profile pages on various services.** Some social media channels offer widgets that visually showcase your products and link to your online store, PayPal, or the equivalent to conclude a transaction.
- **Include a sign-up option for your e-newsletter.** It offers a bridge to sales.

The chart in Figure 1-8 shows the results of a 2015 Small Business Advertising survey that looked at how small businesses use various social media services for generating leads, building brand awareness, or increasing customer engagement.

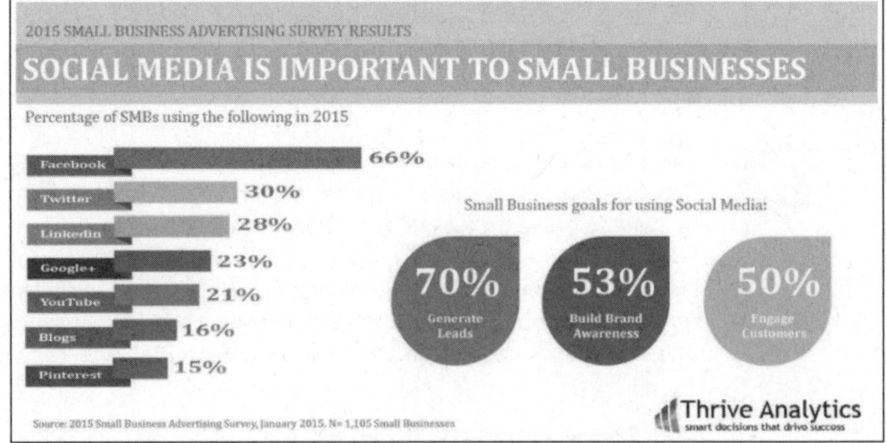

FIGURE 1-8: Small businesses use multiple social media channels to achieve various marketing goals.

Courtesy of Thrive Analytics

TIP

Include sales offers in a stream of information and news to avoid turning your social media site into a series of never-ending advertisements.

Finding alternative advertising opportunities

Although time is money, the magic word is *free.* If you decide to approach social media as an alternative to paid advertising, construct your master social media campaign just as carefully as you would a paid one:

- Create a plan that outlines target markets, ad offers, publishing venues, and schedules for different ad campaigns.
- If necessary, conduct comparative testing of messages, graphics, and offers.
- Monitor results and focus on the outlets that work best at driving qualified visits that lead to conversions.
- Supplement your free advertising with search engine optimization, press releases, and other forms of free promotion.

REMEMBER

Advertising is only one part of marketing!

As you see traffic and conversions building from your social media marketing campaigns, you may want to reduce existing paid advertising campaigns. Just don't stop your paid advertising until you're confident that you have an equally profitable stream of customers from social media. Of course, if your ad campaign isn't working, there's no point continuing it.

Understanding the Cons of Social Media

For all its upsides, social media has its downsides. As social media has gained in popularity, it has also become increasingly difficult to gain visibility among its hundreds of millions of users.

In fact, sometimes you have to craft a campaign just to build an audience on a particular social media site. The process is similar to conducting optimization and inbound link campaigns so that your site is found in natural search results.

TIP

Don't participate in social media for its own sake or just because everyone else is.

By far, the biggest downside in social media is the amount of time you need to invest to see results. You need to make an ongoing commitment to review and respond to comments and to provide an ongoing stream of new material. An initial commitment to set up a profile is just the tip of the iceberg.

WARNING

Keep in mind that you need to watch out for the addictiveness of social media. Individually and collectively, social media is the biggest-ever time sink. Don't believe us? Ask yourself whether you became addicted to news alerts during the 2016 presidential campaign or couldn't take your eyes off live coverage of the terror attacks in Paris. Or maybe you play Candy Crush, Words with Friends, or other video games with a passion, continuously text on your smartphone, or compulsively check email every ten seconds . . . you get the idea. Without self-discipline and a strong time schedule, you can easily become so socially overbooked that other tasks go undone.

As you consider each of the social media options in this book, also consider the level of human resources that is needed. Do you have the time and talents yourself? If not, do other people in your organization have the time and talent? Which other efforts will you need to give up while making room for social media? Will you have to hire new employees or contract services, leading to hard costs for this supposedly "free" media?

Integrating Social Media into Your Overall Marketing Effort

Social media is only part of your online marketing. Online marketing is only part of your overall marketing. Don't mistake the part for the whole.

Consider each foray into social marketing as a strategic choice to supplement your other online-marketing activities, which may include

- **Creating and managing a marketing-effective website:** Use content updates, search engine optimization (SEO), inbound link campaigns, and event calendar postings to your advantage.
- **Displaying your product's or service's value:** Create online press releases and email newsletters. Share testimonials and reviews with your users and offer affiliate or loyalty programs, online events, or promotions.
- **Advertising:** Take advantage of pay-per-click ads, banners, and sponsorships.

REMEMBER

Social media is neither necessary nor sufficient to meet all your online-marketing needs.

Use social media strategically to

- » Meet an otherwise unmet marketing need.
- » Increase access to your target market.
- » Open the door to a new niche market.
- » Move prospects through the conversion funnel.
- » Improve the experience for existing customers.

For example, the website for Fluid IT Services (www.fluiditservices.com) links to its Facebook, Twitter, and LinkedIn sites, as well as its blog (www.fluiditservices.com/blog), to attract its audience. For more information on overall online marketing, see Jan's book, *Web Marketing For Dummies,* 3rd Edition (John Wiley & Sons, Inc.).

To get the maximum benefit from social media, you must have a *hub site,* the site to which web traffic will be directed, as shown in Figure 1-9. With more than 1 billion websites online, you need social media as a source of traffic. Your hub site can be a full website or a blog, as long as the site has its own domain name. It doesn't matter where the site is hosted — only that you own its name, which appears as www.yourcompany.com or http://blog.yourcompany.com. Though you can link to http://yourcompany.wordpress.com, you can't effectively optimize or advertise a WordPress address like this. Besides, it doesn't look professional to use a domain name from a third party.

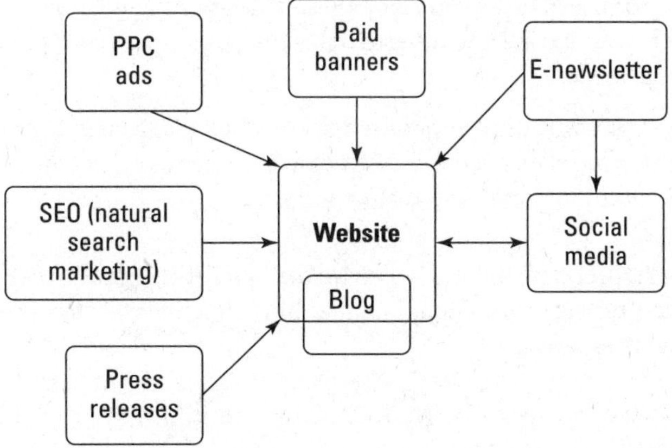

FIGURE 1-9: All social media channels and other forms of online marketing interconnect with your hub website.

Courtesy of Watermelon Mountain Web Marketing: www.watermelonweb.com

Consider doing some sketching for your own campaign: Create a block diagram that shows the relationship between components, the flow of content between outlets, and perhaps even the criteria for success and how you'll measure those criteria.

Developing a Strategic Social Media Marketing Plan

Surely you wrote an overall marketing plan when you last updated your business plan and an online marketing plan when you first created your website. If not, it's never too late! For business planning resources, see the Starting a Business page at `www.sba.gov/category/navigation-structure/starting-managing-business/starting-business`.

You can further refine a marketing plan for social media marketing. As with any other marketing plan, you start with strategy. A Social Media Marketing Goals statement (Figure 1-10 shows an example) would incorporate sections on strategic goals, objectives, target markets, methods, costs, and return on investment (ROI).

You can download the form on this book's website (`www.dummies.com/go/socialmediamarketingaio4e`) and read more about ROI in Book 1, Chapter 2.

Here are some points to keep in mind when putting together your strategic marketing overview:

- The most important function of the form isn't for you to follow it slavishly, but rather to force you to consider the various facets of social media marketing before you invest too much effort or money.
- The form also helps you communicate decisions to your board of advisors or your boss, in case you need to make the business case for getting involved in social media.
- The form provides a coherent framework for explaining to everyone involved in your social media effort — employees, volunteers, or contractors — the task you're trying to accomplish and why.

Book 1, Chapter 3 includes a Social Media Marketing Plan, which helps you develop a detailed tactical approach — including timelines — for specific social media services, sites, and tools.

In the following sections, we talk about the information you should include on this form.

Social Media Marketing Goals

Related to Hub Site (URL): ____________________

Prepared by: ____________________ **Date:** __________

Business Profile

Is the social media plan for a new or established company?

○ New company ○ Existing company, years in business:

Does the company have an existing brick-and-mortar operation?

○ Yes ○ No

Does the company have an existing website or web presence?

○ Yes ○ No

Does the company have an existing blog or social media presence?

○ Yes ○ No

If yes, list all current URLs for social media.

Will your site serve:

○ Business ○ Consumers

What type of business is the website for?

○ Manufacturer ○ Service provider ○ Retailer

○ Distributor ○ Professional

What does the company sell?

○ Goods ○ Services

Describe your goods or services:

What geographical range does the social media campaign address?

○ Local (specify) ○ Regional (specify)

○ National (specify if not US) ○ International (specify)

Social Media Campaign Goals

Rank the applicable goals of your social media campaign from 1-7, with 1 your top goal.

_______ Increasing traffic/visits to hub site

_______ Branding

_______ Building relationships

_______ Improving business process (e.g., customer service, tech support)

_______ Improving visibility in natural search

_______ Increasing sales revenue

_______ Using social media as paid advertising platform

FIGURE 1-10: Establish your social-marketing goals, objectives, and target market definition on this form.

Financial Profile

Social Media Campaign Budget for First Year

Outside development, contractors, includes writing, design, technical $ ________

Special content production (e.g., video, podcasts, photography): $ ________

Marketing/paid ads on social media $ ________

In-house labor (burdened rate) $ ________

Other costs, e.g., tools, equipment $ ________

TOTAL: $ ________

Break-even point: $ ________ Within: ____ ◯ mo or ◯ yr

Return on investment: ________ % Within: ____ ◯ mo or ◯ yr

Sample Objectives

Repeat for appropriate objectives for each goal within time frame specified (for instance, 1 year).

Traffic objective (# visitors per month): ________ Within: ________

Conversion objective: ________ % Within: ________

Sales objectives (# sales per month): $ ________ Within: ________

Average $ per sale: $ ________ Within: ________

$ revenue per month: $ ________ Within: ________

Other objectives specific to your site, e.g., for branding, relationships, search ranking ________ Within: ________

________ Within: ________

________ Within: ________

FIGURE 1-10: continued

Marketing Profile

Describe your target markets. Give specific demographic or other segmentation information. For B2B, segment by industry or job title or both.

What is your marketing tag?

Value proposition: Why should someone buy from your company rather than another?

Name at least six competitors and list their websites, blogs, and social media pages.

FIGURE 1-10: continued

Courtesy of Watermelon Mountain Web Marketing: www.watermelonweb.com

Establishing goals

The Goals section prioritizes the overall reasons you're implementing a social media campaign. You can prioritize your goals from the seven benefits of social media, described in the earlier section "Understanding the Benefits of Social Media," or you can add your own goals. Most businesses have multiple goals, which you can specify on the form.

Consult Table 1-1 to see how various social media services rank in terms of helping you reach some of your goals.

TABLE 1-1 Matching Social Media Services to Goals

Service	Customer Communication	Brand Awareness	Traffic Generation	SEO
Facebook	Good	Good	Good	Good
Google+	Good	Okay	Poor	Good
Instagram	Poor	Good	Good	Poor
LinkedIn	Good	Good	Good	Okay
Periscope	Good	Okay	Okay	Okay
Pinterest	Good	Okay	Okay	Good
Snapchat	Okay	Okay	Good	Poor
Twitter	Good	Good	Good	Good
YouTube	Good	Good	Good	Good

Adapted and interpreted from data sources at aokmarketing.com/wp-content/uploads/2016/06/CMO_Social_Landscape_2016.pdf *and* www.cmo.com/articles/2014/3/13/_2014_social_intro.html.

Setting quantifiable objectives

For each goal, set at least one quantifiable, measurable objective. "More customers" isn't a quantifiable objective. A quantifiable objective is "Increase number of visits to website by 10 percent," "add 30 new customers within three months," or "obtain 100 new followers for Twitter account within one month of launch." Enter this information on the form.

Identifying your target markets

Specify one or more target markets on the form, not by what they consume but rather by who they are. "Everyone who eats dinner out" isn't a submarket you can identify online. However, you can find "high-income couples within 20 miles of your destination who visit wine and classical music sites."

You may want to reach more than one target market by way of social media or other methods. Specify each of them. Then, as you read about different methods in this book, write down next to each one which social media services or sites appear best suited to reach that market. Prioritize the order in which you plan to reach them.

Book 1, Chapter 3 suggests online market research techniques to help you define your markets, match them to social media services, and find them online.

Think niche! Carefully define your audiences for various forms of social media, and target your messages appropriately for each audience.

Estimating costs

Estimating costs from the bottom up is tricky, and this approach rarely includes a cap. Consequently, costs often wildly exceed your budget. Instead, establish first how much money you're willing to invest in the overall effort, including in-house labor, outside contractors, and miscellaneous hard costs such as purchasing software or equipment. Enter those amounts in the Cost section.

Then prioritize your social-marketing efforts based on what you can afford, allocating or reallocating funds within your budget as needed. This approach not only keeps your total social-marketing costs under control but also lets you assess the results against expenses.

To make cost-tracking easier, ask your bookkeeper or CPA to set up an activity or a job in your accounting system for social media marketing. Then you can easily track and report all related costs and labor.

Valuing social media ROI

Return on investment (ROI) is your single most important measure of success for social media marketing. In simple terms, *ROI* is the ratio of revenue divided by costs for your business or, in this case, for your social media marketing effort.

You also need to set a realistic term in which you will recover your investment. Are you willing to wait ten weeks? Ten months? Ten years? Some forms of social media are less likely to produce a fast fix for drooping sales but are great for branding, so consider what you're trying to accomplish.

Figure 1-11 shows how B2C versus B2B marketers assess the ROI of various online marketing techniques. Keep in mind that the only ROI or cost of acquisition that truly matters is your own.

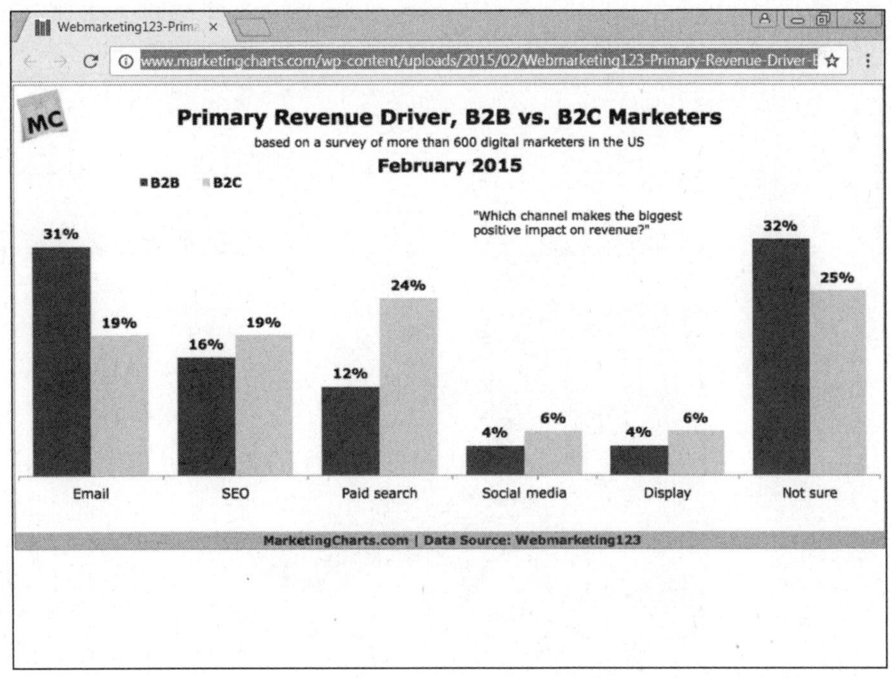

FIGURE 1-11: In spite of the popularity of social media, it is not always the best driver of revenue.

Courtesy of DemandWave

Costs usually turn out to be simpler to track than revenues that are traceable explicitly to social media. Chapter 2 of this minibook discusses techniques for figuring ROI and other financial metrics in detail.

REMEMBER

Whatever you plan for online marketing, it will cost twice as much and take twice as long as anticipated.

A social media service is likely to produce results only when your customers or prospects are already using it or are willing to try it. Pushing people toward a service they don't want is difficult. If in doubt, first expand other online and offline efforts to drive traffic toward your hub site.

SOCIAL MEDIA DELIVERS CUSTOMERS DOOR-TO-DOOR

Door to Door Organics is an online grocery service that simplifies shopping and inspires busy families to achieve a healthier lifestyle. The company delivers fresh, high-quality, organic, natural, and local food directly to homes in 18 states throughout the West, Midwest, and East Coast. According to Andrea Daily, vice president of marketing, the company targets a specific customer: a 25- to 44-year-old well-educated female who is married or living with a partner, has a household income of $75K+, may or may not have children, and is a savvy online shopper seeking convenience. Since launching from its founder's garage in 1997, the company has grown to 500 employees and plans to further expand its geographic reach.

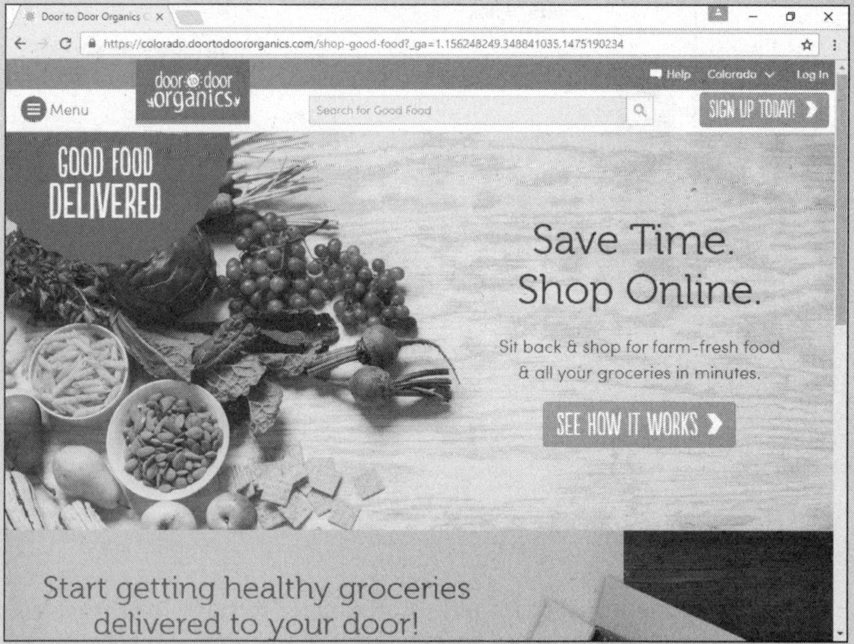

Courtesy of Door-to-Door Organics

Door to Door Organics launched its social media presence in 2009 with Twitter (`https://twitter.com/dtdOrganics`), followed by a Facebook business page (www.facebook.com/DoorToDoorOrganicsColorado/). As Daily explains, "Since the beginning, we viewed these social media pages strategically as customer service channels where we had an opportunity to wow customers with a high level of satisfaction." The company quickly discovered that its target demographic is most active on Facebook.

It wasn't always easy, Daily recalls, "When we first established ourselves on social media, we found ourselves continually explaining what we were and how customers could shop with us. We soon realized there was an opportunity to leverage Facebook to tell that story, creating a specific landing page with an animated video (www.facebook.com/DoorToDoorOrganicsColorado/app/1610975439127108/) that explained how the service works. It continues to be one of our most successful lead generation and conversion tools." Facebook remains the company's top channel for sharing, especially given its combination of unpaid reach through follower engagement, promoted reach through advertisements, and the large number of people on that platform.

Initially, the company's social media growth was organic, with Pinterest added in 2011 and Instagram (www.instagram.com/doortodoororganics/) in 2013 to encourage customers to post images of their food deliveries. The company then began launching a Twitter and Facebook page in each new geographic location it entered to "provide content that was locally relevant, from farm visits and artisan vendor profiles to invitations to join us at events," says Daily. "This presence allowed us to be more authentic in building local communities."

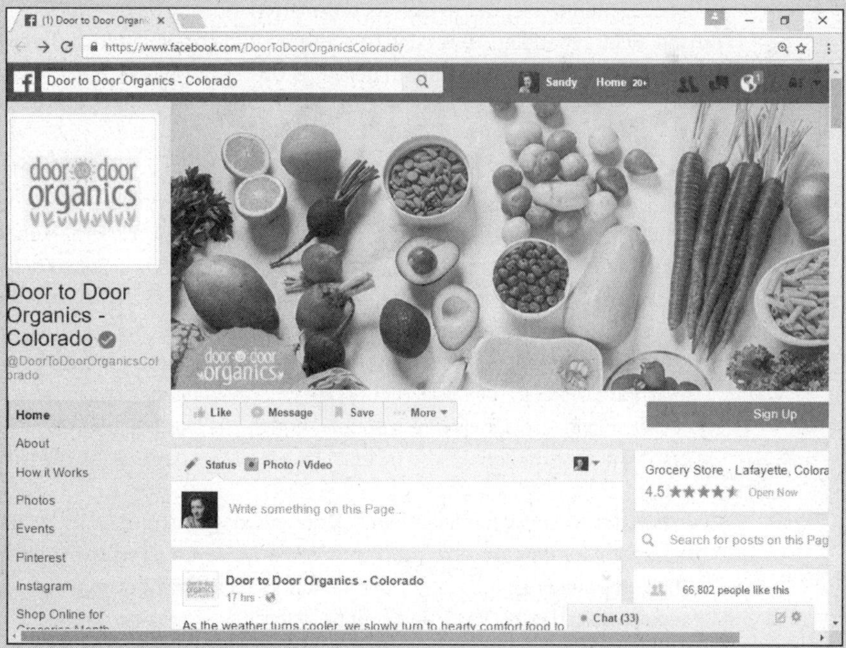

Courtesy of Door-to-Door Organics

(continued)

(continued)

As the company expanded its social media presence, it developed strategic goals for each channel. "We take a balanced approach in leveraging Facebook to drive both engagement and conversions," explains Daily. "Facebook's Audience Insights and targeting tools really allow us to identify not only who is responding to our content, but also to identify new audiences that are likely to respond similarly."

For Door to Door Organics, user-generated content on Facebook has become an important method for letting customers and fans speak for the company and demonstrate their passion for its product. "This content drives engagement, brand awareness, and digital storytelling, as well as sales and conversions."

The company builds engagement on Instagram by writing #JoyDelivered on its boxes and delivery vans with a call to action to "Share Your #JoyDelivered Story." This has led customers to post thousands of pictures on Instagram. The company also uses Instagram for brand building by offering a behind-the-scenes glimpse of company operations, from packers at the warehouse to chefs creating recipes.

Needless to say, all this social media activity requires a fair amount of labor. The company has a social media manager who creates engaging content with a cohesive look and uses advertising to drive brand awareness and new customer acquisition. Meanwhile, the customer care team is actively engaged in community management, responding to fans' questions and concerns seven days a week. The team works with a social media calendar to plan its posting schedule by day, by social media platform, and by target audience, seeking to minimize audience overlap and maximize ad dollars. While its in-house creative team develops content, an outside agency assists with placing advertising on social channels.

To track results, Door to Door Organics uses Google Analytics to understand both traffic to the site and new customer acquisition by platform. Analytics show that Facebook is valuable for customer acquisition, second only to pay-per-click marketing. Daily notes that a significant amount of the firm's marketing budget is invested in digital advertising, with roughly 30 percent of advertising dollars spent on search engine PPC, and another 20 percent spent for advertising on social platforms. She finds these two ad platforms roughly comparable in terms of the volume of new customers they deliver and the cost to acquire them. In the social media category, the vast majority of Door to Door Organics' advertising investment is on Facebook, though it is starting to leverage ads on Instagram. Display and remarketing ads currently take a distant backseat to these two platforms.

In addition to social media and PPC, Door to Door Organics relies on SEO and email marketing for digital reach, supplemented offline with direct mail and terrestrial radio. The company promotes its social media presence almost everywhere, from its website and emails to boxes, vans, and event collateral.

Daily has plenty of advice to offer. First, "be ready for a dialogue; in fact, invite one. It's the best way to showcase your brand and what your company stands for. For us, that means being educational, friendly, and authentic." She doesn't shy away from negative customer feedback, instead seeing it as an opportunity to "try to make it right" and build confidence in the brand.

Second, she urges companies not to be afraid to try new things. "Some of our most successful campaigns were born out of doing things a little differently. If it works for your business, it works for your business. Test, refine, repeat." Finally, she adds that it helps to be an early adopter on a new platform that is gaining traction with your target audience. "Gaining reach is easier and cheaper when there are fewer brands to compete against."

The web presence for Door to Door Organics follows:

- `www.doortodoororganics.com`
- `www.facebook.com/DoorToDoorOrganicsColorado`
- `www.facebook.com/DoorToDoorOrganicsGreatLakes`
- `www.facebook.com/DoorToDoorOrganicsMidwest`
- `www.facebook.com/DoorToDoorOrganicsTriState`
- `www.pinterest.com/dtdorganics`
- `www.twitter.com/dtdOrganics`
- `www.instagram.com/doortodoororganics`
- `www.youtube.com/user/doortodoororganics`

IN THIS CHAPTER

» Estimating the cost of customer acquisition

» Figuring sales metrics and revenue

» Managing and converting leads

» Breaking even

» Calculating return on investment

Chapter 2 Tallying the Bottom Line

In this chapter, you deal with business metrics to determine whether you see a return on investment (ROI) in your social media marketing services. In other words, you get to the bottom line! For details on performance metrics for various types of social media as parameters for campaign success, see Book 9.

By definition, the business metric ROI involves revenues. Alas, becoming famous online isn't a traditional part of ROI; it might have a public relations value and affect business results, but fame doesn't necessarily make you rich. This chapter examines the cost of acquiring new customers, tracking sales, and managing leads. After you reach the break-even point on your investment, you can (in the best of all worlds) start totaling up the profits and then calculate your ROI.

To get the most from this chapter, review your business plan and financial projections. You may find that you need to adjust some of your data collection efforts to ensure that you have the information for these analyses.

TIP

If numbers make your head spin, ask your bookkeeper or accountant for assistance in tracking important business metrics from your financial statements. That person can ensure that you acquire the right data, set up spreadsheets to calculate key metrics, and provide regular reports — and then he or she can teach you how to interpret them.

You don't want to participate in social media marketing for its own sake or because everyone else is doing it. The following sections help you make the business case for yourself.

Preparing to Calculate Return on Investment

To calculate ROI, you have to recognize both costs and revenue related to your social media activities; neither is transparent, even without distinguishing marketing channels.

Surprisingly, the key determinant in tracking cost of sales, and therefore ROI, is most likely to be your sales process, which matters more than whether you sell to other businesses (business to business, or B2B) or consumers (business to consumer, or B2C) or whether you offer products or services.

TIP

The *sales cycle* (the length of time from prospect identification to customer sale) affects the timeline for calculating ROI. If a B2B sale for an expensive, long-term contract or product takes two years, expecting a return on your investment within a month is pointless.

For a *pure-play* (e-commerce only) enterprise selling products from an online store, the ROI calculation detailed in this chapter is fairly standard. However, ROI becomes more complicated if your website generates leads that you must follow up with offline, if you must pull customers from a web presence into a brick-and-mortar storefront (that method is sometimes called *bricks-and-clicks*), or if you sell different products or services in different channels. Table 2-1 provides resource sites that relate to these issues and other business metrics.

REMEMBER

Include the business metrics you intend to monitor in the Business Goals section of your Social Media Marketing Plan, found in Book 1, Chapter 3, and the frequency of review on your Social Media Activity Calendar discussed in Book 1, Chapter 4.

TABLE 2-1 Resources for Business Metrics

Site Name	URL	What You Can Do
Hootsuite	www.blog.hootsuite.com/measure-social-media-roi-business	Measure social media success.
Harvard Business School Toolkit	http://hbswk.hbs.edu/archive/1262.html	Use the break-even analysis tool.
	http://hbswk.hbs.edu/archive/1436.html	Calculate lifetime customer value.
National Retail Federation	https://nrf.com/resources/retail-library	Research, news, and white papers from the NRF's digital retail community.
Olivier Blanchard Basics of Social Media ROI	www.slideshare.net/thebrandbuilder/olivier-blanchard-basics-of-social-media-roi	View an entertaining slide show introduction to ROI.
Panalysis	www.panalysis.com/resources/sales-target-calculator - /calculator	Estimate number of site visitors needed to achieve sales goals.
	www.panalysis.com/resources/customer-acquisition-cost#/calculator	Calculate customer acquisition costs.
Search Engine Watch	http://searchenginewatch.com/article/2079336/4-Steps-to-Measure-Social-Media-ROI-with-Google-Analytics	Set up Google Analytics to measure social media ROI.
SearchCRM	http://searchcrm.techtarget.com	Find information about customer relationship management (CRM).
WhatIs	http://whatis.techtarget.com	Search a dictionary and an encyclopedia of IT-related business terms.

Accounting for Customers Acquired Online

The *cost of customer acquisition* (CCA) refers to the marketing, advertising, support, and other types of expenses required to convert a prospect into a customer. CCA usually excludes the cost of a sales force (the salary and commissions) or payments to affiliates. Some companies carefully segregate promotional expenses, such as loyalty programs, that relate to branding or customer retention. As long as you apply your definition consistently, you're okay.

If your goal in social media marketing is branding or improving relationships with existing customers, CCA may be a bit misleading, but it's still worth tracking for comparison purposes.

The definition of your customers and the cost of acquiring them depend on the nature of your business. For instance, if you have a purely advertising-supported, web-only business, visitors to your site may not even purchase anything. They simply show up, or perhaps they register to download some information online. Your real customers are advertisers. However, a similar business that's not supported by advertising may need to treat those same registrants as leads who might later purchase services or pay for subscriptions.

TIP

The easiest way to define your customers is to figure out who pays you money.

Comparing the costs of customer acquisition

You may want to delineate CCA for several different revenue streams or marketing channels: consumers versus businesses; products versus services (for example, software and support contracts); online sales versus offline sales; and consumers versus advertisers. Compare each one against the average CCA for your company overall. The formula is simple:

cost of customer acquisition = marketing cost ÷ number of leads

Be careful! This formula can be misleading if you calculate it over too short a time frame. The CCA may be too high during quarters that you undertake a new activity or a special promotion (such as early Christmas sales or the introduction of a new product or service) and too low during quarters when spending is down but you reap benefits from an earlier investment in social media.

TIP

Calculate your CCA over six months to a year to smooth out unique events. Alternatively, compute *rolling averages* (taking an average over several months at a time, adjusting the start date each month — January through March, February through April, March through May, and so on) to create a better picture of what's going on.

In Figure 2-1, Rapport Online ranks the return on investment, defined as cost-effectiveness in generating leads, for a variety of online-marketing tactics. The lowest ROI appears at the bottom of the cube, and the highest appears at the top.

Social media marketing runs the gamut of rapport-building options because it involves some or all of these techniques. On this scale, most social media services would probably fall between customer referral and SEO or between SEO and PR/link building, depending on the type and aggressiveness of your effort in a particular marketing channel. Traditional offline media, by contrast, would have a lower ROI than banner advertising.

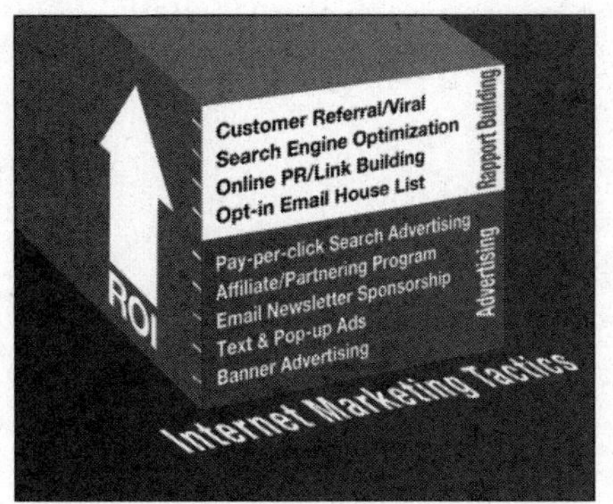

FIGURE 2-1: Social media would fit near the top of the ROI scale for Internet-marketing tactics.

Courtesy of Rapport Online Inc., ROI

REMEMBER

As with performance metrics, business metrics such as CCA and ROI aren't perfect. If you track everything consistently, however, you can at least compare results by marketing channel, which can help you make informed business decisions.

If you garner leads online but close your sales and collect payments offline, you can frame CCA as the cost of lead acquisition, recognizing that you may need to add costs for staff, collateral, demos, travel, and other items to convert a lead.

For a rough idea of your cost of customer acquisition, fill out the cost calculator at `www.panalysis.com/resources/customer-acquisition-cost#/calculator` (shown in Figure 2-2) with your own data. For start-up costs, include labor expense, contractors for content development, and any other hard costs related to your social media activities. Substitute social media costs for web expenses.

To put things in perspective, remember that the traditional business school model for offline marketing teaches that the CCA is roughly equivalent to the profit on the amount a customer spends during the first year.

Because you generally see most of your profits from future sales to that customer, you must also understand the *lifetime customer value* (how much and how often a customer will buy), not just the revenue from an initial sale. The better the customers, the more it's worth spending to acquire them. Harvard Business School offers an online calculator for determining lifetime customer value at `http://hbswk.hbs.edu/archive/1436.html`.

WARNING

Be sure that the cost of customer acquisition (CCA) doesn't exceed the lifetime customer value.

In the 2014 Shop.org/Forrester Research Inc. State of Retailing Online study (`https://nrf.com/media/press-releases/shoporgforrester-search-marketing-tops-online-retail-customer-acquisition`), Forrester finds that retailers continue to invest in digital media, including ads on social media, to acquire new customers.

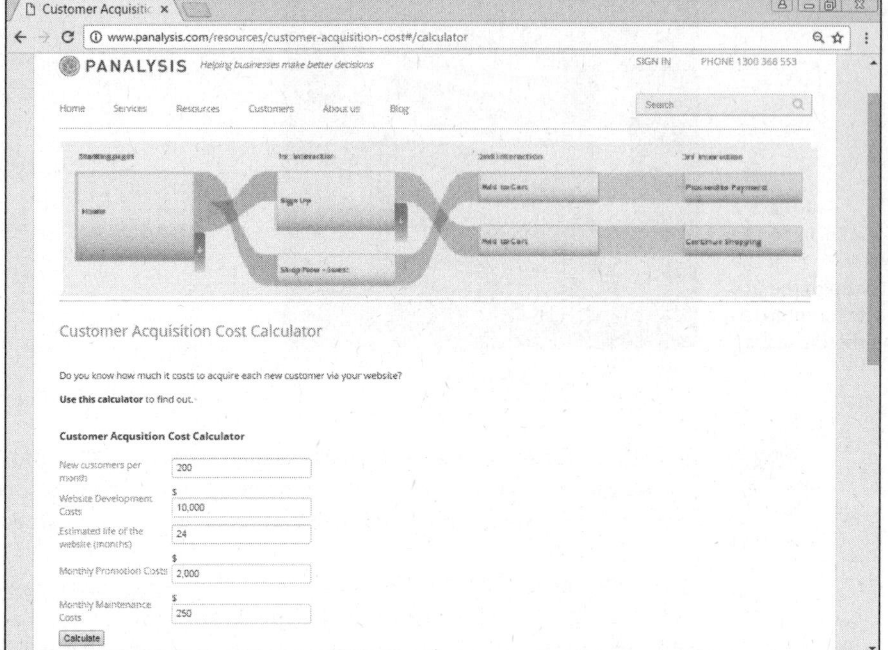

FIGURE 2-2: Compare the cost of customer acquisition (CCA) for social media marketing (SMM) with the average CCA across your entire business.

Courtesy of Panalysis: Marketing Analytics Specialists/goo.gl/ivEOte @PanalysisAU

TIP

Try to keep the total cost of marketing by any method at 6 percent to 11 percent of your revenues; you can spend less after you have an established business with word-of-mouth referrals and loyal repeat customers. Remember, customer acquisition is only part of your total marketing budget; allow for customer retention and branding expenses as well.

Small businesses (fewer than 100 employees), new companies, and new products usually need to spend toward the high end of the scale on marketing initially — perhaps even more than 11 percent. By comparison, mature, well-branded product lines and companies with a large revenue stream can spend a lower percentage on marketing.

Obviously, anything that can reduce marketing costs offers a benefit. See whether your calculation bears out that cost level for your investment in social media.

One is silver and the other gold

You might remember the words to that old Girl Scout song: "Make new friends but keep the old; one is silver and the other gold." To retain customers, apply that philosophy to your policy of customer satisfaction. That may mean anything from sending holiday greetings to establishing a loyalty program with discounts for repeat buyers, from entering repeat customers into a special sweepstakes to offering a coupon on their next purchase when they sign up for a newsletter.

A marketing truism states that it costs anywhere from 3 to 30 times more to acquire a new customer than to retain an existing one. (For details, see `www.linkedin.com/pulse/what-cost-customer-acquisition-vs-retention-ian-kingwill`.) Although costs vary with each type of business, it's common sense to listen to customers' concerns, complaints, product ideas, and desires.

Thus, while you lavish time and attention on social marketing to fill the top of your funnel with new prospects, don't forget its value for improving relationships with current customers and nurturing their involvement with your brand.

The same 2014 Forrester report on retailing online that we mention in the preceding section also noted the critical value of social media in building customer engagement.

Establishing Key Performance Indicators for Sales

If you track ROI, at some point you must track revenue and profits as business metrics. Otherwise, there's no ROI to compute. Unlike the previous emphasis on social media for customer engagement, recent statistics show a rapid increase in social commerce (direct sales from social media), as shown in Figure 2-3. As SmartInsights points out (`www.smartinsights.com/social-media-marketing/social-media-strategy/understanding-role-organic-paid-social-media`), "Social commerce is growing much faster than retail e-commerce," perhaps faster than any other retail sales channel.

Social Commerce Revenues Worldwide. US vs Rest of World, 2011-2015 (Billions)

Year	*US*	*Rest of World*	*Total Revenues*
2011	$1	$4	$5
2012	$3	$6	$9
2013	$5	$8	$13
2014	$9	$12	$21
2015	$14	$16	$30
CAGR (Compound Annual Growth Rate)			93.4% US CAGR

Source: www.smartinsights.com/wp-content/uploads/2016/04/Slide1-700x525.jpg

FIGURE 2-3: Social commerce revenues have grown rapidly since 2011.

If you sell online, your storefront should provide ways for you to slice and dice sales to obtain crucial data. However, if your sales come from services, from a brick-and-mortar store, or from large contractual purchases, you probably need to obtain revenue statistics from financial or other external records to plug into your ROI calculation.

TIP

If you manage a bricks-and-clicks operation, you may want to integrate your online and offline operations by selecting e-commerce software from the vendor who provides the *point-of-sales* (POS) package for your cash registers. That software may already be integrated with your inventory control and accounting packages.

Just as with performance metrics, you should be able to acquire certain key performance indicators (KPI) for sales by using storefront statistics. Confirm that you can access this data before purchasing your e-commerce package:

- You should be able to determine how often customers buy (number of transactions per month), how many new customers you acquire (reach), and how much they spend per transaction (yield).
- Look for sales reports by average dollar amount as well as by number of sales. Plugging average numbers into an ROI calculation is easier, and the results are close enough as long as the inputs are consistent.
- You should be able to find order totals for any specified time frame so that you can track sales tied to promotions, marketing activities, and sale announcements.
- Look for the capability to sort sales by new and repeat customers; to allow for future, personalized offers; and to distinguish numbers for CCA.
- Your sales statistics should include a conversion funnel (as described in Chapter 1 of this minibook). Try to trace the path upstream so that you can identify sales initiated from social media.
- Check that data can be exported to a spreadsheet.
- Make sure that you can collect statistics on the use of promotion codes by number and dollar value so that you can decide which promotions are the most successful.
- Having store reports that break down sales by product is helpful. Sometimes called a *product tree,* this report shows which products are selling by SKU (stock keeping unit) and category.

Table 2-2 lists some storefront options that integrate with social media and offer sales analytics. Unfortunately, not all third-party storefront solutions offer ideal tracking. Many storefront solutions use Google Analytics, shown in Figure 2-4, to track transactions.

TABLE 2-2 **Social Media Store Solutions Offering Sales Statistics**

Name	URL	Type of Sales Stats Available
Google Analytics ECommerce Tracking	`https://developers.google.com/analytics/devguides/collection/analyticsjs`	Google Analytics for e-commerce
Mercantec	`www.mercantec.com`	Google Analytics e-commerce tracking and statistics
Payvment	`www.ecwid.com/payvment`	Integrated storefront that works on social media, mobile, and blog sites
ProductCart	`www.productcart.com`	Google Analytics integration at the product level
Shopify	`www.shopify.com`	Offers its own reports as well as integration with Google Analytics, Facebook pixel, and Pinterest tag
Spreesy	`www.spressy.com`	Social commerce platform that integrates with Google Analytics; works with Instagram, Facebook, Twitter, Pinterest, and mobile sites

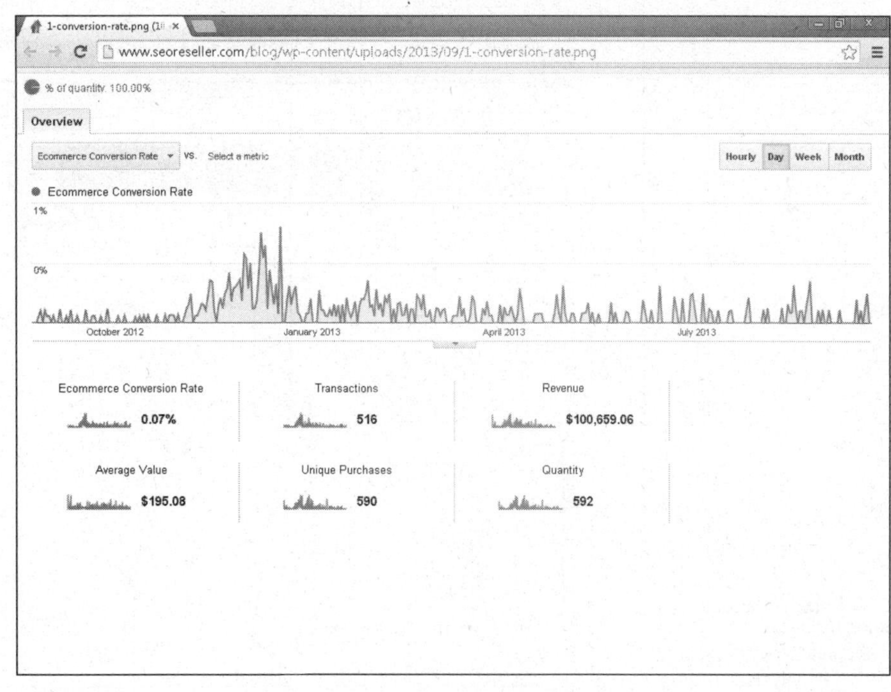

FIGURE 2-4: Typical e-commerce statistics available on Google Analytics.

Courtesy of SEOReseller.com

As the value of social media for generating sales has grown, many social media channels have improved their tracking options for sales completed on a website. In addition to Facebook's long-offered conversion pixel, Pinterest now has a tag code tool and Twitter generates conversion code for placement on a "thank-you" page at the conclusion of a purchase.

If you created alternative SKUs for products sold by way of social media for tracking, be sure to merge them into the same category of your product tree. Using multiple SKUs isn't recommended if your storefront solution includes inventory control.

You can input the numbers from your social media sales metrics into a sales calculator to forecast unit sales needed to meet your goals. Figure 2-5 shows a calculator from Panalysis at `www.panalysis.com/resources/sales-target-calculator#/calculator`. Users enter values for the variables in the fields at the top of the image and click Calculate; different forecasts for monthly revenue appear below the fields.

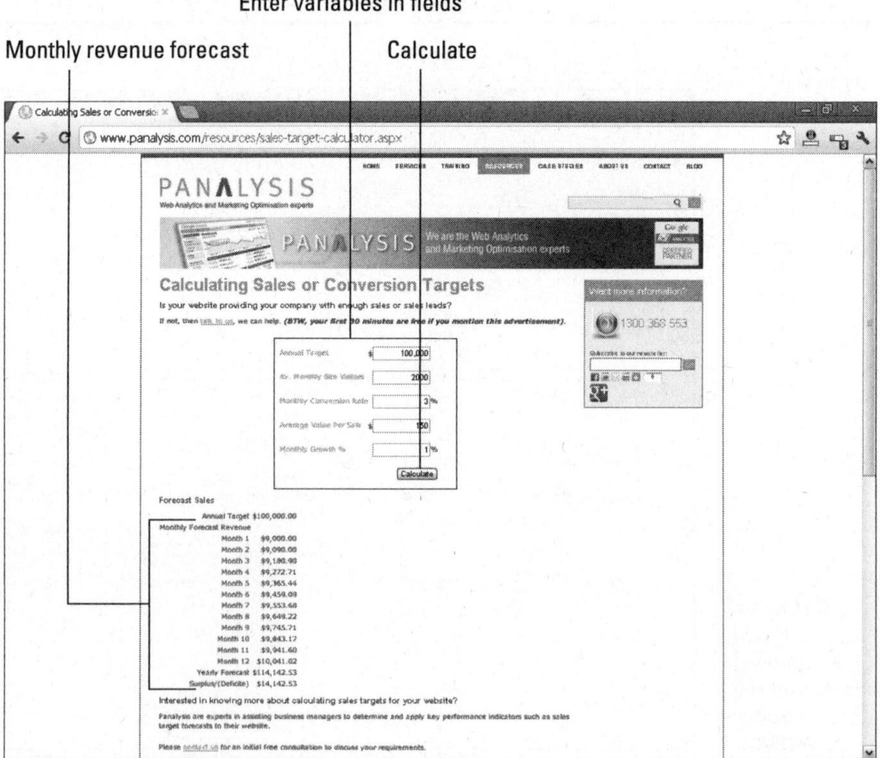

FIGURE 2-5: Sales forecasting calculator from Panalysis.

Courtesy of Panalysis.com

Tracking Leads

Often, your social media or web presence generates leads instead of, or in addition to, sales. If your sales process dictates that some or all sales are closed offline, you need a way to track leads from initiation to conversion. *Customer relationship management* (CRM) software helps you track prospects, qualified leads, and customers in an organized way. A simple database might allow different managers, salespeople, and support personnel to share a client's concerns or track the client's steps within the selling cycle.

The process of CRM and lead management may also include qualifying and nurturing leads, managing marketing campaigns, building relationships, and providing service, all while helping to maximize profits. Table 2-3 lists some lead-monitoring and CRM software options.

TABLE 2-3 Lead-Monitoring and CRM Software

Name	URL	What You Can Do	Cost
Batchbook	`www.batchblue.com`	Integrate social media with CRM	Free 14-day trial with unlimited contacts; starts at $19.95 per month
HubSpot	`http://offers.hubspot.com/free-trial`	All-in-one software; manage inbound leads, lead generation, and more	Free 30-day trial; starts at $200 per month after free trial
LEADSExplorer	`www.leadsexplorer.com`	See who's visiting your website	Free 30-day trial; starts at $42 per month after free trial
SplendidCRM	`www.splendidcrm.com/Store.aspx`	Install open source CRM software	Options range from free open source download to unlimited use for $960

REMEMBER

Although often thought of as the province of B2B companies offering high-ticket items with a long sales cycle, lead-tracking tools can help you segment existing and prospective customers, improve the percentage of leads that turn into clients, and build brand loyalty.

TIP

You can export your Google Analytics results to a spreadsheet and create a similar graphical display.

Understanding Other Common Business Metrics

Your bookkeeper or accountant can help you compute and track other business measurements to ensure that your business turns a profit. You may want to pay particular attention to estimating your break-even point and your profit margin.

Break-even point

Computing the *break-even point* (the number of sales needed for revenues received to equal total costs) helps determine when a product or product line will become profitable. After a product reaches break-even, sales start to contribute to profits.

To calculate the break-even point, first you need to figure out the *cost of goods* (for example, your wholesale price or cost of manufacturing) or *average variable costs* (costs such as materials, shipping, or commission that vary with the number of units sold) and your *fixed costs* (charges such as rent or insurance that are the same each month regardless of how much business you do). Then plug the amounts into these two formulas:

revenues – cost of goods (variable) = gross margin

fixed costs ÷ gross margin = break-even point (in unit sales)

Figure 2-6 shows this relationship. This graph of the break-even point shows fixed costs (the dashed horizontal line) to variable costs (the solid diagonal line) to plot total costs. After revenues surpass the break-even point, each sale contributes to profits (the shaded area on the right).

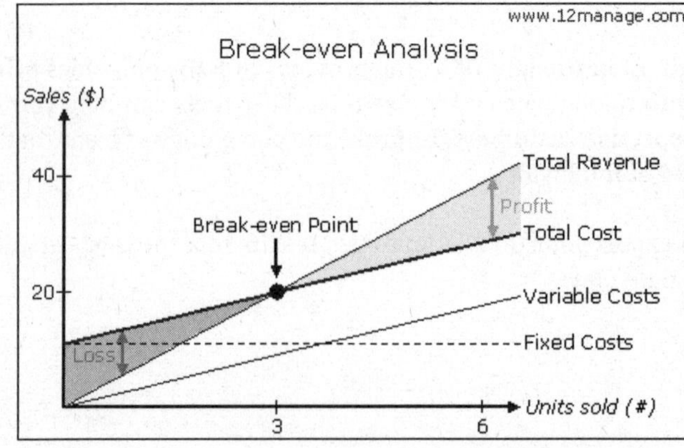

FIGURE 2-6: The break-even chart plots fixed plus variable costs; each sale after the break-even point contributes to profits.

The break-even analysis tool from the Harvard Business School Toolkit (`http://hbswk.hbs.edu/archive/1262.html`) can also help you calculate your break-even point.

Profit margin

Net profit margin is defined as earnings (profits) divided by revenues. If you have $10,000 in revenues and $1,500 in profits, your profit margin is 15 percent (1500 ÷ 10000 = 0.15).

Revenue versus profit

One of the most common errors in marketing is to stop analyzing results when you count the cash in the drawer. You can easily be seduced by growing revenues, but profit is what matters. Profit determines your return on investment, replenishes your resources for growth, and rewards you for taking risks.

Determining Return on Investment

Return on investment (ROI) is a commonly used business metric that evaluates the profitability of an investment or effort compared with its original cost. This versatile metric is usually presented as a ratio or percentage (multiply the following equation by 100). The formula itself is deceptively simple:

ROI = (gain from investment – cost of investment) ÷ cost of investment

The devil is, as usual, in the details. The cost of an investment means more than cold, hard cash. Depending on the type of effort for which you're computing ROI for an accurate picture, you may need to include the cost of labor (including your own!), subcontractors, fees, and advertising. When calculating ROI for your entire business, be sure to include overhead, cost of goods, and cost of sales.

You can affect ROI positively by either increasing the return (revenues) or reducing costs. That's business in a nutshell.

REMEMBER

Because the formula is flexible, be sure that you know what other people mean when they talk about ROI.

You can calculate ROI for a particular marketing campaign or product, or an entire year's worth of marketing expenses. Or compare ROI among various forms of marketing, comparing the net revenue returned from an investment in social media to returns from SEO or paid advertising.

TIP

Run ROI calculations monthly, quarterly, or yearly, depending on the parameter you're trying to measure.

Try the interactive ROI calculator at `www.clickz.com/website-optimization-roi-calculator`, which is also shown in Figure 2-7. You can modify this model for social media by treating Monthly Site Visits as social media visits, Success Events as click-throughs to your main site, and Value of Success Events as the value of a sale. See what happens when you improve the *business metric* (the value of a sale) instead of, or in addition to, improving *performance* (site traffic or conversion rate).

Calculating ROI: Website Optimization
There is value in optimizing your website. How much value? Depending on your desired outcomes, the ZAAZ Calculator is designed to estimate the return on investment. Plug in the numbers and see how it changes the present and future value of your business.
Current Site Behavior
Total Average Monthly Site Visits
5,000
Average Monthly Success Events
Identify specific targeted behavior (lead conversion, sales conversion, etc.)
250
Success Event Conversion Rate
Shows success event conversion from total site visits.
5.00 %
Enter Average Value of a Success Event Visit
Please refer to blogs.zaaz.com or here for more information on calculating this value.
$ 25
Enter the average value associated with a single Average Monthly Success Event Visit. Example: each visit is worth $25 on average.
Potential Improvement
Increase Site Traffic by X%
Enter a value (percentage) of the potential increase in site traffic (example 10%).
10 %
Increase Conversion by X%
Enter a value (percentage) of the potential increase in site conversion (example 10%).
10 %
Estimated Cost to Improve Performance
Enter estimated costs to optimize identified behaviors (e.g., agency fees, marketing and/or operational costs).
$ 3,000
Estimated Impact of Site Optimization
Monthly
Annually
Current Value
$6,250
$75,000
Estimated Future Value
$7,563
$90,750

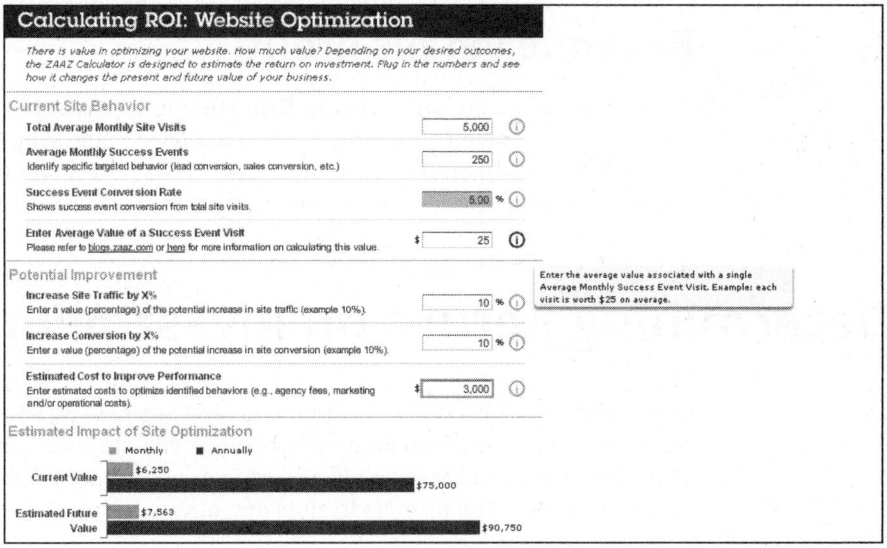

FIGURE 2-7: Play around with variables, such as the value of a sale, and performance criteria.

Courtesy of ClickZ.com

ROI may be expressed as a *rate of return* (how long it takes to earn back an investment). An annual ROI of 25 percent means that it takes four years to recover what you put in. Obviously, if an investment takes too long to earn out, your product — or your business — is at risk of failing in the meantime.

REMEMBER

If your analysis predicts a negative ROI, or even a very low rate of return over an extended period, stop and think! Unless you have a specific tactical plan (such as using a product as a loss leader to draw traffic), look for an alternative effort with a better likelihood of success.

Technically, ROI is a business metric, involving the achievement of business goals, such as more clicks from social media that become sales, higher average value per sale, more repeat sales from existing customers, or reduced cost of customer acquisition.

Many people try to calculate ROI for social media based on performance metrics such as increases in

- The amount of traffic to website or social media pages
- The number of online conversations that include a positive mention of your company
- References to your company versus references to your competitors
- The number of people who join your social networks or bookmark your sites
- The number of people who post to your blog, comment on your Facebook page, or retweet your comments

These measurements may be worth monitoring, but they're only intermediate steps in the ROI process, as shown in Figure 2-8.

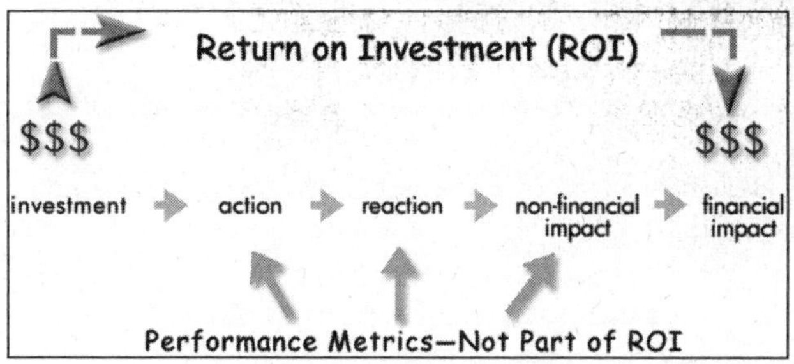

FIGURE 2-8: The relationship between performance metrics and business metrics for ROI.

Source: BrandBuilder, "Olivier Blanchard Basics of Social Media ROI": `www.slideshare.net/thebrandbuilder/olivier-blanchard-basics-of-social-media-roi` (#35)

Here's how to calculate your return on investment:

1. **Establish baselines for what you want to measure before and after your effort.**

   For example, you may want to measure year-over-year growth.

2. **Create activity timelines that appear when specific social media marketing events take place.**

   For example, mark an event on an activity timeline when you start a blog or Twitter campaign.

3. **Plot business metrics over time, particularly sales revenues, number of transactions, and net new customers.**

4. **Measure transactional precursors, such as positive versus negative mentions online, retail store traffic, or performance metrics.**

   For example, keep a tally of comments on a blog post or of site visits.

5. **Line up the timelines for the various relevant activities and transactional (business) results.**
6. **Look for patterns in the data that suggest a relationship between business metrics and transactional precursors.**
7. **Prove those relationships.**

   Try to predict results on the basis of the patterns you see, and monitor your data to see whether your predictions are accurate.

REMEMBER

Improvement in performance metrics doesn't necessarily produce better business results. The only two metrics that count toward ROI are whether your techniques reduce costs or improve revenue.

SOCIAL MEDIA BOOSTS B2B COMPANIES, TOO

HCSS, a Texas-based firm that provides software to the heavy construction industry, allows companies to manage their entire job site from bid to completion on desktop, tablet, or mobile platforms. Over the past 30 years, HCSS has provided software to over 5,000 customers in the US and Canada, and has grown to more than 220 employees.

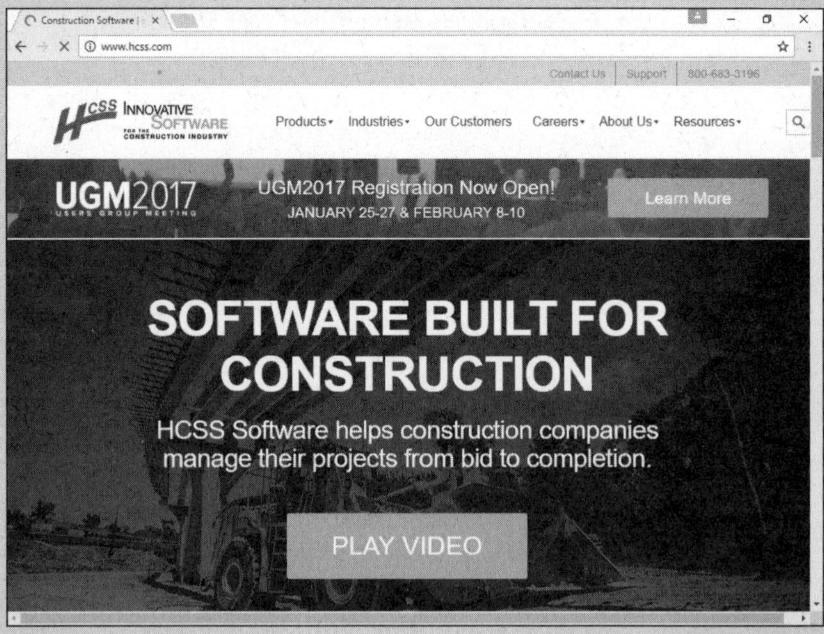

Courtesy of HCSS

With its website well in place, HCSS started posting generic company-style content on standard social media platforms. Beginning around 2013, it took a more active strategic marketing approach to social media, looking for relevant information that its customers would want to read and repost. According to Skyler Moss, director of digital marketing for HCSS, this effort turned its social focus from "'Hey, look at me" to "Hey, here's some helpful info you might like to know.'" By shifting its content from features to benefits, the company starting building a trust relationship with its followers. It took some trial-and-error experiments. "Basically," says Moss, "You have to deliver the content that your audience wants through the social platform they want it on."

As an example, Moss points to the non-profit site I Build America, which HCSS developed to help the industry tell the story of the people, companies, and projects involved in construction. "We found through our social listening that the construction industry was segmented, with 100,000 social discussions going on daily, but on many different mediums, the most active of [which] was Instagram. . . . We found the most popular #s [hashtags] being used, and tagged our photos with them, while also including our own, e.g., #construction, #constructionlife, and #ibuildamerica."

For the first month or two, Moss regularly posted photos on Instagram of real-world construction. From there, the message started to spread organically through the power of cross-tagging. In roughly nine months, the Instagram account for I Build America grew to over 16,000 followers with 100 percent user-generated content. Now more than 300 pieces of individual content are posted each month. "We have created our own conversation around #ibuildamerica by simply trying to tell the story of construction and the people who work in it, rather than making it all about us," claims Moss.

Trying to figure out which platform is best for HCSS to use to achieve different marketing objectives has required a bit of research. Moss discovered the following:

- **LinkedIn-sponsored content placement worked best to generate qualified leads.** Although expensive in terms of cost-per-click, LinkedIn allows the company to target specific buyers and positions at a low cost per lead and a high ROI. Moss recommends knowing much more about your buyer than just a job title. He argues that marketers really need to understand the buyer's persona, from who they are to the types of customers they have and what drives them.
- **To increase site traffic and viral sharing, Facebook proved best.** HCSS runs two major contests every year, the Construction Intern Awards and the Impact Awards. The awards mix an expert judging panel with live voting to increase social awareness and referral traffic. Facebook was the best platform for live voting.

(continued)

(continued)

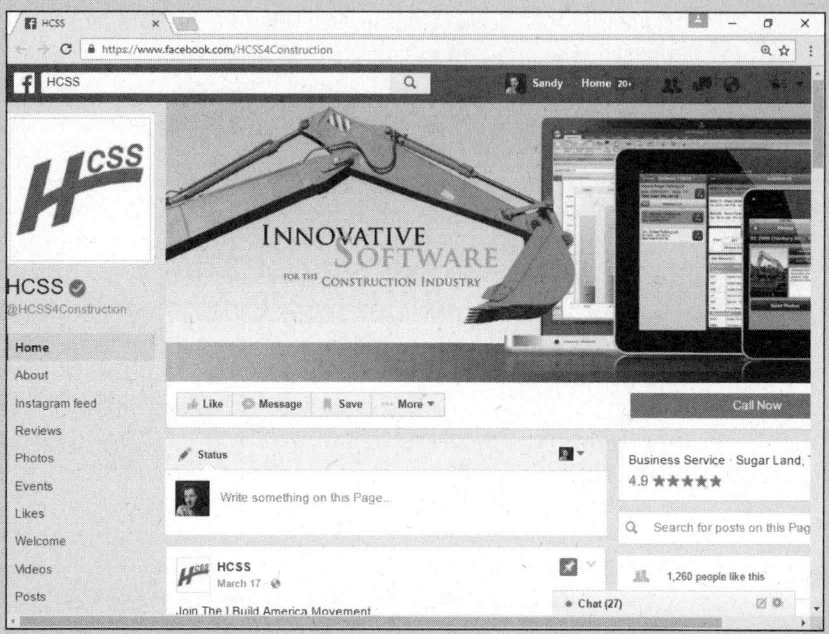

Courtesy of HCSS

At this point, the company's various marketing efforts produce hundreds of leads a month for sales staff to work on. Moss observes that "We've refined our funnel so well that our sales teams only work leads that we deem are qualified through our lead scoring."

HCSS now manages 20 social media accounts split among its core business accounts, career topics, customer support, and the "I Build America" campaign. That's a lot to manage with only two full-time employees, some part-time interns, and Moss leading the effort. To help, they rely on multiple tools. One of the social media interns, Jack Briscoe, has the responsibility of constantly monitoring notifications to see whether an urgent response is required. He uses Google Alerts, Iconosquare to monitor Instagram, and Hootsuite to monitor Facebook and Twitter. Hootsuite is used also to repost construction photos on Instagram, and MeetEdgar is used to schedule cross-posts by category on Twitter and Facebook.

HCSS also uses a variety of tools to track the path from prospect to sale, starting with marketing automation software from HubSpot, which helps with lead scoring. Qualified prospects are then sent to sales using Salesforce. To follow customers' paths through sales funnels, Moss also relies on Google Analytics and Webmaster Tools, as well as Crazy Egg heat maps and video heat-mapping software. (A *heat map* is a color-coded display of data, such as where customers look on a web page or which links they click.) For social media, Moss uses data from Google Analytics and HubSpot to track leads and customer conversions.

"When you know . . . how much you are spending on each social media platform and the value of a customer, you [can] calculate your CPL, or cost per lead. . . . Find the source that produces the best CPL and lowest CPC, cost per customer," says Moss. "That will help you refine your social media spending for ads, sponsored content, or retargeting." However, from his point of view, SEO traffic still retains the lead in ROI.

Moss fervently recommends starting with a persona, so marketers know exactly which marketing techniques will work, and how, when, and where different personas like to engage with content. He pursues that approach by targeting content that specifically addresses different personas' problems, needs, issues, and challenges. For HCSS, this method has led to a 300 percent growth in organic traffic versus branded traffic over the past three years.

Of course, a company this size has a robust marketing mix that also includes email, trade shows, print ads, newsletters, video-publishing platforms, and social media retargeting ads. Although Moss doesn't think that having social media icons on a website matters much now, he does think it helps to cross-promote content among social media channels. For instance, he cross-promotes user-generated images from I Build America to Twitter and Facebook. What makes a difference, he contends, is whether people on Facebook, for example, will share an interesting post with their own followers.

HCSS has also experimented with advertising on social media. It tried a three-month Facebook look-alike campaign and monitored the conversions and CPL. At the end, Moss decided that the CPL for its B2B market was way too high to sustain. On the other hand, a sponsored content campaign on LinkedIn drove more targeted customers at a lower CPL, even though the cost per click was five to ten times as high as on Facebook.

Both Briscoe and Moss have important insights to share. Briscoe reminds people to keep posting and experimenting. "Don't be afraid to not have the perfect content because that doesn't exist. You can't please everyone with just a single post," he says.

Adds Moss, "Always remember that your true north is your customer; they are your guiding compass and will tell you all you want to know. You just have to ask."

(continued)

Following is a list of sites that make up HCSS's web presence:

- www.hcss.com
- http://cia.hcss.com
- www.facebook.com/HCSS4Construction
- www.youtube.com/hcsssoftware
- https://twitter.com/hcss
- https://twitter.com/hcsssupport
- www.linkedin.com/company/hcss
- https://plus.google.com/+Hcsssoftware
- www.ibuildamerica.com
- www.instagram.com/ibuildamerica/?hl=en
- www.linkedin.com/company/i-build-america
- www.youtube.com/ibuildamerica
- https://twitter.com/ibamerica

IN THIS CHAPTER

» Finding your audience online

» Segmenting B2C markets

» Conducting B2B research online

» Planning your strategy

Chapter 3
Plotting Your Social Media Marketing Strategy

In Chapter 1 of this minibook, we talk about making the business case for social media marketing, looking at the question of whether you should or shouldn't get involved. That chapter is about strategy, goals, and objectives — this one is about tactics. It helps you decide which social media services best fit your marketing objectives and your target market.

Let your customers and prospects drive your selection of social media alternatives. To see the best return on your investment in social media, you need to try to use the same social media as they do. This principle is the same one you apply to all your other marketing and advertising efforts. Social media is a new tactic, not a new world.

REMEMBER

Fish where your fish are. If your potential customers aren't on a particular social media outlet, don't start a campaign on that outlet.

In this chapter, we show how to use online market research to assess the match between your target markets and various social media outlets. After you do that, you're ready to start filling out your own Social Media Marketing Plan, which appears at the end of this chapter.

Locating Your Target Market Online

Nothing is more important in marketing than identifying and understanding your target audience (or audiences). After you can describe your customers' and prospects' demographic characteristics, where they live, and what social media they use, you're in a position to focus your social marketing efforts on those people most likely to buy your products or services. (Be sure to include the description of your target market in your Social Media Marketing Goals statement, discussed in Book 1, Chapter 1.)

Because social media techniques focus on inexpensive ways to reach niche markets with specific messages, they're tailor-made for a guerrilla-marketing approach. As with all guerrilla-marketing activities, target one market at a time.

Don't dilute your marketing budget or labor by trying to reach too many audiences at a time. People still need to see your message or brand name at least seven times to remember it. Trying to boost yourself to the forefront of everyone's mind all at once is expensive.

REMEMBER

Focus your resources on one niche at a time. After you succeed, invest your profits in the next niche. It may seem counterintuitive, but it works.

Don't let setting priorities among niches paralyze you. Your choice of niches usually doesn't matter. If you aren't sure, go first for what seems to be the biggest market or the easiest one to reach.

Segmenting Your B2C Market

If you have a business-to-consumer (B2C) company, you can adapt the standard tools of *market segmentation*, which is a technique to define various niche audiences by where they live and how they spend their time and money. The most common types of segmentation are

- Demographics
- Geographic location
- Life-stage-based purchasing behavior
- Psychographics or lifestyle
- Affinity or interest groups

These categories affect not only your social media tactics but also your graphics, message, content, offers, and every other aspect of your marketing.

REMEMBER

Your messages need to be specific enough to satisfy the needs and wants of the distinct subgroups you're trying to reach.

Suppose that you want to sell a line of organic, herbal hair care products using social media. If you described your target market as "everyone who uses shampoo" in your Social Media Marketing Goals statement (see Book 1, Chapter 1), segment that market into different subgroups before you select appropriate social-marketing techniques.

When you're creating subgroups, keep these concepts in mind:

- **Simple demographics affect your market definition.** The use of fragrances, descriptive terms, and even packaging may vary by gender. How many shampoo commercials for men talk about silky hair? For that matter, what's the ratio of shampoo commercials addressed to women versus men?
- **Consider geography.** Geography may not seem obvious, but people who live in dry climates may be more receptive to a message about moisturizers than people who live in humid climates. Or perhaps your production capacity constrains your initial product launch to a local or regional area.
- **Think about how purchasing behavior changes with life stages.** For instance, people who dye their hair look for different hair care products than those who don't, but the reason they color their hair affects your selling message. (Teenagers and young adults may dye their hair unusual colors in an effort to belong to a group of their peers; older men may hide the gray with Grecian Formula; women with kids might be interested in fashion, or color their hair as a pick-me-up.)
- **Even lifestyles (psychographics) affect decisions.** People with limited resources who are unlikely to try new products may respond to messages about value and satisfaction guarantees; people with more resources or a higher status may be affected by messages related to social grouping and self-esteem.
- **Affinity or interest groups are an obvious segmentation parameter.** People who participate in environmental organizations or who recycle goods may be more likely to be swayed by a green shampoo appeal or shop in specific online venues.

Different niche markets are drawn to different social media activities in general and to specific social media service providers in particular. In the following several sections, we look in detail at different online tools you can use to explore the parameters that seem the most appropriate for segmenting your audience and selecting specific social media sites.

For more information on market segmentation and research, see *Small Business Marketing Kit For Dummies,* 3rd Edition, by Barbara Findlay Schenck (John Wiley & Sons, Inc.).

REMEMBER

The most successful marketing campaigns are driven by your target markets, not by techniques.

Demographics

Demographic segmentation, the most common type of market differentiation, covers such standard categories as gender, age, ethnicity, marital status, family size, household income, occupation, social class, and education.

Sites such as Quantcast (`www.quantcast.com`) and Alexa (`www.alexa.com`) provide basic demographic information compared to the overall Internet population, as shown in Figure 3-1. Quantcast also displays the distribution by subcategory within the site. Alexa offers a seven-day free trial, which limits the number of visits per day you can make to Alexa. The three levels of paid plans — Basic ($10/month), Insight ($49/month), and Advanced ($149/month) — offer increasing levels of access to additional tools, such as Keyword Difficulty Tool, Competitor Keyword Matrix, On-Page SEO Checker, SEO Audit Tool, Audience Overlap Tool, and Competitive Intelligence.

As you can see in Figure 3-1, the Quantcast and Alexa sites don't always share the same demographic subcategories or completely agree on the data. However, either one is close enough for your social-marketing purposes.

Use these tools to check out the demographic profile of users on various social media services, as well as your own users and those of your competitors. For instance, by comparing the demographics on Quantcast, you can see that the audience for the popular image site Imgur is younger, more male-dominated, and slightly better educated than the overall population of Internet users.

REMEMBER

Look for a general match between your target audience and that of the social media service you're considering.

TIP

Always check for current demographic information before launching your social media campaign. For details by channel, try `www.pewinternet.org/2015/08/19/the-demographics-of-social-media-users`.

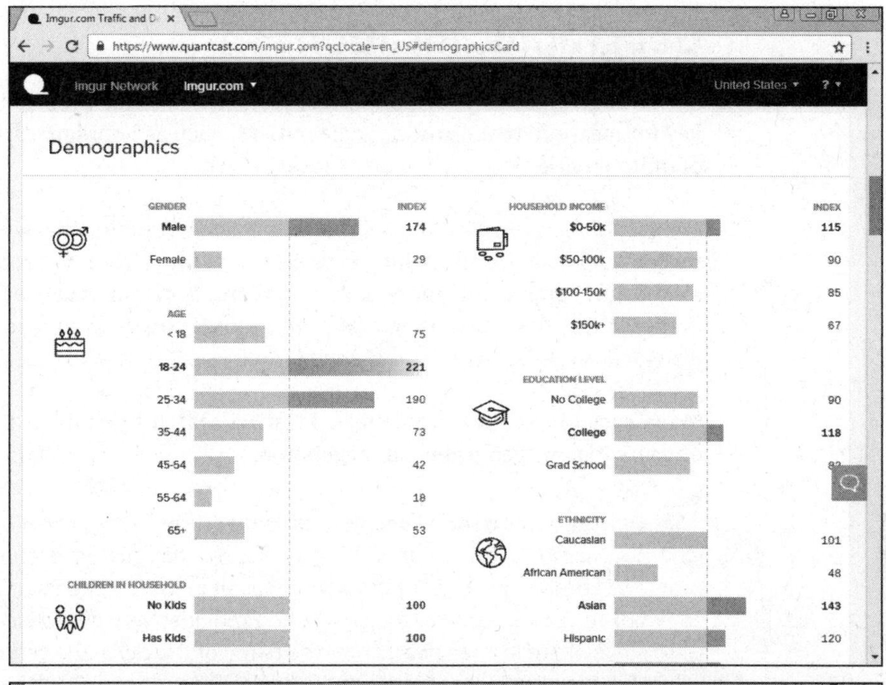

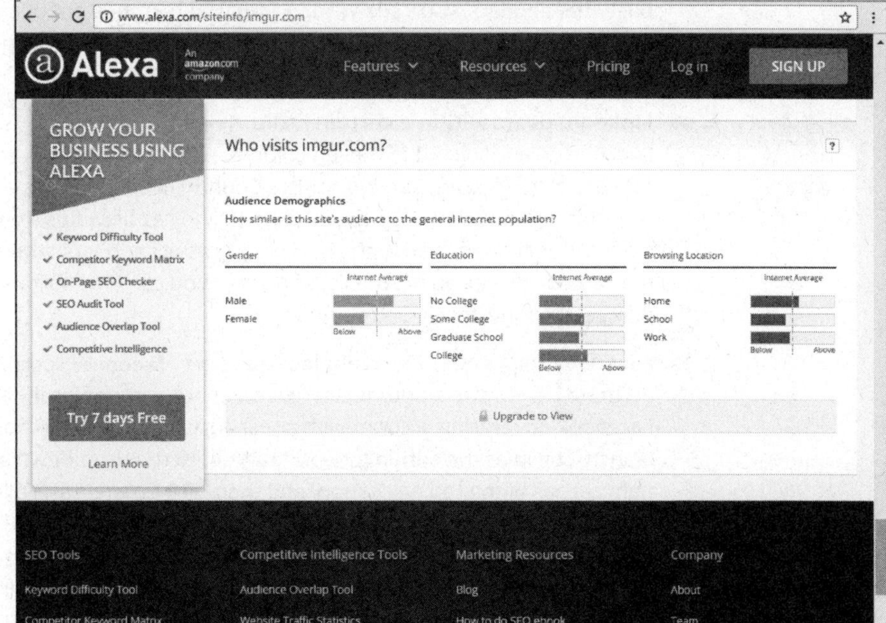

FIGURE 3-1: Quantcast (top) and Alexa (bottom) provide demographic profiles that compare users of a site (in this case, Imgur.com) with the general Internet population.

Geographic location

Marketing by country, region, state, city, zip code, or even neighborhood is the key for location-based social media outlets, such as Foursquare, or any other form of online marketing that involves local search.

Geographic segmentation also makes sense if your business draws its primary target audience from within a certain distance from your brick-and-mortar storefront. For example, geographic segmentation makes sense for grocery stores, barbershops, gas stations, restaurants, movie theaters, and many other service providers, whether or not your social media service itself is location-based.

Many social media services offer a location search function to assess the number of users in your geographical target area:

- **Twitter users near a specified location (**`https://twitter.com/search-advanced`**):** To find users within 15 miles of a designated location, click the Add Location pin under Places. Your current location appears. Click the text box to view a list of several nearby communities, as well as a search field. For somewhere farther away, enter the name of the city in the search field and click the blue Search button at the bottom of the page. On the search results page that appears, you'll see Who to Follow and Trends options in the left column. To alter the 15-mile default distance, change the mileage display in the grey search box at the very top of the results page.
- **LinkedIn users within a certain radius (**`www.linkedin.com/search`**):** In the Location drop-down list in the left column, select Located In or Near. Additional options appear, including a Country drop-down list, a Postal Code text box, and a Within drop-down list, with choices of radius from 10 to 100 miles. After clicking Search, the number of results appears at the top left of the center column, above the list of names. You can filter further by the degree of connection, if you want.
- **Facebook users near a certain location (**`www.facebook.com`**):** The most accurate way to size a potential target audience geographically is to create a Facebook advertising account with a test ad, which you may choose not to launch. Log in as the admin for your page. Click the drop-down arrow in the right corner of the top navigation, and then click Create Ads. Follow the prompts to create an account and choose an objective for an ad. (For audience research, it doesn't matter which objective you select.) Now click Audience in the Ad Set section of the left column that appears. In the center column, choose Everyone in This Location, and specify the geographical region you want. For the total number of Facebook users, avoid setting any demographic or other parameters. At the top of the right column, find the Audience Definition dial display. Below the dial is a numerical value for

potential reach, which is the total number of Facebook users in the location you requested. For more information, see the section on Facebook advertising in Book 5, Chapter 3.

TIP

If you can't determine the number of potential users for a social media channel in your specific geographic location, use the Help function on the social media channel, check the blog, or contact the company.

Several companies combine geographical information with demographics and behavioral characteristics to segment the market more finely. For example, the Nielsen PRIZM system, available from Tetrad (`www.tetrad.com/demographics/usa/nielsen/#tab-prizm`), offers demo-geographic data organized into 66 distinct sub-segments, some of which are described in Table 3-1. (You can download the entire list at `www.tetrad.com/pub/prices/PRIZMNE_Clusters.pdf`.) Various segments, shown in Figure 3-2, can be viewed at the zip code level by using the Claritas tool at `https://segmentationsolutions.nielsen.com/mybestsegments/Default.jsp?ID=20`.

TABLE 3-1 **Top-Level Demo-Geographic Social Groups from Nielsen PRIZM**

Name	Description
Urban Uptown	Wealthiest urban (highest density) consumers (five sub-segments)
Midtown Mix	Midscale, ethnically diverse, urban population (three sub-segments)
Urban Cores	Modest income, affordable housing, urban living (four sub-segments)
Elite Suburbs	Affluent, suburban elite (four sub-segments)
Affluentials	Comfortable suburban lifestyle (six sub-segments)
Middleburbs	Middle-class suburbs (five sub-segments)
Inner Suburbs	Downscale inner suburbs of metropolitan areas (four sub-segments)
Second City Society	Wealthy families in smaller cities on fringes of metro areas (three sub-segments)
City Centers	Low income, satellite cities with mixed demographics (five sub-segments)
Micro-City Blues	Downscale residents in second cities (five sub-segments)
Landed Gentry	Wealthy Americans in small towns (five sub-segments)
Country Comfort	Upper-middle-class homeowners in bedroom communities (five sub-segments)
Middle America	Middle-class homeowners in small towns and exurbs (six sub-segments)
Rustic Living	Most isolated towns and rural areas (six sub-segments)

Reproduced with permission of The Nielsen Company; Source: Nielsen Claritas

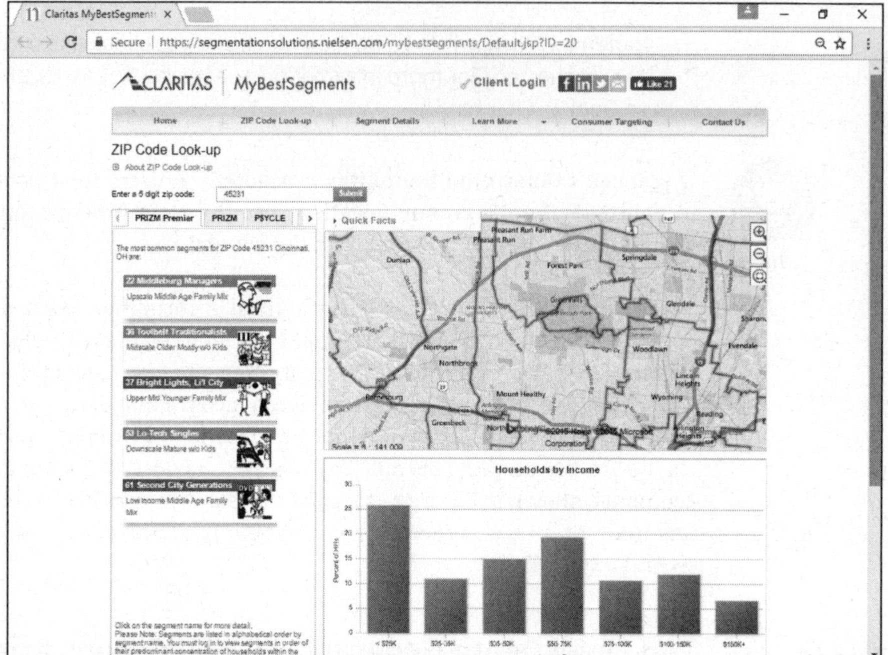

FIGURE 3-2: The My Best Segments tool from Claritas allows you view market segmentation at the zip code level.

Purchasing behavior in different life stages

Rather than look at a target market solely in terms of demographics, *life stage analysis* considers what people are doing with their lives, recognizing that it may affect media behavior and spending patterns.

For interesting details about the demographics of Internet users who access five of the most popular social media channels, visit the Pew Research Center at `www.pewinternet.org/2015/08/19/the-demographics-of-social-media-users`.

Purchasing behavior may also differ by life stages, such as the family life cycle, as shown in Table 3-2. Note that the family life cycle described in the table may not accurately reflect the wider range of today's lifestyles.

REMEMBER

You're looking for a fit between the profile of your target audience and that of the social media service.

REMEMBER

With more flexible timing for going through life passages, demographic analysis isn't enough for many types of products and services. Women may have children later in life; many older, nontraditional students go back to college; some retirees reenter the workforce to supplement Social Security earnings. What your prospective customers do each day may influence what they buy and which media outlets they use more than their age or location.

TABLE 3-2 Stage in the Family Life Cycle

Life Stage	Sample Products or Services They Buy
Single, no children (a.k.a Bachelor Stage)	Fashionable clothing, vehicles
Newly Married Couples, no children	Good furniture, new homes, insurance
Family Nest 1, young children	Baby food and toys, children's items, activities, and education
Family Nest 2, older children	College, possibly travel and furniture
Empty nest, children gone	Vacations, hobbies, savings for retirement
Solitary survivor	Savings, accommodations, medical expenses

Source: Adapted from http://www.marketing91.com/family-life-cycle

For instance, the Pew Research Center found in 2015 that 75 percent of smartphone users access a social-networking site at least once a week (`www.pewresearch.org/fact-tank/2015/04/01/6-facts-about-americans-and-their-smartphones`).

Psychographics or lifestyle

Psychographic segmentation divides a market by social class, lifestyle, or the shared activities, interests, and opinions of prospective customers. It helps identify groups in a social-networking service or other, smaller, social networks that attract users who meet your desired profile.

Behavioral segmentation, which is closely related, divides potential buyers based on their uses, responses, or attitudes toward a product or service. To obtain this information about your customers, consider including a quick poll as part of your e-newsletter, website, or blog. Although the results from those who reply may not be exactly representative of your total customer base — or that of prospective customers — a survey gives you some starter data.

REMEMBER

Don't confuse the psychographic profile of a group with personality traits specific to an individual.

Psychographic segmentation, such as that found at `http://strategicbusinessinsights.com/vals/usframework2015-08.png`, helps you identify not only where to promote your company but also how to craft your message. For instance, understanding your specific target group, its mind-set, and its lifestyle might help you appeal to customers such as the Innovators described at that URL; they might be interested in your high-end line of fashion, home decor, or vacation destinations. Or you might target Experiencers at that URL for a wild new restaurant, a zipline adventure, or an energy drink.

TIP

To develop a better understanding of psychographic profiling, take the quick VALS (Values and Life Styles) survey yourself at `www.strategicbusinessinsights.com/vals/presurvey.shtml`.

Affinity groups

Segmenting by *affinity group* (a group of people who share similar interests or participate in similar activities) fills in the blank at the end of the "People who like this interest or activity also like . . . " statement. Because psychographic segmentation uses activity as a subsection, that approach is somewhat similar.

For example, in Figure 3-3, Quantcast estimates other interests of visitors to Goodreads (`www.goodreads.com`) based on their browsing behavior under the General Interests option. (This data is available only for *quantified sites* — that is, sites for which the site owners have verified the data.) A check mark to the right of the name of the site indicates that it is quantified; otherwise you see the label "not quantified."

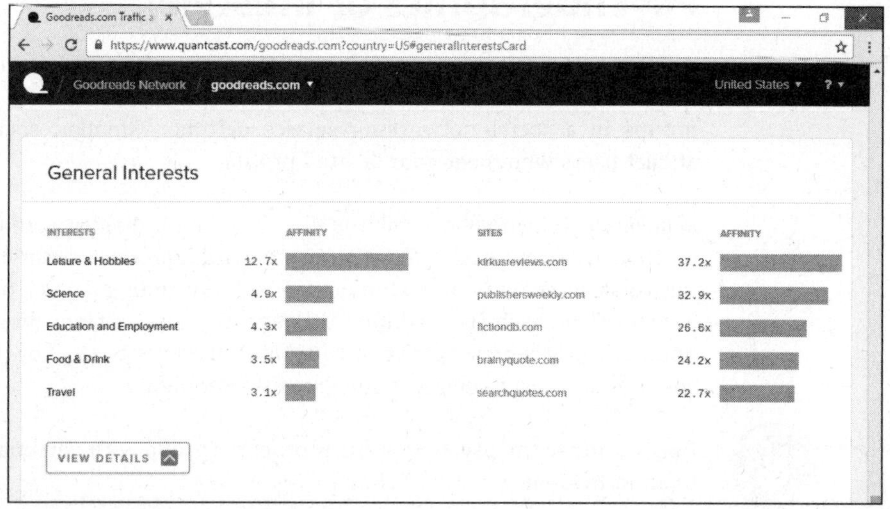

FIGURE 3-3: Quantcast estimates topics that interest users of Goodreads.

On Alexa, scroll down to the Related Links section for a list of the top ten sites related to the target site in various ways, or click Categories with Related Sites to view sites that fit in the same classifications as the target site.

TIP

For information on clickstream analysis (where visitors come from and where they go), see Book 9, Chapter 6.

By using Quantcast and Alexa in this way, you can obtain public information about visits to specific social media services or to your competitors' or other related businesses' websites. You can also use these services to profile your own business, although your website might be too small to provide more than rough estimates. If your business is too small, estimate the interest profile for your target market by running Quantcast for a verified, large corporation that offers a similar product or service.

TIP

Sign up for free, direct measurement of your apps and websites at `www.quantcast.com/user/signup`. Alexa's paid options include Certified Site Metrics, if you want an independent, direct measurement of your site traffic and a more accurate site ranking. To get certified, you'll need to sign up for one of the paid options and install Alexa's Certify Code on your site. You can choose whether or not to display your results to the public.

Otherwise, consider polling your customers to find out more about their specific interests.

You can also use Google Trends (`www.google.com/trends/explore#cmpt=q`) to search by the interest categories shown in Table 3-3. Click All Categories at the top of the page to open a drop-down list. Google Trends uses real-time search data to estimate customer interest in various topics over time. You can select specific keywords, time periods, or locations for additional detail.

TABLE 3-3 Main Categories Available on Google Trends

Arts & Entertainment	Autos & Vehicles	Beauty & Fitness
Books & Literature	Business & Industrial	Computers & Electronics
Finance	Food & Drink	Games
Health	Hobbies & Leisure	Home & Garden
Internet & Telecom	Jobs & Education	Law & Government
News	Online Communities	People & Society
Pets & Animals	Real Estate	Reference
Science	Shopping	Sports
Travel		

Researching B2B Markets

Market research and social media choices for business-to-business (B2B) markets are somewhat different from business-to-consumer (B2C) markets because the sales cycle is different. Usually, B2B companies have a longer sales cycle, high-ticket purchases, and multiple people who play a role in closing a sale; consequently, B2B marketing requires a different social media presence.

In terms of social media, more B2B marketing efforts focus on branding, top-of-mind visibility, customer support, customer loyalty, and problem-solving compared to more sales-focused messages from B2C companies.

TIP

One key step in B2B marketing is to identify people who make the buying decision. Professional social networks such as LinkedIn, Networking for Professionals, or others on www.sitepoint.com/social-networking-sites-for-business may help you research people on your B2B customer or prospect lists.

According to research by the Content Marketing Institute, more than 93 percent of all B2B marketers use some form of social media (http://contentmarketinginstitute.com/wp-content/uploads/2015/09/2016_B2B_Report_Final.pdf). As shown in Figure 3-4, B2B firms may emphasize different forms of social media than B2C businesses. In many cases, the choice of social media varies by company size, industry type, experience with social media, and the availability of budgetary and human resources.

For more information on using social media for B2B marketing, visit one of these links:

- www.business2community.com/social-media/47-superb-social-media-marketing-stats-facts-01431126
- www.socialmediaexaminer.com/wp-content/uploads/2016/05/SocialMediaMarketingIndustryReport2016.pdf
- http://webbiquity.com/social-media-marketing/33-thought-provoking-b2b-social-media-and-marketing-stats
- www.mdgadvertising.com/blog/top-2016-marketing-statistics-marketers-need-to-know-now

HubSpot (www.hubspot.com/marketing-statistics) also offers a range of B2B market research tools, with additional webinars at https://library.hubspot.com/webinar.

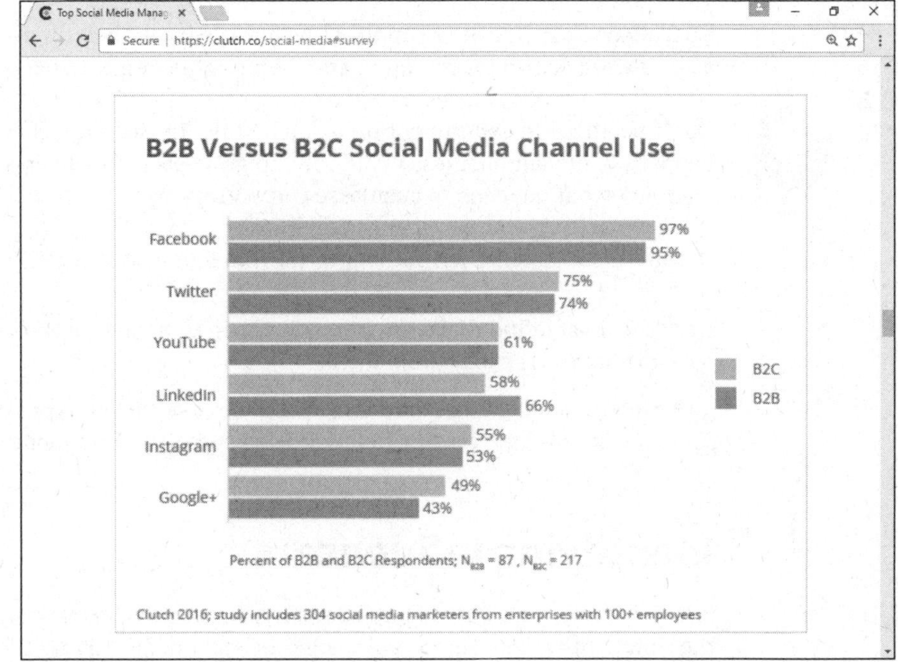

Clutch.co report authored by Sarah Patrick

FIGURE 3-4: B2C (light grey rows) and B2B (dark grey rows) businesses often utilize different social media channels.

As always, the key is ensuring that your customers are using the type of social media you're considering. Use the search feature and group options on major social-networking sites to test your list of existing customers. Chances are good that if a large number of your existing customers are using that service, it will be a good source for future customers as well.

In addition to participating in general market research, you might want to try SimilarSites (`www.similarsites.com`), which not only assists with research on social media alternatives that reach your target market but also helps you find companies that compete with yours.

TIP

Check competing sites for inbound links from other sites, as well as their outbound links, to see how they reach their customers.

Conducting Other Types of Market Research Online

The amount of research available online can be paralyzing. A well-crafted search yields most, if not all, of the social-marketing research you need. You aren't writing an academic paper; you're running a business with limited time and resources. Set aside a week or two for research, and then start laying out your approach.

TIP

Don't be afraid to experiment on a small scale. In the end, what matters is what happens with your business while you integrate social media into your marketing plan, not what happens to businesses on average.

Despite these statements, you might want to touch on two other research points:

- **The most influential sites, posters, or pages on your preferred social media:** You can learn from them.
- **Understanding what motivates people to use certain types of social media:** Make the content you provide meet their expectations and desires.

Identifying influencers

Whether you have a B2B or B2C company, you gain valuable insight by reviewing the comments of *influencers* (companies or individuals driving the conversation in your industry sector). For example, to see the most popular posters on Twitter, use Twitaholic at `http://twitaholic.com` to view by number of updates or number of followers, as shown in Figure 3-5.

You may be surprised to find that the most frequent posters aren't necessarily the ones with the most followers, and vice versa.

For additional tools to identify influencers on various social media channels, check out the lists at Brandwatch (`www.brandwatch.com/2015/02/top-7-free-tools-influencer-marketing`) or Ragan (`www.ragan.com/socialmedia/articles/9_tools_to_find_industry_influencers_47951.aspx`).

These sites can help you identify people you might want to follow for research purposes. You can find more information about tools for identifying influencers for each of the major services in their respective minibooks.

Understanding why people use social media services

The expectation that people gravitate toward different types of social media to meet different needs seems reasonable. The challenge, of course, is to match what people seek with particular social sites.

The Twitaholic.com Top 100 Twitterholics based on Updates

#	Name (Screen Name)	Location	URL	Followers	Following	Updates	Joined
1.	ヴェネティス @VENETHIS			43,394	34	37,771,125	88 months ago
2.	魔剤? @__sa__sa__	[illegible]	[illegible]	79	2	7,099,731	Details...
3.	旧マクロ塾@お受験 @__Soo__	不可視境界線		4,493	292	7,083,295	59 months ago
4.	Twitter Suggests @twittersuggests	Everywhere	[illegible]	113,882	1	6,923,103	Details...
5.	Noticias Venezuela @notiven	venezuela	[illegible]	25,675	207	4,954,477	Details...

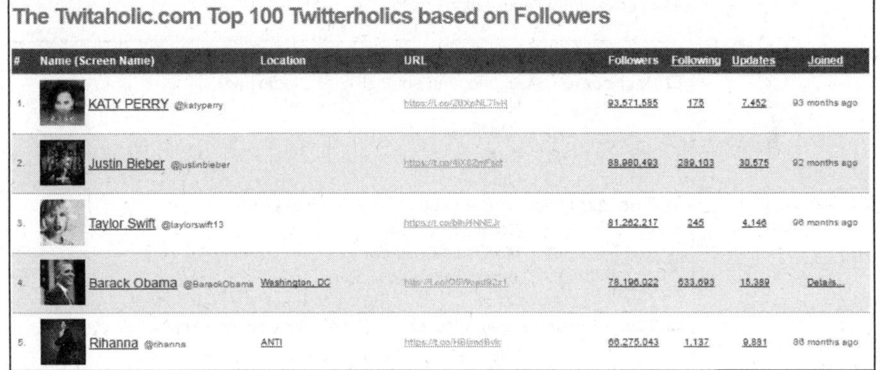

The Twitaholic.com Top 100 Twitterholics based on Followers

#	Name (Screen Name)	Location	URL	Followers	Following	Updates	Joined
1.	KATY PERRY @katyperry		[illegible]	93,571,585	175	7,452	93 months ago
2.	Justin Bieber @justinbieber		[illegible]	88,980,493	289,103	30,575	92 months ago
3.	Taylor Swift @taylorswift13		[illegible]	81,262,217	245	4,146	96 months ago
4.	Barack Obama @BarackObama	Washington, DC	[illegible]	78,196,022	633,693	15,389	Details...
5.	Rihanna @rihanna	ANTI	[illegible]	66,275,043	1,137	9,881	88 months ago

FIGURE 3-5: Twitaholic ranks the most influential tweeters by number of updates (top) or number of followers (bottom).

A review of successful social media models may spark creative ideas for your own campaign.

Setting Up Your Social Media Marketing Plan

You can dive into social media marketing headfirst and see what happens. Or you can take the time to research, plan, execute, and evaluate your approach. The Social Media Marketing Plan, shown in Figure 3-6, is for people taking the latter approach. (You can download the form at `www.dummies.com/go/socialmediamarketingaio4e`.)

REMEMBER

Plan your work; work your plan.

Social Media Marketing Form Tactical Options

Company Name______________________________ **Date**______________

Hub Site(s) (URLs of website or blog with domain name to which traffic will be driven)

____

Standard Social Media Identification Name/Handle______________________

Social Media Project Director ______________________

Social Media Team Members & Tasks ____________ ____________

____________ ____________

____________ ____________

Programming/Technical Team ____________ ____________

Social Media Policy URL ______________________

Select boxes for all applications used.

SOCIAL MEDIA PLANNING

- ❑ **Dashboard** (select one, and enter URL and login info)
  - ❍ Hootsuite
  - ❍ NetVibes
  - ❍ Custom
  - ❍ Other
- ❑ **Calendar** (select one, and enter URL and login info)
  - ❍ Google Calendar
  - ❍ MS Office Calendar
  - ❍ Yahoo Calendar
  - ❍ Other
- ❑ **Social sharing service** (select one, and enter URL and login info)
  - ❍ AddThis
  - ❍ AddtoAny
  - ❍ ShareThis
  - ❍ Other
- ❑ **Social media resources** (enter at least one resource site or blog to follow)
  - ❍

SOCIAL MEDIA TOOLKIT

- ❑ **Monitoring** (select at least one, and enter name, URL, and login info)
  - ❍ Blog monitoring tool
  - ❍ Brand reputation/sentiment tool with fee (e.g., BrandsEye)
  - ❍ Topic monitoring tool (e.g., Google Trends, Addictomatic)
  - ❍ Google Alerts
  - ❍ HowSociable
  - ❍ IceRocket
  - ❍ Mention
  - ❍ Trackur
  - ❍ Twitter monitoring tool
  - ❍ WhosTalkin
  - ❍ Other

FIGURE 3-6: Build a social media marketing plan for your company.

- ❑ **Distribution tools** (select at least one, and enter name, URL, and login info)
  - ❍ RSS/Atom feeds
  - ❍ Buffer
  - ❍ Hootsuite
  - ❍ OnlyWire
  - ❍ TweetDeck
  - ❍ Other
- ❑ **Update notification tools** (select at least one, and enter name, URL, and login info)
  - ❍ Pingdom
  - ❍ GooglePing.com
  - ❍ Other
- ❑ **URL clipping tool** (select at least one, and enter name, URL, and login info)
  - ❍ Bitly
  - ❍ TinyURL
  - ❍ Other
- ❑ **E-commerce tool or widget** (select one, and enter URL, and login info)
  - ❍ Amazon widget
  - ❍ Ecwid
  - ❍ Etsy widget
  - ❍ PayPal widget
  - ❍ Shopify
  - ❍ Storefront Social
  - ❍ Custom
  - ❍ Other
- ❑ **Search engine submissions** (if needed, enter URL, login info, and submission dates)
  - ❍ Automated XML feed
  - ❍ Yahoo!/Bing search engine submission
  - ❍ Google search engine submission
  - ❍ Specialty search submission sites
  - ❍ Other

STANDARD SET PRIMARY KEYWORDS/TAGS

(Enter at least 8 but no more than 30)

- ❑
- ❑
- ❑
- ❑
- ❑
- ❑
- ❑
- ❑

STANDARD SET DESCRIPTION TAG

(Enter 150-character description, preferably including at least 4 of the preceding keywords)

FIGURE 3-6: continued

Plotting Your Social Media Marketing Strategy

SOCIAL MEDIA SERVICES

❑ **Social bookmarking sites** (select at least one, and enter name, URL, and login info)

- ❍ Delicious
- ❍ Google Bookmarks
- ❍ StumbleUpon
- ❍ Y! Toolbar
- ❍ Other

❑ **Social news sites** (select at least one, and enter name, URL, and login info)

- ❍ Digg
- ❍ Newsvine
- ❍ Reddit
- ❍ Slashdot
- ❍ Other

❑ **Social shopping and specialty bookmark sites** (enter name, URL, and login info for all)

- ❍ StyleHive
- ❍ ThisNext
- ❍ Other

❑ **Blogging sites** (enter name, URL, and login info for all)

- ❍ Blog directory submission site
- ❍ Blog monitoring site
- ❍ Blog measuring tool sites
- ❍ Primary blog
- ❍ Other

❑ **Primary social networking services** (select at least one, and enter name, URL, and login info)

Facebook

- ❍ Engagement
- ❍ Events
- ❍ Groups
- ❍ Insights

Twitter

- ❍ Follow Us
- ❍ Hashtags/lists
- ❍ Metrics
- ❍ Tools

LinkedIn

- ❍ Events/answers
- ❍ Groups
- ❍ Follow Us
- ❍ Metrics

Google Plus

- ❍ +1 (ratings)
- ❍ Circles
- ❍ Follow Us
- ❍ Metrics

Pinterest

- ❍ Follow Us
- ❍ Metrics

Specialty networks

Other demographic networks (e.g., Grandparents)

Other professional networks (e.g., Ryze)

Other vertical industry networks (e.g., DeviantArt)

FIGURE 3-6: continued

- ❑ **Social media content-sharing sites** (enter name, URL, and login info for all)
  - ❍ Instagram
  - ❍ Pinterest
  - ❍ Podcasts
  - ❍ Slideshare
  - ❍ Snapchat
  - ❍ Ustream
  - ❍ Vimeo
  - ❍ Vine
  - ❍ YouTube
  - ❍ Other
- ❑ **Social community sites** (enter name, URL, and login info for all)
  - ❍ Forums
  - ❍ Ning
  - ❍ Other
- ❑ **Other social media services** (enter name, URL, and login info for all)
  - ❍ Collective shopping (e.g., Groupon, Living Social)
  - ❍ Geolocation (e.g., Foursquare)
  - ❍ Social Mobile
  - ❍ Other

SOCIAL MEDIA ADVERTISING

- ❑ **Social platforms with paid advertising** (enter the URL and login info for all the options you select)
  - ❍ Facebook
  - ❍ Instagram
  - ❍ LinkedIn
  - ❍ Pinterest
  - ❍ Twitter
  - ❍ Other
- ❑ **Advertising metrics** (be sure to the enter name, account login URL, user name, and password for each social media platform on your spreadsheet)
  - ❍ Click-through rate (CTR)
  - ❍ Cost per click (CPC)
  - ❍ Cost per thousand impressions (CPM)
  - ❍ Conversion rate
  - ❍ Cost per conversion

SOCIAL MEDIA METRICS

- ❑ **Key performance indicators** (enter at least 8, e.g., traffic, CPM, CPC, conversion rate, ROI)
  - ❍
  - ❍
  - ❍
  - ❍
  - ❍
  - ❍
  - ❍
  - ❍
- ❑ **Analytical/statistical tool** (select at least one, and enter name, URL and login info)
  - ❍ Google Analytics
  - ❍ Sitetrail's StatsTool
  - ❍ StatCounter
  - ❍ Yahoo! Analytics
  - ❍ Other

FIGURE 3-6: continued

Courtesy of Watermelon Mountain Web Marketing: www.watermelonweb.com

Depending on your marketing plan's complexity and the availability of support, think in terms of a timeline of 3 to 12 months to complete the following steps. Estimate spending half your time in the planning phase, one-quarter in execution, and one-quarter in evaluation and modification. To set up your own custom social media marketing plan, follow these steps:

1. Do market research and online observation.
2. Draft marketing goals, objectives, and your marketing plan using the form in Figure 3-6.
3. Get your marketing ducks in a row with in-house preparation:
   - Hiring, outsourcing, or selecting in-house staff
   - Training
   - Team-building
   - Writing a social media policy document
4. Complete preparatory development tasks:
   - Designing advertising creatives
   - Content overview (an outline of which marketing messages you want to send out when)
   - Measurement plan and metric implementation
   - Social media tool selection and dashboard development
   - Social media activity calendar setup (see Book 1, Chapter 4)
   - Programming and content modifications to existing website(s), as needed
5. Create accounts and a pilot social media program.
6. Evaluate the pilot program, debug it, and modify it, as needed.
7. Launch and promote your social media campaign one service at a time.
8. Measure and modify social media in a process of constant feedback and reiteration.

TIP

Don't be afraid to build a pilot program — or several — into your plan to see what works.

SOCIAL MEDIA HELPS RAISE THE DOUGH

In 1987, the Cole brothers established a family restaurant in Irving, TX, with a focus on friendly service and simple, handmade. Italian food. Today, i Fratelli Pizza (`www.ifratelli.net`), which now focuses on pizza, has grown to 5 franchise stores, 10 corporate-owned stores, and 400 team members. The company has always valued charitable giving and active involvement in the community.

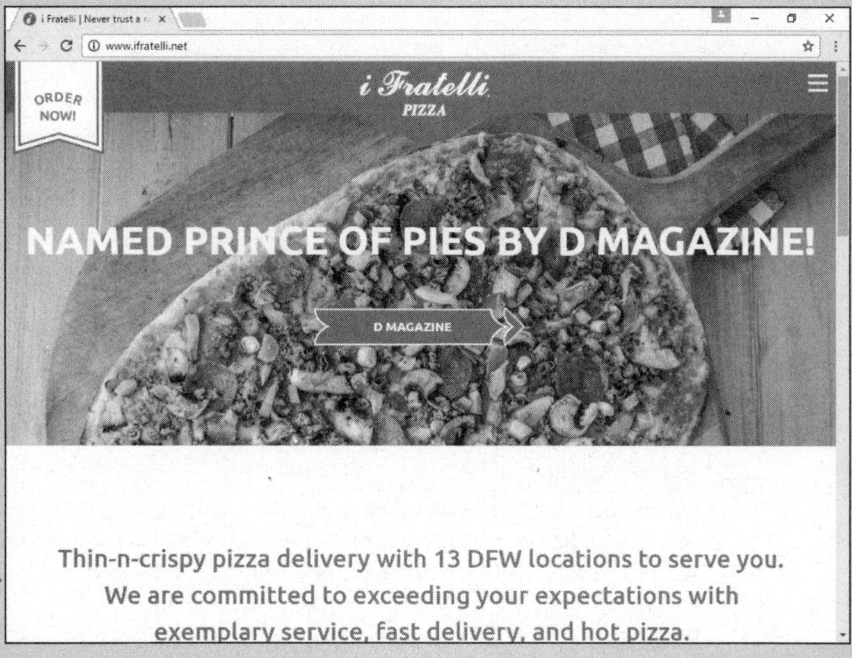

Courtesy of i Fratelli Pizza

The company began using social media in 2010 as a no-cost method for staying "top of mind" with its patrons. Starting with Facebook, i Fratelli soon added a blog called "The Sauce," followed by Twitter and Instagram.

As it approached its 25th anniversary in 2012, the company decided to involve the community in its charity efforts, creating a weekly promotion called Pizza *Dough*Nation. Residents nominate locally based nonprofits, churches, and high school booster clubs to receive 15 percent of the value of orders placed on a specific day using the recipient's name, as seen in the following blog. The blog also includes a description of the program, a nomination form, and tips for organizations to promote their fundraiser themselves.

(continued)

Plotting Your Social Media Marketing Strategy

(continued)

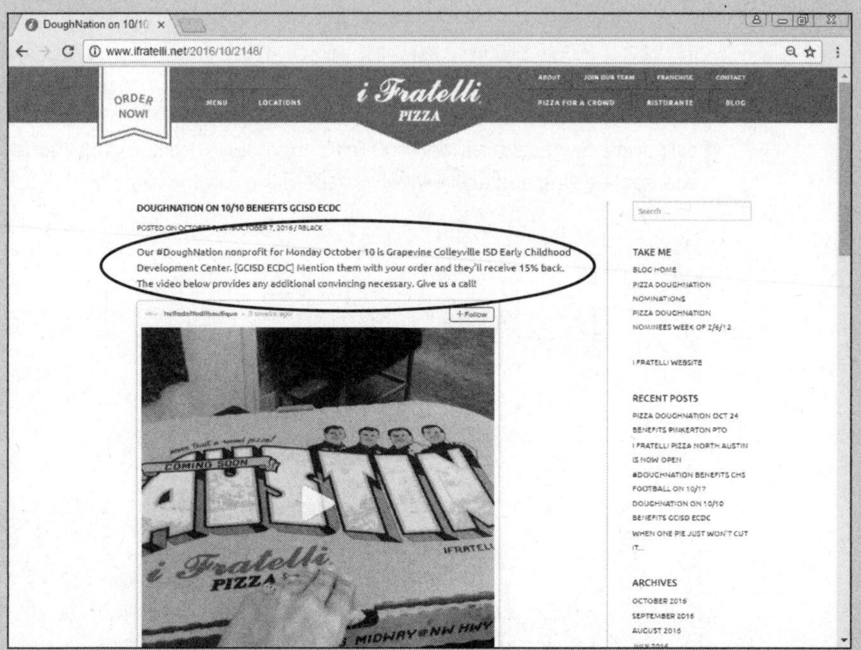

Courtesy of i Fratelli Pizza

The company has done well by doing good. Marketing Manager Rachel Black observes that the company's philanthropic giving has risen as a result of the promotion, now in its seventh year; as of 2016, more than 100 non-profits have benefited.

While giving grew, so did site traffic, Facebook likes, viral sharing, sales, and positive branding. "The *Dough*Nation program allows us to appeal to a new specific market (for example, a congregation or booster club) weekly, plus it gives us content to talk about across all platforms," she explains. The specific results, even in the first few months, were impressive: a tripling of Facebook impressions, a five-fold growth in retweets on Twitter, and a growth in ROI (in terms of increased sales) of more than 300 percent.

The company and the receiving organization both use social media to promote the fundraiser. For i Fratelli, that means using tweets for geotargeted messaging, cross-promoting among Facebook, Twitter, Instagram, and the blog, and identifying influencers to tell the story.

While Black finds that Facebook is the best channel to drive participation in Pizza *Dough*Nation, she always promotes the fundraisers on all its channels. (See an example on its Twitter feed in the nearby figure.) At the same time, the sponsored organization shares the promotional burden by publicizing the fundraiser among its own members and supporters.

Courtesy of i Fratelli Pizza

Black says that the company now spends about 20 hours per week on social media, with one team member creating all the social content in-house for four to five posts per week for the restaurant. Initially, i Fratelli used an outside agency to create and implement the master promotional campaign for *Dough*Nation but now handles that in-house as well.

Although Black uses Google Analytics to monitor a pay-per-click AdWords campaign for the restaurant business, she doesn't actively monitor social statistics. While she occasionally does a Facebook ad campaign to promote a specific sweepstakes or event, Black has spent less than $500 total on Facebook-sponsored posts.

While the *Dough*Nation campaign seems simple, it was carefully planned and executed. Black points out that it's critical to target the correct audience when promoting a fundraiser on social media. "Our *Dough*Nation organizations have specific, sometimes small, groups of supporters, which need to be targeted directly." Organizations get the best results when they use their own platforms to reach their audience and schedule the promotion in advance.

(continued)

(continued)

"It's important to use social media to your best advantage by understanding how others utilize the platforms," Black advises. "For instance, we will tag influencers such as the Convention and Visitors Bureau on *Dough*Nation posts so they can retweet to their followers. The more post and re-post action you can capitalize on, the wider your audience. We also take the time to engage with others' posts weekly; when it comes time for our promotions, we have a captive audience ready to return the favor."

The following list of sites constitute i Fratelli's web presence:

- `www.ifratelli.net`
- `www.facebook.com/ifratellipizza`
- `https://twitter.com/iFratelliPizza`
- `www.instagram.com/nevertrustaroundpizza`
- `http://www.ifratelli.net/blog`

IN THIS CHAPTER

- » Scheduling social media activities
- » Building a team
- » Writing a social media policy
- » Keeping it legal
- » Protecting your brand's reputation

Chapter 4
Managing Your Cybersocial Campaign

After you create a Social Media Marketing Plan, one major task you face is managing the effort. If you're the only one doing the work, the simplest — and likely the hardest — task is making time for it. Although social media need not carry a lot of upfront development costs, it does carry a significant labor cost.

In this chapter, we discuss how to set up a schedule to keep your social media activity from draining all your available time. If you have employees, both you and your company may benefit if you delegate some of the social media tasking to them. You can also supplement your in-house staff with limited assistance from outside professionals.

REMEMBER

For small businesses, it's your money or your life. If you can't afford to hire help to work on social media, you carve it out of the time you've allocated to other marketing activities — unless, of course, you want to add a minimum of another two hours to your workweek.

Finally, this chapter carries a word of caution. Make sure that everyone posting to a social media outlet knows your policy about what is and isn't acceptable, as well as how to protect the company's reputation and confidential material. As you launch your marketing boat onto the churning waters of social media, you should ensure that everyone is wearing a legal life preserver.

Managing Your Social Media Schedule

As you know from the rest of your business experience, if something isn't important enough to schedule, it never gets done. Social media, like the rest of your marketing efforts, can easily be swallowed up by day-to-day demands. You must set aside time for it and assign tasks to specific people.

TIP

Allocate a minimum of two hours per week per platform if you're going to participate in social media, rather than set up pages and abandon them. Otherwise, you simply don't see a return from your initial investment in setup. If you don't have much time, stick with the marketing you're already doing.

Controlling the time commitment

Social media can become addictive. If you truly like what you're doing, the time problem might reverse. Rather than spend too little time, you spend too much. You might find it difficult to avoid the temptation of continually reading what others have to say about your business or spending all your time tweeting, streaming, and posting.

Just as you stick to your initial dollar budget, keep to your initial time budget, at least for the first month until you see what works. After you determine which techniques have the greatest promise, you can rearrange your own efforts as well as your team's.

REMEMBER

Social media marketing is only part of your online-marketing effort, and online marketing is only part of your overall marketing.

Selecting activity days

One way to control the time you spend on social media is to select specific days and times for it. Many business people set aside regularly recurring blocks of time, such as a quiet Friday afternoon, for marketing-related tasks, whether they're conducting competitor research, writing press releases or newsletters for the following week, obtaining inbound links, or handling their social media marketing tasks.

Other people prefer to allocate their time early in the morning, at lunchtime, or just before leaving work each evening. The time slot you choose usually doesn't matter, unless you're offering a time-dependent service, such as accepting to-go orders for breakfast burritos via Twitter.

TIP

Whatever the case, allot time for every task on your Social Media Activity Calendar, followed by the initials of the person responsible for executing the task.

Allowing for ramp-up time

Even if you're the only person involved, allow time for learning before your official social media launch date. Everyone needs time to observe, to master new tools, to practice posting and responding, to experiment, and to decide what works before rolling out your plan.

TIP

Bring your new social media venues online one at a time. This strategy not only helps you evaluate which social media venue works but also reduces stress on you and your staff.

Developing your social date book

There are as many ways to schedule social media activities as there are companies. Whatever you decide, don't leave your schedule to chance.

Larger companies may use sophisticated project management software. Some offer a free trial such as Basecamp (`https://basecamp.com`), Smartsheet (`www.smartsheet.com`), and ProjectLibre (`www.projectlibre.org`), while others are available as freemium proprietary solutions, such as MOOVIA (`https://site.moovia.com`) or as open source programs such as GanttProject (`www.ganttproject.biz`). For more options, see `http://alternativeto.net/software/smartsheet` or `www.techshout.com/alternatives/2013/17/smartsheet-alternatives`. Alternatively, you can schedule tasks using spreadsheet software.

However, the simplest solution may be the best: Calendar software, much of which is free, may be all you need. Paid options may merge schedules for more people and allow customized report formats. Several options are listed in Table 4-1. Look for a solution that lets you

- Choose a display by day, week, or month or longer
- List events or tasks in chronological format
- Select different time frames easily
- Easily schedule repeat activities without requiring duplicate data entry

TIP

If several people are involved in a substantial social media effort, select calendar software that lets you synchronize individual calendars, such as Google, Yahoo!, or Mozilla Lightning. Figure 4-1 shows a sample of a simple social-marketing calendar on Yahoo! The calendar shows the initials of the person responsible. Clicking an event or a task reveals item details, including the time allotted to the task, the sharing level, and whether a reminder is sent and to whom. Figure 4-2 offers an example of an event detail listing in a Google calendar.

TABLE 4-1 **Calendar Software**

Name	URL	Free or Paid
Calendar and Time Management Software for Windows Reviews	`http://download.cnet.com/windows/calendar-and-time-management-software`	Free, shareware, and paid
Connect Daily	`www.mhsoftware.com/connectdaily.htm`	Paid, free trial
EventsLink Network Website Calendar	`www.eventslink.net`	Paid, free trial
Google Calendar	`www.google.com/calendar`	Free
Mozilla Lightning Calendar	`www.mozilla.org/en-us/projects/calendar`	Free, open source
Trumba	`www.trumba.com/connect/default.aspx`	Paid, free trial
Yahoo! Calendar	`http://calendar.yahoo.com`	Free

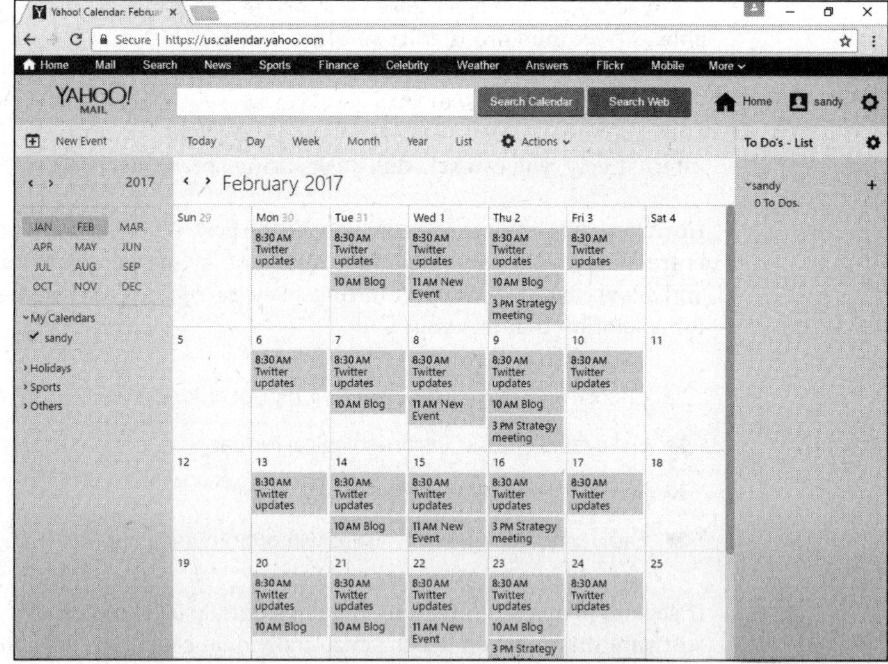

FIGURE 4-1: Using Yahoo! Calendar, you can easily schedule your social media activities.

Courtesy of Watermelon Mountain Web Marketing: `www.watermelonweb.com`

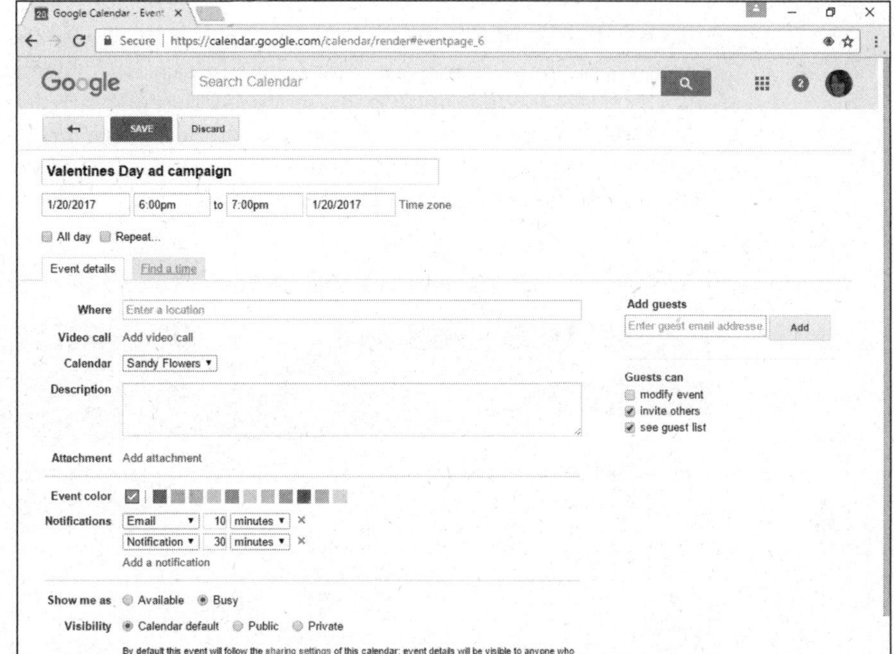

FIGURE 4-2: On the Google Calendar, you can provide specifics for a marketing task by modifying an event detail window.

Courtesy of Watermelon Mountain Web Marketing: `www.watermelonweb.com`

Note: Google and Yahoo! require you to set up an account before you can use their calendars.

REMEMBER

Throughout this book, we refer to this calendar as your *Social Media Activity Calendar*, and we add frequent recommendations of tasks to include on your schedule.

REMEMBER

Set your calendar to private but give access to everyone who needs to be aware of your social media schedule. Depending on the design of your social media program, some outside subcontractors may need access to your calendar to schedule their own production deadlines.

Creating a social media dashboard

Your social media marketing efforts may ultimately involve many tasks: Post to multiple venues; use tools to distribute content to multiple locations; monitor visibility for your company on social media outlets; and measure results by using several analytical tools. Rather than jump back and forth among all these resources, you can save time by using a graphical dashboard or control panel.

Like the dashboard of a car, a social media *dashboard* puts the various required functions at your fingertips in (you hope) an easy-to-understand and easy-to-use visual layout. When you use this approach, the customized dashboard provides easy access in one location to all your social media accounts, tools, and metrics. Figures 4-3 and 4-4 show several tabs of a customized Netvibes dashboard — one for social media postings and another for tools.

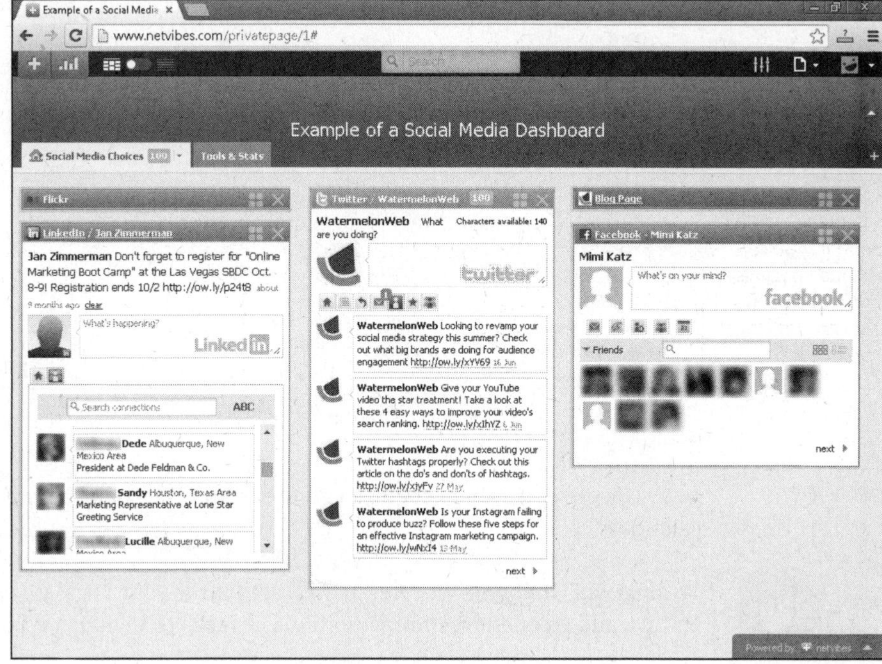

FIGURE 4-3: This mock-up of a social media dashboard from Netvibes gathers the user's various social media services on the Social Media Choices tab.

Courtesy of Watermelon Mountain Web Marketing: www.watermelonweb.com

The items on your primary dashboard may link to other application-specific dashboards, especially for analytical tools and high-end enterprise solutions; those application dashboards are designed primarily to compare the results of multiple social media campaigns.

Table 4-2 provides a list of dashboard resources, some of which are generic (such as My Yahoo!) and others, such as Netvibes and Hootsuite (see Figure 4-5), which are specific to social media.

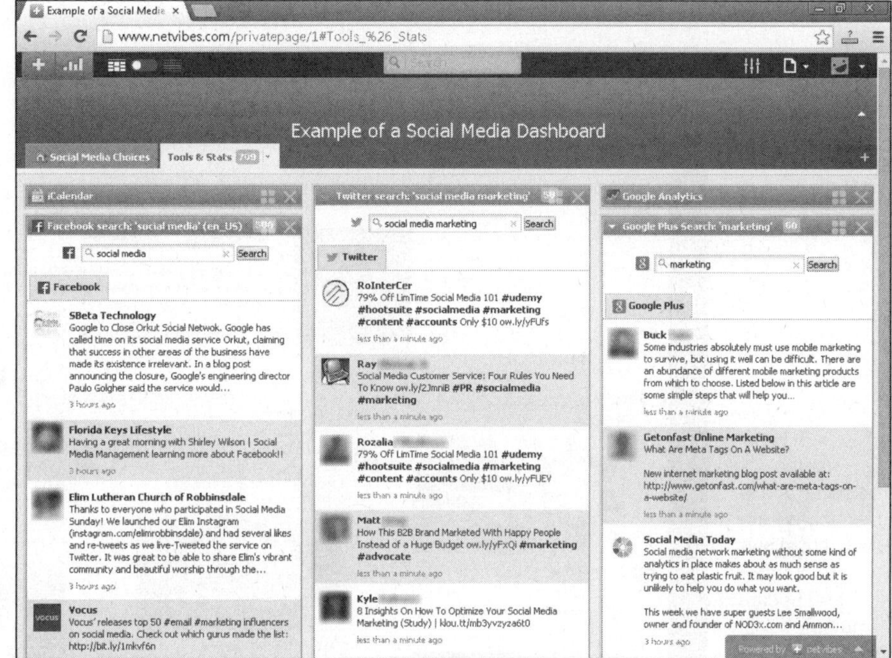

FIGURE 4-4: The Tools & Stats tab of this mock-up Netvibes dashboard displays tools for distributing, monitoring, searching, and analyzing data.

Courtesy of Watermelon Mountain Web Marketing: `www.watermelonweb.com`

TABLE 4-2 **Social Media Dashboard Resources**

Name	URL	Description
Hootsuite	`www.hootsuite.com`	Free, customizable dashboard for social media; paid option available
MarketingProfs	`www.marketingprofs.com/articles/2010/3454/how-to-create-your-marketing-dashboard-in-five-easy-steps`	Instructions for customizing a dashboard (you can close the pop-up window asking you to sign up)
MeetEdgar	`https://meetedgar.com`	A categorized library with smart scheduling; starts at $50/month
My Yahoo!	`http://my.yahoo.com`	Free, customizable Yahoo! home page
Netvibes	`http://netvibes.com`	Free, customizable dashboard for social media
Search Engine Land	`http://searchengineland.com/b2b-social-media-dashboard-a-powerful-tool-to-uncover-key-customer-insights-17839`	Tips on how to use a social media dashboard for B2B

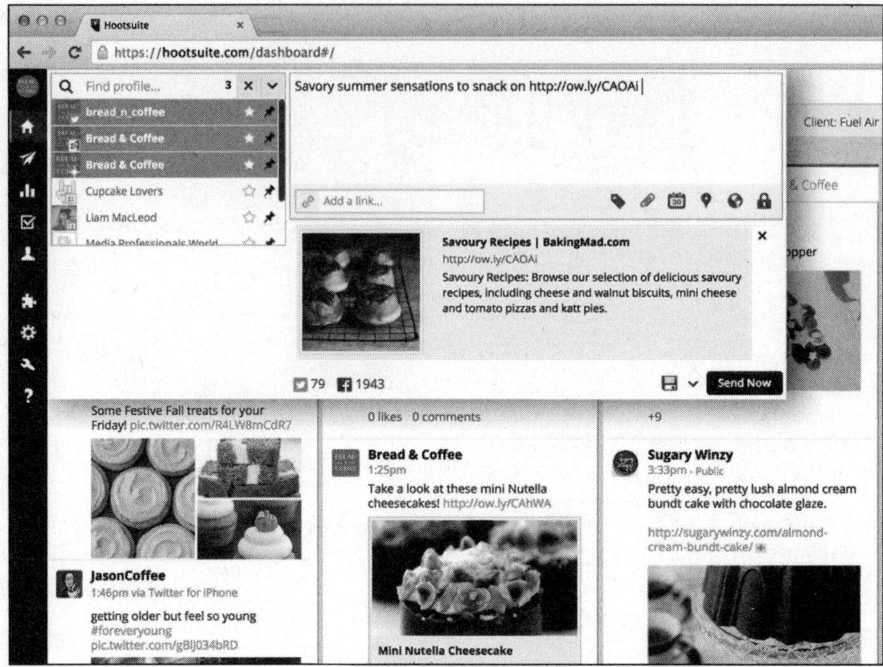

FIGURE 4-5: The social media dashboard from Hootsuite allows you to monitor and update multiple social network services.

Courtesy of Hootsuite

Before you try to build a dashboard, list all the social media sources, services, and reports you want to display, along with their associated URLs, usernames, and passwords. It will help if you indicate whether services are interconnected (for example, note whether you're using a syndication service to update multiple social media at the same time) and how often statistical reports should be updated for each service (hourly, daily, weekly, or monthly).

The more complex your social media campaign, the more functionality your dashboard needs.

TIP

Dashboards sound simple to use, but they can be a bit of a challenge to set up. In some cases, your programmer needs to create or customize *widgets* (mini-applications). Plan to create and test several versions of the dashboard until everyone is satisfied with the results.

Consider implementing password access for approved users to various functions in the dashboard. Some users might be constrained to viewing reports, whereas others might be allowed to change the dashboard configuration.

Building Your Social Media Marketing Dream Team

Just for the moment, assume that you have employees who can — and are willing to — share the burden of social media. If you live a rich fantasy life, assume that you might even hire someone to take the lead.

In a larger company, the nexus for control of social media varies: In some cases, it's the marketing department; in others, corporate communications, public relations, sales, or customer support takes the lead. Some companies disperse responsibilities throughout the company and have tens to dozens of people blogging and tweeting.

If your plan requires multiple employees to leverage LinkedIn profiles for B2B reasons, as well as post on multiple blogs in their individual areas of expertise and tweet current events in their departments, your need for coordination will increase.

Be cautious about asking employees to coordinate links and comments with their personal social media accounts. This task should be voluntary. Alternatively, on company time and on an account that "belongs" to your company (using a business email address), ask employees to develop a hybrid personal-and-business account where their personalities can shine. Now, individual privacy and First Amendment rights are respected on their separate personal accounts, and you have no liability for the content they post there.

No matter who does the bulk of the work — your staff members, contractors, or a combination of the two — always monitor your program randomly but regularly. In addition to getting routine reports on the results, log in to your accounts for a few minutes at various times of the day and week to see what's going on. Most dashboards make it easy for you to review posts on your social media in one convenient place.

Seeking a skilled social media director

A good social media director should have an extroverted personality, at least in writing. This person should truly enjoy interacting with others and take intrinsic pleasure in conversation and communication. You might want to look, based on your chosen tactics, for someone who can

- Write quickly and well, with the right tone for your market.
- Listen well, with an ear for your target audiences and their concerns.

- Post without using defamatory language or making libelous statements about competitors.
- Communicate knowledgeably about your company and your products or services.
- Recognize opportunities and develop creative responses or campaigns.
- Work tactfully with others, alerting them when problems or complaints surface.
- Articulate the goals of social media well enough to take a leadership role in encouraging others to explore its potential.
- Analyze situations to draw conclusions from data.
- Adapt to new social media and mobile technologies when they arise.
- Learn quickly (because this field is extremely fluid).

This combination of skills, experience, and personality may be hard to find. Add to it the need to reach different submarkets for different reasons. Now you have several reasons to build a team with a leader, rather than rely on a single individual to handle all your social media needs.

TIP

You usually can't just add social media to someone's task list; be prepared to reassign some tasks to other people.

Depending on the size and nature of your social media effort, your dream team may also need someone with production skills for podcasting or videocasting, or at least for producing and directing the development of those components. Although this person may not need extensive graphical, photographic, presentation, or data-crunching skills, having some skills in each of those areas is helpful.

Hiring 20-somethings (or younger) because they're familiar with social media may sound like a good idea, but people in this age group aren't as likely to be familiar with business protocol and sensitive to business relationships as someone older and more experienced. You might need to allow extra time for training, review, and revision.

Looking inside

Before implementing a social media plan, speak with your employees to invite their input, assess their level of interest in this effort, evaluate existing skill sets, and ascertain social media experience. Consider all these factors before you move forward; by rearranging task assignments or priorities, you may be able to select in-house personnel to handle this new project.

TIP

Leave time for communication, education, and training both at the beginning and on an ongoing basis.

Hiring experts

Think about using professionals for the tech-heavy tasks, such as podcasts, videocasts, or design, unless you're going for the just-us-folks tone. Professionals can get you started by establishing a model for your staff to follow, or you may want to hire them for long-term tasks such as writing or editing your blogs for consistency.

Many advertising agencies, PR firms, search engine optimizers, marketing companies, and copywriters now take on social media contracts. If you've already worked with someone you like, you can start there. If not, select social media professionals the same way you would select any other professional service provider:

- » Ask your local business colleagues for referrals.
- » Check sources such as LinkedIn and Plaxo. If appropriate, post your search criteria on your site, blog, social media outlets, and topic-related sites.
- » Request several price quotes. If your job is large enough, write and distribute a formal request for proposal (RFP).
- » Review previous work completed by the contractors.
- » Check references.

Creating a Social Media Marketing Policy

Even if you're the only person involved in social media marketing at the beginning, write up a few general guidelines for yourself that you can expand later. Figure 4-6 shows a sample social media policy; you can download other examples from `http://socialmedia.policytool.net`.

To generate a Social Media Marketing Policy customized for your company, click the Start Now button in the bottom right of the page and answer the series of questions that appears.

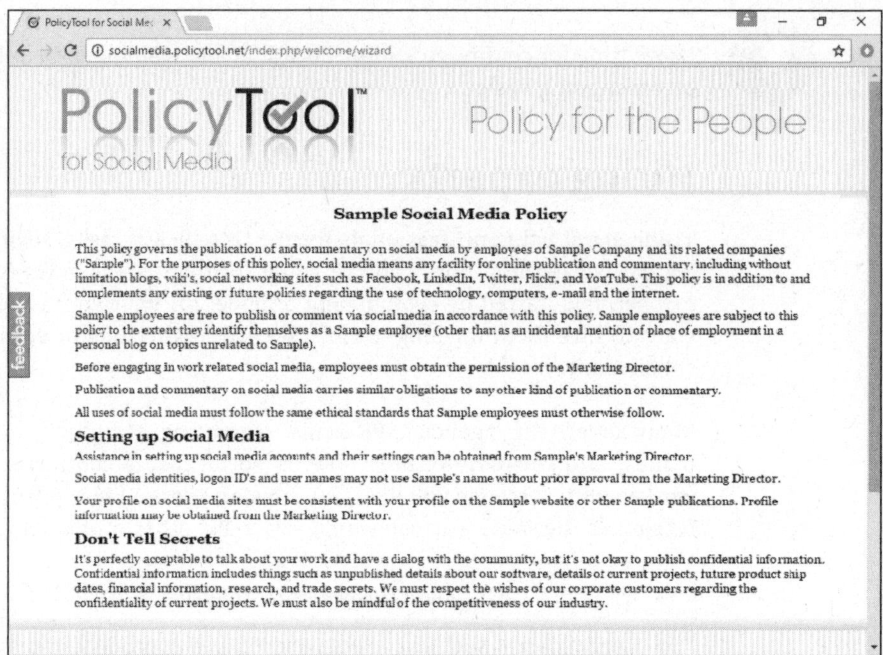

Sample Social Media Policy

This policy governs the publication of and commentary on social media by employees of Sample Company and its related companies ("Sample"). For the purposes of this policy, social media means any facility for online publication and commentary, including without limitation blogs, wiki's, social networking sites such as Facebook, LinkedIn, Twitter, Flickr, and YouTube. This policy is in addition to and complements any existing or future policies regarding the use of technology, computers, e-mail and the internet.

Sample employees are free to publish or comment via social media in accordance with this policy. Sample employees are subject to this policy to the extent they identify themselves as a Sample employee (other than as an incidental mention of place of employment in a personal blog on topics unrelated to Sample).

Before engaging in work related social media, employees must obtain the permission of the Marketing Director.

Publication and commentary on social media carries similar obligations to any other kind of publication or commentary.

All uses of social media must follow the same ethical standards that Sample employees must otherwise follow.

Setting up Social Media

Assistance in setting up social media accounts and their settings can be obtained from Sample's Marketing Director.

Social media identities, logon ID's and user names may not use Sample's name without prior approval from the Marketing Director.

Your profile on social media sites must be consistent with your profile on the Sample website or other Sample publications. Profile information may be obtained from the Marketing Director.

Don't Tell Secrets

It's perfectly acceptable to talk about your work and have a dialog with the community, but it's not okay to publish confidential information. Confidential information includes things such as unpublished details about our software, details of current projects, future product ship dates, financial information, research, and trade secrets. We must respect the wishes of our corporate customers regarding the confidentiality of current projects. We must also be mindful of the competitiveness of our industry.

FIGURE 4-6: A basic social media policy may be enough to get you started.

Courtesy of Ellipsis.Digital, a division of rTraction Canada, Inc.

Most policies address the social media issue both in terms of what employees are allowed to do on behalf of the company and what they aren't allowed to do. For example:

- » Employees may not be allowed to use personal social accounts on company time.
- » Some trained employees may be allowed to post customer support replies on behalf of the company, whereas others are responsible for new product information.

For additional information and examples, see the resources listed in Table 4-3.

TIP

To increase compliance, keep your policy short and easy to read. Try to focus on what people *can do* rather than on what they can't do.

A typical policy addresses risk management, intellectual property protection, individual privacy protection, and the respect of your audience, company, and fellow employees. Given the rapidly changing world of social media, you'll have to keep your policy flexible and update it often.

TABLE 4-3 **Social Media Policy Resource Sites**

Name	URL	Description
American Express	www.americanexpress.com/us/small-business/openforum/articles/employee-social-media-policy	Article titled "Employees Gone Wild: 8 Reasons You Need A Social Media Policy TODAY"
ITBusinessEdge	www.itbusinessedge.com/itdownloads	Social media guidelines, templates, and examples; select Policies in the Type drop-down list, and Social Networking in the Topic drop-down list
LikeableMedia Blog	www.likeable.com/blog/2013/04/5-things-brands-should-consider-for-their-social-media-policy	Article titled "5 Must-Haves For Your Brand's Social Media Policy"
LinkedIn	www.linkedin.com/today/post/article/20140320152546-13721119-how-to-create-a-social-media-strategy-that-actually-gets-read	Article titled "How to create a social media strategy that actually gets read"
Mashable	http://mashable.com/2012/10/06/social-media-policy-update	Article titled "Tips for Updating Your Company's Social Media Policy"
NetSphere Strategies	www.netspherestrategies.com/blog/10-items-to-include-in-your-companys-social-media-policy	Free checklist
PolicyTool for Social Media	http://socialmedia.policytool.net	Free social media policy generator
Rocket Lawyer	www.rocketlawyer.com/document/social-media-policy.rl	Free 1-week trial of social media policy generator
Social Media Examiner	www.socialmediaexaminer.com/write-a-social-media-policy	Article titled "How to Write a Social Media Policy to Empower Employees"
Social Media Governance	http://socialmediagovernance.com/policies.php	Free database of policies for review
TechRepublic	www.techrepublic.com/article/how-to-craft-a-social-media-policy	Article titled "How to craft a social media policy"

Try to incorporate the following suggested concepts, adapted from Hootsuite (`https://blog.hootsuite.com/social-media-policy-for-employees`):

- Hold individuals responsible for what they write.
- Be transparent. Disclose who you are, including your company name and title.
- Recognize that clients, prospects, competitors, and potential future employees are part of your audience.
- Be respectful of everyone.
- Understand the tenor of each social media community and follow its precepts.
- Respect copyright, trademarks, and privacy rights.
- Protect your company's confidential trade-secret and proprietary information in addition to client data, especially trade-secret information under nondisclosure agreements.
- Do not allow personal social media activity to interfere with work.

The complexity of your social media policy depends on the extent of your social media marketing effort and the number of people and departments involved. Generally, the larger the company, the longer the policy.

Staying on the Right Side of the Law

Just about everything in social media pushes the limits of existing intellectual property law. So much information is now repeated online that ownership lines are becoming blurred, much to some people's dismay and damage.

When in doubt, don't copy. Instead, use citations, quote marks, and links to the original source. Always go back to the original to ensure that the information is accurate.

Watch blogs such as Mashable (`http://mashable.com/social-media`) and TechCrunch (`https://techcrunch.com`) for information about legal wrangling. New case law, regulations, and conflicts bubble up continually.

Obtaining permission to avoid infringement

WARNING

You can't (legally) use extended content from someone else's website, blog, or social media page on your own site, even if you can save it or download it. Nope, not even if you include a credit line saying where it came from. Not even if you use only a portion of the content and link to the rest. Not text, not graphics, not compiled data, not photos. Nothing. Nada. Nil. Zilch.

Though small text extracts with attribution are permitted under the fair use doctrine, the copyright concept is intended for individuals and educational institutions, not for profit-making companies. If you don't obtain permission, you and your company can be sued for copyright infringement. In the best-case scenario, you can be asked to cease and desist. In the worst case, your site can be shut down, and you might face other damages.

The way around this situation is simple: Send a permission request, such as the one in the nearby sidebar, "Sample copyright permission."

Be especially careful with photographs, which are usually copyrighted. Here are a few places to find free or low-cost images legally:

- Select from the wealth of material offered under a Creative Commons license (`http://creativecommons.org`). Search for items that can be used for commercial purposes or are in the public domain.
- Search for copyright-free images from the federal government.
- FreeImages (`www.freeimages.com`) has thousands of free photographs.
- Search `http://images.google.com`: Click the Settings link in the bottom-right corner of the window, and then select Advanced Search from the pop-up menu that appears. In the Advanced Search screen that appears, scroll down to the Usage Rights drop-down list and select Free to Use or Share, Even Commercially. Note that these images may still require attribution or have other limits on use; you should still contact the copyright holder for permission.
- Look for stock images from sources such as iStockphoto (`www.istockphoto.com`), Shutterstock (`www.shutterstock.com`), or Freerange Stock (`http://freerangestock.com`).

SAMPLE COPYRIGHT PERMISSION

Dear ____:

Watermelon Mountain Web Marketing wants permission to use your *(information, article, screen shot, art, data, photograph)* on our *(website/blog/social media page)* at *[this URL: WatermelonWeb.com]* and in other media not yet specified. We have attached a copy of the information we want to use. If it meets with your approval, please sign the following release and indicate the credit line you want. You can return the signed form as an email message, a PDF file, a digitally signed document, a fax, or a first-class mail message. Thank you for your prompt response.

The undersigned authorizes Watermelon Mountain Web Marketing to use the attached material without limit for no charge.

Signature:

Printed name:

Title:

Company name:

Company address:

Telephone/fax/email:

Company domain name:

Credit line:

TIP

Trademarks and logos also usually require permission to use, though the logos (icons) that social media companies provide for Share This or Follow Us On functionality are fine to use without permission. If you find an image in the Press or Media section of a company's website, you can assume that you have permission to reproduce it without further permission. Generally, a disclaimer that "all other logos and trademarks are the property of their respective owners" will suffice.

REMEMBER

If it's illegal offline, it's illegal online.

Respecting privacy

Providing a disclaimer about keeping user information private is even more critical now that people sign up willy-nilly online. Individual privacy, already under threat, has become quite slippery with the Facebook Connect sign-in available on all sorts of third-party sites. Facebook Connect may make sign-ins simpler for a user, but it gives Facebook access to user behavior on the web while giving third parties access to users' Facebook profiles for demographic analysis.

Photographs of identifiable individuals, not taken in a public space, historically have required a waiver to use for commercial purposes. When individuals post their images on Facebook, LinkedIn, Instagram, or elsewhere, they may not intend to give permission for that image to appear elsewhere.

Respect a person's space; do not post publicly viewable images of people's faces on any of your social media pages unless you have permission. For a simple photo waiver, see `www.nyip.edu/photo-articles/archive/basic-model-release`.

Revealing product endorsement relationships

Taking aim at companies that were arranging paid recommendations from bloggers, the Federal Trade Commission (FTC) updated its regulations for digital advertising, including blogs, in 2013. The rule (found at `www.ftc.gov/sites/default/files/attachments/press-releases/ftc-staff-revises-online-advertising-disclosure-guidelines/130312dotcomdisclosures.pdf`) and guidelines (at `www.ftc.gov/tips-advice/business-center/guidance/native-advertising-guide-businesses`) require bloggers to disclose whether they've received any type of payment or free products in exchange for a positive review. For more information, see `https://amylynnandrews.com/how-to-disclose-affiliate-links`.

The rule doesn't appear to apply to individuals who post a review on public review sites (such as Epinions, TripAdvisor, or Yelp), but it applies if you review other companies' products on your blog or send products to other bloggers to request a review.

You can find out more about this requirement from the disclosure resources listed in Table 4-4. Some bloggers, offended by the rules, have found humorous or sarcastic ways to comply. Others, such as The Review Stew (`www.thereviewstew.com/p/disclosures.html`), whose blog appears in Figure 4-7, are simply matter-of-fact about it.

TABLE 4-4 Legal Resource Sites

Name	URL	Description
American Bar Association	www.americanbar.org/groups/intellectual_property_law/resources.html	Intellectual property resource lists
BloggyEsq	http://bloggylaw.com/ftc-guidelines-blogger-disclosures	Article titled "FTC Guidelines: Are You Making the Right Blogger Disclosures?"
DisclosurePolicy	http://disclosurepolicy.org	Generate free disclosure policies
Electronic Frontier Foundation	www.eff.org	Not-for-profit focused on free speech, privacy, and consumer rights
Federal Trade Commission	www.ftc.gov/sites/default/files/attachments/press-releases/ftc-staff-revises-online-advertising-disclosure-guidelines/130312dotcomdisclosures.pdf	Federal guidelines for digital media disclosure
FindLaw	http://smallbusiness.findlaw.com/intellectual-property.html	Intellectual property resources
International Technology Law Association	www.itechlaw.org/ask-itech	Online legal issues
PublicLegal from the Internet Legal Research Group	www.ilrg.com	Index of legal sites, free forms, and documents
Nolo	www.nolo.com/legal-encyclopedia/ecommerce-website-development	Online legal issues
Social Media Examiner	www.socialmediaexaminer.com/ftc-2013-disclosures	Article titled "What Marketers Need to Know about the New FTC Disclosures"
US Copyright Office	www.copyright.gov	Copyright information and submission
US Patent and Trademark Office	www.uspto.gov	Patent and trademark information, databases, and submission
Word of Mouth Marketing Association	www.womma.org/ethics	WOMMA Code of Ethics resources

FIGURE 4-7: This blogger sets out a clear acknowledgment policy on product endorsement.

Courtesy of `www.thereviewstew.com`

TIP

Regardless of what you think of the policy, reveal any payments or free promotional products you've received. You can, of course, be as clever, funny, cynical, or straightforward as you want. Feeling lazy? Auto-generate a policy at Disclosure-Policy.org.

Protecting Your Brand Reputation

It's important to start protecting your brand now by registering your company name for social media accounts. To avoid *brandjacking* (others using your company or product brand name on social media for their own purposes or to write misleading or negative things about your company), try to choose the most popular, available handle that will work across multiple sites. Use your company or product name and keep it short.

TIP

Even if you don't plan to do anything else in social media for a year or more, register your name now on Facebook, Twitter, LinkedIn, and Google+ and on any other sites you might want in the future, such as Pinterest or YouTube. You can register your name on every site while you read this book or reserve them all at once.

A number of companies now offer tools that claim to assess the quality of what people are saying about your company, products, or staff. In addition to counting how many times your name appears, they try to assess the *sentiment* of postings — whether statements are negative or positive. Some also offer an assessment of the degree of *engagement* — how enthusiastic or hostile a statement might be.

Some people then take this information, along with frequency of posting, and use their own proprietary formulas to assign a quantitative value to your online reputation, as shown in the example from Trackur (`www.trackur.com/social-media-monitoring`) in Figure 4-8. (Trackur requires that you sign up for a 10-day free trial.)

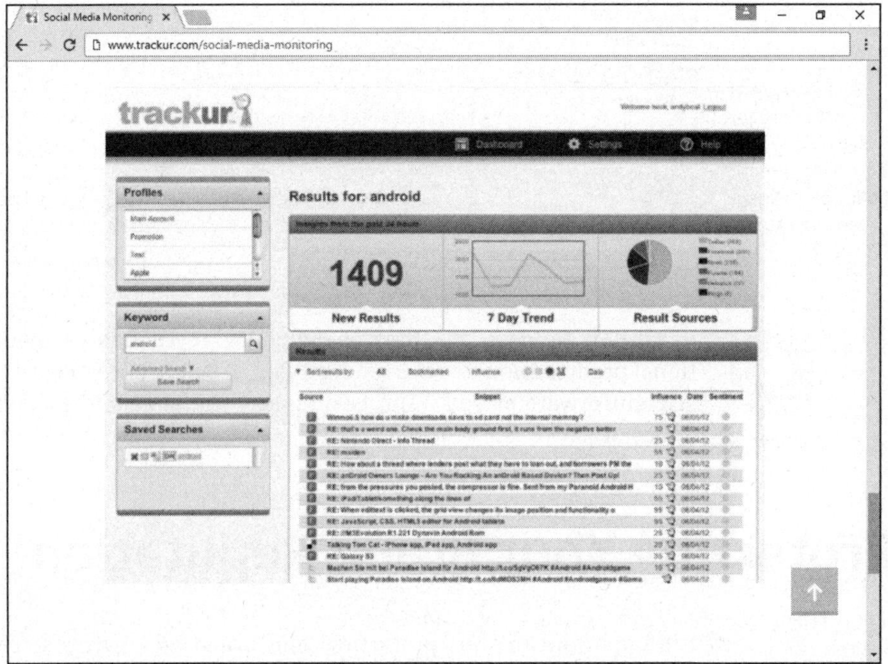

FIGURE 4-8: Trackur offers an inexpensive reputation-management tool that scales up for large companies.

Courtesy of Trackur.com

Be cautious about assigning too much weight to these brand reputation tools, some of which are described in Table 4-5. They may produce widely varying results, and most rely on software that can't understand complex sentences or shortened phrases with words omitted. If you think your dense sibling doesn't understand irony, don't try sarcasm with a computer!

TABLE 4-5 **Brand Sentiment Resources**

Name	URL	Description
Attentio	`http://attentio.com`	Social media dashboard to track sentiment and more; paid
BrandsEye	`www.brandseye.com`	Online reputation tool; paid
Naymz	`www.naymz.com`	Personal reputation on social media
Oracle Social Cloud	`www.oracle.com/us/solutions/social/overview/index.html`	Social relationship management tool
SDL SM2	`www.sdl.com/solution/customer-analytics/social-media-monitoring/learn-more.html`	Social media sentiment tool; paid
Sentiment 140	`www.sentiment140.com`	Twitter sentiment tool; free app
Social Fresh	`http://socialfresh.com/monitoring-your-brand-online-reputation/`	List of social monitoring tools
Trackur	`www.trackur.com/free-brand-monitoring-tools`	Reputation protection tool; freemium model

Notwithstanding the warnings, experiment with one of the free or freemium sentiment-measuring tools in Table 4-5 to see what, if anything, people are saying. (*Freemium* tools offer a free version with limited features; more extensive feature sets carry a charge.) Those results, such as they are, will become one of many baselines for your social media effort. Unless you already have a significant web presence, you may not find much.

Of course, many of these tools are designed for use by multinational corporations worried about their reputations after negative events, such as the Takata airbag recall or the 2016 scandal about Wells Fargo Bank staff who were pushed to create fake customer accounts.

For you, the sentiment results might be good for a laugh or make excellent party chatter at your next *tweet-up* (your real-world meeting arranged through tweets).

2
Cybersocial Tools

Contents at a Glance

CHAPTER 1: **Discovering Helpful Tech Tools** 101
Keeping Track of the Social Media Scene 102
Saving Time with Content-Distribution Tools 104
Snipping Ugly URLs 106
Using E-Commerce Tools for Social Sites. 108
Keeping Your Ear to the Social Ground 118
Measuring the Buzz by Type of Service 124

CHAPTER 2: **Leveraging SEO for Improved Visibility** 127
Making the Statistical Case for SEO 128
Thinking Tactically and Practically. 130
Focusing on the Top Search Engines 131
Knowing the Importance of Search Phrases 132
Maximizing Metatag Muscle 138
Optimizing Your Site and Content for Search Engines 142

CHAPTER 3: **Optimizing Social Media for Internal and External Searches** 159
Placing Search Terms on Social Media. 160
Optimizing Blogs 161
Optimizing Images, Video, and Podcasts. 166
Optimizing Specific Social Media Platforms 167
Optimizing for Mobile Search 173
Gaining Visibility in Real-Time Search. 175
Gaining Traction on Google with Social Media 177
Monitoring Your Search Engine Ranking 178

CHAPTER 4: **Using Social Bookmarks, News, and Share Buttons** 181
Bookmarking Your Way to Traffic. 182
Sharing the News 185
Benefiting from Social Bookmarks and News Services 186
Researching a Social Bookmark and Social News Campaign 187
Submitting to Bookmarking Services 190
Submitting to Social News Services 192
Using Application-Specific Bookmarks. 194
Timing Your Submissions. 195
Encouraging Others to Bookmark or Rate Your Site 201
Using Social Media Buttons 202

CHAPTER 5: **Making Social Media Mobile** 207
Understanding the Statistics of Mobile Device Usage 208
Reaching People on the Move with Social Media 212
Harvesting Leads and Sales from Social Mobile 216
Measuring Your Mobile Marketing Success 220
Counting on Tablets 221
Using Mobile Social Media for Advertising 222

IN THIS CHAPTER

» Keeping current with social media

» Distributing content efficiently

» Giving long URLs a haircut

» Selecting shopping tools that work on social media

» Monitoring the buzz

Chapter 1

Discovering Helpful Tech Tools

In Book 1, you discover that the key to social media success is planning. This minibook reviews useful tools and resources to make your plan easier to execute. Before you start, you may also want to check out Book 9, which focuses on measurement tools for traffic, costs, and campaign performance.

As you select tools and schedule tasks from suggestions in this chapter, remember to enter them on your Social Media Marketing Plan (Book 1, Chapter 3) and Social Media Activity Calendar (Book 1, Chapter 4). You can also download blank copies of these forms by clicking the Downloads tab at `www.dummies.com/go/socialmediamarketingaio4e`.

Try to select at least one tool from each category:

- Resource, news, and blog sites that cover online marketing and social media
- Content-distribution tools
- URL-clipping tools
- Shopping apps or services for social media, if appropriate
- Buzz-tracking tools to monitor mentions of your business

TIP

You can always jump right into the social media scene and figure out these things later, but your efforts will be more productive if you build the right framework first.

Keeping Track of the Social Media Scene

Unless you take advantage of online resources, you'll never be able to stay current with the changes in social media. Here's a quick look at how much the landscape changed in the course of just a few years:

- Use of social media continued its explosive growth. According to the Pew Research Center (www.pewinternet.org/2015/10/08/social-networking-usage-2005-2015), by the end of 2015, 76 percent of all Internet users also used social media. And as amazing as it might seem, Internet users in 2016 averaged more than 5.5 social media accounts each (www.brandwatch.com/blog/96-amazing-social-media-statistics-and-facts-for-2016).
- Social media acquisitions run rampant. Facebook alone purchased Instagram for $1 billion in 2012, Oculus VR, which makes virtual reality headsets, for $2 billion in 2014, and Ascenta, a drone manufacturer, for another $2 billion.
- The 2016 Summer Olympics drew more than 1.5 billion engagements on Facebook (likes, posts, comments, and shares), while Twitter drew 187 million tweets about the event.
- New social media platforms continue to pop up, proving that the power of innovation is still strong. Watch the growth of Periscope.tv (live video streaming), Musical.ly (an instant music video app), and Yikyak.com (a local community sharing app).
- At the same time, other social media services went belly-up. Casualties of the social media wars included Sulia (a subject-matter social media service that connected users to experts), Blab.im (which allowed narrow-casting of video to a defined set of followers), and most notably, Vine.co (the site noted for sharing short, looped videos, which has limited its recording functionality and become mainly a site to review old videos).

To keep current on the changing tides, subscribe to feeds about social marketing from social marketing blogs or news services; check at least one source weekly. Also, review traffic trends on social media services weekly; they're amazingly volatile. Table 1-1 lists some helpful resource sites.

TABLE 1-1 Social Media Marketing Resources

Name	URL	Description
BIgMarketing for Small Business	`www.bigmarketingsmallbusiness.com`	Social media, online, and offline marketing tips
HubSpot	`http://blog.hubspot.com`	Inbound marketing blog about attracting the right prospects to your site and converting them into customers
Marketing Land	`http://marketingland.com`	Internet marketing news
MarketingProfs	`www.marketingprofs.com/marketing/library/100/social-media`	Social media marketing tips, including business-to-business
MarketingSherpa	`www.marketingsherpa.com/library.html`	Publisher of free case studies, research, and training for marketers
Mashable	`http://mashable.com/social-media`	Premier social media guide
SiteProNews	`www.sitepronews.com`	Social media and search engine news
Social Media Examiner	`www.socialmediaexaminer.com`	Online social media magazine advising businesses on the use of social media to achieve marketing goals
Social Media Marketing Group on LinkedIn	`www.linkedin.com/groups/66325`	Professional, non-promotional discussion group
Social Media Today	`www.socialmediatoday.com`	Online community for marketing and PR professionals dealing with social media
TechCrunch	`http://techcrunch.com`	Technology industry blog
TechHive	`www.techhive.com`	Technology news site
Techmeme	`http://techmeme.com`	Top technology news site
TopRank Online Marketing Blog	`www.toprankblog.com`	Blog about online and social marketing
Twitter Marketing	`https://marketing.twitter.com`	Ideas, success stories, and solutions for marketing on Twitter

Saving Time with Content-Distribution Tools

Social media marketing can quickly consume all your waking hours — and then some. Just the thought of needing to post information quickly to Facebook, Twitter, Google+, blogs, Pinterest, and social news services might make any social marketer cringe.

Time to work smarter, not harder, with content-distribution tools to post your content to many places at once for tasks like the following:

- **Routine maintenance:** Use a content-distribution tool whenever you make updates according to your Social Media Activity Calendar. What a timesaver!
- **Quick event postings:** Share information from a conference, trade show, meeting, or training session from your phone by sending short text updates to Twitter and LinkedIn. Or take a picture with your smartphone and send it to Instagram, Twitter, and Facebook. To send something longer, use a distribution tool to post to your blog and Facebook.
- **Daily updates:** Group all social media services that you might want to update with rapidly changing information, such as a daily sale or the location of your traveling cupcake cart by the hour.

REMEMBER

If you have more than three social media outlets or frequently update your content, choosing at least one distribution tool is a must-have way to save time.

Some businesses prefer to craft custom postings for Facebook, Twitter, and other services based on the specific audience and content needs of each channel, while others find this too time-consuming. Do what seems right for your business: Automate *cross-postings* (set up a service so that postings on one social media service automatically appear on others to save time), customize by channel, or mix and match.

In addition to Hootsuite, OnlyWire, and other tools described in the next few sections, you can use Really Simple Syndication (RSS) to feed content to users and to your various social media profiles. Keep in mind, however, that RSS works best with highly technical audiences. For more information about RSS feeds, see `www.whatisrss.com`.

Alternative content distribution services

You can select from several content-distribution services to *syndicate* (copy) your content from one social media service to another. All the services work roughly the same way, but each has its own peculiarities. Choose the one that's the best fit for you.

REMEMBER

Reconfigure your settings on content-distribution tools whenever you decide to add or drop a social media service or create a special-purpose group for marketing.

Buffer

An easy-to-use app, Buffer (https://bufferapp.com) allows you to preschedule content distribution to multiple social media platforms. It uses its own built-in link shortener to gather and compare data about the performance of posts on various channels.

Hootsuite

Self-described as "the leading social media dashboard," Hootsuite (http://hootsuite.com) has expanded from its origins as a way to manage only the Twitter experience. From scheduling to stats, Hootsuite now integrates more than 35 social media channels, allowing multiservice postings from one location to Twitter, Facebook, LinkedIn, Foursquare, Google +, Instagram, YouTube, and your blog, among others.

OnlyWire

OnlyWire (http://onlywire.com) updates up to 50 social networks simultaneously. It also passes updates between WordPress sites, RSS feeds, and social media channels.

OnlyWire also offers several handy mini-apps at http://onlywire.com/tools to facilitate sharing items quickly:

- A developer API to custom-program content exchanges among your social media channels
- A Chrome toolbar add-in that lets you quickly share web pages you like with your Facebook and Twitter accounts
- A WordPress plug-in that automatically submits your WordPress posts to the social media services you've selected
- An app to deliver material from RSS feeds to your selected social media channels

SocialFlow

SocialFlow (`www.socialflow.com`) is a high-end distributor of content and paid advertising across multiple social media networks. The company uses specific data to schedule posts and activities for times when your target audience is active on specific channels.

TweetDeck

Owned by Twitter, this tweet management tool at `https://about.twitter.com/products/tweetdeck` lets you schedule tweets, track engagement, and organize multiple accounts in one convenient location.

UberSocial

If you're on your smartphone all the time, UberSocial (`www.ubersocial.com`) may be perfect for you. This Twitter smartphone app, available for Android, BlackBerry, and iPhone, allows users to post and read tweets. Features vary slightly between the three devices, but all integrate LivePreview, which enables users to view embedded links next to tweets without closing the app and opening a new browser, making it an efficient way to use Twitter on your smartphone. Other features include cross-posting to Facebook, managing multiple accounts, and sending tweets of more than 140 characters.

Snipping Ugly URLs

The last thing you need when microblogging (on sites such as Twitter) is a URL that takes up half your 140-character limit for original text! (Media attachments and retweets no longer count toward the character limit.) Long, descriptive URLs that are useful for search engines are also messy in email, text messages, text versions of e-newsletters, and blogs, and make it difficult to retweet within the limit. The solution is to snip, clip, nip, trim, shave, or otherwise shorten ungainly URLs with a truncating service. Take your choice of those in Table 1-2 or search for others.

The downside is that the true owner of shortened URLs may be a mystery, so it doesn't do much for your branding unless you select the option to create a custom URL. Figure 1-1 shows a typical URL truncating service and the result.

REMEMBER

As always, enter the name of your URL-snipping service on your Social Media Marketing Plan. To make it easier to track URLs and their snipped versions, select just one service.

TABLE 1-2 URL Snipping Services

Service Name	URL	Notes
Bitly	`https://bitly.com`	Free and paid versions, with history, stats, and preferences
Ow.ly	`http://ow.ly/url/shorten-url`	Hootsuite's URL shortener, free
Snipurl	`http://snipurl.com`	Stores, manages, and tracks traffic on short URLs, free
TinyURL	`http://tinyurl.com`	One of the oldest and best-known truncators, free
Twitter	`http://t.co`	Link-shortening service; used only on Twitter, which automatically shortens links in tweets to a t.co link; can still use third-party link shorteners
2 Create a Website	`http://blog.2createawebsite.com/2012/01/09/popular-url-shorteners-for-redirecting-tracking-affiliate-links`	Comparison review article

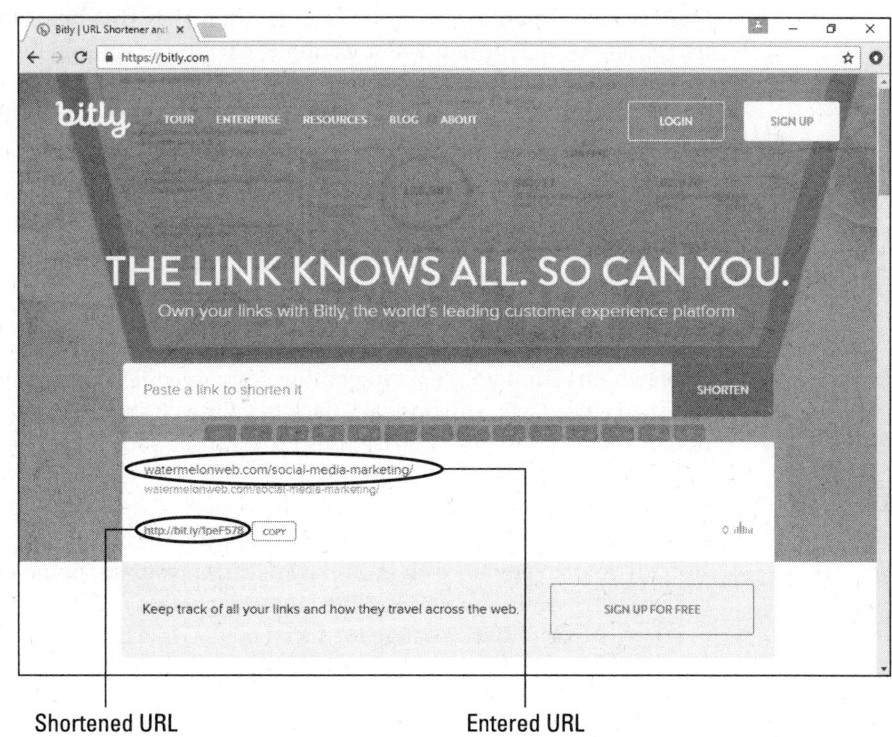

FIGURE 1-1: Enter a long URL at Bitly and receive a shortened URL in return.

Using E-Commerce Tools for Social Sites

If money makes the world go 'round, e-commerce takes the cybersocial world for a dizzying spin. Many options exist for promoting or linking to your online store from blogs and social networks, but several applications now let you sell directly (or indirectly) from social media pages.

REMEMBER

Always check the terms of service on social media sites to be sure you aren't violating their rules. Some services may prohibit selling directly from their site. Check out the possibilities on Facebook, Facebook Marketplace, Etsy, Pinterest, Twitter's Buy Now feature, or with an Instagram third-party add-on, such as Soldsie or Foursixty.

Selling through links

The easiest way to sell from social networks and blogs is simply to post a banner or a text link to your own website or to other sites that sell your products (Etsy, for example). Additionally, you can post images on a site such as Facebook with links to your website or other sites.

Marleylilly is an online boutique that accomplishes this in a sophisticated manner, as shown in Figure 1-2. For example, clicking a featured item on its Facebook timeline (`www.facebook.com/marleylilly/?fref=ts`) takes shoppers to Marleylilly's website at `https://marleylilly.com/product/monogrammed-bracelet-and-earring-set` to fill their carts and check out.

Displaying products on social media channels

If you're looking for a more seamless experience, consider e-commerce tools that display items from your existing online store on your blog or social media pages, and then either link automatically back to your web store to complete the transaction or permit users to purchase directly from the social media page.

E-commerce badges are mini-displays of products; these changeable badges (which appear onscreen as a large button with multiple links) link to an existing web store. If you already have an online store, check your shopping cart or *check stand provider* (the section of your online store that totals orders and takes payments) to see whether it offers a badge for social media, like the one shown in Figure 1-3.

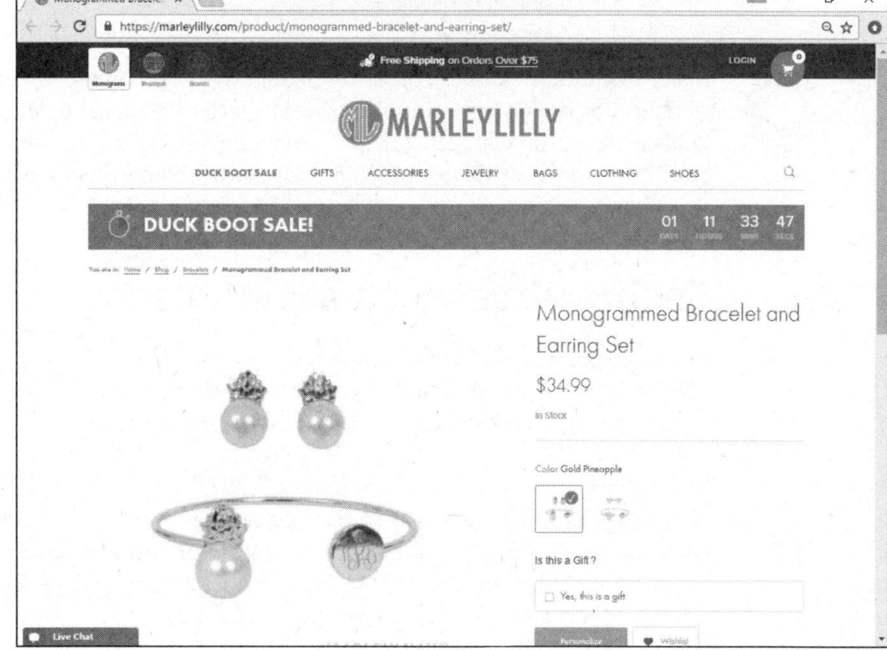

FIGURE 1-2: Product offerings can begin on Facebook (top) and then link to a separate shopping website (bottom).

Courtesy of Marleylilly

FIGURE 1-3: The Etsy mini badge on the right side of this blog drives traffic to the Etsy shop for The Little Dabbler.

Courtesy of the owner of The Little Dabbler

TIP

Many vendors of online stores offer apps with shopping or promotional functionality for use on specific social media services. For instance, 2020AVE uses the Soldsie Have2Have.it feed (`https://have2have.it`) to sell on Instagram (`www.instagram.com/2020ave`) and the Shop Now and comment functions to sell on Facebook (`www.facebook.com/2020ave`).

Selling directly on social media

As we all know, every extra click can cost sales. That's why many businesses choose to sell directly from a social media channel in addition to or instead of linking people to their website, Etsy store, or Amazon store.

This solution can be a very cost-effective one for some B2C micro-businesses with only a few products, at least until they grow large enough to make a dedicated storefront worth the investment. Selling through a social channel may also make sense for introducing new or trending products or generating interest that would drive prospects to a fully empowered storefront.

Marketers for large companies and those with a B2B audience are a bit cautious. Social media channels are not yet flexible enough to handle large inventories or the long-sales cycle generally needed to complete a high-ticket B2B purchase.

WARNING

Another potential downside to selling only from social media is that you can't always land paid search ads on a social media channel. Some PPC platforms, including Google, require that a landing page include the actual URL for the company. If you plan to advertise only on the social media platform from which you are selling (such as Facebook), this is not a problem.

Selling on Facebook

Multiple apps allow shoppers to either complete a purchase directly from your Facebook page or be directed to another website to finish buying. Go to `www.facebook.com/business/help/912190892201033` for more information.

Selling on Pinterest

Pinterest requires merchants to have Buyable Pins to sell on its platform, which attracts a female audience interested in fashion, food, weddings, and home decor. The pins, which grab current products from an existing online store, place a Buy button on each pin you add to Pinterest (see Figure 1-4). There's no charge for sales since payment goes through your established channels. The pins work especially well on mobile devices. At the time of this writing, Buyable Pins were available only to those using specific selling platforms (BigCommerce, IBM Commerce, Demandware, Magento, and Shopify) outside Pinterest, and to established retail partners and US merchants with Pinterest business accounts. However, this policy may change at any time. To sign up for Buyable Pins or obtain updates, see `https://business.pinterest.com/en/buyable-pins` and `https://help.pinterest.com/en/articles/selling-on-pinterest`.

Selling on Twitter

The Buy Now app is required to sell on Twitter. This app, which makes it easy for customers to purchase products from your Twitter timeline, works with a select group of e-commerce providers (BigCommerce, Demandware, Shopify, and Stripe). A Buy Now button is placed on your tweet, which functions as your ad. Basically, this approach lets users grab an item without going through a full online storefront. See `https://business.twitter.com/en/advertising/commerce-on-twitter.html` for additional details.

TIP

For more information about the pros and cons of selling through social media, try these sites: `www.marketingweek.com/2016/03/23/social-commerce-how-willing-are-consumers-to-buy-through-social-media`, `www.trendreports.com/article/social-media-shopping`, and `http://ecommerce-platforms.com/ecommerce-selling-advice/best-apps-tools-use-selling-social-media`.

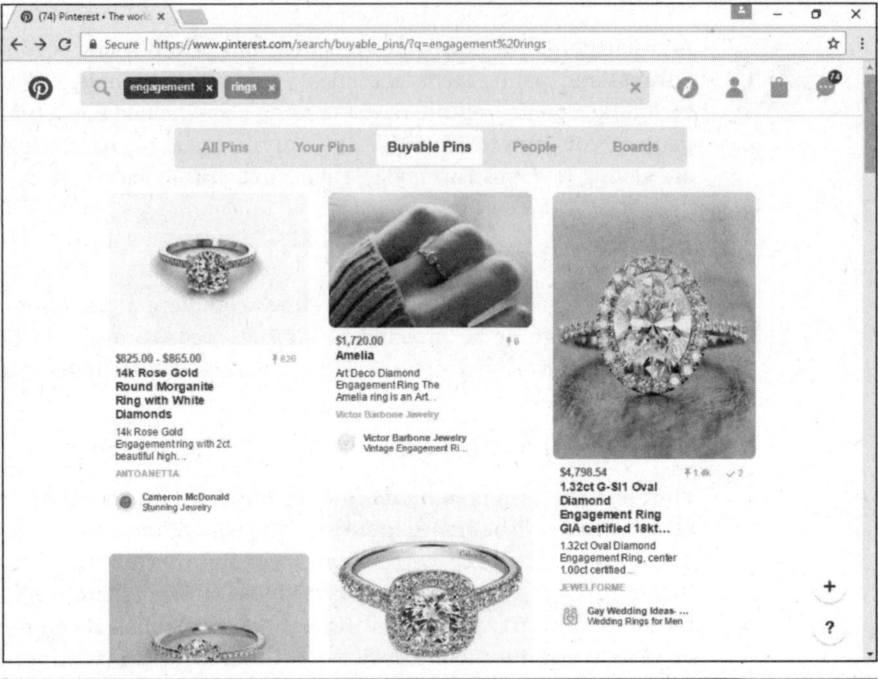

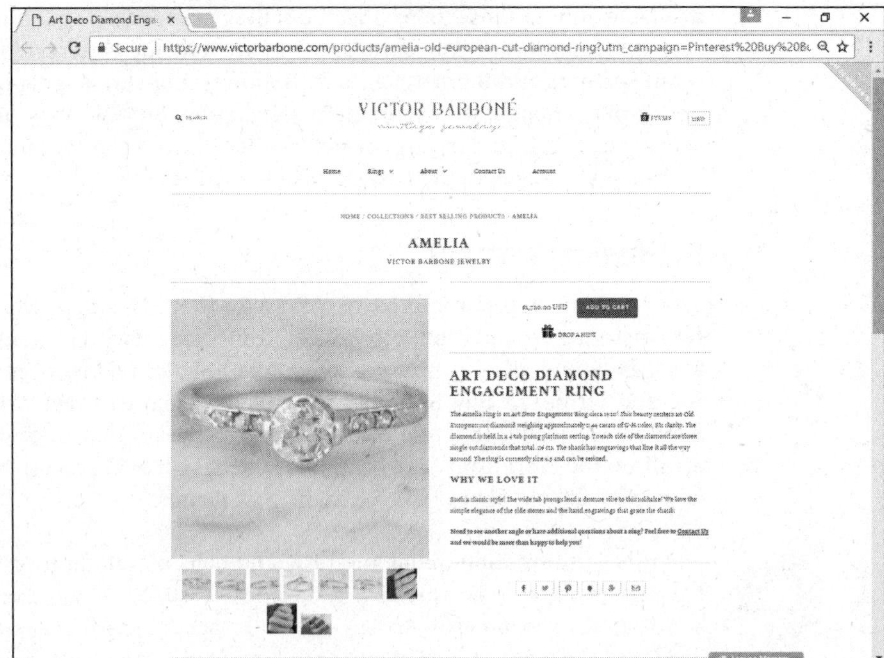

FIGURE 1-4: Victor Barboné Vintage Jewelry uses the Buyable Pins option to sell directly from its Pinterest page.

Courtesy of Victor Barboné Jewelry

MAKING A ROYAL LIVING FROM SOCIAL SALES

Living Royal, whose website appears in the next figure, proudly describes itself as a "funky printed sock company." Started in 2010, the company makes all its socks at its Wheeling, IL, headquarters with a staff of 30 employees.

Courtesy of Living Royal

According to its president, Michael Elyash, "We knew the only way to be successful selling online was to have a large social media following. We started with Facebook, then went to Twitter, Pinterest, and lastly Instagram." Initially, social media was the only source of traffic for the newfound company.

The firm tested just about all social media channels to see which ones would best achieve various marketing goals, from online sales, retail customer acquisition, social following, and email collection to wholesale customer acquisition and branding.

The company found, for instance, that "Facebook was great at getting people to buy product," citing Facebook's capability to tightly target an audience. However, "Pinterest and Instagram were great for spreading awareness about our brand [but] were not as good at converting visitors into customers."

(continued)

(continued)

After additional research, it turned out that Instagram users were having problems finding products on the primary website. To resolve the issue, Living Royal converted to a user-friendly, Instagram-based, direct-purchase program called Foursixty. Elyash particularly liked that it allowed Living Royal to link multiple products per picture compared to other programs, which allowed a link to only one product per picture. Foursixty turned out to be so successful that it now serves as the platform for all purchases on the Living Royal site.

To manage its social media activities, Living Royal takes advantage of an Instagram visual-posting program from Later. "We typically post once a day in the late afternoon," Elyash explains. "A team of [four] people focuses on social [media] from photography to social outreach," with the goal of making the company's social presence as good as possible. To back up their results, the team relies on Google Analytics and Shopify. The get out the word, the team places social media icons on every web page and pushes engagement through various contests and giveaways.

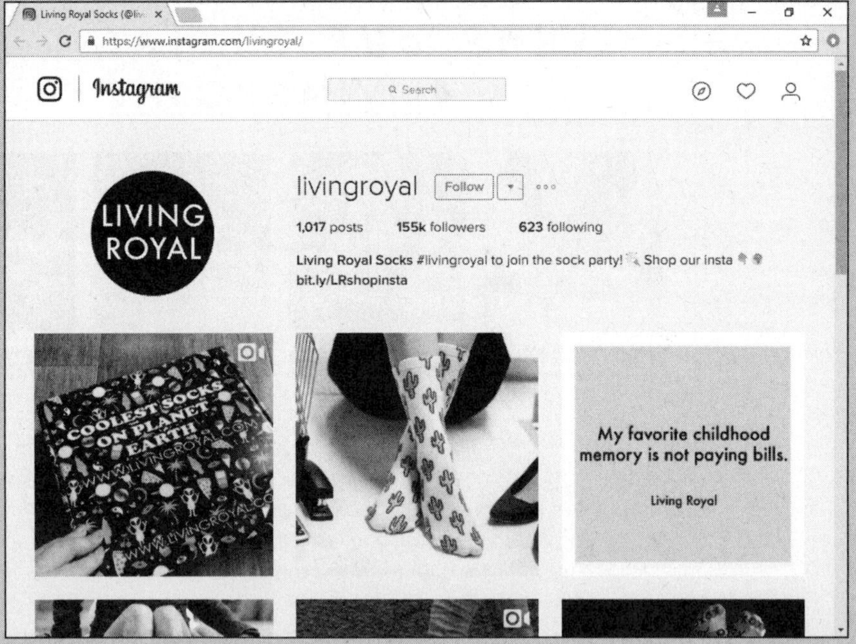

Courtesy of Living Royal

It wasn't always easy, Elyash notes. "Getting the attention of our audience at first was a real challenge. Finding out which style of imagery to get the right conversions also was a big issue for us. [But] if you test anything enough, you will find the right, winning combination."

Following is a list of Living Royal's web presence:

- `www.livingroyal.com`
- `www.pinterest.com/livingroyal`
- `www.instagram.com/livingroyal`
- `www.livingroyal.com/pages/shop-insta`
- `www.foursixty.com/living-royal/127252391`
- `www.facebook.com/Livingroyal`
- `twitter.com/livingroyal`

Reviewing third-party products for selling through social media

The following sections discuss some of the many third-party tools and products available for selling products through social media as an alternative to linking to a storefront on your website or to selling directly using the sometimes limited solutions provided by the social media platform. Instead, most of these solutions link from social media to an independent storefront. Consider these items as examples of the range of products available. You should research and evaluate products to meet your own needs.

Beetailer

Beetailer (`www.beetailer.com`) uses a quick catalog import function to transfer your current product line to Facebook without entering additional information. Unlike some platform-specific solutions discussed previously, Beetailer works with your existing site and storefront. It provides campaign and promotion templates, as well as various reports and trendline predictions.

Ecwid

Ecwid (`www.ecwid.com`) is a complete e-commerce solution for websites, blogs, Facebook, Tumblr, and more. Facebook shoppers complete the entire process, including checkout, on Facebook. Additional social media integration to share purchases and recommend products is also available for Facebook, Twitter, Pinterest, Google+, and Tumblr.

Since the contents of your web store are mirrored on several sites, it's easy to update your product catalog simultaneously at all sites and manage all online locations from one dashboard. Prices range from free for up to ten products to $99 per month for unlimited products. All packages include a free Facebook store.

Shopial

Shopial (www.shopial.com) requires only three clicks to turn your existing e-commerce website into a Facebook store. It also supports conversions from your third-party store on eBay, Etsy, and Amazon. Shopial offers a one-click creation tool for Facebook ads, along with detailed reports on your Facebook sales.

Shopify

Shopify (www.shopify.com) is a full-featured store builder that lets Facebook, Pinterest, and Twitter users browse your catalog and purchase products directly from each of these social media channels. A free Facebook store is included with monthly web-based plans, which range from a $29 starter package to $299 for unlimited storage. If you don't already have or want a web-based store, you can select a Facebook-only plan (www.shopify.com/facebook) with unlimited products starting at $9 per month. In addition, there is a per-transaction credit card fee. All plans have a 14-day free trial.

TIP

When selecting a storefront solution for your website, investigate which ones offer either the capability to use the same solution on social media platforms or provide badges or apps for social media compatibility. Many companies have added this feature in response to demand.

Storefront Social

Made specifically for Facebook, Storefront Social (www.storefrontsocial.com) allows you to sell directly from Facebook using Authorize.net, PayPal, Stripe, or WePay for credit cards. You can forward shoppers to your web-based store to conclude the purchase or to see additional products. Offering a free seven-day trial and flat monthly fees from $9.95 for 100 products to $29.95 for 1,000 products, Storefront Social is an affordable selling solution for small- to medium-size stores.

StoreYa

StoreYa (www.storeya.com) is a cost-effective solution for selling on Facebook, blogs, websites, and in a mobile environment, with links to your primary store to complete a sale. StoreYa allows you to import your products from other e-commerce programs. It includes multiple social media marketing tools to increase sales, as well as store statistics. Pricing varies by the number of products (SKUs) in your catalog, starting with a free version for 20 products and rising to enterprise level, with several affordable levels in between. It offers a free 14-day trial period.

Other resources for selling on social media

Table 1-3 lists other e-commerce widgets, storefronts, and resources you may want to check out.

TABLE 1-3 Social E-Commerce Apps, Storefronts, and Resources

Name	URL	Notes
Amazon aStore	`https://affiliate-program.amazon.com/gp/associates/network/store/main.html`	E-commerce tools for Amazon stores that can be placed on multiple social network, blog, or web pages
Big Cartel	`http://bigcartel.com`	Hosted e-commerce website geared toward artists, clothing designers, and bands; capability to set up freestanding e-commerce sites and add to a Facebook site
BigCommerce	`www.bigcommerce.com/features/sell-on-social/`	E-commerce platform for built-in selling on Facebook and Pinterest
eBay	`https://go.developer.ebay.com`	E-commerce badge for your eBay store; free APIs allow selling on eBay from anywhere online
E-junkie	`www.e-junkie.com`	Cart or Buy Now buttons for social media or blog; fee based on size and volume; handles charges for downloaded items (for example, music or whitepapers)
Etsy	`www.etsy.com/apps/?q=social+media`	List of third-party apps to sell on Etsy from social media; helpful ideas `www.etsy.com/seller-handbook/article/social-media-tips-from-an-etsy-expert/22423398853`
Highwire	`www.highwire.com`	Multichannel storefront for use on your own website, eBay, Facebook, Google, or a mobile site
Mercantec	`www.mercantec.com/google`	Snippet generator that adds a shopping cart to sites, blogs, or social networks; has analytics
PayPal	`https://developer.paypal.com/docs/accept-payments`	Accepting PayPal payments on mobile and social media
Practical eCommerce	`http://search.practicalecommerce.com/search?q=social+media+e-commerce+widgets`	Articles about using e-commerce widgets with social media
Soldsie	`http://new.soldsie.com/how-it-works` `https://web.soldsie.com` `https://have2have.it`	App to sell directly on Facebook and Instagram; Have2Have.It feed lets you sell through links in any social profile

(continued)

TABLE 1-3 (continued)

Name	URL	Notes
Spreesy	`www.spreesy.com`	Social commerce platform that integrates with Google Analytics; works with Instagram, Facebook, Twitter, Pinterest, and mobile sites
Storefront Social	`http://storefrontsocial.com`	Create a Facebook shop in minutes
Wishpond	`http://corp.wishpond.com/social-promotions`	Apps to run promotions, such as coupons, contests, or group sales on Twitter, Facebook, Pinterest, and Instagram

Keeping Your Ear to the Social Ground

The onslaught of data from social media sites can be overwhelming. To garner some value from all the noise, you can take advantage of certain tools to monitor what's being said about your company.

When should you start to worry? Some experts suggest that a negative comment appearing within the first 20 results on a Google search on your name, brand, or product could be a sign of trouble. Don't worry about a one-off negative comment on a minor site.

Social media *monitoring* is about who's saying what. It's about your brand, your products, and your reputation. It's not the same as social media *measurement*, which deals with traffic statistics, conversion rates, and return on investment (ROI). Measurement is covered in Book 9, including chapters about measurement tools specific to particular social networks.

Bring user feedback directly to you. Place a free feedback widget on your site from `http://shoutbox.widget.me`, `http://getbarometer.com`, or `www.makeuseof.com/dir/snapabug-visual-feedback`. This feature takes some programming knowledge; if you're not up to the task, ask your programmer. You can find some monitoring tools for specific types of services in the sections that follow.

Deciding what to monitor and why

If you didn't have anything else to do, you could monitor everything. That situation isn't realistic, so you need to set some constraints. Start with your goal and ask yourself what you want to accomplish. For example, you may want to

- Track what's being said about your company and products, both positive and negative.

- Conduct competitor or market research.
- Stay up-to-date on what's happening in your industry.
- Watch trends in terms of mentions, topics of interest, or volume of comments.
- Gain a competitive advantage.
- Monitor the success of a specific press release, media campaign, or product promotion.
- Monitor infringement of trademark or other intellectual property.
- Obtain customer feedback so you can improve your products and services.

After you decide your goal, it should be obvious what search terms or keywords to monitor. Your list might include

- Your company name
- Your domain name
- Names of executives and staff who speak with the public
- Product names and URLs
- Competitors' names
- Keywords
- Topic tags

Deciding which tools to use

The number of monitoring tools is almost as great as the amount of data they sift through. Research your options and choose at least one tool that monitors across multiple types of social media. Depending on the social media services you're using, you might want to select one from each appropriate service category, as well.

The frequency with which you check results from these tools will depend on the overall visibility of your company, the schedule for your submissions to different services, and the overall intensity of your social media presence. For some companies, it might be a daily task. For others, once weekly or even once per month will be enough.

TIP

If you're not sure where to start, begin with weekly Google Alerts to monitor the web and the 14-day free trial for Mention's daily alerts (plans start at $29/month) to monitor social media. Add one tool each for blogs and Twitter, if you use them actively or think people may be talking about your business on their own. Adjust as needed.

Using free or inexpensive social monitoring tools

Choose one or more of the tools in the following sections to monitor across multiple types of social media.

REMEMBER

Mark your choices on your Social Media Marketing Plan. If the tool doesn't offer automated reporting, you'll need to enter the submission task, as well as the review task, on your Social Media Activity Calendar.

Addictomatic: Inhale the web

Addictomatic (`http://addictomatic.com/about`) lets you "instantly create a custom page with the current buzz on any topic." It searches hundreds of live sites, including news, blog posts, videos, and images, and it offers a bookmarkable, personalized dashboard for keeping track of your updates.

Brand 24

An affordable brand-monitoring tool, Brand 24 (`http://brand24.net`) starts at $49 per month, with a 14-day free trial. It includes both sentiment and data analysis to provide a good sense of the buzz around your product, brand, business, or search term. It covers multiple social media outlets, including Facebook, Twitter, and Blip TV, with alerts daily or more often. Additional features available with more expensive plans allow you to review customer behavior, actions, and posts.

Google Alerts

One of the easiest and most popular of the free monitoring services, Google Alerts (`www.google.com/alerts`) are notifications of new results on up to 1,000 search terms. Alerts can be delivered via email or RSS feed. You can receive results for news articles, websites, blogs, video, and Google books and forums.

You set the frequency with which Google checks for results and other features from your My Alerts dashboard page. Think of Alerts as an online version of a clipping service.

Google Trends

Google Trends (`www.google.com/trends`) is a useful market research tool. It not only provides data on the hottest current searches, but also compares the number of searches on the terms you enter to the total number of searches on Google overall during the same time frame.

Click the menu icon (three bars) to the left of the word *Trends* in the header and select the Explore option in the drop-down list. Type the search phrase that interests you in the Add a Search Term field. From Explore, you can choose to refine your research by selecting options from the drop-down lists under Worldwide (location), Past 5 Years (time frame), All Categories (topic area), and Web Search (content type.)

Select the Subscriptions option in the drop-down list (below the menu icon) to receive email notification of trending searches and stories.

HowSociable

Type any brand name at `www.howsociable.com`, shown in Figure 1-5, to see how visible it is in social media. The free version checks "one brand with 12 different metrics and limited features." The paid upgrade checks 24 more channels. Click any element for additional detail, as shown on the report for the Healthcare.gov in Figure 1-5.

FIGURE 1-5: HowSociable displays social media visibility for Healthcare.gov.

IceRocket

Meltwater's IceRocket (`www.icerocket.com`) is a free monitoring tool that covers millions of blogs, Twitter, and other web documents, in 20 languages. By the way, this is one of the few places left where you can post the URL for your blog to make sure it gets found in search engines.

IFTTT (If This Then That)

If This Then That (www.ifttt.com) is an automation tool that lets you write a script (called an *applet*) to receive notifications and accomplish other tasks online. You can easily use IFTTT to manage your online reputation. It's easiest to browse existing public applets to find one that monitors your desired social media platforms; then tweak the applet to include the search terms you want to monitor.

Mention

Mention (https://mention.com/en) monitors multiple social networks, news sites, forums, blogs, and any web page in 42 languages. It offers several helpful features: one, the capability to export data, filtered by time and source, which allows you to compare your results to competitors' results; and two, real-time alerts plus a daily or weekly digest by email. Its free basic plan allows one user, one alert, and up to 250 mentions per month but doesn't include analytics. Paid versions — which have higher limits on the number of alerts, mentions, and users — start at $29 per month for 2 alerts, 3,000 mentions, and 1 user; all plans include a free 14-day trial.

Social Mention

Social Mention (www.socialmention.com/advanced_search) tracks and measures what's being said about a specific topic in real-time across more than 80 social media services. It provides a social ranking score based on its own definition of *popularity* — which includes self-defined criteria of strength, sentiment, passion, and reach — for every search.

Figure 1-6 shows the results for the term *Mannequin Challenge*, which had received more than 4 million views on YouTube by October 2016. For more information on measuring sentiment, see Book 1, Chapter 4.

You can select to monitor only specific services and choose among service categories of bookmarks, blogs, microblogs, videos, images, or all. Although you can input only one term at a time, the results may go back up to 30 days.

TECHNICAL STUFF

Social Mention also offers real-time widgets (http://socialmention.com/tools) to place on your site or in your browser bar. These widgets are simple plug-ins, but your programmer will need to copy and paste the widget code onto your site.

Sprout Social

A high-end package of social media tools, Sprout Social (www.sproutsocial.com) includes a comprehensive monitoring feature that combines all alerts, messages, and actions into a single stream that can be analyzed to discover trends. You can watch for social media comments about your business, brand, products, competitors, or industry topics in near real-time. Prices start at $99 per user per month, but the company also offers a 30-day free trial.

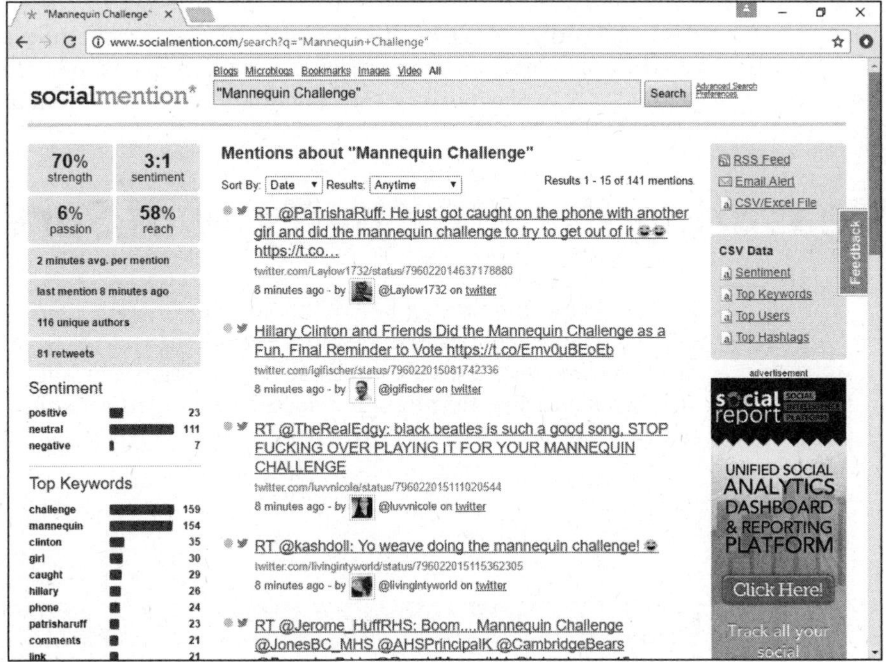

FIGURE 1-6: Social Mention provides a social-ranking score based on its definition of popularity.

Talkwalker Alerts

A comparable alternative to Google Alerts, Talkwalker (`www.talkwalker.com/alerts`) monitors the web for mentions of your brand, competitors, name, events, or other keywords. It provides email updates to your email inbox or RSS reader on a daily or weekly basis. Free for up to 100 alerts, Talkwalker Alerts does not cover social media. However, the paid Pro versions of Talkwalker (`www.talkwalker.com/en/social-media-intelligence`) include multiple social media sources, higher limits on the number of alerts, and other features. Prices start at approximately $700 per month, with a 14-day free trial.

Trackur

Trackur (`www.trackur.com`) tracks all forms of social media, including Facebook, Google+, Reddit, blogs, news, networks, RSS feeds, tweets, images, and video (some sources are available only with paid plans). In addition to displaying conversational content, Trackur presents trends and analyzes any website that mentions a term being monitored. Monthly plans start with 50 search terms at $97 per month. All paid plans come with a free 10-day trial.

WhosTalkin.com

WhosTalkin.com (`www.whostalkin.com`) is another free, real-time search tool. It surveys 60 social media services for current conversations in the categories of blogs, news, networks, videos, images, forums, and tags. It lacks the reporting capabilities of Social Mention, but it does include actual comments. WhosTalkin.com provides results for only one term at a time but offers a browser search plug-in API.

Measuring the Buzz by Type of Service

The number of monitoring tools competing for market share is astonishing. The following tables are not intended to be comprehensive lists; instead, they simply provide some idea of what's out there. Don't forget the "simple" measuring services available directly through a social media platform, such as Twitter's own search function, as seen in Figure 1-7.

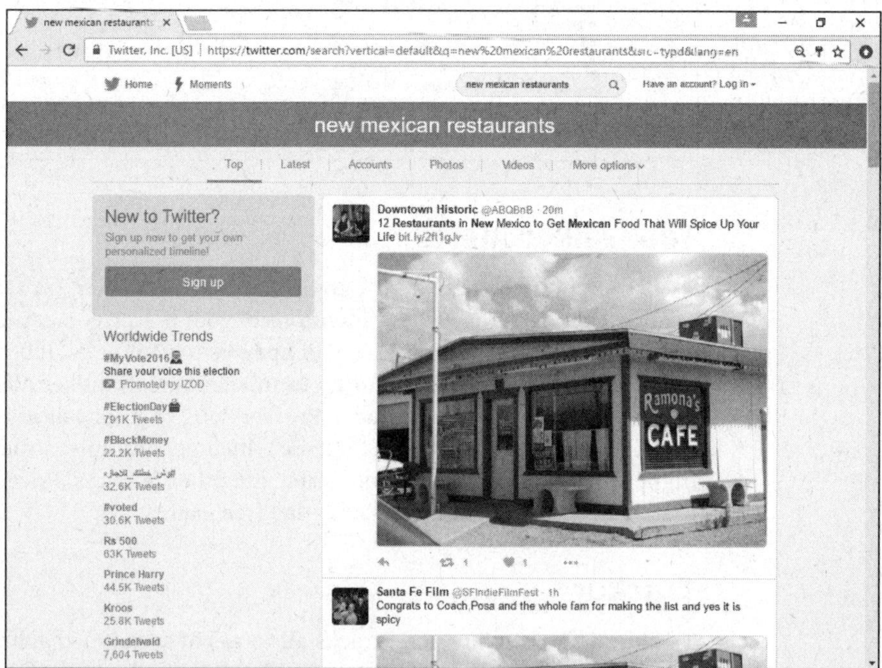

FIGURE 1-7: Results page from a simple Twitter search for *New Mexican Restaurants.*

Table 1-4 lists tools for monitoring blogs and forums; tools for news, RSS, and geolocation sites; tools for Twitter; and some high-end tools at the enterprise level. You can always search for free tools in each category to get more options.

REMEMBER

To ensure that your blog appears in a timely fashion in blog-monitoring tools, submit your blog to each one.

Discovering Helpful Tech Tools

TABLE 1-4 Helpful Monitoring Tools

Name	URL	Description
Blog- and Forum-Monitoring Tools		
Attentio	`http://attentio.com`	A suite of B2B media monitoring and analysis tools; fee.
BlogSearchEngine	`www.blogsearchengine.org/`	Search for blogs by topic area or search term.
IceRocket	`www.icerocket.com`	Trend and buzz monitor for blogs and Twitter.
Sovrn	`www.sovrn.com`	Free tool to help publishers monetize their websites and social media, reach their target audiences, and build relationships. Includes reports on user behavior, demographics, and actions.
Social News and RSS Tools		
Google News	`http://news.google.com`	Keyword search of Google News.
Yahoo! News	`http://news.yahoo.com`	Keyword search of Yahoo! News.
Twitter-Monitoring Tools		
Hashtagify.me	`http://hashtagify.me`	Manage your own hashtags and receive alerts when hashtags are used.
SocialOomph	`www.socialoomph.com`	One-stop shop for multiple tools to monitor and manage many social media channels; freemium model.
TweetDeck	`https://about.twitter.com/products/tweetdeck`	Real-time tool for Twitter organizing, engagement, tracking searches, and activity in one interface.
Twitter Search	`https://twitter.com/search-home` `https://twitter.com/search-advanced?lang=en`	Twitter's own search filter with advanced queries on multiple parameters.
Fee-Based, Enterprise-Level Monitoring Tools		
BrandsEye	`www.brandseye.com`	Paid service tracks online conversations with monitoring and insight tools.
eCairn	`www.ecairn.com`	Integrate and analyze multiple social media sources for marketing and PR pros.

(continued)

TABLE 1-4 ***(continued)***

Name	URL	Description
Sysomos Heartbeat	`www.sysomos.com/products/overview/heartbeat`	Monitor and measure buzz and sentiment in real time.
Lithium	`www.lithium.com/products-solutions/social-media-analytics`	Monitor community engagement as part of an integrated social media management package.
Nielsen Online	`www.nielsen.com/us/en/solutions/measurement/online.html`	Measure and analyze online audiences for social media, advertising, video viewing, consumer-generated media, word of mouth, and other consumer behaviors.
Salesforce Marketing Cloud	`www.salesforcemarketingcloud.com/products/social-media-listening`	Detailed monitoring of social media buzz about industry, competitors, and/or brand. Analyze customer desires, evaluate content engagement, and assess campaign reaction.

IN THIS CHAPTER

» Understanding why SEO still matters

» Looking into the top search engines

» Focusing on the SEO basics of keywords and metatags

» Optimizing your web presence for search engines

Chapter 2 Leveraging SEO for Improved Visibility

No matter how popular social media may be, search engine optimization (SEO) must still be a part of your toolkit for a successful, broad-spectrum web presence. The goal of SEO is to get various components of your web presence to appear near the top — preferably in the top ten — of search results on general search engines or specific social media services.

You accomplish this by selecting appropriate search terms or keywords and then optimizing content, navigation, and structure to create a web page or profile that's search friendly for your selected terms. At the same time, you maximize cross-links from social media to increase the number of inbound links to your primary website.

Fortunately, you can optimize social media, from blogs to Facebook, very much the same way that you optimize a website. Some people call this social media optimization (SMO), referring to the application of SEO techniques to social media. SMO has become even more critical with search engines such as Google moving toward personalization and semantic analysis, which skews users' results on the basis of location and past searches.

If you do a good job optimizing multiple components of your web presence — your website, blog, Facebook page, Twitter profile, and more — they may all appear near the top of search engine result pages (SERPs) on selected terms, increasing your company's share of that premium screen real estate. As mentioned in Book 1, Chapter 1, improving search engine ranking is one strategic justification for implementing a social media campaign in the first place.

Making the Statistical Case for SEO

News of the publicity about social media usage sometimes overshadows the actual numbers. For instance, comScore's Unique Visitor Table (`www.comscore.com/Insights/Rankings`) for November 2016 showed that Facebook (208.9 million unique visitors) fell behind Google sites (246.1 million) but remained ahead of Microsoft sites (188.7 million) and Yahoo! sites (205.6 million) in terms of visits.

Although more than 1.18 billion people worldwide (almost 85 percent outside North America) were called daily active Facebook users in September 2016, that doesn't mean they were using it to search for information that might lead them to your company.

In fact, a survey in January 2015 by the Local Search Association asked how consumers search for products and services. The results showed that most consumers prefer search engines, followed by company websites. Both options significantly outnumbered social media or other sources, as shown in Figure 2-1.

At the moment, no social media alternative covers as wide a base of web pages or as commanding an algorithm for assessing relevance as search engines. What will happen in the future? Get out your crystal ball or watch eMarketer and other sites for more data. One thing about the web is for sure — like the world, it's always changing.

Given these statistics, do you still need to bother with search engine optimization techniques for your hub website, as we discuss in Book 1, Chapter 1? Absolutely. Here's why:

- Although the younger subset of Internet users is attracted to searching for trending topics on social media or relying on friends' recommendations of products, not all members of your target audience are active users of social media — especially if you have a business-to-business (B2B) company or target an older consumer audience.
- After you optimize your hub website or blog, registered under your own domain name, you can quickly transfer the techniques, tools, and results to social media, especially to blogs and tweets.

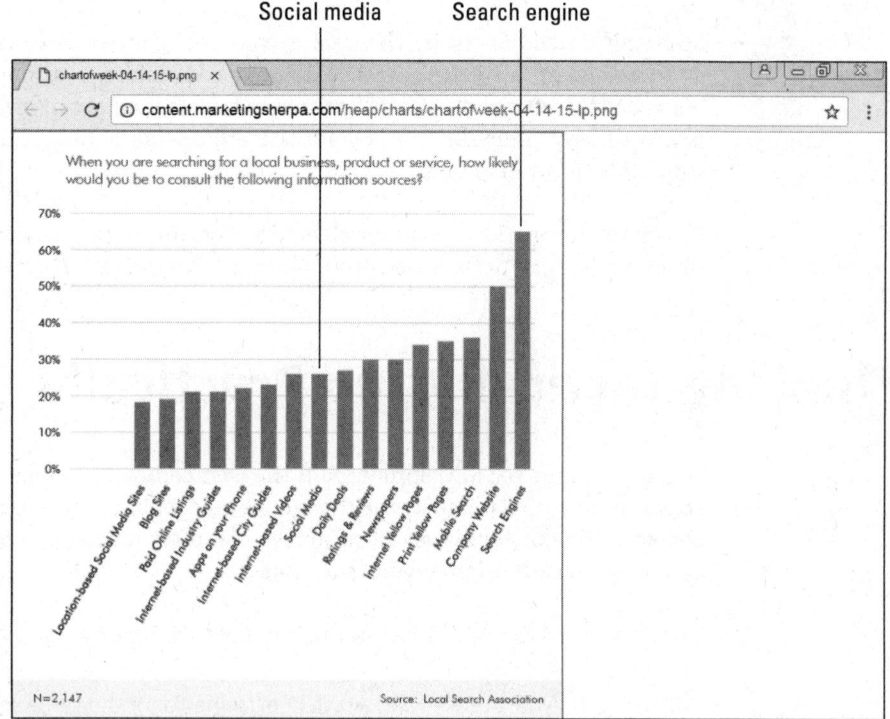

FIGURE 2-1: In 2015, consumers still favored search engines over social media to find products and services.

Courtesy of Local Search Association and Marketing Sherpa

- Inbound links to a hub website remain a key to high ranking in search results, especially on Google. Your social media pages are a rich source of these links. Google treats posts and profiles on social media channels, which are written in HTML, just like any other sites on the web for ranking and search.

  REMEMBER

  Google can't review social media pages that have been set to private, no matter how much traffic or engagement those pages may have.
- Most social media services still aren't as flexible as a full-fledged website when it comes to handling e-commerce, database applications, forms, or other myriad features involving real-time data entry. Most third-party apps on social media that offer some of this functionality can't give you the same degree of control as you have on your website.
- Your website or blog benefits from links to your site from social media pages. In particular, make sure your profile is public and contains links to your site.
- SEO remains necessary, though not sufficient, method of ensuring site visibility based on a method other than the number of friends, fans, or followers you have. You're chasing profits, not popularity.

REMEMBER

SEO isn't an end in itself. The goal is to draw qualified visitors to your website so that you can turn them into customers and clients. A strong SEO foundation helps direct traffic to your full-featured hub from your social media presence. SEO is a necessary component of a complete online-marketing strategic plan, but it shouldn't be the only one.

For more information about search engine optimization, see *Search Engine Optimization All-in-One For Dummies*, 3rd Edition, by Bruce Clay (John Wiley & Sons, Inc.).

Thinking Tactically and Practically

The best results for SEO sprout from the best content — and so does the largest stream of qualified prospects. Although we talk about many SEO techniques in this chapter, none of them will work unless you offer appealing content that draws and holds the attention of your audience.

Two schools of thought drive SEO tactics for social media:

- Optimize your website and all your social media for the same search terms, occupying the first page of results with one or more pages of your web presence.
- Use your social media pages to grab a good position for some relatively rare search terms that your website doesn't use.

TIP

Get greedy. Go for the best of both worlds. Use your standard search terms on social media profiles and the more rarely used terms on individual posts, photo captions, or updates.

Use a free trial at sites such as `http://seosuite.com`, `www.webseoanalytics.com/free/seo-tools/keyword-competition-checker.php`, or `http://moz.com/tools` to see how your site ranks on different search terms. Your tactical decisions about keyword selection may depend on those results, as well as on the goals and objectives of your social media campaign.

In the later section "Choosing the right search terms," you discover how to select terms that people are likely to use and ones that give you a chance of breaking through to the first page of search results.

SEARCH ENGINE JARGON

Help yourself by mastering the terminology you see on search engine resource sites or in articles:

- **Natural or organic search** refers to the type of search results produced by a search engine's *algorithm* (set of rules) when indexing unpaid submissions.
- **Paid search results** are those for which a submission fee or bid has been paid to appear as sponsorships at the top of a search results page, in pay-per-click (PPC) ads in the right margin, or in some cases at the top of the list of search results.
- **Search engine marketing (SEM)** combines both natural and paid search activities.
- **Search engine optimization (SEO)** is the process of adjusting websites, web pages, and social media pages to gain higher placement in search engine results.
- **Social media optimization (SMO)** is the process of adjusting social media profiles and postings to gain higher placement in search engine results.
- **Spiders, crawlers, and robots (bots)** are automated programs used by search engines to visit websites and index their content.

Focusing on the Top Search Engines

Ignore all those emails about submitting your site to 3,000 search engines. You need to submit to only the top two: Google, and Yahoo!/Bing (which share the same algorithm). When you submit to Bing, you're also listed on Yahoo! However, the results pages may not always be identical, particularly on local searches.

Table 2-1 tells where to submit your sites to those search engines.

TABLE 2-1 Submission URLs for Key Search Engines

Name	URL	Search % February 2016
Google	`www.google.com/webmasters/tools`	64.0
Yahoo!	`www.bing.com/toolbox/submit-site-url`	12.2
Bing	`www.bing.com/toolbox/submit-site-url`	21.4

Source: comScore Explicit Core Search Share Report February 2016
`www.comscore.com/Insights/Rankings/comScore-Releases-February-2016-US-Desktop-Search-Engine-Rankings`

According to comScore, these three search engines accounted for 97.6 percent of all searches in February 2016, with Google executing about three times as many searches as Bing, its closest search competitor. All remaining search engines together accounted for the remaining 2.4 percent of searches. Primary search engines spider the web incessantly. You don't need to resubmit your site routinely. But you should resubmit your site to trigger a visit from the arachnids if you add new content or products, expand to a new location, or update your search terms.

TIP

Different search engines use different *algorithms* (sets of rules) to display search results, which may vary rapidly over time. To complicate matters further, different search engines tend to attract different audiences. Optimize your site for the search engine that best attracts your audience. Here are some facts about the top search engines and their audiences that might affect your SEO, posting, and online advertising tactics:

- Compared to the overall population of Internet users, Google users are slightly more likely to be male, whileYahoo!/Bing users are more likely to be female
- The search engines skew by age, with users younger than 35 more likely to use Google and older users more likely to use Yahoo!/Bing.
- Consistent with usage location, Google users tend to search during work hours on workdays, while Yahoo!/Bing users search early mornings or on weekends.
- Google users are night owls, hitting the keyboards from 8 p.m. to midnight. In contrast, users of Yahoo!/Bing are morning doves, with prime usage from 4 a.m. to 7 a.m or 10 a.m to 3 p.m.
- Mobile searchers are more likely to use Google; tablet searchers gravitate to Yahoo!/Bing.
- The Yahoo!/Bing search engine is popular in households with children and households with more than $75 thousand in household income.

Knowing the Importance of Search Phrases

Users enter search terms in the query box on a search engine, website, or social media service to locate the information they seek. The trick to success is to identify the search terms that your prospective customers are likely to use.

REMEMBER

For good visibility on a search term, your site or social media profile needs to appear within the top ten positions on the first page of search results for that term. Only academic researchers and obsessive-compulsives are likely to search beyond the first page.

Fortunately or unfortunately, everyone's brain is wired a little differently, leading to different choices of words and different ways of organizing information. Some differences are simple matters of dialect: Someone in the southern United States may look for *bucket*, whereas someone in the north looks for a *pail*. Someone in the United Kingdom may enter *cheap petrol*, whereas someone in the United States types *cheap gas*.

Other differences have to do with industry-specific jargon. *Rag* has one meaning to someone looking for a job in the garment industry, another in the publishing business, and yet another meaning to someone wanting to buy a chamois to polish a car.

Other variations have to do with spelling simplicity. Users will invariably spell *hotels* rather than *accommodations*, or *army clothes* instead of *camouflage* or *khaki*. And users rarely type a phrase that's longer than five words.

TIP

The predominant length of a search query in English is currently between two and three words. With personal search and location-based search now built into engines such as Google, many users don't bother to include as many words in searches as they used to. However, because people are using voice to query their smartphones, search queries may become longer and are often phrased as a question, rather than as a noun phrase. Now you need to think of search phrases in terms of not only what your content includes but also what your user might intend (take out your mind-reader hat) and how various concepts in your content relate to one another. Longer search queries, which are sometimes called *long-tail keywords*, are more likely to land people on a specific page or post. Therefore, lengthy queries, while rarely used, may be more likely to lead to conversions.

Choosing the right search terms

We recommend trying to come up with a list of at least 30 search terms that can be distributed among different pages of your website (more if you have a large site). You must juggle the terms people are likely to use to find your product or service with the likelihood that you can show up on the first page of search results. Here are some tips for building a list of potential keywords:

- Brainstorm all possible terms that you think your target audience might use. Ask your customers, friends, and employees for ideas.

- Be sure your list includes the names of all your products and service packages and your company name. Someone who has heard of you must absolutely be able to find you online.
- Incorporate all industry-specific search terms and jargon you can think of.
- If you sell to a local or regional territory, incorporate location into your terms: for example, *Lancaster bakery* or *Columbus OH chiropractor*. It's very difficult to appear on the first page of results for a single word, such as *bakery* or *chiropractor.*
- For additional ideas, go to Google, enter a search term, and click the Search button. Then select the Related Searches option in the left margin. You may be surprised by the other search phrases that users try.
- If you already have a website, look at your analytics results to see which search phrases people are using to find your site.
- Use one or more of the free search tools listed in Table 2-2 to get ideas for other keywords, how often they're used, and how many competing sites use the same term.
- Figure 2-2 displays results and synonyms from the SEMrush.com keyword overview tool for the phrase *cake decorating supplies.*
- You can also try the Google AdWords Keyword Planner Tool at `https://adwords.google.com/home/tools/keyword-planner`. Intended to help buyers of Google AdWords, this tool is also useful when you're brainstorming search terms. However, to access this tool, you need to sign into an existing AdWords account or create one by clicking the links on the Keyword Planner page.

TIP

You'll get more accurate, detailed numbers if you also sign up for Google Search Console (formerly Webmaster Tools). You or your programmer should do this anyway at `www.google.com/webmasters` or `http://g.co/SearchConsole`.

- Check your competitors' search terms for ideas. Visit your competitors' sites and right-click to view the page source, or look in the browser toolbar for something like View⇨Source. The keywords are usually listed near the top of the source code for a page. If you don't see them, use the Find command (Ctrl+F) to search for *keyword.*
- Not sure who your competitors are? Enter one of your search terms to identify similar companies appearing on the first page of search results. Then you can go look at their other keywords, too.
- Look at the tag clouds for topics on social news services or blog search engines such as `www.icerocket.com` to assess the relative popularity of different search terms. *Tag clouds* visualize how often keywords appear in specific

content or how often they're used by searchers, with the most popular terms usually appearing in larger type. (You can find more on tag clouds in the section "Understanding tags and tag clouds," later in this chapter.)

- Avoid using single words except in technical fields where the word is a term specific to a particular industry, such as *seismometer* or *angiogram,* with only hundreds of thousands, instead of millions, of competing pages. Not only will you have too much competition on generalized single words, but results for single words also produce too wide a range of options. People simply give up.

TABLE 2-2 **Keyword Selection Resources**

Name	URL	Description
Google AdWords Keyword Planner	https://adwords.google.com/home/tools/keyword-planner	Free keyword generator and statistics available to holders of Google and AdWords accounts; better results for paid accounts
Google Trends	www.google.com/trends	Research on trending search terms
KGen	https://addons.mozilla.org/firefox/addon/kgen https://chrome.google.com/webstore/detail/kgen/jkpcelefglapiahikhocfdcigfpaagcl	Shareware add-on for the Firefox and Chrome toolbars showing which keywords are strong on visited web pages
SEMrush	www.semrush.com	Research keywords used by competitors for Google and Bing organic searches
Ubersuggest	http://ubersuggest.org	Free keyword suggestion tool
WordStream	www.wordstream.com/keywords	Basic keyword tools; 30 free searches
Wordtracker	www.wordtracker.com	Keyword suggestion tool; free 7-day trial

Crafting a page, blog post, or social media profile for more than four or five search terms is difficult. Break up your list of terms into sets that you think you can work into a single paragraph of text while still making sense.

TIP

Optimizing for search terms that real people rarely use doesn't make sense. Sure, you can be number one because you have no competition, but why bother? You will show up on these words anyway. The exceptions are your company and product names and terms highly specific to your business.

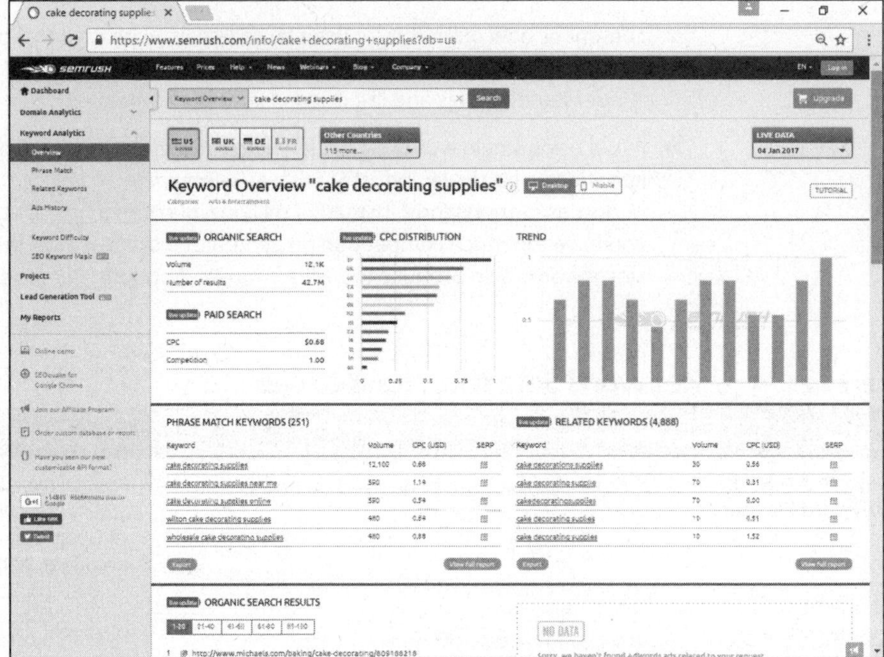

FIGURE 2-2: The SEMrush keyword tool estimates the volume of requests for related search terms and the cost per click for a term.

Courtesy of Oleg Shchegolev, CEO of SEMrush Inc.

REMEMBER

Always test your selected search terms to be sure that sites like yours show up in the results for that term. For instance, entering *artificial trees* as a search term yields inexpensive artificial Christmas trees, especially at the holiday season, and perhaps some silk palm trees. However, that term doesn't produce appropriate results if your company offers $30,000 tree sculptures designed for shopping malls, zoos, or museums.

Where to place search terms on your site

Sprinkle your keywords throughout the content that visitors will see. Although Google searches the entire page, it's a good idea to include search terms in the first paragraph of a page.

Opinions vary, but some experts recommend generally constraining your use to three to five search terms per page, aiming for a keyword density of 2 to 6 percent. The longer your content, the more search terms you can include on a page. Just be careful that the language remains readable!

WARNING

If your keyword density is too high, your content may not read well and Google will ding you for it.

Your home page should include your most important search terms and your brand names; you may want to include as many as eight terms. As you drill down in the navigation, the nature of the search terms may change. For instance, give your *category pages* (additional pages in the top navigation), which have general overview information, two to four general, short phrases.

Detailed pages that describe your products or services generally appear at secondary or tertiary levels in your navigation. Keep the search terms on these pages focused on one topic per page, and optimize for one to three brand names or longer search terms related to your topic.

TIP

You generally don't get much mileage from search terms on boilerplate pages such as your privacy policy, terms of service, or contact us page unless you modify the content to include relevant information.

Understanding tags and tag clouds

We want to dispense with one major source of confusion. *Tags* are the social media equivalent of search terms (several keywords together, such as *New Mexico artists*). Tags are commonly used on blogs, social media, and content-heavy sites other than search engines to categorize content and help users find material.

Tag clouds are simply a way to visualize how often keywords either appear in specific content or are used by searchers.

Keywords in a tag cloud are often arranged alphabetically or with common terms grouped and displayed as a paragraph. The more frequently used terms (minus common elements such as articles and prepositions) appear in the largest font, as shown in Figure 2-3.

Tag clouds can help you quickly grasp the popularity of particular topics, the terms that people most often use to find a topic, or the relative size or frequency of something, such as city population or usage of different browser versions.

When you submit your site to social-bookmarking or social news services (as we describe in Chapter 4 of this minibook), you're often asked to enter a list of helpful tags so that other people can search for your content. The first rule is to use tags that match your primary search terms and ensure that those terms appear in your text.

TIP

You can quickly generate a tag cloud for content by using a tool such as TagCrowd (`http://tagcrowd.com`) or Wordle (`www.wordle.net`). Simply paste in text from your website or enter the URL for your site and click to create a tag cloud. You can then enter the most frequently appearing words as the tags when you submit content to a social media service.

FIGURE 2-3: This tag cloud from TagCrowd shows the frequency (popularity) of words used on the home page for PenningtonBuilders.com.

Courtesy of Pennington Builders

Some social media services display tag clouds created on a running basis to identify trending topics. Use these tag clouds on social media to help determine the popularity of various topics while you decide which content to post. You can also modify the tags you use to categorize your postings. Include or default to commonly used tags when you make your submission to increase the likelihood that your posting shows up in search results.

Maximizing Metatag Muscle

Search engines use the title and description metatags to help rank the relevance of a website, blog, or social media page to a search query. Historically, engines needed many types of *metadata* (data that describes a web page overall) to categorize a website, but now search engines need only the title and description metatags for that purpose. Search engines can automatically detect the rest of the information they need, and too many metatags just slow them down.

WARNING

The keyword metatag is no longer used by search engines, which rely on the appearance of search terms within readable text. While the keyword metatag may be useful for human beings to track which terms were optimized, some experts recommend omitting it.

Title and page description tags have become even more important with the advent of social media. Facebook and some other platforms will pull content from these tags when a URL is shared.

Don't confuse the term *metatags,* which refers to specific entries that appear in page source code, with the term *tags,* the label used to refer to assigned keywords in blogs, or the term *hashtags,* which is used for categorization purposes on many social media platforms.

To view metatags for any website, choose View ⇨ Source in Internet Explorer; look for a similar command in other browsers. (You can also right-click a web page and choose View Source from the pop-up menu that appears.) A display appears like the one shown in Figure 2-4 (top), which shows the primary metatags for Pennington Builders (`www.penningtonbuilders.com`).

Note that the first paragraph of text shown in Figure 2-4 (bottom) is optimized with some of the same search terms that appear in the keyword tag and title tag. Note also the page title above the browser toolbar, which also includes two of the search terms. We talk more about the title metatag in the next section "Tipping the scales with the page title metatag."

If you don't see page title or page description metatags in the page source for your own site, you may be in trouble. That could partially account for poor results in search engines.

You can usually insert metatags and <alt> tags for photos quite easily if you use a content management system (CMS) to maintain your website or if you use blog software. If you don't, you may need to ask your programmer or web developer for assistance.

Tipping the scales with the page title metatag

Perhaps the most important metatag, the page title appears above the browser toolbar when users are on a website. (Refer to Figure 2-4, bottom, to see where the output of the title tag appears on the screen.) A good page title metatag includes one or more keywords followed by your company name. Select one or more search terms from the set of keywords you've assigned to that particular page.

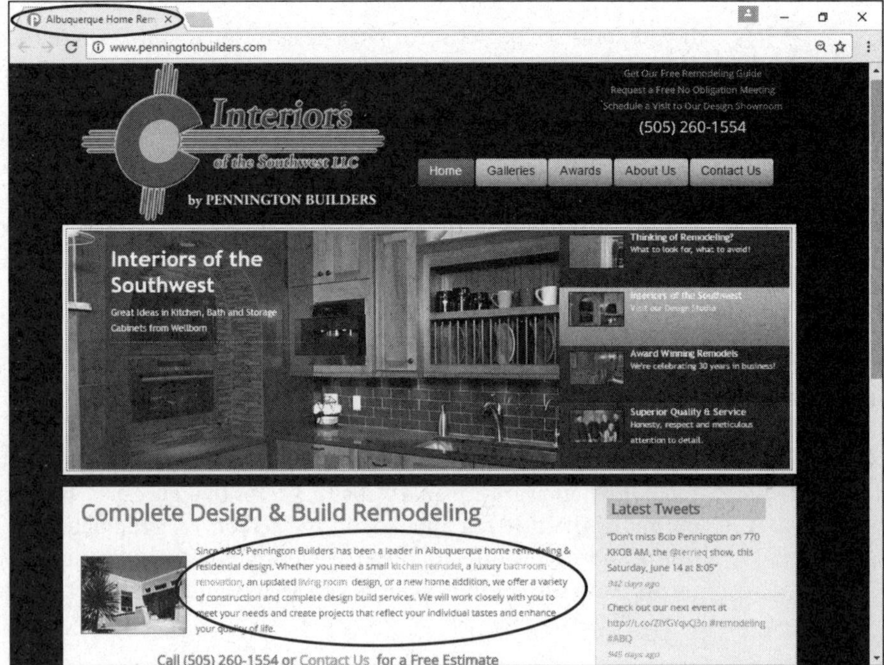

FIGURE 2-4: The page source (top) for the home page of Pennington Builders (bottom).

Courtesy of Pennington Builders

Because browsers may truncate the title display, place the search term first. Although you can use a longer title tag, we suggest an average length of seven to ten words and fewer than 70 characters. Some search engines may truncate title tags that are more than 55 characters anyway. A long, long time ago, way back in the dinosaur age of the Internet, page names were used to index a website. That method is now unnecessary; it's a waste of time to use a phrase such as *home page* rather than a search term in a page title. It's almost as big a waste of time as having no title tag. The portion of the <title> metatag (Albuquerque Home Remodeling & Residential Design) that appears in Figure 2-4 (compare top image to bottom) is typical.

TIP

Because longer, more descriptive title tags may work better for social sharing, don't obsess about length. It's always better to write a title tag that gets clicks!

Google and other search engines dislike multiple pages with identical metatags. Changing the <title> tag on each page is one of the easiest ways to handle this preference. Simply pull another relevant search term from your list of keywords and insert it in front of the company name in the <title> tag.

Pumping up page description metatags

The page description metatag appears as several sentences below the link to each site in natural search results. It's important to write an appealing page description because you may want to repeat this tag in all your social media profiles.

Some search engines truncate description metatags after as few as 115 characters, although you are generally safe at 150-160 characters. In 2016, Google experimented with allowing title tags up to 70 characters and description tags up to 276 characters, but the final status on character counts remains uncertain. Just in case, front-load the description with all the search terms from the set you've assigned to that page. Search engines display the first line of text when a page description metatag isn't available.

TIP

Why pass up a marketing opportunity? Just because your site appears near the top of search results, you have no guarantee that someone will click through to your site. Write your page description metatag as though it were ad copy, including a benefits statement and a call to action.

Figure 2-5 displays natural search results on Google with the page description for the home page of Pennington Builders. Note the inclusion of search terms *(kitchen remodel, home remodeling)* from the keywords metatag in Figure 2-4 (top).

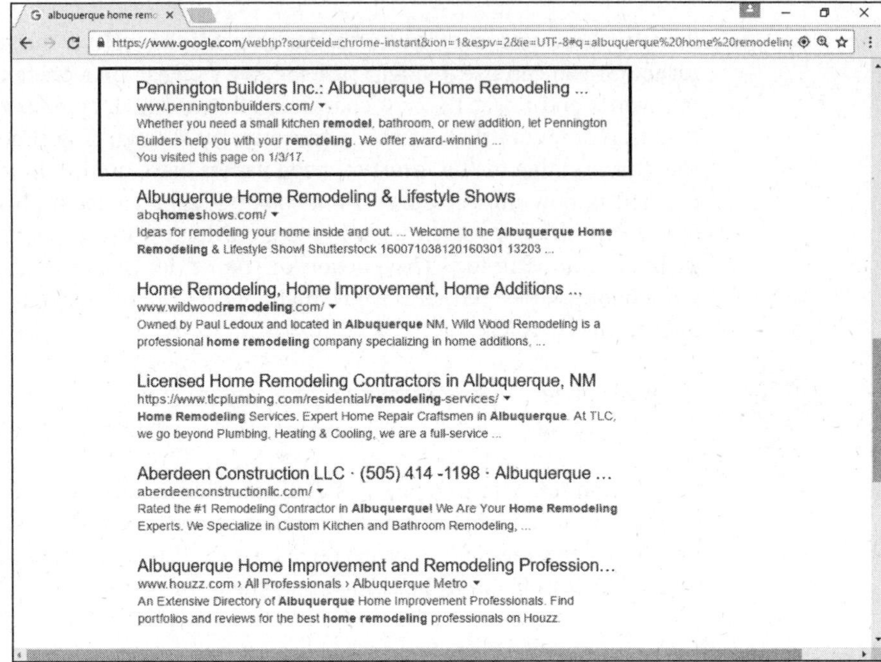

FIGURE 2-5: The page description metatag for the home page of the Pennington Builders site appears on the first page of the natural search results for the term *albuquerque remodeling*.

Courtesy of Pennington Builders

Optimizing Your Site and Content for Search Engines

Optimization is the process of adjusting your site, blog, or social media profiles to play well with search algorithms. You optimize primarily by having plenty of relevant content, updating it often, and making sure that your web presence is easy for general and on-site search engines to discover with their spiders. We cover a few of the most important tricks of the trade in the following sections. For additional information on search engines and site optimization, check out some of the resources listed in Table 2-3.

TECHNICAL STUFF

Google has such a habit of modifying its search algorithms that the changes have been called *dances*. The 2016 version of the Penguin algorithm change devalued bad inbound links and resulted in a shake-up of search engine rankings.

TIP

Because Google algorithm changes unfold over time, your best option is to watch your search engine results weekly and take action as needed. To stay up to date on Google's jitterbugs, waltzes, cha-chas, quick-steps, and other dances, you might want to bookmark `https://moz.com/google-algorithm-change`. You can also monitor any of the sources in Table 2-3 for news.

TABLE 2-3 Search Engine and Optimization Resources

Name	URL	Description
Google Search Console	`https://static.googleusercontent.com/media/www.google.com/en//webmasters/docs/search-engine-optimization-starter-guide.pdf`	Guidelines and suggestions for site optimization and SEO information for webmasters
	`https://support.google.com/webmasters/answer/35291`	
Moz	`http://moz.com`	SEO learning resource with tools and community support.
MozBar	`https://moz.com/products/pro/seo-toolbar`	All-in-one SEO toolbar with rankings
Search Engine Guide	`http://www.searchengineguide.com/marketing.html`	Search engine articles, blog, marketing
Search Engine Journal	`www.searchenginejournal.com/seo-101-resources-learn-with-guides-tutorials-and-more/35740`	Best practices for URLs and SEO
Search Engine Land	`http://searchengineland.com`	Search engine news
Search Engine Watch	`www.searchenginewatch.com`	Articles, tutorials, forums, blogs, SEO articles, and tips
UrlTrends	`www.urltrends.com`	Suite of SEO tools and reports

Writing an optimized first paragraph

First and foremost, use the search terms you've assigned to each page in the first paragraph of text or the first paragraph of a blog posting. Although search engines now check the full pages of entire websites or blogs, it helps to have search terms visible near the beginning of the page's text for faster indexing.

TIP

There's nothing like on-site social media, such as a blog or a forum, to generate keyword-rich content for search engines to munch on. Best of all, other folks are helping you feed the beast! Generally speaking, keep your word count per article to at least 300 for SEO purposes. While longer articles can increase opportunities for SEO, they may also turn off readers.

Figure 2-6 shows a well-optimized posting (top) and its source code (bottom) from InjuryLawyerNM.com. Archibeque Law Firm owns the blog. This entry (at `www.injurylawyernm.com/top-things-your-albuquerque-personal-injury-lawyer-needs`) includes the phrase *personal injury lawyer* in its URL, post title, and text. Note the social media chiclets in the header. The source code uses the same term in the keyword and page description metatags.

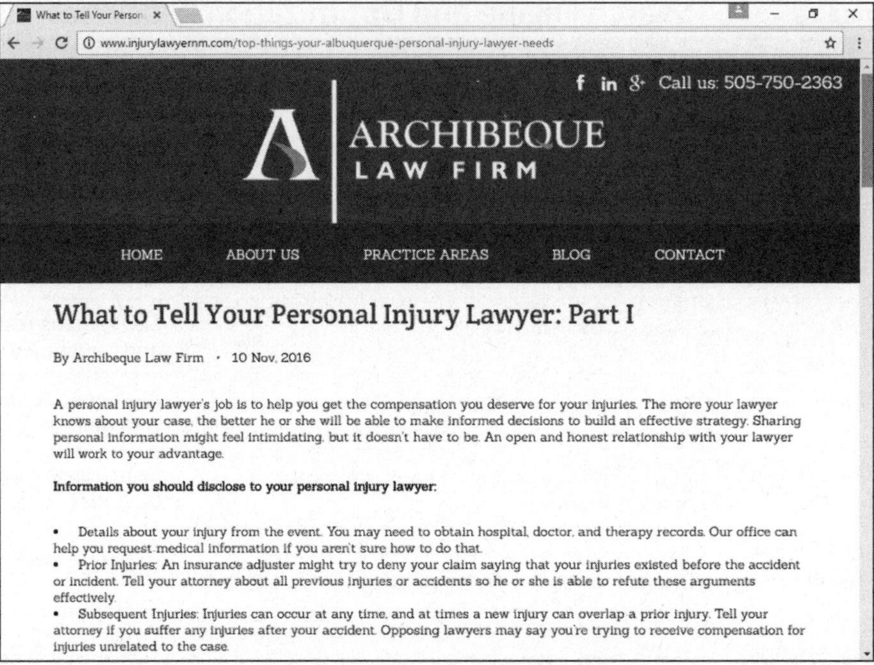

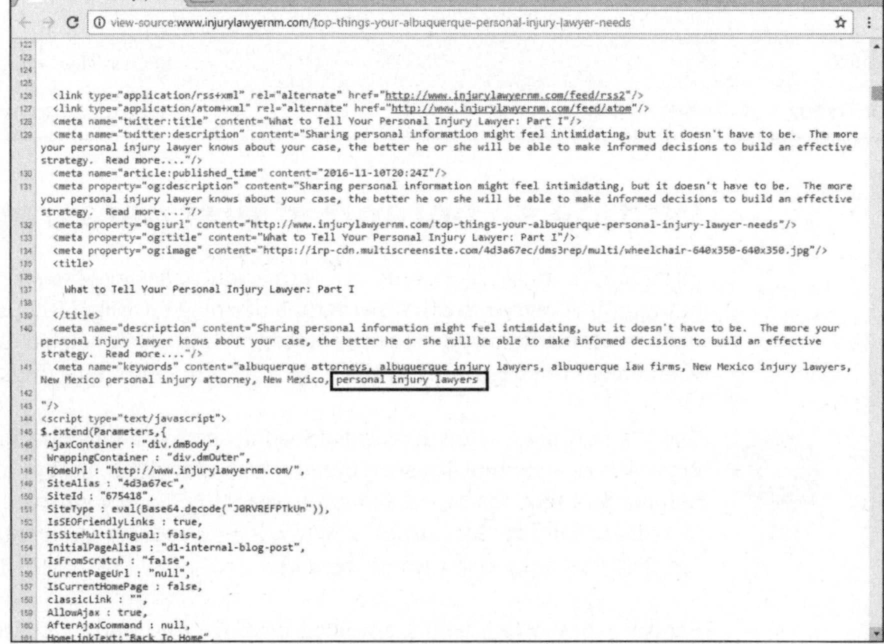

FIGURE 2-6: Compare the blog post (top) — which uses the keyword phrase *personal injury lawyer* in its title, page URL, and text — to the source code (bottom).

Courtesy of Archibeque Law Firm

TIP

Try to arrange your navigation so every page on your site is accessible with no more than three to four clicks from any other page.

Don't try to force more than a few terms into the first paragraph. If another phrase or two fits naturally, that's fine. Trying to cram more words into your text may render it unintelligible or jargon-loaded to human readers.

TECHNICAL STUFF

No matter where the first paragraph of text appears on the page, place the text near the top of the source code. The text should appear above any tags for images, video, or Flash.

Updating often

Search engines, especially Google, love to see updated content. Regular updates are a sign that a website is loved and cared for, and easily updated content is one of many reasons for having a blog or content management system on your site. If changing content is simple and free, you're more likely to do it.

At least once a month, change a paragraph of content on your site. Include this task on your Social Media Activity Calendar. (See Book 1, Chapter 4.) If you can't commit to this task, at least ask your programmer to incorporate some kind of automatically updated material, whether it's a date-and-time stamp, a quote, or a syndicated content feed, for example.

TIP

If you follow no other search optimization tips in this chapter, make sure that you follow at least these two: Update often and optimize the first paragraph of text on every page.

Guess what? You score extra jelly beans in the relevance jar if your search terms appear in particular places on your website, in addition to your <title> and page <description> metatags. Follow these tips to optimize your web page or blog for your selected set of search terms. However, if they don't work naturally, don't force them:

- **Links:** Use the words from your set of search terms as *text links* or *anchor text* (words that form an active link to another internal page or external site). Link liberally within text, but don't waste valuable real estate on meaningless phrases such as *Learn more* or *Click here.* They don't do a darn thing for your search ranking. Make sure that internal links open in the same window, while external links open in a new window so users don't lose track of your site.

TIP

If a clickable image opens another page, such as a product detail page, add a clickable caption that includes a search term or the product name. Score some points!

» **Headings:** Headlines and subheads help organize text and assist readers who are skimming your copy for the information they want. Headings that include your search terms can also improve your search engine ranking.

Onscreen, these words usually appear in bold and in a larger font size or different color (or both) from the body copy.

TECHNICAL STUFF

Headings must carry the <h1> to <h6> tags, which define HTML headings, rather than appear as graphics. Search engines can't "read" words embedded in a picture.

» **Navigation:** Search terms that appear as navigational items, whether for main or secondary pages, also earn extra relevance jelly beans. Like with headings, navigation must be in text, not graphic, form.

» **URLs:** Include search terms in understandable URLs for your pages. URLs not only help with search engines but also are often used as link text elsewhere on the web — for example, when shared on social media.

» **Body text:** Use search terms intelligently in your content. Above all, make sure that the content makes sense to a human reader and is rich in information.

WARNING

Avoid *keyword stuffing:* Don't overload a page with repetitive search terms or a long list of different terms in an effort to juice your standing on search engine results pages. Not only do words out of context ring an alarm bell for Google, they make readers very unhappy. If you stick with well-written, natural English and useful content, you'll do just fine in both human and search engine results.

» **Images and <alt> tags:** Not only may your images appear in image search results, they can also help with search engine results. The title, filename, caption, nearby text, and <alt> tag (the text that appears when hovering your cursor over an image on a PC) can contribute to a better ranking when they include a search term.

Sometimes you have to weigh the design considerations or limitations of your CMS or blog against search engine optimization needs. Some designers prefer the greater control and flexibility of font styles available in a graphic. Unfortunately, text in graphics is not readable by search engines. Ultimately, only you can decide what matters more to you.

WARNING

Under no circumstances should you implement *black hat* techniques, which are scams promoted as the search engine equivalent of a get-rich-quick scheme. For instance, don't even think about hiding search terms in the same color as the background, installing magic pixels, or any other shifty tricks. These techniques might get you blacklisted from search engines.

Making your site search engine friendly

In addition to trying the techniques in the preceding section, which apply at the page level, you can take specific actions to make your site, as a whole, friendly to search engines.

Avoiding elements that search engines hate

If you expect a search engine to rank your site or blog favorably, you have to give it something to work with. Computers may be getting smarter all the time, but they can't yet "read" pictures, videos, or soundtracks, let alone minds. They need to be fed a rich diet of words. The list of search engine detestable content is short, but each of the following items can be avoided without harming your message:

- **Graphics without descriptions:** As much as artists and photographers love pages without words, search engines hate them. Simple solutions can make your pictures search engine friendly: Provide an <alt> tag, a caption, or both, have text appear below the fold (as long as the text appears near the top of the code), or include a descriptive paragraph near the image. For an extra boost, include keywords in the filenames for photos.
- **Flash animations:** Whether developers provide Flash animation because it's lucrative or because their clients demand it, not all search engines can index Flash content. (Not to mention that Macs and mobile phones detest it.) Although Google can "read" Flash files, your best bet is to incorporate Flash much as you would incorporate a video — as an element on a page, not as an entire page.
- **Parallax scrolling site design:** You may be familiar with the currently popular design trend to use large images, minimal text, and long scrolling pages on websites. Adapted from video game design, this approach often incorporates parallax design, in which the background and foreground move at slightly different rates. While this can provide an illusion of depth and lovely design effects, it also leads to slower load times (a downer for SEO) and makes it difficult to optimize text for search engines. In particular, it does not work well on mobile devices, an increasingly important factor in search ranking. With some extra effort by your programmer, you can still get decent search ranking, but it may not be worth the sacrifice. For more information, see `https://moz.com/blog/parallax-scrolling-websites-and-seo-a-collection-of-solutions-and-examples`.
- **Substantially duplicate content at different URLs:** The content may not be malicious; maybe it's just printer-only versions of your website. Be sure to delete old versions of pages that have been replaced. Even if they sit in archives, search engines may try to index these pages and reduce your page rank for duplicate information. Have your programmer read the directions at `https://support.google.com/webmasters/answer/66359` about how to

handle this situation. On the other hand, if Google thinks the duplication is deliberate, your site may be penalized or removed from the index.

- **Splash pages:** This misguided attempt to design a website as though it were a book with a cover may harm site traffic. Generally, a site loses half its audience every time a click is required. Why cut your prospect list in half before you even have a chance to explain your benefits? Splash pages often consist of beautiful images or animations that make a statement about a company but carry no content or navigation. If you use rich media on a splash page, make sure to include a regular HTML link to a text-based page for search purposes.

  Often found on sites of companies specializing in entertainment, web development, architecture, arts and crafts, or graphic design, splash pages usually offer viewers an option to skip the introduction and an arrow cuing them to click to enter the real site. The simpler solution is to not include a splash page on your site. For more about the pros and cons of splash pages, see `http://webdesign.about.com/od/navigation/a/aa020303a.htm`.

- **Mobile friendliness:** It's now critical that your website be mobile friendly. Google will penalize sites that aren't mobile friendly in search results while promoting friendly ones. Mobile-friendliness extends beyond simply resizing the screen to the smaller width of mobile devices. Pages must be downloadable in less than one second; the font must be large enough to read on a mobile screen; links must be far enough apart for distinct finger taps; and the amount of data transferred must be minimized. To test your site, enter your URL at `https://search.google.com/search-console/mobile-friendly`. Read the results carefully for suggestions! We talk about search optimization for mobile devices in the next chapter.

TECHNICAL STUFF

If you insist on having a splash page or an entry page, at least don't annoy your visitors. Direct the navigational link for Home to the main page of real content, not to the splash page. With a bit of clever naming, you may be able to get search engine spiders to crawl over the first page of content and ignore the splash page.

Configuring URLs

The best URLs are readable and might include one of your search terms or a descriptive title: www.*yourdomain*.com/social-media-small-businesses. Using a search term from your set of keywords for your web or blog page earns you another point for relevance and lets users know what to expect. At least try to keep the URLs as readable text, as in www.*yourdomain*.com/pages/socialmedia/article1234.htm.

If the content in this entire section makes your eyes glaze over, just hand this chapter to your developer!

TECHNICAL STUFF

Problems with page URLs tend to occur when they're automatically assigned by a content management system (CMS) or when the pages are created dynamically. Those URLs tend to look like gobbledygook: `www.`*`yourdomain`*`.com/shop/AS-djfa-16734-QETR`. Although search engines can review these URLs, these addresses do nothing for your search engine ranking and aren't helpful to users.

You can improve your URL configuration several other ways:

» Use hyphens to separate words instead of using underscores, spaces, or plus signs.

» Keep your URLs as short as possible. Make your URL easier to copy and paste by minimizing the number of words and trailing slashes.

» Don't use database-generated URLs or pages created on the fly (called dynamic URLs) that include multiple non-alphanumeric characters. Search engines are less fussy than they used to be, but many still have problems indexing URLs that have more than four non-alphanumeric characters. Google recommends using a robots.txt file to prevent search engines from trying to spider URLs that generate search results or have infinite spaces (such as calendars). Send your programmer to `https://support.google.com/webmasters/answer/76329?hl=en` for Google's detailed recommendations.

REMEMBER

Be careful when redesigning a blog or website, especially if you're changing developers or platforms. If the existing site is already doing well in search engines, try to preserve its URLs. Not all transitions to a new platform accommodate this strategy. Ask your programmer before you begin.

A badly configured URL may simply not be indexed. This problem can become significant with product databases on e-commerce sites, especially when you want every individual product detail page to appear in search engines. Note that this doesn't apply to tracking ID numbers appended following a ? to identify the source of a link. (For more on tracking URLs, see Book 9, Chapter 1.)

TECHNICAL STUFF

Fortunately, a technical fix exists. You (or your programmer) can implement the Apache Mod_Rewrite module or ISAPI Rewrite for Microsoft, which convert URLs on the fly to a format that's search engine friendly. Have your programmer review `www.digitalocean.com/community/tutorials/how-to-set-up-mod_rewrite` or `www.helicontech.com/isapi_rewrite`, respectively, for more information.

Indexing a site

You can easily create a virtual path to ensure that search engines crawl your entire site. A virtual path of links is especially important in two cases:

- When the top and left navigational elements are graphics, making it impossible for search engines to know which pages are really on the site
- When you have a large, deep, database-driven site without links to all pages easily available in the navigation

For a small site that has graphical navigation, you have a couple of simple fixes. You can create a parallel series of linkable main pages in the footer of your site or create a navigational breadcrumb trail at the top of the page, as shown in Figure 2-7. Either way can help both search engines and human beings know where they are within your site structure.

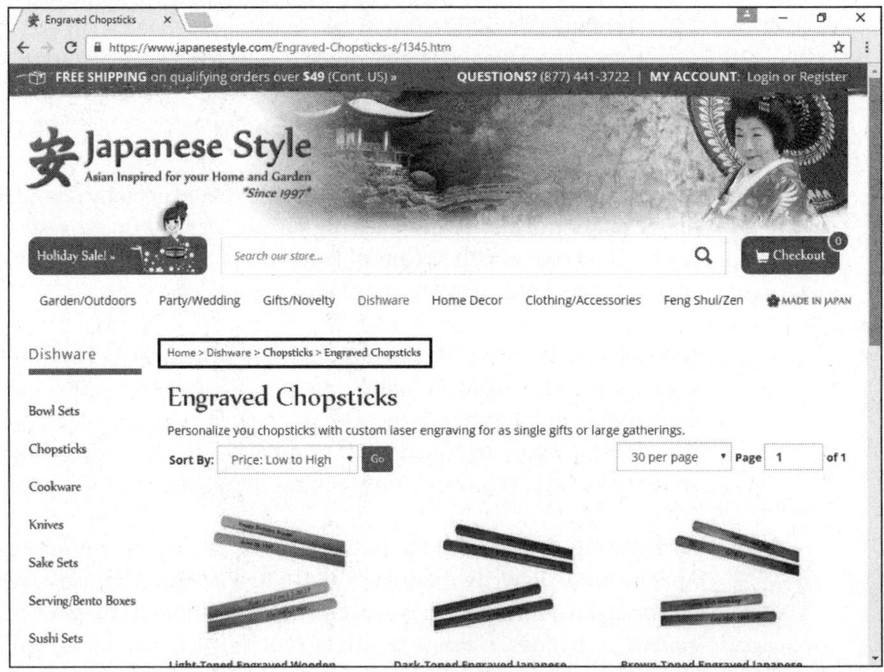

FIGURE 2-7: Breadcrumb trails help both search engine robots and real people navigate your site.

Courtesy of Japanese Style (portrait in header graphic from www.flickr.com/photos/paulsynnott/3406065635/in/album-72157616258070704/ via Creative Commons license https://creativecommons.org/licenses/by/2.0)

A *breadcrumb trail* (think Hansel and Gretel) helps users track where they are on a complex website. It typically consists of a series of page links that extend horizontally across each page, just above the content. Breadcrumb trails, which may either display the site structure or the actual navigation path a user has followed, usually look something like this:

```
Home page &gt; Main section page &gt; Internal page &gt;
  Detail page
```

TECHNICAL STUFF

Put these links in a Server Side Include (SSI) in the footer to ensure that links are displayed consistently on all pages. You then make future changes in only one place (other than in the site itself, of course).

For a site that has a significant number of pages, especially on several tiers, the best solution is to include a linkable site map or site index, as shown in Figure 2-8. It looks a lot like a junior high school outline, which is a perfectly fine solution for both search engine friendliness and site usability.

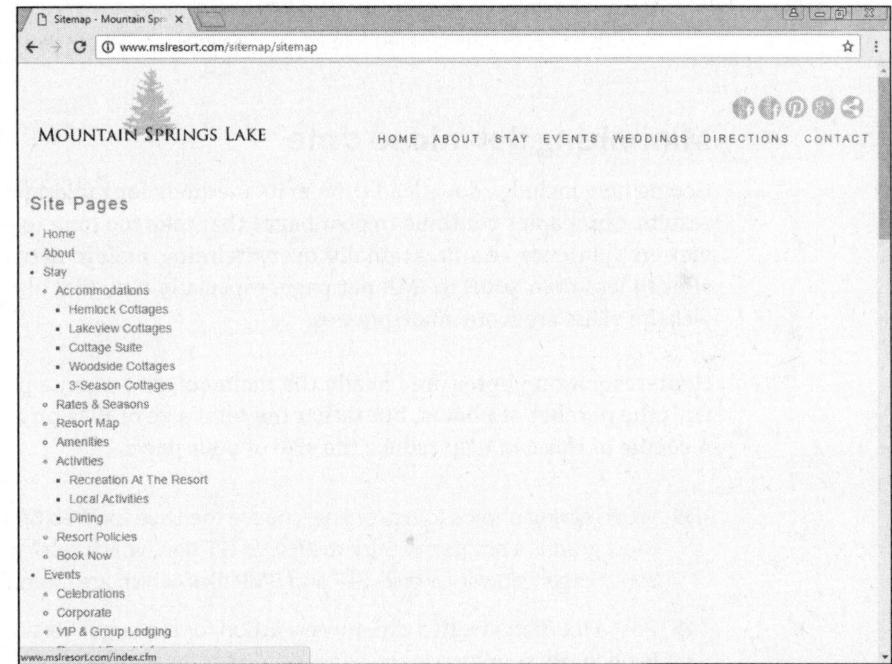

FIGURE 2-8: Page links on a site index provide easy access to all pages on the site.

Courtesy of the Lodge at Mountain Springs Lake Resort

TECHNICAL STUFF

Another solution exists for very large database-driven sites and large stores. Sitemap (XML) feeds that connect directly to Google or Yahoo!/Bing provide current content to all your pages. Direct your programmer to `www.xml-sitemaps.com`, `https://help.smallbusiness.yahoo.net/s/article/SLN19495`, `www.bing.com/webmaster/help/bing-xml-sitemap-plugin-f50bebf5`, or `https://support.google.com/webmasters/topic/4581190` for more information. If content on your site doesn't change very often, you can update these feeds manually every month. If you have continually changing inventory and other content, have your programmer upload these feeds automatically, at least once a day, using RSS.

If you want to index your site to see what pages you have, try one of these free tools:

- **Bing Webmaster Tools:** Use the Index Explore tool in the Reports & Data section to view how Bing sees your site (accessible in the top navigation after you log in).
- **Google Index Status page:** This tool provides stats about which URLs Google has indexed for your site over the past year. To get to this tool, sign in to the Google Search Console at `www.google.com/webmasters/tools/home`.
- **Xenu's Link Sleuth (for PCs only):** Download and run this link verification program (at `http://home.snafu.de/tilman/xenulink.html`). In the results, click the link labeled Site Map of Valid HTML Pages with a Title.

Minimizing download time

Google now includes download time in its methods for ranking websites in search results. Companies continue to post pages that take too long to download, testing viewers' patience and occasionally overwhelming mobile networks. Try to keep sites to less than 500K to 1MB per page, especially now that almost 39 percent of website visits are from smartphones.

High-resolution photos are usually the main culprits when a page is too large. It isn't the number of photos, but rather the total size of files on a page that counts. A couple of tips can help reduce the size of your page:

- When saving photos to use online, choose the Save for Web option, found in most graphics programs. Stick to JPEG or GIF files, which work well online, and avoid larger, slower-to-load TIFF and BMP files, which are intended for print.
- Post a thumbnail with a click-to-view action for the larger version in a pop-up window. Be sure to save the larger image for the web. (Refer to the first bullet.)

TIP

Check the download size and time for your home page for free at sites such as `www.websiteoptimization.com/services/analyze`, or check out `www.compuware.com/en_us/application-performance-management/performance-test-center.html`, which tests both mobile and web download times. Call your developer if changes are needed.

Optimizing for local search

Local search has obvious value for brick-and-mortar retail businesses using the web and social media to drive traffic to their stores. However, it's just as valuable for local service businesses such as plumbers or even for non-local businesses seeking online customers from a particular region.

Local optimization is needed for your site to appear near the top of results in spite of geolocation devices on smartphones (not always turned on), geographic tagging of images on Flickr and other photo-sharing sites, or the localization settings on Google results.

REMEMBER

Chances are good that your business is not the only one of a particular type in your city or neighborhood. Localization is absolutely critical for restaurants, tourism, hospitality, and entertainment businesses.

The concepts used for local optimization on websites apply equally well to social media:

- **Optimize search terms by city, region, neighborhood, or even zip code.** Rather than use a locality as a separate keyword, use it in a search term phrase with your product or service.
- **Include location in any pay-per-click ads.** This is equally true whether your ads appear on a search engine, Facebook, or other social media.
- **Post your business on search maps.** These maps include Google My Business (`www.google.com/business`), Bing Places for Business Portal (`www.bingplaces.com`), Yahoo! Localworks for $30/month (`https://smallbusiness.yahoo.com/local-listings`), and Yext.com (`http://www.yext.com/products/location-cloud/`), which is another paid site, Consider using one or more of your social media pages as site link extensions (additional links that appear following your page description in search engine results). Appearing on search maps is critical for mobile search, as discussed in the Chapter 3 of this minibook.
- **Take advantage of local business directories, events calendars, and review sites to spread the word about your company and its social media pages.** In some cases, you might want to use one of your social media pages instead of your primary website as the destination link. Most directories are also excellent sources of high-value inbound links.
- **Use specialized local social media with a geographic component.** These options include social channels such as Meetup and Everplaces. You can find more on these social media services in Book 8, Chapter 2.

You may want to view or manage search results for a location other than the one in which your computer is located, such as to view search results where various franchise customers are located. First do any search, such as for *grocery stores*. Scroll down to the bottom of the results page, where you will see the location Google is currently using. The simplest way to view search results for another place is to modify your search query to include the location you are looking for. As an alternative, use the Google AdPreview tool, at `www.google.com/AdPreview`. Enter your desired location in the first field on the left and your search phrase in the search box at the top.

OPTIMIZING FOR PERSONALIZED SEARCH

From a marketer's perspective, all bets are off with personalized search on Google. Google now defaults to a customized list of search results based on your past searches, location, and the results you clicked. In theory, these search results, derived either from a cookie or web search history, are continuously refined to become more relevant to your needs.

Google claims that with searches determined by location, visitors may be more likely to find new businesses in their area to support. Supposedly, the user's search history will remind her of links she has clicked previously, and those links will continually rank higher and higher in search results (because they aren't competing with the full pool of all relevant companies). In Google's mind, this process allows for repeat messaging, better branding, and increased customer loyalty for local business owners.

In practice, that relevance is debatable; users tend to see results that are more of the same, distorting the reality of what's out there and reducing the likelihood of receiving new information. (This algorithm, inadvertently or not, produced havoc during the 2016 presidential election.)

Most users don't even know that personalized search exists, let alone how to turn it off or how to delete repeatedly occurring, undesirable sites from results to make room for new ones. (The latter option requires logging into your Google account to personalize settings for your Web History.) For more information, see `https://support.google.com/websearch/answer/54068`.

Unfortunately, the algorithm for personalized search tends to produce results reflecting a philosophy of "Them that has, gets." Your website may have more difficulty breaking through to new prospects or achieving a presence on the first page of some individuals' search results. Sadly, you can do nothing about it. Whether those users who see your site are more qualified as prospects, and therefore more likely to buy, remains to be seen.

TECHNICAL STUFF

For a more sophisticated search filter, follow the directions at http://searchengineland.com/localize-google-search-results-239768. You'll find three other ways to localize search results for places other than where your computer or mobile device happens to be.

TECHNICAL STUFF

To turn off Google's personalized search, you must first sign out of Google. If you are signed in, click on your personal icon in the upper-right corner and select Sign Out. Then click the three-dot icon in the upper-right corner of any search results page and select History from the drop-down menu. In the pop-up dialog box that appears, select History. Then select the box for Clear Browsing Data. Do all your future searching while signed out. This step will also remove localization from search results, which is very useful for managing SEO.

Getting inbound links from social sharing, social bookmarks, and social news services

Leverage your social marketing activities to increase the number of inbound links to your site. If it's permissible, post your site to some of the social-sharing, bookmarking, shopping, and news services described in Book 2, Chapters 1 and 4. (Not all social bookmarks allow you to submit your own site, so you may need to ask a friend to help.) You're generally required to include either your domain name or a specific page URL with your submission.

These links encourage both inbound links and traffic. Some of these sites pass *link juice,* which refers to the increased value your site achieves when it receives an inbound link from another site that already has a high ranking on search results. In Figure 2-9, you can see an example of a site that benefits from inbound links from multiple social media channels. Link juice is more valuable if you have multiple links from social news sites back to different news stories or content on your main site. For more information, see Chapter 4 of this minibook.

TECHNICAL STUFF

Not all link shorteners are equal. Choose ones that will pass link juice with a 301 redirect. The link shorteners Bitly, Ow.ly, goo.gl, and TinyURL are safe bets. Of course, surround your links with relevant keywords. Just like with inbound-link campaigns for search engines, don't link everything from social-bookmarking, news, or shopping services to your home page. For example, multiple product recommendations on social-shopping sites should link to the appropriate product detail pages in your store.

TIP

Cross-link by submitting especially good blog entries to several social news services or by linking from one product recommendation to another on social-shopping sites or from one review site to another.

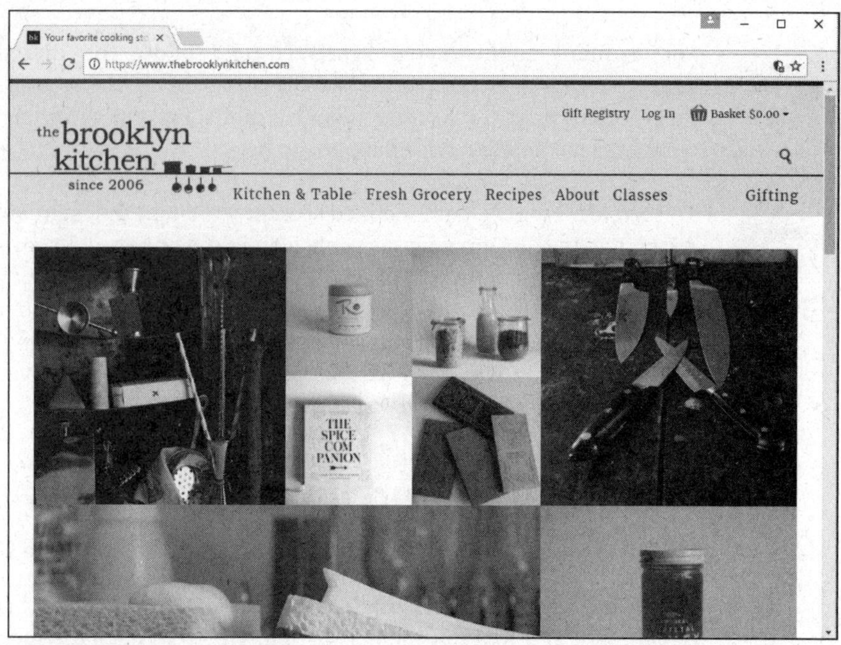

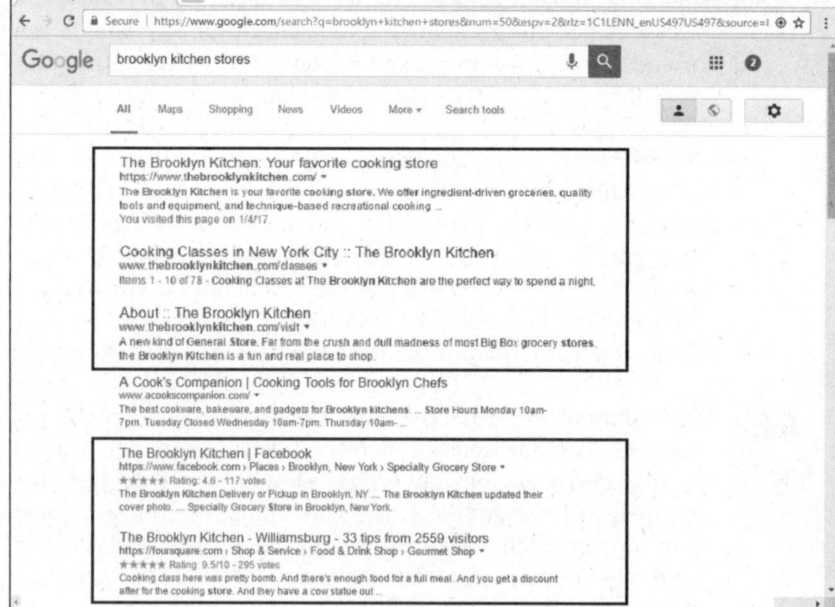

FIGURE 2-9: The Brooklyn Kitchen (top) earns high placement in Google search results (bottom) with inbound links from Facebook and Foursquare, which supplement the rankings of its own site.

Courtesy of the Brooklyn Kitchen

Reaping other links from social media

Inbound links can win you points in Google search results as an indication of your web relevance. One easy way to build inbound links is to distribute *(syndicate)* content, as described in Chapter 1 of this minibook. By repurposing content on multiple social media sites, you increase not only your audience but also the number of inbound links.

Taking advantage of the many places to post links on social media pages not only drives traffic to multiple elements of your web presence but also improves your search engine rankings in the process.

REMEMBER

Somewhere on your website or blog — at least on the About Us or Contact page — display a list of links to all your profiles on social media services, along with buttons for ShareThis and Google's +1. As best practice, these links of chiclets should be on every page. This form of passive link building can pay off big-time with improved ranking in search results.

The more places these links appear, the better. You can also repeat text links to your social media pages in your linkable footer.

TIP

Don't be shy! Include calls to action to share your web page in the body copy of ads or e-newsletters. These links don't always have to hide their charms in the header or footer.

Here are a few other ideas for laying down a link:

- Every profile on a social network has a place to enter at least your web address and blog address, if you have one. If possible, link to both. The links in profiles usually provide link juice, but the ones in status updates usually don't.
- Include your web address when you make comments on other people's blogs, post reviews on recommendation sites, or submit someone else's news story. You may have to work it into the content. Use at least *yourcompanyemail address@yourdomain*.com for branding reasons!
- Include your company name for branding and your web address for linking when you post to groups on any social networking site, as long as it's appropriate, relevant, and not too self-promotional.

WARNING

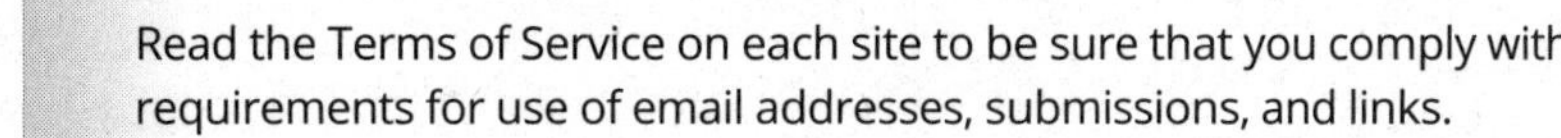

Read the Terms of Service on each site to be sure that you comply with requirements for use of email addresses, submissions, and links.

- Post events on LinkedIn, Twitter, Facebook, and elsewhere with a link to your site for more information.

» Include a Share button, described in Chapter 4 of this minibook, to encourage additional distribution. People who receive content they like often pass it along or link to it from their own pages or blogs.
» Be sure to post cross-links on newsletters and on all your social media profiles to all your other web pages, including to your primary site and your blog.

REMEMBER

Now that social media is included in ordinary search results, using search terms consistently can help you occupy more than one slot in search engine results pages.

IN THIS CHAPTER

» Placing search terms on social media sites

» Improving search ranking for blogs

» Optimizing images, audio, and video

» Optimizing for internal searches

» Improving ranking on external search engines

» Optimizing for mobile and real-time search

Chapter 3
Optimizing Social Media for Internal and External Searches

Keep in mind that when we talk about optimizing social media for search, we're talking about two separate types of optimization. The first is getting found in a social media channel, which has become increasingly difficult as the number of members reach into the millions or, in the case of Facebook, billions. The second is using your presence and posts on social media to improve your company's ranking in organic search results on Google, and Yahoo!/Bing.

Here's the good news: Everything we cover about using SEO for your website or blog applies to other social media, too. (See Chapter 2 of this minibook.) Whew! You still have to implement the techniques, but you can save time by reusing search terms, metatags, inbound links, and optimized text.

In this chapter, we go through various social media platforms one-by-one, providing explicit directions for internal and external search optimization on blogs, multimedia, Twitter, Facebook, Google+, Pinterest, and LinkedIn. We also address the specific challenges of being found on real-time search, including social media specific search engines, and the complications introduced by optimizing for localized search on mobile devices.

Placing Search Terms on Social Media

Start by reviewing your research for keywords and phrases. Decide on a primary set of four to six terms that best describe your company. Because your search terms must still relate to your content, you may want to reuse other sets for individual posts from your SEO research, mix them up, or include additional terms not optimized on your primary site.

You can place these types of terms in many locations:

- **Tags:** *Tags,* which are the social media equivalents of keywords, are assigned to specific content. Because many social media services place a limit on the number of tags that can be assigned to a given piece of content, choose a few from your primary set of search terms and select others (for example, brands, products, market, or competition) from your secondary list or elsewhere that are specific to your content.

  TIP

  If you're pulling tags out of thin air, remember to confirm which synonyms are most popular with the users of that service. For example, do people search for *Yule* or *Noel* or *Christmas*? Use a keyword selection tool for websites (see the table in Chapter 2 of this minibook on keyword selection resources) or check a tag cloud (see Chapter 2), if it exists, on the service you're using for the latest trends in tag usage.

- **Hashtags:** #search, #now what, #huh? Words or phrases preceded by the pound sign (#) are called *hashtags.* Used on social media to designate a search term or topic, hashtags facilitate internal searches on that platform. When people click on or search for a hashtag, they receive a page or stream of compiled posts using that hashtag. Twitter, Facebook, Instagram, YouTube, Google+, Tumblr (blog), Pinterest, and other social networks all support the use of hashtags.

  Alas, it's difficult to determine what similar hashtags might already be in use, let alone which of the similar hashtags are the most effective. Sometimes you can effectively transpose hashtags to different platforms and sometimes you can't. For starters, try creating hashtags for your company name, brand names, and search terms that are part of your standard suite of keywords. Test the terms you use to see whether they're popular or rarely used.

For more on hashtag etiquette and best practices, see `http://sproutsocial.com/insights/how-to-use-hashtags` or `https://blog.hubspot.com/marketing/hashtags-twitter-facebook-instagram`.

- **Profiles:** Just about every form of social media asks you to establish an account. Most profiles ask for a brief description of your company and location, as well as the URLs for your website and blog. Work your primary set of keywords and brands into your profile and any other place you can comfortably integrate them, including featured products, department names, the marketing tagline, and staff bios.

  Occasionally, a service requests only your email address. Of course, use the one with your domain name in it.

TECHNICAL STUFF

  If you haven't already set up email to forward from *you@yourdomain*.com to whatever email address you have from your ISP, do so now. Most hosting packages include at least five free email addresses. Email from @*yourdomain*.com not only makes you look more professional but also adds to brand value.

- **Page content, status updates, and comments:** Obviously, you should include search terms in the first paragraph of text for each blog post. They don't need to be part of your primary set of terms, so you have some creative flexibility. Incorporate search terms in updates and comments, too, to increase the likelihood of being found in on-site search results.
- **Metatags, titles, and headlines:** Use search terms from your list in the title of your blog or page name; in the title of your post; in <alt> tags, captions, or descriptions for images; and within metatags if you have a separate URL for a blog. Each service handles these elements a little differently, as we discuss in the later sections on individual services.

REMEMBER

Every search engine has its own rules. You may need to tweak your terms for not only general search engines, but also internal search engines on specific social media services.

TIP

Once upon a time (until 2014), you used to pay a bit of a performance penalty on Facebook by using an automated service such as Hootsuite or Sprout Social to update multiple social media channels at once. This is no longer true. However, long, duplicate posts might set off warning bells on Google, as will auto-generated content that appears to have been created by a software tool simply to include search terms.

Optimizing Blogs

Because blogs (discussed in Book 3, Chapter 2) are basically websites in a different format, the same principles of site optimization and configuration apply, including the need for inbound links and cross-promotion on social media services. Hard-learned lessons and best practices truly pay off because search engines crawl frequently updated blogs at least daily.

REMEMBER

Integrate your domain name with your blog URL (http://*yourblog.yourdomain*.com) or buy a separate, related domain name (http://*yourcompanyblog*.com, even if a third-party server hosts your blogs. For SEO purposes, you must own your own blog domain name. A blog at www.*mycompanyblog*.blogspot.com or www.typepad.com/*mycompanyblog* isn't acceptable.

Blogs are primo link bait. The casual sharing of relevant, text-based links in posts, the use of *blog rolls* (bloggers' linkable recommendations of other blogs), and related thematic material attract inbound links like black jackets attract white cat fur. With all that link juice, plus rapidly updated content, many blogs quickly zoom to page one in search engine results.

REMEMBER

Review all requests for inclusion on your blog roll or reciprocal link offers. Make sure that the requesting site is relevant, has a decent page rank, and is one that you feel good about recommending.

Different blog platforms operate somewhat differently, leading to confusion on the part of bloggers trying to optimize sites for search engines. Whatever your platform, the same methods you follow for websites still apply, with a multitude of additions:

- Include keywords from your primary list in your blog name, such as http://*yourcompany*.com/social_media_blog. The blog name should appear with an HTML <h1> tag on only the front page. On other pages of your blog, the heading level can be as low as <h3>.
- Include keywords in individual titles for each post. Use these keywords in the <title> tag in the source code for that entry, as well as in the page URL. Put those titles at the HTML <h1> level.
- Include primary keywords in the first sentence of content, which becomes the page <description> metatag by default, unless you write one manually. Use your secondary keywords in the body of your post.
- Fill out the tag box with your keywords, but do so judiciously. You don't need to bloat your blog tags with synonyms or terms you don't need to rank on.
- Incorporate search terms in anchor text for links on your blog.
- Use <alt> tags, captions, and descriptions with search terms for any images or media you upload to your blog.
- Post rich, appealing content with search terms regularly and often.

- Make sure the search engine spiders can crawl your blog easily by including a side navigation column on all pages and by offering access to archives and previous posts from all pages of your blog.
- Include a linkable breadcrumb trail that includes keywords without reaching the point of overstuffing.
- Provide internal text links to your own related posts, especially to relevant ones that are already ranking well.
- Submit your blog to blog directories and syndicated submission sites. Two excellent lists are at `http://web-marketing.masternewmedia.org/rsstop55-best-blog-directory-and-rss-submission-sites` and `www.toprankblog.com/rss-blog-directories`.
- Use your blog roll as a resource — just having a blog roll isn't enough. Contact other bloggers to request a backlink or offer a reciprocal appearance on your blog roll in exchange for a backlink. Just be careful that you don't inadvertently create a link farm. For more on blog roll links, see `www.britmums.com/2014/07/blogs-sidebar-blogroll-yet`.
- Get backlinks to your blog with *trackbacks* (an automated way of notifying other bloggers that you've referenced their blog) or by posting comments on other blogs. Not all blogging hosts support trackbacks.
- Create an XML site map and submit it to search engines, just as you would for your website.
- Use *permalinks* (permanent links) to maintain blog URLs permanently.
- Use analytics tools to monitor traffic and user behavior.

TIP

If you need quick suggestions for good blog keywords, install the Wordtracker Keywords Tool (it offers a free seven-day trial) at `www.wordtracker.com/find-the-best-keywords`. It sits next to your blog editor on the screen so that you can consider tag suggestions while you write. Alternately, return to Google's free AdWords Keyword Planner, as described in the section "Choosing the right search terms," in Chapter 2 of this minibook.

TIP

If you're an experienced blog writer, your posts are probably already written with one designated search term in mind. Review your top 10 to 15 most-viewed posts, make a list of the keywords you used for them, and use that list as input into the AdWords Keyword Planner.

TECHNICAL STUFF

Long blog pages with a lot of responses, including those from spammers, may end up with too many outbound links. Ask your programmer to place an HTML nofollow attribute in the code just before links from comments to discourage people from leaving fake comments that include links to their own sites in hopes of increasing their own search rankings.

Optimizing WordPress

Although plug-ins for WordPress templates can be set to automatically generate title and page description metatags, you may want to tweak the automated SEO results for important posts. Auto-generation is fine for mundane posts or when you're short on time. For more information on selecting plug-ins, see Book 3, Chapter 2.

For more flexibility and additional optimization features, try the Yoast SEO plug-in at `http://wordpress.org/plugins/wordpress-seo` or the All in One SEO Pack at `http://wordpress.org/extend/plugins/all-in-one-seo-pack`.

TIP

Make your WordPress life easier by searching the list of WordPress plug-ins for items you need at `http://wordpress.org/plugins`. Compare plug-ins carefully — they're not all alike.

Here are a few things you can do to optimize your WordPress blog posts:

- **Swap elements of the blog post title.** Reverse the WordPress plug-in default arrangement by putting the post title first, which contains keywords, followed by the name of your blog.
- **Use a consistent format for keyword-rich page titles on all pages.** You can set up the format once in your template and apply it everywhere by using the Yoast or All in One SEO Pack plug-ins.
- **Insert a longer title description, with more search terms, into the image title field.** WordPress automatically uses the title you give an image as its <alt> tag. Unless you insert a longer title description with more search terms into the Image Title field, WordPress uses the filename as the image title.

When you write a post and add tags, WordPress automatically adds your tags to its global tag system. The global system determines the WordPress list of hot topics in real time. Users can click any word in the real-time tag cloud to view the most recent posts for that tag.

TECHNICAL STUFF

WordPress, like other blogs, often duplicates content by showing the same posts on archive, author, category, index, and tag pages. To remove duplicate content, which can have a negative effect on SEO, create a robots.txt file. See `www.problogger.net/archives/2013/08/14/how-to-stop-your-wordpress-blog-getting-penalized-for-duplicate-content`.

Optimizing Blogger

Contrary to myth, Google doesn't necessarily give preference to blogs hosted on its own service, Blogger. However, Blogger poses some unique advantages and challenges:

- Blogger templates place <h1> through <h6> tags into the source code through the What You See Is What You Get (WYSIWYG) interface, thereby helping with SEO. You can easily adjust page titles and blog names for the correct heading level in page templates.
- Blogger lacks theme-related categories, which makes it a little more difficult for you and for theme-based SEO. To overcome that problem, create permalinks that include your categories or directory names. We discuss permalinks in the following section.
- Because Blogger doesn't provide a related-links feature, create that list of related text links within or at the bottom of each post. These links should lead to your other postings on the same topic. Or take advantage of unlimited sidebar space to create a separate section for related links above your blogroll.
- Use labels on Blogger to categorize your posts. On the page where you're writing a post, click the Settings tab in the right column. Select Labels from the drop-down menu. In the box that appears, enter the terms you want to use, separated by commas, and click Done. For future posts, just click Labels in the drop-down menu. All the terms in the box appear below your post when it's published.
- Blogger defaults to weekly archiving, but the time frames for archiving are malleable. Adjust the time frame based on your volume of posts and comments to maintain good keyword density. If you post only weekly, it might make more sense to archive monthly. For an extremely active blog, you might want to archive daily.
- Creating text links is easy, so use your keywords in links whenever possible.

Assigning permalinks

Because most blogs are created on dynamic, database-driven platforms, their posts don't have fixed web addresses. Links to individual posts disappear after the posting is archived and no longer available on a page. Obviously, that's bad news for inbound links and SEO.

Permalinks (short for *permanent links*) solve that problem by assigning a specific web address to each post. Then individual posts can be bookmarked or linked to from elsewhere, forever.

Most blog software programs, such as WordPress and Blogger, already offer this as an option; you just have to use it. If your blog doesn't offer it, you can generate permalinks at `www.generateit.net/mod-rewrite`, although you may need help from your programmer to install them. Try to avoid links that look like this: `www.`*`yourblog`*`.com/?p=123`. Instead, choose an option to use one or more keywords, such as `www.`*`yourblog`*`.com/contests/summer-travel-sweepstakes`.

If you prefer to customize your permalinks, use the Permalink option in the Post Settings box. On the page where you're writing a post, click the Settings tab in the right column. Select Permalink from the drop-down menu that appears. Then you can create a URL that's different from your title, which you might want for search term reasons.

TECHNICAL STUFF

To generate WordPress permalinks, open the Settings option in the Admin panel, which appears in the left navigation. From there, select Permalinks from the second-tier navigation and choose either the Common Structure option or the Custom Permalinks option to enter your own structure. (For example, you might want to insert a category.) For new blogs, that's it; for existing blogs, you may need to use the Redirection plug-in, as well. For more information, see `http://codex.wordpress.org/Using_Permalinks`. For directions about creating permalinks on Blogger, visit `https://support.google.com/blogger/answer/2523525`.

Optimizing Images, Video, and Podcasts

Because search engines can't directly parse the contents of multimedia, you must take advantage of all opportunities to use your relevant search terms in every metatag, descriptive field, or <alt> tag. You can find more about podcasts and video in Book 3, Chapter 3.

Make these fields as keyword- and content-rich as you can. In these elements, you can often use existing keyword research, metatags from your website or blog, or optimized text that you've already created:

- **Title and <title> tag for your content:** This catchy name should include a search term.
- **Filenames:** Using names such as *image1234.jpg* or *podcast1.mp3* doesn't help with SEO; names such as *PlushBrownTeddyBear.jpg* or *tabbycats-sing-jingle-bells.mp3* are much more helpful. Use terms also in category or directory names.
- **Tags:** Use relevant keywords, just as you would with other social media.
- **<alt> tags:** Use these tags for a short description with a search term, for example, *Used cat tree for sale*.
- **Long description metatags:** Follow this example: *longdesc=for sale-gently used, gray, carpeted 6 foot cat tree with 4 platforms.*
- **Content:** Surround multimedia elements with keyword-rich, descriptive content, especially in caption fields.

» **Transcriptions:** Transcribe and post a short excerpt from a keyword-loaded portion of your video or podcast.

» **Anchor text:** Use keywords in the text link that opens your multimedia file.

» **Large images:** Upload large versions, as well as the thumbnails that are visible on your blog or website.

» **RSS and XML:** Expand your reach with media RSS and site maps.

For more information on indexing multimedia, see `https://support.google.com/webmasters/answer/114016`.

TIP

Even though search engines can't read watermarks, you may want to mark both videos and large images with your domain name and logo to encourage visits, for branding, and to discourage unauthorized copying.

Optimizing Specific Social Media Platforms

Each social media platform offers specific opportunities to optimize content for internal and external searching. They all share one thing in common: a section for a company profile. Profiles offer a rich opportunity for external SEO; they are invariably searched by Google and Yahoo!/Bing. Let's take a look at optimizing major social media platforms one-by-one.

Optimizing Twitter

In addition to adhering to the standard admonishments about providing good content and using well-researched keywords, you can follow a few extra guidelines to improve search results on both internal Twitter searches and on external searches:

» **Your name on Twitter acts like a <title> tag.** If you want to benefit from branding and to rank on your own or your company name, you have to use it! If you haven't already done this, log in to your Twitter account, click your profile picture on the top right, and then select the Settings link. Then change your name.

  Your username, or Twitter *handle,* should relate to your brand, company name, or campaign and be easy to remember. It can include a keyword or topic area.

» **Pack your one-line bio with keywords.** Your Twitter bio serves as the page <description> metatag and is limited to 160 characters. Use resume-style language and include some of your primary search terms. Talk about yourself or your company in the third person.

From the drop-down list at the top-right of the page (under your profile icon), select View Profile. After you click on the Edit Profile button, you can edit your profile photo, header graphic, name, business description, location, website URL, and theme color. Remember to click the Save Changes button when you finish.

- **On your Profile page, use your business address as your location.** Doing so helps with local searches. Remember to save your changes.
- **Brand your Twitter cover (header) image.** Use your standard business logo, logotype, or a photo showing one of your products or services, resized to the current cover dimensions of 1500-x-500 pixels.
- **Include keywords and hashtags in your tweets and retweets whenever possible.** That way, you offer search engines more than a time stamp. With its 140-character limit on text, Twitter might be a good place to use those single-word terms. Use keywords in your Twitter #hashtags, too.

REMEMBER

Twitter no longer counts multimedia attachments, links, quoted tweets, or @names against the 140-character limit on a tweet.

- **Remember the importance of the initial 42 characters of a tweet.** They serve as the <title> tag for that specific post. Search engines will index the full tweet, however, and Twitter will include the entire post in the <title> tag if users click on an individual post.
- **Format your retweets.** Because a quoted tweet doesn't count against your character limit, you probably want to keep the original tweet intact. Use the Retweet button to paste the content into a new tweet box. Add the letters RT and the @*username* of the original author. However, you can insert your comment as long as it's less than 140 characters. Finally, click Tweet to post the retweet.
- **Maximize retweets as a measure of popularity.** Write interesting content or share good articles, especially when the direct link to detailed content goes to your own site.
- **Increase your visibility.** When linking to your Twitter profile from other sites, use your name or company name rather than your Twitter handle as the anchor text for the link. (Search engines don't handle well the @ in a Twitter handle, for example, @watermelonweb.) If you happen to have a tweet with great keywords and hashtags, you can pin your tweet to the top of your timeline.

TECHNICAL STUFF

Because Twitter adds a nofollow attribute to links placed by users, linking to your site from Twitter won't help your ranking on search results pages. Truncated URLs (such as the TinyURLs described in Chapter 1 of this minibook) behave just like their longer-version cousins because they're permanent redirects.

However, links from Twitter still boost branding and drive traffic to your site. More traffic to your site improves your ranking at Alexa (`www.alexa.com`), which in turn improves one of the quality factors Google uses for search engine results position. It's all one giant loop. For more information on Twitter, see Book 4.

Optimizing Facebook

Take advantage of myriad opportunities to gain traffic from your Facebook pages by applying optimization techniques. Next to blogs, Facebook pages offer the highest number of opportunities to use SEO on social media to reach people who don't already know you. Fortunately, Facebook search engines can index all shared content on Facebook.

REMEMBER

Every social network has different rules for its account names and profiles. Although consistency is preferable for branding, follow the rules carefully. When you first create a Facebook page for your business, as described in Book 5, try these techniques:

- Use an easy-to-remember version of your business name alone or combined with a search term as your business's Facebook page name. If possible, use the same username on both Twitter and Facebook for branding reasons. Facebook doesn't like generic names.
- In the Website field on the About page, enter your primary domain name. In the description box, list all your other relevant domain names, including other websites, your blog, and other social media pages. Later, you can also place links to your website or blog or another type of social media in your posts. Generally, it's easier to use the actual URL than to implement anchor text.
- Place keyword-loaded content in the first paragraph of each of the remaining boxes under About Us. The boxes may vary depending on the type of page you elected to create. Include your contact information in the Company Overview box; address information also helps with local searches. Your page <description> metatag may work well in the Short Description box because it's already optimized for search terms. Try to include your site URL, even though this field is limited to 157 characters. Be sure to include all your brand names and all the products or services that you offer in the Products or Long Description boxes.
- More search term opportunities abound if you use iFrame-based solutions (customizable sections for your Facebook pages) to create HTML boxes. These additional iFrame boxes or apps can display text, images, and more links. Be sure to use a good search term in your box app's tab name (which is limited to ten characters) and include text links in your content. It's a bit of a pain, but you can do this on your own.

If you're a page administrator, you might want to explore other third-party apps found at www.socialmediaexaminer.com/15-types-of-facebook-apps to enhance your Facebook presence.

For more information on creating a Facebook account and business pages, see Book 5.

Optimizing Google+

Not surprisingly, the rules for optimizing Google+ track well with the principles for optimizing websites for Google. To maximize your search engine visibility on Google+, SEO Hacker recommends the following:

- Optimize the tagline feature in Google+ with a keyword.
- Claim your custom, branded URL. You need more than ten followers, a profile photo, and a page that's at least 30 days old. Go to https://support.google.com/plus/answer/2676340.
- Because the Introduction in the Story section serves as the body of your Google+ page, you can use the same keyword-optimized content that appears as the first paragraph on your home page or on other essential pages of your site. If you have multiple Google profiles, visit https://aboutme.google.com to view and edit them. You can toggle among accounts by clicking your avatar in the upper-right corner.
- Add links to your website and other social media profiles to your Google+ profile under the Sites section.
- Like with your main website, update your Google+ page every two to seven days to indicate activity. When appropriate for marketing reasons, linking to your Google+ page can help boost your search rankings. It's just another example of Google's self-love!
- Publish to your Google+ page what you're already publishing to other social channels.
- Get your Story straight. You might want to reuse content from the About section of your website as part of the Story section of Google+. Your Story should include an introduction to your business, what sets you apart, and of course, some search terms.
- Optimize the first 45 to 50 characters of your posts. They become the post's page title in Google search results; in other words, include one of your prized search terms.
- Even on social media, pictures are worth 1,000 words, maybe more. Include a lot of photos, videos, graphics, or GIF animations.

- For more suggestions on optimizing Google+ pages, see `www.socialmediaexaminer.com/use-google-increase-search-rankings` or `www.semrush.com/blog/boost-local-seo-rankings-google-plus`.

Optimizing Pinterest

With its visual content, Pinterest is perhaps the most challenging social media option to optimize for search engines. Start by creating a business account or converting your personal one at `www.pinterest.com/business/create`, as described in Book 7, Chapter 1. Then take advantage of several tried-and-true techniques to give your Pinterest site some search oomph:

- Verify your website by clicking the Verify Website button next to the Website Text field. Follow the directions in the pop-up window so that your site will show up on profile and search results. For more details, see `www.pinterest.com/settings`.
- Optimize your username or business profile name or both to include your company name and a search term describing what you sell or what business category you're in (unless you're a well-known brand). For instance, instead of listing only *Pretty Puppy*, use *Pretty Puppy Play Clothes for Puppies*.
- Use your four most important search terms and your page <description> metatag in the About You section of your company profile (under Settings).
- Optimize for local search by including your city, state, and zip code in the Location field of the profile. Of course, include the URL for your website or blog or both in the Website field.
- Click Settings (gear icon), choose Business Account Basics, and set the Visibility option to Off in your Profile; you *don't* want to hide your Pinterest profile from search engines. Click Settings, choose Social Networks, and be sure to select the cross-link options to Twitter and Facebook. Also, upload your logo graphic by clicking Settings and choosing Profile.
- Use a descriptive filename that includes a keyword for each of the images you pin from your website or blog. The source link for each image will go back to your website or blog to increase your inbound links and drive traffic to specific pages. If you have optimized images on other photo-sharing sites, you can use that URL as the image source for a pin.

  TECHNICAL STUFF

  Unfortunately, Pinterest adds the nofollow attribute to the originating URL for pinned images themselves, thus diminishing the value of those links as repins. No link juice — sigh! However, Google and Bing still note your presence on Pinterest; it becomes a subtle signal when it comes to ranking your site's usefulness and popularity.

Optimizing Social Media

» Include keywords in the title *and* description for each board and pin, whether the boards are employee headshots, photos of your company at trade shows, or images also used on your blog. For local optimization, include your city. You might want to structure boards by customer type, product, service, or brand name to maximize the search terms you use. Just remember to keep your descriptions captivating. They need to be more than a collection of search terms to engage Pinners.

» If you create data charts or infographics, be sure to include keywords in the title for your charts or graphics. (Try the infographics tool at `http://piktochart.com`, which offers a limited free account.)

» Remember to add the linkable Pinterest icon and link to your suite of social media buttons on your website, blogs, and other social media pages.

For more ideas, visit `https://business.pinterest.com/sites/business/files/best_practices_02_en.pdf`.

WARNING

Use only images you own or have permission to use on Pinterest. You're liable for any copyright infringement. Respect the use of any credit lines required by Creative Commons or the owner of the image.

Like with other social media, Pinterest is a back-scratching site — you like me, and I'll like you. To increase traffic to your Pinterest posts (and eventually to your website), follow other Pinterest users and boards related to your company, repin relevant images, and click their Like buttons.

TIP

Pinterest offers a great new tool called *rich pins*, which allow you to incorporate additional information on the pin itself. There are rich pins for movies, recipes, articles, apps, places, and products. For more about rich pins, visit `https://business.pinterest.com/en/rich-pins`.

Since its inception as a visual scrapbooking network, Pinterest has evolved into a visual search engine for the millions of competing images found on its own site. (Compare to Google Image Search.) As with every search engine, you can take advantage of certain techniques to help Pinterest users discover your pins among the wealth of images. For details on on-site optimization, see `https://searchenginewatch.com/2016/04/08/11-tips-on-how-to-optimise-pinterest-pins-for-seo`.

For more information on creating and using Pinterest for marketing, see Book 7, Chapter 1.

Optimizing LinkedIn

LinkedIn (discussed in Book 6) doesn't offer quite as many options for SEO as other forms of social media. Start by including search terms in your profile text, in the descriptions of any LinkedIn groups you start, and in postings to a group. Just keep it gentle and unobtrusive. Follow these steps to optimize your profile and to pass along some SEO credibility:

- » Use your name or company name in your LinkedIn URL (www.linkedin.com/in/*yourcompanyname*. Because search engines look at keywords in URLs, this technique makes your company easier to find.
- » LinkedIn's company pages are a bountiful gift for SEO. Google displays up to the first 156 characters of the text on a company page. Therefore, you can use content similar to your page <description> metatag within the first paragraph of your LinkedIn profile. It should already be loaded with some of your primary search terms.
- » Like links from Twitter, links from LinkedIn to other sites don't carry link juice. You can have as many as three links on your profile. Set one to your website and another to your blog. Use keyword-based link text on a third link to drive traffic to another page on your site or to another of your social media pages. Nothing says that all links have to lead to different domains.
- » For successful search results within LinkedIn, make it easy for LinkedIn members to search for companies like yours. Be sure your description includes search terms for your business, industry sector, experience, and expertise.

For more optimization ideas, see www.linkedin.com/today/post/article/20140320151331-142790335-11-seo-tips-for-your-personal-linkedin-profile or www.socialmediaexaminer.com/7-ways-to-improve-your-linkedin-company-page.

Optimizing for Mobile Search

The rapid adoption of smartphones and tablets is stunning: comScore estimates that nearly 80 percent of all US adults owned smartphones as of January 2016.

Other usage statistics provide all the more reason to optimize for mobile search. Here are some percentages for how people use their smartphones, according to the Pew Research Center (www.pewresearch.org/fact-tank/2016/01/29/us-smartphone-use/ft_01-27-16_smartphoneactivities_640):

- » 90 percent use their phones to get directions or other location-based information.

» 73 percent of users under 29 buy a product from their phone.

» 67 percent listen to music or radio services such as Pandora or Spotify.

Combined with rapid technological advancements in location-based and integrated real-time search, this trend in smartphone adoption pushes business owners to ensure that their sites appear just as high in mobile search results and on mobile social media as they do on desktop computers. Not so fast. Alas, the process of optimizing for mobile search is not quite the same as for desktop search.

Users see even fewer results on mobile search than they do on a larger screen. With all that competition, you need to take every possible step to improve your rankings in results, including the local optimization techniques mentioned in the preceding section.

Here are a few techniques to incorporate:

» **Mobile site ranking is much more susceptible to technical performance characteristics than desktop site ranking.** According to Bruce Clay, Inc. (`www.bruceclay.com/seo/mobile-seo.htm`), your mobile site needs to be friendly for mobile search browsers based on such characteristics as usability, download speed, and screen rendering. Broken links or poor navigation will reduce your ranking in results. If you render a large site in responsive design, it might look fine but take so long to download that no one will wait.

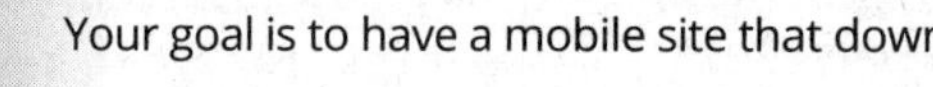

Your goal is to have a mobile site that downloads in less than one second!

» **Your mobile site must work on all brands of smartphones.** It should use standard HTML coding. Better yet, incorporate next-generation languages such as HTML5 to enhance the performance of your mobile site, leading to higher rankings.

» **Apply SEO optimization and localization techniques from earlier in this chapter to your mobile site.** Use appropriate keywords in headlines and text. It's critical to use geographically targeted terms such as state, zip code, town, or neighborhood. That may be the only content scanned to produce mobile search results. Location and timeliness matter much more than search terms for mobile users.

» **Aim at the top of the funnel with your mobile home page.** Try to reach many new prospects with keyword-focused content that explains who you are and the benefits of what you offer. On secondary pages, include content that adds value to the sale process, such as product specs, ratings, schedules, business hours, and prices. Also, include frequently updated offers, entertainments, and competitions that help build the business relationship.

» **Take advantage of the unique features of mobile devices.** Provide your visitors with click-to-call, mobile coupons, store locators, barcode scanners or

QR codes, easy ways to share and recommend your business, and new mobile payment tools.

- **Incorporate outbound links to relevant sources and other elements of your social media presence.** Mobile users constantly consume social media, especially Facebook, Instagram, and Twitter. If your prospects are using mobile media, you might want to pay particular attention to incorporating and optimizing these channels in your social media strategic plan.
- **If you have a separate mobile site, include links to it in e-newsletters, text messages, and social media.** According to emailmonday (`www.emailmonday.com/mobile-email-usage-statistics`), about 55 percent of email is opened on a mobile device; mobile users can share links quickly with their friends.

Search behavior on mobile sites is somewhat different from search behavior on a desktop in the home or office. Mobile searchers are highly focused on the task at hand and want results — often local ones — quickly. They may not have the time or patience to search beyond the first two or three results.

Well-optimized mobile sites can increase traffic, enhance brand loyalty, and improve revenue. It's worth the time investment. For more on mobile social media, see Chapter 5 of this minibook.

Gaining Visibility in Real-Time Search

All the emphasis on social media has forced search algorithms to adjust accordingly. Search engines vary in how they handle social media services in natural search results. Google and Yahoo! note your social media presence but don't include individual tweets or posts in results because they're private. You may find that you need to resort to specialized search sites such as `www.socialsearch.com` (shown in Figure 3-1) to see near real-time search results for Twitter, Instagram, and YouTube.

Bing displays the results of topical posts from influencers and public figures in regular search results without users needing to connect to their social media accounts. Dedicated real-time search engines are available for different services, such as Facebook, Twitter, syndicated (RSS) feeds, and blogs. These engines, some of which are listed in Table 3-1, may also index comments and other elements found only on a particular social media service.

You can't benefit from real-time search unless you're active on Facebook, Twitter, and other services. Looking for something to say? Add your twist on the latest trends in your market sector. For ideas on current topics, use Google Trends (`http://google.com/trends`) or the hot-topic searches on most social media services.

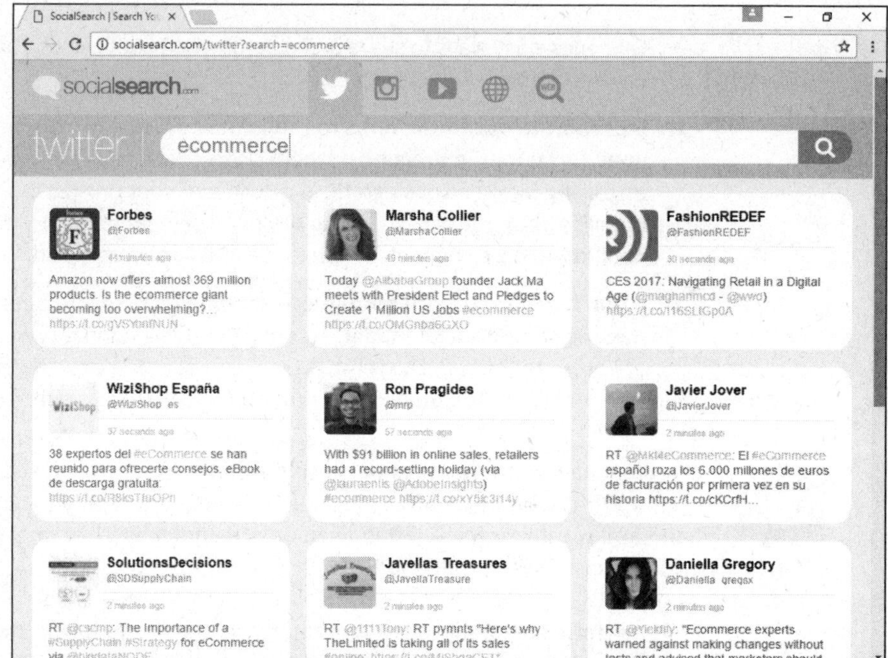

FIGURE 3-1: Use tools such as SocialSearch to find real-time posts on Instagram, Twitter, or YouTube.

TABLE 3-1 Real-Time and Specialty Search Engines for Social Media

Name	URL	Description
Facebook	`http://search.fb.com`	Search Facebook people, pages, places, groups, apps, events, and web results.
Google Plus	`https://plus.google.com`	Search for people, pages, or posts on Google+.
IceRocket	`www.icerocket.com`	Real-time search of Twitter, Facebook, or blogs, or a combination of all three.
LinkedIn	`www.linkedin.com/search`	Real-time search built-in for people, jobs, answers, groups, companies, universities, and posts.
Twitter Search	`http://search.twitter.com`	Real-time Twitter search.
Yahoo!	`http://search.yahoo.com`	Real-time search from Yahoo! (includes Twitter, Yahoo! News, Yahoo! Shopping, and several video channels).

Gaining Traction on Google with Social Media

Sigh. Nothing ever stands still in the social whirl — or maybe social tornado is a better description.

Regular Google search results for the past hour may include near real-time results from Twitter, Facebook, Google+, or social media channels such as blogs and press release sites (see Figure 3-2). To view these, enter your search term on Google as usual. On the search results page, click the Search Tools tab and then choose Any Time⇨Past Hour. If you're more concerned about time than content, switch from the default to Sorted by Date on the Sorted by Relevance sub-tab that appears.

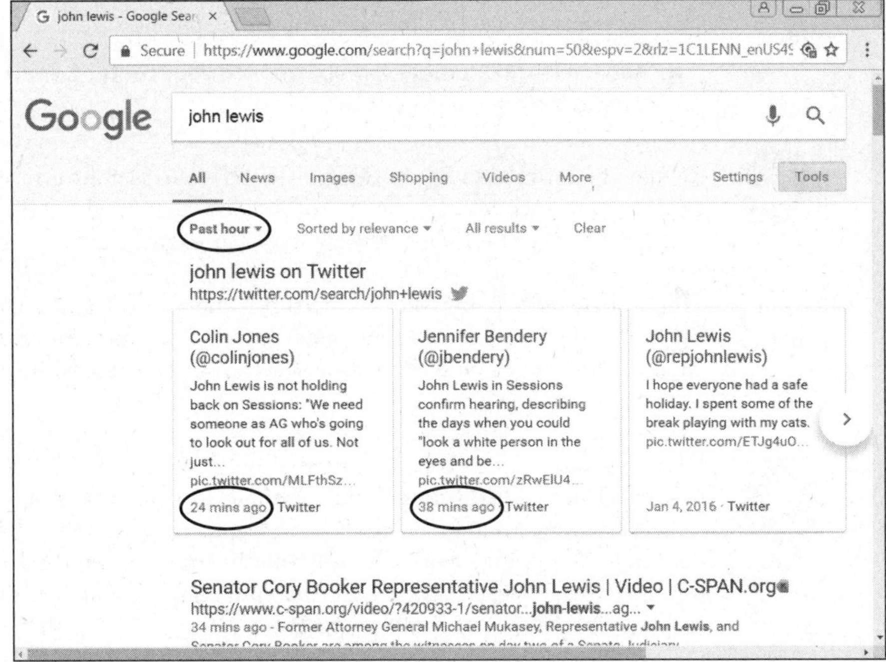

FIGURE 3-2: Posts on Facebook, Twitter, and other social media are included in Google search results when you search by time.

Google doesn't evaluate engagement on any social media platforms except Google+. It is aware of inbound links and search terms that appear in posts and profiles. Take action based on this information:

- **Post early, post often.** Real-time search creates pressure to update frequently on social media so that you can stay near the top of the results stream. Multiple recent posts can tip the scale in your favor. Schedule times on your Social Media Activity Calendar (see Book I, Chapter 4) to post to your blog, add to your Facebook timeline, or send tweets at least twice a day. Use management tools like those described in Book I, Chapter 4 to make this process easier.

- **Share and share alike.** Post a lot of appealing, keyword-rich content on social media, and explicitly invite others to link to it. Good content on social media may draw a lot of likes, but the number of links to that content pushes up search results.
- **+1 +1 = 3, or maybe 30.** Put Google +1 buttons anywhere and everywhere — on your social media, your website, your newsletters, your forehead. Google incorporates +1 buttons but doesn't evaluate engagement (such as likes, follows, and comments) on other social media.
- **Pin your hopes to Pinterest.** The Google spider now crawls Pinterest pins and boards, looking for relevant keywords in descriptions. Use hashtag keywords for each pin for extra SEO-om-pa-pa.
- **Add Pin It and StumbleUpon buttons to your content.** For referral traffic, these two sites offer special value.

TIP

To view real-time results in Google+, enter your search term in the Search text box. When you see results, click the option for Most Recent at the top of the results list. From then on, relevant posts will appear in real time.

Think about which messages are truly time-critical and save your real-time efforts for them. On your Social Media Activity Calendar, enter the times that you expect your target market might be searching, such as first thing in the morning or right before lunch.

TIP

Get some sleep! There's no point tweeting in the middle of the night when your customers are in bed (unless you're selling to insomniacs or international customers halfway around the world). Your tweets may be long buried by tweets from dozens — if not hundreds — of others by the time the sun rises. Better yet, schedule your tweets ahead of time with Hootsuite, Buffer, Netvibes, or other dashboard tools for specific social media channels.

Monitoring Your Search Engine Ranking

If you're serious about SEO, you'll want to monitor how well you're doing. Table 3-2 lists some search engine ranking software that shows where your site appears on search engines by keyword or page. Most ranking software carries a charge, but some offer a free trial or will rank a limited number of pages, keywords, or engines for free.

TABLE 3-2 **Search Engine Ranking Services**

Name	URL	Starting Price
CheckMoz	`www.checkmoz.com/`	Free bulk moz rank checker
mozRank Pro Checker	`https://moz.com/tools/rank-tracker`	Free 30-day trial; starts at $99/mo for up to 5 sites
Rank Tracker	`www.link-assistant.com/rank-tracker`	Free download; licenses $125–$300
Search Engine Rankings	`www.mikes-marketing-tools.com/ranking-reports`	Free
SERank	`www.ragesw.com/products/search-engine-rank.html`	$99.95 $149.95 (other tools also available)
ZoomRank	`www.zoomrank.com`	Fee; contact representative for pricing

SEO is a long-term strategy to deliver solid traffic over time to your hub website or blog. It takes time for your investment in SEO to pay off, and results can vary unpredictably from one week or month to the next. Generally, after you have everything set up and running smoothly, monitoring once per quarter should be enough, except for exceptionally large and constantly growing sites.

REMEMBER

Enter your preferred SEO tools in your Social Media Marketing Plan and insert the tasks into your Social Media Activity Calendar.

IN THIS CHAPTER

- **Differentiating between social bookmarks and social news**
- **Submitting to social-bookmarking sites**
- **Submitting to social news sites**
- **Using social share buttons**

Chapter 4

Using Social Bookmarks, News, and Share Buttons

Social bookmarks and social news services are essentially peer-to-peer referral networks. Each one is an expansion of the former tell-a-friend call to action. Rather than email a link to a site or some content to one or two people, users can notify many people at a time. Advocates of these recommendation services often argue that they filter the avalanche of websites that appear in standard search engines. Because social bookmarks and social news services rely on popular input from real people, rather than from algorithms, some Internet users place a greater value on these search results.

Hundreds of these services exist, which you can see on `www.qdtricks.net/free-high-pr-social-bookmarking-sites-list`. In this chapter, we discuss the benefits of using these services, including higher search engine ranking, more traffic, and free visibility for minimal effort. We also emphasize using share buttons to encourage viral sharing of social media and website content.

TIP

Search engines recognize inbound links from many (but not all) of these services, so appearing on them can improve your search engine ranking. See Chapters 2 and 3 of this minibook for more information on search engine optimization.

Bookmarking Your Way to Traffic

You most likely already know how to bookmark sites in a browser. Social-bookmarking services work in much the same way, but you save bookmarks to a *public* website rather than to an individual computer. Then, users of bookmarking services can easily share links to their favorite sites and can easily share content with friends or colleagues (or with the world) while enjoying convenient access to their own bookmarks from any browser, anywhere.

Social bookmarks act as testimonials from one amorphous group of web users to many others. Bookmarking services, such as StumbleUpon (shown in Figure 4-1) and Delicious, recommend websites, blogs, videos, products, or content. At StumbleUpon, among other things, users can view bookmarks from their own list of favorites, friends' favorites, or everyone in the StumbleUpon database of submitters. Several subsets of bookmarking services are specific to certain applications (blogs only, for example) or activities (shopping only, for example).

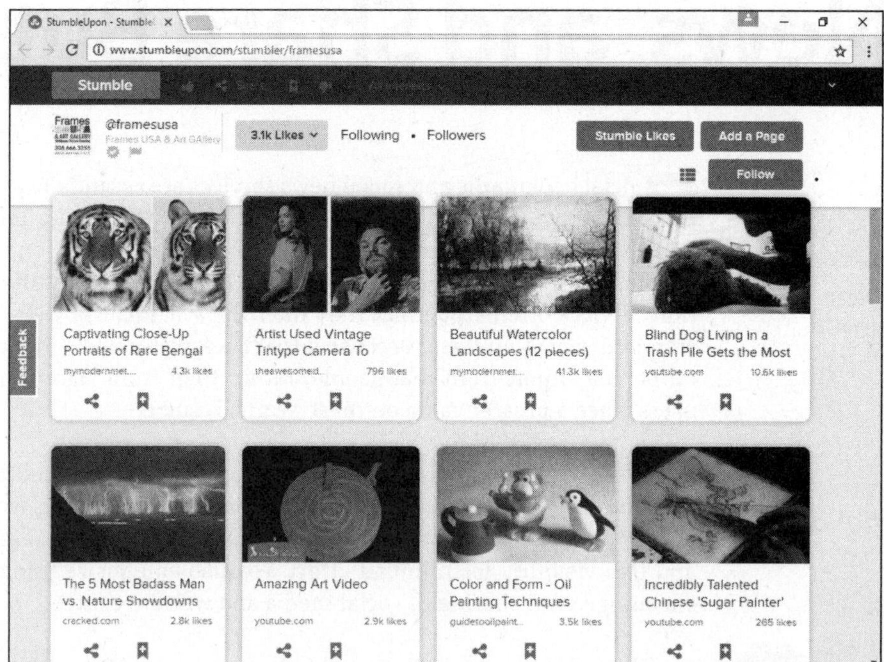

FIGURE 4-1: Use bookmarking services such as StumbleUpon to recommend websites.

REMEMBER

Participating in social bookmarking is a no-brainer. Even if you do no other social media marketing, you should submit your site to several social-bookmarking services, if they permit it, as part of your search engine optimization (SEO) efforts. Note that some services may not permit direct submission but will allow you to include a badge on your site to encourage your viewers to submit the site.

Users generally search for listings by *tag* (keyword), category, most recent, most popular, or individual submitter. Bookmarking services rank items by the number of people who have cited them.

Table 4-1 lists some of the dozens of popular social-bookmarking services and shows whether you're allowed to submit your own site. The Passes Link Juice column indicates whether search engines recognize a link from that service, as discussed in Book 2, Chapter 2.

TABLE 4-1 Popular Social-Bookmarking Services

Name	URL	Allows Self-Submission	Passes Link Juice
Bing Toolbar	www.bingtoolbar.com	Yes	No
Delicious	http://delicious.com	No	No
FolkD	http://www.folkd.com	Yes	No
Google Bookmarks	www.google.com/bookmarks	Yes	Yes
Linkroll	www.linkroll.com	Yes	No
StumbleUpon	www.stumbleupon.com	No	Yes
Yahoo! Toolbar	https://toolbar.yahoo.com	No	Yes

TECHNICAL STUFF

The visibility of your website on search engines improves when you have inbound links from a site that already has a high ranking in search results, but only if it passes link juice. Search the site's source code to see whether it contains a <nofollow> tag. Sites with a <nofollow> tag do not pass link juice. Without that tag, links follow by default.

TIP

You can find more information about the sites in this list and helpful lists of more social media bookmarking and other platforms at `www.ebizmba.com/articles/social-bookmarking-websites` or `www.searchenginejournal.com/death-social-bookmarking/171061`.

The two largest search engines (Google and Yahoo!/Bing) also have bookmarking services. However, bookmarking on Yahoo!/Bing is available only through toolbars.

Later in this chapter, we discuss how to research bookmarking services, decide which ones to use, and then submit a site.

Pinterest, the online-scrapbooking site, functions in many ways as a meta-bookmarking site. (For more information on Pinterest, see Book 7, Chapter 1.)

The site attracts huge audiences and drives traffic to commercial websites, especially in the areas of weddings, home décor, women's apparel, cooking, do-it-yourself, and shopping. The Shade Store, a custom window treatment firm, is an example of a company using Pinterest (see Figure 4-2).

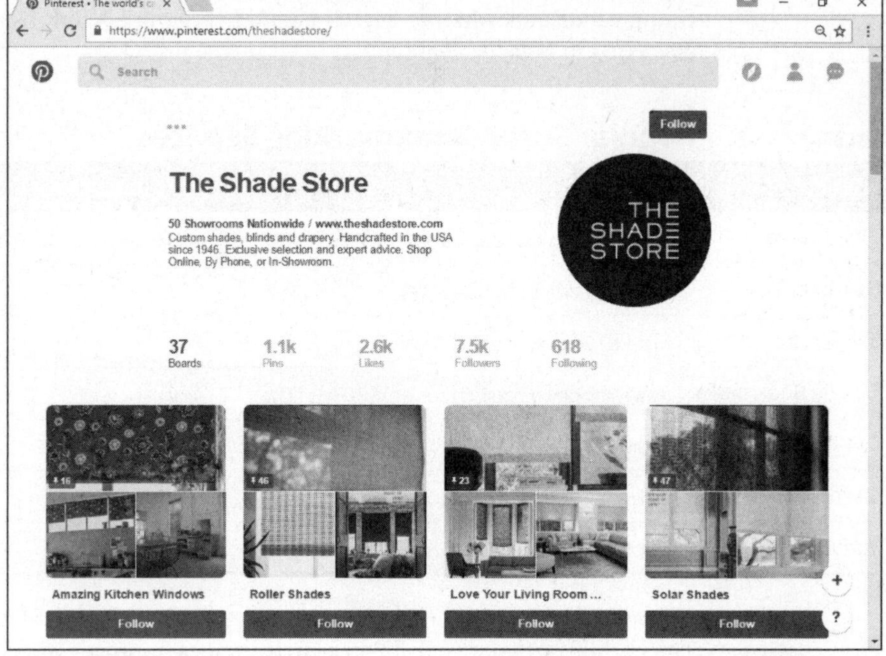

FIGURE 4-2: At Pinterest, companies can use different boards (categories) of images (pins) based on product lines and users' interests.

Courtesy of the Shade Store

By October 2016, Pinterest surpassed 150 million active users per month, with 100 million loyal users logging in daily for almost one-quarter of an hour on average. According to Social Drift (`http://socialdraft.com/ten-pinterest-stats-all-marketers-need-in-2016`), the demographics are a retailer's dream: Although the number of men using Pinterest is increasing, about 85 percent of users are women. And, according to Pew Research Center (`www.pewinternet.org/2016/11/11/social-media-update-2016`), women with higher household incomes and higher educational levels are more likely to use the site.

TIP

Traffic has skyrocketed for vendors specializing in home, lifestyle, apparel, food, and weddings, as users follow pins back to their source. If these are your target markets, start pinning!

Sharing the News

In comparison with social-bookmarking services, social news services such as Reddit and Digg (shown in Figure 4-3) point to time-sensitive individual postings and articles. Whereas bookmarking services look at sites without reference to timeliness, social *news* services focus on what's news now.

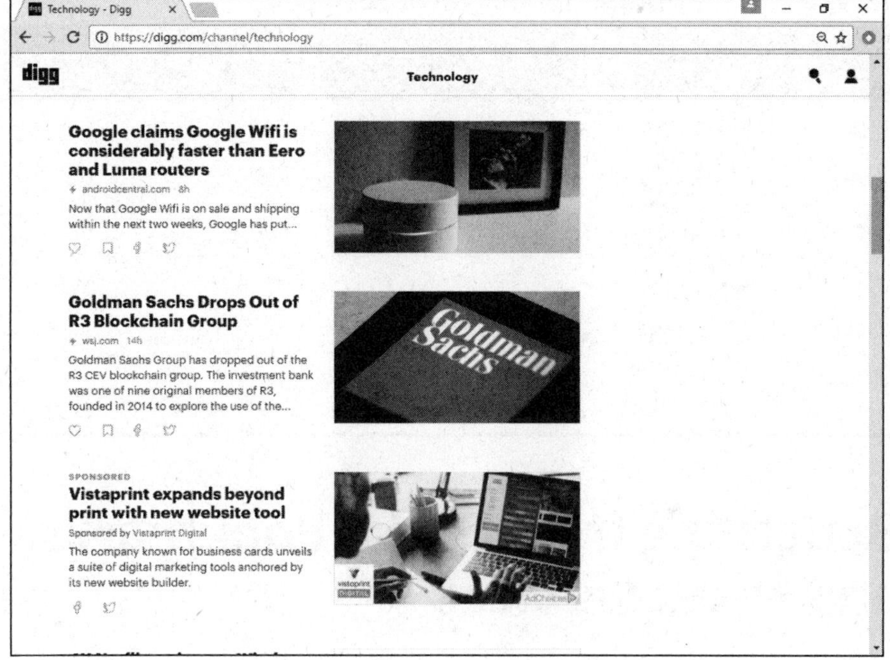

FIGURE 4-3: Digg shows links to individual articles submitted by hundreds of thousands of Internet readers.

Users can recommend dozens of different content pages on a particular website to a social news service, quickly driving significant amounts of traffic to the originating site. Many social news services rely on users to vote on submissions, with more popular results appearing on the service's front page. Unlike bookmarks, social news services aren't designed to share a list of recommendations with friends.

Figure 4-3 shows recently posted popular articles in the Technology channel on Digg. Although most entries link to standard news sources, business press releases and even special offers may appear.

REMEMBER

Peer-based recommendations aren't always golden. Because they reflect whoever randomly happens to have posted, these posts may be volatile, biased, and nonrepresentative. They certainly don't reflect scientific results. In fact, you may find some recommended articles shocking or disgusting. Watch the articles that appear for a few days to be sure you feel comfortable with the quality of what people recommend.

Table 4-2 lists some popular social news sites and whether you can submit your own site or press releases. The Passes Link Juice column indicates whether search engines recognize a link from that service.

TABLE 4-2 Popular Social News Services

Name	URL	Uses Popularity Voting	Allows Self-Submission	Allows Press Releases	Passes Link Juice
Digg	`www.digg.com`	Yes	Yes	Yes	Yes
Fark	`www.fark.com`	No	Yes	Yes	No
MetaFilter	`www.metafilter.com`	Yes	Yes	Yes	Yes
Newsvine	`www.newsvine.com`	Yes	No	No	Yes
Reddit	`www.reddit.com`	Yes	Yes, but not often	Yes	No
Slashdot	`www.slashdot.org`	No	Yes	Yes	Yes

Benefiting from Social Bookmarks and News Services

Social bookmarks and news services offer multiple benefits. To start with, they're free, which is quickly becoming unusual in the social media world. Free is always a positive factor for online guerrilla marketers. In addition, you may benefit in many other ways by using these services:

- **Improved search engine ranking:** By using your primary search terms in tags and other elements of your submissions, you may improve your overall web presence in general search engines. The appearance of your content on these services supplements your own site in general search results.
- **Increased inbound links:** Inbound links from social-bookmarking and social news services may dramatically improve your position on search engine results pages, as well as deliver visitors directly to your site.
- **Increased brand visibility and traffic:** The more people who see your website or content listed on one of these services, the more people will

remember your name and visit your site. Like many other social-marketing techniques, bookmarks and news services help fill the conversion funnel.

- **Increased readership and membership:** If you're a writer, pundit, professional speaker, or consultant, these services can be extraordinarily valuable. After you establish a reputation on a service, you may find that you have loyal followers, as well as many new readers, subscribers, clients, and speaking gigs.
- **Increased earnings:** You can consider people who visit your URL from social-bookmarking and social news services as prequalified prospects, pushing them farther down the funnel toward likely-buyer status. Be sure that your site validates the ratings it has earned, though.
- **Triggered more influentials:** Many online influentials watch social-bookmarking and social news services to spot trends and decide whether to mention a site or an article in their own blogs or tweets. Of course, submissions by these influential people carry additional value in the eyes of their followers.

REMEMBER

Monitor comments about your site to confirm that recommended pages, content, or products continue to appear and that links still work. Visitors shouldn't see 404 File Not Found messages.

Your task is to ensure that your business is listed in the appropriate services and shows up near the top of results. Always review a potential social news service to check that it's not just a spam aggregator, to make sure that postings are recent, to see what's permitted in its Terms of Use, and to discover how it ranks on Google. Sounds a lot like the process of finding inbound links in Chapter 2 of this minibook, doesn't it?

In the following sections, we talk about researching social news services, selecting the right ones for your business, and submitting to them.

TIP

For more social news sites, check out `http://addthis.com/services/all?c=social_news` and `http://newinternetorder.com/get-backlinks-social-news-sites`.

Researching a Social Bookmark and Social News Campaign

Listing your website, blog, or content initially is easy. You, or others, can post your site on as many services as you want. Being listed high in the rankings is a more difficult task, though.

WARNING

Check the Terms of Use on these services; in some cases, you can't submit your own site or content. Many news services have more constraints on the voting process than on submissions.

Here's how to post your site to the right services:

1. **Research appropriate social-bookmarking and social news services.**

   For an overview, try Quantcast or Alexa to review the user base, demographics, and traffic statistics for each prospective service. You can check sites such as Popurls (`http://popurls.com`) for the most popular daily headlines on the Internet. Generally, you're looking for services that

   - Receive a lot of traffic
   - Specialize in your market niche
   - Attract your target market

2. **Visit each site to confirm that it fits your needs and attracts your audience.**

   To understand more about the kinds of people who use a particular service, look at other top sites bookmarked in your category or at the content rated most favorably. Are the businesses and articles complementary to yours? To your competitors? Are the users of each service likely to try the products or services you offer?

   TIP

   You can sometimes tell whether an audience might be receptive to your offerings by looking at who's paying for ads on particular pages.

3. **Sort by the names who submitted postings to see which individuals or companies are responsible for most of the public listings.**

   Don't be surprised if the results follow the 80/20 rule: 80 percent of posts will come from 20 percent of users. The top ten submitters are likely to be the influentials on that service.

Executing your plan

Because a distinct effort is involved in recruiting other people to submit your site to social-bookmarking and social news services, select just a few services from your research to begin. Start with the popular ones listed in Table 4-1 or 4-2 to see whether readers will vote for your content or repost your links on smaller services, saving you the effort.

Some groupthink takes place on these services. If you have a popular post on Digg, for instance, someone may copy it to Reddit or StumbleUpon for you.

Some services display a list of icons above every story for readers to share elsewhere.

Most users select only one social-bookmarking service because they want only one place for their own favorites. That behavior complicates your task because you may need to submit to multiple services to obtain broad coverage. Strive for a realistic balance between coverage and the level of effort you can commit. If you're short of time, don't worry. Start small — you can always do another campaign later.

After you select your list of appropriate services, write them into your Social Media Marketing Plan (found in Book 1, Chapter 3) with a schedule for regular postings and review. Then create an account and a profile, if appropriate, for each selected service. Finally, submit the URLs for your site (or sites) or content, as appropriate. Your schedule will probably reflect

- An initial mix of multiple one-time submissions to social-bookmarking services
- Regular, repeat submissions to one or two social news services, within the constraints of their Terms of Use
- Occasional additions to your social bookmarks
- Regular monitoring of links to your site and mentions in the cybersocial whirl

Watch for scam services offering hundreds of automated social bookmark submissions. You don't need hundreds, any more than you need hundreds of search engines. Besides, you could end up blacklisted for using sites such as Social Marker, SocialAdr, or TribePro.

Many services offer a toolbar add-in to help users easily submit sites or content whenever they find something they like. You might find it handy to install toolbar add-ins for the specific services you expect to use regularly. Better yet, install a share button (see the section "Using Social Media Buttons," later in this chapter) on your site and use the button to access your suite of accounts.

Monitoring results

As we discuss in Book 9, you always need to monitor the results of all your marketing techniques. Watch traffic statistics to identify which services produce the most referrals and when you see spikes in traffic. Stick with the services that become good referrers, of course — especially if they eventually lead to qualified prospects and sales. Replace the ones that don't work.

Consider trying a tool designed for monitoring appearances on social-bookmarking and social news sites, including when others have recommended or rated you. You can use these monitoring tools to assess these elements:

- The success of your social-bookmarking and social news campaign
- The efficacy of one posting compared with another
- The unauthorized use of trademarks
- The effectiveness of a specific press release or sales promotion
- The appearances of your competitors on social bookmarks and news services

Book 2, Chapter 1 discusses multiple tools for monitoring mentions of your business or website on social networks and blogs. Many of those tools also monitor bookmarking and news services. You might also want to try

- **Alltop (`www.alltop.com`):** Collects current headlines and lead paragraphs from websites and blogs and sorts by topic
- **BuzzFeed (`www.buzzfeed.com`):** Monitors hot stuff online to share
- **Popurls (`http://popurls.com`):** Aggregates current headlines from the most popular sites on the Internet
- **Social Media for Firefox (`http://addons.mozilla.org/en-US/firefox/addon/social-media-for-firefox-7888`):** Status bar add-on that displays how many votes content has at Digg, StumbleUpon, Twitter, Delicious, and Reddit
- **WhosTalkin (`www.whostalkin.com/`):** A free topic search for multiple social media sites

Submitting to Bookmarking Services

Consider submitting URLs to bookmarking services from a personal, rather than business, address or have friends or employees use their personal email addresses as the submission source. Use neutral, non-promotional language in any comment or review. Figure 4-4 shows how to submit a site to Delicious, a popular social-bookmarking service. Submitting to social-bookmarking services is usually very simple: Create an account and submit a URL with a brief description.

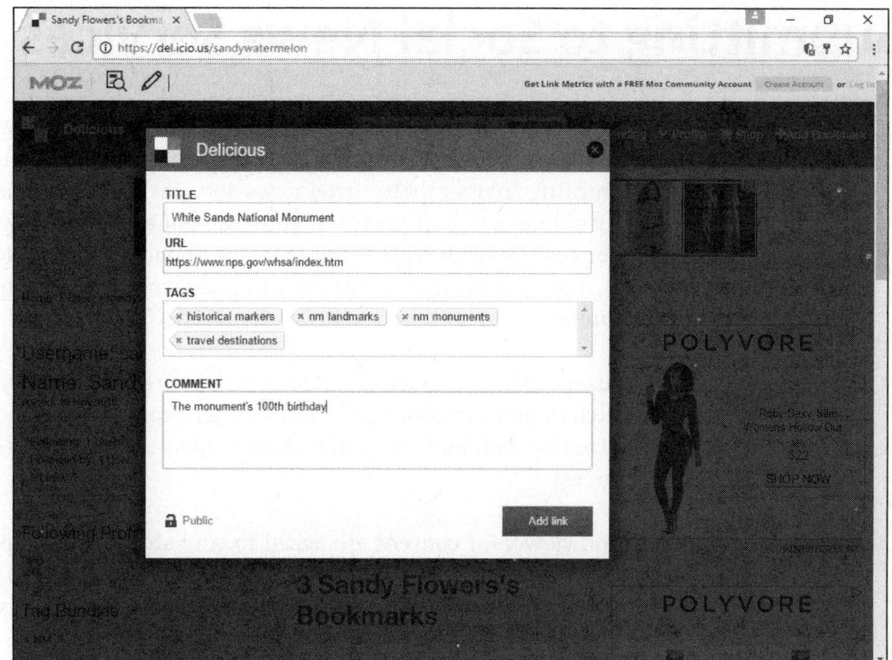

FIGURE 4-4: A submission to Delicious, the social-bookmarking service.

Try to use appropriate search terms in category names, tags, text, or titles when you submit your site. Select terms that searchers are particularly likely to use. Generally, you can find those terms in traffic statistics for your website or in *tag clouds* (a graphic display of search terms that appear in an article, with the most frequently used terms appearing in a large font) from the target service. (Read about tag clouds in Book 2, Chapter 2.) Enter your site in as many categories as possible.

If you have separate domain names or subdomains for your blog or community site, submit a few of them as bookmarks, along with your primary website, as long as the number is reasonable (say, less than six). You can also post social bookmarks to where links are permitted on Facebook, LinkedIn, or other social networking pages to further enhance your visibility. Just don't personally submit too many of your own pages to one bookmarking site lest you become marked as a spammer.

WARNING

Be discreet. Don't spam social-bookmarking or news services with multiple frequent submissions. Although you can organize a few submissions from others to get the ball rolling, don't set up multiple accounts per user on a social news service to vote for yourself or use automated submitters, which not only might have malware but also might be prohibited. Like regular search engines, these social services act aggressively to detect and blacklist spammers. Read the Terms of Use on every site if you have questions.

Submitting to Social News Services

Think of social news services as peer-reviewed indexes to short-term, contemporary articles, whereas social bookmarks are more useful for longer-term content. Submitting frequently to social news services is not only acceptable but also practically obligatory, particularly if your site generates news within a particular industry or geographical region or if your livelihood is content dependent. Generally, with most social news services, you must create an account first and then submit content.

Because users are in and out of these services often, you always need new content to catch their attention. These users prefer peer-recommended stories versus ones selected by staff editors or that appear in an unfiltered syndicated feed from other sources.

People who view your content are asked to vote stories up or down and are often given an opportunity to comment, as well. You generally need to create an account to post, vote, or comment on stories, but anyone can read the listings.

Always select appropriate categories for your material, such as technology, world news, politics, business, entertainment, lifestyle, or environment. Avoid vague categories such as general, other, or miscellaneous — they're deep, dark pits from which your content may never escape!

TIP

On Reddit, you can create niche subject communities called *subreddits*. Subreddits, which have their own rules and must be approved by a moderator, offer the opportunity to maximize attention for your business area. There are 50 default subreddits and more than 10,000 others, plus local subreddits. For more information, read the case study story in this chapter, or visit `http://maximizesocialbusiness.com/design-subreddit-business-service-program-17369`, `http://maximizesocialbusiness.com/subreddits-care-12544/#`, or `www.reddit.com/r/help/comments/2yob6r/creating_a_subreddit`.

Selecting content for social news services

Content choice is critical. Not every item on your blog or website will entice readers to submit or rate an article. Generally, the ones that drive the most traffic to your site will have timely content, such as breaking news, or entertainment, humor, or quality resource information not found elsewhere.

Keep the following in mind when deciding what to post on social news services:

- **Remember that social news services are culturally dependent.** If you're trying to reach an international market, you may need to submit your content in languages other than English. Note that other countries and languages might have their own localized social-bookmarking and news services. Visit `www.searchenginejournal.com/death-social-bookmarking/171061` or international search engines to identify the appropriate, remaining social news services.

- **Avoid out-of-date material.** If you must submit older stories, look for such items as features, interviews, how-to's, and essays that have longer-lasting interest. Those items are good for social-bookmarking sites, too.
- **Match your content submissions to sites where readers like the types of stories you want to recommend.** Look at the tag cloud for frequency of use on tags similar to yours over the past 6 to 12 months.
- **Select the services with features that best match the content you offer and the audience you're trying to reach.** Some social news services allow links to images, video, and audio; others accept only links to text.
- **Think tactically.** Initiate posts for specific pages, posts, or articles that have the potential to lead to traffic, prospects, or sales, not for your everyday internal company news update.

REMEMBER

If you get a reputation for posting meaningless items or using the comment space for hard-sell language, you might find it hard to gain traction on these sites; you might even be banned for posting junk.

Preparing social news stories for success

Although you might be tempted to splatter social news services with your stories, just give them a little thought. Set up tags, titles, and lead lines carefully. Follow these online journalistic tips for improved results:

- **Write a catchy headline, not an academic title.** Keep headlines short and memorable. Try to use vivid verbs (not just nouns) and active voice. Instead of "New social media app created by local company" for your star-gazing app, try "AstroWare's New App Rockets to the Stars."
- **Write a good lede.** The headline and first line of a story (the *lede*) are often the only elements that viewers see. Set a hook to catch readers and make them want to link back to your original content. Tell people what's in it for them or how they'll benefit by reading the story.
- **Write a good description, comment, or summary.** Keep it short (20 to 25 words!) and focus on benefits.
- **Check your facts, spelling, and links.** If you make errors, someone is likely to post a negative comment. If your links don't work, you lose potential

traffic — a primary reason you're using social-bookmarking and news services in the first place.

» **Prepare your site for success.** Just in case, be sure to structure your site to take advantage of new traffic. Links to related articles on your site or blog give interested readers more than one story to explore, thus increasing the number of page views per visit. To increase conversion rates, use calls to action and visual reminders to sign up for syndicated feeds and newsletters, subscribe to a paid publication, or make a purchase.

» **Serve up your site.** Be sure that your hosting package allows for increased traffic. Traffic from social bookmarks tends to build slowly, but an appearance on the front page of a social news site can flood your server with more traffic than it's set up to handle. A quick call to your host or IT department should confirm your preparations.

TIP

These writing tactics not only help attract the kind of viewers who are more likely to click-through but also help increase the time users spend on your blog or website.

Using Application-Specific Bookmarks

Some bookmarking and social news services are constrained to specific types of content, such as blogs or video, and others are specific to topic, or activity, such as shopping or product reviews. Table 4-3 provides some examples.

TABLE 4-3 Bookmarks for Specific Applications

Application	Name	URL
Blogs	BlogCatalog	`www.blogcatalog.com`
	Feedly	`www.feedly.com`
Reviews	Epinions	`www.epinions.com`
	SnapFiles	`www.snapfiles.com/userreviews/latest.html`
	TripAdvisor	`http://tripadvisor.com`

Application	Name	URL
Shopping	Fab	http://fab.com/
	Lyst	www.lyst.com
	Stylehive	www.stylehive.com
	Sumally	http://sumally.com/
	ThisNext	www.thisnext.com
	Wanelo	http://wanelo.com/
Video	MyVidster	www.myvidster.com
	Simfany	www.simfany.com

You can find more shopping bookmark sites at www.pcmag.com/slideshow/story/293956/the-rapid-ascension-of-pinterest-and-social-shopping-sites/1. In addition, search for *topic area + bookmarking site* on any search engine to find specialty bookmarking services.

Timing Your Submissions

Like with search engines, getting yourself on the first page of social-bookmarking and social news services can be difficult. You generally have only a 24-hour window on social news services to attract enough attention for either lasting value or timeliness. Remember that you may need to coordinate submissions by others to get things started.

There's no point in posting in the middle of the night, when many people are asleep on one side of the country or both. Generally, posting between 10 a.m. and 4 p.m. US central daylight time works well, with an anecdotal peak of best results around 3 p.m. Workdays are generally better for generating traffic, although weekends see less competition. Of course, you need to adjust submission times if getting a scoop is critical or if you seek visibility on an international site.

On the other hand, if you're posting to specific bookmarking services (such as social-shopping or sports-bookmarking sites) that aren't time-dependent, weekends may find more of your audience available. It's a lot like scheduling an e-newsletter delivery or press release, both of which are audience dependent.

TIP

For lists of additional social-bookmarking sites with a high page rank, visit the following:

» `www.socialcliff.com/sites/free-high-pr-dofollow-social-bookmarking-sites-list.php`

» `www.qdtricks.net/free-high-pr-social-bookmarking-sites-list`

» `http://alltipsfinder.com/free-high-pr-dofollow-social-bookmarking-sites-list`

Your best bet is to experiment. Note that timing for news sites is not the same as timing posts for major social media channels. Based on HubSpot data (`http://blog.hubspot.com/marketing/best-times-post-pin-tweet-social-media-infographic - sm.0005sbiqt19ejdart8v2fyj1r3rns`), the best times to post on social media to ensure maximum engagement are as follows:

» **Facebook:**
  - Saturday and Sunday from 12 p.m. to 1 p.m.
  - Wednesday from 3 p.m. to 4 p.m.
  - Thursday and Friday from 1 p.m. to 4 p.m.

» **Twitter:**
  - Monday through Friday from 12 p.m. to 3 p.m.
  - Wednesdays from 5 p.m. to 6 p.m.

» **LinkedIn:**
  - Tuesday, Wednesday, and Thursday from 7:30 a.m. to 8:30 a.m., at 12 p.m., and from 5 p.m. to 6 p.m.
  - Tuesday from 10 a.m. to 11 a.m.

» **Pinterest:**
  - Every day from 2 a.m. to 4 a.m. and evening hours
  - Friday at 5 p.m.
  - Saturday from 8 p.m. to 11 p.m.

» **Instagram:**
  - Monday through Thursday anytime except from 3 p.m. to 4 p.m.

Try submitting the same post to different services at different times of the day, or try submitting different posts to the same service at different times. Monitor traffic to your site by the hour and day, and adjust your plans accordingly.

ARCADIA ALES BREWS SUCCESS WITH SOCIAL MEDIA

Founded in 1996 in Battle Creek, MI, Arcadia Brewing Company now encompasses Arcadia Kalamazoo and Arcadia Battle Creek under the umbrella URL Arcadia Ales, with about 100 employees. The company relaunched its original website (`www.arcadiabrewingcompany.com`) in 2009 with the domain name `arcadiaales.com`; in 2015 that site was redesigned as shown in the figure.

Courtesy of Arcadia Ales

"The growth of our social media platforms has definitely been organic," says Marketing Coordinator Karmene Hassell. Growing apace with the expanding role of social media in building relationships between industries and customers, Arcadia Ales quickly developed a marketing philosophy for its use. "We've been firm believers that it is better to utilize social media deliberately versus having a presence on all platforms and not using them effectively."

The decision to use the social news site Reddit grew serendipitously from the strong local Reddit community in Kalamazoo (`www.reddit.com/r/kzoo`). A marketing intern from Western Michigan University who was familiar with the Reddit community felt it would be a good place for genuine local feedback. Once she posted the informal survey seen in the

(continued)

following image, a long-term relationship was established. Arcadia Ales Kalamazoo now serves as the location for many meet-ups, including the 2015 Reddit Day Meetup (www.reddit.com/r/kzoo/comments/3b76tk/reddit_meetup_day_results).

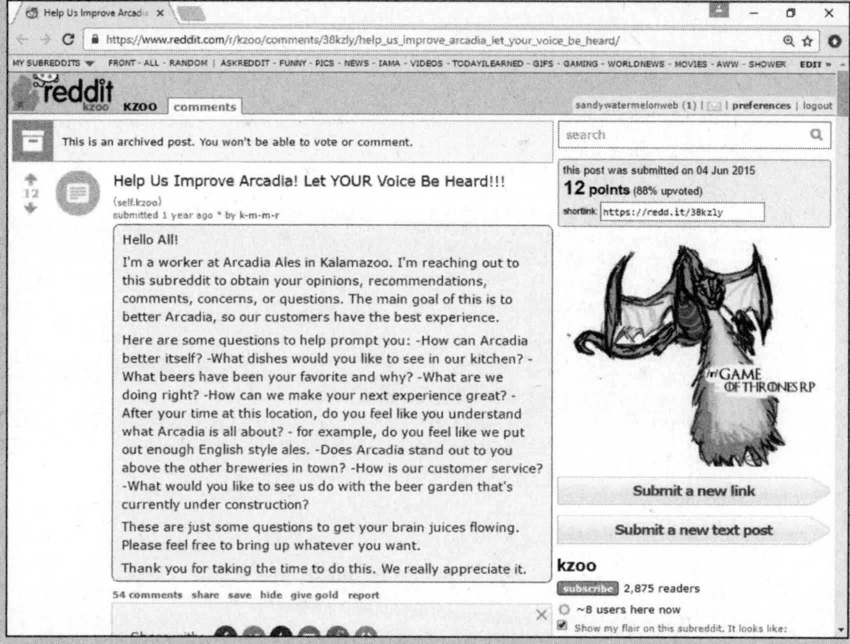

Courtesy of Arcadia Ales

"Reddit has been a great place to get an inside peek as to what is important and relevant within in our social community," Hassell observes. (See the tip following this story for more information about local Reddits.)

While Reddit is a fantastic resource, it is one of many platforms Hassell uses. For example, the company advertises in Michigan through organizations such as the West Michigan Tourist Association and Pure Michigan, as well as on local online platforms such as Discover Kalamazoo and Revue. It also posts its events on multiple sites, including www.evensi.us, www.eventsinusa.net, and www.everydayevents.org.

The company is also an enthusiastic member of the craft beer community in Michigan. As a member of the Brewers Association since its creation, it has access to many other brewery-centric platforms, such as www.craftbeer.com and www.brewbound.com, and cross-promotes actively with retail outlets on their social media. Perhaps as a reminder that social media needs to be sociable in real life as well, Hassell notes that the craft beer community has its own natural and extremely supportive culture that promotes itself.

In spite of all the activity on niche social media, Hassell still finds the most success on the "majors," maintaining strong Facebook pages and a thriving Instagram presence. But it's no surprise that Arcadia Ales has found that different platforms work best for different marketing goals. "It's been most helpful to know what market we're trying to reach or what message we're trying to send." For instance, the company shows more behind-the-scenes media and real-time images on Instagram, while customer education and engagement are the goals for Facebook.

Managing all this social media activity takes some coordination. The company uses Facebook's scheduling capability for posts that notify followers of upcoming events, tastings, and beer dinners, but relies on Hootsuite for cross-posting. Hassell appreciates Hootsuite's overview capability, which lets her see everything going on with all Arcadia Ales's social media platforms at once. She also takes advantage of Hootsuite's educational tools and webinars to stay up-to-date on social media trends.

While Arcadia Ales relies on the individual analytics offered on most social media channels, it also compiles them to see a bigger picture. "[Analytics] shows us whom we aren't reaching and helps us find new ways to promote our brand. We've even used analytics to help us come up with new beer styles to brew!" she exclaims.

Hassell emphasizes that "just because there's a variety of social apps out there, it doesn't mean you have to be on all of them. Which work best for your business? On which can you most effectively share your message and vision? Which platform gets you in touch with your customer base? It's better to do a few things well than to do a lot of things poorly."

She adds one more often-overlooked piece of advice: "Be mindful of your voice on social media. You are representing the company at all times. . . . If there's ever any question if [something] is right to post, don't do it. The social network doesn't have an "undo" button. . . . Maintaining good brand representation . . . is applicable to all platforms but especially platforms like Reddit."

The following URLs represent Arcadia Brewing Company's web presence:

- `www.arcadiaales.com`
- `www.facebook.com/arcadiaales`
- `www.facebook.com/arcadiakalamazoo`
- `www.facebook.com/arcadiabattlecreek`
- `www.facebook.com/twistedtailbbq`
- `www.instagram.com/arcadiaales`

(continued)

(continued)

- www.yelp.com/biz/arcadia-brewing-company-kalamazoo-kalamazoo
- https://twitter.com/arcadiaales
- https://untappd.com/arcadiaales
- https://in.pinterest.com/arcadiabrewing
- https://foursquare.com/v/arcadia-brewing-company-kalamazoo/534ed62d11d2d11c601da928

Generally, social bookmarks drive traffic to your site slowly as people find your URL, but you can generate a spike in traffic by pushing your site on social news services (if they permit it). You can ask several people to submit your site, but leave it to others to vote it up or down.

Try to get 15 to 25 people to submit your posting within the first few hours of its publication. That's usually enough to get attention from others and build momentum for votes. Receiving 25 recommendations within a few hours means a lot more than receiving 25 recommendations within a week!

While your visibility on the service rises, so, too, does traffic to your site.

REMEMBER

For all the value these services may have as recommendation search engines, the traffic on them is nothing compared with traffic on major search engines, such as Google and Yahoo!/Bing. Optimization for general search engines is still absolutely necessary, as discussed in Book 2, Chapter 2, and forms the basis for your success.

TIP

Local Reddits work differently than other subreddits. Take advantage of your local Reddit to market both location-specific topics and locally related posts for subjects and events, from marathons to meals. Always remember to link directly to your local Reddit in posts on any other subreddits. And don't forget to check Reddit's traffic stats to estimate how many Reddit readers live in your community. For a list of all local Reddits, visit www.reddit.com/r/LocationReddits/wiki/index. If your community isn't listed, request a listing from the moderator. For more ideas for Reddit marketing, see www.socialmediaexaminer.com/reddit.

Encouraging Others to Bookmark or Rate Your Site

Like most political campaigns, the popularity contest on services that rely on votes or frequency of submission can be managed to your advantage. It just takes a little planning. Although illegal vote-rigging and outright manipulation are forms of cyberfraud, the following techniques are valid ways to encourage others to submit or rate your site:

- **We all get by with a little help from our friends.** Always have other people submit your material; on some services, submission by others is required. One easy way is to email a circle of employees, colleagues, and friends to help when you post a new page or content, or help them set up syndicated feeds from your selected services. Ask them to submit or comment on your posting within a few hours after being notified.
- **Scratch backs.** In addition to posting your own stories, recommending material on other sites that complement yours (as long as you don't drive traffic to your competition) is good practice. If you help others increase the ratings on their stories through your repostings and votes, they're more likely to return the favor. These practices establish your reputation as a fair-minded individual who's interested in the topic, not just in sales.
- **Be a courteous responder.** You make friends and influence people by responding to comments on your stories and commenting on others. Again, one good turn deserves another. Consider it as building your cyberkarma.
- **Become known as the go-to poster.** If you frequently post interesting material on one service, you may develop a reputation and a following, with readers watching for new items from you. They will happily rate or rank items you suggest.
- **Ask.** People who visit your site might be willing to let others know about it, but you need to remind them. Put a call to action or share button at the end of a story or post, reminding them to tell a friend or share your content publicly. If you've decided to focus on a particular service, display its icon with a link (see the later section "Using Social Media Buttons"). You might even include a call to action to install a toolbar.

REMEMBER

Don't confuse *popularity* — a subjective and manipulated quantity — with the *quality* of leads that a bookmark or social news mention may generate. Popularity is a means, not an end. Ultimately, you're better off with fewer but higher-quality visitors arriving at your site.

Like exchanging reciprocal links to improve search engine ranking, exchanging bookmarks has become common practice. Like linking, bookmark swapping can be done honestly, but it has a darker side.

Follow the same principles that you do with links:

- Don't exchange bookmarks with spamlike junk sites — only with ones that offer value.
- Be suspicious of people who offer to sell bookmarks or votes.
- Look for relevance, including shared tags or search terms, as well as traffic rankings on the exchanging site.

Because submitting too many of your own pages to a bookmarking service can tag you as a spammer, you can participate in a service in which members bookmark each other. These are similar to some of the old link exchanges, banner exchanges, and web rings. Be cautious. Avoid anything that looks illegitimate.

If you have no friends or colleagues to help you out, you might examine the option of Piqqus (`www.piqqus.com`) for exchanges between Digg and StumbleUpon.

WARNING

Avoid automated submission services or scripts. The safest way to participate in social bookmarking is the old-fashioned way: individually, by hand.

Using Social Media Buttons

Social media buttons have two functions: Follow Us buttons cross-link visitors to multiple elements of your web presence; share buttons enable visitors easily to share your content or website with others. Place buttons consistently near the top of a page or an article, where you place key information.

When you repeat smaller versions of the buttons at the end of each post on your blog, users can share a specific item instead of the entire blog. Social media buttons can also be placed on e-newsletters and on multiple social media networks. Anecdotal evidence from some companies that tried organized campaigns shows dramatic increases in traffic on their social media sites.

Follow Us buttons

Follow Us buttons — sometimes called *chiclets* — link visitors to other elements of your social media presence, such as to your Facebook profile, Twitter page, or blog. In Figure 4-5, the chiclets above the top navigation on every page of the site for the San Francisco Theological Seminary (`www.sfts.edu`) encourage users to link to the school Facebook page, Twitter page, donation page, and email.

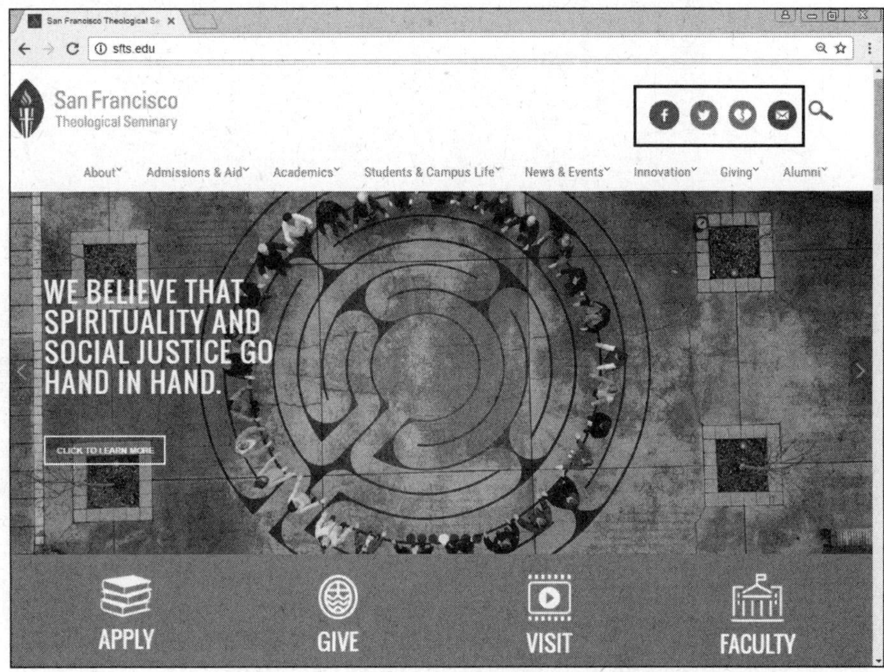

FIGURE 4-5: On every page of its website, San Francisco Theological Seminary includes chiclets that link to its social media pages.

Courtesy of San Francisco Theological Seminary: SFTS.edu

Almost all services offer free standard icons along with code to insert them. Alternatively, you can search for creative icons online at sites such as `www.evohosting.co.uk/blog/web-development/design/more-free-social-media-icons` and `www.designsrock.com/free-social-media-icons` and create your own link, or use a social bookmark links generator, such as Keotag (`www.keotag.com/sociable.php`).

Share buttons

Social share buttons from services such as AddtoAny offer a drop-down list that gives the user sharing options, as shown in Figure 4-6. This approach lets visitors easily share content by linking them to the sign-in page for their own accounts on other social-sharing services.

FIGURE 4-6: Social share buttons encourage visitors to pass along your site or content through their own accounts.

Courtesy of Dede Feldman Co.

In an interesting variation, Shareaholic (`www.shareaholic.com/publishers`) offers buttons that appear as you mouse over an image. Several sources for other social share buttons are listed in Table 4-4.

TABLE 4-4 **Sources for Social Share Buttons**

Name	URL
AddThis	`http://addthis.com`
AddToAny	`http://addtoany.com`
HubSpot article titled "How to Create Social Media Buttons for All the Top Social Networks"	`http://blog.hubspot.com/blog/tabid/6307/bid/29544/The-Ultimate-Cheat-Sheet-for-Creating-Social-Media-Buttons.aspx`
Ridiculously Responsive Social Sharing Buttons	`http://kurtnoble.com/labs/rrssb`
Shareaholic	`www.shareaholic.com`
ShareThis	`http://sharethis.com`
SmartAddon	`www.smartaddon.com`

These free, easy-to-install buttons allow users to transfer content quickly to their own profiles, blogs, preferred social-bookmarking service, instant messages, email, or text messages. You can even use a special widget, albeit for a fee, from Elegant Themes (`www.elegantthemes.com/preview/Monarch/automatic-pop-up`) that facilitates sharing products or pages from your site, as shown in Figure 4-7. This is viral marketing at an epidemic level!

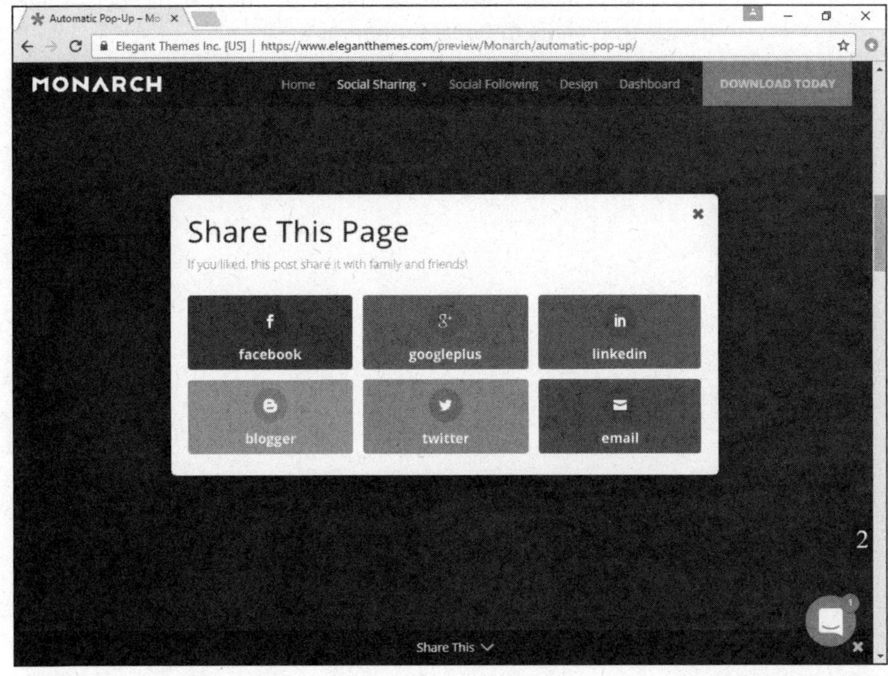

FIGURE 4-7: This widget from Elegant Themes enables users to quickly recommend products or pages from your site.

Courtesy of Elegant Themes

Register for free analytics on sharing services that offer it to see how and where users elected to share your material or site. You can often find a toolbar add-on for each service on the site. You may want to install the ones you need in your browser and offer that option to your users in a call to action.

REMEMBER

Always include Print, Email, and Favorites (for personal bookmarks) in your set of social share buttons. Some people like the convenience of the old stuff.

TECHNICAL STUFF

If you aren't comfortable inserting code on your site, ask your web developer or programmer to do it for you. Sometimes even your hosting company can help. Specify which Follow Us or share buttons you want to have visible and ask to have the buttons appear on every page of your site.

If all these tasks seem overwhelming, plenty of providers are willing to help you for a fee. Most SEO firms, press and public relations firms, online-marketing companies, specialized social marketing ad agencies, and copywriters who specialize in online content now offer assistance with social bookmarking, social news, and other forms of social media marketing. Try searching for *social media services, social media agencies, digital media marketing,* or *social media marketing.*

We discuss more advanced methods for integrating social media into your overall marketing plans in Book 8, Chapter 4.

IN THIS CHAPTER

» Understanding mobile media users

» Marketing with social media sites on mobile devices

» Marketing with text messages on smartphones

» Advertising on mobile social media

Chapter 5 Making Social Media Mobile

Social media is no longer confined to a standard computer of any size. The proliferation of smartphones and apps, 5G networks, more affordable data plans, built-in web browsers, and mobile-ready websites have all contributed to the growth of mobile social activities. Most devices (except old feature phones) can use either a cellular network or Wi-Fi for wireless Internet access.

The integration of social media with mobile devices creates more opportunities to reach your target audience in addition to challenges for managing and integrating your marketing campaigns.

As a social media marketer, try to tap the potential that these mobile devices offer: incredible marketing opportunities to reach both retail and business prospects at the moment they seek information about the product or service you offer, wherever they are. You don't have to wait for them to get back to their desktop computers. Of course, the social media marketing techniques you select may depend on the platforms that your target market uses. In this chapter, we look at how rapidly advancing mobile technology allows you to use social media to reach people on the go.

REMEMBER

Mobile social marketing gives you many new ways to reach with your message. The challenge, of course, is that everyone else is trying to do that, too. Your efforts have to cut through an increasing amount of clutter.

Understanding the Statistics of Mobile Device Usage

To understand why mobile social marketing is so important, you must first acknowledge the explosive growth in the use of mobile devices, as shown in Table 5-1. ComScore estimates that the crossover point when mobile usage exceeded desktop usage occurred in 2014.

TABLE 5-1 Number of Global Users in Millions (Desktop versus Mobile)

Device Usage	2012	2015
Desktop	1,550	1,750
Mobile	1,400	1,900

Source: `www.smartinsights.com/mobile-marketing/mobile-marketing-analytics/mobile-marketing-statistics`

With nearly 80 percent smartphone penetration of the US market by population as of March 2016, consumers increasingly use smartphones to search for local information, research products, and send messages, as shown in Figure 5-1. The trend extends beyond research, with mobile transactions now accounting for more than 15 percent of all digital commerce dollars.

Exploring mobile use of social media

According to Marketing Land (`http://marketingland.com/facebook-usage-accounts-1-5-minutes-spent-mobile-171561`), nearly 80 percent of the time users are engaged with social media is now spent on some form of mobile device, not desktop (see Table 5-2). As you would expect, the increased use of mobile devices means that social media channels are seeing explosive mobile usage. According to Statista (`www.statista.com/statistics/294445/minutes-spent-on-us-media-sites-by-platform`), Facebook and Twitter enjoy significant majority usage on mobile platforms, while Pinterest, Snapchat, and Instagram are used almost exclusively on mobile platforms. Only LinkedIn and Tumblr are still used primarily on desktops.

Apple's iOS and Google's Android operating systems are highly competitive. According to Parks Associates, Apple iPhones had a 43 percent market share in the US in fourth quarter 2016, compared to a 30 percent for Samsung (see Figure 5-2). The remaining 27 percent of the market is split among multiple Android smartphone brands. Worldwide, Android's lead is a substantial 82 percent.

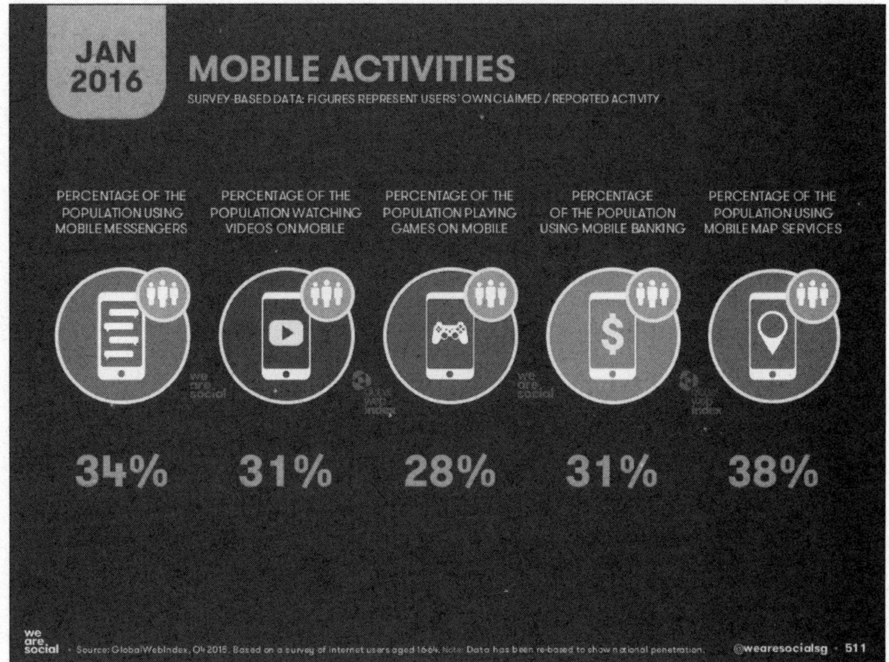

FIGURE 5-1: How people in the US used their smartphones in January 2016.

Courtesy of We Are Social

TABLE 5-2 **Share of Time Spent on Social Media across Different Platforms**

Platform	2013	2014	2015
Desktop	33%	26%	21%
Smartphone app	53%	53%	61%
Smartphone web	3%	4%	6%
Tablet app	10%	13%	9%
Tablet web	0%	3%	3%

Source: `http://marketingland.com/facebook-usage-accounts-1-5-minutes-spent-mobile-171561` *with data from comScore Media Metrix Multi-Platform & Mobile Metrix US, Dec 2015/Dec 2014/Dec 2013 (Whitepaper downloadable at* `www.comscore.com/Insights/Presentations-and-Whitepapers/2016/2016-US-Cross-Platform-Future-in-Focus`*)*

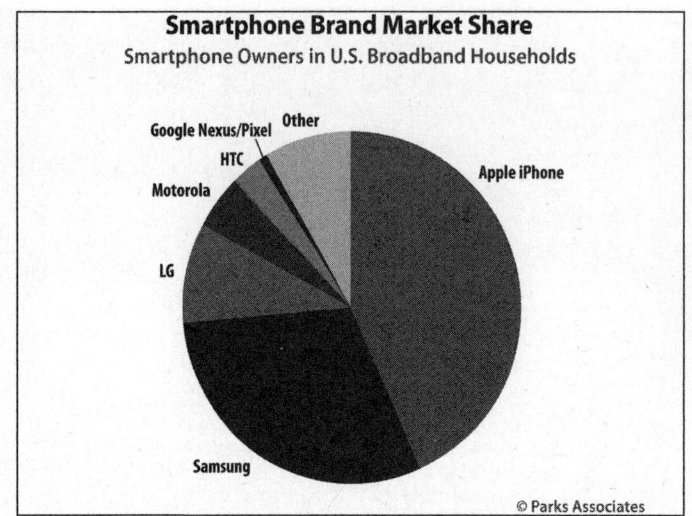

FIGURE 5-2: Market share for smartphones by brand in the US, fourth quarter, 2016.

Courtesy of Parks Associates; source: www.parksassociates.com/blog/article/pr-02102016-mwc

REMEMBER

In terms of social media marketing, the question of platform affects only the development of mobile apps, which need to be created for specific operating systems. Mobile sites, mobile advertising, and social media channels are generally operating-system neutral from a marketer's point of view (unless you're marketing your own app to users of a specific platform).

Why bother your marketing head with all this mobile information? You need to get your social media message across on the specific social media channels that your target audience uses, no matter how they access those channels. Your social content should be optimized visually and for ease of use on mobile platforms.

Demographics of mobile users

An October 2015 study by the Pew Research Center (www.pewinternet.org/2015/10/29/the-demographics-of-device-ownership) showed that 70 percent of US adult men and 66 percent of women owned a smartphone as of January 2015. The report also showed that the smartphone user population spans racial categories: 66 percent of whites, 68 percent of blacks, and 64 percent of Hispanics now use smartphones.

The biggest variation in smartphone use is by age, with 86 percent of those age 18 to 29 using smartphones; 83 percent of 30- to 49-year-olds; 58 percent of those ages 50 to 64; and 30 percent of those 65 and older.

Household income is a second differentiator: Only 52 percent of households earning less than $30,000 annually have a smartphone, but 69 percent of those earning $30,000 to $49,999 have one, as do 76 percent of those earning $50,000 to $74,999 and 87 percent of those earning more than $75,000.

Getting a handle on mobile activities

Mobile users check email, weather, traffic, maps, directions, and headlines. They also search for companies and products (especially local ones), compare prices, review entertainment schedules, access social media sites, watch videos, check review and ratings sites, sign up for alerts and coupons, and play games online. In other words, they are avid users of just about every social media channel.

As you can see in Figures 5-3 and 5-4, a well-optimized mobile site looks quite different from its desktop equivalent, even if the desktop site is done with responsive design to adjust for different page widths.

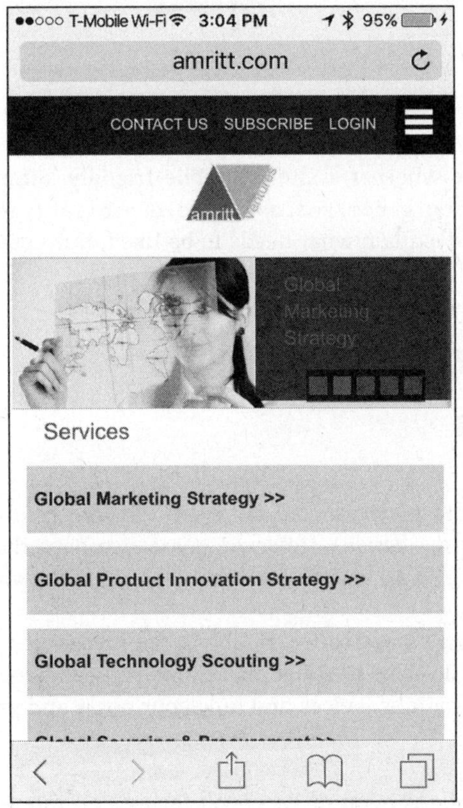

FIGURE 5-3: The dedicated mobile website for Amritt.com.

Courtesy of Amritt, Inc.

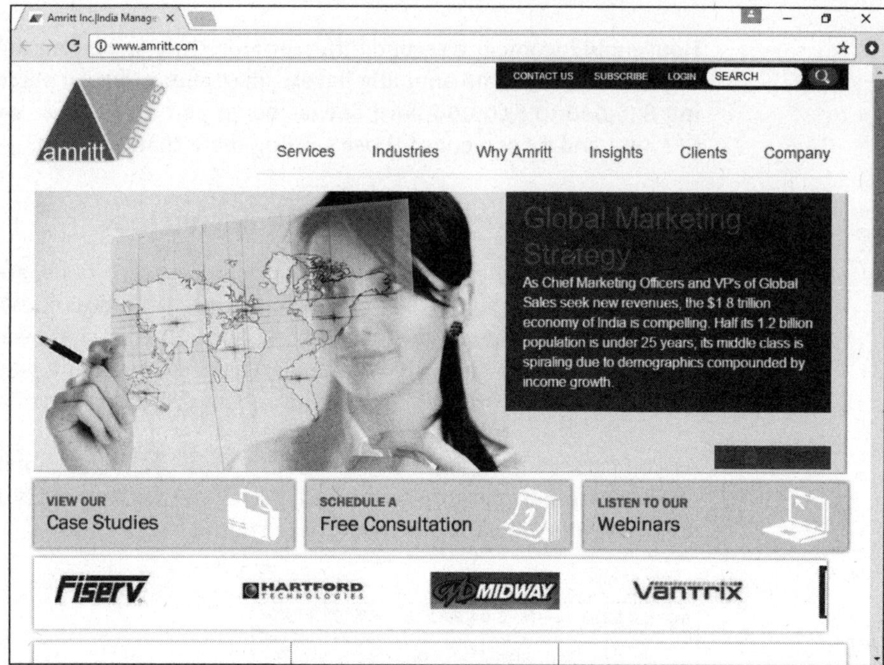

FIGURE 5-4: Amritt's standard website as it appears in a desktop environment.

Courtesy of Amritt, Inc.

TIP

It's easy to determine whether a site is mobile friendly. Simply enter the URL at `https://search.google.com/search-console/mobile-friendly`. Google will provide the results and explain what needs to be fixed, if necessary.

Reaching People on the Move with Social Media

Almost all social media services now automatically reconfigure their sites for mobile devices *(responsive design)*. However, most also have their own app optimized for mobile usage (both smartphone and tablet), as shown in Table 5-3.

In either case, you don't have to worry about the mechanics of changing your page or post. But you do have to think about how you can benefit from reaching people who are using mobile devices and how your posts and profiles will appear in these formats.

For example, the mobile version of Facebook focuses on interactivity. Users can view their news feeds and post their own updates, comments, videos, and images.

TABLE 5-3 Mobile Apps for Social Media

Name	URL to Download App	Mobile Site (Responsive Design)	Vanity URL
Digg	`https://itunes.apple.com/us/app/digg/id362872995` `https://play.google.com/store/apps/details?id=com.diggreader&hl=en`	`http://m.digg.com`	None
Facebook	`https://itunes.apple.com/us/app/facebook/id284882215` `https://play.google.com/store/apps/details?id=com.facebook.katana`	`https://m.facebook.com`	`www.facebook.com/mobile`
Flickr	`http://itunes.apple.com/us/app/flickr/id328407587` `https://play.google.com/store/apps/details?id=com.yahoo.mobile.client.android.flickr`	`https://m.flickr.com`	`www.flickr.com`
Foursquare	`http://itunes.apple.com/us/app/foursquare/id306934924` `https://play.google.com/store/apps/details?id=com.joelapenna.foursquared`	None	`https://foursquare.com/download`
Google+	`http://itunes.apple.com/us/app/google+/id447119634` `https://play.google.com/store/apps/details?id=com.google.android.apps.plus`	None	`www.google.com/mobile/+`
LinkedIn	`http://itunes.apple.com/us/app/linkedin/id288429040` `https://play.google.com/store/apps/details?id=com.linkedin.android`	None	`www.linkedin.com/mobile`

(continued)

TABLE 5-3 *(continued)*

Name	URL to Download App	Mobile Site (Responsive Design)	Vanity URL
Pinterest	`http://itunes.apple.com/us/app/pinterest/id429047995` `https://play.google.com/store/apps/details?id=com.pinterest`	None	None
Twitter	`https://itunes.apple.com/us/app/twitter/id333903271` `https://play.google.com/store/apps/details?id=com.twitter.android`	`https://mobile.twitter.com`	`https://twitter.com/download`

Even Twitter, which has cellphone DNA in its genes, has revamped its mobile appearance with an app. The app offers an easy-to-use layout, with navigation that allows you to visit your timeline, discover trends or people, view your own profile, search for people or tweets, and of course, send out a tweet.

So what does all of this mean for your business while you develop social media messages for users who are always on the run? Keep in mind the following points:

- Pin your posts to the top of the news feed stream because only the first several posts will be displayed on mobile screens.
- Use analytics to make sure your posts are relevant to the demographics and behavioral patterns of the users of that particular social channel.
- Before publishing, always double-check the appearance of your posts and other content on smartphones and tablets to be sure everything looks right.
- If you have links, be sure they go to mobile-friendly pages; links to your website should go to a mobile-specific site or to a page built with responsive design.
- Make it easy for users to share your content on other social media from their mobile devices via text, email, and share buttons.

Compare the mobile app version of the Hacienda Nicholas Facebook page in Figure 5-5 with the desktop version of its Facebook page in Figure 5-6.

TIP

Always check your Facebook page, LinkedIn profile, and Twitter stream on various smartphone and tablet operating systems to see how they appear; adjust as needed.

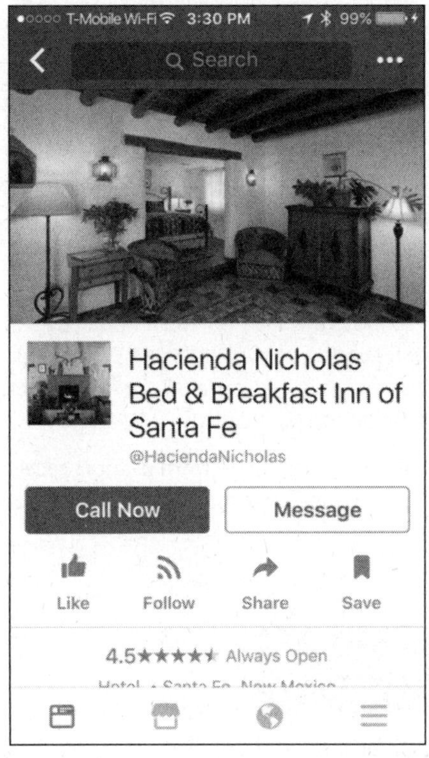

FIGURE 5-5: The mobile app version of the Facebook page for Hacienda Nicholas.

Courtesy of Hacienda Nicholas

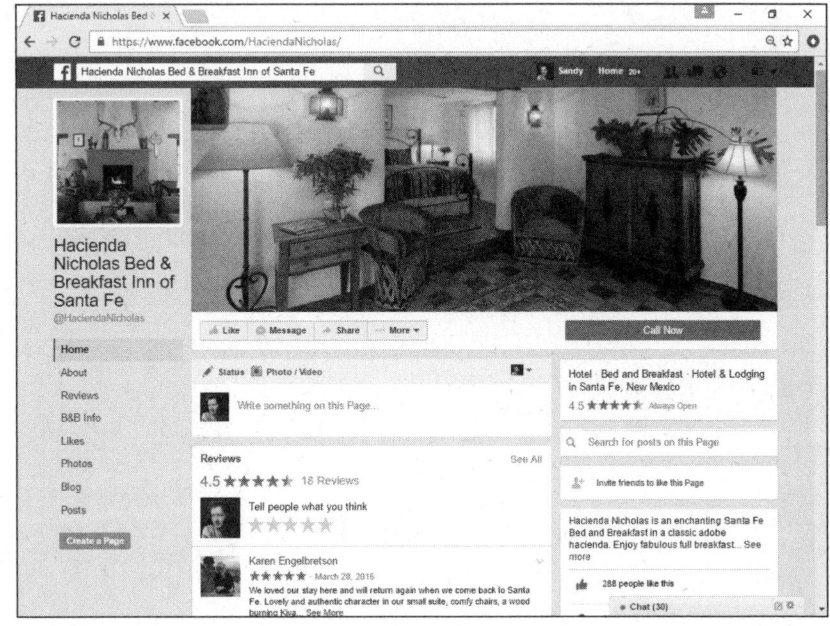

FIGURE 5-6: The desktop version of the Facebook page for Hacienda Nicholas.

Courtesy of Hacienda Nicholas

Harvesting Leads and Sales from Social Mobile

You can find as many applications for marketing via mobile social media as you can imagine. Keep in mind the areas described in this list, whatever the device or market segment you target:

- **News and updates:** Distribute this type of information to your Twitter, Facebook, and LinkedIn followers, as well as to people on your prospect list and your newsletter subscribers. (See Figure 5-7 for an example of updates distributed on the mobile version of Twitter.)
- **Emergency information:** Warnings range from product recalls to weather hazards. Short message service (SMS) is a cost-effective way to send out these messages.

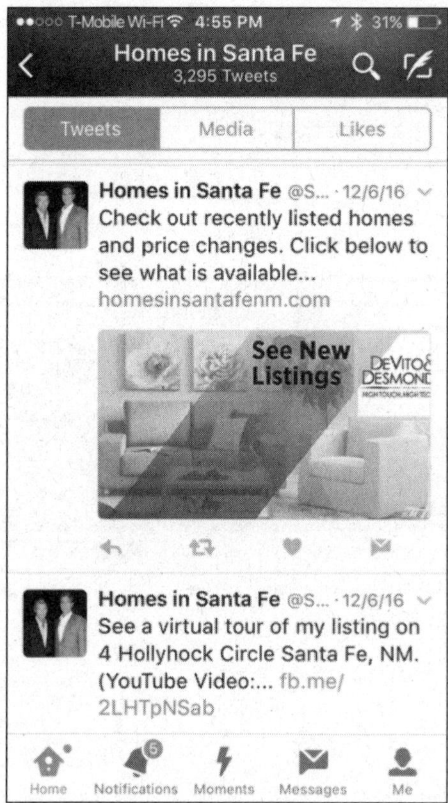

FIGURE 5-7: Homes in Santa Fe distributes recent listings and price changes on its Twitter mobile feed.

Courtesy Homes in Santa Fe NM

- **Comparison shopping:** Provide information so that Facebook, Twitter, Instagram, and Pinterest shoppers can compare by price and feature and learn about sales.
- **Local business announcements:** Announce coupons, deals, and special offers across all your social media channels, including SMS.
- **Video distribution:** Video is one of the most successful formats in social media. In addition to posting on YouTube, post short versions of your videos (or at least a link) on all your social media platforms and vice versa, especially Facebook, Instagram, and Snapchat. Although you can't post YouTube videos on Periscope (Twitter's app for live video streaming), you can post from Periscope to YouTube.
- **Customer service improvements:** For instance, use Twitter to let customers place a pickup order and find out when their order is ready. Use QR codes so people can quickly determine your competitive products, features, and prices.

  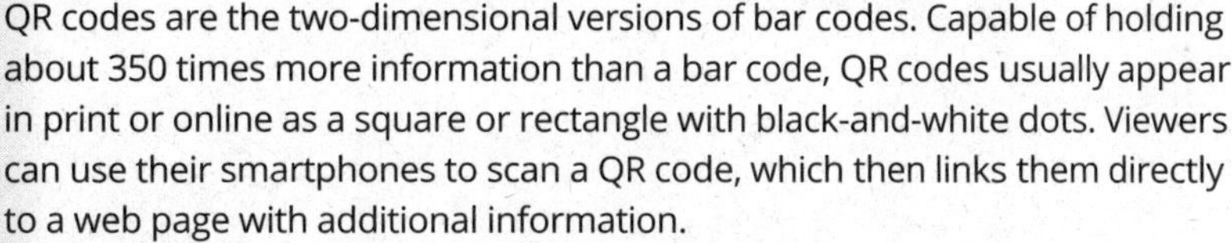

  TECHNICAL STUFF

  QR codes are the two-dimensional versions of bar codes. Capable of holding about 350 times more information than a bar code, QR codes usually appear in print or online as a square or rectangle with black-and-white dots. Viewers can use their smartphones to scan a QR code, which then links them directly to a web page with additional information.
- **Event publicity:** On Twitter and Facebook, consider providing real-time logistical information.
- **Integration of mobile marketing and social media:** Post updates on the fly and use real-time services, such as Instagram, Twitter, or Snapchat (described in Book 7, Chapter 2), especially if your business targets younger, local customers.

Don't let the obvious business-to-customer (B2C) value of mobile devices blind you: Mobile marketing has a place in business-to-business (B2B) strategies, as well. For example, sales people are using the technology for competitive research, tracking sales calls, and demonstrating their products and services to prospective customers. According to Google, 42 percent of B2B buyers use a mobile device during the purchasing process.

TIP

Consider using SMS (short message service) as a form of mobile marketing to maximize your reach, especially to younger audiences. Use SMS to provide coupons, encourage repeat visits, or announce special time-limited offers to customers who have already signed up to receive your text messages. It's less expensive than a custom mobile app! Be sure to promote sign-ups for your SMS option on all your social media, website, and retail locations, just as you promote sign-ups for an e-newsletter.

GETTING A HANDLE ON SNAPCHAT'S MOBILE MOMENTS

In July 2008, 16 Handles opened its first, pioneering, self-serve frozen yogurt shop in Manhattan's East Village neighborhood. Its popularity encouraged 16 Handles to franchise the concept, leading to 40 current locations in six states up and down the east coast and the Middle East. 16 Handles created its dedicated mobile site in 2013 (as seen next); now most of its web traffic comes from mobile devices or from its recently launched mobile app.

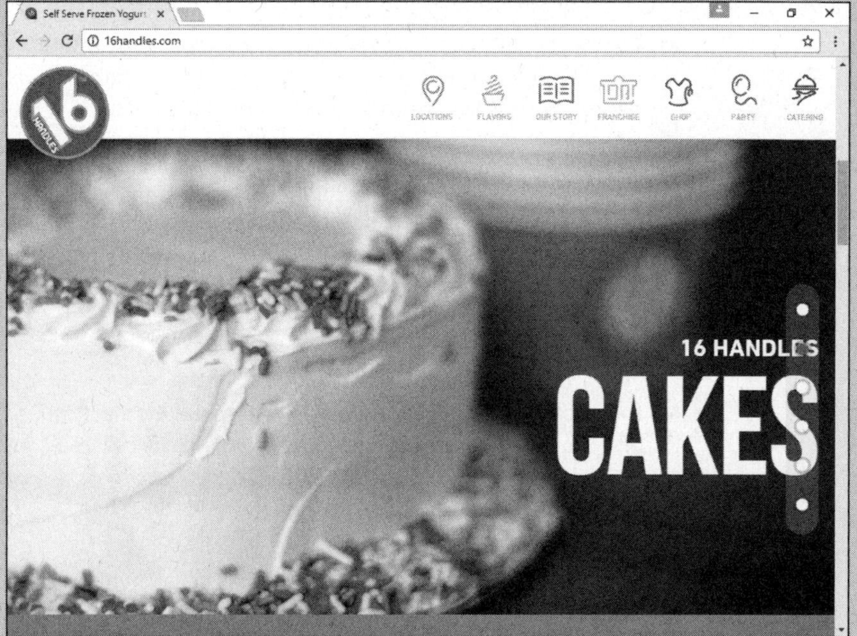

Courtesy of 16 Handles

According to CEO Solomon Choi, 16 Handles grew its social media presence organically, starting with Facebook and Twitter, and adding Instagram, Snapchat, LinkedIn, and YouTube over time. The company is strategic in its application of social media channels, using different channels for different purposes:

- Facebook: to post events and for interactive customer relationship management
- Twitter: to post micro-blogs
- Instagram: to post content and images

- Snapchat: to reach the younger generation
- LinkedIn: to post in the CEO's voice, to talk about the industry, and to reach a B2B audience
- YouTube: to post flavor-launch videos

In 2013, 16 Handles became the first retail brand to use Snapchat to offer coupons, as seen in the next image. When shoppers snapped a picture of themselves enjoying a frozen yogurt, the company snapped back a discount coupon for a surprise amount to be used for another treat. Based on an idea from the community manager at the time, the Snapchat coupons offered a unique opportunity to generate added purchases and build customer loyalty. It was a quick success, producing about 100 redemptions within a week of launch. Although the Snapchat coupon was a one-time promotion, 16 Handles continues to experiment with Snapchat marketing as an added fun element for in-store events. In 2017, it plans to use Snapchat alongside Instagram Stories to promote video content.

Courtesy of 16 Handles

To promote its Snapchat activity, the company's Snapchat account (Love16Handles) is linked on all its other social channels. Occasionally, the marketing department will include a call to action on its Facebook, Twitter, or Instagram posts for users to "Follow Love16Handles" on Snapchat. 16 Handles also recently adapted Uber's "Ride with Uber" links on its location pages, which appear only on mobile devices.

(continued)

(continued)

"Social media is a large focus of our [marketing] time," explains Choi, "since it's one of the primary ways our consumers interact with each other and with our brand." This active social media presence is managed by a team of several people who are always hands on with social media accounts. Posts are based on research showing when the company's audience is most likely to see and engage with 16 Handles' content. Engagement data are determined from social-media-specific analytics, as well as Google Analytics.

The company supplements its social media with paid online advertising, email marketing, music service advertising, and in-store marketing, including TV, slides, videos, and printed marketing collateral, such as flyers, table tents, and window clings.

Choi offers succinct advice for promoting with Snapchat. "The key," he says, "is to tap into the app's ephemeral nature, and to know your audience. The majority of people using Snapchat are very young, so promotions and messaging should be tailored to their demographic."

Following is a list of 16 Handles' web presence:

- `www.16handles.com`
- `www.linkedin.com/company-beta/2557813?pathWildcard=2557813`
- `www.instagram.com/16Handles`
- `twitter.com/16Handles`
- `www.facebook.com/16Handles`
- `www.youtube.com/user/16handles`
- Snapchat user name: Love16Handles

Measuring Your Mobile Marketing Success

As with all analytics, which elements you measure depends on your goals and objectives. Of course, your choices depend on whether you're measuring intermediate performance indicators (for example, the number of Likes on your Facebook page from mobile versus desktop users) or your return on investment in a mobile advertising campaign, a new mobile app, or increased foot traffic to your brick-and-mortar store.

You can segment mobile visitors by using the available tools in Google Analytics to track behavior on a mobile site or on your regular website (or both). You might want to set up a separate conversion funnel for mobile users. Watch for variations between mobile and web visitors on traffic to your social media pages, links to your mobile website, qualified prospects, and leads that turn into sales.

See Book 9, Chapter 5 for additional information about analyzing mobile social metrics and comparing them to metrics for social media in a standard environment.

Counting on Tablets

Use of e-readers, iPads, and other tablet computers is exploding. Given the convergence of high technology with usability, portability, mobility, and affordability, it may represent a true paradigm shift in computing.

By October 2015, roughly 45 percent of US adults owned tablet computers. Although the rate of purchase of tablets has slowed as larger screen smartphones have become more powerful, they remain popular with many businesses that need to display large inventories or product details. Social media channels are omnipresent on both Apple iPads and Android-based tablets, as well as on smartphones.

Like with smartphones, tablet owners use their devices for many purposes: research, shopping, news, customer reviews, and yes, social media. Once again, the Pew Research Center (`www.pewinternet.org/2015/10/29/the-demographics-of-device-ownership`) comes through with essential insights:

- Tablet use doesn't differ too much by gender or by race and ethnicity any more. The percentage of American adults with tablets hovers at 47 percent for whites, 38 percent for blacks, and 35 percent for Hispanics. In terms of gender, 43 percent of men and 47 percent of women own a tablet.
- The highest adoption rate is by users ages 30 to 49 (57 percent), followed closely by the younger cohort of 18- to 29-year-olds (50 percent). Both have significantly higher usage than 50- to 64-year-olds (37 percent) and those over 65 (32 percent).
- As you might expect, the higher their education level, the more likely it is that adults own a tablet: 62 percent of college graduates, 49 percent with some college, and 35 percent of those with a high school degree but no college education.
- Also quite predictably, ownership rises with household income, ranging from 28 percent of those with less than $30,000 in annual income, to 44 percent with annual income in the $30,000-and-$50,000 range, 51 percent with incomes between $50,000 and $75,000, and 67 percent for those with a household annual income of $75,000 or more.

TIP

As smartphones become larger and tablets become smaller, the challenge of developing sites that will work in both environments may disappear for some businesses, but not for companies that need to offer mobile access to large amounts of information.

Obviously, larger high-resolution tablets make viewing videos on tablets more appealing than viewing them on smartphones, leading to even greater popularity for video-sharing sites such as YouTube and Vimeo. Figure 5-8 shows a YouTube site on a tablet.

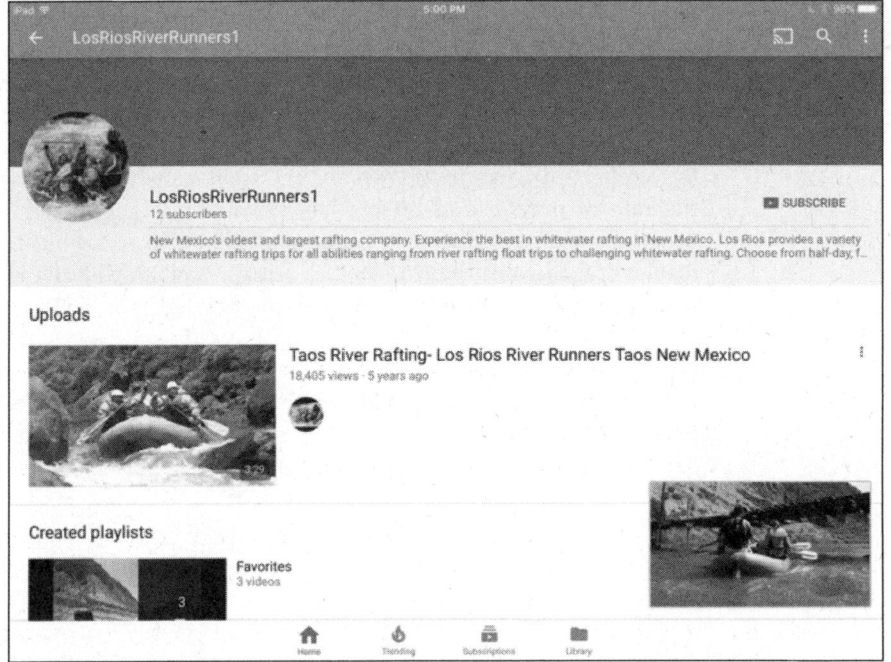

FIGURE 5-8: The YouTube page for Los Rios River Runners displays well on a tablet.

Courtesy of Los Rios River Runners

Using Mobile Social Media for Advertising

Statista (`www.statista.com/statistics/271259/advertising-revenue-of-social-networks-in-the-us`) projects that the overall social advertising market will grow from $11 billion in 2015 to more than $23 billion in 2018, representing more than 21 percent of all digital ad spending in the US.

Mobile social media represents a major share of those advertising dollars. About 84 percent of Facebook's ad revenue, 86 percent of Twitter's, and 60 percent of

Google's now derive from ads that appear on mobile pages (including YouTube). Facebook, Twitter, and other social media channels mine their huge populations of users to deliver extremely targeted audiences for advertising based not only on context, hashtags, or search terms, but also on behavior and likely action. As an advertiser, you can now follow users as they research products, compare prices, and make purchases in near real-time from their mobile devices.

Facebook's mobile advertising network allows you to publish ads not only on Facebook's mobile pages but also on approved third-party apps and mobile websites outside Facebook, much like Google's display ad network does.

For more information on Facebook mobile advertising, see *Facebook Marketing All-in-One For Dummies*, 3rd Edition, by Andrea Vahl, John Haydon, and Jan Zimmerman (John Wiley & Sons, Inc.), or visit `www.facebook.com/help/714656935225188` to get started.

Twitter, which acquired the ad network MoPub in 2013, has taken a similar approach, allowing you to target your audiences by device, as well as by interest area, geographical region, and keyword. For more about Twitter mobile advertising, visit `https://business.twitter.com`. Pay special attention to the use of mobile advertising to encourage people to download your apps directly from a tweet at `https://business.twitter.com/solutions/drive-app-installations-or-engagements`.

3 Content Marketing

Contents at a Glance

CHAPTER 1: **Growing Your Brand with Content** 227
Introducing Content Marketing 228
Determining the Best Content Platform for Your Needs. 231
Selling Your Brand through Content Marketing 232
Making Your Content Stand Out 233

CHAPTER 2: **Exploring Content-Marketing Platforms** 237
Building a Blog 238
Using Podcasts and Video on Your Blog or Website 243
Sharing Images 249
Using Social Media Platforms for Online Content 254
Guest Blogging to Grow Awareness and Expertise 258

CHAPTER 3: **Developing a Content-Marketing Strategy** 263
Determining Content Goals 263
Putting a Strategy on Paper 270

CHAPTER 4: **Getting Your Content to the Masses** 275
Creating an Editorial Calendar to Keep Content Flowing 276
Finding the Right Mix between Evergreen and Timely Content 278
Executing Your Content Strategy 279
Sharing Your Content with the Public. 280
Measuring the Success of Your Content Strategy. 281

IN THIS CHAPTER

- » Discovering the world of content marketing
- » Considering your content platform choices
- » Using content to sell your brand online
- » Developing content that stands out from the crowd

Chapter 1
Growing Your Brand with Content

Everything you see online is content — the written word, images, podcasts, radio, video, infographics, charts, and even social media updates on Facebook and Twitter. Content can amuse or teach, but it's also a powerful tool for catching the attention of search engines and the people who are looking for whatever it is you do. Many businesses are achieving positive results by using different types of content to reach customers and raise brand awareness.

In this chapter, we discuss content marketing. In particular, we define content marketing and discuss the importance of having a content strategy in place.

TIP

Don't get overwhelmed thinking about all the different kinds of content you have to create. The important thing to remember is that you don't have to use every content platform available. Instead, master one or two platforms and see where that takes you.

Introducing Content Marketing

Today is a wonderful time to be in business. Thanks to the web, you can use endless tools to promote your business or brand, and many of these tools are free.

You don't have to have a way with words or a flair for the dramatic to sell your product or service online. All you need to do is tap into your creativity. Using online content to promote your personal or business brand can mean the difference between local and global recognition.

Defining content marketing

If you're dabbling in social media to help market your business, you may have heard the expression *content marketing*, which is the practice of using blog posts, podcasts, videos, and images to promote your product or service. For example, if you own a farmer's market and you wish more people could find information about your business when they search online, you can create content that is attractive to search engines, making it easier to find your store online.

Think about the type of content people who visit farmer's markets are searching for online. For example, they might be looking for articles on how to choose the best strawberries, or the times of year when different fruits and vegetables are in season. When readers land on your blog posts, they'll see other links to more of your content, as well as your location, special events, sales, and other items of interest posted at your website. Content marketing drives people to a particular location, helping you achieve your goals.

Examining how content marketing can help your business

Content marketing serves several purposes — first and foremost is to drive traffic and sales. Relevant content helps your business get a better ranking in search engine results. So if your business initially showed up on page 10 of a Google search, content marketing, if done right, can help your business move to the first or second page for many different *search terms* — the words and phrases entered into the search engines.

Content marketing isn't only for the benefit of search engines, however. It's also a way to connect with your customers and community, and share expertise to build better brand recognition. When you create good content, something wonderful happens: People don't just read your content; they also leave comments to participate in the conversation, as shown in Figure 1-1.

Speak Your Mind
Logged in as Deb Ng. Log out?
POST COMMENT
Google Custom Search
SEARCH

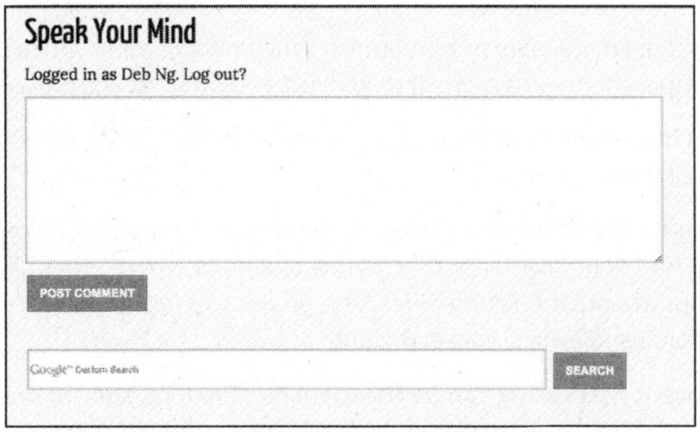

FIGURE 1-1: Use the comment area to have a conversation with customers and potential customers.

People also share your content with their friends and online followers, as shown in Figure 1-2. Next thing you know, other people are reading, sharing, and commenting. Even though they're not actively promoting your brand, you're getting wonderful brand recognition because the more people who share your content, the more people are seeing your logo, brand name, and other recognizable features.

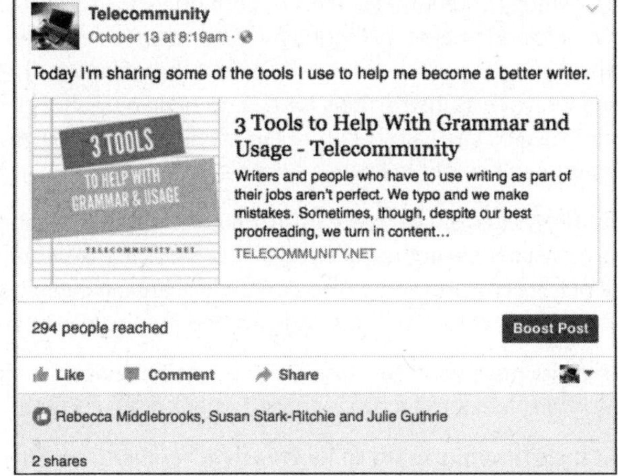

Telecommunity
October 13 at 8:19am ·
Today I'm sharing some of the tools I use to help me become a better writer.
3 TOOLS
TO HELP WITH GRAMMAR & USAGE
TELECOMMUNITY.NET
3 Tools to Help With Grammar and Usage - Telecommunity
Writers and people who have to use writing as part of their jobs aren't perfect. We typo and we make mistakes. Sometimes, though, despite our best proofreading, we turn in content…
TELECOMMUNITY.NET
294 people reached
Boost Post
Like
Comment
Share
Rebecca Middlebrooks, Susan Stark-Ritchie and Julie Guthrie
2 shares

FIGURE 1-2: When you create useful content, others will want to share it, which leads to better brand visibility.

Here are some additional ways that content marketing can benefit your company:

- **Your company has a voice.** Content marketing allows you to present your business in a positive light. In addition to creating helpful educational content, you're also able to address customer concerns, competitor messages, and both bad and good reviews.
- **You establish expertise.** Are you really good at something, or is your brand known for being the foremost expert in its field? Content is an excellent way

to share your expertise with others. When people think you're smart and transparent, they're more likely to trust you, which leads to sales.

- **You increase brand visibility.** The more content you share, the more your name is seen online.
- **Your local business can become global.** Online content helps a business that had only local connections grow to a place where more people can learn about what that business does. This access to a wider audience can mean national and even global exposure.
- **Content marketing can be inexpensive.** Creating and sharing content doesn't have to be expensive. If you or your team is creative, you can even handle content creation in-house. The types of content you create can be anything from a blog post, which doesn't cost anything, to a highly produced video, which can be costly. Both methods work.
- **Any business can to use content marketing.** It doesn't matter what your business does. If you have an existing customer base, you can create content to communicate with them and reach even more customers.
- **People can find your business for as long as your content remains online.** Creating content that's relevant both now and in the future, however, means your brand's name will continue to come up in searches — both now and in the future. *Evergreen content* — content that people will always be searching for, such as instructions for how to build a treehouse or how to maintain a healthy lawn all season — has staying power. We go into detail about evergreen content in Book 3, Chapter 4.

TIP

- **Content allows people to make informed decisions.** The more information you share with people about your product or service, the better able they are to make purchasing decisions. Your content will enable customers and potential customers to make comparisons and purchase with confidence.
- **You can repurpose your content.** Content can be reworked and rewritten to add new information and make existing content more current.
- **Content inspires your team to be creative.** Your entire team can help plan the content and suggest ideas for blog posts, articles, videos, podcasts, and more.

TIP

People enjoy consuming content. They like to watch videos that teach and entertain, and they enjoy reading enlightening articles. If your content provides a valuable service and shares good information, it has the potential to be seen by many people.

Determining the Best Content Platform for Your Needs

You can choose from plenty of content platforms, and it's easy to become overwhelmed if you're not sure which method to start with. The important thing to remember is that you don't have to do everything at once, nor do you have to create content on every single platform or social network. It's better to choose a couple of platforms and build content and community there over time, rather than spread content out in many different places.

The content platforms you choose depend on several factors:

- **Goals:** What are some of the reasons you're creating content? Is it for SEO? Sales? Authority? Knowing why you want to attract customers will help you to determine which content and social media platforms to use.
- **Budget:** Some brands pull out all the stops to create a viral video, while others put very little money into a blog post. Figure 1-3 shows a WordPress blog post, which costs only as much as you're willing to pay for web hosting. Interestingly, both blogs and videos can achieve the same result. Sometimes low-budget content goes viral, and sometimes high-budget content tanks.

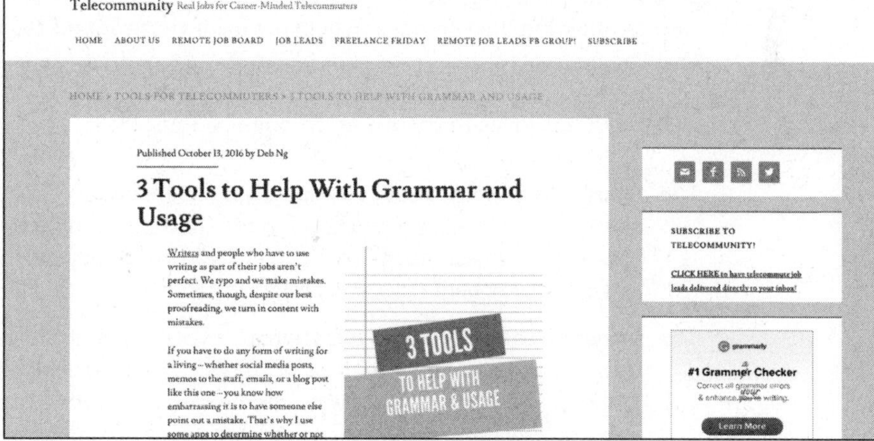

FIGURE 1-3: Many businesses choose blogs to start their content-marketing strategy because they're inexpensive and simple.

- **Expertise:** If you create your content to teach, choose a platform that best illustrates your knowledge.
- **Talent:** Do you have a talented team of writers? Is someone on staff handy with a camera, or technically equipped to set up a podcast? Choose a platform

that your team has the experience to use. You can still experiment, but your first effort should be something you and your team are comfortable doing.

» **Demographic:** The age and interests of your customers and community matter when choosing a content platform. Content should be tailored to that age and on a platform people in that demographic are mostly likely to use. For example, teens and people in their early 20s don't spend a lot of time on Facebook, and seniors don't often spend time on YouTube.

Don't dive into content creation blindly. Take some time to learn about your community and create a strategy. Marketers who have a plan in place are the ones who succeed. We talk more about content strategy in Book 3, Chapter 3.

Selling Your Brand through Content Marketing

So how do you go about selling your brand online through your content? The secret is to look like you're not selling. People don't like someone who's pushy and are turned off by obvious sales pitches. However, when you share important information, you build trust with your readers and customers. They appreciate learning about what your brand has to offer, and next time they have a need for a product or service like yours, they'll contact you — not only because your brand is now familiar but also because they know from your content that you're a resource that can be trusted.

Here are a few ideas to try selling through content:

» **Share information about your product or service.** Whether you're using blog posts or video, content allows you to show how your product works and how to get the best results. With content, you can go beyond the product label and discuss benefits, risks, and proven results.

» **Answer frequently asked questions.** Do your customers have questions? Do some questions arise more than others? Your content allows you to answer common questions your customers and potential customers have about not only your products and services but also your competitors'.

» **Create links that lead to your product or service.** For every piece of content that you post online, you should, at the very least, also post a link to related sales pages.

» **Offer free content in exchange for a newsletter sign-up or registration.** The reason so many businesses use newsletters is because they're collecting email addresses so they can send their customers sales pitches. Many brands even use content to entice newsletter signups. For example, they'll give a link to download a free e-book for every registration.

- **Address known issues through your content.** If people are leaving negative reviews or comments about specific issues with products or services, don't ignore them. Use your content to talk about the issues and put rumors to rest.
- **Tell your brand's story.** People love history, and they especially enjoy feeling as if they're part of history. If you or your brand has a unique story, use content to share your history, your mission, and your goals. This type of honesty builds trust, and people shop where they trust.
- **Open up lines of communication.** Content enables you to have a conversation with your community. For example, any questions or comments posted to Twitter, Pinterest, a Facebook page, blog posts, or YouTube are an opportunity for you to have a conversation with your customers.

None of the preceding suggestions look like selling. There is no call to action, nor is there an obvious sales page. However, your content took care of the hard part of the sales process: It got people to your website.

REMEMBER

Not all content is created in the same manner. For example, blogs are usually text or image heavy, while podcasting and video require recording equipment and a little more technical knowledge. However, all are doable and easy to maintain, and all have the capability to drive traffic and sales, as well as raise awareness for your product or service.

Making Your Content Stand Out

All this content creation is for naught if no one sees it. If you want to have the kind of content that people read or view, and then share, you have to take steps to ensure that your content stands out from the rest. Despite what you see on Facebook, you don't have to bring cats into your content for it to be well received.

TIP

For your content to stand out, it has to be useful and appealing. Answer this question: What value will your customers and potential customers receive from viewing your content?

What follows are some considerations for creating the type of content people respond to. Content should

- **Have a purpose:** Don't create content for the sake of creating content; otherwise, it will be bland, redundant, or confusing. Content should have both a plan and a purpose. For example, content should teach, or drive traffic or sales. Even content created solely to go viral has a purpose. When you understand why you're creating the content, it will be easier for you to write, photograph, or video-tape.

- **Provide value:** If a video makes someone laugh, it has value. If a blog post teaches people something, it has value. If a tweet breaks news, it has value. In other words, don't create content that doesn't offer anything to the viewer or reader.
- **Answer a question:** If people are searching for information and land on an article on your website, will they stay to read the whole thing, or will they move on after a quick scan? Your content should answer a question, even if the question is simply, "What am I doing here?"
- **Be unique:** What perspective can you give to your niche that no one else has covered? Content that stands out does so because it's different — not the same old, same old.
- **Be easy to relate to:** People like to read a blog post or watch a video, and then nod their head in agreement. For example, a funny video from a car-cleaning service that shows kids dropping food in the car or scribbling on the back seat with a permanent marker might have parents sharing the content because they've been in the same situation.
- **Be visual:** A vibrant or intriguing photo will catch the eye, and readers will want to know how it relates to the content.
- **Have variety:** Mix up your content with new, timely, and evergreen information. Experiment with photos, videos, and written content, too.
- **Be entertaining:** Entertaining content isn't necessarily slapstick or pet tricks. Entertaining content might be educational, interesting, or intriguing. If content entertains, consumers will want to see more content from you and may even want to learn more about your product or service.
- **Be inspiring:** You want to create content that encourages reaction. Whether it's a call to action, a link to more information or a sales page, or an invitation to comment and share, your content should give readers and viewers the idea to do these things. It should make them want to take action.
- **Be scannable:** People consume content differently on the web than they do in print. Whereas they'll read books and consume newspaper and magazine articles in their entirety offline, most people have short attention spans on the web. So break up all content into easily digestible pieces with images, headings, subheads, bullet points, and numbered lists. (Sort of like what we're doing here!) If you present the content in this way, people can scan it and still take something away from it.

» **Have an intriguing title:** You don't have to create a scandalous or shocking headline, but your content should have a title that will immediately capture attention and encourage readers or viewers to want to learn more.

WARNING

By all means be entertaining and use a catchy headline. However, it's best to avoid *clickbait,* or content that draws people in with a shocking, intriguing, or scandalous headline but doesn't deliver much in the way of value or substance. In other words, focus more on content that provides a helpful or educational purpose and avoid driving traffic for traffic's sake.

» **Be shareable:** It's great when someone likes your content; it's even better when they like the content so much they want to share it with others. The more people who share your content, the more recognizable your brand. Shareable content is great marketing.

» **Be compatible:** Make sure your content can be read and viewed easily across mobile platforms. Because so many people are consuming content on smartphones and tablets, it won't do to have content that doesn't work on every mobile platform.

» **Be published with some regularity.** You don't have to publish content every day, but if you post consistently, people have something to look forward to. For example, if you post to the corporate blog every Tuesday, regular readers will stop by every Tuesday to see your new content. In Book 3, Chapter 4, we discuss working with editorial calendars, which can help in planning regular content.

REMEMBER

The web is flooded with content that's inaccurate or fluffy and that doesn't really share solid information. By creating content that's valuable and that serves a purpose, you're cutting through the clutter and noise to become a trusted resource. This content creation may not seem like selling, but when it comes time to buy, potential customers will remember you for providing quality content and equate it with a quality product or service.

IN THIS CHAPTER

» Creating and sharing professional content

» Guest blogging for fun and profit

» Getting social

Chapter 2
Exploring Content-Marketing Platforms

As we discuss in Chapter 1 of this minibook, content encompasses a wide variety of platforms, and every platform is beginner-friendly. After all, we all have to start somewhere. However, you may find that you're more comfortable using some platforms over others, which is perfectly normal. Your content strategy can include one platform or all of them. As you become familiar with the different options, you can determine for yourself which work best for your needs.

Take a look at some of the different platforms available to you:

- **Blog:** Informal, conversational, articles.
- **Podcast:** Audio files akin to an online radio show. A podcast can be a single person discussing issues or ranting, or interviews, music, or news updates.
- **Video:** Videos can be used to promote, sell, entertain, and enlighten.
- **Image:** Use photographs in blog posts or alone to tell a story.
- **Social media:** Facebook, Pinterest, Twitter, Instagram, Snapchat, Vine, and other social-networking sites can be used as content — that is, to create your own post or to share relevant content that someone else created.

In this chapter, we explore some of the available platforms and talk about ways that you can use them all as part of your content-marketing strategy.

Building a Blog

Blogs, such as the one shown in Figure 2-1, are no longer link-heavy, personal journals used to describe one's day or give a daily rant. Businesses use blogs as marketing tools to share updates and industry-related news and to offer tips, recipes, or ideas for using products and services.

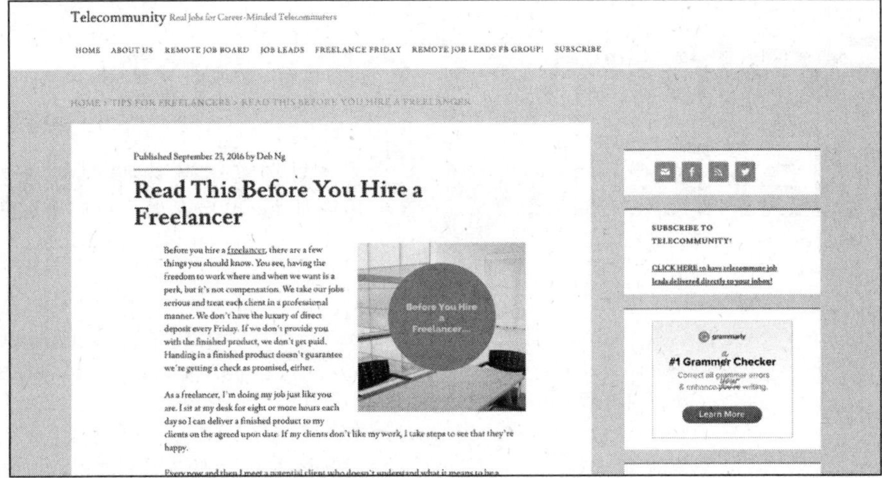

FIGURE 2-1: Use a blog to promote your business.

The good news is that even if your background isn't in writing or web design, you can easily maintain a regular blog. All you need is a way with words and the ability to write in a conversational tone. The conversational aspect sets blogs apart from more newsy and antiseptic articles.

Understanding how blogging can benefit your business

People enjoy reading blogs because of the simple language and the ability to add their own comments. At the other end of the spectrum, blogs allow businesses to engage with their customers or community in a new way.

Additionally, blogging has the following features:

- **Catches the attention of search engines:** If you're looking for a heavier Internet presence, you most likely want people to be able to find you when they're searching Google, Yahoo!, Bing, or other search engines. Blogging is perfect for this purpose. With the right content and regular updates to your blog, there's no reason why you shouldn't land in the top results for any number of search terms.
- **Catches the attention of the people using search engines:** With the right headlines, *keywords* (the words and terms people use when using search engines), and images, web searchers are intrigued enough to land on one of your pages. If your blog is informative, they may even be intrigued enough to explore several different pages.
- **Is shareable:** When people find something they like online, they share it via email or on one of the social networks. When a blog post touches on an interesting or sensitive topic, your readers will likely want to pass it on.
- **Allows everyone to join the conversation:** Most blogs allow for comments at the bottom of each blog post. Readers love to comment because it gives them the opportunity to add their own thoughts and opinions and to share experiences.
- **Allows you to manage your reputation:** Sometimes people say something about a business or brand that isn't nice. Sometimes rumors fly. Sometimes you just need to set the record straight. Blogging allows you to speak to your community at a time when you need them most.
- **Builds expertise:** When you share tips on a regular basis, you're seen as someone who is knowledgeable in your field. You may even get a reputation as someone who really knows his or her stuff.
- **Can make you the go-to person for the subject matter:** With regular blogging, journalists, authors, conferences, and even other bloggers are likely to contact you for interviews and speaking engagements and to write articles or guest blog posts so that you can share your knowledge with their communities.
- **Enables you to grow your community:** When you have regular readers who comment on your blog and share your blog posts, they become your online community. Your community advocates for you and helps spread the word about your brand, product, or service. (We talk more about building an online community later in this chapter.)
- **Is inexpensive:** Most blog platforms don't cost anything to use. Your biggest expense will be web hosting and possibly hiring someone to help with content creation and design. Blogging is one of the least expensive marketing tools you can use.

- **Allows you to update thousands of people at one time:** As your community grows and more people read your blog each day, it will become a place where you can update your customers on promotions, news, updates, and new product information.
- **Allows you to connect with other businesses, brands, and experts:** Blogs are wonderful networking tools. They allow you to link to people you respect and receive links back in return. You may even discover that influential people in your niche are following your blog and participating in your conversations.
- **Allows you to add personality to your business:** The beauty of blogging is the conversational tone. Because the writing is more casual than news articles, you can add humor and personality to your blog posts. Readers appreciate this lighthearted approach because they don't feel as if they're being talked down to. Besides, everyone likes to share entertaining content.
- **Builds trust:** When you keep your community updated and use your blog as a two-way communication tool, you build trust among your customers and community. People won't feel you have something to hide if you're open and honest on your blog, which gives them a good feeling about using your product or service.
- **Is easy:** After you set up your blog and it's ready to roll, maintaining it is easy. In most cases, all you need to do is type the day's blog post and add the necessary links, images, or other bells and whistles.

What types of businesses can benefit from blogs? Just about anyone with a story to tell or a product to sell can benefit from having a blog, but some brands benefit more from this form of content than others. For example, blogs are perfect for product-oriented brands.

Some items that product-oriented brands can blog about include the following:

- **Ingredients:** If you take pride in using wholesome ingredients, you should talk about it often. It's an important message and strong selling point. In fact, each individual ingredient can be turned into at least one blog post — probably more.
- **Recipes:** If you add two parts water to your household cleaning product, can it be used to clean stains on a rug? Can your brand of peanut butter be used as the base for a number of different dishes? Blog about it!
- **Uses for the products:** Vinegar has at least 100 different uses; how about your product? If your product can do a variety of different things, talk about it.
- **Launches and product news:** Do you have a new product on the horizon? Are you opening up shop in a new location? These items are worthy of a blog post.

» **A behind-the-scenes peek:** Your customers and community would love to know that you and the other people who work for your brand are real. Announce promotions. Take photos around the office. Show your employees hard at work or goofing off . . . er, team-building. Make your community feel as if they're in on a secret.

TIP

A common mistake brands make when blogging is to assume every update has to be a sales pitch or product-oriented content. The best blogs barely sell. Instead, they focus on the benefits of the product. Go beyond the obvious, and you'll have a blog people want to read.

Deciding if blogging is right for you

Any business or businessperson can benefit from regular blogging. If you have something to say or something to sell, blogs are a simple, cost-effective solution to reach many people at once.

REMEMBER

Building a blog takes time. You have to update it often and monitor it at least once per day for comments. You also have to promote new content on social networks or in newsletters so that your community can learn when you publish new blog posts. Don't expect to see massive traffic when you're just starting out, though. Most new blogs show a slow, steady growth rate.

Setting up your blog

Before choosing a blog platform, decide whether you want to host the blog on your own domain or on a blog platform's subdomain. While a hosted blog through platforms such as WordPress or Blogger is free to use and maintain, most bloggers and business owners agree it's more beneficial to put out the money and purchase your own domain and hosting. Even so, it doesn't have to be an expensive endeavor, and it's well worth the investment.

REMEMBER

Hosting on a blogging platform's subdomain means you have limited design and customization choices, and you may not be able to support advertising.

Setting up a blog can be as easy as you need it to be. Because you're using your blog for marketing, we're going to go ahead and assume that you prefer to self-host your blog. A self-hosted blog means you pay for the hosting yourself and handle blog installation and design.

It's much better SEO to have traffic come to your own website (and brand) than someone else's, anyway. A self-hosted WordPress blog (as opposed to the free blog that is hosted on the WordPress subdomain) is the marketer's blogging tool of choice because it's so easy to use and to adapt to your needs.

Some hosts — for example, Bluehost — allow you to easily set up a WordPress blog with little effort. All you have to do is click a button, such as the one shown in Figure 2-2, and follow the simple step-by-step instructions. See `www.bluehost.com/` for more details.

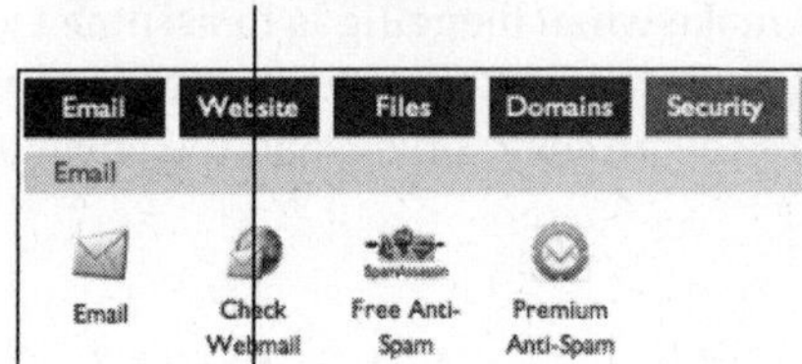

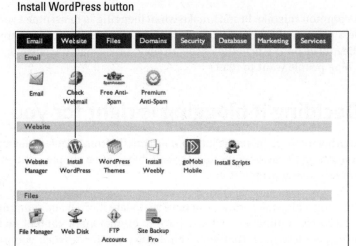

FIGURE 2-2: Some web-hosting companies, such as Bluehost, enable you to set up a blog on WordPress with a mouse click.

If you already have a website for your business, you'll want to host your blog there, with a link to the blog in the site's navigation menu. Your webmaster can install a WordPress setup in less than an hour. Or if you want to find out how to do it yourself, check out *WordPress Web Design For Dummies*, 3rd Edition by Lisa Sabin-Wilson (John Wiley & Sons, Inc.).

As for design, you can look up WordPress themes online and upload one to your blog, or you can hire a designer for a more custom look. Most brands choose to have their blogs blend in with their website and match their logos, so they opt for a custom design.

Here's a look at the components of a successful blog:

- **Dashboard:** Your blog's *dashboard* is its control center. From here, you can choose to add a new post, upload plug-ins, customize the design, add a new static page, or take care of any blogging business.
- **Blog post:** A *blog post* is an individual article. Each time you create content for your blog, you're adding a blog post. The blog is the entire setup; the post is an individual article. In your dashboard, you can set up how many blog posts

you want to appear on the blog's home page. Blog posts are generally listed in date order. Eventually, the oldest blog posts are no longer on the home page, but users can search the categories or the blog itself for older posts.

- **Static page:** Similar to a blog post, a *static page* is a page of content that stays in place, rather than falling off the home page when new content is added. The blog's navigation usually has a link to the static page. One example of a static page is an About page that lists information about your company, a sales page that offers a look at products and services, or a pricing menu.
- **Categories:** You can set up categories to make it easier for your readers to find specific content. For example, if your company is a dairy farm, your categories might be Products, Recipes, and Events. You can place categories in your blog's sidebar navigation.
- **Search:** A search bar can help your readers and customers find specific content.
- **Comments section:** By enabling comments at the bottom of each post, you're inviting your customers and readers to share their own tips and anecdotes.
- **Sidebar:** Your blog's sidebar houses important information. For example, information about you and your brand, the menu of categories, the search bar, Follow buttons for Facebook and Twitter, and links to sales pages.
- **Share buttons:** Each of your blog posts should have share buttons so that readers can share the blog posts with their friends on Facebook, Twitter, and other social networks. You can set up a share button by downloading a plug-in.
- **Plug-ins:** Plug-ins allow your blog to have some wonderful bells and whistles. For example, you can use plug-ins to keep spam out of your comments section, share your content, and configure advertising. To search for plug-ins, simply use the search function in the Plug-In section of your blog's dashboard.

TIP

The beauty of blogs is how easy they are to customize. You can do almost anything with a blog, such as sell products or tell a story. You can even use a WordPress blog setup to create an entire website. Take some time to explore all the options to make your blog stand out from the competition.

Using Podcasts and Video on Your Blog or Website

Text isn't the only game in content marketing. Many brands are now taking advantage of creating podcasts and video blog posts to add variety to their written content. In the following sections, we explore the benefits of creating podcasts and video and how you can add them to your content-marketing plan.

Deciding if podcasting is right for you

With social media, you don't have to join every network or pontificate from every platform. Some people love podcasting, but others would rather type than talk. Is podcasting right for you?

Podcasting doesn't necessarily have to entail the use of a lot of expensive equipment. Many hard-core podcasters do have their own studios, while others get by with a simple microphone. Sound quality is important, however, and if you host hard-to-listen-to podcasts full of static and feedback, folks are going to stay away.

REMEMBER

You don't want to spend lots of money on expensive equipment if you're not into podcasting. Definitely try podcasting a few times to be sure there's interest — not only from you but also from your community.

You also have to consider editing. All those perfect podcasts you watch or listen to aren't necessarily first takes, especially if you're just starting out. You're bound to have some fits and starts, and even a few "uhms." Your options are to leave them in or edit them out — and editing out can be time-consuming.

We don't mean to discourage you from podcasting, but we also don't want you to enter into it blindly. Here are a few things to consider before launching your first podcast:

- **Is podcasting something you want to do on a regular basis?** Will you want to record a podcast once a week and then edit and upload the podcast? For newbies, this process can take several hours.
- **Will you be able to handle the technical aspects?** Blog platforms are mostly intuitive, and most people can figure them out without much effort. Editing a podcast isn't difficult, per se, but it's not as easy as clicking a Send button.
- **Will you have listeners?** Do you know people will tune **in?** Will podcasting be worth the effort? Some communities aren't into regular podcasts. Also, the success of your podcast depends on the brand. For example, if you're a laundry detergent manufacturer, do you think you can come up with enough interesting material to bring in listeners each time you upload a podcast?

- **Will you be able to bring in listeners?** Although you're using podcasting as a marketing tool, you'll have to do a fair amount of marketing yourself to bring in listeners. Where will you find them, and how will you get them to listen?
- **What do you hope to achieve by podcasting?** Determine your reason for podcasting before you begin so that you can tailor your podcast to the right people. For example, if you're raising awareness for a cause, you wouldn't talk about the same thing as if you were selling a product.
- **Where will you host your podcast?** Will you post your podcast to your blog, website, or another area? If you host the podcast on your blog or website, your site will receive more traffic. If you host through iTunes, you may have more listeners. And there's nothing wrong with using a combination of both.

Not everyone has the time or even patience to read long, lengthy articles and blog posts. Having content that people can listen to at their convenience is another great option for spreading your message and can open you up to a new audience. Many people enjoy downloading podcasts to their smartphones and listening to them in the car or at the gym. Podcasting can be more convenient than text or video because you can listen much in the way you listen to music while you're going about your day. There's nothing to print, and you're not chained to your laptop.

REMEMBER

Because your listeners hear your voice in a podcast, you build a different type of relationship. When they can hear your voice, and your emotion and passion as you talk about your favorite topics, you add another element of trust to your message. They laugh with you at jokes and know when you're dead serious. In text, your audience can easily misread tones and inflections. The content of a podcast is more engaging because it's more emotional.

Unlike written content, podcasts aren't scannable. Although people can fast forward as needed, most people are more focused when they're listening than when they're scanning a blog post.

Podcasts also allow you to expand upon your expertise. When you write a blog post, brevity is important. You have to say what you have to say in 500 to 1,000 words, or you run the risk of losing your reader. On the other hand, podcasts allow you to talk until the talking is done. Many podcasts run 30 to 60 minutes. Another beautiful thing about podcasts is how you can interview another person of interest and ask as many questions as you want.

TIP

For more information on podcasting, check out David Jackson's School of Podcasting website and podcast at `http://schoolofpodcasting.com/`.

Using podcasts to drive traffic and land sales

When you think about traditional marketing tactics, very few brands considered broadcasting regularly to appeal to more people. Perhaps they'd advertise on a popular program, but they didn't really want to commit staff or cover the cost for 30 minutes or an entire hour of programming. It's different today, though. Many brands are discovering how podcasting appeals to a whole different group of people. As long as your podcast isn't a long sales pitch, you definitely have the ability to drive sales.

Here's how podcasting drives traffic and sales for your brand:

- **Your host page always leads to an action page.** Whether you host your podcast on a blog or website, it should always be embedded on a page offering listeners an opportunity to take further action. It's not enough to embed your podcast. List bullets of the podcast's main points to draw in readers and offer a link to a More Information page for listeners who want to find out more.
- **If you host a good podcast, others will recommend it.** If you have informative, actionable, engaging content, new listeners will not only come back but also tell others about it.
- **Search engines pick it up.** Podcasting pages also catch the attention of search engines. Use your search terms on your podcast's host page; folks looking for podcasts on your topic or to find out more about your topic will stop by for a listen.
- **Choose buzz-worthy content, which always brings in more listeners.** When you podcast an interesting discussion, with notable guests, you'll bring in regular listeners. Regular listeners also bring in new listeners, either with share buttons or word-of-mouth recommendation. This traffic, in turn, can lead to action, whether it's sales, awareness, or another goal.
- **Get it on iTunes.** When you get your podcast on iTunes, you're opening yourself up to a new listener base. Many people browse iTunes each day to find new podcasts to listen to on their morning drive or while working out.

Creating viral videos

Sometimes videos go *viral* — that is, they're shared and viewed thousands (and sometimes millions!) of times on the web. Videos go viral for different reasons, and it's not always an accident. Some brands create videos in hopes that they'll catch the attention of the masses and the press.

TIP

Just about every viral video has one thing in common: It's entertaining. Your video blog about Top 10 Reasons to Buy Organic isn't going to go viral because that's just not exciting or interesting to most people. Viral videos are funny or heartwarming, but more importantly, the people who view viral videos look at them and immediately want to share them afterwards.

Videos can also turn into viral sensations when they

- **Are parodies:** People like to see brands or celebrities poke fun at something, and self-deprecating humor always goes over well. When you poke fun at yourself, your brand, or your genre, people appreciate your ability to keep it real. Just be careful not to be mean and insult the people you're trying to reach.
- **Are something people can relate to:** When people see a video that resonates with them, they're likely to share. Common household mishaps, children being children, bad acting or singing, and a humorous look at the things people go through during their regular routines are especially appealing.
- **Appeal to our emotions:** Charitable organizations or campaigns to raise awareness often use unfortunate but real situations to tug at heartstrings and get people talking.
- **Are not too deep:** When people have to think about what they're watching or if they just don't get what they're watching, they're not going to stick around. If you have to touch on a deep or intellectual topic, try doing so with humor so that you don't lose your audience.
- **Are unique:** You know what makes a video *not* go viral? When it copies other viral videos. Come up with some ideas no one else is doing, and you'll have more viewers.
- **Show something remarkable:** Many viral videos show talented people. Singers, athletes, musicians, and others have gone viral.
- **Are not staged:** Videos that are staged to look spontaneous usually don't look anything close to spontaneous.

REMEMBER

Although some brands or individuals create videos with the intention of them going viral, the truth is most viral videos weren't intended to be that way. They had a real quality to them that people appreciated and shared. What can you create that people will want to share?

Interviewing experts on camera

People love video interviews. They have more of an effect than text and even audio because viewers can see the faces of both the interviewer and interviewee and see reactions to questions. It's that trust thing again. Videos can show sincerity or catch someone in the middle of a lie. Plus, it's just nice to place faces with names and voices.

Because you're interviewing on camera, your flaws, imperfections, and mannerisms are open for scrutiny. If you're always smoothing your hair or rubbing your nose, it may be a source of embarrassment if you're not mindful of your quirks during the interview. Also, if you're not prepared for your interview, it's more difficult to wing it.

The following tips help you host an awesome video interview:

- **Do your research.** Know as much about your interview subject as possible so that when you're live on camera, you can get more personal, if needed.
- **Don't get too personal.** The last thing you want is to make the person with you feel uncomfortable. It leads to a bad interview, your viewers may also be uncomfortable, and you may have problems finding future interview subjects.
- **If you're reading from notes, don't make it obvious.** Place bullet points off camera where you can sneak a glance, but don't spend your interview time reading. It looks unprofessional.
- **Be mindful of your "uhms."** Sometimes people don't notice their own little habits, but boy, do they show up on camera! It takes some practice, but do pay attention to throat clearings, "uhms," and other habits that don't show well on camera.
- **Make eye contact.** If you're not looking at the person you're interviewing, look at the camera. Looking off to the side or down at your lap makes you look distracted and not really interested in what's going on around you.
- **Talk into the camera.** If you're talking to viewers, look at the camera so that they feel as if you're talking to them.
- **Create your list of questions beforehand and share it with your interview subject.** Always know what you're going to talk about ahead of time. Winging it sometimes leads to a lapse in the conversation and looks unprofessional. Also, if your interview subjects know what questions to expect, they can provide some good information, statistics, and other facts to help back up their point of view.

» **Don't let your interview subject take control.** If you're not careful, the person whom you're interviewing will take the lead and talk about only what she wants to talk about or start selling her latest book or blog post. After you lose control of an interview, it's hard to get back on the right track. Take the lead and keep the lead.

» **Ask to expand upon one-word answers.** Nothing turns off viewers more than a boring interview. You'll find most people enjoy talking about themselves or what they do. However, now and then, you'll come across someone who is shy or unpolished. They may even feel "yes" or "no" is an adequate response. It's up to the interviewer to bring out the best in the guests by asking open-ended questions and directing the conversation.

Sharing Images

Images are an important part of content creation. They help illustrate a point, break up text, and add more to the conversation. But using an image in your content isn't as simple as pilfering a photo from Google Images and adding it to your blog post. In addition to choosing a photo that helps to enhance your content, you also have legal and copyright considerations.

The following sections explore how to add great images to your content without breaking the law.

Using images for your online content

A picture doesn't always say a thousand words, but it often gives your content a little extra something-something. People like images; their eyes are drawn to them. If it's not the headline that makes them take notice, your image can be the one-two punch. Because online content works best when it's scannable, images give the reader another area to focus on, as well.

TIP

Images are also good search engine optimization. When you take the time to add keywords to your image and caption the photo, search engines will pick up the search terms. Your images then show up in image searches, such as Google Images.

You can also use images for other reasons. For example, you can invite your community to "caption this" on your Facebook page or create a Twitter discussion by sharing a photo and inviting discussion. Images are another way to provide content and bring in readers, build community, and (we hope) drive sales.

Legalities: What you need to know about sharing images

Adding a photo to your blog isn't as simple as downloading an image. People who take photos own the copyright to them. Just because you see a photo online doesn't mean that you have permission to use it. Also, just because you don't see a copyright symbol doesn't mean that the image isn't copyright protected.

WARNING

Some people feel that because something is posted on the web, it's in the public domain. This assumption isn't true, either. It's always important to check each and every image for the available rights and usage. You can tell whether you can use a photo by reading all the details around it. The different types of rights and usage are explained in the following list:

- **All Rights Reserved:** The photo isn't available for use unless you contact the author for permission. If you receive permission to use the image, you may embed it into your blog post as long as you provide attribution. The photographer may also require a link back to the original content. Please note that this requirement usually means that you're granted only one-time usage for that specific blog post or content. You don't have permission to use the photo as often as you want.

  In addition, most images require a fee to use: If you want to use an image more than once, you'll have to pay extra. Make sure that any agreement between the photographer and you is clear, and that you have a good understanding of how many times you can use the image and what other requirements she may have for its use.

- **Some Rights Reserved:** The agreement between you and the photographer isn't as strict, but it also means you should read all the fine print to find out exactly what rights you have when using the image. You may have unlimited use but have to attribute to the photographer each time. It also may mean that you can use the image on a personal blog but not for commercial use.
- **No Derivative Works:** You're not allowed to take the photo and alter it in any way and publicly post it as your own. You can't add anything to the photo, nor can you change colors or retouch it using Photoshop. If you do use the photo, be sure you're using it with the proper permission and attribution.
- **Creative Commons:** You're welcome to use the photo if you follow the listed guidelines, as shown in Figure 2-3. Although, in many cases, Creative Commons photographers allow others to share their photo, usually royalty-free, it doesn't mean that the images are free to use any way you like. Read all the fine print. The photographer may require specific credits, limited usage, and a link back to the original content.

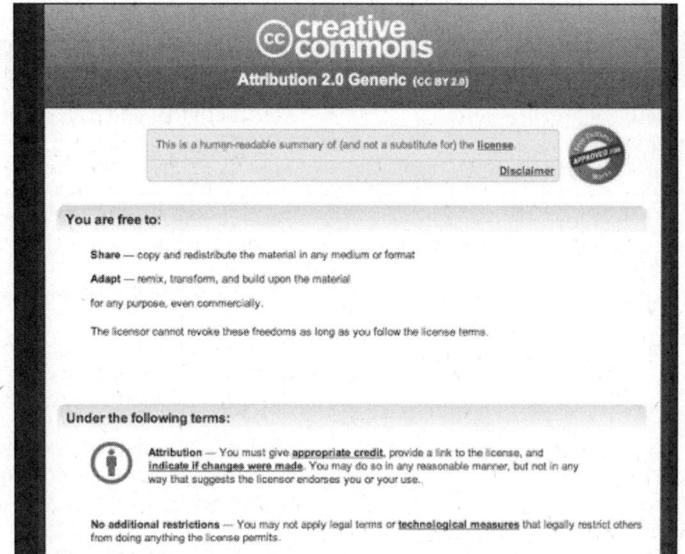

FIGURE 2-3: Always check for image rights and ask permission before using a photo.

REMEMBER

Even if no specific requests are made, the right thing to do is to offer attribution to the photographer. Using a photo is the same as quoting another blogger on your blog or sharing someone else's text on your blog. If you post someone else's photo and pass it off as your own, even if that's not your intention, you're not only violating copyright laws, but you're sharing in an unethical manner.

WARNING

A good general rule for anyone looking to use a photo found online (or offline!) is, "When in doubt, ask." In some cases, photographers discovered years later that bloggers had used their images, and the photographers successfully sued for back royalties.

Finding images online

Don't let all this talk about rights and usage discourage you from finding photos to use for your content. Finding photos to use isn't difficult, and the rights are usually laid out for you below each photo.

TIP

Instead of typing keywords into your favorite search engine's image search, which can lead to confusion about rights, it's a better idea to become a member of photo-sharing sites. Table 2-1 lists some popular photo sharing sites and indicates whether the sites are free or require a monthly or per-photo fee.

TABLE 2-1 **Popular Photo -Sharing Sites**

Site	URL	Description
123RF	www.123rf.com	Offers both free and paying options.
Bigstock	www.bigstockphoto.com	Requires a subscription fee.
Creative Commons	http://creativecommons.org	Allows for the posting and sharing of Creative Commons works.
Dreamstime	www.dreamstime.com	Offers both free and paying options.
Flickr	www.flickr.com	Images often fall under Creative Commons, but check the right sidebar of each image page to view rights for each photo.
Freeimages	www.freeimages.com/	Offers a wide variety of free-to-use images, but be sure to check the restrictions. (Formerly called stck.xchng.)
iStockphoto	www.istockphoto.com	Requires a subscription fee.
Morguefile	www.morguefile.com	Offers free photos that are mostly taken by amateur photographers and aren't always professional quality.
Pinterest	www.pinterest.com	Enables you to search images on the site and then contact the original photographer to find out whether you can buy a copy of the photo.
Shutterstock	www.shutterstock.com	Subscription-based service.
Wikimedia Commons	http://commons.wikimedia.org	Offers royalty-free and free photos.
Wylio	www.wylio.com	A search engine featuring free images for bloggers. A nifty feature of this service is that you can format your image right on the website to cut and paste into your blog post.

Some sites allow you to use photos for free as long as you follow certain guidelines, such as notifying the photographer and giving attribution. Notifying the photographer, though, isn't the same as asking permission. If the site requires you to notify the photographer, it simply means the photographer has given permission already; he or she just wants to know where it's going to be used.

Also, some photographers won't allow their images to be used on certain sites — for example, pornography, political, religious, or any other sites where the image may be taken out of context or use of it will reflect poorly on the photographer. However, the photo-sharing site you choose explains these limitations for each photo.

REMEMBER

Many of the photos shared for free online, even on image-sharing sites, aren't shot by professional photographers and can sometimes look a little rough or amateurish. However, you can still find plenty of professional-quality photos.

Most stock-image sites require you to pay a fee. It can either be a monthly fee, where you're granted permission to use a set amount of photos, or a per-photo fee. You may also be required to attribute the photo to the photo-sharing site so that everyone knows where the image came from.

Sharing images on photo-sharing sites

Images aren't useful only for illustrating your content. They're also handy as a marketing tool. When you share and upload your own images, you can reach a whole new audience. For example, if you like to photograph local architecture, you can post your images to a photo-sharing site, such as Flickr (see Figure 2-4), and catch the eye of people who are also into architecture. They may end up following you on Twitter or Google+ because they enjoy your take on the subject matter.

FIGURE 2-4: Use a photo-sharing site, such as Flickr, to help market your brand.

TIP

When you allow others to use your images, you also create an opportunity for backlinks. When users attribute a photograph to you and link to your website, they're alerting search engines, which is always a very good thing. Moreover, others will follow the attribution to your blog or website, and some may even become members of your community.

Sharing photos is also a way to establish expertise. For example, foodies often share images of their latest culinary creations or a wonderful dinner out. If your business is an auto dealership, sharing images based on the cars you sell can help bring in new business. If you sell cosmetics, sharing before-and-after makeover pictures can lead to sales. If you tag people in images on your Facebook page, their friends might see those photos. In this sense, tagging can lead to new customers and community members.

Often times, when you post an image on a social network devoted to image sharing, others will comment. Those comments lead to a whole new way to grow your community.

Smartphone users like using Instagram and Snapchat to share images. See Book 7 for more on visual social sharing.

TIP

When you share an image on photo-sharing sites, make sure to leave contact information. This is helpful in case someone wants to share the image or find out more about you.

Using Social Media Platforms for Online Content

Most people don't usually think of social media updates such as Twitter or Facebook as "content." However, social media is an important part of any content-marketing strategy. (See Chapter 3 in this minibook for the lowdown on developing your content-marketing strategy.) Not only are all your posts and updates considered content, but you can also use social media as a marketing tool for your blog posts, videos, and podcasts.

Although we're going to cover the nitty-gritty details of how to use Facebook and Twitter later in this book, we'd be remiss if we didn't at least share here why you need to include social media in discussions about content and content marketing.

Why social media? Here are some reasons:

- **Social media can be good SEO.** Public social media updates can appear in searches.
- **Your customers and potential customers are on the social networks.** It makes sense to go where the people are. If your customers are using Facebook and Twitter, it's well worth your time to spend time talking to them on those platforms.
- **Social media can help more people to see your content.** Not everyone will see your blog or video updates. Sharing on social media not only puts your

content in front of more eyeballs, but your customers may also share that content, giving it even more exposure.

- **Social media is a good way to update customers and community.** If you have quick updates, using Twitter, Google+, or Facebook will share your news without having to invest a lot of time creating.
- **Social media is affordable.** The social networking platforms are all free to use.

Deciding which social media platforms to use

Social media encompasses a broad range of platforms. For example, blogs, video, image sharing, and podcasting all fall under social media's wide umbrella. Social media also includes the different social networks such as Facebook, Instagram, Pinterest, Twitter, and Google+.

Like all other content-marketing platforms, you don't have to have a presence on every social media platform available. When brands sign on for too many platforms, at least one of them ends up in neglect. It's much better to have a presence on a few platforms than to have dead space and old news on an existing platform. Try building up one platform at a time rather than spreading yourself thin on a variety of social networks.

How do you know which platforms to choose? Here are some questions to help you determine the best platform(s) for you:

- **Where are your customers?** Before you sign up for a social media platform, understand the platform's demographics and how that platform relates to your customers' and clients' demographics. For example, if your brand is hoping to attract teens, you have a better chance of doing so on Instagram or Snapchat than on Facebook. If you sell crafting or home design products, Pinterest is your game.
- **What platforms are your competitors neglecting?** We hope you are investigating your competitors' social media use. If so, there are two items to note:
  - Are they dominating a particular platform? This means that your customers are using that platform, too, and you want to get in on it.
  - Do you see an opportunity for growth and outreach on another platform that your competitors aren't using? It might be worth your while to consider testing the waters there as well, so that you can be the dominant force for your niche.

» **Which platforms are you best equipped to handle?** Can you write better than you can take photos? If so, Facebook is probably a better place to begin than Instagram.

» **What is your budget?** Can you spend money on your social media efforts? You have a better chance of having your content seen on Facebook if you purchase an ad for your Facebook page. Twitter and LinkedIn also offer more visibility to those who pay to play. These aren't deal breakers, however, and you can still reach your customers and community in a smaller capacity without a big budget.

» **What kind of content will you be sharing?** If you prefer to share photos over words, you'll want to choose a more visual platform like Instagram or Pinterest. However, Facebook lends itself better to having a conversation around a video or blog post.

REMEMBER

Don't spend too much time agonizing over a high friend or follower count on the social networks. The numbers aren't as important as making quality connections and cultivating existing relationships. The quality over quantity route is infinitely more rewarding than random Follows just to up your numbers.

Creating and sharing content with social media

Social media serves a dual purpose in your content-marketing strategy. You can use it as a way to create content, but also as a way to share content.

We start with using social media as a content-creation platform. What's interesting about the social networks is how many different things you can do with them. Here are some ideas:

» Use Twitter to tell 140-character stories about your brand.

» Use Instagram to create a *meme* (a viral photo people use to write and share funny captions) using your photos. Also, use Instagram to share tips, for example, when styling shoes, jewelry, or accessories with an outfit. (If yours is a brand that does this sort of thing.)

» Use Snapchat to create visual stories about your business.

» Use Pinterest to share design tips and how-to's. If you handle marketing for a hair or nail salon, or sell products to the same, use Pinterest to share different hair or nail style tips.

» Use Facebook to share product information, unique recipes, and photos of attractive place settings. Food product manufacturers would do well to share original recipes on Facebook.

» Use LinkedIn's blogging platform to share tips for professionals.

In addition to using social media as a tool for content creation, it's also a terrific tool for sharing content on different platforms. Every bit of content you post online should have the capability to be shared on the social networks as well. So if you publish a blog post, you'll also want to share the link on all the social networks in which a brand has a presence.

TIP

You want to give your online community the opportunity to share your content as well. For example, you might notice blog and online articles have buttons near the top or bottom of the content where the author invites readers to share the post on Facebook, Twitter, YouTube, and even LinkedIn. See Figure 2-5 for an example of share buttons.

FIGURE 2-5: Use share buttons to make it easy for others to share your content.

You'll find that when your brand has a loyal online community, they will want to share your content with others. Having share buttons allows them to do that with just a couple of clicks.

Understanding the importance of community

Many businesses and brands are now discovering the importance of cultivating an *online community.* Everyone who comments on your content, follows your brand on Twitter, and belongs to your Facebook pages and groups is part of your online community. How you decide to leverage your community is up to you.

It's important to consider your community when planning content because they are the people who will consume and respond to your online content. Without your online community, all your content-marketing efforts will be for nil.

There's a difference, however, between customers and community. Customers are people who use your service or buy your product. On the other hand, community members rally around your brand. They feel good about you because they're spending time with you online, which can lead to some terrific brand advocacy and word-of-mouth marketing.

Online communities are important because they create trust. When a brand is interacting on a regular basis with the people who use their products or services, the people feel as if they're privy to something special — as if they're part of the brand. Plus, interaction and conversation don't feel or look like selling. Because your members are enjoying their time with you, they have a good feeling about buying your product or hiring your service.

REMEMBER

Business is no longer local. Thanks to the Internet, you're global and your online communities can help spread the word even further. Your members are your staunchest allies and advocates.

Your online relationships can lead to partnerships, collaborations, and fame. Even more important, online communities enable you to find out about the people who use your product or service and how you can improve. In fact, online communities are so important, one of your authors wrote an entire book devoted to their intricacies. Check out *Online Community Management For Dummies* by Deborah Ng (John Wiley & Sons, Inc.).

Guest Blogging to Grow Awareness and Expertise

Another way to use content to drive traffic to your website is through guest blogging. *Guest blogging* enables you to create content to showcase your expertise, but you're posting it to someone else's blog. This might seem counterproductive, but there's a definite purpose to guest blogging.

Figure 2-6 shows the Type-A Parent blog with a guest blog post. With guess blogging you can do the following:

- **Share your perspective with a new audience.** The purpose of guest blogging is to find people who don't hang out in the usual places. You're expanding your network.
- **Grow backlinks for your blog.** Guest blogging is terrific SEO. When another blog links to your blog, you now have what are called *backlinks*. Backlinks are important for driving traffic and catching the attention of the search engines.
- **Sell to people who you might not have reached otherwise.** Because you're reaching out to a new community, you've expanded your selling base. Guest blogging can lead to new fans, newsletter sign-ups, and even sales.

FIGURE 2-6: Guest blogging gives you the opportunity to reach a new customer base.

Understanding guest blogging

Guest blogging is a form of content marketing in which you're writing articles for someone else's blog or website. Even though your content is on a blog that isn't owned by you, you still reap many benefits. As you discover in Book 2, Chapter 2, having other blogs link to your site attracts people to your site and helps your site rank higher on search engines.

Just as when writing content for your own blog, guest blog posts have to offer something of value. You won't have many people inviting you to guest blog if you share only fluff. Guest blogging content should teach, inspire, or cause people to take action. However, guest blog posts should never sell. Nothing turns off readers more than a blatant sales pitch.

Something else to know before you write your first guest blog post is that you shouldn't write an article filled with links to your blog or website. Most blog owners allow a link in a bio, where you can describe your expertise and link back to your business. Some bloggers also allow a relevant link in the body of the guest blog post. It's best to ask each blogger his or her policy on linking back to your site. Everyone who accepts guest blog posts does so with the knowledge that there will be at least one link back to the guest blogger's site of choice.

TIP

Don't limit yourself to a particular subject or demographic. Think about all the types of websites that can benefit from your content. For instance, if you are a writer, reach out to a variety of businesses in which writing is relevant to what they do. For example, you might create a guest post for a marketing company on writing sales copy or calls to action, or one for a real estate school on writing effective home descriptions.

Finding relevant blogs and pitching your content

If you'd like to include guest blogging as part of your content strategy, it's important to put together a list of relevant blogs and websites so you know to whom you should pitch your guest blog post:

Consider the following when looking for relevant blogs for your content:

- **Relevant subject matter:** You don't have to stick to the exact subject matter, but the topics should be someone related. It wouldn't do to submit a post on the benefits of free-range chickens to a vegan recipe blog, for example.
- **Search engine ranking:** Do your best to choose blogs that rank high on search engines. For example, *Huffington Post* is a favorite for people who want to submit guest blog posts because it ranks so high in searches.
- **An engaged community:** Find blogs with active readers. If a blog has many active discussions going on in its comments section or on social networks, your guest post might receive the same attention. This attention can drive interest to your own blog, which can result in action.
- **Traffic:** It makes no sense to post to a blog that receives no traffic. Research each blog to make sure it has a good flow of traffic to both blogs and social networks.

- **A positive reputation:** Make sure the blog fits your own rules for engagement. For example, if you provide a family atmosphere, you don't want to risk your reputation by posting to an adult-oriented blog.

After you have an idea of whom you'd like to share a guest post with, it's time to work on your pitch.

TIP

Nothing makes bloggers less inclined to accept your guest blog post than a cookie-cutter pitch. If you tailor each pitch to fit the individual blog, you'll have a better chance of acceptance.

Consider the following questions when pitching to another blogger:

- **Who is the blogger?** Make sure you know exactly to whom you're pitching. Use a name when reaching out and make it clear you know who the blogger is and what he or she does.
- **Do you understand the subject matter?** In your pitch, it's important to show that you know the focus of the other person's blog and how your business — and guest blog post — are related.
- **What will readers learn or take away from your blog post?** Why should someone else give up precious bandwidth for your post? Your pitch should detail talking points and takeaways so that the blogger has a good idea of the value you offer to his or her community.
- **What is your end result with guest blogging?** Why are you guest blogging? Are you promoting a product? Are you launching your business? Do you want to establish yourself as a thought leader? Make your intentions clear.

REMEMBER

Your writing is reflected in your pitch. Be sure to proofread; you don't want to create a bad impression with typos or grammatical errors.

Promoting your guest blog posts

When you pitch a guest blog post, make sure the person you're pitching to knows that you are going to help promote it.

For example, you can do the following:

- **Share the blog post on social networks.** Post your guest blog post on Facebook, Twitter, LinkedIn, and anywhere else you feel your readers will benefit from the link.

» **Link to the blog post on your own blog or website.** You can link to your guest blog posts in different places, including a bio page, an About page, or a media page (where you list all your online contributions), or even as a relevant link in articles or blog posts.

» **Share the blog post in your newsletter.** Don't forget to share your guest blog post on your newsletter. Many people subscribe to newsletters so that they don't have to become members of online groups or fan pages.

Guest blogging is a two-way street. Don't assume you're being allowed to submit guest blog posts because the other bloggers are kind. They would like you to also drive traffic to their own website. Make sure you promote your guest blog post in a way that benefits everyone involved.

IN THIS CHAPTER

» Thinking about what you want to achieve with your content

» Developing a content strategy

» Outlining your strategy on paper

Chapter 3

Developing a Content-Marketing Strategy

All content needs a plan. It's not enough to write something and post it to your blog platform; you also want to take the time to plan your content so it makes sense. If you're just posting without any clear direction, your content can become confusing, and your customers won't know what actions to take.

Having a clear content-marketing strategy is even more important than the content itself. Without a plan, you won't be able to see the big picture and you'll be creating and posting without a result in mind. Having a strategy in place allows you to focus on traffic, sales, and growth. A strategy helps you know what kind of content to create and how to achieve the desired growth with that content.

In this chapter, we talk about putting a content-marketing strategy together to achieve your objectives.

Determining Content Goals

Because you're reading this section, you're probably thinking about starting a blog, podcast, or video series, and you want to learn how to do so to achieve a particular result. Knowing why you're creating content is the first — and the most important — step in your content-marketing strategy.

Here's a look at many of the goals that businesses and business people hope to achieve with their content strategies:

- **Drive traffic.** Your content will help to bring new traffic to your blog or website.
- **Make sales.** If you have a product or service to promote, sales is probably your top reason for wanting to learn more about content marketing. Content is terrific for selling because you can drive traffic directly to your sales page or website.
- **Build brand recognition.** By putting out content regularly, you're increasing readership or viewership. After you have an audience, you're creating brand recognition. If you're recognized as sharing useful or entertaining content, people will know your brand and your logo. When it comes time to buy, your business will come to mind because you already have an online presence.
- **Establish expertise.** Content can be educational. You can use your content to share product information, details, and usage tips, or you can use your content to establish expertise for your personal or professional brand. If you share useful and important information, your community will see you as somewhat of an expert.
- **Improve search engine rankings.** Plenty of good-quality content can help your business land on the first or second page of the top search engines.
- **Build trust.** Your content enables you to be transparent with customers and community. When you're honest about what you do and keep an open line of communication, people have trust in the brand. Trust equals sales.
- **Inspire customer loyalty.** Content that informs and rewards customers can also inspire customer loyalty. Your customers will not only make return visits to your content channels but also share your content with others.
- **Generate subscriptions and registrations.** Content can lead to newsletter sign-ups or website registrations. For example, you can direct traffic to a specific page or offer premium content (such as an e-book) in exchange for a sign-up or registration. We describe how content can help drive sales and grow your mailing list in the "Collecting leads with your content" section, later in this chapter.
- **Engage customers.** Content allows your customers to chat with you. Whether it's friendly banter on Twitter or a more opinionated discussion on your blog, they'll appreciate having a voice.
- **Build links to your content.** A content-marketing strategy is a link-building strategy. As long as you're providing valuable content to your consumers, other businesses and professionals will link to your content so that they can

share it with their own communities. All those backlinks are good search engine optimization (SEO).

- **Generate leads or new opportunities.** Smart content leads to smart opportunities. For example, if you regularly blog on important topics in your industry, those blog discussions can land you new clients or speaking engagements.

Not everyone uses his or her content for the same purpose, so you can't count on doing what everyone else is doing online. Take some time to outline your goals before you begin.

In the following sections, we describe several of these content goals in more detail.

Driving traffic

Traffic is a top goal in most content-marketing strategies. Businesses want to bring traffic to their websites that they can divert to sales or other sign-up pages, but they aren't sure how to drum up interest. By producing relevant, valuable content, you're catching the attention of the search engines.

When you're working out how to use your content to drive traffic, consider the following:

- **Guest blog posts:** Your content doesn't have to be only on your own pages or platforms. You can also consider writing a guest blog post for another blog. There are great benefits to guest blogging, including backlinks and creating brand visibility. Target the most influential blogs in your niche and read several posts before pitching to make sure you're a good fit. If you think that blogger's audience can benefit from your expertise, send the blogger a note describing the post you'd like to write and asking if he or she is interested. We talk in depth about guest blogging in Book 3, Chapter 2.
- **Viral videos:** If you create a great video, others might want to share it on the social networks. You don't have to make a video that's a big sales pitch, but do put your company's information at the end of the video and link to your website or sales page in the video page's description. The interesting thing about viral videos is that if everyone is sharing it, they'll mention your name. "Hey, check out this funny video from XYZ brand."
- **How-to content:** People are always searching online to learn how to do things. If you create useful how-to content that includes descriptive steps to complete a certain task, people will find it online via the search engines and land on your website. If it's truly useful, they may even stick around and read a few more pages or see what you have to sell.

- **Lists:** List blog posts come in many shapes and sizes, and they serve a variety of purposes. You can create a list of influential professionals in your niche or list steps to achieving a specific goal. You can even create funny lists such as those at BuzzFeed. The beauty of the list post is how it gets shared. If people enjoy your list or find it useful, it has the potential to go viral, which can lead to a lot of traffic and backlinks.
- **Calls to action:** If you want to get people to take a specific action, lead them there with a *call to action* (CTA). For example, if you're posting a link to your content on Facebook, give a call to action such as, "To learn more about building treehouses, see over 150 plans with step-by-step instructions for each at our website."
- **Optimized content, including photos:** Use your keywords to attract search engines. Don't make the words repetitious and annoying, but do insert keywords and key phrases as needed. Save photos with keywords as well, so that you can bring in traffic from users searching images online.
- **Social networks:** Sharing links to your content with a brief call to action will send traffic from Facebook, Twitter, and all the social networks you use to share with your community.
- **Easy sharing:** Using share buttons on all your content will inspire others to post your content to their Facebook news feeds or Twitter streams, or to email that content to friends who might have an interest.
- **Relationships with influential people:** Use your content to build relationships. For example, profile or interview influential people on your blog. They'll share that content in return, possibly bringing in a few new sales.

TIP

Content marketing isn't about advertising or spamming. Calls to actions shouldn't be overly "pitchy." The idea behind content marketing is that your content will be so interesting and useful, it will catch the attention of search engines, as well as the people who can benefit from such content.

Making sales

Okay, to be honest, even though you don't want content to seem as if you're selling, you want sales — otherwise, you wouldn't be marketing so hard. People who consume your content know this. For example, people know a brand such as Starbucks has a great social media presence to sell its products, and no one holds it against the company. The only thing they would hold against a brand is obnoxious sales tactics.

So, how do you sell through content without being pushy? Here are a few ideas that might help:

- **Use a call to action.** Have a call to action at the bottom or end of your content. For example, suppose your content is a how-to project for building a birdhouse, and you list all the materials and steps needed to create a beautiful birdhouse. At no time during the tutorial itself should you sell. However, when it's all over, you can post a relevant link with this call to action: "Stop by our website to purchase plans and materials needed to complete this project." You didn't sell at all, but you did give a suggestion at the end. Even if people don't buy right then, they now know where to go when it comes time for them to build their birdhouses.
- **Use newsletters.** Another way businesses use content to sell is through a newsletter sign-up. For example, through calls to action on blogs, websites, and social networks, brands invite their customers and community to subscribe to their newsletters. Many businesses even offer something of value in exchange for the newsletter sign-up — for example, a coupon for significant savings or an e-book. Each week, the brand sends subscribers a newsletter that features tips and news and also links to sales and discounts. Many of the discounts are offered only to subscribers.
- **Answer questions.** You can also try answering questions. If you notice customers or potential customers ask the same questions, address those questions in your content, giving your customers the ability to buy with confidence.
- **Follow the one-percent rule.** Content should follow a 99:1 ratio. That is, only 1 percent of your content should be a sales pitch. The rest of your content should focus on helping, educating, and entertaining. Your customers will prefer to support you by reading your content and buying your products or services, as needed, rather than to read spiel and jargon all the time.
- **Focus on your customers' needs.** Your content should have a purpose. For example, it can answer common questions that your customers may have. You can also use it to teach how the product or service works and establish expertise in a niche.
- **Provide proof.** People have to know that what you're selling works. Create *infographics* (images listing facts) and case studies, or share reviews from existing customers.

REMEMBER

Although traditional advertising and marketing still has its place, selling today is less about heavy block letters and lots of exclamation points. Instead, people are inspired to buy after consuming content and feeling as if they can trust a person or brand.

Establishing expertise

Content marketing allows both businesses and individuals to share expertise in a niche or topic group. For example, an author or independent contractor can use content to prove to her potential readers or clients that she knows her topic.

Some of the methods used for establishing expertise include the following:

- **Blog posts, articles, case studies, online reports, and white papers:** Text-based content is excellent for sharing tips, knowledge, facts, demographic information, and anything written that highlights your particular expertise.
- **E-books and traditional books:** Books enable you to expand beyond the blog post. You can offer a book as a perk to entice people into buying, sell it to earn some side cash, or offer it for free to gain name recognition.
- **Videos:** You can use video for interviews, product demonstrations, case studies, and even mini-webinars. Video allows you an opportunity to connect with your audience because they can hear your voice and see your facial expressions.
- **Guest blog posts:** Reach out to influential bloggers in your niche and ask them if you can offer a guest post for their blogs or if you can exchange blog posts. Appearing in another person's blog gives you an opportunity to expand your reach.

REMEMBER

If you want people to see you as an expert in your field, use content marketing.

Growing your online community

Another common content-marketing goal is for online community growth and development. Your content gives you an opportunity to open up the channels and communication between you and your customers. Through your content, you also have the ability to foster loyal relationships, the kind that lead to word-of-mouth marketing. What follows are some ways content helps to grow your online community:

- **Have a dialogue.** Your content opens up a two-way line of communication. Through your content, you can address a variety of consumer- or product-related issues, and through comment areas and social media, your customers can respond.

» **Collect and respond to feedback.** When you give your customers a chance to talk to you via your content, you have a wonderful opportunity to learn how they truly feel about your product or service. They'll share the bad and the good, which can help you improve. When your online community sees you responding to their comments and concerns, it builds trust. Trust equals sales.

» **Build brand loyalty.** All the trust you establish means customers who care about your product or service. That loyalty means they stay with the brand and recommend it to others.

» **Grow your social media presence.** When you share content online, your community will want to follow you on all online platforms. You can also use social networks to discuss content. For example, if you post an article to Facebook, your Facebook community can have a conversation about the article in the comments section of the same Facebook post.

» **Share promotions and discounts.** Through your content, you can offer special sales for your online customers, and also offer coupon codes and other discounts.

Collecting leads with your content

Your content has another important purpose — lead generation. Building your mailing list is an essential part of your content-marketing strategy and should be one of your top goals.

Having customers and potential customers sign up for a newsletter or other type of online subscription can drive a lot more sales than if you had relied on content marketing without incorporating email contact. A database of email or even snail-mail addresses means you can share your content directly.

How do you get people to sign up or subscribe without a heavy sales pitch? By offering them something of value for free. For example, many brands create e-books, white papers, case studies, and in-depth reports that they offer for free if their customers register for their newsletter using a valid email address.

First, you have to convince your community that they will receive something of value. In addition to the free content, regularly send them a newsletter in their email inboxes. Make sure these newsletters contain tips, ideas, news, and discounts — discounts that lead to sales.

Putting a Strategy on Paper

When you have a good idea about the types of goals you hope to accomplish with your content-marketing strategy, put your strategy on paper in an order that makes sense to you and your team. If you don't take the time to list all your goals, as well as the steps needed to achieve those goals, you may forget an important step along the way.

Understanding the elements of a content-marketing strategy

Components of a successful marketing strategy include the following:

- **Definition of goals:** Define goals so everyone who reads and uses the strategy has a clear picture of what you're hoping to achieve with content marketing.
- **Core message:** What message are you trying to share with your customers and community? Is it a sales message? Are you trying to raise awareness for a cause? Do you want to share details for a new product? Keep your core message in mind while you plan your strategy.
- **Target audience:** Knowing whom you're trying to reach can help you to focus on content and platform.
- **Keywords:** Pinpoint the words and phrases people are using to lead to your website and your competitors' websites. Discuss ways you can use these keywords in your strategy.
- **Content platform and types of content:** Your strategy should include a plan of action for each different platform, which can include blogs, websites, images, and the social networks.
- **Editorial calendar:** An editorial calendar should list the content you're releasing each week, as well as deadlines for all. (We talk about putting together an editorial calendar in Book 3, Chapter 4.)
- **Task delegation:** A strategy is made up of tasks. Delegate tasks as part of the strategy, complete with deadlines, or nothing will get done.
- **Reporting and analytics:** Keeping careful records is essential to any strategy so that you can know what works and what doesn't, and how to tweak next time around.

Doing a content inventory

What content do you have already, and what have you done with it? For example, do you have a blog? If so, are you only posting once a week? Consider the steps needed to get people to view your content. Also, what unpublished content do you have that might be useful to your community? For example, you can repurpose internal reports and demographic information into content to share with your readers.

TIP

Make a list of all the content that's available to use and the different ways you can use it. (A spreadsheet is especially handy for putting together these lists.) Using existing content can save time and resources, as compared to creating content from scratch.

You can format a content inventory on a spreadsheet as described in Table 3-1.

TABLE 3-1 Outlining Your Content Inventory on a Spreadsheet

Column	Notes
Type of content	Note whether the content is an article, an e-book, a video, or another form of content. When you're planning your editorial calendar, mix around the types of content you're using. For example, don't release five videos in the same week. Having a list of the types of content available can help you avoid doubling or tripling up on the platform.
Name of content	When choosing a title for your content, think of something that is eye-catching, reflects the content itself, and has the type of keywords that will attract search engines. A good rule of thumb for headlines is, "If I saw this, would I want to learn more?"
Date published, if published	You want to space out the topics so that you're not publishing a repurposed bit of content soon after you published the original.
Description of content	Arrange the list so that you can see, at a glance, what the content is about so that you can plan your editorial calendar accordingly.
Ways to repurpose original content	For example, if someone wrote a blog post that wasn't used, how can you transform it into something that you can use? Also, what previously published content can you rework into something new? List all the different ways your content can be used — or reused.
Notes	Is there anything your team should know about the content? Do you have thoughts about how it should be published? Also, if it was previously published, note whether it was well received or poorly received.

Now that you have the components of your strategy and a content inventory, it's time to think about what's missing:

- Do you want to cover a topic, a how-to, an editorial, or another type of content that you don't already have as inventory? If so, make a list so that it can become part of your strategy.
- What are competitors doing that you're not? List all the ways you can take inspiration from people who have a similar business.
- Is there content you want to create that, as far as you know, no one else is doing? It doesn't hurt to suggest taking a risk.

Taking steps to achieve your goals

A *strategy* is a plan you put into place to achieve your goals. It lists all the steps you need to complete, along with an explanation of why each step is necessary. You have to sell your strategy to your team, put ideas into place, and assign each task to the best person for the job.

Here's an example of how you might put your content strategy on paper:

1. **Give an overview of your content strategy.**

   You use your overview to sell your content strategy to your team or anyone who has a stake in the business. Talk about why the strategy is necessary and what you hope your result will be. Discuss the problems you hope this strategy will solve and why you feel it would benefit the business and the community as a whole.

2. **Outline your goals.**

   List your goals for the strategy and how the strategy will help you to achieve your goals.

3. **Discuss your customers and community.**

   Whom are you writing for? Profile typical members of your community and customer base. Discuss how your different types of content will appeal to the different demographic groups.

4. **Share your ideas for content.**

   List a clear plan for your content. Include titles, keywords for each title, a platform for each title, and how you plan to share each title on the social networks.

5. **Discuss how you'll share each piece of content.**

   For example, if you record a podcast that features an expert interview, you should share it not only with your community but also with the expert's community. Discuss a strategy for sharing on your pages and the expert's pages (with that expert's input) and targeting mutual influential friends who can also help share.

6. **Talk about cost.**

   Consider how much this will cost. Be honest about the investment involved, what you consider a necessary expense, and what kind of return on investment (ROI) you expect in the long run.

7. **Provide a call to action.**

   The most essential part of your content strategy is the call to action. Whether you're driving traffic, sales, or brand recognition, you need to guide people to the end result.

8. **Attach an editorial calendar.**

   Create an editorial calendar, and include it with your strategy so that your team can see what you have planned in the upcoming months. You'll probably need to tweak the calendar after everyone has a look because they'll all have suggestions and ideas. We discuss how to create an editorial calendar in more detail in Chapter 4 of this minibook.

9. **Set a follow-up date.**

   You're going to have to do a bit of reporting in three to six months to discuss the results of your content strategy. You have to prove it worked and discuss things that went well, things that didn't work, and how to move forward.

TIP

After you have your strategy in place, you or another person on your team will have to keep detailed records, including an analytics report to see whether campaigns and keywords are driving traffic, and a sales report to see whether sales did, indeed, go up.

Delegating tasks

If you're part of a team and not handling the content strategy and all the tasks included on your own, be sure that tasks are matched to the correct person and that you have accountability in place to ensure that everything is performed on time.

REMEMBER

Sometimes, management thinks that social media tasks can be handed off to the intern because, after all, it's just a bunch of tweeting, isn't it? Although we think social media can be an entry-level position, you should hand the tasks surrounding content marketing to people who have the knowledge and experience to do the job correctly.

A content strategy can't work without the right people behind it. Here are some of the roles you may need to create when putting together your team:

- **Project manager:** Have a project manager in place to make sure that every task is being performed properly and on time.
- **Content creators:** Choose content creators who are talented and know your audience. Writers should understand how to write clean copy in a tone that best represents your brand and your customers. Podcasters and video people should speak in a confident manner and know how to handle all the technical aspects of recording and video equipment. If script writers are needed, that's another task for delegation.
- **Correspondent:** You may also need to have a member of your team handle correspondence with industry experts so you can gather quotes and book interviews.
- **Editors:** You need editors to make sure the writing is clean and coherent.
- **Marketing team:** Hand off promotion to the marketing team. They'll handle email marketing, social media marketing, advertising, and more.

TIP

You should distribute tasks with the utmost care. However, it's not enough to assign tasks — you also need accountability. Project management software such as Basecamp (`https://basecamp.com`) or Teamwork (`www.teamwork.com`) can help you assign tasks, assign deadlines, request progress reports, and share files. Because everyone has access to the software and has his own accounts with tasks, reminders, and deadlines, no one can say he missed something.

IN THIS CHAPTER

» Planning content

» Creating content with staying power

» Putting your content plan into play

Chapter 4 Getting Your Content to the Masses

Think about content marketing like the old tree-falling-in-the-forest joke. If you put your content online and no one sees it, does it really matter that you took the time to create it? Why invest all that time into writing or creating an awesome video, just to let it languish?

Taking the time to put an editorial calendar into place, as well as a plan for sharing your content, can help to get as many eyes on that content as possible.

TIP

Content promotion is equally as important as content creation. Without promotion, no one will know about your blog posts, videos, and other content.

In this chapter, we talk about how to get your content seen. Some of the methods we discuss may not be visible to the public (that is, they happen in the background) and may not seem important, but they really do make a difference.

Creating an Editorial Calendar to Keep Content Flowing

You might wonder what an editorial calendar has to do with getting people to view your content. The more organized you are, the better your strategy and your content will come together. An editorial calendar keeps your content team on track and ensures that fresh content is flowing on a regular basis, as shown in Figure 4-1.

FIGURE 4-1: An editorial calendar can help keep your content organized and prioritized.

Exploring the benefits of an editorial calendar

Scheduling content ahead of time is important for several reasons:

- **Allows the marketing team to plan accordingly:** If your content is part of a particular campaign, or if a campaign is being created around your content, the team has enough time to work rather than plan a hasty, last-minute campaign.
- **Ensures you won't be duplicating content:** Seeing a month's worth of content on a calendar can help keep you from becoming repetitive and redundant.
- **Enables you to plan seasonal or timely content:** If you're posting seasonal content, do it at least six weeks in advance to be available for search engine results. With an editorial calendar, you can set reminders to post seasonal content.

- **Gives everyone deadlines to meet:** With an editorial calendar, everyone can verify when content is due and when to post content online.
- **Enables you to post content with regularity:** Editorial calendars keep things consistent. You can see when you last put content online and how long it has been between postings.

Deciding what to include on your calendar

Here are some of the items to list on your editorial calendar:

- **Content:** The title of the content and a description, if you feel it's necessary.
- **Types of content:** Blog post, video, podcast, social media updates, newsletter, and so on.
- **Authors and producers:** Assign the tasks.
- **Editorial tasks:** If writing needs proofreading or videos need cleaning up, note it on the editorial calendar.
- **Marketing tasks:** Posting content or links to content on the social sites, creating email newsletters, and any other promotional tasks.
- **Deadlines:** The day the content is to be completed by the author or producer.
- **Reminders:** If you need to think about items such as seasonal content or a product launch, put those reminders on the calendar.
- **Date of publication:** The day that the content go live.
- **Publication location:** Where you are posting the content.
- **Reporting:** If you have to provide accountability to management, note the day reports are due on the editorial calendar.

TIP

Google Calendar is free to use and is stored online. You can share the calendar, so your entire team will have access to it, and you can allow others to add to it. Google Calendar also enables users to set reminders in the form of an email or a pop-up message.

WARNING

Don't load up your editorial calendar with so many details that it's hard to read. The calendar should act only as a reminder. You can go into greater detail in your content-marketing strategy and with your project management program, if you're using one.

Finding the Right Mix between Evergreen and Timely Content

When you write a news analysis, do a product review, launch a product or service, or discuss an industry trend, this content gets more or less dated as time passes. It may bring in some eyeballs when the news first breaks, but after a while, searches for these news items or product news will trickle to a stop.

On the other hand, evergreen content has the potential to be searchable indefinitely. A blog post titled "How to Change a Tire" is a good example of evergreen content. Some other examples of evergreen content follow:

- How-to's
- Histories (even if it's the history of a certain product or service)
- Biographies
- Informational posts (for example, "The Health Benefits of Bananas")
- Etiquette (for example, "The Etiquette of Commenting on Blogs")
- Rules (for example, "Rules of Grammar")

Achieving a good balance with your content is important. You want both trendy and evergreen content. If not, you'll receive spikes in traffic here and there but not a steady rise, which is what you really want.

WARNING

Many bloggers go for shocking headlines and controversial content in hopes of snagging the retweet crowd. This approach works sometimes, but your content and page traffic will spike and drop off. To keep traffic numbers high all the time, make the content consistent and appealing to searchers and readers for months, if not years.

Evergreen content is highly linkable as well. With the right kind of content, you'll always have something to link to internally. Plus, other content creators can use your content as a reference for their own blog posts. Also, consider how evergreen content works for all platforms: text, video, and audio.

TIP

If you write three blog posts per week, try writing one evergreen post once during that week. Soon, you'll see regular, steady streams of traffic rather than one-off spikes like you'd get with scandalous news or controversy.

Executing Your Content Strategy

After you receive approval for your content strategy, it's time to put the wheels in motion. What was once on paper now has to go to work in real-time.

Follow these steps to execute your content strategy:

1. **Schedule and assign tasks.**

   Get your content strategy going:

   a. Add all necessary items to your editorial calendar.

   b. Assign tasks in your project management system.

2. **Make sure all aspects of your content strategy are working as planned.**

   Your strategy needs to be on target and on time:

   - *Request periodic updates or progress reports.* Check on each task halfway through. If you're using a project management system such as Basecamp, you'll find areas where you can communicate with your team, as well as receive notifications and reminders when something is due or past due.
   - *Make sure things are on track and on schedule.* Check to make sure everything is going according to schedule. If someone is falling behind, see what needs to be done to meet your deadlines.

     REMEMBER

     Be strict with deadlines; otherwise, no one will adhere to them.

3. **Make sure all your team's hard work is paying off.**

   Keep tabs on how things are going:

   - *Review your measurement tools.* You have to know whether all your team's efforts are working. Keep an eye on your analytics to see whether you're achieving your goals.
   - *Report any findings.* Keep records and set up regular reports — weekly, monthly, quarterly, and annually. Compare numbers and note trends.
   - *Make recommendations to improve your content strategy.* A content strategy isn't a static document. It's requires updating and reworking.

REMEMBER

Don't rest on your laurels. As long as there's an Internet, you need to put out content. Keep repeating the cycle and tweaking as needed.

Sharing Your Content with the Public

You're going to have to do more than set it and forget it when it comes to your content. This is where the *marketing* part of the content marketing strategy comes in.

Social media is a wonderful tool for sharing. Don't be afraid to use the different platforms, but don't share only links to your own content. If you're overly promotional and only toot your horn, you'll lose friends and followers rather than earn new members of your community.

Here are some suggestions for sharing your content with the public:

- **Share your content with Facebook fans.** When you share your content on Facebook, it shows up in your fans' news feeds. If they like the content, they'll share it with their friends, and so on and so forth. This is how content goes viral. (Figure 4-2 shows how readers share content they feel is entertaining or informative.)

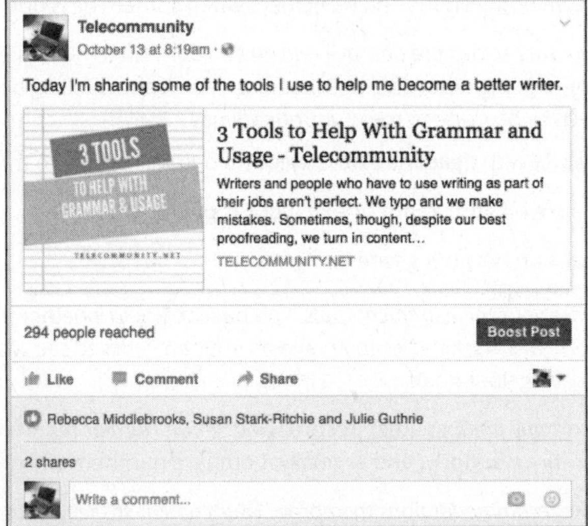
Telecommunity
October 13 at 8:19am ·
Today I'm sharing some of the tools I use to help me become a better writer.
3 TOOLS
TO HELP WITH GRAMMAR & USAGE
3 Tools to Help With Grammar and Usage - Telecommunity
Writers and people who have to use writing as part of their jobs aren't perfect. We typo and we make mistakes. Sometimes, though, despite our best proofreading, we turn in content...
TELECOMMUNITY.NET
294 people reached
Boost Post
Like
Comment
Share
Rebecca Middlebrooks, Susan Stark-Ritchie and Julie Guthrie
2 shares
Write a comment...

FIGURE 4-2: Sharing your content on Facebook gives it the potential to go viral.

- **Share links to your content on Twitter.** Sharing links to your content on Twitter means the links will show up in your followers' feeds. If they like the content, they'll retweet it to their followers.
- **Share your content on other social networks, such as LinkedIn and Pinterest.** You want your content to be seen by as many people as possible.

- **Share content in your regular newsletter.** Does your business have a regular newsletter? (If it doesn't, it should!) Include a brief excerpt (a paragraph or two) of new content with a link to the full article, video, or image.
- **Reach out to influential professionals.** If you know of influential professionals in your niche who have a good reach via social media or an email newsletter, see whether you can build up some sort of relationship in which you share each others' content.
- **Share and share alike.** When you share content from other people and brands, some will happily reciprocate.

TIP

Create the kind of content people want to share: People don't share boring content. Instead, they want to read or hear or watch content that educates, inspires, and entertains. Before publishing any content, ask yourself, "Would I want to share this?"

TIP

Pay special attention to activity times on social networks. For example, if you notice that you receive the most engagement on Facebook at 10 a.m., continue to post Facebook content at that time, while avoiding off-peak hours.

Measuring the Success of Your Content Strategy

An analytics program tells you how and why people are coming to your site. Without it, you know little about your customers, your community, or the content they're consuming.

TIP

The type of analytics program you use depends on your needs, but most bloggers are comfortable with the free, tried-and-true Google Analytics (available at `www.google.com/analytics` to anyone with a Google account). Use Google Analytics to see how many visitors are coming to your pages and what they're doing after they arrive.

Analytics programs are simple to install and come with detailed, easy-to-follow instructions. You upload a plug-in or place some code on your blog or website. We discuss analytics programs in more detail in Book 9.

Here is what you can discover from your analytics program:

- **Number of people who visit your content:** Your analytics program lists how many people visit on a given day, week, month, or even hour. This information enables you to pinpoint traffic trends. Knowing the most popular times of the day or week for readers can help you plan content and sales campaigns.
- **Your most popular content:** Your analytics program offers a rundown of how many people read your pages, letting you know which content went over well and what people weren't interested in reading.
- **Bounce rate:** The *bounce rate* is the amount of time people spend on a page. A high bounce rate means people leave your site quickly, and a low rate means folks are staying for a while and consuming your content. If you have a high bounce rate, you want to work on having the kind of blog and content people want to read.
- **Keywords and search terms:** You need to know who's visiting your blog and why. Your analytics program can show you which keywords people are searching for through search engines before landing on your site. When you know these often-used keywords, you can use them in your content to attract even more readers.
- **Response to advertisements and sales pages:** Many analytics have *heat maps,* which allow you to see specifically where most people are spending their time on each page. As a result, you can place ads in the right spots and see whether folks are reading and reacting to your sales pages.
- **Top traffic referrers:** Your analytics program shows you whether your Twitter or Facebook campaign is working. In fact, if anyone is sharing or talking about your content, you can follow the trail using your analytics program.
- **Page views:** You can discover how many people read a page and move on to read more pages, or leave after reading only one page. Page views are different from bounce rates in that *page views* tell how many individual pages each person spends time on at your blog or website, and bounce rates tell you only how long someone stays on your website before leaving.
- **Whether your content is driving sales:** Your analytics program shows you whether your content is leading folks to sales pages and how many people are taking action on those pages.

All this information can help you refine your marketing strategy because it gives you deeper knowledge about customers and the online community. It's like you're spying on their habits, in a noninvasive way. When you know how, when, and why people are consuming your content, you're better able to tweak it for maximum potential. This knowledge can lead to more sales and visibility.

TIP

In addition to checking to see whether your content is driving more customers to your blog or website, you also want to notice other trends:

- **Sales:** Have you noticed higher sales since beginning your content strategy? Is your content driving people to the right pages? Note trends in sales, especially what's driving people to buy.
- **Sign-ups and subscriptions:** Check the number of people who are signing up for a service, product demo, or offered freebies, as well as subscriptions to the company newsletter. Did your content lead people to take action?
- **Social media engagement:** Do you have more friends, fans, and followers? Are more people talking about your brand online? Are more people sharing your content and visiting your social media pages?
- **Visibility:** Is your personal or professional brand being talked about in a positive way?

REMEMBER

There will always be people who want to read blog posts, listen to podcasts, watch videos, share images, and interact on the social networks. If you're looking to grow your business, it makes sense to go where the people are. Content helps you sell without looking like you're selling, while building trust among your customers and community.

4
Twitter

Contents at a Glance

CHAPTER 1: Using Twitter as a Marketing Tool 287
Deciding Whether Twitter Is Right for You.................. 288
Communicating in 140 Characters 290
Promoting without Seeming like You're Promoting............ 291
Researching Other Brands on Twitter 296
Knowing Quality Is More Important than Quantity 297

CHAPTER 2: Using Twitter as a Networking Tool 299
Finding the Right People to Follow 300
Finding Out Who Is Talking about You on Twitter 301
Responding to Tweets 302
Searching on Twitter...................................... 303
Tweeting like a Pro 304
Sharing on Twitter....................................... 305
Following the Twitter Rules of Etiquette 310
Hosting a Tweet-Up....................................... 311

CHAPTER 3: Finding the Right Twitter Tools.................. 313
Customizing Your Twitter Profile Page...................... 314
Pinning Tweets... 317
Using a Twitter Application 318

CHAPTER 4: Social Listening with Twitter..................... 321
Using Twitter to Listen to Your Customers 321

CHAPTER 5: Hosting Twitter Chats............................ 327
Benefiting from Twitter Chats 327
Finding a Hashtag for Your Chat........................... 328
Keeping Track of Who Says What 329
Finding Guests for Your Twitter Chat 331
Promoting Your Twitter Chat.............................. 332
Hosting Your Twitter Chat 333

IN THIS CHAPTER

» Understanding the benefits of Twitter for your brand

» Embracing brevity

» Checking out the competition

Chapter 1
Using Twitter as a Marketing Tool

Twitter took the world by storm in 2007. At first, the social media and blogging communities mostly embraced Twitter, but soon brands began appreciating its value. Today, Twitter is mainstream.

At first glance, Twitter looks like a lot of people dropping links and talking about nothing important. But before you write this microblogging site off as a lot of noise, consider the benefits of Twitter and how you can use it as a valuable marketing tool — because, make no mistake, Twitter can totally make a brand.

In this chapter, we discuss the benefits of Twitter and how you can use it to raise brand awareness and drive traffic and sales.

TIP

For more information, check out *Twitter For Dummies,* 3rd Edition by Laura Fitton, Anum Hussain, and Brittany Leaning, or *Twitter Marketing For Dummies,* 2nd Edition by Kyle Lacy both books published by John Wiley & Sons, Inc.

Deciding Whether Twitter Is Right for You

Even if you've never used Twitter (see Figure 1-1), you've probably heard about this online social-networking service. The Twitter icon, with its famous blue bird, is everywhere, from cable news broadcasts to your local supermarket. Everyone wants you to follow them on Twitter.

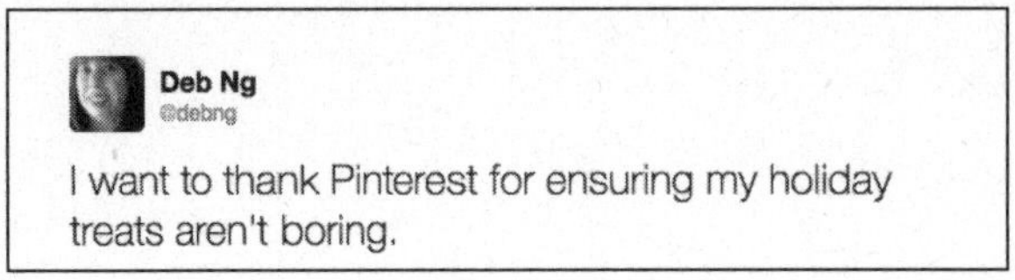

Deb Ng
@debng

I want to thank Pinterest for ensuring my holiday treats aren't boring.

FIGURE 1-1: Twitter allows you to communicate in only 140 characters.

Before you post the Twitter icon on your blog or website, or add your Twitter handle to your business cards, you need to know what exactly Twitter is and whether it's the right marketing platform for you.

Twitter is a microblogging social network. We get into the microblogging aspect more in the following section of this chapter, but suffice it to say that everything you post has to be short and simple. Believe us: Communicating in a short form isn't as easy as it sounds, especially if you want to get a message out. Still, millions of people are using Twitter, and many brands are finding success.

People use Twitter to do the following:

- **Build a community.** The best reason to join any social network is to grow a community of friends and advocates. Your community consists of the people with whom you build trust and relationships because they view you as being accessible. These people are the ones who will have your back.
- **Find new customers.** Thanks to the Internet, you now have the ability to reach a global market. With Twitter, you have the ability to reach millions of new people. Each person you interact with has the ability to reach people, as well. You can leverage all that reachability into sales.
- **Have a conversation.** The best part of Twitter and other social networks is the capability to sell without sounding like you're selling. It's called *conversational marketing,* and it's exactly what it sounds like. When you have a conversation with your friends and followers, people get to know who you are and what you do. When they have a need for someone who does what you do, they're more likely to call on you. They may even like you so much that they decide to buy what you're selling just to support a friend.

» **Ask questions.** The best way to learn about your customers and potential customers is to ask questions. We're not saying that you need to have a Twitter poll (unless you want to), but there's nothing wrong with dropping a question now and then to find out about a demographic or habit (see Figure 1-2).

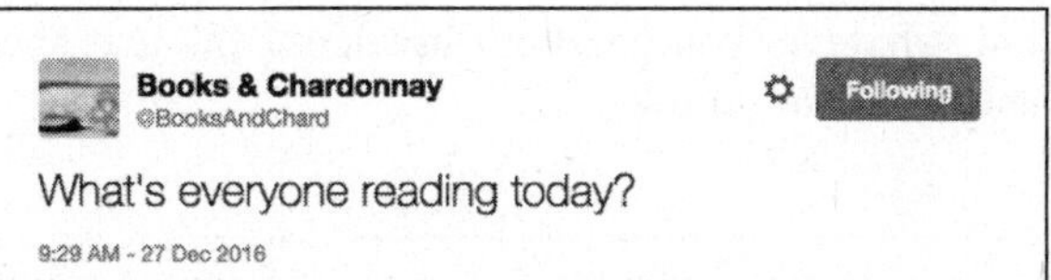

Books & Chardonnay
@BooksAndChard
Following
What's everyone reading today?
9:29 AM - 27 Dec 2016

FIGURE 1-2: Use Twitter to ask questions and learn about your brand's community.

Using Twitter as a Marketing Tool

» **Offer customer support.** Many people like to reach out to their favorite brands on Twitter to ask questions about a product or service, or to ask for direction or technical support. Twitter is another way to be accessible to your customers. You can also use Twitter to search and make sure your customers aren't having issues.

REMEMBER

» **Discover what people are saying about you.** It's important to receive feedback, especially unsolicited feedback. Sometimes folks are talking about your brand online, and you definitely want to know about it.

» **Promote your content.** Did you just write up a killer blog post? Are you releasing a new video? Do you want to let folks know about a new product launch? Twitter is an awesome tool for promoting new items.

» **Host Twitter chats.** Twitter chats allow you to discuss topics at length or bring in special guests. They're another way to interact with your community. See Chapter 5 of this minibook for an in-depth look at Twitter chats.

» **Promote brand visibility.** When people see your logo on Twitter and they see you communicating with customers and other Twitter friends, they feel confident in the brand. They like the human element and especially knowing that when they reach out to you on social networks, you'll be there to respond.

» **Give out perks.** Some brands share Twitter-only discounts and freebies as a way to reward their followers. Lucky recipients will no doubt share these perks with their own followers.

REMEMBER

Twitter is a commitment. Networking on Twitter isn't as simple as sending a tweet and expecting to bring in the masses; it's also a matter of building relationships, getting to know people, and holding a conversation.

Communicating in 140 Characters

Possibly the most challenging part of Twitter is the 140-character limit. This amount may seem like a lot at first — until you try to post something pithy or clever and realize you can't fit everything you want to say. Once you start deleting characters, your sentence can lose all meaning.

Don't fret and, whatever you do, don't break out the text speak (see Figure 1-3). Brevity is easier than you think.

FIGURE 1-3: Using text speak hurts the eyes and looks unprofessional.

WARNING

You may notice that a lot of people use shortened words, such as *u* instead of *you* or 2 instead of *too* or *to*. The problem is that using acronyms or abbreviations is unprofessional and hurts people's eyes. Ditto running words together to fit them in the space. A good general rule is that if people can't read your sentence at first glance, you'll lose them.

Here are a few tips for getting the most out of your 140 characters:

- **Make every word count.** Use words that show an action or make an impact. Avoid filler words, such as *that.*
- **Use short words when at all possible.** Try short, eye-catching words over longer words. Just about every "big" word has a shorter counterpart.
- **Punctuation matters.** You may be tempted to skip your periods and commas to fit in more characters. Run-on sentences don't look pretty, and they're hard to read. Do your best to use proper grammar and punctuation.
- **Use humor.** Do you know what gets lots of retweets and responses? A funny tweet. That isn't to say every post needs to be slapstick, but don't be afraid to say something funny now and again. Your community will enjoy it.
- **Get to the point.** Don't take the scenic route; get right to the point. You have only 140 characters to work with, so say what you have to say without mincing words.
- **Grammar counts.** Don't use poor grammar simply because you think it fits the tweet. Grammatical errors turn people off from wanting to do business with you because they feel you're unprofessional.

» **Use sentence case.** All uppercase letters make people feel as if you're yelling at them, and all lowercase letters look as if you're too lazy to press the shift key. Make a good impression by rocking the uppercases and lowercases.

» **Give value.** Being silly and fun on Twitter is okay, and it's fine to say something frivolous, as well. Just be sure to add value into the mix. If you're using Twitter to promote your business, share your expertise, as well.

» **Don't always make it about you.** Don't make every tweet about you or your business. Visit with your community. Participate in other conversations, ask questions, and share links to other people's stuff.

» **Don't break up your tweets.** Be careful dividing up tweets to continue a thought. A lot of people will see only the first or second half of the tweet and have absolutely no idea what you're talking about.

» **It's okay to use characters.** Even though we discourage text speak, feel free to replace the word *and* with an ampersand (&). Replacing a word with an accepted character isn't considered unprofessional.

TIP

Before you get started with tweets, research other brands that are having success using Twitter and observe how they're interacting with their communities. You may come away from the experience with some good ideas for interacting with your own communities. (See the upcoming "Researching Other Brands on Twitter" section.)

Twitter recently changed guidelines regarding its 140-character rule. Links and photos are no longer counted as part of your 140 characters. Although you should still shorten links before posting to Twitter, long links no longer mean you have to shorten your description.

Twitter has also waived the 140-character rule when quoting a retweet. Now a retweet will show the entire quote and you can add commentary within the 140-character limit.

Promoting without Seeming like You're Promoting

REMEMBER

On social networks, there's a delicate balance between promoting and spamming. If everything you do is calling attention to you or your business, you'll find yourself losing followers faster than you can bat an eye. The beautiful thing about conversational marketing is that you can talk to your friends and followers about anything in the world, and it still has the potential to drive business.

Your first course of action is to follow the right people (see Chapter 2 of this minibook). After all, why be on Twitter if you're not reaching people? Don't worry about starting out slowly at first; your numbers will grow if your tweets offer value, and you gain a reputation for being interactive and engaging. The tricky part is to get people to like what you do without turning them off with spam or over-the-top sales tactics.

You can easily be overly promotional on Twitter, especially when you see others do nothing but drop links. Because of the 140-character limit, many people feel it's more important to fit in a link than some interesting text. The problem is, many of the people who drop too many links either lose their followers, don't gain new follows, or end up ignored by their existing followers.

What follows is a list of do's and don'ts for promoting your brand on Twitter without looking like you're promoting your brand on Twitter:

- **Do follow the people who will receive the most value from your tweets and your brand.** You may be tempted to follow everyone you can simply to receive a follow-back in return, but this approach leads to a cluttered, hard-to-follow Twitter stream with people who don't care about you or your brand. Be selective with your follows for the best level of engagement. Go for quality over quantity.
- **Don't auto-follow everyone who follows you.** You may be considering paying for an *auto-follow program* — that is, an app that automatically follows everyone who follows you or who follows a specific Twitter account or keyword. An auto-follow program isn't a good idea. You won't know everyone in your Twitter stream, and people who auto-follow are easy to spot because they have a high ratio of people they follow versus people who follow them. This ratio imbalance is usually the sign of a spammer, and it drives followers away.
- **Do search for specific keywords and topics.** By all means, use your search function to find the people who follow a specific keyword or talk about a particular topic.
- **Don't spam everyone who is talking about those topics and keywords.** Do you know what people who use Twitter regularly hate? They can't stand it when they mention a word, and then all these spammers come out of the woodwork. For example, mentioning "iPad" on Twitter leads to a flurry of hopeful salespeople bombarding the unsuspecting tweeter with links to discounts on tablets. You'll find yourself reported as a spammer if you spam.

TIP

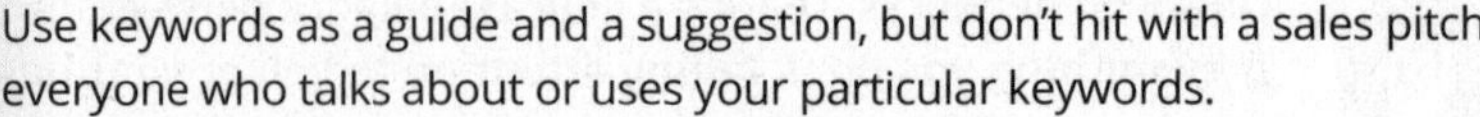

Use keywords as a guide and a suggestion, but don't hit with a sales pitch everyone who talks about or uses your particular keywords.

- **Do ask questions.** Get some interaction going with your Twitter community by asking questions. Keep in mind that you won't get a response every time, but sometimes some great conversations ensue. Also, don't be afraid to use question time to solicit feedback — both positive and negative.

- **Don't respond to each question with a link.** If people reach out to your brand on Twitter, you may at times respond with links and at other times avoid them. For example, if they can't find a sign-up page for your newsletter, by all means respond with a link. If they ask a general information question falling within your area of expertise, don't respond with your latest blog post. That'll get old and spammy after a while.
- **Do be sure to inject your personality into your tweets.** Don't be afraid to use humor, slang (that isn't vulgar or offensive), or any other words that show off your personality. You want to show your human, endearing side. The people who are most successful on Twitter aren't afraid to show their personality and fun, playful side.
- **Don't rely solely on the scheduled tweet.** Scheduling your tweets, usually through an app such as Hootsuite, helps to make sure that you post announcements throughout your day. However, when all you post are announcements, links, or sales pitches, you're broadcasting, not interacting. If it helps, go ahead and schedule those announcements, but do stick around in case someone has questions. Try to have back-and-forth interaction through your tweets.

WARNING

It's common etiquette to remove scheduled marketing tweets in the face of a tragedy or a catastrophic event so as not to seem insensitive. A brand that uses a tragic event to promote or sell is seen as newsjacking and it might create a backlash. For example, if you manufacture umbrellas, it would be bad form to schedule a tweet offering to sell umbrellas during a hurricane.

- **Do answer questions and respond to comments.** If folks are reaching out to you on Twitter, it's a good thing. It means they're putting their faith in you and find you accessible. Make sure to check Twitter throughout the day for questions and comments so that you can address everything in a timely manner.
- **Don't ignore a tweet because you don't want to draw light to negativity.** All feedback is good feedback, even the bad stuff. Answer questions even if they relate to a negative experience, especially because people are watching. If you'd rather not talk about such things with so many people in attendance, invite the tweeter to take it offline with a phone call or email.
- **Do share links to your stuff.** Have a great promotion? Share the link! Did you write a great blog post? Share the link! Does someone else have something cool to promote? Share the link! After all, if you're using Twitter as a promotional tool, you're looking for a result for your ultimate goal, a goal that you can't meet without the link. Don't let all our warnings about spamming make you afraid to share.

» **Don't only drop links.** If your Twitter stream is nothing but links and self-promotional spamminess, you'll drive everyone away. Make sure that links are a small percentage of what you share on Twitter.

» **Do share links to other people's stuff.** Social networks aren't only about you. Highlight other people's achievements, and they'll be more likely to highlight yours. Remember, though, a "you scratch my back, and I'll scratch yours" mentality gets a bit old.

» **Don't share or retweet a link unless you know what it's about.** Have you ever seen a popular tweeter share a link and instantaneously receive hundreds of retweets in return? It's a good bet many of those retweeters didn't even click the link to read what it's all about. Blind faith is cool and all, but what if the tweeter was linking to a post that is a lie or something offensive or inappropriate? A retweet is an endorsement, and it's in the best interests of your brand to know exactly what you're putting out there.

» **Do tweet every day.** Consistency is key to social media success. Put yourself out there every day so that you're a visible presence. When folks know when to expect your tweet, it's a good thing.

» **Don't let your Twitter account become a ghost town.** People feel better knowing that their favorite brands are socially engaged. When they look up a brand on Twitter and there haven't been any tweets since 2014, it tells everyone the brand isn't interested in what their community thinks.

» **Do take conversations private.** Not everything has to be out in the open. Nothing is wrong with offering to take an in-depth conversation offline or private. Sometimes, a one-on-one conversation best because you don't want to exclude everyone else in your stream. Also, if you're dealing with a negative situation, there's little you can resolve in 140 characters, so taking the conversation private is the way to go.

» **Don't auto-DM.** Avoid sending auto private or direct messages (DMs), as shown in Figure 1-4. Some apps instantaneously send *thank you* or *follow this link* private messages as soon as someone follows you. Auto-DMs and spam DMs are a sure way to receive an immediate unfollow. DMs are considered a private area, and most tweeters don't want their privacy invaded.

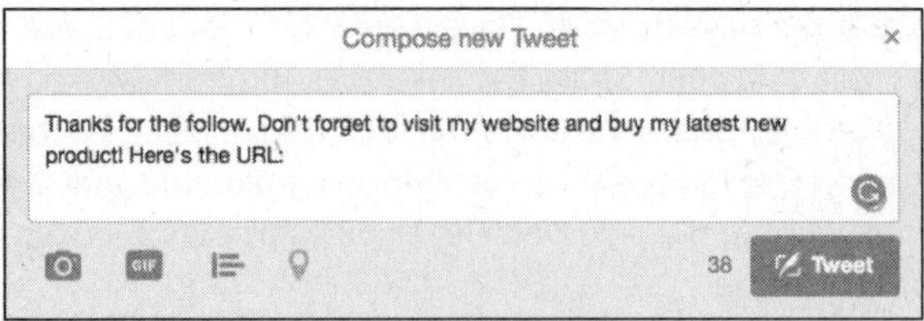

FIGURE 1-4: Sending spammy auto-DMs to your new followers will cause most of them to immediately unfollow you.

- **Do talk about yourself and your brand.** You're going to hear and read a lot about how social networks aren't for self-promotion and how it's all about the conversation, and that's true. However, it's silly to think that you're spending all your time on Twitter or Facebook and can't even promote your brand.
- **Don't talk only about yourself and your brand.** It's all about balance. Go ahead and promote your stuff, but make sure that you have a good ratio of conversational tweets versus promotional tweets. Different experts have a good idea of what that ratio should be, but usually trial and error determine what works best for you. Try tweeting one to two promotional tweets out of every ten tweets.
- **Do find topics of interest.** Try introducing a different discussion topic or question to your community each day. See whether you find any news that will interest your niche, or talk about the latest tools and techniques. Find something discussion-worthy and go for it.
- **Don't be corporate and boring.** People don't always want to discuss the brand. While they do enjoy some transparency from time to time, you'll lose people if your tweets are all about the corporate shareholder meeting. Do share some company business, but all work and no play will make you a very dull tweeter.
- **Do talk to everyone.** If your Twitter account has 2,500 followers, 2,500 people are interested in learning about you or your brand. Of course, you can't reach out to everyone by name every day, but ensuring that many of your daily tweets apply to everyone is almost as good as reaching out to everyone. At times you'll want to reach out to individuals, but you'll lose followers if your Twitter account is a hotbed of exclusivity.
- **Don't reach out to only the big names.** Many people feel that if they reach out to the big names on Twitter, they'll receive more attention. When someone with thousands of followers retweets your link or mentions you on social networks, you're bound to get more followers and interest in your brand. However, if you're only reaching out to the big names, it won't be long before you gain a reputation for pandering to famous people. Your biggest advocates aren't the people with a huge following; they're the people who use your brand and interact with you every day. Collectively, they can have a bigger reach.

TIP

Many parts of this laundry list of action items and things to avoid make it sound as if you're not promoting at all, and that's the point. On social networks, people don't want to be pitched to, unless they invite it. They want to enjoy a conversation and share interesting items they find online. If you turn it from a heavy sales pitch to a conversation between friends, you may find that you land more sales.

Researching Other Brands on Twitter

Finding out more about how other brands are using Twitter can help you formulate your own Twitter marketing plan. Many brands achieve success on social networks because they're interesting and engaging. Scope them out and learn by their example.

First, get off Twitter and get on Google. Do a Google search to find the brands that have been successful on Twitter. So many case studies online talk about brands that are doing Twitter right. Read the case studies and follow the brands to see them in action. Note the following:

- How often are they tweeting each day?
- What are they tweeting about?
- How are they handling customer comments, inquiries, and complaints online?
- How often are they dropping links?
- Are they offering discounts, freebies, or other perks to their followers?
- In what way are they bantering good-naturedly with both brands and individuals?
- What is setting their Twitter apart from the rest?

Next, you want to determine how brands similar to yours are using Twitter. You may love certain aspects of their community outreach and not agree with others. This contrast is good because it means you won't be tempted to flat-out copy their approach.

Finally, research cases of companies that made mistakes —you can find plenty of these case studies and stories online. For example, some brands haven't reacted well to negative feedback; others have dropped a personal tweet from the company account.

TIP

When you learn about the way others are using Twitter and learn from their mistakes, you'll become a positive case study yourself.

Knowing Quality Is More Important than Quantity

Too many people on Twitter worry about numbers when they should be thinking about other things. For example, sometimes brands don't feel as if they're successful unless they have tens of thousands of followers. True, it's great to have such a large reach, but the truth is, a brand can't interact with all those people. By all means, strive for the big numbers, but don't obsess over them. Instead, worry about building up quality followers: the customers and members of your community who truly believe in the brand and will advocate for you online. Build a core follower base, and the rest will fall into place.

WARNING

You may also be tempted to follow thousands of people right off the bat so that they'll follow you in return. Before you do so, keep in mind that all these people are going to show up in your Twitter stream. Adding thousands of people is much easier than removing them.

Although nothing is wrong with following so many people, sometimes seeing what people are saying in your Twitter stream is hard because so many people are talking at once. Following so many friends can make it difficult to find the quality conversational tweets through all the links and spam. Also, if Twitter thinks that you're randomly and blindly following people, it will suspend your account pending investigation.

By all means, continue to add new followers, but do it slowly so that you know whom you're following and are better able to have a conversation.

You may also be wondering how many tweets you should send out on any given day. While it's true people don't want to see only you in their Twitter streams, it's also true that we can't give you a set-in-stone rule regarding the amount of tweets you should be sending out. Spontaneity is what leads to success, and if you're counting, planning, and scheduling tweets, you're going to lose a lot of the element of fun and surprise many successful brand accounts have. Do what feels right. If you're deep in conversation with others, you're going to be sending out more tweets than you would on a slow day. Also, if you're launching a new product, you're probably going to spend more time on social networks than you would on a normal day.

Finally, many brands and individuals are concerned about the number of links they share on a given day. Of course, you don't want to spam links all day; but again, it depends on the day and what you're sharing. Always do your best to add balance and have more conversational tweets than link tweets — you don't want to be known only for dropping links.

REMEMBER

Don't obsess over numbers. Succeeding on Twitter is more about tweeting quality information to quality people than about going overboard with followers or worrying about whether or not you tweeted enough in one day. Good, organic growth always trumps big numbers.

IN THIS CHAPTER

» Following and reaching out on Twitter

» Using Twitter etiquette

» Socializing on Twitter

Chapter 2
Using Twitter as a Networking Tool

The people who do nothing but drop links on Twitter are missing out on some amazing opportunities. That's because Twitter is not just a useful promotional tool but also an important networking tool.

Before the Internet, most people had to join professional organizations and attend networking events on a regular basis. While that's still the case now, all that in-person networking can be expensive. Many people who are just starting out in their fields can't afford to put out the money to attend a lot of events or join many professional groups.

The beauty of Twitter and other social networks is the capability to reach so many people without spending a lot of money. With millions of people on Twitter at any given time, you have ample opportunity to reach out and be reached out to. Make no mistake, Twitter may force you into brevity, but the opportunity to grow your professional network is there.

In this chapter, we take a look at how to use Twitter as a networking tool and a few best practices for making the most of your experience.

Finding the Right People to Follow

The first step in your Twitter marketing journey is to spend time with the people who make up your community and enjoy their company. To do that, you have to build up a follower base.

The best way to find followers on Twitter is search Twitter for the people who are most likely to support your brand. Here are some ideas for getting started:

- **See how many of your existing customers are online.** If you're already in business, you probably have a list of people with whom you do business. They may also be on social networks. Use your mailing lists to find people to follow on Twitter. Most business people now have their Twitter accounts on their business cards and email signatures. You can also use Twitter's search function.
- **Find your friends and followers from other social networks.** If you already have a Facebook, Google+, or brand page set up on one of the other social networks, see whether those same friends are on Twitter and give them a follow.
- **Follow other professionals you know from your respective space.** If you share tips or interact online with other professionals, follow them on Twitter, as well.
- **Use Twitter search to find people with similar jobs or brands to yours.** Use the search function located at the top of your Twitter page or Twitter app, or go to `http://twitter.com/search-home`. Search for similar brands and interests.
- **See who follows brands similar to yours.** When you find brands that do the same as or close to what you do, follow their followers.
- **Use your keywords in Twitter search.** Take the keywords you use to optimize your pages and search for them.

TIP

Starting a Twitter follower base is as easy as following someone first. Once you start following people, most will follow you in return.

WARNING

Be careful with randomly following dozens of people at once. Twitter has tools to detect a huge bulk following and can suspend your account pending further investigation. If Twitter checks your history and feels you're adding people only so they'll follow back so you can spam them, they'll close your account. Conversely, Twitter also prohibits mass unfollows. So if you're only following for the follows, and plan on unfollowing people after they follow your account, you might get banned.

Finding Out Who Is Talking about You on Twitter

Nothing is voyeuristic or wrong about observing conversations on Twitter. Most people who tweet are hoping others will notice and join the conversation. If they didn't want a public conversation, they'd send a direct message (DM) or use some other form of communication. They also wouldn't mention or @reply you unless they wanted you to know what they're saying. So if you see a complaint or @reply (see Figure 2-1), it's in your best interest to respond, even if it's just to say, "Thank you."

FIGURE 2-1: To get someone's attention on Twitter, use an @reply.

As a brand (personal or professional), you always want to keep your ear to the ground. With Twitter, you can easily monitor the conversation and respond to comments and queries.

Many times, if someone is talking about or to you, he will @reply you. This means that person is putting an @ in front of your Twitter screen name to get your attention. Without the @, there's a chance you won't see the tweet, unless you do a search on your name, your company name, or specific keywords. Also, if you're reaching out to someone, you have to put an @ in front of his screen name, or the tweet will get lost among the thousands of other tweets.

It's good customer service to find out what people are saying about you on Twitter. It gives you an opportunity to learn about problems or concerns and shows your customers and community you're accessible.

TIP

Make time each day to explore Twitter and see who is talking and what they're saying. Don't shy away from criticism or critique. Instead, thank the other party and take it as valuable feedback.

Responding to Tweets

To monitor the conversation so that you can find out whether people are tweeting about you or your brand, keep a Twitter app, such as Hootsuite, Sprout Social, or TweetDeck, open on your computer's desktop. You can set up these apps to ping you every time you receive an @reply or when someone posts a specific search term, including your name or that of your brand. (We cover apps in Chapter 3 of this minibook.)

You need to set up these searches to reach out or respond to the people who are talking about or to you. For example, if you work for a restaurant chain and someone tweets out a picture of one of your dishes and talks about how much she enjoyed her meal, you want to acknowledge the tweet by thanking the other party and encouraging her to visit again. If someone tweets that a meal was subpar, you want to respond with an apology and perhaps even offer a discount or coupon for another meal to make things right.

WARNING

Avoid public negativity at all costs. If people are saying negative things about you or your brand, do reach out to them publicly to ask if you can help, but also ask if you can take it private via phone, email, or IM so that you can discuss without feeling pressured to respond to the whole world. Be especially wary of trading barbs or disparaging remarks, or using rude language. This behavior can harm your brand beyond repair and lead to a public relations nightmare. A good rule of thumb is to never post anything online you wouldn't want to see on the front page of *The New York Times*.

TIP

When you @reply someone, the comment doesn't show up for the masses, only people with whom you're both friends. It's not a private conversation — anyone who is searching can find it — but it's not mainstream, either.

If you want everyone to see comments you make when you @reply people, put a period in front of it; now everyone can see it. For example, if you wanted everyone to see an @reply to Deb, it would read .@debng (see Figure 2-2).

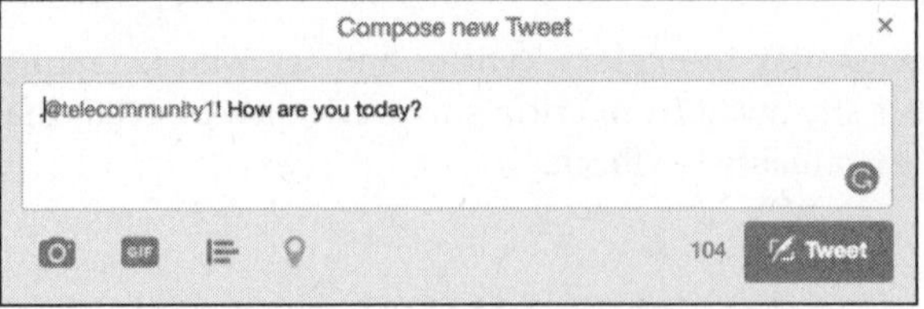

FIGURE 2-2: Put a period in front of an @reply if you want everyone who follows you to see it.

Searching on Twitter

Twitter is an excellent search tool. As discussed in the preceding section, you can use it to discover who is talking about you or your brand. However, you can use Twitter also as an awesome search engine to find people to follow or reach out to, to find similar brands, and to see what's going on with specific keywords, search terms, hashtags, and news items.

TIP

Traditionally, Twitter isn't considered to be a search engine, but that doesn't mean you can't treat it like one. If you're looking for something, anything, there's a very good chance you'll find it on Twitter.

What follows are some of the ways to use Twitter's search function or the search engine at `http://twitter.com/search-home` as a search tool. You can find the following:

» **People:** Search specific names, Twitter handles, professions, or hobbies. Don't forget to give them a follow so that you can connect.

» **Brands:** Use Twitter to search for similar brands to see how they're using the platform.

» **Clients:** Search terms will help you find potential clients. Also, consider the types of people you seek out offline to drum up business, and search for the same types of people online.

» **Jobs:** You can search for job-specific hashtags and keywords to find job openings on Twitter. Moreover, many job boards tweet out job opportunities.

» **Hashtags:** The Twitter search engines help you follow your favorite hashtags.

» **Search terms:** When you use a Twitter search for particular search terms and keywords, you'll find everyone who is talking about those words and phrases.

» **Your brand:** Discover what others are saying about your brand.

» **Your passion:** Search your favorite subjects.

» **News:** Whether you want to go local, international, or niche-oriented, you can search for the latest news on Twitter.

TIP

Take advantage of Twitter's trending topics: Discussions might be happening that can benefit you or your brand. Simply use the trending hashtag to ask questions or respond to people who are already chatting using that hashtag. Don't spam or get into hashtag jacking. Be sure to stay on topic if you're getting involved in a hashtag conversation, and avoid sharing links unless they're specifically requested.

TIP

Find trending hashtags at `https://twitter.com/search-home`. Also, when you log into Twitter, you'll also see trending topics and hashtags in the left sidebar.

Tweeting like a Pro

There's a difference in the way someone wanting to do business uses Twitter as opposed to a teen who only wants to tweet out to her friends. Just as you conduct yourself in a professional manner at offline networking events, you'll also want to conduct yourself as a professional on social networks. People really do pay attention.

Articulating in 140 characters

Text speak, using abbreviations and shortened words to shorten a cellphone text message, is difficult to read and unprofessional when used while representing your brand on any platform. Because Twitter allows for only 140 characters, you may be tempted to use abbreviations or shortened words to fit in everything you want to say, but we don't recommend it.

What follows are some tips for making every character count. (We provide more details in Chapter 1 of this minibook.)

- **Spell out every word.**
- **Use punctuation.**
- **Practice the art of brevity.**
- **Let your personality shine through.**

REMEMBER

Using social networks isn't a reason to forget you're a professional. When you're using your brand account, conduct yourself in the same manner in which you'd conduct yourself at an offline business event.

Using the hashtag

When you put a pound sign (#) in front of a keyword, you're using a *hashtag*. The hashtag makes it easy to follow a conversation centered on a keyword or topic. For example, if yours is a sausage brand and you want to create a recipe contest around your world-famous kielbasa, you might use #kielbasarecipes as your hashtag. The benefits to using a hashtag over an @reply abound:

- **Hashtags catch the attention of others.** Sometimes people aren't necessarily part of a conversation but join in after espying a catchy hashtag in their Twitter streams.
- **Hashtags add longevity to a conversation.** An @reply can die in a busy Twitter stream, but following the hashtag will allow you to view all tweets in a conversation at one time.
- **Hashtags allow tweets to appear in a stream even if the other party doesn't @reply you.** Often during Twitter chats or hashtag campaigns, participants in the conversation don't use an @reply to catch your attention but instead rely solely on the hashtag. When you view a hashtag chat using an app such as Hootsuite or TweetChat, you can better view the entire conversation at one time.
- **You can measure the results of a hashtag.** Several apps and services, such as Radian6 or Hashtracking, offer not only a transcript of a hashtag but also data from all the people who use the hashtag — for example, how many people viewed the hashtag (who didn't necessarily participate in the conversation), how many people clicked links, and which people are the most influential ones using the platform.

When you use hashtags, you can take your Twitter conversations to a new level. Hashtags allow you to have, keep track of, and measure a conversation, something important to anyone marketing a brand.

TIP

Be careful about sharing too many links or promotional tweets on someone else's hashtag, an activity called *hashtag jacking.* Hashtag jackers spam popular or trending hashtags to drive traffic to their own interests, and it's considered a serious breach of Twitter etiquette.

Please see Book 4, Chapter 5 to discover the benefits and best practices of hosting a hashtag chat.

Sharing on Twitter

The beauty of Twitter is how awesome a tool it is for sharing. The people who use Twitter love to discover new articles, videos, and people. They're quick to offer a recommendation or review, and they especially enjoy when you ask for their opinions. If they like what you say, they'll even give you a retweet.

Knowing when to @reply and direct message

For the most part, your responses to other tweeters will be public unless someone specifically reaches out to you via direct message (DM). Sometimes, though, you want to take public messages private because you don't want to expose some things to the entire Twittersphere:

- **Long conversations between you and someone else:** Yes, Twitter is all about public conversations, but you also don't want to clutter up your friends' Twitter streams with a long conversation you're having with someone else. For something expansive, you may want to offer to take it private.
- **Complaints:** If someone has a complaint about your brand or is reaching out in a negative manner, let him know you're sorry for the inconvenience and offer to take it to a phone call, email, or DM so that you can better handle the situation. You don't want to sweep the complaint under the rug, nor do you want to ignore it. However, you don't necessarily want to air all your brand's negativity to the masses, either.
- **Personal details:** It should go without saying that private email addresses, phone numbers, addresses, and other personal details shouldn't be available to the public. If you need to share this information or need to request that others share it with you, it's best to take it private.
- **Information that isn't meant for public consumption:** Sometimes there are details you'd like to share with people but can't put it out to the public yet. By all means, use a Twitter DM.
- **Something that may embarrass someone:** Perhaps a negative situation is the result of customer or client error. The last thing you want to do is shame that person on the social networks. If you need to talk to someone because of a potentially embarrassing error, take it private.

For the most part, your Twitter updates are public. However, use your best judgment. Every now and then, you may need to take things private. Something else to consider: In 2010, it was announced that tweets were going to be archived in the Library of Congress. Although this hasn't come into fruition as of this writing, it's something to think about when you're crafting tweets.

Retweeting and being retweeted

For many people on Twitter, getting retweeted is part of their marketing plan. It may not seem like much, but a retweet can go a long way. For example, if you tweet out a link to your latest blog post and someone else retweets it, more people are likely to view your blog post. The more retweets you get, the further your reach.

If you're on Twitter for any length of time, you may notice that certain famous tweeters and those with the most followers get retweets every time they post something. What follows are some tips for retweeting other people's tweets and also for writing the types of things people will want to retweet:

- **Say something people want to share.** If you're tweeting links to your food or talking about the weather, your content isn't very shareable. The type of content people share is usually funny, unique, profound, or interesting.
- **Share something others want to share.** Don't share for the sake of sharing; share because you think an item has interest or value. Before tweeting a quote or link, ask, "Will this interest my community enough that they want to share it with others?" Think about why you felt compelled to share it and whether your community will feel the same way.
- **Don't write for the retweet.** Usually tweets fall flat when people are trying hard to be clever or funny. Retweetable tweets are usually organic and spontaneous, not forced or flat.
- **Don't retweet just because someone famous said something.** Many people retweet well-known people in hopes of catching their attention. If you retweet celebrities all the time, it tells your community you don't care about them as much as you do famous people. If the Kardashians have nothing to do with you and your community, and the celebrities aren't saying anything all that great, save your retweet for someone more deserving.
- **Say "thank you" for retweets.** When people retweet something you said or share links to your blog posts, be sure to say "thank you." It shows them you appreciate the community effort.

WARNING

Avoid the *vanity retweet* — when someone tweets something nice about you and you retweet it. For example, if someone tweeted "@debng is the most brilliant blogger in the world" and I retweeted it, I'd look like a fool. Most people think a vanity retweet is bragging and roll their eyes at those who do it.

Blocking people

It's going to happen. Some people on Twitter are so abusive or spammy that you have no recourse but to ban them. First, don't feel guilty. We all have a list of blocked tweeters, even if we don't talk about them. Second, understand that no one has to put up with abuse.

What does it mean to *block* your tweets? Simply, it means the person you block shouldn't be able to see or respond to your tweets.

Here are some reasons you might want to block people from viewing your tweets or participating in your conversation:

- Every time they respond to a question or comment, it's with a link to a sales page.
- Every time you post, they respond with something snarky.
- Someone uses vulgarity and profanity on a regular basis, and that's not your thing.
- Someone is abusive to you and your followers.

TIP

If someone isn't being nice on Twitter, or if someone is using your conversations as an excuse to sell stuff or drive traffic to his site, go ahead and block that person. Your community will probably applaud you.

Creating a successful Twitter campaign

Your Twitter campaign takes careful planning. It's not enough to shoot out a tweet every now and then. You also want to put a strategy in place. If you don't go into it with a specific plan and goal, your tweets may be sporadic and haphazard, and you won't achieve the success you were hoping for.

Here are some tips for creating a successful Twitter campaign:

- **Plan a follower strategy.** Determine the types of people you want to follow and have follow you in return. Consider a mix of people who are customers, have the potential to be customers, and work in similar jobs, as well as brand accounts that may have a tie-in with your community. (For more on this topic, see the section "Finding the Right People to Follow," earlier in this chapter.)
- **Plan a content strategy.** Think about the types of tweets you want to post each day. Consider a mix of humor, news, questions, retweets, and a few promotional tweets with or without links.
- **Plan a hashtag strategy.** Hashtags can be a lot of fun. You can have a regular hashtag chat (see Book 4, Chapter 5 to learn more about hashtag chats) or use a hashtag in contests, news, and updates about your brand and more. Plan for at least a couple hashtag updates per day. (See the earlier "Using the hashtag" section for details.)

- **Don't make every tweet a sale.** Plan a balanced content strategy so that your tweets feature more than selling. Perhaps publish two links or sales for every ten tweets.
- **Don't make every tweet about your brand.** Share non–brand-related thoughts and ideas so as not to make everything about you.
- **Ask questions.** Ask questions not only about your products and services, but also about news items, trending topics, and topics geared toward individual members of your community.
- **Share other people's stuff.** Share links to blog posts, images, news articles, and videos by a variety of people.
- **With all that said, don't be afraid to share your own stuff.** There's no shame in sharing your own blog posts, news, and even links to sales and discounts. Again, it's all about balance.
- **Think outside the box.** Think about ways to reach your community on Twitter that are different from the same old, same old. Plan content or campaigns that few people are using. Research some unique ways brands are using Twitter, and then put your own spin on them. (For more on researching brands, see Chapter 1 of this minibook.)
- **Use Twitter with other platforms.** Plan content and campaigns that span the platforms. Use teaser tweets to draw attention to blog posts or Facebook content, for example. (For more on marketing with Facebook, see Book 5, Chapter 1.)
- **Call out your community.** If someone in your community has a milestone, offer public congratulations. Wish happy birthdays and anniversaries, and offer condolences or congratulations. Don't forget to use the @reply so that the other party knows you're offering good wishes.
- **Seek assistance.** If you have any technical questions or would like recommendations on the latest gadgets and gear, reach out to your community. Try to have at least one question per week because your community appreciates seeing your human side.
- **Create discount codes for your community.** Although you don't want to be spammy, offering perks to your community is a nice gesture. Why not create discount codes for only your Twitter members to thank them for their support? Try for at least one discount per month.

TIP

- **Be transparent.** Be honest with your community. If you're asked questions, don't tap dance around an issue or fudge numbers — it's sure to backfire on you.

Using keywords in your tweets

With 140 characters, you need to choose your words wisely, so we don't always recommend that you use keywords in your tweets. However, you can make your Twitter content more searchable by using keywords in some of your tweets. Your keywords should make sense and work in a sentence, and others should be searching for them online.

Try writing your keyword tweets ahead of time, playing with the words so that they make sense. If you're using keywords to make announcements, perhaps take an hour or two to write up a list of appropriate tweets. When you try to tweet keywords off the cuff, it often doesn't come out as intended.

To make your tweets even more searchable, use your keywords as hashtags. Using hashtags makes it easy to refer to them later to see who else is using them. A hashtag is different from a keyword; a hashtag is used to hold a conversation rather than make your tweet visible in a search.

WARNING

Don't use keywords for every tweet. If your community feels like you're using Twitter only to drive traffic or sell something, you're sure to lose followers.

Following the Twitter Rules of Etiquette

Like everything else online, Twitter has certain unwritten rules of behavior.

What follows is a list of accepted Twitter practices. Most of these items are common courtesy, and some are things that aren't as intuitive to new Twitter users. While most of these items won't get you booted off Twitter, not following certain rules of etiquette can cost you some followers:

- **Don't spam.** If a potential follower takes a peek at your Twitter stream and it's nothing but preprogrammed links, she's going to turn tail and run. If you post sales or traffic driving links all day, you're going to lose community. If you talk only about yourself, your brand, or your product, you'll never enjoy a good conversation. Balance your promotional tweets with conversational tweets.
- **Be positive.** There's a time and place for negativity, and Twitter usually isn't it. Avoid rants, profanity, and depressing woe-is-me type topics. If you're bringing down the mood of the community, they won't feel the love anymore and will unfollow.
- **Don't use all caps.** TYPING IN ALL CAPS IS CONSIDERED YELLING. It hurts the eyes, too. Avoid it at all costs.

- **Don't swear unless you're sure that your community isn't easily offended by profanity.** Some people don't mind a little cursing, but others do. If you're going to go the edgy route, make sure that your community is comfortable with it.
- **If you're joining a Twitter chat, let your community know.** When you participate in a Twitter chat, you generally have more tweets in your stream than usual. Give a tweet before beginning to let everyone know that you're joining a chat and will tweet more than normal for the next hour or so.
- **Don't feel you need to follow everyone who follows you.** Not everyone who follows you is a good fit. Don't feel compelled to follow everyone who follows you first. By the same token, don't be afraid to unfollow someone who doesn't sit well with you or your brand's message and tone.
- **Give credit where it's due.** If you're sharing a tip, quote, or link you saw someone else share, give that person credit. You don't want a reputation as someone who steals other people's thunder.
- **Don't hijack someone else's hashtag.** Don't use someone else's hashtag to promote your stuff. It's wrong and will turn off both old and new followers.
- **Don't respond to a tweet with a sales push.** If someone is reaching out to the community for assistance, don't respond with a link to something promotional. It makes you look insincere. Instead, reach out with genuine, helpful information.
- **Avoid private jokes.** If you can't share with everyone, don't share at all.

REMEMBER

When using Twitter, follow your best practices for business in the offline world. Sure, it's a more casual form of communication, but you're still looking to make a good impression.

Hosting a Tweet-Up

Enjoying Twitter? Feel like taking your show on the road? Why not grow your community offline with a tweet-up?

Tweet-ups are Twitter community get-togethers. You see them at many blogging, business, and social media conferences, though they're also held often in cities, as well. They don't take much effort to plan, they don't have to cost much money, and promoting them is as simple as getting everyone you know to tweet.

Many brands host tweet-ups to meet their community offline. They invite the people who follow them on Twitter to join them at a pub or restaurant to meet them face to face. Sometimes the brand buys a round of drinks or provides food, and other times it's up to individuals in attendance to provide their own refreshments. It's usually more about the people than what's being served.

Tweet-ups are easy to set up. Just follow these steps:

1. **Plan a time and place for your tweet-up.**
2. **Contact the venue in advance to make sure that it can accommodate a small gathering.**
3. **Start tweeting out the details of the tweet-up at least two weeks in advance.**
4. **Invite your community to share the details with their friends.**
5. **Show up at the designated date and time, and meet and greet your community.**

Tweet-ups can be low-maintenance gatherings, or you can invest money in putting on a full-fledged spread. Either way, your community will be happy to spend time with you.

IN THIS CHAPTER

» Personalizing your page

» Creating your profile

» Using Twitter apps

» Tweeting from your devices

Chapter 3

Finding the Right Twitter Tools

Twitter has evolved over the past few years to highlight users and their interests. Visitors to your Twitter home page now find an eye-catching header image that draws the attention to your avatar and bio. This setup is especially helpful for users who want to find people to follow who have common interests. The Twitter page now allows users to add personality and passion to their profiles.

Despite a striking header image, you don't have to spend all your time at Twitter.com itself. Tools and applications, or apps, enhance your experience and take your page from ho-hum to something that's intriguing, personal, and unique — and the best part is that you don't have to be on Twitter to use them.

In this chapter, we discuss the tools that can help make your Twitter experience even better, and we also suggest ways to take your Twitter profile page to a whole new level.

Customizing Your Twitter Profile Page

Don't overlook customizing your Twitter profile page. Otherwise, it's just a page with no personality, giving others no reason to follow you. You see, unless potential followers know you, they don't have much to go on. They'll want to click your profile page and know immediately whether you're worthy of a follow.

On your website, you take the time to create an About page that's representative of you and your brand (see Book 3, Chapter 2). Your Twitter profile page, shown in Figure 3-1, should be no different.

FIGURE 3-1: Your Twitter profile page offers little space to make a big impression.

The following elements make up your Twitter profile page:

- **Header photo:** A large background image that best represents you or your brand
- **Avatar:** A photo or logo that you feel best represents your brand
- **Bio:** A few lines telling who you are and what you do
- **URL:** A link to your blog or website
- **Location:** Where you're based

Your profile page also lists the number of people you follow and how many people follow you. These numbers tell people how popular your Twitter account is and can indicate whether you're a spammer.

WARNING

As we mention in Book 4, Chapter 2, following more people than you have followers is a sign of someone who uses auto-follow software, which is usually an indication that you're spammy or heavy into sales. People tend to stay away from those who don't organically grow their followers.

Your most recent tweets are also listed on your profile page. The number of recent tweets is important because it shows potential followers that your account is still active.

The following sections explain how to add a header photo and avatar to your Twitter profile page.

Creating a header photo

Generic Twitter pages are boring. By creating a custom header photo (see Figure 3-2), you're offering a better opportunity for potential followers, customers, and members of your community to find out more about you. A picture is worth a thousand words, right? You're also proving you're a real human being and not some spammy bot. People who make up accounts for the purpose of pushy selling or spamming don't take the time to create a custom header image because they know they'll probably be banned soon. Your background not only represents you as a brand, but it also tells folks you're legit.

FIGURE 3-2: A header photo can highlight personality and passion.

REMEMBER

Use the space in your Twitter header image to define your brand and entice people into wanting to learn more about you.

Before you create your header image, take a look around. Visit other people and brands to see how they're customizing their Twitter pages and get some ideas. If you're technically challenged and not sure that you can create the right type of header image, hire someone to put together something representative of you or your brand. If you're representing a personal brand — for example, if you're a freelancer — your photo should say something about you and your interests or expertise. If you're placing a header photo on a brand page, the image should be representative of your brand and customers.

Deciding what to include in your header

Consider putting these elements into your background image:

- **Your brand's logo:** Your logo doesn't have to be front and center, but incorporating it helps with brand recognition.
- **An image representative of your brand:** For example, if you work for a beer company, consider a frosty mug of one of your premium beers as a header image.
- **Your fans and community:** Showing how people who are passionate about the brand are using the brand is a great sales tactic.

Uploading a header image

After you create a header image, you're ready to upload to your Twitter page:

1. **Click your avatar in the upper-right corner of your Twitter profile page and click View Profile.**

   You see your profile page.

2. **Click the Edit Profile button, located below the position where your cover shot should be.**

   You see a camera icon over your profile and cover photo areas.

3. **Click the cover photo camera icon, and select the option to upload a new photo or remove an existing photo.**
4. **Click Save Changes.**

   You now have a custom Twitter header that shares information about you and your brand, and (you hope) reflects the message you're trying to share.

Creating a custom Twitter avatar

Your Twitter *avatar* is the small image next to your @name that your followers see every time you tweet. If yours is a personal brand, you may want to use an image showing your likeness. If you're managing a professional brand, consider using a logo for your avatar.

Uploading an avatar is simple. Just follow these steps:

1. **Click your small avatar in the upper-right corner of your profile page, and select View Profile.**

   You see your profile page.

2. **Select Edit Profile.**

   A camera icon appears over your profile photo.

3. **Click the camera icon, and choose to upload an avatar photo or remove an existing photo.**
4. **Click Save Changes.**

WARNING

Feel free to change your header to reflect the seasons or holidays, but make sure your avatar remains familiar to your community. If you change your avatar more than people change shoes, your brand isn't going to be very recognizable on Twitter.

Pinning Tweets

Did you tweet something especially important, amusing, or newsworthy? Is your brand currently running a promotion? Twitter now offers the ability to *pin* tweets to the top of your Twitter profile page so they remain there, even after you add other tweets. As Figure 3-3 illustrates, the pinned tweet stays at the top of your profile page, so it's the first thing people read when they access that page.

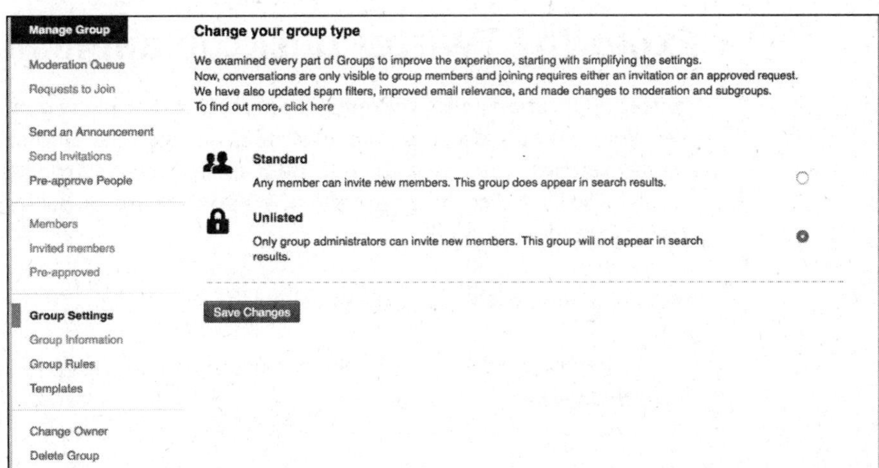

FIGURE 3-3: Pinning tweets keeps them at the top of your profile page.

To pin tweets, follow these steps:

1. **Open your profile page.**
2. **Select the tweet you want to highlight.**

   That tweet appears in its own page.
3. **Select the More option (which looks like an ellipsis).**
4. **Select Pin to Your Profile Page from the pop-up menu that appears.**

Keep in mind that if you have a tweet that is already pinned, you'll have to unpin it first. Twitter only allows you to pin one tweet at a time.

To unpin a tweet, follow the preceding steps, but choose the Unpin option in Step 4.

Using a Twitter Application

Twitter applications (or apps) help enhance your experience. They allow you to manage multiple accounts or see several different search terms or hashtags at a glance. They can also tell you whether you're using Twitter effectively and how well your followers are responding to your tweets, and even help you upload images to your account.

If you're looking to spend any amount of time on Twitter to market your brand and interact with your customers and community, a Twitter app is essential.

Exploring Twitter desktop applications

Twitter applications are programs and websites that allow you to do more things with your Twitter account. For example, an app like Hootsuite or TweetDeck enables you not only to see all your followers' tweets and the messages you tweet, but also to see direct messages and any search terms or hashtags you follow, all at the same glance.

Here are some Twitter apps to consider:

- **TweetChat (`http://tweetchat.com`):** Allows you to keep up with busy hashtag chats.

- **Hootsuite** (`http://hootsuite.com`) **and TweetDeck** (`www.tweetdeck.com`)**:** Enable you to see all your followers, as well as search terms and hashtags. You can also manage several different Twitter accounts at a time, follow and update your Facebook accounts, and even schedule your tweets. Hootsuite also offers a premium (paid version) where you can access reports and statistics.
- **Sprout Social** (`http://sproutsocial.com`)**:** A tool that allows you to handle multiple Twitter, Facebook, Google+, and other social accounts. In addition to scheduling tweets, Sprout Social offers insights and analytics so that you know how well your social media campaigns are working.
- **TweetCaster** (`http://tweetcaster.com`)**:** Manage multiple accounts from your smartphone.
- **Buffer** (`https://bufferapp.com`)**:** Schedule your tweets so you can have them go live at a specific time, even if you're not online.
- **Instagram** (`http://instagram.com`)**:** Although it's a separate social network on its own, the Instagram app on your smartphone can also post your photos to your Twitter account, if you're so inclined. (See Book 7, Chapter 3 to learn more about using Instagram.)

TIP

Literally thousands of Twitter apps are available. To find out more about Twitter apps, do a web search — you can find plenty of roundups of the available tools. Just be sure to check the date on the reviews because some of the tools from, say 2012, aren't available today, and many new ones have been added to the mix. Also, ask your friends and followers for recommendations. Everyone has favorites.

Tweeting from a gadget

Thankfully, we don't have to stay chained to our desks anymore. We can still market our brands online from the beach, grocery store, or coffee shop using our favorite gadgets. In fact, you can use some of the same apps for tweeting online to tweet from your devices.

You can download Hootsuite, Sprout Social, or TweetCaster for your iPhone or Android app, enabling you to manage several accounts at once and still follow keywords and hashtags.

Instagram, the popular photo-sharing app for smartphones, allows for sharing on Twitter, leading to more visual engagement with your community.

WARNING

What's important to remember is that thumb typing isn't an excuse for poor business practices. Some people feel that because they're not typing on a full-size keyboard, they have carte blanche to misspell words or use text speak, which isn't the case. These things are considered unprofessional no matter where you're tweeting from.

TIP

If you're marketing your brand, treat your mobile tweeting seriously, just as if you were working from your home or office computer. Don't just broadcast, engage. Because sending links from a full-size keyboard is easier, schedule these types of tweets if you'll be away from your desk for an extended period of time and use your mobile devices to have conversations with your followers.

Here are a few tips for tweeting from a mobile device or tablet:

- **Proofread.** People tend to make more typos from gadgets.
- **Set up notifications.** If you're away from your desk, your notifications will let you know whether people are engaging, and you can respond in kind. You can set your notifications up to make noise or just to send an email.
- **Install an app for easy tweeting.** Use a Twitter management app, such as Hootsuite, for mobile tweeting. You can use this app with your regular Twitter account and pull all your stats together.
- **Use an app that allows you to manage several different accounts at once.** If you have more than one Twitter account (for example, business and personal), find an app that will manage both accounts. This way, you don't have to do a lot of logging on and off.
- **Check back as often as you can.** We're not saying that you should tweet from a wedding or funeral, but if you're not in the middle of an important obligation, do check your mobile Twitter app several times a day to be sure you're not missing out on an engagement.

IN THIS CHAPTER

» Discovering what your customers are saying about you

» Selling by helping

Chapter 4 Social Listening with Twitter

Social media has opened up countless opportunities for businesses to connect with their customers. Social networks present brands with a valuable opportunity to hear what their customers are saying, providing an unprecedented peek into their lives. Using social media to monitor conversations is called *social listening,* and it's something all businesses should take advantage of daily.

In this chapter, we discuss the benefits of social listening, and how to use Twitter as a tool to monitor — and participate in — important conversations.

Using Twitter to Listen to Your Customers

These days, businesses can't sweep complaints under the rug. Before everyone was online, it was easy to ignore negativity. Nowadays, customers can take their complaints public, and if businesses aren't careful, those complaints can go viral.

Because so many people are on Twitter, it's one of the best places to go to hear what customers are saying. Before we get into the nitty-gritty of how to use social listening, let's first discuss some of the benefits. Here are some important reasons to use Twitter to monitor your customers' online conversations:

- **Gain insight into how customers feel about products and services.** You can search Twitter to learn who is talking about your products and services. By monitoring these conversations, you can discover how people are using your products, what type of experiences they're having, and what, if any, improvements need to be made.
- **Respond to customer questions.** Many customers find it easier to reach out on Twitter and ask 140-character questions than to commit to email. Sometimes, instead of reaching out to the brand, they'll ask other people about their experiences and whether they recommend using your brand. Monitoring these conversations allows you to listen in — and even participate.
- **Handle customer complaints.** Much to the chagrin of businesses everywhere, customers take their complaints online when they are disgruntled. Although no one ever wants to see her company associated with negativity, it's a chance to show off customer service skills and gain new customers as a result.
- **Grow your online community.** By monitoring conversations where people are discussing topics related to your brand, you can share wisdom, expertise, and product information, growing your online community and customer base in the process.
- **Gauge the effectiveness of your customer service.** By monitoring online conversations, you can see how your customer service teams are handling online inquiries. Moreover, you can also see what customers and potential customers are saying about them on Twitter.
- **See how campaigns are working.** One way to gauge how sales and marketing campaigns are working is to see how people are responding to them on Twitter. You can monitor to see what kind of buzz is happening and whether people are sharing.
- **Collect important demographic information.** Use Twitter to determine important information about your customers. For example, do the people who talk about your brand fall into a certain age group?
- **Track sentiment on a regular basis.** Start a spreadsheet and take note of sentiment for specific days, weeks, months, and years.
- **Learn your customers' frequently asked questions about your company.** Knowing what your customers are asking helps you to shape your campaigns, content, and business.

- **Note competitors.** Monitoring Twitter chatter is a good way to gauge the popularity of competitors, how their campaigns are working, how they interact with their customers online, and online sentiment towards their brands.
- **Meet potential brand advocates.** As your brand and Twitter account gain in popularity, you'll notice a few diehard fans. These are your brand advocates. When you communicate and share discounts with them, they'll continue to sing your praises online.
- **Improve upon products and services.** Because people like to air grievances on Twitter, you can use social listening as a way to gather information and use it to make your products and services even better.

Twitter gives you a wonderful opportunity to move beyond customer service 800 lines and online support tickets. Many of today's customers don't have the patience to navigate a phone menu or wait for someone to respond to an email complaint. In fact, they might feel Twitter is the best avenue to get a response because they know businesses don't want to see online negativity.

TIP

The best way to monitor Twitter conversations is with Twitter tools and third-party apps. Using apps such as Hootsuite or TweetDeck enables you to set up different columns for different search terms so you can see all your information at a glance. To learn more about Twitter tools, please see Book 4, Chapter 3.

Here are some searches to consider:

- **Your brand name:** Always search for conversations centered on the name of your company. If several brands are under your company's umbrella, search for all those names as well.
- **Searches related to your brands product or service:** For example, if yours is a cereal brand, you might want to search for *nutrition, breakfast,* and *recipes.*
- **The keywords people use to search for your brand, product, or service:** When people land on your website, what search terms are they using? Use these words and phrases when you search on Twitter. They might not necessarily be talking about your stuff, but you might find a good conversation starter and attract new people to the brand.
- **Your competitors:** It's always a good idea to see what people are saying about your competitors, what your competitors are sharing, and what new products they're introducing.

» **Related searches that aren't necessarily brand specific:** Sometimes you can grow your online community by searching outside the box. For example, if you work for an umbrella brand, you can do obvious searches for *umbrellas* and *rain,* but also look to see what people are saying when they talk about *weather, sunshine,* and even *vacations.* (No one likes to be stuck in the rain unprepared while on vacation!)

After you begin searching, it's time to take notes and take action. For example, if people are mentioning an aspect of an item that frustrates them, you can pass the information on to your design department so they can make the necessary changes. Also, if you see people complaining about not receiving an item or being charged the wrong price, you can delegate to the customer service department so they can reach out and rectify the situation.

REMEMBER

Many of the people who complain on social media are hoping to catch a brand's attention. Use that moment to do the right thing so you can turn a disgruntled customer into a long-term advocate.

Responding to questions and complaints

It's not enough to monitor and listen to Twitter conversations. It's also important to respond. How and when you respond can make all the difference in the world. You'll find that if you're kind and responsive, you'll not only help one customer but also show others you care about the people who buy your products and services. People appreciate good customer service, and it gives them confidence in the brand. Thus, a public customer service strategy helps the customer in need while giving your brand a positive image in potential customers' minds.

However, responding to customers doesn't necessarily mean the public has to be privy to every conversation a brand has with people online. It's also important to know when to take it private. A 140-character tweet is not enough to solve most problems or give in-depth responses to questions. With that in mind, let's now explore some best practices for responding to questions and complaints on Twitter:

» **If you can help in 140 characters, by all means, do so.** Brevity is fine, but people prefer to have problems handled properly, character count be damned. It's fine to answer general questions in a tweet if you're able to do so. You can even break your answers down into several tweets — as long as it doesn't become too convoluted and difficult to read. However, if a question or complaint requires more than a brief answer, find a platform that enables you to use more words.

- **Use a name when you can.** If you can determine a first name from a Twitter account, it's good practice to use it. Using a first name makes the response personal instead of looking like a canned response.
- **Be kind and respectful.** When responding online, it's always a good idea to remember you're representing your brand. Anything perceived as being uncaring or unkind is a reflection on your brand.
- **When possible, take it private.** A private message on Twitter can be as long or short as you'd like. Nothing is wrong with responding to a comment or question with "Hi, John. Let's take this to DM so I can give your answer the attention it deserves." When you're private, you can even ask for a phone number so you can resolve the issue voice to voice.
- **You don't have to handle it all on Twitter.** Although the conversation starts on Twitter, it doesn't have to end on Twitter. A tweet is a good starting point, but you can also use private message, email, phone, Skype, or another platform that's convenient for both of you.
- **Never share private information on Twitter.** Never ask for information such as a phone number or address on Twitter. Save the personal details for a private message, a phone call, or communication on another platform that isn't available for public consumption.
- **Don't leave people hanging.** If someone reaches out to your brand's Twitter account with a question or customer service issue, respond as soon as possible. Many brands with a strict Twitter policy like to respond within an hour. When you don't respond promptly, it sends a negative message. Even responding by writing "I'm looking into that" is better than nothing.
- **Do your best to avoid online negativity:** Back and forth, tit for tat negativity can harm a brand's image. It's better to take the high road during an angry conversation than say something that can cause a loss of sales — or even your job.
- **Don't ignore legitimate negative feedback.** Many times, negativity comes with truth. Always hear what people are saying. If people are angry, let them know you heard them and invite them to converse privately so you can rectify the issue. If they respond with abuse, move on. If there's a legitimate issue, do your best to clear it up so the negativity doesn't continue.
- **Always follow up.** If you help one of your Twitter customers, a good practice is to follow up in the next few days to see if everything is now rectified. Your customers will appreciate the additional care.

TIP

Collect positive tweets and use them for testimonials. Share them on your website and promotional materials to inspire others to get behind your brand.

TIP

Turn on the Receive DM's from Anybody option so people don't necessarily have to follow you to send you a direct message. Here's how to do so:

1. **Click your profile photo in the upper-right corner, and choose Settings from the drop-down menu.**
2. **Select Privacy and Security.**
3. **Scroll down until you see the Privacy section. Choose Receive Direct Messages from Anyone, next to the Direct Messages option.**
4. **Scroll to the bottom and click the Save Changes button.**

Gaining new customers by being helpful

The beautiful thing about Twitter is how you can use it to bring in new customers without even using a sales pitch. All you have to do is be helpful.

When you're making your rounds monitoring the conversation, don't look only for people who are asking questions or talking about your brand. Note what people are saying about the brand and respond in a helpful manner. You can have conversations that have nothing at all to do with your business.

It doesn't matter if someone is reaching out to your brand specifically. When people ask a question publicly on Twitter, they're inviting responses from anyone who is available for conversation.

For example, say the social media manager for a rainwear company is making the rounds on Twitter. While looking at the different conversations, she notices someone asking what the weather will be like. This is a great opening for a raingear company. The social media manager can respond with a weather report. If there's room, she can also tweet, "I know where you can get a great raincoat if you need one!" Here's another example: A company selling cold-weather gear notices a certain area is going to receive a significant amount of snow. The social media manager can send a tweet reminding people snow is coming and offer a discount code for snow boots.

TIP

Using Twitter for customer service involve more than answering questions and complaints. Look for opportunities to be helpful as well. Doing so leaves a favorable impression of your company, which means people are more likely to use your product or service when there's a need.

IN THIS CHAPTER

» Reaping the benefits of Twitter chats

» Creating a hashtag

» Using Twitter chat tools

» Promoting and hosting a Twitter chat

Chapter 5
Hosting Twitter Chats

Twitter chats are a way for people with similar interests to come together and discuss relevant information regularly. Generally, Twitter chats happen at consistent intervals (usually weekly). Twitter chats, when done well, are an excellent way to build and maintain community.

This chapter helps you determine whether a Twitter chat matches your business goals and needs, explains how to choose the best hashtag for your chat, and introduces you to tools to help you manage your chats effectively. If you're concerned that no one will show up to the chat, don't worry: We also share some ideas about where to find guests and how to promote your chat so that more people will come (and tell their friends). Finally, we give you a complete step-by-step run-through of how to host a Twitter chat.

Benefiting from Twitter Chats

Many brands are hosting Twitter chats as a way to connect with their communities. Hosted regularly, usually once per week, Twitter chats enable a brand to discuss issues everyone in the community has to deal with, and share tips and ideas.

Twitter chats have many benefits:

- **Create brand awareness.** When you have an engaging presence on Twitter, people remember you.
- **Get people talking about you.** Your hashtag will get people noticing what you're talking about. Moreover, if your community has a good time at your regular chat, they'll share with others.
- **Help others learn about your community.** Twitter chats enable you to interview guests or pose questions to your community. This way, you find out about their likes, dislikes, and needs, even if you aren't directly surveying them about a product or service.
- **Allow a conversation among like-minded people.** Suppose you're a real estate professional and host a Twitter chat to share tips and ideas and discuss issues pertaining to real estate professionals. You're not only establishing your name and expertise but also allowing those in your profession to rally around a specific topic.
- **Grow your follower base.** When people participate in a Twitter chat, the hashtag shows up in their Twitter streams, which attracts the attention of others who might also follow your brand and participate.
- **Provide valuable networking opportunities.** Through your Twitter chats, you can meet other professionals, customers, clients, collaborators, and friends.

Hosting a regular Twitter chat is a commitment because you have to provide value every week at a designated date and time, so don't enter into them lightly. First, try having a Twitter party, a one-off hashtag chat to see whether there's interest on both ends. If you enjoy the experience and have a decent turnout, you can then determine whether continuing the effort will be worthwhile.

Finding a Hashtag for Your Chat

The hashtag, the most important part of the Twitter chat, appears next to each and every post and on all promotional tweets, blog posts, and Facebook updates. Everyone who participates in the chat will use the hashtag, which means it has the opportunity to be viewed by millions. Take your time and determine the best hashtag for your chat.

Don't go overboard trying to figure out something hip. If you overthink your hashtag, you'll fall short. The most popular Twitter chats use obvious hashtags. For example, #blogchat is a chat about bloggers and #speakchat is a chat for public speakers.

You also want your hashtag to reflect your niche or your brand. For example, if yours is a soap manufacturer, do you want your hashtag to be #soapchat or #suds-chat, or would you rather it was #JoesSoapChat? Be careful, though. Although it's a good thing to throw in branding, a long hashtag takes up precious character space.

TIP

By the way, in case you haven't noticed, make sure the word *chat* is attached to the end of your hashtag so that folks on Twitter know a chat is in session (see Figure 5-1). The first part of the hashtag (before *chat*) usually stands for the name of the brand or the topic of the chat.

FIGURE 5-1: Attach *chat* to the end of your hashtag word.

Keeping Track of Who Says What

If a lot of people are participating, your Twitter chat will go by fast. You won't just be interviewing a guest; everyone who participates will be talking at once. All this conversation can be a lot to keep up with, and your usual Twitter app won't do.

Some tools can help make your Twitter chat experience work a little better. For example, the TweetChat platform, shown in Figure 5-2, enables you to view only the tweets for one particular hashtag at a time so that all the other conversations on Twitter don't get caught up in a confusing stream. TweetChat also allows you to respond and retweet to everyone who is taking part.

TIP

A platform such as TweetChat is much more manageable than Hootsuite because TweetChat updates more quickly and shares every tweet by those using the hashtag. You can also set it to refresh every five seconds or slow it down so that tweets appear a bit more slowly.

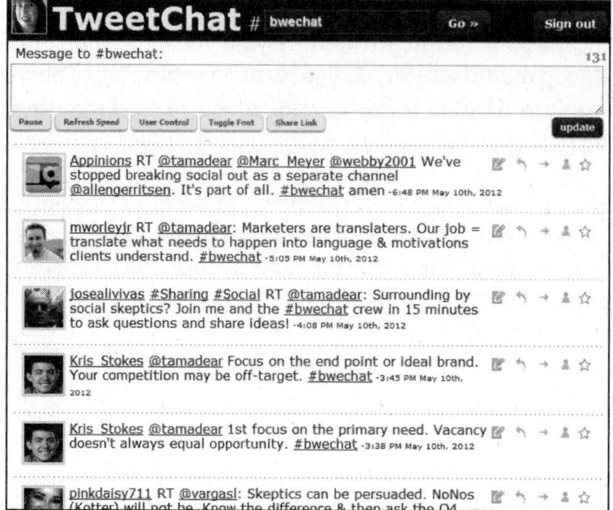

FIGURE 5-2: A Twitter chat management platform, such as TweetChat, can help you follow a busy chat.

WARNING

Not all of your followers will enjoy watching you participate in a Twitter chat, especially if you're a prolific chatter. Although most people gain followers after a Twitter chat, you may also find you lost a few regular followers because you're taking up too much of their Twitter stream. It's customary to let your followers know that you'll be participating in a Twitter chat for the next hour and apologize in advance for excessive tweeting.

Another important Twitter chat tool is Hashtracking, shown in Figure 5-3. With Hashtracking, you can generate a transcript of the chat to share with other. Plus, you receive statistics for each chat so that you know how many people participated, who the most influential people were in the chat, and how many people you reached through the chat.

TIP

Before hosting your Twitter chat, take some time to research the best tools for your needs. They'll make a world of difference.

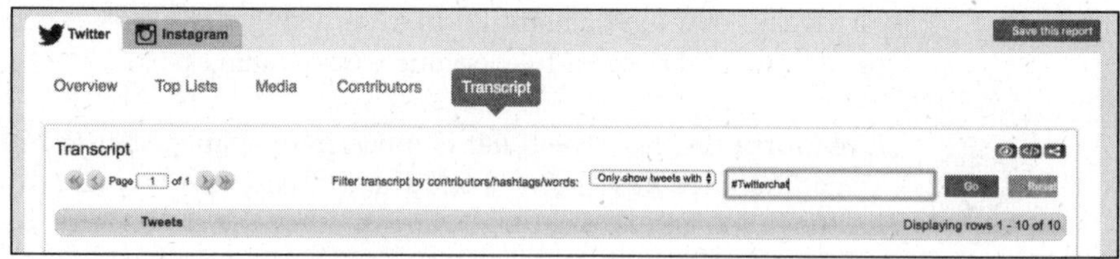

FIGURE 5-3: Use a transcript tool to share the chat with members of your community who can't make the chat.

Finding Guests for Your Twitter Chat

Twitter chats can take on a couple of different formats. You can host a town-hall type format where it's just you and your community, or you can invite special guests to participate. We get into how to host both types of chats in the section "Hosting Your Twitter Chat," later in this chapter. For now, we focus on how to find guests for your chat.

The beautiful thing about the online social media world is how many people fancy themselves experts and have something to promote. Authors, bloggers, independent musicians, online talk show hosts, podcasters, and a variety of professionals are interested in sharing their knowledge online. What follows are some ways to find these people:

- **Social networks:** The people you follow on social networks and those who follow you have interest in your topic. How many of them are experts or have something to share or promote to your community? Many times, you don't have to look further than the friends, followers, customers, and brands who are sharing with you online.
- **Public-speaking networks:** Speakers love to share their expertise both online and offline. Many of them are happy to participate in Twitter chats.
- **Publishing companies:** Book publishers want their authors to succeed. See who has anyone of interest. Many times, if you follow publishers on Twitter or Facebook, you can discover which authors they're promoting. See who is a good fit.
- **Brand pages:** Similar brands also have experts who like to share. Don't be afraid to reach out — it can be the start of a beautiful collaboration.
- **Colleges:** Teachers and professors are a gold mine of information and enjoy sharing with others. Invite them to take part in your Twitter chats.
- **Web searches:** Search Google or Yahoo! to find the movers and shakers in your world and invite them to chat.
- **Crowdsourcing:** Ask your community members who they'd like to see as a #chat guest.

When you interview people or invite them to participate in a community project, it's always a good idea to let them know what's in it for them. If you can present your chat as something of value, they're less likely to say no. Here are some of the ways to sell a Twitter chat:

- **Visibility:** Let your guests know that your community has great reach. Each person who participates in your chat has the ability to reach hundreds of people, depending on the number of followers. If you estimate all your participants by the number of people who follow each, the number of people who view the hashtag can number in the thousands — the bigger chats average millions of views.

- **Promotion:** Let guests know that you'll allow time at the end of the chat for them to plug books, products, services, and so on. Sometimes your guests may even have special discounts or offers for your Twitter chat community.
- **Stats:** If you use a service such as Hashtracking to put together your Twitter chat stats, share some of these stats with potential guests so that they can see the value. Let them know the average number of participants, the reach, and how many new followers you gain after each track.
- **Influential participants:** Every niche has its influential members. If you have influential regular participants, do share this information with your guests. But don't look like you're name-dropping because that can be a turnoff.

If you can't find a guest for a particular week's chat, don't sweat it. You can find plenty of things to talk about with your community. Sometimes the community-driven chats are livelier than those involving guests.

Controversy can attract negativity. If you're bringing in a guest with controversial views or an infamous reputation, be prepared for some people to tweet negative comments. Sometimes a controversial chat can erupt into a free-for-all of bashing, such as what happened when author E.L. James hosted a Twitter chat to promote her new book.

Promoting Your Twitter Chat

Twitter chats are easy to market and promote. If you have a network and a platform, you have the ability to tell people about your chat:

- **Blog:** Use your blog to announce each Twitter chat. Touch on the discussion topic and announce any special guests. Be sure to link to your guest's blog, website, or Twitter account, which will catch her attention and encourage her to share the link with her own community.
- **Twitter:** Announce your chat at least once or twice per day. Although you're limited in characters, try to name the topic and guest, and don't forget the hashtag, as shown in Figure 5-4.
- **Facebook:** Try announcing the time, hashtag, and date at least once per day.

- **Google+:** Share with everyone in your circles.
- **LinkedIn:** Career-oriented chats are especially of interest to the folks on LinkedIn.
- **Your community:** Ask your community to help spread the word. Don't spam them, but do say "please share" when tweeting, blogging, or putting it out on the other social networks.
- **Your guests:** Ask your guests to help promote the event to their communities.
- **A community calendar:** Create a shareable calendar listing all the #chat dates, topics, and guests. Plan at least a month in advance.

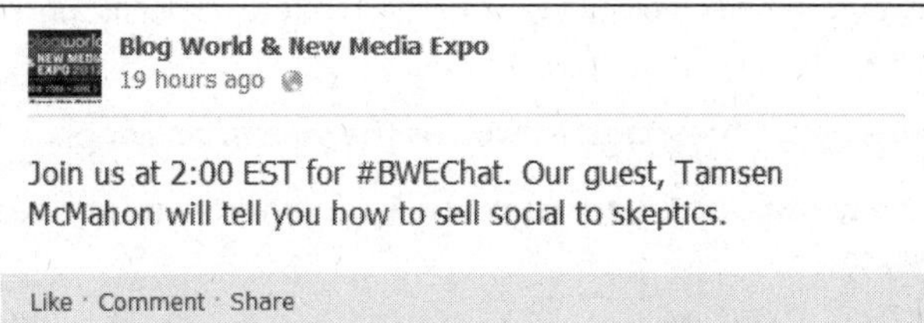

Blog World & New Media Expo
19 hours ago
Join us at 2:00 EST for #BWEChat. Our guest, Tamsen McMahon will tell you how to sell social to skeptics.
Like · Comment · Share

FIGURE 5-4: Promote your chat on social networks.

Promote your Twitter chat in the same way you promote your business. Share it with your community without being pushy, smarmy, or spammy. Invite them to participate and share with their communities.

REMEMBER

You're not going to get the same interest in every topic every week, but you'll find that you do have at least a few loyal community members who show up each time. Use participation to gauge the types of things your Twitter community enjoys talking about.

Hosting Your Twitter Chat

Most Twitter chats follow the same format. The host asks questions, the guests and community respond, and conversation ensues. However, put forth in that manner, chaos will also ensue. That's why Twitter chat hosts follow a numbered format for questions and answers. Twitter chats can be fast and busy. If they're not organized, no one will be able to follow the chat, and you won't gain a very strong community of participants.

Try following this format for hour-long Twitter chats:

1. **Welcome community members to your chat and invite them all to share a little about themselves.**

   Allow about three to five minutes for this.

2. **Introduce the format.**

   For most Twitter chats, each question will be prefaced with a `Q1` for Question 1 (see Figure 5-5). Those who answer the question will respond A1 for Answer 1. This way, there's no mistake about which questions are being answered because some people come late but start at the beginning.

   TIP

   When questioning your guest, always @reply the guest's name — for example, *@debng, Q1. What is your favorite ice-cream flavor?* If you have no guests, don't worry about the @reply unless you reach out to a specific person. (Refer to Figure 5-5.)

3. **Retweet your questions, as well as the guests' answers.**
4. **See what responses your community is sharing and retweet the best of those, too.**
5. **After about 10 or 15 minutes, ask the next question.**

   Most hosts share four to six questions. Just time them accordingly so that you have enough space for responding.

6. **(Optional) Save the last ten minutes for the community to ask the guests questions.**
7. **Three minutes before the hour is up, thank your guests and ask them whether they have anything to plug or promote.**
8. **End the chat with any announcement you need to make, including the next week's guests.**

FIGURE 5-5: Following a numbered format will help keep your chat more organized.

TIP

Don't be afraid to ask questions of your community when you see an opportunity during the discussion. If you'd like for people to expand upon their answers or to keep the chat flowing between numbered questions, it's fine to throw out some non-numbered questions for your participants.

Here's a bonus tip for you: If you're intrigued by the idea of starting your own Twitter chat, check out some of these popular chats to see how they're handled:

- **#BlogChat:** For bloggers; hosted every Sunday at 9 p.m. EST.
- **#CMWorld:** Devoted to content marketing; every Tuesday at noon EST. Although most brands use *chat* in their Twitter chat hashtags, Content Marketing World chose not to for consistency.
- **#MMChat:** For marketers; Monday at 8 p.m. EST.
- **#BrandChat:** About digital marketing and promotion; Wednesdays at 11:00 a.m. CT.

5 Facebook

Contents at a Glance

CHAPTER 1: **Using Facebook as a Marketing Tool** 339
Understanding the Appeal of Brands on Facebook 340
Branding with Facebook Pages 341
Examining the Components of a Facebook Page 342
Making the Most of Your Facebook Page. 345
Understanding Your Facebook Administrative Functions 348
Filling Out What You're About 349
Using a Custom URL for Your Page. 350
Inviting People to Join Your Community 351
Liking Other Brands 353
Creating Facebook Events 354

CHAPTER 2: **Creating and Sharing Content on Facebook** 357
Creating a Facebook Content Strategy. 358
Sharing Your Brand's Story 359
Creating Content That Sings 361
Sharing and Being Shared 362
Bringing Your Community into the Mix 365
Using Closed or Secret Groups 368
Learning through Insights 370

CHAPTER 3: **Advertising on Facebook** 373
Reaching More Fans with Ads 374
Measuring Your Ad's ROI 379

CHAPTER 4: **Streaming Live Video on Facebook** 381
Understanding the Benefits of Live Streaming 382
Setting Up Your Live Stream 384
Engaging with Your Community via Facebook Live 388
Brainstorming Ideas for Live Videos. 389

IN THIS CHAPTER

» Using Facebook pages

» Setting up your Facebook presence

» Making the most of likes

» Using Facebook events

Chapter 1
Using Facebook as a Marketing Tool

Facebook is the world's most popular social network, where people of all ages, professions, and backgrounds gather to stay in touch and share cute cat photos with friends, present and former colleagues, old classmates, and family.

Having millions of people gathered in one place is the perfect opportunity for any brand to raise awareness and grow a community of customers and advocates. If you're not on Facebook already, you're missing out on a huge opportunity. Simply put, Facebook is where the people are — and you have to be where the people are if you want to succeed in business.

In this chapter, we explore how Facebook pages work and how you can make them work for your brand.

TIP

For more in-depth coverage, find a copy of Facebook Marketing *All-in-One For Dummies*, 3rd Edition by Andrea Vahl, John Haydon, and Jan Zimmerman (Wiley).

Understanding the Appeal of Brands on Facebook

People who *like*, or give a thumbs-up to, a brand on Facebook are more likely to buy from that brand. *But they're not liking you to buy from you.* They're liking you to find out more about you and to receive updates and news regarding products and services. They may have had a positive experience with the brand and want to engage more. In any event, it's important to know why people are so willing to like a business on a social network.

Everyone knows plenty of people who like brands on Facebook. Friends and family come to Facebook each day to enjoy the company of others, but not necessarily to engage in a lot of deep reading or thinking. So why are people following brands on Facebook? Here are several reasons:

- **They are seeking a discount.** The majority of people liking your brand's Facebook page are hoping to receive some sort of benefit. This doesn't mean you have to give discounts and freebies every day, but if people know at some point they'll receive coupons, codes, or other perks, they're more likely to sign up and remain active members of your Facebook community.
- **They are looking for updates and news.** Fans follow television shows, bands and musicians, and other forms of entertainment to learn about showtimes and dates, new releases, and more.
- **They want to interacting with like-minded people.** People enjoy following local businesses, news stations, politicians, movies, television shows, and other businesses on Facebook to talk about those things with other enthusiasts.
- **Their friends are doing it.** When someone likes, shares, or comments on a brand's Facebook page, many of that person's friends will see that action. The power of suggestion can lead others to like a brand page, if only because they know other friends are fans, as well.
- **They are following a recommendation.** When people feel good about a brand, they leave positive comments on their timelines and tell their friends, hoping that the friends then enjoy the same positive experience. If their friends also enjoy the experience, those friends in turn invite their friends and family, and so on.
- **They want to express their loyalty.** Customers who enjoy the brand offline often seek out the brand to enjoy online. In addition to receiving freebies or updates, they're mostly interested in showing support to a name they believe in.
- **They are seeking entertainment.** If your content is stale with only the occasional business-like updates, you're not going to keep your Facebook fans.

However, if your content is entertaining and fun, and keeps folks coming back to see what you're going to talk about each day, your community will continue to grow.

- **They have a question.** Your community has many questions, but they may not want to call a customer service line and wait on hold. Being able to reach out via Facebook gives people a way to connect without having to invest a lot of time.
- **They want to give feedback.** Many people follow a brand on Facebook so they can leave feedback regarding a product, service, or experience.

REMEMBER

Many people who like your Facebook page won't interact further on it. They'll read your updates on their news feeds and may even take advantage of discount codes or calls to action, but they won't comment or communicate. That's fine; marketing to the silent members of your community is still important.

If your brand's Facebook page is engaging and the person running it is funny, knowledgeable, and patient, your Facebook community will evolve into something wonderful. Some followers will comment on posts, others will vote in polls — and, yes, a number of folks will buy when you have sales or offer discounts.

WARNING

Although this chapter explores all the ways a brand can benefit from using Facebook to reach its customers, remember that Facebook is continuously evolving and changing its algorithm. It's not as easy for brands to reach their Facebook fans as it used to be, and social media marketers are encouraged to stay on top of Facebook updates and changes. If you don't keep apprised of Facebook news, your brand can be penalized for not following specific rules or understanding how specific changes will reflect on the brand's Facebook page. Also, you may not receive as much traffic to your page if you don't know how the latest algorithm works. This is why it's important keep apprised of Facebook news and updates. Checking the Facebook section of Google News (under Technology) will alert you to any changes and recommendations for handling said changes.

Branding with Facebook Pages

You may think you know Facebook pretty well because you have a personal account, but Facebook pages for brands (formerly called *fan pages*) and your Facebook profile have major differences. Facebook pages have to follow specific rules to avoid coming across as overly spammy. For example, you have to follow specific guidelines for selling or running contests. (For more on these guidelines, see Chapter 2 in this minibook.)

The purpose of the Facebook page is simple: to promote a brand. The goal of most brands is to have as many individuals like them as possible to best get their message to the masses. Some brands (such as Coca-Cola, with more than 100 million followers) can reach more people with one Facebook update than with a television commercial — and it's cheaper, too. So a major brand's goal is to make its Facebook page as interactive as possible to get those likes.

After your brand has accumulated fans and followers, a variety of interactions can occur. A representative of the brand posts an update in hopes of getting as many likes, comments, and shares on that post as possible. When people like or comment on a public post, or share a status update or an image, their friends can see that action, which means it's exposed to even more people.

If a brand's update gets liked or shared or both by hundreds of thousands of people, it has the potential to be seen by millions of people. This visibility leads to higher brand recognition, even if the people who viewed the update didn't share it in return. You want as many people as possible to at least know about your brand on Facebook.

TIP

If your page is truly interactive and offers some cool perks, your community will be inspired to invite others to like the brand, as well. So another purpose of the Facebook page is to create a community of brand advocates and word-of-mouth marketers.

REMEMBER

Facebook pages are a way to humanize your brand and make you seem more real to your customers or community. If you take the time to answer inquiries, post updates, and make them feel as if they're part of the brand, too, your fans will put their faith and trust into you and are more likely to support your efforts.

Brands are taking advantage of Facebook pages because they're a way to reach people honestly and effectively. The most successful brands on Facebook aren't shouting "Buy Me!" or posting only product updates. They're having conversations with their communities, and it's working.

Examining the Components of a Facebook Page

A Facebook page has several components, which you'll want to be familiar with before launching your own page:

- **Profile photo:** Most brands use this space to post their logo or something that's regularly associated with the brand. Your profile photo isn't the biggest photo on your page, but it's visible at eye level for whoever visits your page. (See Figure 1-1.)

Make sure that you properly prepare your graphic so it doesn't end up distorted when Facebook places the image into its presized box. Facebook recommends the image be at least 180 pixels wide.

FIGURE 1-1: Use your brand's logo for the profile photo.

- **Cover photo:** The biggest photo on your page, this cover photo can be a touching, amusing, or scenic image that best represents your brand and what it stands for.
- **About:** Includes your company's message, mission statement, or a brief bio of who you are and what you do. Your About page should be compelling and written in an engaging style. For more on your About page, see the section "Filling Out What You're About," later in this chapter.
- **Contact info:** This section, found on the About page, should list all the ways people can get in touch with you. At the very least, it should include email addresses where your community can offer feedback. You should also include your Twitter handle, blog, or website.
- **Visitor posts:** Posts to the brand page by others in your online community. You can delete posts if they're inappropriate, highlight them if they're something you feel everyone should see, or disable this feature so that no one else is publishing to your page. If you do nothing, posts by others will remain in a small, out-of-the-way area, in the sidebar.
- **Liked by this page:** Brand pages that your brand's page follows in order to show support to another brand.
- **Settings page:** Your Settings page (see Figure 1-2) is also your admin panel and is where you discover how many new likes you have each week, how many people are sharing on your page, what countries people are visiting from, and more. From your Admin panel, you can learn about your community, and you can also update the content and design of your Facebook page.

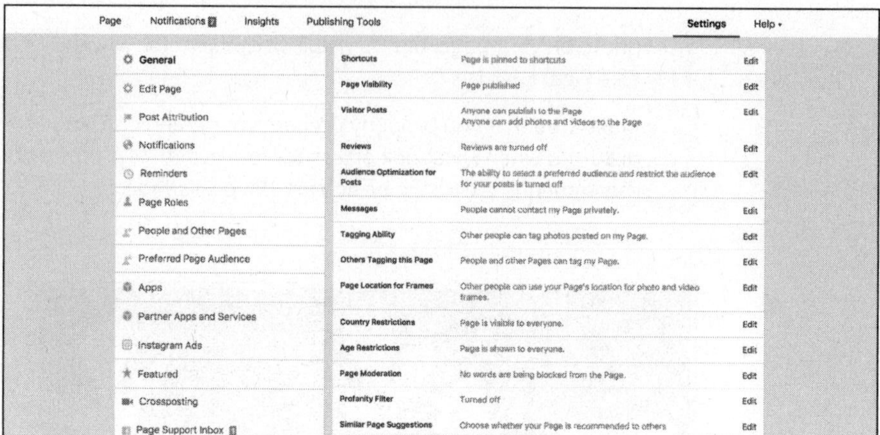

FIGURE 1-2: Your Setting page is your Facebook toolbox.

» **Timeline:** Your brand's public-facing Facebook page, shown in Figure 1-3, is where you post content.

» **Pinned posts:** Posts you want to keep front and center on your timeline.

» **Tabs:** Extras your community can click to engage with the brand. Polls, quizzes, photo albums, video, as well as hundreds of apps and other fun items are accessed through tabs.

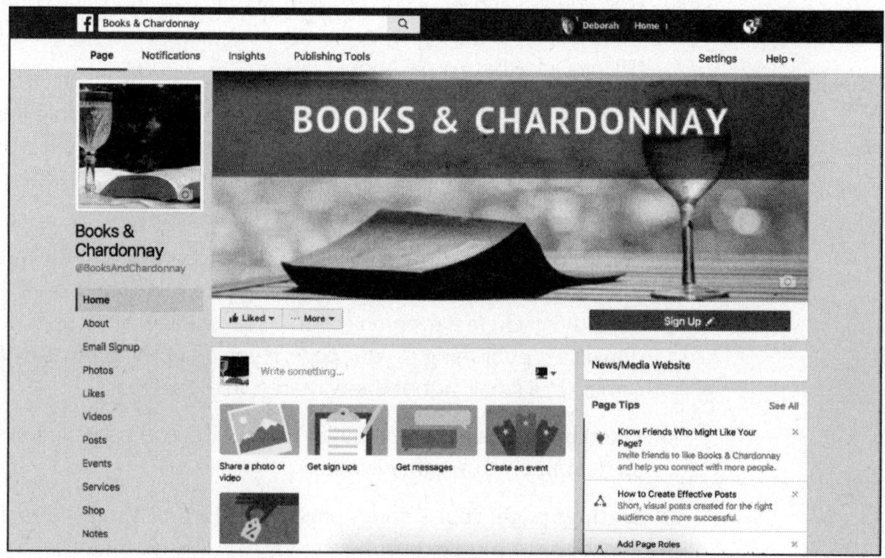

FIGURE 1-3: Your timeline is where you and your community interact.

Making the Most of Your Facebook Page

Setting up your timeline is simple and can take as little or as much time as you want, depending on how many bells and whistles you add to your profile.

Because the timeline is so visual, it's the perfect opportunity for you to share your company's story. In fact, with your timeline, you can go back in time to your brand's beginning and share milestones, articles, photographs, videos, and more — all in chronological order.

Some interesting features of the timeline include the following:

- **Private messaging:** Allows your community to reach out and ask questions privately and then receive a personal response in return. Please note that some brands turn off the messaging feature because they'd rather not receive private messages. You can turn off the private messaging feature, but you'll miss valuable community feedback because not everyone wants to publicly post to your wall.
- **Notifications:** A number on the Admin panel tab, shown in Figure 1-4, shows all your new notifications so that you can welcome new members by name, see who's messaging you, know who's posting to your timeline, and find out who's talking about you on their own timelines.
- **The capability to pin key events and photos:** You can make certain content "sticky" to highlight key dates, milestones, and events.
- **Posts from your fans:** Allowing others to post on your timeline enables your brand to interact with its customers and community.

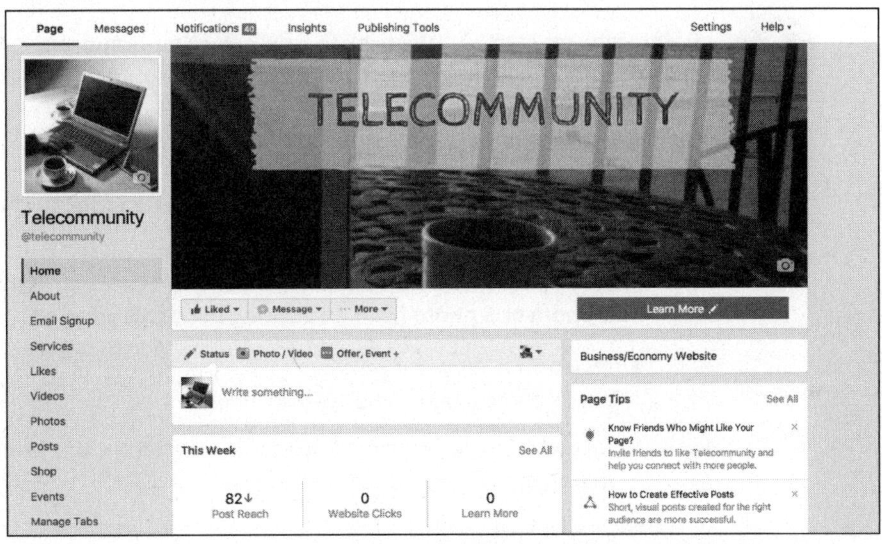

FIGURE 1-4: The number next to Notifications signifies new interactions and updates.

Adding a profile picture

To set up your timeline, the first step is to upload a profile picture. Your profile picture is the small photo on the left, usually a brand logo.

To upload your profile photo, follow these steps:

1. **Hover your cursor on the profile image area and click the Update Profile Picture function (camera icon) that appears.**

   A pop-up window appears, enabling you to choose from a variety of options.

2. **Choose the Upload Photo option.**

   Alternatively, you can choose a photo that's already been uploaded to Facebook or take an image using Facebook's camera function.

3. **Assuming that you're going to upload your brand's logo, choose the file you want to upload from the File Upload window that appears.**
4. **Save your profile photo.**

Adding a cover photo

Your next step is to choose your cover photo. This is the large background photo appearing at the top of your timeline (refer to Figure 1-1) and the first thing people will see when landing on your brand's page. Your cover photo is more than just a picture; it's a representation of your brand. You have a wonderful opportunity to illustrate your brand, product, or service in any way you want — and you want to make a lasting impression. Many top brands, such as Ben & Jerry's, Ford, and Coca-Cola, take great care in designing their timeline images.

TIP

Before you get started, take time to research other brands on Facebook to see how they're using their timelines. This may give you some good ideas.

To add a cover photo to your timeline, follow these steps:

1. **Select the camera icon located on the image and click to change your cover photo.**
2. **In the pop-up menu that appears, choose whether you want to upload a new photo or a photo from an existing photo album.**
   - *Choose from Photos:* If you want to use a photo that already resides in your page's photo albums, choose this option.
   - *Upload Photo:* If you want to upload an image from your computer, choose this option.

After you choose a photo, you can reposition it by clicking the image and dragging it up or down.

3. **Click Save Changes.**

This helpful link has information for working with the cover photo: `www.facebook.com/help/timeline/cover`.

TIP

Keep in mind that your timeline cover image doesn't have to be permanent. You can change it as often as you see fit. Change with the seasons or to coincide with product launches.

To change your timeline cover image or profile photo, follow these steps:

1. **Select the camera icon located on the photo.**
2. **Choose where you want to get your photo from.**

   You have these choices:

   - *Choose from Photos:* If you want to use a photo that already resides in your page's Photo Albums, choose this option.
   - *Upload Photo:* If you want to upload an image from your computer, choose this option.
   - *Reposition:* For only a cover photo. You can keep your current cover photo and simply reposition it by clicking and holding the cover photo, and then dragging it to its new position.
   - *Remove:* You can remove the cover or profile photo with this option. You don't have to remove the current photo to change it. Instead, you can just choose one of the first two options.

3. **Click Save Changes.**

Adding finishing touches

If you went through the steps in the preceding sections, your Facebook timeline is pretty much set up except for a little tweaking. From here, you can do the following:

» **Pin content.** Make certain posts or images *sticky,* meaning they'll stay in the same location until you unpin them. Pinning content is a good way to highlight sales events, announcements, and promotional campaigns. The pins last for only a week, unless you unpin or pin another item before the seven days are up. Please note that Facebook allows you to pin only one item at a time.

To pin a post: After you post an update, select the arrow located at the upper-right side of the published post. From the drop-down menu, select Pin to Top of Page.

- **Share your brand's story.** Because Facebook's timeline allows you to upload content in chronological order, you can now go back to the day your brand launched, even if it was 100 years ago. Scan old newspaper articles, advertisements, photos, and more. Give your community a transparent look into your brand's past.
- **Explore apps.** Make your brand's page even more interactive with apps that allow you to poll your community, share videos, share slides from presentations, post testimonials from customers, connect your Twitter account, share your blog posts, and so much more.

TIP

Don't go overboard with the bells and whistles. When you have too many items pinned to your timeline, or if your page is nothing but Twitter updates and blog feeds, your brand's account becomes too cluttered and confusing. Take the time to research the best apps for your community and use them in a way that doesn't assault the senses.

Understanding Your Facebook Administrative Functions

Facebook allows you to have a detailed look at the activity on your brand's page with several administrative features. The features include settings and Insights, which give you the information needed to provide your Facebook community with a positive user experience.

Here are some of the things you can discover when you access your administrative functions:

- **New likes:** The number of new likes for the current week is posted in the right sidebar next to your cover photo.
- **Post reach:** When you access your Insights dashboard, you'll see the reach of all current posts (as well as other handy analytics), which tells you how many people viewed your Facebook posts for the week.
- **Private messages:** If you choose to have the messaging option available, your fans can send you messages that no one else can see. Your notifications tab will tell you when you have a new message.

- **Notifications:** When there's new activity on your page, a red button appears at the Notifications link at the top of the page. The button also displays a number indicating how many activities have occurred.

The Insights section shares important details for Facebook page administrators. Those details include the following:

- **Likes:** In which you can see how many new likes your page received and view a graph showing your page's likes over time.
- **Advertising Insights:** The Promotions area gives a rundown of how many people saw your brand's Facebook ad and what actions, if any, they performed.
- **Overview:** Analyzes your Facebook content, helping you to determine the best types of content to post, as well as the best times of day and days of the week to post.

TIP

Before launching your brand's Facebook page, take some time to explore all administrative features and learn how to use them. The last thing you want to do is fly blindly.

Filling Out What You're About

Your About page, the spot where you share a brief story or description about your brand, is essentially your business profile. You should be able to tell people what your brand is about while not overwhelming them with details.

TIP

Your Facebook page is a vehicle in which to drive traffic to your website or sales page. Keep your profile information brief but intriguing so that readers seek out more information from your home page.

Here are some important details to include in your brand's business profile:

- A brief explanation of what your company does and perhaps your mission statement. This information shouldn't be a sales pitch; focus more on what you believe and what your brand can offer the community.
- A link to your blog or website or both.
- Links to other social media profiles — for example, Twitter and Google+.
- Contact information.

TIP

The purpose of your brand's Facebook page is to engage with your community and share your brand's story. Therefore, don't make the About section of your profile a long historical manifesto. Instead, keep it brief so that you don't lose page visitors before they get to a link where they can learn more.

Using a Custom URL for Your Page

You have the option to have a custom URL for your brand's page. A recognizable URL means better search engine optimization, and people are more likely to remember this address over an address featuring a lot of random numbers and letters.

To create your custom URL, follow these steps:

1. **Click your page's About section, in the left sidebar.**
2. **Scroll down to Username, and click the link that asks Create a Web Address for This Page?**
3. **In the pop-up that appears, type the name you want in the URL (see Figure 1-5).**
4. **Click Create Username.**

   If that name is available, you're all set. If the name is taken, you'll have to choose another name.

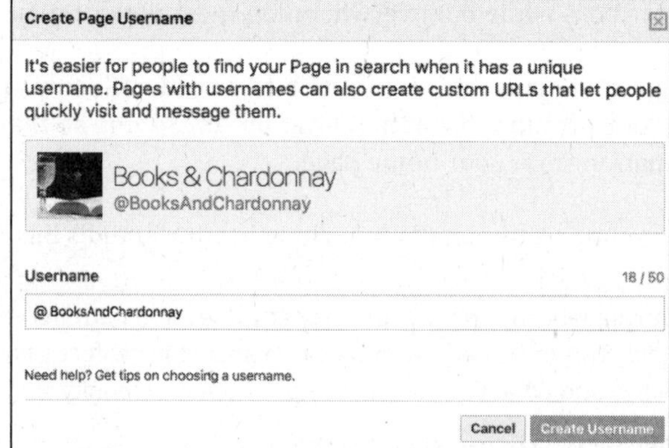

FIGURE 1-5: Choose your brand's name for your custom URL.

It should go without saying that it's a good idea to choose your brand name as your username. However, if your brand name is common, someone may have already beaten you to the punch. If that's the case, see whether you can add another word to your brand name so that you still have that recognizability.

WARNING

Choose wisely! You can go back and change your custom URL only once. Thus, the name used on your custom URL should be something you're comfortable using well into the future.

Inviting People to Join Your Community

The most important aspect of having a Facebook page isn't compelling About information or the perfect timeline cover photo. Instead, it's the community of people who will become your biggest advocates. If you're like most brands, you want to have as many people interacting on your wall as possible.

Before you begin inviting folks to join your community, keep in mind a couple of things:

- » You can invite only people you're friends with. (We discuss how to attract people who aren't your friends in the section "Getting likes from others," later in this chapter.)
- » Facebook frowns upon blatant attempts to get likes on specific posts and takes measures to make sure you're not like-baiting by having people like your page in exchange for a perk.

Using Facebook as a Marketing Tool

Inviting friends to like your page

When choosing friends to invite to like your page and participate, take care to choose those who will really appreciate being part of that community. When you randomly and regularly invite people who don't care to be a part of the brand, they might get annoyed at having their Facebook experience interrupted with brand messages, and this can cost you a Facebook friendship.

To invite friends to like your Facebook page, follow these steps:

1. **Locate the Build Audience pop-up menu at the top-right of your Facebook page, as shown in Figure 1-6.**
2. **Select Invite Friends.**

   A list of all your friends appears.

3. **Choose the Search All Friends option.**
4. **Click the Invite button next to each friend's name.**

   Your friends receive an invitation to like your brand's page. Not all will accept your invitation, so please don't take it personally. Some people simply don't want to follow brands on Facebook.

See Pages Feed
Posts from Pages you've liked as your Page
Invite friends to like this Page
118 post reach this week

FIGURE 1-6: Use the Build Audience menu to invite friends to join your community.

Getting likes from others

In addition to inviting friends to like your brand on Facebook, you can also try some of these methods for raising brand awareness and getting likes:

- **Use your brand's Twitter, Google+, and Pinterest accounts to bring in new community members.** Without spamming, invite people to join your Facebook page from time to time. If space permits, also share the benefits of becoming a member of your Facebook community.
- **Invite your community to share.** Although Facebook frowns upon contests and events in which people have to like a page to participate, nothing is wrong with inviting your community to share content they like.
- **Create the type of content your community will share.** Have you ever logged in to your personal Facebook account to find that your friends are sharing a funny video, a provocative image, or an informative article? This is the type of content people enjoy sharing on their walls. A Facebook page that is nothing but brand updates is not compelling. Instead, share informative or fun items with your community, and they will not only share in return but may also inspire others to like your brand.
- **Place share buttons on your blog and website.** If you want people to share your content, you have to give them a way to share. Having a Facebook share button, like those shown in Figure 1-7, on your blog or website will encourage readers to like your page. You can also place individual share buttons on the bottom of each post so people can share your content.

FIGURE 1-7: Use share buttons on your content.

- **Be consistent.** If you post engaging or compelling content every day, folks are more likely to like your brand. If you're sporadic and haphazard with your content, you won't receive many likes in return.
- **Place share information in offline content.** If you have offline content — for example, if yours is a supermarket brand with a weekly flyer or a retail shop with posters on the windows — be sure to let shoppers know how they can follow your brand on the social networks. If you're a restaurant, add the URL for your social networking channels on the back of your menus or have postcards handy for customers.

REMEMBER

Unlike the popular movie tagline, if you build it, they won't necessarily come. You have to give everyone a reason to want to show up each day. Everyone has a favorite brand of detergent or applesauce, but few people love these brands so much that they want to receive updates from them every day. It's not enough to have a presence; give everyone a reason to like you.

Liking Other Brands

One step you shouldn't overlook in your Facebook marketing campaign is to like other brands, even competing brands. Many people are afraid to like competitors because they feel they'll lose community to someone else. This fear isn't true at all. People who like brands on Facebook like many different brands, even if some are similar.

Here are some of the benefits of liking brands on Facebook:

- **Using your brand account, you can participate in discussions happening on other pages.** Your comments may inspire others to check out your brand's page and like you.
- **It puts you on the other brand's radar, which may be a good thing.** They may want to use and recommend your product or service one day or collaborate on a promotion.

- **It creates brand awareness.** The more people who see your logo, the better. When people see your logo on the social networks, it instills trust. They feel you're more accessible.
- **It helps to establish your expertise.** When you participate in discussions and respond to comments and inquiries in a knowledgeable manner, people see you as an authority and are inspired to follow you on the various social media channels.

WARNING

Be sure to follow the rules of social media etiquette and avoid dropping links on another brand's page unless you're invited to do so. The last thing you want is to have a reputation as a spammer. Also, if Facebook feels you've been spammy, you could lose your account.

Creating Facebook Events

The power of community is a wonderful thing. A tight-knit community will rally around the brand for all occasions. They'll comment on blog posts and social networking updates, respond to promotions and discounts, and attend events. In fact, a good way to gauge community interest is to create an event.

What is an event? Events include the following:

- Sale
- Party
- Tweet-up (a real-world meet-up organized on Twitter)
- Conference

Events can also be online affairs, such as the following:

- Webinar
- Contest
- Twitter chat

When you create an event using Facebook, you have the opportunity to invite everyone who likes your brand's page to attend.

Creating events doesn't take much time at all, and they're simple to set up. Just follow these steps:

1. **Choose the Create an Event box (under the text box where you post content).**

   A pop-up screen appears.

2. **In the box that appears, enter information and take any necessary actions.**

   You might enter the event name, date, time, and location, and a few words about the event. You can also upload a cover photo, include a link for tickets (if tickets are involved), and determine who can invite people to your event.

3. **After you're finished, click the blue Publish button.**

   Your event page appears.

4. **Invite people to attend.**

   Click the blue Share button, at the top right of the page. You can invite friends, post your event to the brand's Facebook page, and send an invitation via Facebook messenger.

   You also have the option to select whether you want your invitation page to show who has been invited to the event. Most people like to see who will be attending events, so it's a good idea to select this option. People can also see who has declined and who's a maybe. Because you don't want to have an invitation page filled with declines, don't create events for every move your brand makes. Instead, send invites to events you know will receive a positive response.

WARNING

Don't use events as invitations to spam. If you send out invitations every other day to drive traffic and sales, you're going to lose your community and possibly your Facebook account.

IN THIS CHAPTER

» Planning a Facebook content strategy

» Coming up with shareable content

» Creating a community with groups

Chapter 2
Creating and Sharing Content on Facebook

Your brand's Facebook page, just like everything else you do for your brand both online and off, requires a strategy and a set of goals. Plan what you hope to achieve with Facebook, as well as how you hope to achieve it, before you make your first post or upload your brand's cover photo. Just as you would take time to plan a marketing or advertising campaign, so should you also think through your Facebook campaign.

Facebook may look like a random bunch of comments and images, but it's much more than that. For your brand page, it's a way to create the type of content people want to both digest and pass along to others. However, creating interesting content isn't necessarily your most important objective. Most marketers use Facebook as a way to engage with customers, to sell, or to raise brand awareness. The content is a way to make that happen.

In this chapter, we discuss how to create the type of content that inspires your Facebook community to react.

TIP

See Book 3, Chapter 3 for a more in-depth look at planning and implementing a content strategy for all platforms, including Facebook.

Creating a Facebook Content Strategy

Many brands set up a Facebook account without any idea of what to do with it. Just like with a blog, website, or even a Twitter account, you have to have a plan. To just randomly post topics and hope they stick will lead to inconsistency and confusion.

WARNING

Facebook is constantly changing the rules for brands and brand pages, and to enter into Facebook marketing blindly without any planning and research on your part can mean Facebook will penalize your page — or even your personal account. A poorly executed brand page can reflect badly on you, as a social media marketer, and on your brand.

Take some time to put together a plan before you get started. If you already have a Facebook account for your brand and it needs an overhaul, pretend you're starting from scratch and plan a strategy anyway.

The first item to check off your list is your goal. What do you hope to achieve with your Facebook account? You won't be able to plan the right types of content without listing your goal first. For most brands, the goal is to build a community of advocates, which will lead to traffic to the main company website and, hopefully, sales.

After you know your brand's goal, you want to plan the type of content that will help lead to that goal. Now, this doesn't mean if you're looking for sales, every Facebook post should be selling something. However, you should post with sales and the people who help you achieve your goal in mind. (For more on creating content, see the section "Creating Content That Sings," later in this chapter.)

What follows are some ideas for the types of goals you might want to achieve with your Facebook page, as well as the content to help you best achieve each goal:

- **Drive sales.** Your content should inspire a sale but not necessarily be a sales pitch. For example, has one of your customers been in the news as a result of using your product? If so, share that story. Do the ingredients in your products have health benefits? If so, talk about them and share other healthy living tips. Do you offer a business-oriented coaching service? If so, use your Facebook page to share tips and best practices. In this manner, you're not exactly selling, but you are putting the idea of the sale in people's minds.
- **Increase your community.** Your updates should be more conversational. The people who join your Facebook page will do so because of the engaging content, which will help to establish trust. This trust leads to community growth and sales through customer loyalty and word-of-mouth marketing.

- **Grow your mailing list.** Do you want more people to sign up for your newsletter? If so, offer sneak peeks of what they'll receive if they sign up.
- **Create brand awareness.** When you share news and updates regarding your brand, it shows up in news feeds belonging to the people who are Facebook fans of your brand. When they like or comment on your public posts, those actions can show up on their friends' and families' news feeds, as well. When people share your content, it helps to turn your brand into a household name.
- **Establish expertise.** Use Facebook to share facts and drop tips. This approach is especially useful in selling books, providing informational products and services, and promoting blogs.
- **Receive feedback.** Use Facebook to create polls, ask questions, and pick the brains of the people who use your product or service. Just be sure you're ready to receive some brutally honest answers.
- **Drive traffic.** Link to your blog posts and web articles, and create discussions around the day's topics.
- **Have multiple goals.** Most brands have multiple goals for their Facebook pages. Mixing and matching content to serve many different purposes is okay. Be mindful of sharing too many links, however, because it can be perceived as spammy.

TIP

You may not necessarily see your timeline cover photo as a sales tool, but as the first thing people see when they land on your Facebook page, that's exactly what it is. The photo may not be of your product or service, but it should inspire the sale. You're not allowed to use your timeline cover photo as a call to action, but that doesn't mean it can't inspire action. (For more on setting up your timeline cover photo, see Chapter 1 in this minibook.)

Take time to understand your community. Watch them interact on the various social networks and watch how they interact on Facebook with you. Use your Facebook Insights and analytics to observe the types of content they best react to and what they shy away from. When you know your community, you can plan the most successful types of content. See the last section in this chapter for more information on Insights.

Sharing Your Brand's Story

Facebook's timeline for brands is created so you can share your brand's story from the very beginning. This chronological approach is a beautiful opportunity for your customers to find out more about your milestones and feel connected to your history.

Your community enjoys being made to feel as if they're part of the brand, even learning some secrets about your brand or being regaled with tales from back in the day. When your customers feel connected to you, they're more likely to share your stories — and products or services — with their friends and family. The more stories you share, the more brand loyalty is inspired.

Some items you may want to include on your brand page include the following:

- **A brand logo:** Use your logo as the profile photo — it helps to promote brand awareness.
- **A cover photo representative of your brand:** Your timeline cover photo is designed to catch the eye of anyone landing on your page.
- **A blurb describing your brand:** You have the opportunity to grab the attention of potential customers with a couple of forceful sentences under your profile photo.
- **A longer brand description in the About section:** Use your timeline's About section to tell potential customers what you do and how your product or service will benefit them.
- **Links to your website and social media pages:** Your Facebook community isn't network-exclusive. Many of your customers enjoy interacting at your blog or on Twitter, too. Be sure to include links to all the different places folks can follow you.
- **Contact information:** Include your email address in your timeline's About section. Also consider including other important contact details, including a customer service phone line and address.
- **A specific action:** In the area where you post, you'll see boxes enabling you to take specific actions. For example, you can write a note, which gives you the ability to create a longer blog post type of message. You can also create an offer to share a discount with your customer or a post to drive newsletter subscription sign-ups.
- **Events:** Are you having a special sale? Throwing a gala? Having a Twitter chat? If so, use the events function. You can invite people individually, and also have the event show up in your timeline. Use events sparingly, however. No one wants to be hit up with an event invite every day.
- **Photos and videos:** Your online community is especially receptive of photos and videos. You can share images of your team and offices, old historic photos, and even videos of your company's old television commercials. The options are endless. Photos and videos are shared more often than any other content, as well.

- **Tabs:** You can create a variety of tabs for your Facebook timeline, including events, polls, and FAQs. To learn more about tabs, see the section "Creating polls, quizzes, and contests," later in this chapter.

Creating Content That Sings

If you create a Facebook content strategy, then you should have some idea of what to talk about with your Facebook community. Planning content by using an editorial calendar or a spreadsheet can help to keep you from posting stale updates because you don't know what to say.

TIP

Before creating content for your Facebook page, visit some successful pages to see how those brands handle content. Seeing how other brands are engaging their communities can inspire you to do some neat things of your own. Also, visit competitors to see what they're doing right, and also what they're missing. There may be an opportunity to fill a void with some much-needed content.

REMEMBER

Your content isn't about the sale, but rather the conversation and engagement that may lead to the sale. Make sure to provide a mix of fun questions, photographs, videos, and informative articles and blog posts.

What follows are some tips for creating good content for your Facebook page:

- **Don't make everything serious and deep.** It's best to keep brand interaction light. Although thought-provoking questions and discussions are part of a good content strategy, don't forget to add humor to the mix.
- **Brevity counts.** Although you can be wordier than when using Twitter, Facebook isn't your blog. Keep updates brief. Too many words, and people lose interest. Write for the short attention span.
- **Stay on topic.** When you write about a mishmash of things that have nothing to do with your niche, people get confused. If yours is a cereal brand, your community expects topics centered on cereal — for example, nutrition and recipes. If you start talking about cross-country skiing or barbecue grills, people are going to wonder what any of that has to do with your brand.
- **Try to create content that's open-ended.** Give your community opportunity to respond. Ask questions or talk about the sorts of things that provoke a discussion. Make sure everything you post is inviting a response.
- **Let your comments be your guide.** What kinds of questions does your community ask on your page? What posts do they most respond to? When

they do respond, what do they say? Look to your community for topics. If certain topics stir up more interest than others, plan more of those types of topics.

- **Proofread everything you post.** When you don't take the time to read over everything and eliminate errors and typos, it tells your community you don't care enough about them to communicate error-free.
- **Look to your blog or website traffic for ideas.** If people are using search terms, phrases, and certain topics to land on your content, use these same topics when creating content for your Facebook community.
- **Be careful of TMI:** Although you should use a personal touch on a brand page, there's such a thing as too much information. Avoid making your brand page about you as a person, unless the brand page is for your personal brand.
- **Don't be afraid to court controversy.** You don't want to always have negativity and squabbles on your Facebook page, but the occasional controversial topic does wonders to create a discussion.

WARNING

When you post too many controversial topics or allow a lot of negativity on your brand page, eventually the only people who come around are those who thrive on drama and negativity. A positive attitude, with positive content, will inspire positive results.

Sharing and Being Shared

Sharing is an important part of brand page interaction. Creating the right types of content means that same content may be seen by thousands of eyes. When your community and others share your content, it generates brand recognition and word-of-mouth marketing. If you're known for creating interesting and creative content, you gain even more fans on your Facebook page, which means more potential sales.

REMEMBER

Be careful not to write for Facebook, an inanimate thing, instead of people. Too many brands make the mistake of creating content for its ability to go viral, as opposed to making content that resonates with people. When all your content is obvious click-bait, your fans will grow wary of all the shocking headlines and exclamation points.

TIP

People like to feel as if they discovered something wonderful. Sharing items with their friends and family sometimes can make them feel as if they created that content themselves.

When someone clicks the Share button below something you posted, it means your content is going to show up in the news feeds of that person's friends, as well. If a dozen fans with 200 friends each share your content, your post has the potential to be seen by 2,400 people. Out of all those people, it would be terrific if ten new fans like your page as a result. However, even if they don't, sharing is creating brand recognition.

REMEMBER

If you're recognized for putting out shareable content, more people will follow and use your brand and your brand will be seen as a respected authority in your field.

Posting content that followers will want to share

So what types of content do people want to share?

- **Photos:** People share more photos than anything else. Make sure that your photos are relevant, thought-provoking, discussion worthy, and even amusing, but don't make them offensive. People see photos before they see words, so put some thought into the photos you share.
- **Funny or amusing content:** People like to share content that makes them laugh. Post tasteful but amusing photographs, blog posts, or videos.
- **Heartwarming stories:** People love a good success or comeback story. They enjoy hearing tales of folks who beat the odds. People share inspiration.
- **Relatable content:** Ever read an article and think, "Oh my gosh. This happens to me all the time!"? People respond well to content they can relate to. Create content based on experiences everyone in your community may share.
- **Discounts:** Most people who follow brands do so in hopes of receiving special perks that they can share with their friends and family.
- **Viral videos:** Admit it; you love to share a funny video. That's how videos go viral. Post relevant, fun videos on your page for more shares.
- **Live video:** Facebook's Live feature enables businesses and individuals to share news and events as they happen.
- **Lists, tips, and how-to's:** People enjoy sharing learning experiences. Share tips or steps to success.

TIP

Say thank you to the people who share your content. When they're called out in a positive manner, they're more inclined to continue with the support. If another brand page shares your content, try to do the same for continued cross-promotion.

Don't sit around waiting to be shared, however. Do some sharing of your own. Take some time each day to visit other Facebook accounts and find content relevant to your community to share. This goodwill toward other brands puts you on their radar, and they may want to reciprocate. In addition, your community will appreciate your finding discussion topics or images to share with them. This especially works if you switch your Facebook identity to that of your brand page and not your personal account.

TIP

You don't have to limit shared content to Facebook posts or your own content creation. Sharing blog posts, images, videos, and podcasts by others will help create goodwill among different communities and will bring in more awareness of your brand page.

Using hashtags in your posts

Hashtags make topics searchable without having to use a search bar or search engine. When you use a hashtag in your Facebook post, it's visible to all who search for the topic used in your hashtag. For example, if you're posting a healthy recipe using the grain quinoa, you can use the hashtag #quinoa, #recipes, or even #healthy. Now everyone who's searching for that same hashtag will see your post.

Here are some best practices for using hashtags:

- **Use hashtags sparingly.** Too many hashtags hurt the eyes. Try for one or two — any more than three is too many and makes your update look cluttered and confusing.
- **Hashtags should make sense.** Don't use a hashtag because it's popular or trending. Use one that works with the content. The last thing your brand wants is to be accused of *hashtag jacking,* or spamming a hashtag with your irrelevant content.
- **Hashtags are all one word.** Avoid spaces and hyphens when using hashtags. They're all one word, usually all lowercase.
- **Do a search before using a hashtag.** If you have a hashtag you want to use, do a search of that hashtag first. It could be in use or could have previously held inappropriate content.
- **Don't worry about uppercase or lowercase.** Hashtags are usually all lowercase. Don't worry about making sure words are separated by capital letters.
- **It's okay to use a unique hashtag.** Don't be afraid of making up your own hashtag. A unique hashtag can help your brand stand apart.

Bringing Your Community into the Mix

Every tip you read about Facebook will come to nil if you don't have a positive, productive community. The more people who like your brand page, the more people you have responding to and commenting on your posts and campaigns. You want your community members to feel good about participating, and when they feel good, they share and they buy.

The last thing you want is a timeline filled with random updates. Take some time to explore the different Facebook apps to find out how to better interact with people. When you share in different, unique ways, your community will grow, and so will sales and brand recognition.

Selling on Facebook

Most of the people on Facebook aren't there because they want to buy or find a good bargain. They're there to visit with their friends. This mindset shouldn't discourage you from selling, however. With the right campaign, Facebook can become your community's equivalent of the supermarket impulse-item aisle. Facebook offers the perfect social shopping opportunity because people can socialize, shop, and share. In fact, people are more likely to buy something they see their friends buying.

Facebook has specific rules about what brands can present to their communities, especially when it comes to selling, promoting, and holding contests. If not kept in check, Facebook can become a haven for spammers, so regulations are necessary. It's a good idea to familiarize yourself with Facebook's Terms of Use for brands before selling; go to `www.facebook.com/page_guidelines.php`.

Facebook requires the use of specific apps for selling and promotions to keep spammers out of the mix and to ensure that all opportunities are legitimate. So, to sell on Facebook, you have to do so the right way.

Here are a couple of apps to help you sell on Facebook:

- **Facebook Store:** This feature gives you the opportunity to create a shopping experience on your timeline. The app appears as a tab and allows you to display merchandise or sell products and services. Your store can have as many items as you like.
- **Facebook Marketplace:** This app allows your advertisement to appear in classified advertising format. Because most Facebook users don't really know about this app, you may find it results in a low level of buying and engagement. However, some brands have found success.

To find specific apps on Facebook, type the name of the app or a description of the type of app you're looking for in the search bar at the top of the page. When the results page appears, click Apps (at the top right) to see all the apps within your search terms.

TIP

Facebook advertising is a terrific way to sell products and reach people who share similar likes and interests. Check out Chapter 3 in this minibook for more about using Facebook advertising.

REMEMBER

Not all your selling on Facebook has to be via apps and widgets. You can also create action terms and phrases to post on your timeline that lead your community to your website. Sharing news about a sale, new merchandise, or a discount is fine, as long as you're not spamming.

Creating polls, quizzes, and contests

For a truly interactive experience, you have to give your Facebook community the tools to get the party going. Asking questions or posting links is only a small part of growing your Facebook network. To truly tap into the power of the people, create some other fun experiences.

Polls

Polls can be fun and frivolous, or you can use them to collect information about the consumer. People like to participate in polls because they feel as if they're part of a campaign. Plus, creating a poll isn't a big-time commitment; a simple click of the button, and you have the user's vote.

Facebook's poll app, available at `www.facebook.com/simple.polls`, allows participants to add comments about why they voted as they did, and you can also configure the poll to allow participants to add their own items for folks to vote on.

TIP

Test out a free app such as the one found at `https://apps.facebook.com/my-polls` to see how your community responds to Facebook polls. Sometimes polls just aren't a good fit, and you'll want to play around a bit before investing money.

WARNING

Polls are best advised for bigger, active Facebook communities. When smaller communities put out polls and have a poor showing, they may receive only a couple of responses. The last thing you want is to promote something publicly and have a poor showing.

Quizzes

For even more community interaction, try creating quizzes. Quizzes aren't necessarily a way to gather information from your community, but if the quizzes are entertaining, the people who take them will share them with others in the community.

Facebook features several quiz-building apps such as QuizMaker (found at `www.facebook.com/games/quizmaker/`), and they're intuitive enough that even the most technically challenged people can create a quiz. See whether you can put something together representative of your brand. For example, if you're representing an Italian restaurant, create a quiz seeing how many Italian words and phrases your community recognizes. If yours is a car brand, list the parts of the car and see whether your community knows what each part does or where it's located. At the end of the quiz, have a ratings score for expertise. These quizzes are frivolous, but fun and extremely shareable. They're also great community-building tools.

Contests

Contests are another way to perform community outreach and raise awareness of your brand. However, like with selling, Facebook has specific rules about contests. You don't have to download a special app to host contests, but Facebook does have specific rules as to what is and what isn't allowed.

An app such as My Contests (`https://apps.facebook.com/my-contests/?fb_source=search`) can help you to create the type of Facebook-friendly contests that appeal to Facebook fans.

TIP

Before running a contest on Facebook, read Facebook's promotions policy. Check the policy each time you run a contest because the rules often change, and you don't want to be caught unawares. See Facebook's Terms of Use for pages at `www.facebook.com/page_guidelines.php#promotionsguidelines`.

WARNING

When planning fun content for your Facebook page, keep in mind that Facebook is cracking down on *like bait,* or the practice of asking Facebook fans to like, share, or comment on posts. Facebook is also cracking down on *click bait,* or the practice of using sensational headlines to bring likes and shares to specific posts. For example, be careful using headlines that say *and you won't believe what happened next!* as a way to draw in readers.

Offering discounts to your community

One of the main reasons people follow brands on Facebook is because they're interested in receiving bargains, freebies, or discounts. In fact, these types of perks are a terrific way to reward your community for their loyalty.

When you offer discounts and perks that are available only to your Facebook community, it makes people feel special and inclined to share your brand with others. Discounts are what fans share the most when it comes to brands.

You can offer discounts in a variety of ways:

- Set up a unique code for your Facebook community only.
- Link to discounts on your website.
- Use the Facebook offers feature, which enables you to post your discount and an image (and they then appear in your fans' news feeds). This feature is found in the status update box when you select the Create an Offer option below the box where you post content.

TIP

Do be careful not to spam your Facebook page with discount codes and sales pitches. Although your community is interested in receiving bargains, they're not interested in reading spiel and jargon every time they see an update from you. Balance your discounts with other content and don't post sales or discounted items more than once per day.

Using Closed or Secret Groups

Facebook enables users to create closed groups and secret groups for more intimate discussion. There are times people want to share their opinions but aren't comfortable doing so because liking or commenting on a public page can mean their Facebook friends might see what they're doing. Closed and secret groups allow Facebook groups to participate without having to worry that friends and family are watching.

Closed versus secret groups

Both closed and secret groups are private. However, they do vary in a couple ways:

- **A closed group shows up in a Facebook search, and anyone can request membership.** The group's administrator can approve membership requests or set the group up so that anyone can approve new members. With closed groups, you can also see a list of all members of that group, even though you can't see any of the messages, images, or other interaction.
- **A secret group doesn't show up in a search, and members must be invited to join.** You (or another member) have to be Facebook friends with a person to invite him to join a secret group, and all membership is approved by the group's administrators. In fact, many families use secret groups to keep in touch and share photos without having to worry about outsiders viewing their

personal family details. If you're not a member of a secret group, you can't see that group's updates or member list, and you can't access the group at all without an invitation from a member.

WARNING

Although secret groups are great for private interaction and they keep out spammers, some feel they promote exclusivity and cliquishness because only select people are part of the group, which may not be a good idea for a popular brand.

REMEMBER

Content posted to a secret or closed group isn't available for public search (for example, on Google), nor can it be shared outside the group.

TIP

Brand pages and groups are different in that pages are for fans to have conversations and learn about a brand, whereas groups allow like-minded people to interact and have conversations on a more expansive basis. Although you wouldn't have dozens of conversations going each day on your brand page, you can have many conversations going at the same time in a group, where members can opt in. The downside to groups is that Facebook caps the amount of people who can join to 5,000 members, whereas your brand's Facebook page can host millions.

Creating a Facebook group

Facebook groups are a way to have more interaction with your customers or fans, and to encourage them to interact with each other. People tend to let their hair down more in a group than on a public Facebook page. Some active groups are updated often throughout the day. Groups turn fans and customers into a thriving community of participants.

To create a Facebook group, follow these steps:

1. **Click the Groups function, in the left sidebar of your Facebook profile.**
2. **Click the green +Create Group in the top right of the page.**

   The Create New Group dialog box appears.
3. **Determine your Group name, invite members, and select your privacy options.**
4. **Click Create, and you're good to go.**

TIP

Don't create a group unless you already have people to invite. Facebook won't allow you to create an empty group.

After you start your group, you can do a few things to make it interactive and appealing. For example, you can upload a cover photo that's representative of the group. You can also pin a welcome message or group rules to the top of the page.

Groups allow you to share photos and even upload documents and files, so be sure to spend some time exploring all the different features.

WARNING

When creating separate discussion groups on Facebook, don't allow them to turn into cliques. If members feel excluded, they won't feel as strongly about your brand. Continue adding members to your groups to keep the interaction fresh. See Book 3, Chapter 3 for more on creating communities, not cliques.

Learning through Insights

Facebook continues to evolve, with the rules for brands changing all the time. Although some social media marketers aren't thrilled with many of the changes, most are reluctant to move away from Facebook because it's still where most of their customers converge.

No matter how they feel about Facebook's changes to both algorithms and rules for brand pages, marketers can't deny the benefit of using Facebook's *Insights,* or analytics panel, to learn more about their customers and online community.

TIP

The more you use Facebook Insights to analyze your page's content, the more your page will grow. The information on your Facebook page offers a valuable look into your Facebook community's habits. When you know how they behave while they're on Facebook, you can create the type of Facebook content that they will best respond to. When you plan your Facebook content strategy, make sure to allow time to analyze all the data that comes with Facebook Insights.

Getting the scoop on your fans through Insights

Facebook Insights is an analytics tool for your brand page that enables you to see what your community is up to and keep track of likes, unlikes, and comments. You can even access downloadable reports for in-depth analysis. In short, Facebook Insights gives you a peek into what people are doing when they land on your page.

Through Insights, located at the top of your brand page, you can determine your Facebook page's success. You can find out the following information about your visitors:

- **How many people liked your page each day, week, and month:** In addition to finding out how many people liked your page on a daily, weekly, and monthly basis, Insights also breaks down the likes by demographics.

A downloadable spreadsheet shows these numbers over time, enabling you to gauge growth and loss.

- **How many people unliked your page:** Don't just measure likes. Learning how many people unliked your page is important, too. It helps you determine how your Facebook community is reacting to your content and the amount of updates you're serving up each day. Knowing which topics and content lead to the most unlikes can help you to share only content that provokes a more positive response.
- **Organic likes versus paid likes:** Learn whether the likes you received were achieved via people who landed on your page on their own or who were brought in through paid advertising. If you find that most likes are via paid advertising, analyze your content to see why it might not be bringing in many organic views.
- **Where your likes happened:** Insights tells you whether likes were achieved by a computer or a mobile device. If more people are viewing your brand's page through their smartphones, be sure to provide the type of content that's easy to view on a smaller device, and maybe offer some sort of coupons or perks for people who might be on the go.
- **Your page's reach:** Because likes, shares, and comments can be seen by people who aren't fans of the page, each post has the capability to reach many people. Insights will let you know your Facebook page's true reach.
- **Engagement per post:** Insights breaks down each post and lets you know how many comments, likes, and shares it received.
- **Types of posts:** You can find out which types of posts do better than others — for example, if a humorous image gets more engagement than a link to a blog post or straight-up text.
- **Pages you watch:** You can watch Facebook pages via your brand's Facebook page. That is, you can keep an eye on competitors' pages and see how their most popular pages are performing by using the Pages to Watch feature in the Overview section of Insights.
- **Information about external referrals:** Insights details which outside websites are sending people to your Facebook page, such as if you're receiving traffic to your page from a search engine or a link from a website.
- **Details on demographics:** Facebook Insights offers a variety of demographics, including age, gender, and location.

Putting Insights data to good use

Now that you have all this information about your Facebook community, what are you going to do with it? The reason Facebook provides Insights for pages is because they know how important it is for you to see whether Facebook offers good *ROI*, or return on investment. By analyzing the data offered in Insights, you can make any needed improvements and drive even more traffic and engagement to your Facebook page.

Take some time each week to check out your Facebook numbers and make note of the following:

- **If your likes are going up:** You're doing something right! When people like your page, it means they're interested in your brand. It also means the promotion you're doing on behalf of your Facebook page is working, and you're creating the type of content folks are responding to and sharing. Continue doing what you're doing — but don't be afraid to add different types of content to see what your Facebook community best responds to.
- **If your likes are going down:** You could be losing Facebook fans for a variety of reasons. Maybe you're updating too many times a day. Two to three times per day is optimal. Any more than that, and people are going to tire of seeing you in their news feeds. It can also be that you're not offering the type of content they find interesting. Experiment with different types of content to see what they react to most.
- **If your likes aren't doing anything:** You want your page to receive new likes daily, and if this isn't happening, you have to step up your game. Try changing your timeline photo to see whether you can find one more appealing to your community. See what you can do to find the type of content or images that appeal at first glance to the people landing on your page.
- **If people are responding well to certain types of content:** Take note. If people are commenting, liking, and sharing certain content on your Facebook page, this is the type of content you want to continue to provide. Do still create a good mix of different types of content, but give the people what they want, as well.
- **If your demographic is made up of people of a certain age:** If your community is made up of 20- or 30-year-olds, tailor most of your content to appeal to people in these age groups.
- **If specific types of content receive more engagement:** If you notice photos and videos get more shares and comments than a simple post with a few sentences of text, add more visual content to your Facebook page.
- **If no one is responding to certain types of content:** If you post certain types of content and no one is responding, your community isn't interested. Avoid posting this type of content in the future.

TIP

Facebook provides Insights so that you can better understand the people who are interacting on your page or show interest in your brand. When you know how they react to your content, you can plan the types of campaigns they best respond to. Because you're given the additional benefit of demographics, you can also target your content so it appeals to a particular gender, age, or even locale.

IN THIS CHAPTER

» Paying to reach more people

» Choosing specific people to target

» Boosting your Facebook posts

» Understanding if advertising is working for you

Chapter 3
Advertising on Facebook

With recent changes to Facebook's algorithm, marketers have noticed a decrease in traffic and engagement with their Facebook pages. Facebook has made changes to the way brands operate for a few reasons. The first is that they don't want brands to spam the Facebook community. So, although they don't mind brands selling on Facebook, they don't want sales pitches and pleas for interaction to make for an unpleasant experience for users.

TIP

Facebook changes its algorithm often to best serve the needs of its users. Be sure to be aware of these changes and how they might affect brand pages such as yours. Also keep apprised of changes to how most users view and consume Facebook content.

Facebook is also a free service, which means it has to make its money somehow. Brands that pay for advertising on Facebook can find they reach more people, achieve more interaction, and even drive traffic to their websites.

In this chapter, we cover the basics of Facebook advertising so that you can determine whether it's worthwhile to pay for more fans and interaction.

Reaching More Fans with Ads

Should you pay to play on Facebook? Many brands are asking this very question. Because of the aforementioned changes to Facebook's algorithm, fewer fans are seeing your Facebook posts in their news feeds. If you're trying organic methods for growing your fans and interactions (for example, viral or more visual content) and those methods aren't panning out, advertising might be worth looking into.

The good news for small businesses is that it's not expensive to advertise on Facebook. You can invest as little as $5 in an ad or boosted post, or as much as hundreds of dollars, as shown in Figure 3-1. The more you spend, the more people you reach.

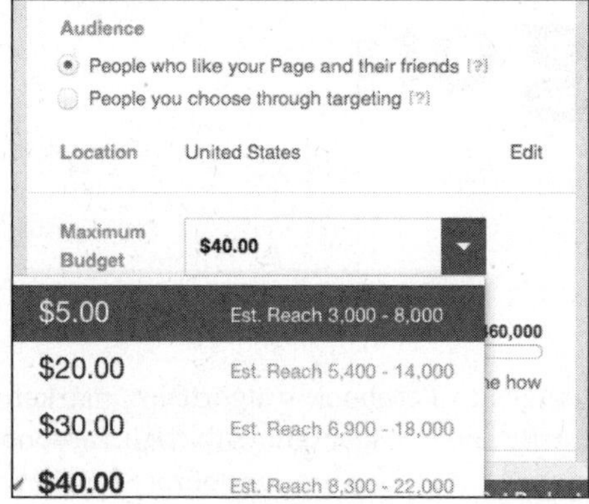

FIGURE 3-1: A Facebook ad doesn't have to cost a lot of money.

TIP

If you're wary of spending money on a Facebook ad, try testing the waters with a small amount. Boosting a post (we talk about that in the section "Targeting your fans," later in this chapter) for as little as $5 or $10 is a good way to gauge if you want to advertise on Facebook on a more regular basis without putting out a large investment. You can set the price for a boosted post. So even if you have a small advertising budget, you can still see results with a lower priced boosted post.

Facebook offers different ad choices, so it's important to put money into the right campaign for your needs. Just as it's important to have a Facebook content strategy (see Chapter 2 of this minibook), it's equally as important to have a plan for advertising.

Deciding whether you want to invest in an ad

First, you need to determine what you hope to achieve with your Facebook ad. What follows is a look at some of the reasons people invest in Facebook advertising:

- **More engagement on your brand page:** If you have fans but no one is communicating by likes, shares, or comments, they might not be seeing your page in their news feeds. An ad can help to reach more people and up the engagement.
- **More likes to your brand's page:** Sometimes a brand needs a boost to get started. Using Facebook advertising is a good way to gain new fans who wouldn't have known your brand has a Facebook page otherwise.
- **More traffic to your website:** When your posts appear in more fans' news feeds, more fans will click your blog posts, articles, and other shared web pages.
- **More people to attend your event:** Facebook advertising can help your events reach more people.
- **More app downloads:** A Facebook ad can direct users to your mobile app download page.

Taking out a Facebook ad means more visibility for your brand. On your own Facebook news feed, much of the brand content isn't shared by your friends — you're seeing it because that page's manager used advertising. Advertising can be targeted to people who have similar interests or friends of fans, which means more views and actions on your Facebook page.

WARNING

People can control what they see in their Facebook feeds. For example, if they find an ad offensive or annoying, they can opt to not see the ad. They can also opt to not see any posts from your brand. So try to share content that is educational, entertaining, and visually pleasing. When people enjoy your advertised content, they'll like your page so they can see more.

Choosing the right Facebook ad for you

Different types of Facebook ads can help marketers achieve a variety of goals. Familiarize yourself with your choices so you can see which ones best suit your needs.

What follows is a sampling of Facebook ad types:

- **Boosted post:** When you *boost* a Facebook post by clicking Boost Post, as shown in Figure 3-2, that post appears higher in your fans' news feeds. A single post or update can have a wider reach than a post you didn't boost. For example, if a single post normally gets 200 views, you can boost a post so it receives 2,000 views.

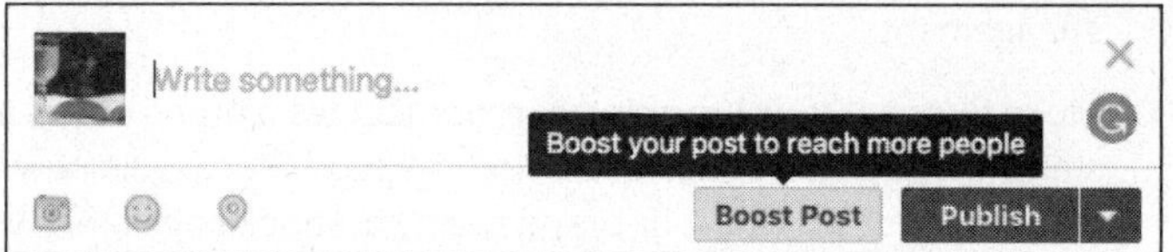

FIGURE 3-2: You can boost a post on Facebook to give it more visibility.

- **Click to website:** These ads are geared toward driving traffic to your website. A specific article or page on your website is highlighted, so when the reader clicks to learn more, he or she is taken to your website instead of your Facebook page.
- **Events:** Create invitations and share them with your fans. Paying for the ad makes sure the invite gets in front of more eyes than if you created a Facebook event invitation without an ad.
- **Page post engagement:** Like a boosted post, these ads give a little push to single posts so they're seen by more people, but they're designed so they receive more likes, shares, or comments. For example, instead of seeing an advertised post in your news feed, there will be a call to action to like the post or the page.
- **Page likes:** Page like ads advertise the page itself, with a Like button included so viewers can like directly from their news feeds. You can choose to target this (and other) ads to a specific demographic or send it to friends of fans.
- **Offer claims:** When you use Facebook's Offer function on your brand's page, you can also pay to boost that offer so more people can take advantage of it.
- **Multi-product carousel:** Enables you to showcase several featured items in one ad.

The cost of a Facebook ad is up to you. Whether you choose to spend $5 to put your ad in front of several hundred people or hundreds of dollars to have your ad put in front of thousands of people, you set a cost you can live with.

TIP

Before investing in a Facebook ad, take some time to familiarize yourself with Facebook's guidelines for advertisers at www.facebook.com/ad_guidelines.php. The last thing you want is to have your ad pulled or declined because it wasn't in compliance.

Creating an ad with Ads Manager

Facebook's Ads Manager is your one-stop shopping destination for Facebook ads.

To create an ad by using the Ads Manager, follow these steps:

1. **Access the Ads Manager at** www.facebook.com/ads/manage/accounts/.
2. **Click the Ads Manager account you want to access, as shown in in Figure 3-3.**

   Your account summary appears.

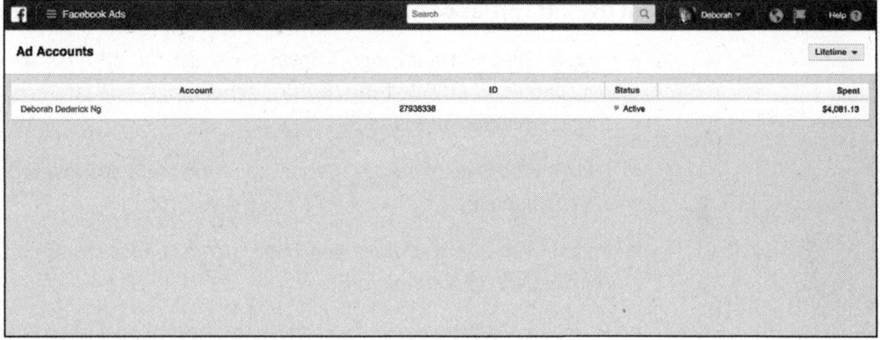

FIGURE 3-3: Facebook's Ads Manager can help you get started.

3. **Click Create Ad to get started.**
4. **Choose a marketing objective for your ad.**

   For example, you can choose to reach more people who are already fans, boost an existing Facebook post, or add to your existing fan base. When you select a scenario, you're taken to a window where you're asked to perform a series of actions. For example, if you're selecting the option to boost a post, you then select the brand page account you want to use and the post you want to boost. You're also asked to name your campaign, select various demographics to target your ad to, and choose your budget.
5. **Fill in all the required information about your campaign.**

6. **Select the option at the bottom to review your order.**
7. **If everything is to your liking, click the Place Order button.**

After you create your ad, you can use the Ads Manager to access analytics, print reports, and see your page history, among other functions. For example, you can see at a glance how many ads you've purchased and how each is performing.

Targeting your fans

One of the nicest features about Facebook advertising is the capability to target fans — or potential fans. For example, if you want to boost a post, you can target your audience as follows:

1. **After you create your post, click the Boost Post button, located to the left of the Post button on your status update (refer to Figure 3-2).**

   A dashboard of sorts appears.

2. **In the left corner of the Boost Post dashboard, select an Audience option:**
   - *People You Choose through Targeting: Choose this option if you want to reach new people. Then Select the country, gender, age, and interests you want to target, as shown in Figure 3-4.*
   - *People Who Like Your Page: Choose to market to only those who follow your Facebook page.*
   - *People Who Like Your Page and Their Friends: Choose this option if you want to reach existing Facebook fans.*
   - *Previously targeted fans: If you chose to target people through a previous boosted post, you'll have the option to do so again. This option appears on the under the name you titled the post.*
3. **Under Budget and Duration, determine the amount of money you want to spend and how long you'd like the ad to run.**
4. **Choose your payment method.**

   You can pay by credit card or PayPal.

5. **Click Set Budget to publish your post.**

REMEMBER

Your ad won't start running immediately. Facebook has to review the ad first to make sure it's in compliance. This review doesn't take long; in most cases, your ad will run within a couple of hours.

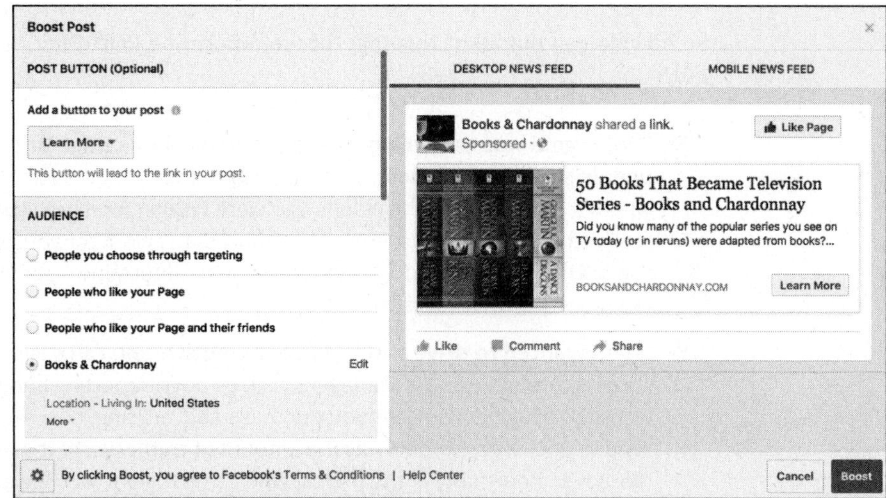

FIGURE 3-4: To reach the right people, target your ads.

Measuring Your Ad's ROI

It's important to know how well your Facebook ad is performing, and Facebook has the tools to help you with this. Whether you use your page's Insights dashboard (described in Chapter 2 of this minibook) or the Ads Manager dashboard, you can determine whether your investment is working.

What follows are a few of the ways to determine your ad's return on investment:

- **Regular posts versus paid posts:** When you select Posts on your Insights dashboard, you receive an overview on how your posts are performing. You can also see whether a post is paid or unpaid, enabling you to make a comparison.
- **Likes:** When you select likes on your Insights dashboard, you can compare likes achieved during paid campaigns with organic likes.
- **Reach:** When you select Reach on your Insights dashboard, you can see at a glance how much of a boost a paid post received and how many people were reached as a result of that boost.
- **Engagement:** On your Ads Manager dashboard, you can see a list of your advertising and how much engagement each received. You can even see the cost per engagement.

So how do you put all of this together to determine ROI? First, it depends on your goals:

- **If your goal was to receive likes to your Facebook page or to have more people see a specific post,** you can analyze the numbers and determine whether you achieved the results you were hoping for. If you spent $100 and received one like, your campaign probably didn't work for you. But if you spent $100 and received 50 likes, you have to determine if spending $2 per like is a worthwhile investment for you.
- **If you wanted to drive traffic to your website,** you can easily measure your success through the Ads Manager's click-through reporting and your own website's analytics. On days you purchased advertising, how much traffic did it send to your website, and was the amount of traffic worth the money spent? Moreover, how many of the people who came to your website as a result of the ad will continue to visit in the future? Measure traffic over time and see whether you have a nice steady rise and repeat visits as a result of your ad.

  You can also measure sales. If you receive traffic and no sales, the ad might need to be reworked or retargeted or maybe Facebook ads aren't a good fit. In this case, consider trying more than once, just to make sure. However, if you notice a rise in sales as a result of your Facebook ad, continue with this investment.

REMEMBER

It's important to determine whether a Facebook ad campaign is worth the investment. If you don't take time to analyze the numbers and determine whether you're meeting your goals, you're throwing away money.

IN THIS CHAPTER

» Delving into video

» Getting creative with a live stream

» Going live!

Chapter 4
Streaming Live Video on Facebook

Social media has presented marketers with new ways to communicate with customers and potential customers. They're able to move beyond the written word or a simple photograph, to audio, two-way communication, and video. In the past, live streaming was a technical, expensive consideration, but it no longer has to be. Thanks to tools such as Facebook Live, the capability to bring a brand to life is easier than ever. You don't need fancy equipment or a crew to follow you around. Live streaming is now as simple as using a smartphone and a Facebook app.

Facebook Live doesn't present a one-sided video experience, either. People who watch Facebook Live streams in real time are able to communicate in the form of comments or reactions, such as a thumbs ups, smiley faces, and hearts. The best part is that the person who is doing the live stream can see these interaction and respond.

If some viewers miss the live part of the live stream, they still have the ability to watch again later. They can't participate as the event is taking place, but that doesn't mean they're not going to benefit from the experience. A live stream can last forever.

Facebook Live is available to everyone who has a Facebook account. It's available to both brand pages and individual pages.

Some of the types of businesses and professionals that regularly use Facebook Live follow:

- **News organizations:** Many newspapers, broadcasters, and other news organizations go live with breaking news updates, interviews, and event coverage.
- **Teachers:** Educators use Facebook Live to share homework tips, read books, and share learning experiences.
- **Fitness and sports coaches:** Physical fitness professionals are sharing fitness tips and workout demos.
- **Musicians:** Entertainers are using Facebook Live to perform.
- **Product manufacturers:** Manufacturers are sharing demos, product information, and even behind the scenes looks at their factories.
- **Bloggers:** Facebook Live is a terrific extension of a blog — many bloggers use it to share their passion and communicate their readers.
- **Entertainment venues:** Local theaters use Facebook Live to share backstage secrets and introduce performers.
- **Restaurants:** Chefs use Facebook Live to put up cooking demonstrations or to show how popular dishes are assembled.
- **Retail chains:** Shops and stores use Facebook Live to live stream sales events, give product demos, and share news and promotional information.
- **Charitable events:** Charities and causes are using Facebook Live to stream 5Ks, for basket auctions, and to show viewers how and where funds are need and allocated.

As you can see, with Facebook Live the possibilities are endless.

TIP

Search for examples of how some of your favorite brands are using Facebook Live. Seeing how it works in action can inspire some fresh ideas of your own.

Understanding the Benefits of Live Streaming

Using a live streaming tool such as Facebook Live isn't just another social media vanity project. It's a way to humanize your business and interact with your customers and online community. You don't even have to appear on your live video if you're camera shy; train the camera on an event or an item of interest and narrate without appearing on screen. Because Facebook Live encourages a reaction, it's not a one-way effort. In fact, the engagement with your viewers is a favorite part of a Facebook Live stream.

The benefits of Facebook Live abound. Here are some reasons to take your Facebook experience live:

- **Show a human side to a brand.** Live streaming allows you to go talk, see you in action, or understand how something works in person.
- **Interact with viewers.** Because Facebook Live gives viewers the capability to comment or react, you're able to respond live to their questions, comments, or other interaction.
- **Bring new ideas to life.** Sometimes it's easier to illustrate or demonstrate a point with video than with words on a page. Facebook Live gives you an opportunity to make your actions speak louder than words.
- **Reach more people than with written posts.** As all brand page managers know, it can be a struggle to reach as many people as possible with a Facebook post. However, Facebook gives preference to live video, so more of your Facebook community sees video over your usual posts. Moreover, when more people see video posts, it gives a boost to future posts.
- **Send a notification to everyone who likes your page.** Unlike your regular posts, everyone who subscribes to your brand page receives notifications when you go live. This gives you the ability to reach as many fans as possible. Moreover, if your fans are enjoying the video, they can share it with friends and family, so you can reach even more people.
- **Show events as they happen.** If your company is doing something interesting or important, you can show those events in real time. This gives everyone an opportunity to feel as if they're there.
- **Continue to provide the content.** Your Facebook Live videos can stay on Facebook for as long as you want them to. Now anyone can see those videos any time they want. Moreover, if people search for a topic that you live streamed about, they can find your video, which might lead to new customers.
- **Get Facebook preference.** Marketers are always looking for ways to boost their Facebook posts, and Facebook's algorithm can make it difficult for people to see brand posts in their feeds. However, Facebook's algorithm gives preference to Facebook Live videos, so more people see the live stream than other (non-boosted) posts.
- **Live stream in Facebook groups.** You can use Facebook Live in private, closed, or public groups, allowing you to target a specific audience without making a public video.

- **Use Facebook Live on event pages.** If you have a Facebook event posted, you can live stream from that event page. Event streaming enables people who couldn't attend to see the action, and attendees can look back on the videos after the event.
- **Broadcast in the moment.** When you use Facebook Live you don't have to wait an hour for the video to render, there's nothing to upload, and you get to share the action live, as it happens.
- **Eliminate the need for fancy equipment.** Don't worry about purchasing expensive recording equipment. With Facebook Live you need only your smartphone.
- **Target specific viewers.** Facebook Live doesn't have to be a public live stream. You can target specific demographic and interest groups.
- **Add a call to action.** You can put information at the end of the video that encourages viewers to perform a particular action. For example, you can ask them to visit a sales page, donate to charity, or subscribe to your company newsletter.
- **Seek out users of all levels.** Facebook Live isn't only for developers or advanced users, nor is it only for people who run brand pages. Anyone who has a Facebook account can use Facebook Live.
- **Showcase and educate.** Facebook Live provides marketers with an opportunity to showcase products and services, or teach a how-to project, or offer other forms of education.

As soon as you go live on Facebook, you'll be able to see how many people are viewing the video stream at any given time. You can also see the names of people who are viewing so you can say hello by name. Knowing who is watching and when viewership picks up and drops off enables you to fine-tune your video content so it appeals to the most people.

TIP

A favorite feature of Facebook Live is the capability to engage with your community. Definitely take advantage! If someone comments, read the comment on the air and respond. If people give you a heart, thumbs up, or smiley face, call them out and let them know you appreciate that they took the time out to show their approval. Many of the people who engage during Facebook Live streams are hoping for a shout out.

Setting Up Your Live Stream

Ready to give Facebook Live a whirl? Is your smartphone handy? Let's get started!

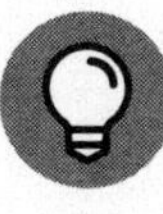

TIP

To practice, set privacy preferences to Only Me, so that no one else can see your video. You can practice using your private account instead of your brand page. To learn more about Facebook Live, read the official Facebook Live page at `https://live.fb.com/about/`.

Use Facebook Live in the same manner in which you'd post a photo or written update:

1. **From your brand page, tap the Publish option.**

   You now have the ability to do a variety of tasks, including add a photo, check in to a location, or go live, as shown in Figure 4-1.

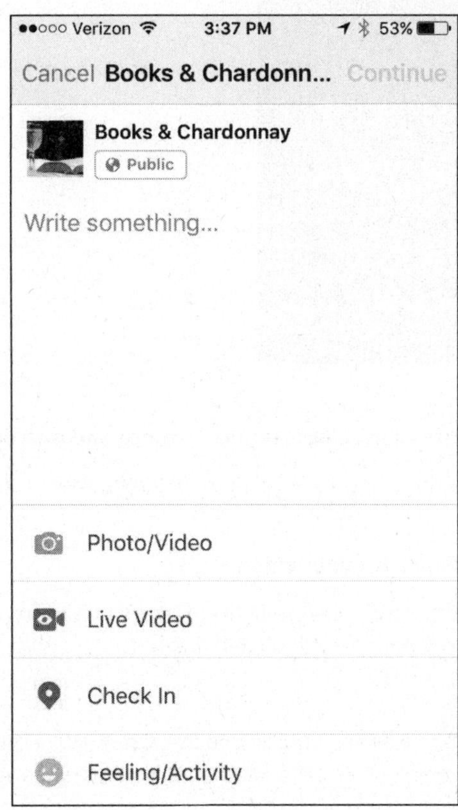

FIGURE 4-1: Using Facebook Live is as easy as posting to your brand page!

2. **Select Live Video.**

   You're taken to a live screen, as shown in Figure 4-2.

3. **Describe your video, and then tap Go Live.**

   Type a title of the video or a description of what your viewers will be seeing.

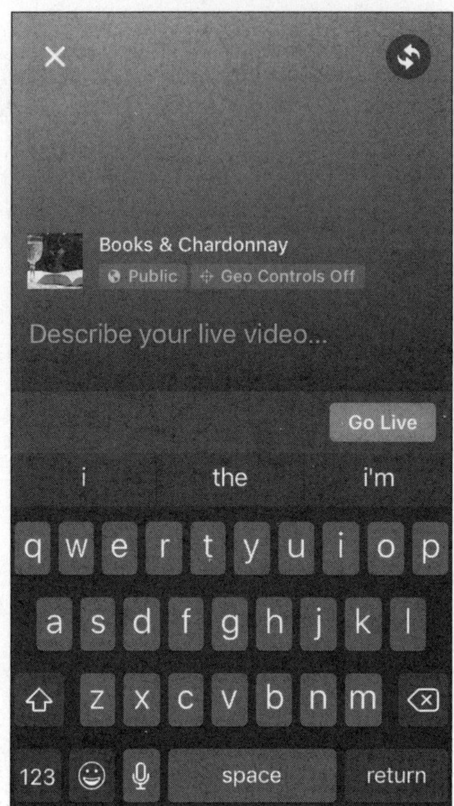

FIGURE 4-2: Describe your video, set your permissions, and determine your audience.

4. **Give Facebook permission to access your camera and microphone.**

   You need to give permission only once. Facebook remembers you for future videos.

5. **Determine an audience for your video.**

   Most brand pages choose a public audience. Tap the Public drop-down menu to change the privacy options for this video.

6. **Tap Go Live.**

   You get a three-second warning until you go live. Once you're live, you can begin! You see a red recording icon and the number of viewers when you're live.

7. **Record your video.**

   Don't forget to engage with your audience!

8. **To end the video, tap Finish.**
9. **To save the video, tap to toggle the button next to Save Video to Your Camera Roll.**

TIP

To edit the video description, delete the video, or change your privacy options, simply click the Edit Post function next to the video post on your timeline.

WARNING

Don't click Go Live unless you're ready to go live. The last thing you want is to be caught unaware. Get your camera set up and pointed at your target, alert any interview subjects or anyone else who is live with you, and make sure you're camera ready.

After your live stream, you can gauge how well your video did with your online community. Discover how many people were in your live audience, how many minutes were viewed, the amount of people reached, and more. You can also access a graph to see your viewership over time, which will enable you to see where peak viewership happened during your video.

Take these steps to view your video analytics:

1. **At the top of your brand page, click Insights.**
2. **Tap the Video option, to the left.**
3. **Scroll down and tap the Video Library option.**
4. **Select the video.**

Here are a few more things to know about Facebook Live:

- Live streams can last up to 8 hours.
- Make sure you have a strong signal before recording. The last thing you want is to lose your stream because of a slow connection.
- Facebook doesn't mind if you give a brief call to action at the end of your video. You might want to direct your viewers to a special web page or to a sign-up page.
- After recording, you can edit your video's description to add a URL if needed. This is especially helpful if you use a call of action or want to give people a place to go to get more information.
- Videos should be at least 10 minutes. The longer you broadcast, the more viewers and engagement you'll have. Short video snippets don't get much in the way of viewership or interaction.

TIP

Consider announcing live events so you'll have more viewers. Surprises are fun, but if your Facebook community knows you'll be broadcasting from a specific place at a specific time, they'll be waiting for you. You have an opportunity to reach more viewers by advertising your live event.

Engaging with Your Community via Facebook Live

A favorite aspect of Facebook Live is the capability to interact with viewers. Give and take between the viewer and the person producing the video provides a more authentic experience and can endear a brand to its community.

When you take time out to pay homage to the people who are watching your video, you're telling them that they're a part of the event and that you value them and the experience.

TIP

You can engage with your Facebook Live viewers in several ways. By talking *with* them instead of *at* them, you're encouraging participation. So it's important to notice who is viewing your video at any given time. In turn, viewers will communicate in the form of comments, or by reactions such as those shown in Figure 4-3.

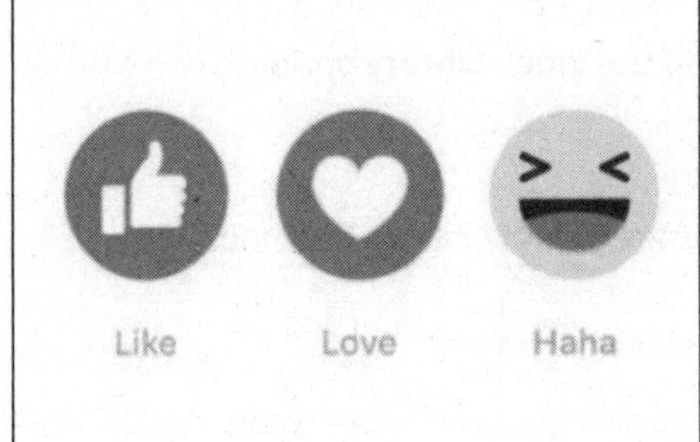

FIGURE 4-3: Viewers can interact by asking questions or by using reactions.

Here are some tips and best practices for engaging with your Facebook community:

- **Respond to comments and interaction by using names.** Respond, by name if possible, when people post comments and use reactions. When you use names, you're making the viewers feel special and important.
- **Encourage questions.** Invite your viewers to ask questions so you can respond.
- **Ask questions.** Ask questions so your viewers can respond. Read their responses out loud so they know you see them.
- **Welcome new viewers by name.** When new viewers join the live stream, call them out by name. They'll appreciate being noticed.
- **Take requests.** Ask your viewers what they would like to see during the live stream. They'll enjoy helping to shape your content.

REMEMBER

It's important to make your viewers feel as if they're an important part of the live streaming experience. When you call them out by name, they feel as if you value their viewership, input, and time.

Brainstorming Ideas for Live Videos

Like all other Facebook content, you'll want to have a plan in place for all your Facebook Live videos. Unlike a regular Facebook post, it's not as easy to go back and edit your video. If you struggle with finding the right thing to say or don't have talking points before you shoot your video, there may be lag time or uncomfortable pauses in the action, causing you to lose viewers.

If you want to use the Facebook Live feature regularly, put together an editorial calendar for ideas and dates. For each item on your editorial calendar, include the video's description, the people who will be involved, the shooting location, and any other pertinent details. Work on a script, talking points, or interview questions before your broadcast.

Your video content should be reflective of your brand, even if it's loosely related. Take steps before airing to make sure the content is entertaining or informational. Treat Facebook Live content as you would any other content. Be creative, be entertaining, and have fun.

Here are some creative ways to use Facebook Live:

- **Book readings:** Launch a book by reading a chapter.
- **Recipe demos:** Share knife skills, talk about specific ingredients, and offer tips for food presentation. Facebook Live is the perfect platform for foodies!
- **Physical fitness:** Showcase exercises and offer tips for keeping fit and doing exercise in a proper, safe manner.
- **Nutrition:** Share ideas for proper eating habits. Show off food swaps, present flavorful, healthy choices, and demonstrate how to cook delicious healthy food.
- **Listening parties:** Preview a new song, promote a concert, or showcase new talent.
- **Product manufacturing:** Bring customers to a factory or plant, or from the farm to the table. Seeing how something is made is a good way to get your customers to trust the brand and product.
- **Product demos:** Show how a newly launched product works.

- **Behind the scenes:** Share what goes on behind the scenes. For example, you can show planning meetings or introduce your Facebook community to staff.
- **Recording studio:** Get a tour of a recording studio or watch a favorite band record a new song.
- **Theaters:** Provide tours or theaters and previews of performances.
- **Teaching:** Teach people how to do what you do. For example, a math teacher can share algebra shortcuts and a science teacher can demonstrate experiments.
- **Interviews with notable people:** Conduct interviews with the people who are doing amazing things or have insight to share with your Facebook community.
- **Q & A with your online community:** Do an online town hall. Invite your Facebook community to ask questions of you and your team. This two-way conversation brings others into the video and makes them feel as if they're part of the brand.
- **FAQs:** Answer the questions you're asked the most (FAQs, or frequently asked questions).
- **Online charity auctions or telethons:** Raise money for a favorite cause.
- **Life hacks:** Share relevant tips for easier living.
- **DIY projects:** Share tips for building a birdhouse, restoring furniture, repairing a wall, or installing drywall.
- **Real estate:** Provide a video tour of a new house on the market.
- **Interior design:** Present tips for furniture spacing, accessory placement, and color examples.
- **School events:** Live stream a school's concerts, plays, and sporting events.
- **Town events:** Promote local events such as parades and sporting events or visit and highlight local businesses.
- **Art projects:** Show off works in progress, with fans watching as the artist finalizes the product.
- **Job openings:** Announce job opportunities, showing where the chosen candidate will be working and what the job entails.
- **Safety tips:** Share tips of fire safety or water safety.

We hope you're inspired by some of these ideas to come up with a few of your own.

WARNING

Avoid negativity or depressing topics, if possible. If people are made to feel uncomfortable or bad about themselves, they'll stay away from future live streams.

6 LinkedIn

Contents at a Glance

CHAPTER 1: **Promoting Yourself with LinkedIn** 393

Exploring the Benefits of Using LinkedIn 394
Creating an Online Resume 395
Understanding Recommendations and Endorsements 402
Using LinkedIn Messages 407

CHAPTER 2: **Promoting Your Business with LinkedIn** 409

Exploring the Benefits of a Company Page 410
Creating a LinkedIn Company Page 410
Selling and Promoting with LinkedIn Showcase Pages 414

CHAPTER 3: **Starting a LinkedIn Group** 417

Exploring the Benefits of LinkedIn Groups 417
Growing a Community with a LinkedIn Group 418
Growing Your Group 422
Moderating Your LinkedIn Group 424

CHAPTER 4: **Using LinkedIn as a Content Platform** 429

Blogging on LinkedIn 430
Promoting Your LinkedIn Posts on Other Social Channels 433

IN THIS CHAPTER

» Using LinkedIn as an online resume

» Highlighting your career

» Endorsing and being endorsed

» Private messaging with LinkedIn

Chapter 1 Promoting Yourself with LinkedIn

LinkedIn sometimes gets a bum rap because people aren't sure how to use it, or because they don't see the same type of interaction as they do on Facebook, Twitter, and Pinterest. However, different social networks serve different purposes, and thus they're used differently. Don't write off LinkedIn just because it's more about business than cat photos. If you use it on a regular basis, it can be a formidable part of your marketing plan — not just in finding work but also in making important connections.

LinkedIn isn't merely a place to post your resume. Use it to connect with old business associates and meet new associates. You can share your achievements, recommend colleagues, find jobs, and join discussion groups filled with like-minded people. You can also use LinkedIn to promote your brand with brand pages or groups. Many businesses are using LinkedIn to connect with a more professional crowd.

In this chapter, we show you how to set up a profile that attracts the attention of potential employers and clients while highlighting your expertise. We also show you how others can help highlight your achievements and how you can recommend others in return.

Exploring the Benefits of Using LinkedIn

LinkedIn has many features for the brand and social media marketer. You can establish your expertise through the LinkedIn content platform (you find out more about blogging with LinkedIn in Chapter 4 of this minibook), interact with your community via brand pages and groups, and reach out to others via LinkedIn messaging.

Also, LinkedIn offers opportunities to network every day. You can expand your business connections through LinkedIn far more than by using Facebook or Twitter.

You need to be on LinkedIn for the following reasons:

- **Recruiters and human resources professionals are on LinkedIn.** People who are hiring are looking at your profile on LinkedIn. In fact, if you're not on LinkedIn, it may lead them to speculate why. For example, are you not Internet savvy? If you're looking for a job, it's expected you'll be on LinkedIn.
- **LinkedIn has extensive job listings.** If you're looking for work, you can take advantage of LinkedIn's job search engine. Many top brands are using LinkedIn as a way to find suitable candidates through job listings, and there are plenty of listings exclusive to LinkedIn.
- **Receive (and give) endorsements and testimonials.** LinkedIn enables your peers to endorse your skills and write up recommendations, and you can do the same for them. People who are searching for networking connections or job candidates will take these recommendations into consideration. (We discuss endorsements and testimonials in more detail in the section "Understanding Recommendations and Endorsements," later in this chapter.)
- **Make important business connections.** You get to choose whom to connect with on LinkedIn. For example, you can connect with past co-workers, employers, and Fortune 500 executives. You never know who will accept your invitation.
- **Join professional groups that include like-minded people.** LinkedIn hosts thousands of online groups, enabling professionals to network within their respective niches.
- **Reach out to the people who are viewing your profile.** LinkedIn tells you who's viewing your profile, which opens the door when it comes to meeting new people and making important connections. For example, if someone you're interested in working with has viewed your profile, you can contact him, saying, "I noticed you viewed my profile. I'd love to chat." We talk more about contacting the people who view your LinkedIn profile in Chapter 4 in this minibook.

- **Updating an online resume is easier than continuously updating a paper resume.** With LinkedIn, you don't have to worry about formatting documents or hiring a professional resume writer. You just have to click the Edit button and enter your desired information. The formatting is done for you. (However, you still have to worry about spelling and grammar.)
- **Establish your expertise by using the LinkedIn content platform.** LinkedIn invites users to create content, as well. Posting articles on LinkedIn can help to establish your expertise.
- **Read news from your connections.** Your connections post news, tips, and updates, which you can look over to stay current on industry trends and timely topics.
- **Research other businesses.** A lot of businesses are on LinkedIn. If you're interested in working with a particular business, you can use LinkedIn to read its business profile, connect with people who work for that business, and more.
- **Introduce others to your books, websites, blogs, and more.** Your profile has spots where you can list books you authored and links to your blog, website, or other online content. This drives more traffic (and sales) to your interests.

REMEMBER

On LinkedIn, your community members aren't called friends or followers; instead, they're considered *connections.* You have varying degrees of connections: The closer you're connected to a person, the more ways you can interact with him or her. For example, you can't send a private message to someone who isn't a first-degree connection.

Creating an Online Resume

Something interesting is happening in the world of hiring. Many employers are now accepting LinkedIn profiles instead of resumes. In fact, many online job applications even offer an option to link to a LinkedIn profile rather than to upload your resume.

Even if you're not looking for work, someone may be looking for you. Recruiters visit LinkedIn daily, throughout the day. They are always looking for fresh prospects, and LinkedIn enables them to see new, qualified people.

LinkedIn is also a way for sales people, customers, and potential clients and job candidates to learn about a business.

REMEMBER

Keep your LinkedIn profile updated because you never know who's going to come calling.

Projecting a professional image on LinkedIn

LinkedIn isn't your usual social network. Most people aren't on LinkedIn to find friends; they're looking for professional connections, so how you present yourself is very important. Whereas you may be a little more casual with your profile photo and bio on Facebook, for example, the type of photo you use on LinkedIn and the information you share on your profile should be of a more professional nature.

Here are a few things to consider before creating your LinkedIn profile:

- **Your title or headline is front and center.** Your title is the second thing people view after your headshot. Choose a title that represents you and what you do in the most professional manner. If you want to attract clients, for example, use a title that best highlights both you and your business.
- **Participate in groups.** Many people say they're not on LinkedIn to socialize; rather, they want to have an online resume. Don't discount the importance of joining groups, however. Not only are they important networking tools, but when you join a group, those groups show up on your profile. Group membership shows potential connections that you're looking to continuously learn and network.
- **Make sure your career summary is professional, but personal.** Your summary should sum up your career in a businesslike tone but should also feature elements of your personality. For example, nothing is wrong with adding elements of humor, as long as you aren't raunchy or over the top.
- **Spelling and grammar matter.** You wouldn't hand out a paper resume that contained misspellings, and neither would you want people to view an online resume riddled with errors. Clients want to know you'll take care with their product or service. A resume with errors says you don't pay attention.
- **Ask for recommendations.** Your colleagues and former colleagues can give testimonials as to how you work. Don't be afraid to ask them to recommend you on LinkedIn — and don't forget to reciprocate.
- **Use relevant keywords.** Keywords help recruiters and potential employers, clients, and connections find you.
- **Decide whether you want to browse LinkedIn publicly or anonymously.** When you view another member's profile, that action shows up in the person's Who Viewed Your Profile section. You may not mind making it known you looked at someone's profile, but it can lead that person to contact you to

see whether she can help with anything or to make a connection. However, if you go anonymous, you can't see who viewed your profile, or any of the statistics LinkedIn offers regarding the people who viewed your profile. To browse anonymously, go to your privacy settings as outlined in the next bullet point. Then select Privacy (at the top of the page), choose Profile Viewing Options, and choose Private.

- **Check your privacy settings so that your activities aren't broadcast to the world.** When you update your resume or add experiences, your connections may receive notifications of those updates. This can be a problem if you don't want your current employer or clients to know you're in the market for something new. Adjust your LinkedIn privacy settings, as shown in Figure 1-1, if you don't want others knowing you're making changes.

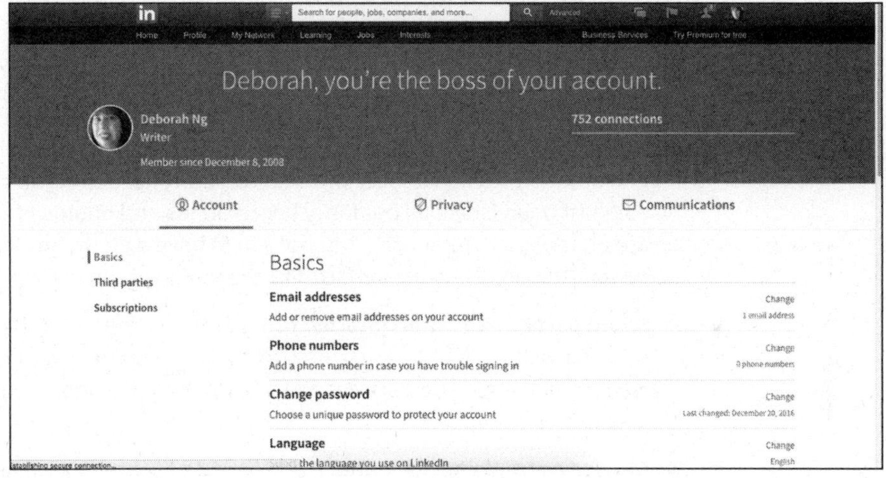

FIGURE 1-1: Pay attention to your privacy settings.

- **Add media to your profile.** You can add video, images, and presentations to your LinkedIn profile. Take advantage of these tools to show off your creative side.
- **Reorder skills so the most important skills are at the top.** You can set up your skills so they're in the order you feel goes from most to least important.
- **List places you volunteer.** Clients, employers, and other connections like to know the people they work with are doing some good in the world. List your charitable endeavors.
- **Don't skimp on the achievements and accolades.** You may find it to be a humble brag to talk about the great things you do, but it's perfectly acceptable in your LinkedIn profile. Go ahead and list all your important achievements and awards received.

Choosing and uploading a profile photo

According to LinkedIn, a profile with a photo receives 14 times more views than a profile without a photo. It also holds true many professionals won't connect with people on LinkedIn unless he has a photo on his profile. Photos add an element of trust. It also tells others you care enough about your professional profile to make sure you have all the necessary elements. If you can't take the time to present yourself in the best light, how can a business trust you to present them in the best light?

WARNING

Choose the right type of photos for your LinkedIn profile. Because your photo is the first view of you people see on LinkedIn, if you choose an inappropriate photo, a potential client may wonder what other bad choices you make. Thus, take the utmost care with your LinkedIn profile photo.

Choosing a profile photo

Here are a few guidelines for choosing a profile photo:

- **Headshots are fine.** Most professionals on LinkedIn choose to go with a headshot. Some even have headshots done professionally for their LinkedIn and other professional social profiles. You don't have to break the bank to post a headshot on LinkedIn, but fancy backgrounds and photos of your entire body are unnecessary. Although it's important to have a photo on LinkedIn, most people just want to see your face, like the profile photo in Figure 1-2.
- **Avoid party or vacation photos.** Your LinkedIn profile isn't the place to post personal photos. Don't post an image of you in a bikini or with beer in hand. Neither type of picture portrays you as a professional and can even cost you a job.
- **Choose a simple background.** If you have a photo with a white background, or with nothing going on in the background, it's a better choice than a photo that has a lot going on.

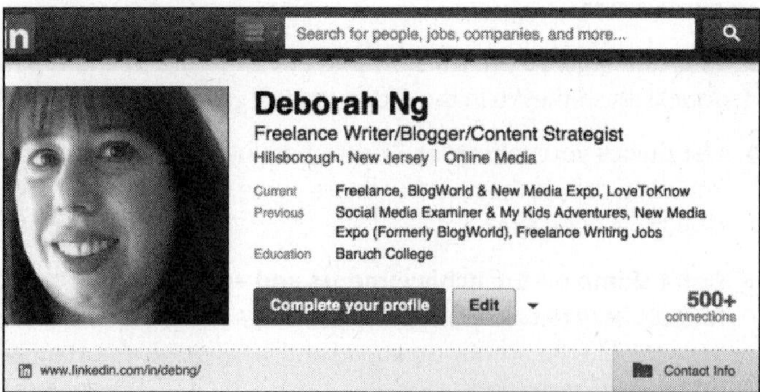

FIGURE 1-2: Choose a photo that portrays you in a positive, professional manner.

» **Avoid photos with others.** Don't post group photos or photos with a significant other, kids, or friends. It's not professional, and people won't know which person is you.

» **Choose an up-to-date photo.** The photo should reflect what you look like now. This way, if professional connections see you in real life, they can recognize you instantly. For example, if your profile shot has you with long brown hair, but you now sport a bright pink Mohawk, that might be a deal breaker for an image-conscious employer who wouldn't have invited you in for an interview had he or she had known you what you really look like.

» **No selfies.** There's a time and place for selfies. LinkedIn isn't it. Selfies aren't considered professional.

» **No wedding photos.** You may be over-the-top blissfully happy because you're a newlywed, but if you choose a profile photo in a wedding dress, it might lead to a potential client or connection feeling you're too focused on the wedding or marriage to concentrate on anything else.

» **Avoid pets or objects.** Using a photo of pets or objects, instead of a photo of yourself, will lead others to wonder why you're being vague about your professional appearance. Do you have something to hide?

» **Avoid blurry images.** A blurry profile photo indicates you don't pay careful attention to what you're putting out there.

» **Avoid a logo unless you're setting up a brand page.** Logos are fine for brand pages, but few people will want to ask you to represent their brand if your own brand is front and center.

REMEMBER

Your LinkedIn photo is the first thing people see when they access your profile. Choose wisely. As the saying goes, you never get a second chance to make a good first impression.

Uploading a profile photo

To upload a photo to LinkedIn, follow these steps:

1. **Click Profile, and then select Edit Profile from the drop-down list that opens.**

   Your profile page opens.

2. **Hover your cursor over your profile photo and click Change Photo.**

   You'll also see a camera icon.

3. **In the Edit Photo pop-up window that appears, click Browse.**

   A File Upload pop-up window appears.

4. **Select the photo you want to use and then click Open.**
5. **Click and drag the photo as desired. To crop the photo, move the yellow square until the photo is centered the way you want it.**
6. **Click Save to save your photo.**

Uploading a background photo

You can elect to have a background image on your LinkedIn profile. This should be an image that's representative of you as a professional or of your brand. The background photo appears underneath the text on your profile.

To upload a background photo such as the one shown in Figure 1-3, follow these steps:

1. **Hover your cursor over the cover shot area. Click the Edit Background button that appears.**
2. **In the Upload File pop-up window that appears, choose an image and click Open.**
3. **Click and drag to reposition the image, if you want.**
4. **Click Save to add this picture as your background photo.**

   You can instead select Change Image or Remove Image if you've changed your mind. Selecting Change Image reopens the Upload File pop-up window in Step 2. Remove Image leaves you with no background image displayed.

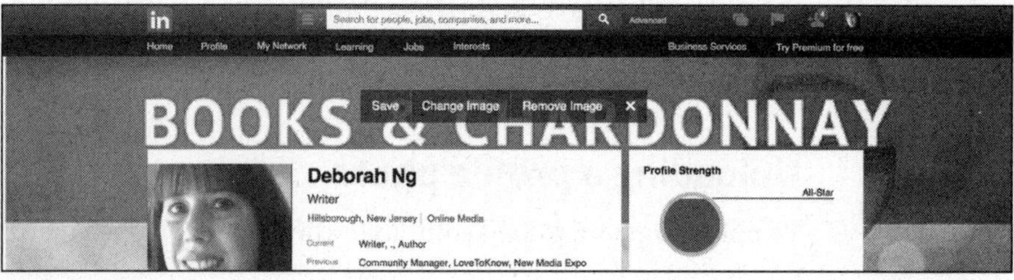

FIGURE 1-3: Choose a background photo that says something about you as a professional.

Filling out your profile

What should you include in your LinkedIn profile? Considering it's an online resume, include your work history, achievements, accolades, and anything that portrays you and your career in a positive light.

To fill in all the appropriate items on your LinkedIn profile, hover your cursor over the sections you want to edit, as shown in Figure 1-4. You'll notice a pencil icon next to each item that is available for editing. Click the pencil, and you're now in edit mode for that item. Make your changes and updates, and then click Save. You'll also notice you have to click the appropriate pencil to edit each individual section and save those sections separately as you finish updating the items you want to edit.

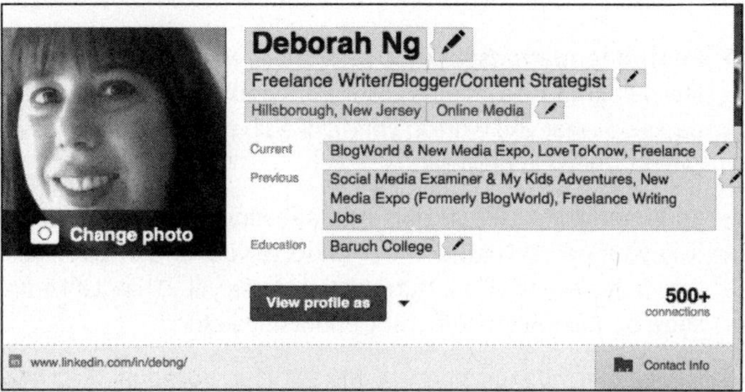

FIGURE 1-4: Hover your cursor over each section you want to edit.

You can edit the following profile sections:

- **Summary:** Summarize your experiences and achievements. This is often the second place people look after your photo. What you say in your summary can determine whether a LinkedIn connection or potential connection will read on or look for another candidate.
- **Experience:** Just like you would on your resume, list your employment history. Click Add Position to add a new job. You can also use the arrows to arrange your past and present jobs in date order, with the most current job first just as you would list it on a paper resume.
- **Projects:** If you're working on something amazing in your spare time or took part in an important project, list it here.
- **Publications:** This is where authors can list and link to their books, articles, or other publications.
- **Featured skills:** You can add skills to your profile to highlight your strengths and areas of expertise.
- **Education:** List high school and college education, and all degrees and honors.

TIP

Don't set up your LinkedIn profile once and forget about it. Just like you evolve in your career, so should your online resume. Take care to keep it updated.

Understanding Recommendations and Endorsements

LinkedIn offers the opportunity to receive recommendations and endorsements from your peers:

- **Recommendations:** Like job references. People you work with can write a few paragraphs to attest to your skills and expertise. Having testimonials backs up what you write in your LinkedIn profile and acts as proof that you can do what you promise.
- **Endorsements:** Like check marks attesting to your skills. LinkedIn occasionally asks your peers whether they'll endorse you for particular skills. If they agree, they only have to click a button to endorse you. Their LinkedIn profile photos show up next to the skills they endorse you for.

  Having many people endorse you for your individual skills helps to establish your expertise. Moreover, it has benefits for the person who endorsed your skills, as well, because when her profile photo shows up in your Skills area, others can click it to see her profile.

The beauty of recommendations and endorsements is that they save you from having to keep files of references to hand over to potential clients and employers.

In the following sections, we cover the benefits and basics of recommendations and endorsements so that you can have social proof of all your career achievements.

Receiving recommendations

Don't underestimate the importance of LinkedIn recommendations. It's essential to back up your experience with other peoples' experiences in working with you. A potential client or employer can look at testimonials on LinkedIn, saving himself a lot of time researching your skills and helping him see that you're someone who's trustworthy, and that you can get the job done.

REMEMBER

Recommendations aren't visible in public LinkedIn pages. Instead, they're visible to only first-, second-, and third-level connections who are logged in. Therefore, people who aren't familiar with your industry and don't have many of the same connections in common can't just stumble upon your recommendations.

Here are some tips and best practices for receiving recommendations:

- **Don't be afraid to ask.** Just like you ask employers, clients, and co-workers for reference letters, don't be afraid to ask them for recommendations on LinkedIn.
- **Request many recommendations.** The more, the merrier. If you have many stellar references, it means many people appreciate your work. Get as many on your LinkedIn profile as you can.
- **Do some back scratching.** Offer to trade recommendations. Give a recommendation to get one.
- **Offer to write it yourself.** Sometimes people don't have time to write a recommendation. Offer to write a recommendation that the person can approve and post at her convenience.
- **Use LinkedIn's Ask to Be Recommended feature.** LinkedIn offers a way for you to ask your connections for recommendations. When you select this option, shown in Figure 1-5, your connections receive a message asking for a recommendation.

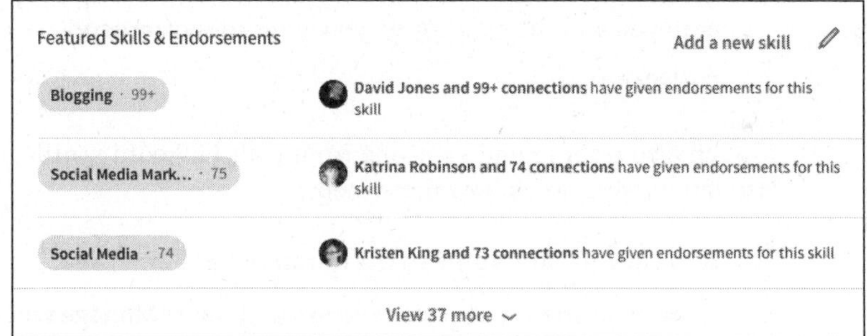

FIGURE 1-5: Your connections can endorse you based on your skills.

TIP

Don't request a recommendation from a client or colleague with whom you may have had a stormy relationship. Even though you might have done stellar work, bitterness can show through in a recommendation.

Giving recommendations

You should also give recommendations to deserving colleagues and connections. They'll appreciate the recommendations because it makes their LinkedIn profiles look good.

Recommending others strengthens your relationships with those people, and it also helps to add more visibility to your profile because your recommendation will appear in other profiles.

To give a recommendation to a LinkedIn connection, follow these steps:

1. **Go to the profile of the person you want to recommend.**

   Under the profile photo is a blue box with a Send Message button.

2. **Hover your cursor over the Send Message button's drop-down menu, and choose Recommendation from the drop-down list that appears.**

   The Recommendations screen appears.

3. **In the Write a Recommendation text box, enter your recommendation and then click Send.**
4. **(Optional) In the Your Message to *Connection* text box, create a personalized message for the person you're recommending.**

   You can also just leave the standard message that LinkedIn provides.

5. **In the What's Your Relationship drop-down list, make a selection.**
6. **Select from the What Were Your Positions at the Time drop-down lists for both you and the connection you want to recommend.**
7. **Click Send.**

You can also recommend someone from your LinkedIn profile, using the Recommendations section. Follow these steps:

1. **Scroll down your profile to the Recommendations area.**
2. **Hover your mouse over this section and select Manage when it appears in the upper right of the Recommendations section.**
3. **Select Give Recommendations, located just below Recommendations.**
4. **In the Who Do You Want to Recommend text box, type the person's name.**
5. **Fill out the appropriate information and write the recommendation.**
6. **Click Send.**

TIP

Don't wait to be asked to give recommendations to people whose work you respect. You can recommend anyone at any time. Providing recommendations gives your profile more visibility and sets you up as an influential person. You're also doing something nice for someone else.

Asking for endorsements

Endorsements (see Figure 1-6) are a way for your connections to attest to your skills without having to write out a recommendation. They can respond to a prompt generated by LinkedIn asking if you're good at particular skills, they can respond to a request from you, or they can even offer an endorsement out of the goodness of their hearts.

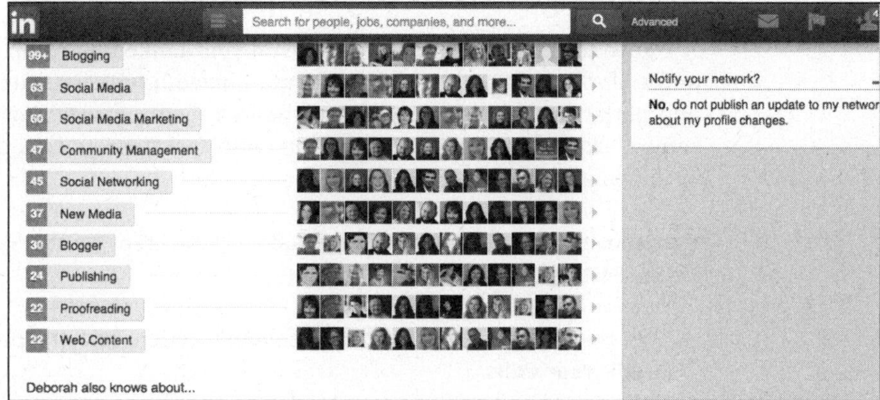

FIGURE 1-6: More endorsements mean more people are attesting to your skills.

The most popular way to receive endorsements is when LinkedIn prompts your connections to do so. For example, every now and then when you log into LinkedIn, a prompt appears at the top of your page listing several of your connections and asking you if those people are skilled in a particular topic. You can endorse by clicking Yes to answer the question, or click X or skip to not respond.

REMEMBER

Endorsements show others that you have the skill set to back up your profile. Make sure that the skills listed and endorsed on your profile are the best representation of you.

Adding skills to your profile

You can add endorsements so that your contacts know for which skills you want an endorsement. To add skills to your profile, follow these steps:

1. **On your profile page, scroll down to the Featured Skills and Endorsements section.**
2. **Click Add a New Skill.**

   A pop-up screen appears.

3. **In the Skills text box, enter the skills you want to highlight.**

   As you type, different skills will appear. Click the skills that best describe your expertise to automatically add them to your profile.

4. **Repeat Steps 2 and 3 for each skill you want to add.**
5. **After you enter all your skills, click Save.**

Removing skills from your profile

It's good to show you're well rounded on your LinkedIn profile with a lot of skills and endorsements. Sometimes, though, LinkedIn will generate skills that aren't appropriate, but your friends may endorse them anyway. Fortunately, you can remove skills from your profile if you don't feel them to be a good fit, or if they aren't what you want to be known for.

To remove skills from your profile, follow these steps on the Skills and Endorsements Settings screen:

1. **In the Featured Skills and Endorsement section, click the pencil icon to edit your skills.**
2. **Click the X next to the skills you want to remove.**
3. **Click Save.**

Reordering skills

You can also reorder your endorsements so that the most appropriate and important skills appear on top of your skills list, and the stuff you're not as great at appears at the bottom.

To reorder skills, follow these steps on the Featured Skills and Endorsements Edit screen:

1. **Under Reorder, click the box all the way to the right for the skill you want to move. Drag it to the desired location in the group of skills.**
2. **Repeat as necessary.**
3. **When you have your skills in the order you want, click Save.**

Opting out of endorsements

You may not even want to have endorsements on your LinkedIn profile. Although they're nice to have, they're optional.

To opt out of receiving endorsements, follow these steps on the Skills and Endorsements Settings screen:

1. **For the I Want to Be Endorsed option, select the No option.**
2. **Click Save.**

Using LinkedIn Messages

LinkedIn provides a way to send and receive private messages that you can access in your LinkedIn mailbox. You can send and receive private messages only with first-level connections. However, other levels of connections can choose to pay for a LinkedIn Premium account to use InMail, which runs upwards of $39.95 per month. So anyone can send you a message if he wants to badly enough. Fortunately, you receive messages mostly from connections.

Why would you want to send a personal message to a connection? Maybe you don't have that person's email address and need to get in touch with her. Or you might want to request an endorsement or recommendation, which you can do via private message. You can also reach out to someone from a group you participate in to further a discussion or ask to connect.

To send a LinkedIn message, follow these steps:

1. **At the top right of any LinkedIn page, click Messaging (envelope icon).**
2. **Next to All Messages, click the Create New Messages button.**
3. **In the To text box, type your connection's name.**
4. **In the Type Your Message field, enter your message.**
5. **Click the Send Message button.**

TIP

For a more in-depth look at using LinkedIn, check out *LinkedIn For Dummies*, 4th Edition, by Joel Elad (Wiley).

IN THIS CHAPTER

» Using a LinkedIn company page

» Showcasing products with LinkedIn

» Putting together a showcase page

Chapter 2
Promoting Your Business with LinkedIn

LinkedIn isn't merely a social network for job seekers to get their resume to the right people. It's also a wonderful marketing tool for businesses. LinkedIn company pages enable you to connect with a different kind of audience — a more businesslike audience.

The people who network on LinkedIn are professionals — yes, some are looking for work but many are looking to meet and learn from other professionals. These same professionals are using LinkedIn also to research businesses because they want to work for or with the brand or they want to become a customer of the brand. You don't want to miss out on an important opportunity because you didn't start a company page on LinkedIn.

In this chapter, we delve into some of the things you can do with a LinkedIn company page so that you can gain better brand visibility, highlight your products and services, grow your business, and drive traffic to your website and sales pages.

Exploring the Benefits of a Company Page

A *company page* on LinkedIn is different from a business page on Facebook or Google+, especially in the content being shared. Everything on LinkedIn is geared toward businesses and professionals, which presents a different atmosphere than other social media sites. You also have a unique opportunity to create specific pages that showcase your different products, services, events, and brands.

Why does your business need a LinkedIn company page? Here are a few reasons:

- **Share job openings.** You can set up your LinkedIn company page so that it lists open positions with your business. In addition to viewing the listings, candidates can also learn more about your business from the information you put forth on your company page.
- **Use showcase pages.** You can create special pages for products, services, and events. These showcase pages enable you to share in-depth information and engage with a target audience.
- **Share content.** Share blog posts, articles, and more with the LinkedIn community.
- **Share news.** You can share news — for example, product launches — with your LinkedIn community through your company page.
- **Increase your searchability.** Increase your business's visibility on both LinkedIn and the search engines.
- **Engage with your community.** Use your company page to chat with your followers.
- **Increase opportunities for your team to network.** People who list your business as their place of employment on their LinkedIn profiles will also show up on your company page as working for your brand, which gives them more opportunities to network.

Creating a LinkedIn Company Page

A LinkedIn company page gives your brand a strong presence on an important business and career-oriented social network. As such, you don't want to just slap together any old page and be done with it. Put time and care into your page — it's well worth the effort.

Here are some tips and best practices for your LinkedIn company page:

- **Choose a background image that represents your brand.** Just as with Facebook and Twitter, your LinkedIn company page encourages the use of a large cover image, in addition to a smaller profile shot, such as a logo. Choose an eye-catching background image that shows off your company in the best possible light.
- **Ask your team to give recommendations.** Is your company a great place to work? If so, ask the people who work with you or for you to give your brand a recommendation. Showcasing your brand as a good place to work is good for business, as well.
- **Take advantage of the career page.** If you have job openings in your company, you can highlight them on your career page. Those jobs have the potential to appear in front of many more qualified professionals than if you simply took out an ad. Your page will show up in a job search on LinkedIn, adding even more brand visibility.
- **Optimize your page for search.** Use relevant keywords to attract searches within and outside LinkedIn.
- **Check your company page every day.** Engage with your community on a daily basis. Posting new content each day ensures traffic every day, as well.
- **Use image and video.** Mix up your content to keep interest going on your page.
- **Stay on topic.** Make sure to share content relevant to your brand.

TIP

Before setting up your LinkedIn company page, look around to see how other brands are using LinkedIn. You may walk away with some good ideas for your own page, as well as see how your competitors are interacting with the community.

Setting up your brand's profile

A company page on LinkedIn is an important marketing tool. Because people will be researching your brand and interacting with you online, you definitely want to take advantage of the opportunity to connect with others on LinkedIn.

WARNING

You have to have an existing personal LinkedIn account to create a company page. If you make up a fake account and LinkedIn suspects you're using a fake account, you receive notification and your page may become unpublished.

It doesn't take much time to set up a LinkedIn company page. Just follow these steps:

1. **Select Interests, located at the top of any LinkedIn page.**
2. **From the drop-down list that appears, select Companies.**
3. **In the right sidebar's Create a Company page section, click the Create button.**

   The Add a Company screen appears.

4. **Fill in your company name and your business email address in the appropriate text boxes, as shown in Figure 2-1.**

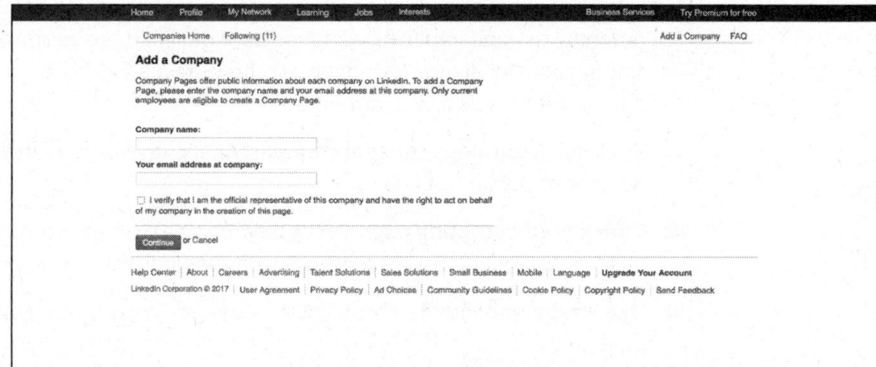

FIGURE 2-1: Use your company information to set up your LinkedIn company page profile.

5. **Select the I Verify That I Am the Official Representative of This Company check box.**
6. **Click Continue.**
7. **In the text box that appears, fill in your company information.**

   For example, you'll be asked to provide a description of your company, a company name, the size of your company, and the type of company.

8. **Click Publish.**

Adding and removing administrators

You may want to appoint an administrator or two for your LinkedIn company page. Most businesses let the marketing or social media department handle LinkedIn updates.

REMEMBER

You must be connected to the person whom you're appointing as an administrator. Invite that person to connect if you haven't done so already.

To add an administrator, follow these steps:

1. **On your company page, click the Edit button at the top right of the page.**

   Your company's Overview page appears.

2. **Scroll down to find the Company Pages Admin function, near the bottom of the page.**
3. **In the Designated Admins section, type the name of the person who will be handling the company page.**

   If you want to remove someone as an administrator, click the X to the right of the person's information in the Designated Admins section.

4. **Click Publish, located at the top right of the page.**

Sharing your brand's content

Of course, you shouldn't have a company page and not do anything with it. Just like you would on Facebook, Twitter, and Google+, you should share content on LinkedIn.

Some types of content that do well on LinkedIn include the following:

- **Company news:** Share new hires, product launches, event announcements, promotions, and anything of note happening with your company.
- **Industry news:** Share news of interest or related to your niche.
- **How-to's and tutorials:** Show how to use your product or service, or offer tips for others in your industry.
- **Business-oriented images and videos:** Don't forget to add visual elements to your company page.
- **Blog posts and articles:** If your business has a blog, share posts on LinkedIn. Also, share related content from other brands.

WARNING

Be mindful of how often you post. If you batter your LinkedIn community with a constant barrage of updates, they'll consider you too spammy to follow. Most brands update one to three times per day at most, with updates spaced out several hours apart.

Selling and Promoting with LinkedIn Showcase Pages

LinkedIn provides you with the perfect opportunity to highlight products and services with showcase pages. *Showcase pages* are stand-alone pages that you can use to announce product launches, websites, events, and any kind of product, service, or opportunity (see Figure 2-2).

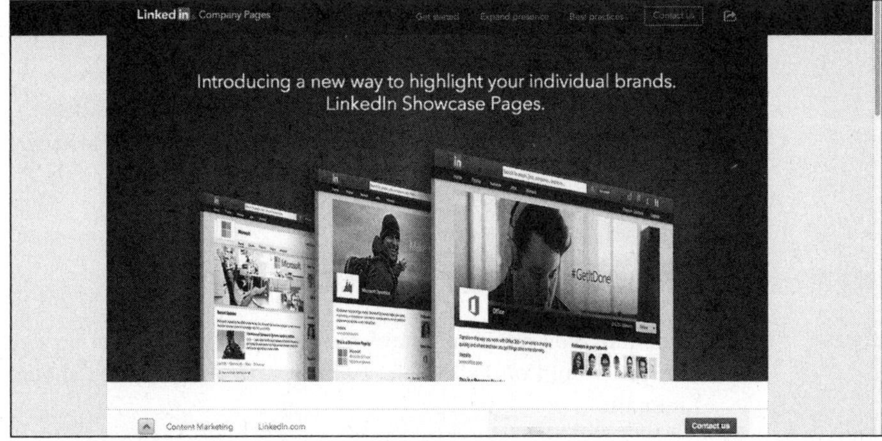

FIGURE 2-2: Use showcase pages to highlight individual products, events, or services.

Basically, a showcase page is an additional LinkedIn business page where you can engage your community and share a particular aspect of your business. For example, if your company has several smaller brands, you can use a company page as your main page with the smaller brands highlighted in the showcase pages.

Highlighting your products and services

People enter showcase pages through the right sidebar of your company page or a link on each individual showcase page. For example, each showcase page links to all of your brand's other showcase pages (if you have more than one). So people can see at a glance what's being showcased whenever they visit any of your pages. Best of all, people can follow the pages that interest them without having to follow all pages.

What are the benefits of showcase pages? Use them to do the following:

- **Share in-depth information about your brand.** Rather than a brief status update, showcase pages enable you to share any and all necessary information with your LinkedIn community.
- **Share with a target audience.** Because people follow only the showcase pages that interest them, you're interacting with people who truly want to be there. The audience is more targeted, and you don't have to sell as much on your company page.
- **Answer questions and receive feedback regarding the showcased element of your business.** When people have questions regarding your product or service, they can ask on the appropriate showcase page. Talking with you or your team can increase their confidence with the brand, making them more likely to buy. Moreover, you can use this opportunity to receive valuable feedback.
- **Increase engagement.** Multiple showcase pages mean multiple opportunities for having a conversation with your now well-informed LinkedIn community.

TIP

You can create ten showcase pages for each company page. And you can delete a showcase page if you need to make room for another. If your brand has a lot of things going on, choose the most important items to highlight. You might want to save one or two pages for new product launches or events, instead of using all ten at once.

Showcase pages

Only a company page administrator can create showcase pages. Before you begin, you need to know the following:

- The name of the showcase page
- A short and sweet description — up to 200 characters
- The industry your page falls under
- The name of at least one showcase page administrator assigned to each page

You also need to have a *hero image* (a cover image) for your showcase page, preferably one highlighting the showcased item, as well as two logo images.

Here are the specifications for your showcase page's images:

- **Hero image:** A minimum of 974 x 330 pixels in PNG, JPEG, or GIF format. You can play around and crop the image after you upload it.
- **Logos:** 300 x 300 pixels. If the size is slightly off, LinkedIn will resize it to fit.

WARNING

Before you create your Showcase page, it's important to understand that you can't easily unpublish a LinkedIn showcase page. To remove a page, you have to contact and ask LinkedIn to remove it for you. Choose wisely when it comes to the products and services you're showcasing because you can't delete at will.

To create a showcase page, follow these steps:

1. **While on your company page, click the down-pointing arrow next to the Edit button and then select Create a Showcase Page from the list that appears.**

   A Showcase Page pop-up appears.

2. **Click the yellow Get Started button.**
3. **In the appropriate fields, enter the showcase page's name (for example, the name of the item you're showcasing) and the person who will be administrator.**
4. **Click Create Page.**

   You can now see what the page will look like. If you're happy, go on to the next step. Otherwise, make any necessary edits.

5. **Click Publish to make the showcase page go live.**

LinkedIn provides you with some wonderful tools to promote your business and drive sales. Don't miss this opportunity to reach a whole new audience.

IN THIS CHAPTER

» Engaging with like-minded people through LinkedIn groups

» Growing a LinkedIn community around your brand

» Moderating LinkedIn groups

Chapter 3
Starting a LinkedIn Group

A LinkedIn group is much different than a company page or an individual profile. A group is less about your brand and more about growing a community and engaging people about a specific topic or niche. Creating a group doesn't promote your business in an obvious way, nor does it give you a place to sell — however, a group can be a wonderful place to learn more about your online community and your niche, which can help with the sales process.

LinkedIn groups provide you with a way to extend your brand's reach without selling. When you spend time with your online community, you gain their trust, and trust leads to sales. In this chapter, we talk about how to rock a LinkedIn group so that it's the place everyone wants to be.

Exploring the Benefits of LinkedIn Groups

LinkedIn *groups* are like forums where the members of your group can ask and answer questions and share ideas. You can have up to 20,000 members of your LinkedIn group, so it gives you an opportunity to reach many people.

The benefits of a LinkedIn group abound:

- **Establish expertise.** By participating in discussions, you're showing off your knowledge.
- **Learn about the people who are interested in your brand or niche.** Having ongoing discussions outside of your company page gives you an opportunity to learn about the people who are part of your online community.
- **Understand what questions your community might have.** Knowing what people have questions about can help you shape your content, as well as your products and services.
- **Drive traffic to your website and sales pages.** By putting a link to your website in the group description, you're driving traffic to your interests.
- **Create subgroups.** LinkedIn offers the capability for groups to break off into subgroups. You can use this feature to focus on specific topics without having those topics dominate the entire group.
- **Send weekly messages.** Group owners can send messages once a week to everyone in the group. For example, you can create a newsletter especially for your LinkedIn group community, sharing company information, content, and product updates. Consider your LinkedIn group to be an extension of your mailing list.
- **Make new connections and expand your reach.** The people who participate in groups may want to connect with you — and vice versa.
- **Hold in-depth discussions.** A group enables you to delve deeply into topics, rather than simply putting a quick update on your company page.

Growing a Community with a LinkedIn Group

Business people like to network. They want to have career-related discussions with others and ask questions while also establishing their own expertise and making new connections. By participating in a LinkedIn group, they're helping to make that happen.

In the following sections, we discuss how to set up a LinkedIn group, as well as how to set guidelines and restrictions for it.

Setting up a LinkedIn group

You can set up your LinkedIn group in a matter of minutes. Follow these steps to create your group:

1. **At the top of any LinkedIn page, click Interests and then select Groups from the drop-down list that appears.**

   The Group Highlights page appears.

2. **At the top of the page, select My Groups.**
3. **In the left sidebar, select Create a Group.**
4. **Fill in all necessary information about your group, including group name, summary, website URL, and description.**

   Be as descriptive as possible about the purpose of the group, so you have the right type of networking happening in the group.

5. **(Optional) Upload a logo or photo.**
6. **Select the Unlisted box if you want your LinkedIn group to be unlisted.**

   Otherwise, your group will be open to the public.

7. **Click to accept the Terms of Service.**
8. **Click the blue Create Group button.**

Congratulations! You now have your very own LinkedIn group. However, you need to go through a few more steps before you start sharing.

After your group is created, you see the Send Invitations page. You can send invitations to your LinkedIn connections, and you can also email anyone you'd like to invite to your group.

Either way, you can preapprove those people for your group so you don't have to go through the approval process later. To do so, click the yellow Pre Approve People button in the left sidebar of the Send Invitations page. On the page that appears, you can enter the names of LinkedIn connections and email addresses you want to preapprove.

If you don't want to preapprove or send invitations, click the Skip This Step link at the bottom of the page.

You're now ready to set up and manage your group. Take some time to familiarize yourself with the available management tools and group settings.

Choosing a standard or unlisted group

LinkedIn offers two options for types of groups. In a *standard group:*

- Members can invite others to join the group.
- Discussions show up in search engine results.

In an *unlisted group:*

- Discussions don't show up in search engine searches.
- Only members can view discussions.
- Only administrators can invite and approve new members.
- The group is indicated by a padlock icon.

Basically, a standard group is an open group, and an unlisted group is a private group. Keep in mind that having an open group can be a good thing because it's more visible and more people can see brand interaction. The downside is that some people might shy away from participating in an open group.

You can share conversations that you have with open groups with your other online communities. For example, if your group is having an interesting discussion, you can post a link to it on your Facebook page and invite your community to join the discussion. This link can lead to additional membership. With a private group, you're less likely to see additional membership because anyone who isn't a member can't access the link.

Both open and unlisted groups have their benefits, and some top online brands have no problem managing either.

TIP

Having an unlisted group and the ability to control membership can help reduce spam and keep out trolls. But it could also mean that the group doesn't grow. Set up your group so that you approve all new members regardless of how you invited them.

To edit your LinkedIn group settings so that your group is standard or unlisted, follow these steps:

1. **While in the group, select Manage, located at the top right of the group page.**

   You see a menu in the left sidebar with all your group administration options.

2. **In the left sidebar, select Group Settings.**

   You're taken to the Group Settings page, which has a variety of options for managing your LinkedIn group.

3. **Select either the Standard or Unlisted option.**
4. **Scroll to the bottom of the page and select Save Changes.**

Establishing group guidelines

Don't overlook your group rules (see Figure 3-1), which set some guidelines for members so they know what's expected and what behavior won't be tolerated. For example, LinkedIn groups can be a hotbed of spam if not moderated properly. Members always want to share links to their blog posts and articles, and this can be a turnoff to other members because your group will soon resemble a spammy link farm.

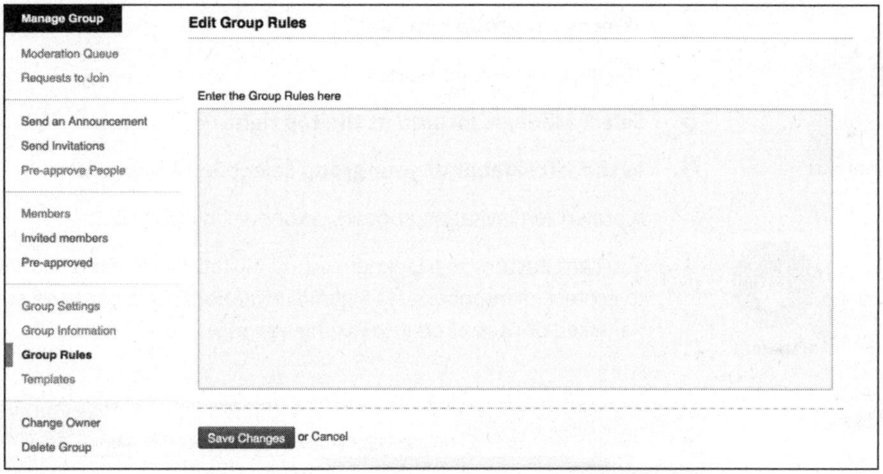

FIGURE 3-1: Group rules help to make a positive experience for everyone.

So, in your group rules, you can let everyone know where you stand on allowing members to post links.

You can set up your group rules by clicking the Group Rules function in the left sidebar of your LinkedIn group. Type your rules, and click Save Changes. ***Note:*** You'll need to access your group management page to edit group rules.

You might also set a few gentle guidelines for how members treat each other. For example, if you'd prefer not to have members swearing in their comments, you can mention this restriction in your group rules.

TIP

If you're already a part of some existing LinkedIn groups, read their group rules for ideas about what to include in your own group rules. If you're not a member of any groups, check out a few open groups to see how they handle group rules.

Growing Your Group

After you create a group, you need members. You can increase your membership by inviting connections or approving requests to join.

Inviting others to join your group

To invite other LinkedIn members to join your group, follow these steps:

1. **At the top of any LinkedIn page, hover your mouse over Interests and then select My Groups from the drop-down list that appears.**

   The Your Groups page opens, displaying a menu of groups you belong to or own.

2. **Select your group's name.**

   The group's page appears.

3. **Select Manage, located at the top right.**

4. **In the left sidebar of your group Select Send Invitations.**

   A prewritten invitation appears, as shown in Figure 3-2.

REMEMBER

You can't customize a LinkedIn group invitation. LinkedIn has it set up this way to protect its members. It's a gentle invitation, not a hard sell, so no one feels harassed or pressured into joining a group.

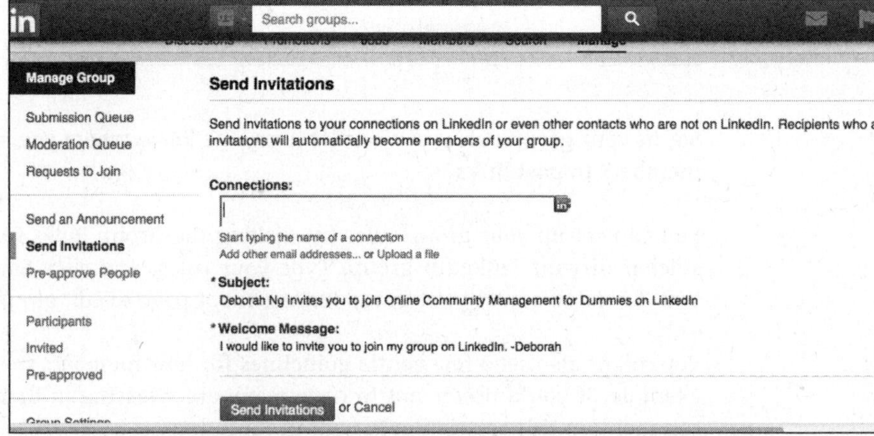

FIGURE 3-2: Invitations for LinkedIn groups are prewritten so that you don't spam your community.

5. **Click the In icon to the right of the Connections text box, and select the name of the person you want to invite from the list of connections that appears.**

Alternatively, you can enter in the text box the email address of anyone you're not connected to.

TIP

Take care in selecting connections to invite to your LinkedIn group. Not everyone you're connected to will want to join your group; select only those you feel will have an interest.

6. **Click Send Invitations.**

   The invited people will see a notification at the top right of their LinkedIn page, indicating an invitation. If their email is set up to sent LinkedIn notifications, they will also receive an email invitation.

Everyone you invite through a LinkedIn invitation or email is preapproved to join your group. No further approval is necessary for these connections.

Approving or preapproving group members

In addition to receiving an invitation, potential group members can find your group by doing a search on LinkedIn for groups in a particular topic. You can set up your group for auto join, where group members don't need approval to join the group. However, this setting opens the door for spammers and abuse.

You can and should set up your group so that individual membership has to be approved, which helps you keep out spammers and fake accounts. For example, if a profile has only vague information, few or no connections, or no headshot, it may be a fake account, and you can elect not to allow that person in the group.

To edit your group settings so that members can join automatically or have to request to join, follow these steps:

1. **While in your group, select Manage.**
2. **Select Group Settings, located in the left sidebar.**
3. **Select one of the following:**
   - *Standard:* Members are allowed to invite others.
   - *Unlisted:* You as the administrator must approve all new members.

   An example is shown in Figure 3-3.
4. **Scroll to the bottom and select Save Changes.**

TIP

Don't be afraid to share your group on your other social channels. Many people with whom you're not connected via LinkedIn might follow you on another social network. If they follow you on Facebook or Twitter or subscribe to your newsletter, they might be interested in joining your LinkedIn group as well.

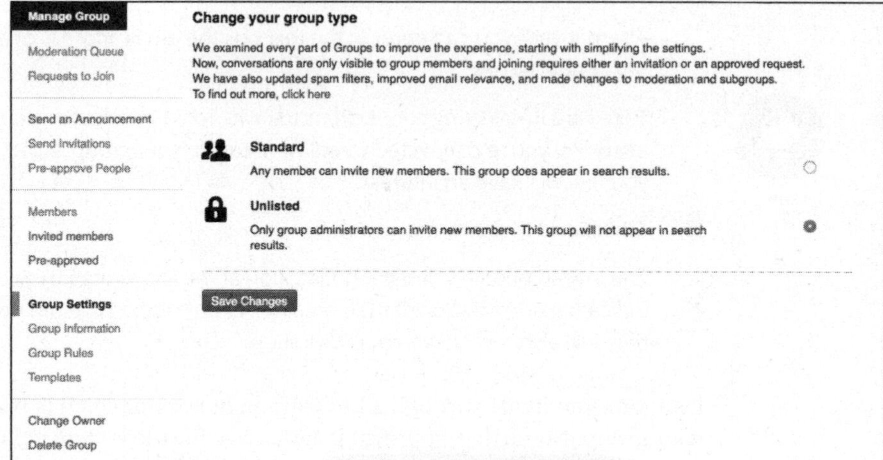

FIGURE 3-3: You can set up your group to preapprove invited members or to not allow new members without your permission.

Moderating Your LinkedIn Group

Have at least one person in place to moderate or manage your LinkedIn group. Without someone in charge, anarchy can ensue. Managers can make sure that your community members are treating each other respectfully and that no one is spamming with links and sales pitches.

Appointing a manager or moderator

Before you appoint someone to watch over your LinkedIn group, understand the roles available for managing LinkedIn groups:

- **Owner:** The person who created the group. Controls moderators, membership, and all aspects of group administration. Ownership can be transferred if the group owner is moving on.
- **Manager:** Can perform the same duties as the owner, except the group manager can't transfer ownership.
- **Moderator:** Can feature discussions as Moderator's Choice (located in a feature box at the top of the group), moderate conversations, and manage posts held in moderation.

Smaller groups might not require heavy moderation, but if your group has thousands of members, you might want to appoint at least a couple of people in moderator or manager roles so that nothing falls through the cracks.

REMEMBER

For someone to become a member or moderator, he or she must already be a member of the group.

To appoint a moderator or manager, follow these steps:

1. **While in your group, select the Manage option at the top of the group.**
2. **In the left sidebar, select Members.**

   You're taken to a page with the following tabs: Admins, Members, Blocked, and Requests to Join. The Participants options in Figure 3-4 appear.
3. **Select Members.**
4. **Select the check box to the left of the member you want to add as moderator or manager, and then click Change Role.**

   A drop-down menu appears with two options: Manager and Moderator.
5. **Select your desired role: manager or moderator.**

   The person will receive notice that he or she has been promoted in the group.
6. **Click Save.**

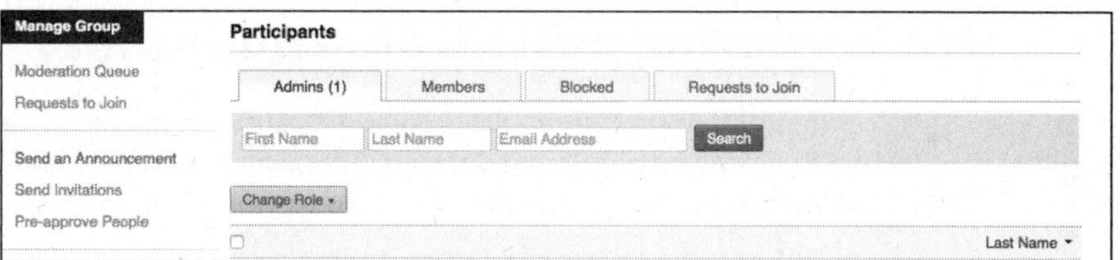

FIGURE 3-4: Appoint a manager or moderator to make sure everyone in your group is playing by the rules.

Managing a moderation queue

At the top of your group, in the top-right corner of Manage, a red number appears (as shown in Figure 3-5), telling you the number of notifications for your group. Notifications let you know whether a post is being held in moderation, usually because it contains links.

FIGURE 3-5: If items are in your moderation queue, a notification number appears at the top of your dashboard.

Here's how to manage your moderation queue:

- **To handle a post that's held in moderation:** Select the box to the left of the post, and then choose the link to approve it, delete it, or move it to a different area.
- **To handle requests to join:** Click the Requests to Join function in the left sidebar, which takes you to a list of anyone who's waiting for approval. Select the box next to people's names, and then click the link to approve, decline, delete, or block those people from your group.
- **To delete a post because it doesn't fall within your group's guidelines:** Click the down-pointing arrow at the top right of the post and select Delete from the list that appears.

TIP

You don't have to be militant in your moderation. Just make sure people are following the rules. You'll find that most group members are happy to comply. However, if a member does drop in a link, delete the offending post and send him a nice message in private to let him know you did so and why. Most are testing the waters and probably will be apologetic. If you establish that links aren't allowed, your group members will comply.

Featuring posts from community members

To highlight a community discussion, feature it at the top of the group page. This is a nice way to single out interesting discussion topics and bring attention to individual community members.

To feature a discussion, select the More button (three dots) at the top-right corner of the post you're highlighting, and select the Feature option from the drop-down menu that appears. The post will be showcased to all members.

Some managers like to highlight a few different discussions each week so that each member has a chance to be featured.

Adding a Jobs tab to your group

You can add a Jobs tab to your group to create sections for members to post jobs that their business currently has available.

You can allow your members to post relevant jobs in the Jobs tab. You have to police this area because, again, it can be a haven for spammers; but your community may appreciate your allowing job opportunities to be posted. Jobs are posted in the same way you post a discussion topic — but in a different area.

If someone posts a job in the main group, you can choose to delete or move it to the Jobs tab — just click the down-pointing arrow in the upper right of the post and select Move to Jobs from the drop-down list that appears.

Sending a weekly email to your group

Many company page managers see the option to send a weekly email, or *announcement*, to group members as a way to reach potential customers. Some brands think of it as a weekly newsletter, but others use it only if they have something particular to share. These announcements are sent by email, not by LinkedIn messaging.

Group managers can send announcements for many reasons, such as the following:

- **Highlight discussions or group members.** Sharing links to the week's discussion is a way to bring some members back to the group because not everyone checks out your LinkedIn group every day.
- **Share news.** If something important is going on with your brand, you can share it in your weekly announcement.
- **Launch products or events.** Share new releases.
- **Link to blog posts.** If you have a company blog, you can share links to blog posts and articles in the weekly announcement.
- **Reiterate group rules.** It doesn't hurt to give reminders from time to time. (We talk about group rules in the section "Establishing group guidelines," earlier in this chapter.)

WARNING

Because you can send only one email each week, make note of the time and date you send the email. If you sent the last email at 4 p.m. on Friday, you can't send another email until the next Friday at 4 p.m.

Avoid turning your weekly announcement into spam. Try to mix up the content so it is pertinent to the group and highlights some of the goings-on of your business, or your group's niche or interest area, in addition to news and links.

To send a weekly announcement, follow these steps:

1. **Click Manage (at the top of the group) to access your group's administrative area, and select Send an Announcement in the left sidebar.**

   A page with the Send an Announcement text window appears, as shown in Figure 3-6. LinkedIn adds a generic subject line to your announcement automatically.

2. **(Optional) Change the subject line, if you want, by clicking in the Subject text box and entering your subject.**

   We recommend that you change the subject line to something more engaging and personalized.

3. **In the Message text box, type or paste your message.**

   Although you can post links in your message, you can't anchor a hyperlink to text. That is, your members can't click text to access the link. They have to see the link written out in all its glory.

4. **(Optional) To receive a test email, select the Send Test box.**

   You can use this test email to see how it arrives in your own email, to give it a last proofread, and to check formatting.

5. **If you're satisfied with your message, click Send Announcement.**

Send an Announcement

Send an announcement to all your members who are currently accepting notifications from this group. You may send up to one announcement per week. Sending an announcement sends an email as well as posts the announcement as a discussion. **Please note**: For groups over 100,000 members, this process may take up to minute. For additional troubleshooting please refer here.

* **Subject:**

Now hear this!

* **Message:**

FIGURE 3-6: LinkedIn allows you to send one announcement per week to your group.

TIP

Don't send an announcement just to send an announcement. If you don't have anything of interest to share with your community, you can skip a week or two — or more, if necessary. Your community would rather receive sporadic announcements that offer something of value rather than a boring email or just spam with links every week.

Keep in mind that this chapter touches on the basics of a LinkedIn group. You can do so much more with LinkedIn groups, such as creating subgroups for different topics. For information on using LinkedIn groups for business, see *LinkedIn For Dummies*, 4th Edition, by Joe Elad (Wiley).

IN THIS CHAPTER

» Blogging with LinkedIn

» Sharing your LinkedIn content across platforms

Chapter 4

Using LinkedIn as a Content Platform

LinkedIn offers members the opportunity to showcase their expertise by publishing long-form content on the LinkedIn platform. Even if you have a blog or a website where you share content, you might still want to consider writing on LinkedIn, at least occasionally.

Having a post on LinkedIn enables you to reach a new, more professional social network — and what could be a whole new audience.

TIP

Everyone has the ability to publish an article or a blog post through the LinkedIn content platform. Use it to showcase your expertise and foster brand recognition.

In this chapter, we discuss the benefits of using LinkedIn as a content platform, plus a few of the basics for posting and promoting your content.

Blogging on LinkedIn

With all the content platforms available, why publish on LinkedIn when you can use your own blog or website, keeping all the traffic to yourself? Although you don't receive direct traffic to your website when you publish to LinkedIn, it does provide you the capability to drive traffic. If you share informative content, people will want to learn more and look up your website, blog, and other projects.

Some of the benefits of using LinkedIn as a content platform are

- **Your posts appear on your profile.** As you can see in Figure 4-1, when you publish a post, it's listed on your professional profile. Therefore, anyone who views your profile may also click through to read your content.

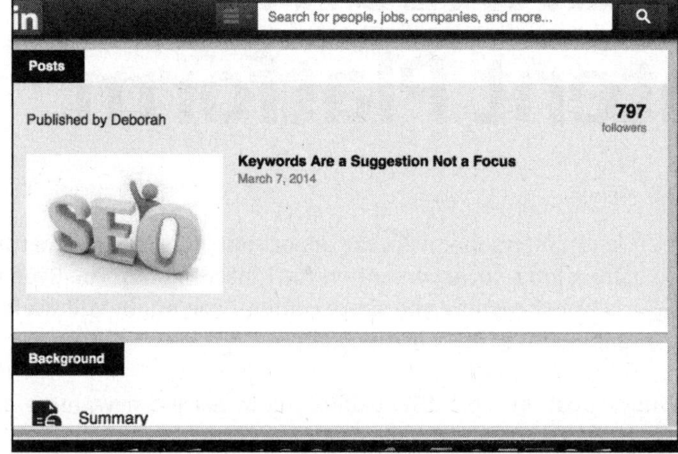

FIGURE 4-1: Your published posts appear in your profile, further establishing your expertise.

- **Your posts can be seen by your entire professional network on LinkedIn.** When you publish a post, your connections receive notification via the flag icon at the top of their LinkedIn pages. The bigger your network, the more people can potentially view your content.
- **People with whom you're not connected can see your posts, leading to new connections.**
- **If you don't already have a blog, you can use the LinkedIn platform.** Everything is already set up for you, and it's free.

» **LinkedIn members can follow your content without having to follow you.**

» **You increase the chances for engagement with other professionals.** Readers can comment or like your posts.

Creating your first post

You can create your first or any post from your LinkedIn home page. Follow these steps:

1. **At the top left of any LinkedIn page, click Home.**

   Your LinkedIn home page appears. This page includes updates from connections and a space for you to add your own updates, as shown in Figure 4-2.

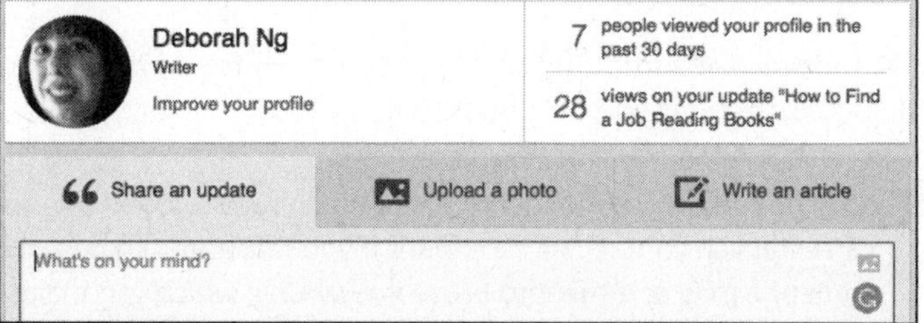

FIGURE 4-2: Access your LinkedIn blogging dashboard from your home page.

2. **At the top of the page, click Write an Article.**

   A blogging dashboard like the one shown in Figure 4-3 appears.

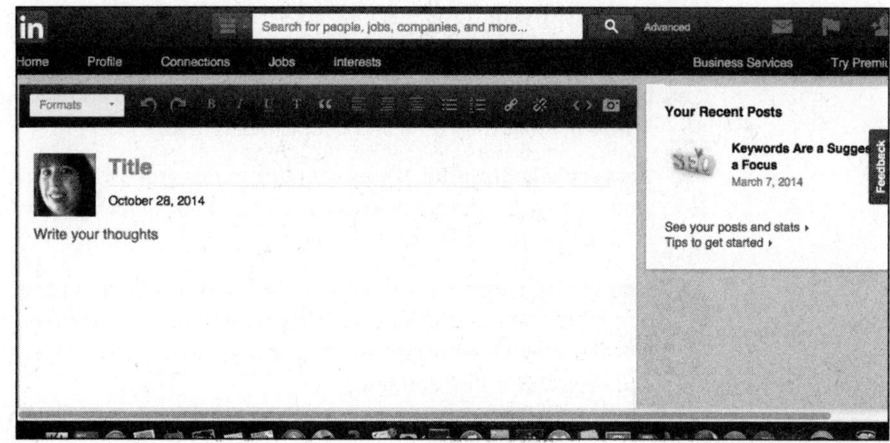

FIGURE 4-3: Start writing your post in the LinkedIn blogging dashboard.

3. **In the Title area, fill in your title.**
4. **In the Write Here area, write or paste content.**

   You can use the formatting buttons as needed.

5. **Click Publish, located at the top right of the page.**

TIP

Proofread! Giving your post one last read-through and format check before publishing ensures that you have no spelling, grammatical, or formatting errors; those mistakes can make you look unprofessional.

Writing in a professional voice

Because LinkedIn is considered a platform for professional, career-oriented people, you have to write in the proper tone. Although you can still use a casual blogging style, do be mindful of your words and topics.

What follows are some tips and best practices for writing in a professional voice and successful blogging on LinkedIn:

- **Stay in your area of expertise.** Stick with topics you know well so that you can establish yourself as an expert. If you talk about things you're unsure of, someone may comment to prove you wrong, which can make readers lose faith in your expertise.
- **Solve problems and answer questions.** What do people want to know about your industry and what you do? Make sure your content serves a purpose. Readers like posts that teach and guide.
- **Give advice to others starting out in your profession.** Young professionals are reading your posts on LinkedIn. What can you tell them that you wish you knew when you were just starting out?
- **Brevity counts.** Word count should fall between 500 and 800 words. Anything more than that, and people begin to lose interest.
- **Respectfully disagree.** If you're writing to disagree with another blogger or writer, be respectful in your disagreement. Make your points without finger-pointing, name-calling, or accusation.
- **Respond to comments.** If readers ask questions, share tips, or add to your discussion, be sure to respond. If they know you're likely to respond, and they feel as if their opinion matters, they're more likely to become regular readers and even share your content.
- **Link thoughtfully.** Add links as needed, but only if they add to the discussion. Don't write a post that contains nothing but links.

- **Know your demographic.** Understand whom you're writing for. You may have to do a little research and learn more about your connections, the people who visit your LinkedIn company page, or those who use your product or service.
- **Think carefully about your headline.** Try to avoid overly inflated headlines. Keep them brief and professional. If it looks like it belongs to a tabloid, you're on the wrong platform.
- **Use rich media.** Don't forget to add a visual element to your posts. LinkedIn enables you to use images, as well as embed videos from YouTube and presentations from SlideShare.

TIP

If you're still not sure about whether to write on LinkedIn's platform, take some time to look at some other blog posts there. Seeing how well it works for other professionals may inspire you to create some content. At the very least, try one post to test the waters.

Promoting Your LinkedIn Posts on Other Social Channels

Almost every content platform offers a way to share your newly created content with others, and LinkedIn is no different. In fact, it provides share buttons for LinkedIn, Facebook, Twitter, and Google+ right on your published post so that you can share as soon as you publish.

To share a post, follow these steps:

1. **Click the share button for the content platform you want to use, as shown in Figure 4-4.**

   A window appears for that social network.
2. **Fill in some brief descriptive text in the text window.**
3. **Click Share.**
4. **Repeat Steps 1 to 3 for each platform on which you want to share.**

TIP

Don't share your post more than once per platform; otherwise, it can be considered spam.

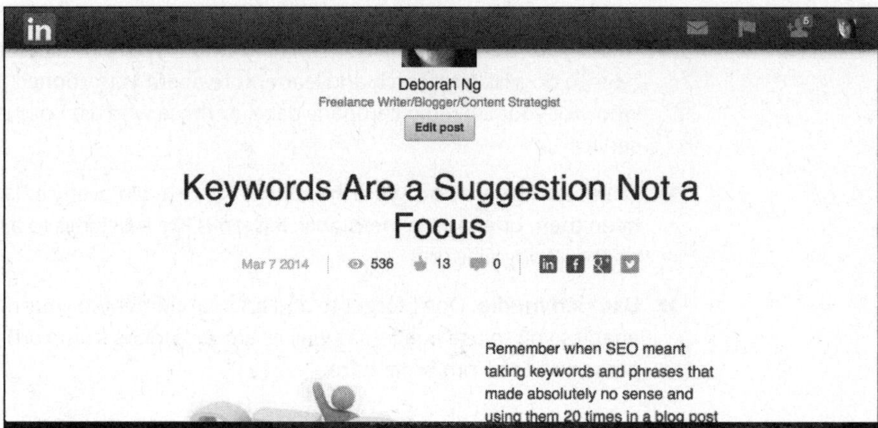

FIGURE 4-4: LinkedIn allows you to share your posts on other social networks.

Creating content on LinkedIn is another way to tell your brand's story, share tips and news regarding your industry, and increase your personal and professional brand visibility. The best part is that your posts have the potential to be seen by a vast professional community. How could you not take advantage of the opportunity?

7 Getting Visual

Contents at a Glance

CHAPTER 1: Pinning Down Pinterest 437
Understanding Pinterest 438
Getting Started. 439
Joining Pinterest. 441
Getting on Board 445
Pinning on Pinterest 448
Following on Pinterest 452
Sharing on Pinterest 453
Driving Traffic with Pinterest 455
Building Your Pinterest Community 459

CHAPTER 2: Snapchatting It Up! 463
Getting Started with Snapchat. 463
Taking Your First Snap 470
Telling Your Snapchat Story 471

CHAPTER 3: Getting Started with Instagram 477
Promoting Your Brand on Instagram 478
Creating and Using Your Instagram Account 479
Determining What Is Photo-Worthy for Your Brand 484
Using Hashtags in Your Instagram Posts 485
Finding Friends and Fans on Instagram 487
Using Instagram Stories 488

IN THIS CHAPTER

- » Understanding Pinterest
- » Setting up your Pinterest account
- » Creating boards, pinning pins, and growing your Pinterest community
- » Driving sales with Pinterest

Chapter 1 Pinning Down Pinterest

What is it about Pinterest that's so attractive? Is it the mouthwatering food images, the inspiring island-getaway shots, or the humorous jokes?

The answer is all of the above. Pinterest is a social network that enables you to share content, but with a twist: You can't see the text beyond the caption that the pinner adds when pinning the image to his or her board. Because Pinterest pulls only the images from blog posts and web articles, the site is very visually appealing. It's not an eye-catching headline that pulls you in, but rather colors and creativity.

One complaint people have about the various social networks is that everyone is sharing the same things across all the networks. They're making the same comments and sharing the same links and videos. Pinterest takes that sharing to a new level. It's not the same old, same old. Instead of seeing nothing but links, you're seeing vibrant, enticing images.

Pinterest is the perfect place to plan a vacation, redesign a kitchen, or landscape a backyard. By creating boards for all your interests, you're also saving images you might want to refer to later.

In this chapter, you find out about Pinterest, why it's so popular, and how you can use it to grow your online community and drive sales.

Understanding Pinterest

Pinterest is a social network based on images. Users upload photos (called *pins*) to create *boards*, or groups of images centered on a common theme. Members of the Pinterest community use Pinterest for different reasons. Some just like to share pretty photos or recipes, and others share images in hopes that those viewing the photos will click through and drive traffic to their blogs or website. Because it's a visual site, it's perfect for product-based retailers who are hoping to drive sales.

Pinterest is the perfect social network for clothing retailers, interior designers, foodies, landscapers, travel professionals, and members of any profession who can benefit from telling a story with an image. Although the US user base is primarily female, men are also using Pinterest to share funny images, sports-related photos, gadgets, and the great outdoors. Knowing how the different demographics are using Pinterest is important, especially if you're reaching out to a global market.

Before you dive into the Pinterest deep end, be familiar with these common Pinterest terms:

- **Pin:** An image or a video that you or someone else has uploaded to a board on Pinterest, such as the one shown in Figure 1-1, is a *pin.* When you enter a URL or upload an image to one of your boards, you're pinning to that board.
- **Boards:** Each time you add a pin, you assign it to a category of your creation called a *board.* In essence, you're creating virtual pin boards. For instance, you can create a board named Funny and pin images that make you laugh, or you can make a board named Knitting Patterns to pin images from relevant how-to articles.
- **Pinner:** Someone who uses Pinterest.
- **Repin:** When you *repin* something, you add something pinned by someone else to one of your boards. (The Save It button appears at the top of a pin when you hover your mouse pointer over that pin.)
- **Comment:** You can discuss pins by commenting in the area below the pin.
- **Like:** If you enjoy someone's pin but don't necessarily want to repin it, you can show approval by liking it. Hover your mouse pointer over the pin and then, in the top right of the pin, click the like button (which looks like a heart).

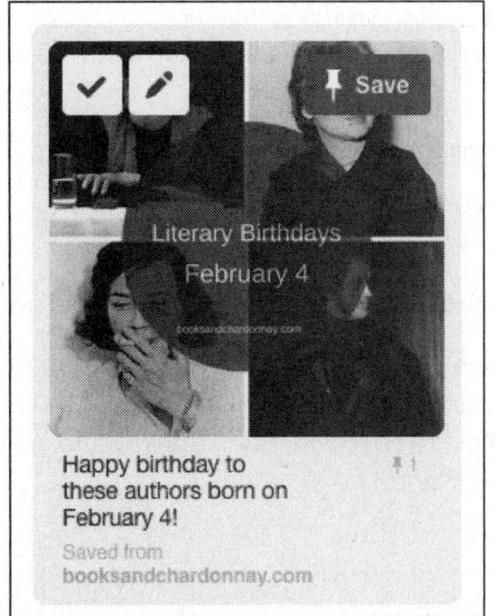

FIGURE 1-1: Each pin includes buttons for sharing or repining, liking, and commenting.

Getting Started

Before launching your Pinterest account, take some time to see what a few brands are doing on Pinterest. Whole Foods Market is a great example of a business that effectively uses Pinterest. Its boards tell the story of who it is without being overly promotional.

To search for a specific brand on Pinterest, follow these steps:

1. **In the Search box at the top of the page, type any company name and (see Figure 1-2), and then press Enter.**

   As you type, a drop-down menu appears with suggestions and items with that brand's name. You can choose the brand itself from the drop-down menu. Or you can choose one of the keyword options. If you do this, a results page appears, displaying every pin that uses that search term.

   At the very top of the page, you see more keywords. Choose one if you want, or browse the pins to see if one of those has what you are looking for.

2. **Click any button that appears above the search results to focus your search:**

   - *All Pins:* Shows all pins that contain the search term. This is the page you land on by default.
   - *Your Pins:* Shows pins you added to Pinterest that fall within the search term.
   - *Buyable Pins:* Showcases products people can buy directly on Pinterest.

- *People:* Shows all users who have that search term in their username or profile description.
- *Boards:* Shows all boards that have a title that includes the search term.

You can see the examples of keywords, as well as the five ways to sort your search results, in Figure 1-3.

3. **Click the Boards link to see the boards and the pins they contain.**

   Check out boards that have a good variety of pins and start thinking of ways your brand can incorporate pinning. If you're looking at brand examples for inspiration, it's probably best to check out boards the brand itself is pinning to, rather than pins about the brand.

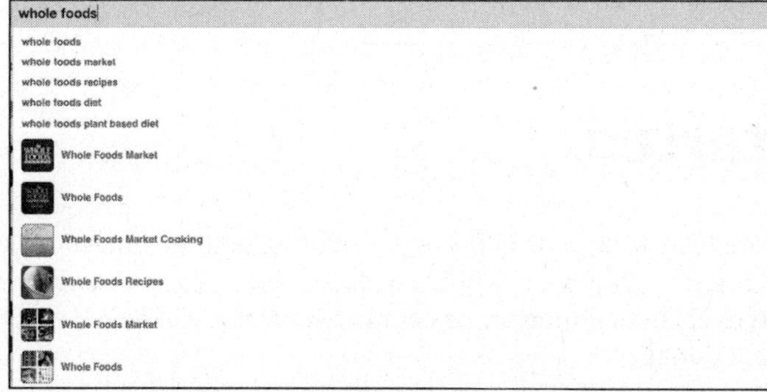

FIGURE 1-2: Type the name of the brand you're searching for in Pinterest's search engine.

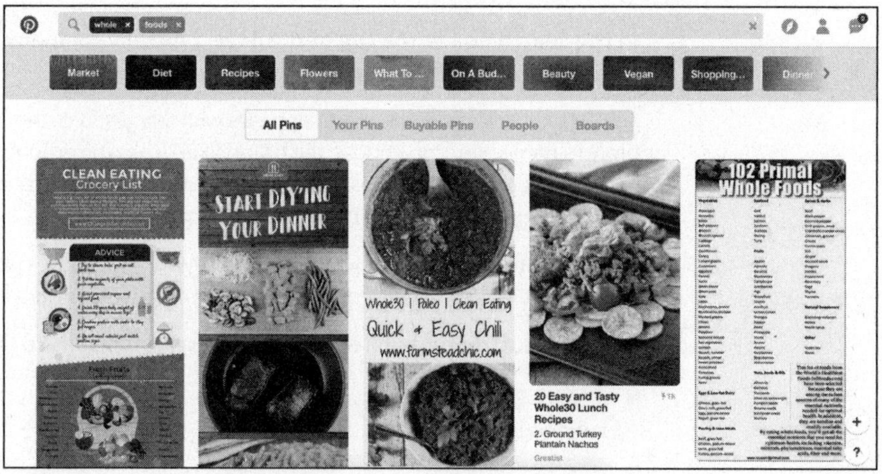

FIGURE 1-3: The five ways to sort your search results.

Joining Pinterest

To join Pinterest, head to `http://pinterest.com` and follow these steps to create an account:

1. **On the Pinterest home page, do one of the following:**

   - *Type your email address and desired password in the appropriate text boxes, and then click the red Continue button, as shown in Figure 1-4.*
   - *Sign in using your Facebook account by clicking the Continue with Facebook button.* When you log in with Facebook, you also have the option to follow your friends from that network after you provide your profile details.

   Next, a page appears that asks you what you're interested in, with many options to check off as interests.

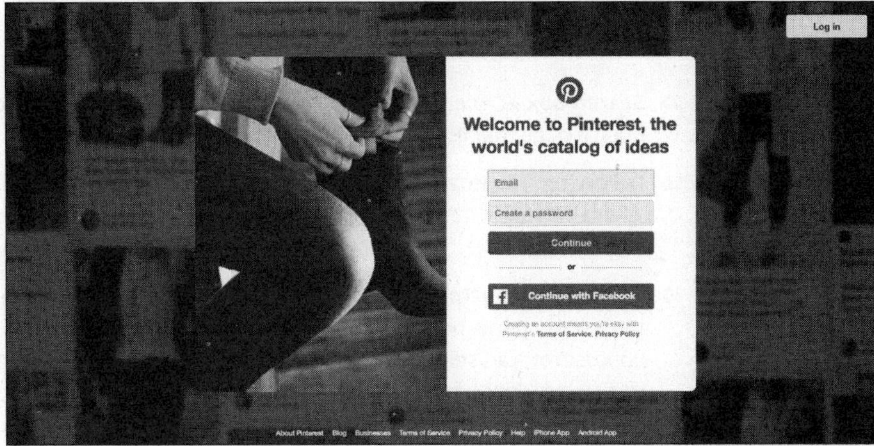

FIGURE 1-4: Sign up for Pinterest.

2. **Select the categories you like the most.**

   Don't worry, though, you can tweak and fine-tune your account any time.

3. **If you're signing up with email, do the following:**

   a. *Type your name.*

   b. *Select whether you are male or female.*

   c. *Type your age.*

   d. *Select the Continue as a Business link below the red Continue button.* (This set of steps is about brand pages, not a personal account.)

e. Type your email address, password, and business name, and select your business type from the drop-down menu. You can also list your business URL.

f. Click Create Account.

4. Click Follow.

Now you have some pins to look at.

After you get an account, the easiest way to log in is by using the same method you used to create the account: by Facebook or by typing your email address. After you log in, you can get started.

Navigating Pinterest

You have to know your way around Pinterest so that you can pin like a pro. Whenever you log in, you see the most recent pins added to the boards you follow.

Your Pinterest home page is organized as follows:

- **Search box:** At the top of the page is a Search box. Type a search term to open a page that lists pins associated with your search term.
- **Following:** The images you see on your Pinterest page are from pinners whom you follow. For each pinner, you can follow specific boards or all the person's boards.
- **Plus sign (+) button:** Click the plus sign (+) button, in the top right of your screen, to open a pop-up menu that you can use to add pins to your own boards. You can select the options Upload a Pin (to open the Upload an Image pop-up window, which you can use to locate an image file on your computer), Save from a Website (which opens the Add a Pin from a Website pop-up window), or Create Ad (to promote a pin).
- **Explore button:** At the upper right of the screen is the Explore button, which looks like a compass (see Figure 1-5). Click Explore to see new pins — not necessarily by people you already follow — in a variety of categories. The Explore button gives you a way to learn about new followers and topics.

Setting up your Pinterest profile

As with any social network, first impressions are important. They're especially important if you're using the social network as a marketing tool. Your Pinterest profile page is where pinners stop by to find out more about you. To get to this page, click your person icon in the top-right corner of any Pinterest page and select Settings from the drop-down menu. The profile page contains your profile image and a few words about you, links to drive traffic to your website and social networking accounts, and your boards.

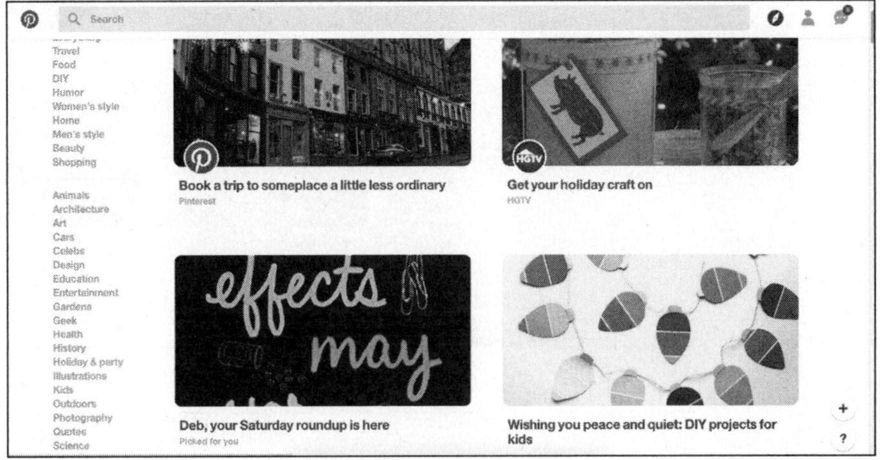

FIGURE 1-5: The compass icon gives you a way to search for new topics and pinners.

Before you get started on filling out your profile, get to know the elements of the Pinterest profile page, as shown in Figure 1-6:

- **Profile image:** The image you want to display that best represents your brand. Most brands use their logo or a photo of their product.
- **The profile itself:** The profile page shows your business name, information about your business, your location, and a link to your website.
- **Edit Profile:** Enables you to add your profile photo, bio, and links.
- **Settings button:** When you click the Settings button (gear icon), you see a variety of options, including Account Settings, Promoted Pins, Tips for Your Business, and Analytics.
- **Boards:** All your boards appear on your profile page, and you can see how many boards you have at the top of your profile page.
- **Pins:** Shows how many pins you have.
- **Followers:** The number of people who follow your boards on Pinterest.
- **Following:** The people and boards you follow on Pinterest.
- **Notifications:** The red Notifications button shows a number to tell you when people follow you or like your pins. (See Figure 1-7.) It also notifies you if someone has repinned your pins or added your pins to other boards.

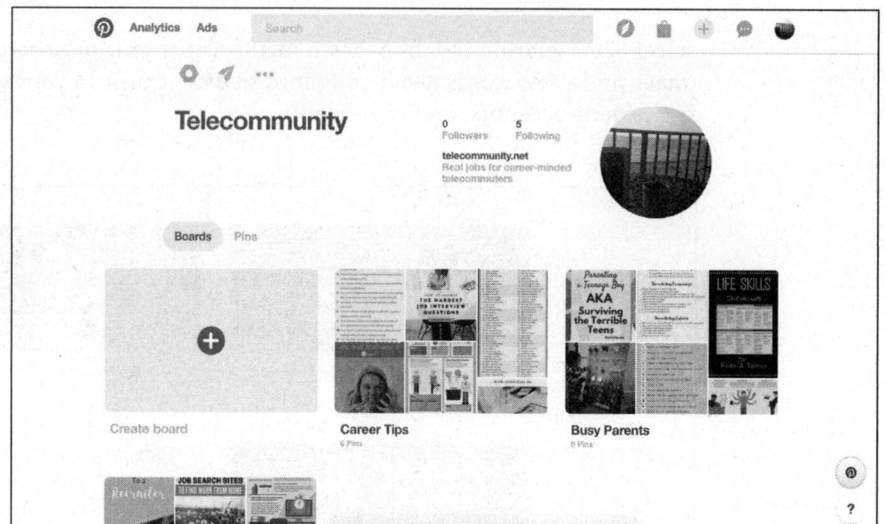

FIGURE 1-6: Your Pinterest profile page.

FIGURE 1-7: The Notifications button is located at the top right of the page.

Make sure your profile gives a positive impression to your Pinterest community, as well as any potential community members or customers, by filling out your profile information. Follow these steps to set up your profile page:

1. **Click your name or the person icon at the top right of any Pinterest page.**

   Your profile page appears.

2. **Click the gear icon, as shown in Figure 1-8.**
3. **Under Account Basics, click Profile.**
4. **Fill in all pertinent information and upload your profile photo.**
5. **Click Save Settings.**

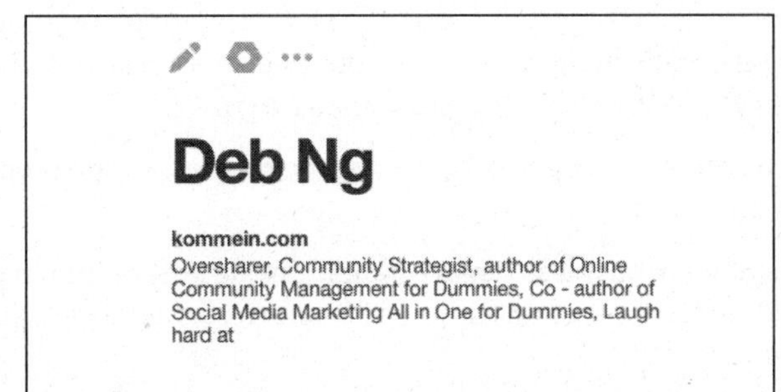

FIGURE 1-8: Click the gear icon to set up your profile page.

Getting on Board

Pinterest organizes users' content in *boards*, which resemble a series of bulletin boards hanging on a wall. Each board has its own label, as shown in Figure 1-9.

FIGURE 1-9: Pins are organized into topics called boards.

Boards organize your pins into categories of your choosing. However, if you treat your Pinterest boards as mere categories, you end up with a bunch of random generic groupings. If you treat boards as a marketing tool for your product, brand, or business, you can create content that people want to follow, encouraging them to find out more about what your brand is all about.

Basic boards can accomplish any number of goals, such as the following:

- **Show steps in a process.** For example, create a craft project and visually list the instructions.
- **Reflect different elements of planning.** Highlight party or wedding planning; kitchen and bath renovations; or food, drink, table settings, and theme ideas.
- **Provide an industry overview.** Pin the clothing styles, designers, and fabrics of the fashion world.

- **Show how something works.** Point out all the moving parts of a vehicle and how they come together to make the vehicle go.
- **Offer a recipe.** Provide pins illustrating the process of food preparation, from beginning to end.
- **Highlight your business departments.** Include images from meetings or production facilities, as well as news items, awards, accolades, and online mentions.

Planning your initial boards

Before you start pinning, you want to have several boards in place. You'll create new boards while you progress on Pinterest, but do plan the first few. Following are suggestions for your first boards:

- **History of your brand:** Go back to where you began and show how things have changed throughout the years. Pin promotional material or product labels from prior years to show how they've evolved.
- **History of your products:** Have your products received a makeover over the years? Has the packaging changed? Or maybe you have an archive of print ads spanning back through the decades. Use these items to create historic boards. When viewers see how long your product has been around, it tells them you have a product and a name worthy of their trust.
- **Brand showcase:** Entice people into buying by showing them how they can use your product or service. You can even pin unusual or uncommon uses. Additionally, community members love it when they're highlighted on brand pages. Ask your community members to send photos of themselves using your product or service.
- **Who you are:** A Pinterest board can make a great About page. Use it to highlight your team members, location, mission, and products or services.
- **Tips, how-to's, and DIYs:** Use your pins to teach. For example, if you're a writer, give tips for creating headlines and hooks. If you're a carpenter, share tips for creating projects that don't look homemade.
- **Gift ideas:** Product-oriented brands can benefit from pinning gift ideas. Take it even further by pinning a series of gift boards.
- **Books:** Recommend books that relate to your field. Lead a discussion in the comments section.

TIP

If you're at a loss as to the types of boards you can create, go through your company's archives, photo albums, and old files. You might find some literature from back in the day, memos and announcements, storyboards, and all kinds of inspiration.

Creating your first board

To create a board, follow these steps:

1. **On your company profile page, click the red button with the +, in the Create a Board box.**

   The Create a Board pop-up window appears.

2. **Fill in the Name text box.**

   Choose a name that will describe what your board is about, but in a way that catches the eye so other pinners will want to learn more.

3. **In the Description text box, enter a description of your board.**

   Add a brief paragraph or two describing your board and what makes it so unique.

4. **Select an option from the Category drop-down list.**

   Your category options include Architecture, Photography, Art, and Wedding & Events. Choose the one most representative of your board and your brand.

TIP

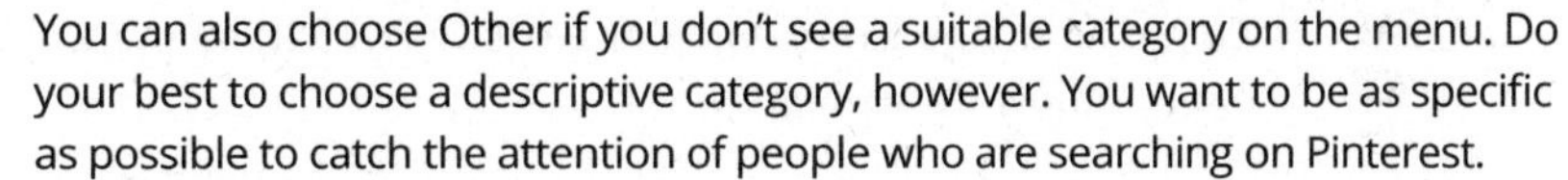

   You can also choose Other if you don't see a suitable category on the menu. Do your best to choose a descriptive category, however. You want to be as specific as possible to catch the attention of people who are searching on Pinterest.

5. **If you want to keep your board a secret, click the Keep It Secret option so that it displays Yes.**

   This option is set to No by default. If you're using Pinterest as a marketing tool, you most likely don't want yours to be a secret board that no one can see. However, if you're using Pinterest for research or to plan an event and don't want the world to know, you can select this option to make a secret board.

6. **If you want to add collaborators (pinners to contribute pins) to your board:**

   a. *Click the + sign next to your profile when you're on the page for that particular board.*

   b. *Add the collaborator's name and email address, or invite a person from your contacts.*

   If you want to be the only pinner, don't change a thing.

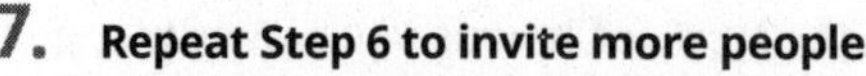

7. **Repeat Step 6 to invite more people.**

TIP

A collaborative board is a wonderful way to find out how others see your brand or niche and to get people excited about what you do.

8. **Click the Create button.**

You arrive at your newly created, and sadly empty, board. Go add some pins!

Pinning on Pinterest

Pinning can be addictive. Many pinners admit to spending hours pinning and finding items to like and repin. From a brand perspective, it may not look or feel like marketing because you're not doing, say, creating eye-catching headlines. (You *will* need a way with words for your descriptions, however.) But instead of those attention-grabbing headlines, you're using images and videos to capture the attention of the Pinterest community. That's why your content has to be appealing and colorful, and it needs to make folks want to learn more.

Pinning an image

Pinterest is a huge traffic driver. Funny and vivid images can capture the attention of thousands of people. To start, go ahead and pin something.

To pin an image from a blog or website (which, by the way, also links back to the blog), follow these steps:

1. **To pin something, click the plus sign (+) button, at top of the page.**

   A dialog box appears, containing a text box where you can enter a URL.

2. **Enter the URL of the item you want to pin, and then click Next.**

   Pinterest automatically pulls images from the website and displays them in the Choose a Pin page that appears.

3. **Click the arrow to cycle through the images to choose the one you want to pin.**

   Make sure you select a photo that's eye-catching and properly showcases what you're trying to show.

4. **Hover your mouse over the picture you want to pin and click the Save button that appears.**

   The Pick a Board dialog box opens.

5. **In the Board drop-down list, and select the board you want to pin to.**

   Alternatively, you can create an appropriate board. We discuss creating new boards in the section "Getting on Board," earlier in this chapter.

6. **In the Description text box, create a description of up to 500 characters.**
7. **Click the Pin It button at the bottom of the dialog box.**

   Your pin now appears in the feed on your main page, as well as on the feeds of everyone who follows that particular board.

WARNING

Some websites and blogs have blocked the capability to download or share their images because they don't want them reposted on Pinterest. If you come across a photo that has sharing disabled, seek permission before pinning the image. Don't violate a copyright.

Pinning the right images

At first glance, Pinterest might seem like a random bunch of images. On a typical Pinterest feed, most users see dozens of photos, and many of the same pins are repinned over and over.

Being random and repetitive might be okay for personal users, but a brand must make sure its pins are well thought out. Keep these points in mind when selecting an image to pin:

- **Images shouldn't conflict with the message you're trying to send.** You want the viewer to be clear, not confused, about what you pin. For example, it wouldn't make sense for a ravioli manufacturer to post pictures of vehicles — unless they were delivery trucks or made out of ravioli.
- **Images should make people feel good or evoke emotion.** You want people to see the images and react with a comment, a like, or a repin. Just like with Facebook posts or Twitter tweets, you want to know your Pinterest community is paying attention.
- **Images must be eye-catching, engaging, and unique.** You want your content to stand out, and you have only a few seconds for your pin to catch someone's attention. If a viewer's response isn't positive and immediate, chances are your pin won't get a second look.
- **Images should support your goals.** If you want to drive sales, create pins with sales in mind. Create a board of images showing happy people using your product or the result of using your service.

WARNING

If you want to drive traffic to a particular website, create one board with pins that link to the site. If every board you create and every image you pin is a link to your blog or website, you'll lose followers — fast — because they want to view wonderful images without feeling like they're being sold to all the time.

The rest of your boards should represent what you do without pushing sales or traffic.

Pinning the wrong images

You can come up with many ideas for what to pin, but there are plenty of types of pins you need to avoid. Because Pinterest is visual and pins appeal to emotions, pinning one of the following can lead to unfollows:

- **Out-of-focus photos:** Images should be sharp and vivid.
- **Photos that have no rhyme, reason, or purpose:** Although not every pin should be about your brand, if you have too many pins that are off topic, you might confuse your followers.
- **Repins that everyone is repinning:** If you pin the same things everyone else is pinning, Pinterest users have no reason to follow you.
- **Rude and offensive photos:** Be considerate of your community. Leave swearing and vulgarity out of it, lest folks get the wrong message about you and your brand. If you wouldn't say something to a customer in person, don't say it on Pinterest.
- **Constantly spamming with sales messages:** Few people use Pinterest to receive sales messages. Avoid pitching to the Pinterest community. Instead, let your images be your pitch. If you're known for making it all about the sale, no one will want to follow you.
- **Bait-and-switch images:** Don't mislead your followers. If you pin an image and it refers to an article called "10 Reasons to Paint Your Bedroom Purple," that's what people should see. Don't reference one thing on Pinterest only to have users click through to something different, such as a sales page.

TIP

Whenever you repin someone else's pin, make sure the pin is legitimate: Test the pin by clicking through to the website. There's nothing worse than to repin something only to find out later that it's one of those hated bait-and-switch pins.

When you first start with Pinterest, it may be frustrating to wait for people to comment on your pins. It takes a while to grow a community and start receiving comments. Use the following tips to create the types of pins people feel inclined to comment on:

- **Appeal to emotion.** Whether it's laughing out loud or choking back tears, people talk about pins that inspire emotion. Before you pin something, ask yourself how you feel about it. If the answer is indifferent, consider finding something more thought-provoking.
- **Pin items your target audience can relate to.** It's important for you to stay on topic with your Pinterest community. For example, if you're marketing to parent bloggers, your pins should reflect items of interest to parents. If you're an automotive dealership, consider posting photos of cars or funny street signs. You want your community members to relate to you. If you go off topic, that only confuses people. If they're relating to your pins, they'll comment to tell you why.
- **Nothing is wrong with controversy from time to time.** Don't post negative pins, but don't shy away from discussion-worthy topics simply because they're hot topics.
- **Be different.** There may be times when you look at your feeds and notice that everyone is repinning the same thing. It's great for the original pinner if something goes viral, but after a while, seeing the same image over and over gets boring. Go against the grain and find something different. Search Pinterest for pins that are compelling and unique, or create unique content and share that.
- **Find out what people are responding to.** Take a ride around Pinterest. Which types of pins are getting the most comments and why? Is it the type of pin? The types of friends? How is the pinner interacting? Take notes.

Tagging

Tagging on Pinterest is similar to tagging on Facebook or Twitter. You *tag* people, or type their name so it links to their account, to call their attention to your pins. For example, you can tag someone if he's in the photo you're pinning or if the topic is of interest to him. When you call someone's attention to your photos through tagging, she might be inclined to share your pins with her communities too.

Here's how you tag someone on Pinterest: In the description area of the pin, put an @ symbol in front of the name of the person you want to tag. If that person is a friend (see the following section for a discussion of following people on Pinterest), a menu of pinners' names appears from which you can select. If that person isn't a friend, you can't tag him.

When a person is tagged, she is notified that you've tagged her in a pin. Tagging is a great way to call a person's attention to a particular pin. For example, suppose you have a client who loves Italian food. If you're connected to him on Pinterest, you can let him know you posted a delicious recipe for him to consider. He'll appreciate that you were thinking about him!

Following on Pinterest

What fun is it to create boards and share pins when there's no one to share them with? To make friends, you have to first follow others. Following is similar to friending on Facebook. When you *follow* someone, you're choosing to have her boards and pins show up in your feed, which can help you find people you want to know more about and inspire others to follow you in return.

Determining the types of people you want to follow and want to have follow you requires some strategy. Although your goal is to reach a wide variety of people, you also want to target the people who will do the most good. And by *good,* we mean those who will follow through with liking, commenting on, and repinning your content.

Following friends

Because you're representing a brand, you definitely want to appeal to the people who already follow your brand on Facebook, Twitter, and other social networks. However, you don't want to solely rely on your loyal existing online community to make up your Pinterest community. The reason you join any social network is to grow your community, and you can't grow it by following (and being followed by) the same people on every platform.

Definitely announce on your blog, Twitter, Facebook, Google+, and other social media services that you've started a Pinterest page. But to build up the number of pinners you follow and who follow you, also contact social-networking connections directly and let them know you want to connect on Pinterest.

Following folks you don't know

After you exhaust all your known contacts, it's time to branch out to make new friends to follow. To find new friends to whom you aren't already connected, use the Search box located at the top of any of your Pinterest pages. You can also use the Categories drop-down list above Pinterest feeds, and then browse the categories that appear to find pins and pinners that would be a good fit for your community.

Before randomly following everyone who pins, make sure you share common interests and that your brand page fits the types of pins they post and the interests discussed in their personal profiles.

Also, before you begin following others, have some boards already created. This way, when people follow you in return, they have something to look at, as well.

TIP

If you're worried about being overwhelmed by too many images in your feed, you don't have to follow every board by a particular pinner. You have the option to follow only the boards that interest you.

Don't randomly follow people. Make a list of the types of people you want to follow and the keywords and phrases you can use to find them, including the search engine optimization terms you use for your website or other social-networking profiles. Search for existing customers so that they can continue to support you by sharing your pins.

Sharing on Pinterest

Many marketers who were skeptical about Pinterest at first now admit that it's a great source for sharing information about brands, products, and services. With the right image and the right descriptive text, a picture really is worth a thousand words.

Sharing other people's pins

When you share another person's pin in your feed, you *repin* it. Similar to a Facebook share or Twitter retweet, a repin tells the original pinner you liked what she posted so much, you also wanted to share.

To repin a pin that you like, follow these steps:

1. **Hover your mouse pointer on the pin that you want to share, and click the red Save button that appears in the top left of the pin.**

   The Choose board window pops up with the pin on the left and board options on the right. The Description section automatically populates with what the original pinner wrote.

2. **From the Boards drop-down list, select the board to which you want to repin the image.**

   You have the option to select a board you already have or create a board. As soon as you select a board, it will save your pin.

3. **(Optional) Change the description.**

   If the description contains helpful information, such as the name of a particular food dish, we recommend leaving it as-is.

Note: You can also click the pin, which takes you to the pinner's page and to the pin itself. You can like the pin from there in the same manner. Click the pin image one more time to be taken to the original website where the image came from.

Using share buttons

Ultimately, you want others to share your content on Pinterest. The ideal situation is for other people to read your blog or view one of your photographs and pin it, inspiring dozens of repins. However, you have to make it easy to do so.

Most people who read content online won't share the same content if sharing isn't made easy for them. Although it doesn't take more than a few seconds to cut a link and paste it into the Pinterest Add function, it's too much trouble for most. They want to be able to share at the click of a button and not have to leave their current page.

Share buttons enable the people who view your content to share it without visiting Pinterest. The user simply clicks the Pin It button, fills in the description, and chooses a board, and your content is pinned to his board. If you're not logged in to Pinterest already, you're taken to the login screen so you can do so first.

Here are a few features and plug-ins to look into:

- **Pin It:** Available from Pinterest at `http://pinterest.com/about/goodies`, the Pin It button enables you to embed code on your blog or website so that others can pin your content. Pin It is available for WordPress blogs and even Flickr so that you can share your photos with others.
- **Pinterest Follow button:** You can add this button to your blog or website. Grab the code at `https://developers.pinterest.com/tools/widget-builder/?type=follow` and paste the code where you feel it will do the most good. Most people like pasting the code into their right sidebars at eye level. Share buttons should never be difficult to find.
- **Sumo.me Image Sharer:** This WordPress plug-in, at `https://sumo.com/app/image-sharer`, enables the user to share visual content on Pinterest, Instagram, and elsewhere.
- **ShareThis:** Another plug-in that enables social share buttons. When you activate this plug-in, share buttons appear at the top or bottom of the page. You can find it at `https://wordpress.org/plugins/share-this`.

Although DiggDigg and ShareThis aren't specific to Pinterest, these popular share buttons are used to share content on Pinterest and other social networks. People who use one of these plug-ins have the option to tweet, pin, post on Facebook, and so on. Because DiggDigg and ShareThis feature all the social networks, the majority of bloggers who use share buttons on their content use these plug-ins rather than installing a bunch of individual ones.

Driving Traffic with Pinterest

Did you know that Pinterest drives more traffic to individual blogs and websites than YouTube, Google+, and LinkedIn combined? That's a force to be reckoned with, and it's why Pinterest, unlike some of the other emerging social networks, is something anyone marketing a brand needs to take seriously.

Here's how the traffic flow works. If you're following proper Pinterest etiquette, you're sharing a good mix of content (which can be both images and video). Some of that content is from your own sources, such as your blog or website. The rest of your content is from other content, including repins and other people's blog posts or videos. In fact, most of the items you pin shouldn't be your own content. Unless an image is uploaded directly, most images are links from external sources. Most people who are marketing with Pinterest do so because they want pinners to click their links. However, it isn't as simple as sharing a link and hoping people visit your website; you have to be strategic.

Consider the following when creating and sharing content on Pinterest:

- **Select images with Pinterest in mind.** Your most important goal when creating pin-worthy content is to select an image that represents the article and entices others to click through to the originating site. Don't go through the motions and select some random stock photo. Use colorful, thought-provoking, and awe-inspiring photos. Pinterest automatically gives image options when you're preparing to pin something from a site, so take advantage of that opportunity to select the best pin! Photos that tell a story will inspire others to click to learn more.
- **Be descriptive.** On Pinterest, brevity is essential. With that said, you should write a description worthy of the image. It's not exactly a headline but, similar to a headline, you want to use the description to capture attention. Share one or two sentences describing the image but leave most of the details to the imagination.
- **Tag when possible.** Tagging all your friends every time you post a pin is annoying. However, if a pin reminds you of someone or if you want to give

credit to a particular pinner, do tag. The person being tagged, more often than not, will like or share your pin, and that helps get your brand on other people's radars. Individual followers appreciate the shout-out and will be encouraged to share as well.

- **Give others the opportunity to pin your content.** Use share buttons on your blog posts, articles, images, and videos so that others can share with their friends.
- **Use keywords and search terms.** In your descriptions, use the words and phrases that people are searching for. People also search for images online, so optimize your photos for search to help others find them. We talk about keywords in the section "Using keywords," later in this section.
- **Grow your community.** Keep finding new people to follow and interact with. While you grow your Pinterest community, you also grow traffic. We talk more about community later in this chapter, in the "Building Your Pinterest Community" section.
- **Be consistent.** Pin on a regular basis. If people never see anything new from you, they have no reason to continue to follow your pins.
- **Get nichey.** Cater to your niche. Appeal to the people who are most likely to use your products or services.
- **Use humor.** People love to share funny pins, and humor is a great way to break up the themes of your regular pins now and again.
- **Pay attention to your board categories.** Don't be generic. Your boards should be as eye-catching as your images. Take special care with the names you use for your boards. Pinterest suggests names, but those are only suggestions. Don't be afraid to change them. Be creative and imaginative, and explore how other brands are using boards.
- **Be strategic when arranging your boards.** Don't have a random mishmash of boards. Arrange them in an order that puts the most important boards first. If your goal is to sell, place the board with pins relating to your products or services first.

REMEMBER

When we talk about sharing content and arranging boards, not every pin has to be your content or from you. You can use other people's content on your boards and in your pins.

Being descriptive but brief

The descriptions you include with pins are just as important as the images. The words you use to describe an image, not the image itself, brings in search traffic.

If you're a travel agent and are posting a photo taken in Bora Bora, for example, you should let the viewer know where the image was taken, but you also need to tell the viewer that you can arrange vacations there. Write a description such as, "This gorgeous vista is Bora Bora. Now doesn't it make you want to plan your next tropical getaway there?" With this description, you also appear in searches for *Bora Bora*, *tropical*, and *getaway*. Did you notice that we didn't state directly that we can plan the vacation for the viewer, though? Drive traffic with your pin but avoid appearing too "selly" to the viewer. You want the viewer to come to you.

Pinterest doesn't allow descriptions to break text into paragraphs, which means descriptions can become one long-winded block of text if you're not careful. Make sure your message comes across in a few clear, concise sentences.

Finding the right words

Because you're using Pinterest as a sales or marketing tool, you want to be visible to search engines. You also want to create a description so enticing that pinners click through to your website when you pin your own items.

What follows are a few best practices for creating the best descriptions for your pins:

- **Use search engine optimization (SEO).** We talk about SEO a lot in this book because it's so important to catch the attention of the search engines. By all means, use search terms in your pin descriptions, but don't make it obvious. The terms you use should flow naturally. Think about what words people use, or words you want them to use, to land on your brand in Pinterest. Use those words or terms in a way that doesn't look silly.
- **Use words that paint a picture.** A description should, well, describe. If you pinned an image of a hen holding a flag, avoid stating the obvious. *This is a hen holding a flag* is descriptive but kind of boring. Calling the hen *patriotic* is less boring and describes the hen without insulting the intelligence of the reader.
- **Use words that stimulate discussion.** Try to phrase sentences so they're open ended. When you ask questions, request more information, or make a statement that leaves room for interpretation, you're more likely to receive comments.
- **Use titles if they benefit you.** If you're pinning from a link to an article or a blog post, nothing is wrong with using the original title as your description. However, there's also nothing wrong with *not* using the title and instead describing the image using words that benefit your brand and bring searchers to your board or pin.

» **Let your personality show.** Don't be afraid to be funny, perky, or anything else that helps you and your brand shine. Avoid bland, general terminology and Internet slang. Use words that show your personality instead.

» **Avoid negativity.** Don't use words that evoke negative images or connotations. Always go for a positive point of view. But be appropriate and authentic. If your business sells Goth items, for example, dark words might be expected by the audience.

Finding pinners to emulate

You can get help from the top pinners in your community to see which pins are receiving the most attention. Just click Categories (compass icon) at the top of any Pinterest window, and then select the pins that will best suit your needs. Each pin shows how many likes and repins it receives. If a pin is going viral — you see the pin more than once — look for the pin's original source.

Using keywords

After you find the top pinners (discussed in the preceding section), read a sampling of their pins. Think about the descriptive words and phrases you would use to find them. Are they using the same keywords? For example, if a bedroom set has gone viral, read the description to note if it's a *girl's bedroom set* or a *blue bedroom set.* Those descriptive terms are keyword phrases. Consider the words and phrases people are using to find pins and use those words and phrases in your own pins.

What follows are some best practices when using keywords on Pinterest:

» **Keywords and phrases should sound natural.** People don't type information into search engines in the same way they speak. For example, they would type *wet iPhone* instead of *How to dry a wet iPhone*. When pinning, use phrases that sound natural. Pinterest is a visual platform, and the words should be as pleasing as the photos.

» **Avoid creating pins with keywords in mind.** Write for the people, not the platform. Definitely use keywords in your pins, but don't put up any old photo just because you want to use a keyword.

» **The keyword or phrase should match the pin.** Don't use a keyword unless it describes the pin. You'll lose followers if you're known to bait and switch.

» **Use keywords for board titles.** Rather than using Pinterest-suggested titles for your boards, use your own titles that include keywords. This way, both boards and pins will appear in a search.

Building Your Pinterest Community

Even though you're using Pinterest as a marketing tool, make no mistake: Building a community on any of the social networks is more about others than it is about you. Your Pinterest community is made up of people who share like-minded interests. They visit Pinterest for their own reasons. They may be pinning to promote books, learn about particular topics, or market their own businesses. They want you to be part of their communities, too. That's why interaction and participation are so important.

A variety of people make up your Pinterest community. As with the other social networks, you follow and are followed by friends, co-workers, family, new friends whom you met online, and strangers. When you harness the power of your community, you're turning online friends into loyal customers and creating word-of-mouth marketing.

REMEMBER

Driving traffic isn't about typing *CLICK MY LINKS* in big, bold letters. It's about giving people a reason to want to learn more about you. Driving traffic is more about creating the right types of content and building your community than it is using a sales pitch. When you take on a warm tone over marketing speech, you have a better chance of winning them over.

Collaborating with group boards

A great way to connect with your community is to collaborate on boards. Pinterest lets pinners participate in *group boards*, where like-minded people add pins around a common theme. For example, crafters can contribute to a board featuring current projects, or LEGO enthusiasts can pin their latest creations.

Here are a few reasons pinners are collaborating:

- **Exposure:** You're marketing your brand, and others are doing the same. Having pins on a collaborative board means more exposure. Moreover, some of the pins you share will lead to your blogs and websites.
- **Community:** If you consistently post intriguing pins, others will want to see more of your Pinterest pins and boards. Group boards are a terrific community-building tool.
- **Camaraderie:** Some pinners just enjoy planning boards around a theme in the spirit of fun collaboration.

To create a group board, you essentially follow the steps to create a regular board. See the "Creating your first board" section, earlier in the chapter. After the group board is created, those who are invited to collaborate receive a notification and can begin pinning immediately.

TIP

Check your notifications — the number in the red box at the top of your screen indicates how many you have.

Here are some additional things to consider about group boards:

- **Invite people you trust.** Be sure group pinners have your best interests at heart and won't spam the boards.
- **Invite people who are knowledgeable about the topic.** When you plan a board, choose people who know the subject matter. If you don't, your board will be a mishmash of items instead of a visually, informative resource.
- **Establish clear guidelines.** You want to establish some guidelines for pinning to your group board so there's no inappropriate content. You can provide this information in an email before you invite pinners — in either a heads-up that an invite is on the way or, better, a request asking whether it's okay to send the invite.
- **Stay on topic.** If the board is meant to share the architecture of New York City and someone pins an image of the St. Louis's Gateway Arch, you'll probably want to alert the pinner to remove it unless it's germane to the discussion.

Liking pins

The fun isn't contained to only your boards. Showing approval for other people's boards and pins by liking them tells the pinner that he's on the right track. And if you like pins by people you don't know, they might want to look at your pins and subsequently follow you in return.

Likes show the Pinterest community you do more than pin and that you're not just on Pinterest to pimp out your own stuff. When others land on your page and see that you like a lot of images, they might be inclined to friend you so that you can like their stuff, too. When people see photos with a lot of likes to them, they want to see what all the fuss is about and click through for more information.

To like a pin, hover your mouse pointer on the pin's image. The Save Send, and Like buttons appear. Click the Like button (heart icon) to show the pinner you like her pin.

Commenting on pins

You may think the fun is in the pinning, but that's not it at all. The fun is in the conversation.

Don't wait for people to make remarks on your pins to engage with your community. Go ahead and comment on other people's pins. Do you have an opinion on a particular image? Tell the pinner how you feel! Does an image evoke emotion? Share that emotion with the person who pinned. Do you have questions or concerns? Share those, as well. Conversations ensue when others comment.

To comment, click the pin. That pin now fills your entire window. Scroll down to the bottom of the page where you see your picture or logo. Right next to that is a Comment drop-down link. Because it's white on white, the text box can get lost on the page; but if you remember that it's next to your picture towards the bottom of the page, you'll find it. Type in your comment and press Enter.

REMEMBER

Always be polite in your comments. Some people on the Internet are looking to start fights by posting rude and negative comments. Don't give them the pleasure of knowing they've gotten under your skin by responding. Take the higher road.

Playing nice

Every social network has its own set of etiquette rules, and Pinterest is no exception. Most social networking etiquette is in place so you don't annoy others, but most of it is common sense and courtesy.

Keep in mind that etiquette isn't made up of hard-and-fast rules; rather, it's a series of best practices most pinners follow to keep Pinterest free of spammers, trolls, and people who make the experience more difficult by causing arguments. Here's a list of Pinterest etiquette tips:

» **Give credit where credit is due.** If you're sharing another person's pin, always give a shout-out to the original source. For example, after uploading a pin and sharing it in your feed, type *via @name* at the bottom of your description.

When sharing online content, some photographers or websites want you to ask permission before posting their images on Pinterest. You may feel you're doing a third party a favor by linking to that party's work, but because Pinterest pulls the image and you gave Pinterest permission to use your content, the original source may want compensation or recognition.

TIP

Be safe; follow the intellectual property rules laid out in the About Pinterest page. `https://about.pinterest.com/en/copyright`.

» **Fill out descriptions for all your pins.** It's not always easy to tell what the pin is about. For example, not everyone will know the name of a recipe or the location of an island scene. It's a courtesy to your friends to let them know what you're pinning.

» **Avoid over-pinning.** We know that pinning is addictive. However, don't flood your friends' streams with dozens of photos at once. Pace yourself. If they see only your pins all the time, and everyone else's pins are lost, your friends are going to stop following you.

» **Don't spam.** Mix up your pins so they provide a variety of content. For example, share other people's blog posts, web articles, and images (if you have permission). Don't make everything link back to your own website or sales page.

» **Keep your pin descriptions brief.** If your description is filled with all the details that are in the pin's original link, why would anyone click through to the pin's site for more information? See the earlier "Driving Traffic with Pinterest" section for tips on writing a tantalizing pin description.

REMEMBER

Most rules of etiquette are good common sense. If you think something you do might make others uncomfortable, it probably will. Also, take some time to test other people's links before sharing to make sure they are still active and lead to appropriate content.

IN THIS CHAPTER

» Setting up a Snapchat account

» Telling your brand's story

» Engaging with your Snapchat community

Chapter 2

Snapchatting It Up!

Snapchat is taking social business by storm. Like Instagram, Snapchat is a mobile app, so you can't schedule posts from your computer. However, many brands are finding benefits from having a mobile account and sharing their Snapchat stories with their online communities. Unlike other platforms, Snapchat isn't about sharing links and directing people to a specific page with a text call to action. Instead, brands use Snapchat to share photos and brief videos called *stories* with their Snapchat community.

In this chapter, you find out how to join Snapchat as well as the basics of using Snapchat for your brand.

Getting Started with Snapchat

Here are some reasons to consider using Snapchat for your business:

- **You can target a new audience.** Snapchat is the social media platform of choice for Millenials and teens. If you're looking for a way to reach a younger, hipper demographic, try Snapchat.
- **Sharing is visual.** The only content you have to write is a caption, so you don't have to commit a big block of time to creating content.

- **Posts and stories are brief.** Snaps are either a photo or a 10-second video. Sharing with your community is quick, so you can free up your time for other campaigns and platforms.
- **Chat with individuals.** Snapchat makes it easy to have a private conversation with the members of your brand's Snapchat community.
- **Snaps aren't permanent.** Snaps and stories are permanently deleted after 24 hours.
- **Snaps are real time.** You can't upload to Snapchat. Photos and videos are spontaneous and in the moment.
- **There's no public feed for brands.** People can't access your snaps unless they have the Snapchat app. Moreover, they have to subscribe to your snaps to see them.
- **Snaps appeal to those with short attention spans.** Your customers don't have to commit to watching 15 or 30 minutes of video to learn about your latest product or service. Snapchat videos are only 10 seconds long.
- **Branded filters are available for occasions and events.** Snapchat enables brands to use geofilters, company-branded frames for their snaps, events, launches, and more.
- **Snapchat has more than 300 million monthly active users.** With so many active users, it makes sense to go where all the people are.

TIP

As with other social media platforms, take some time to see how other businesses are using Snapchat. Doing so will not only give you a sense of what Snapchat is all about but also inspire creative ideas for your own business.

Setting up an account

Snapchat is an app available only for smartphones. You can't use Snapchat on a tablet, laptop, or computer. To set up a Snapchat account, first head to your App store (for Apple products) or Google Play Store (for Android) to download the Snapchat app.

Then, to set up your account, follow these steps:

1. **Open Snapchat on your smartphone, and select Sign Up, as shown in Figure 2-1.**
2. **Enter your first name and last name, as shown in Figure 2-2, and then tap Sign Up & Accept.**

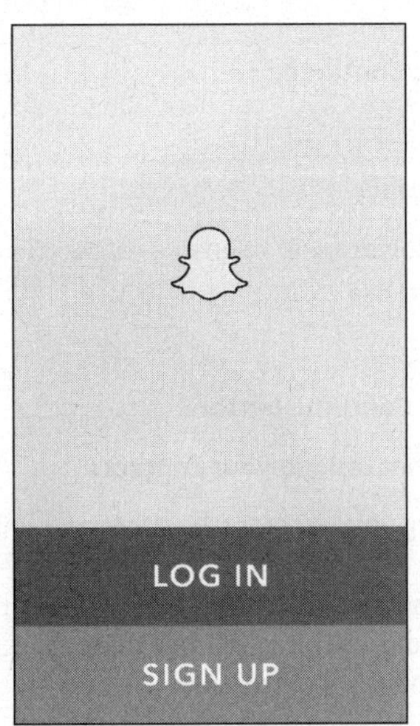

FIGURE 2-1: Sign up to use Snapchat.

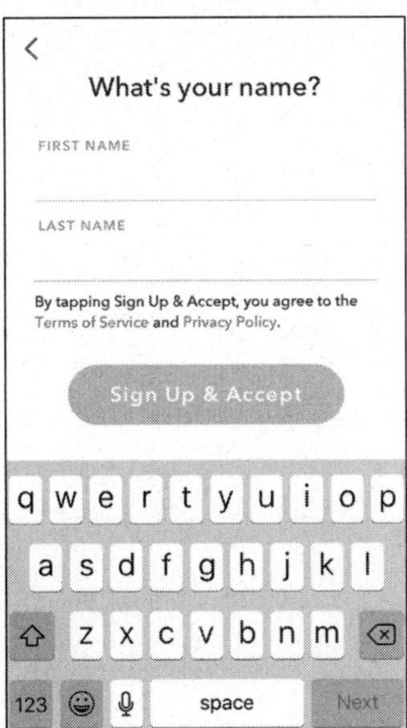

FIGURE 2-2: Type your name.

3. **Enter your birthday.**

   By doing so, you verify that you're old enough to use Snapchat.

4. **Choose a username that's at least three characters and tap Continue.**

   Use your company name or a name that best represents your business. Choose wisely!

5. **Enter your password and tap Continue.**
6. **Enter your email address.**
7. **Enter your mobile phone number.**

   Snapchat sends you a verification number to ensure that you're not a spammer, a scammer, or another unsavory type of person.

8. **Enter the verification code.**
9. **Once you're verified, tap the Continue button.**
10. **Decide whether to let Snapchat upload your contacts.**

    It's up to you if this is something you want for a business account.

Now that your account is set up, add a selfie as your Snapchat profile image. Click the white ghost icon, at the top of your screen, and take a series of photos that best represent your brand, as shown in Figure 2-3.

FIGURE 2-3: Tap the ghost icon to upload your selfie or logo.

TIP

Profile photos are a sequence of shots instead of just one, so Snapchat takes a series of rapid-fire shots. Don't move the phone away from its intended target.

Understanding the lingo

Before we get any further along in the process, it's time to learn the lingo. Here are the terms you should know if you want to use Snapchat:

- **Snap:** A photo or a 10-second video you take using Snapchat.
- **Story:** A photo or a series of photos set up to last 24 hours before disappearing.
- **Chat:** Comments back and forth with you and other members of your community.
- **Score:** The number under your profile photo. Your score indicates the number of snaps you've shared and viewed.
- **Lens:** Special effects such as a crown or a wreath that you can add to your selfies when you take your photo.
- **Memories:** Published snaps saved to a special place so they live longer than the 24-hour viewing period.
- **Filter:** Add to snaps to commemorate an event, such as a frame of garland to adorn your picture for a holiday snap.
- **Geofilter:** Used for location-based events. For example, if you're attending a music festival that is taking place in only one location, you can use a geofilter set up by the festival's organizers. It might have a date, logo, and location.
- **Snapcode:** Similar to a QR code, it's used to add friends with the touch of a button.

Touring the Snapchat screens

Now let's talk about some of the bells and whistles you can find in Snapchat. From the Snap screen, shown in Figure 2-4, you see the following:

- **Chat button:** Have a private conversation with your friends.
- **Stories button:** View your story or your friends' stories. When you tap this button, you see the following options:
  - *Your Stories:* A chronological display of all your stories available for viewing.
  - *Your Friends' Stories:* Stories from your friends that are available for viewing.
  - *Recent Updates:* Updates from friends and brands you follow.
  - *Discover:* A place where you can discover new people and brands to follow.
- **Image/Video button:** Use the round button to take a photo or a video.

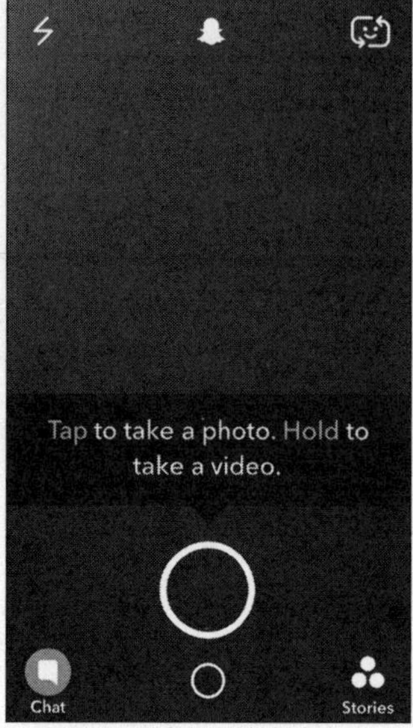

FIGURE 2-4: The Snap screen is where you take photos or video or access Chat and Stories sections.

From the Profile screen, shown in Figure 2-5, you see the following:

- **Share:** Share snaps via message or social networks.
- **Create Bigmoji:** Create your own emoji.
- **Settings:** The wheel icon allows you to access a dashboard, where you can edit your information, ban users from viewing your snaps, access Snapchat support, or log out.
- **Added Me:** Display which friends added you and gave you access to their snaps.
- **Add Friends:** See a variety of options for adding friends, such as by Snapchat username (if you know it), contacts, or Snapcode. No one can view your snaps without your approval.
- **My Friends:** Get a list of all your friends.
- **Snap button:** The round button takes a photo or video.
- **Trophies:** Users are awarded trophies based on Snapchat usage. See yours when you click the trophy.

FIGURE 2-5: Other Snapchatters see your Profile screen when they follow your account.

Tips for adding followers

What's the point of sharing all your wonderful stories if no one is around to view them? Snapchat doesn't have a public feed. You share either with individuals or with everyone who follows your account. And your snaps can't be viewed by someone who doesn't have the Snapchat app and whom you haven't approved.

With a business account, it's in your best interests to add as many relevant followers as possible. Don't just hope people will request to follow your brand. Take the initiative to seek out followers.

To add or find friends to grow your Snapchat community, do the following:

TIP

- **Use the Snap code.** At public events, encourage your customers to use the Snap code so you add each other to Snapchat.
- **Use the Add Friends feature.** Tap the ghost icon at the top of your screen, and then tap Add Friends. You will now see a variety of ways to add friends as well as suggestions for people to follow.
- **Encourage your community to Add your brand.** In addition to adding people on your own, share your Snapchat information with your online community, much in the same way you share your Facebook and Twitter details. Add Snapchat information to your marketing materials, signage, website, newsletter, and other promotional campaigns.

One more thing before you take your first snaps. Notifications tell you when people comment on your snaps, send you a private message, or want to be your friend. To view your notifications, go to the Profile screen. On the bottom left of the screen is a square with a number, indicating the number of pending notifications. Tap the number to access notifications.

Taking Your First Snap

You can take two types of snaps: a photo or a quick video. The steps are almost identical:

1. **On the main Snapchat screen (refer to Figure 2-4), set your smartphone to face the subject.**

   For example, for a selfie, point the camera at yourself using the camera-with-arrow button at the top of the screen. For a different subject, turn the camera away from you. The camera icon in the upper right can turn toward you or away from you. Tap it to change direction.

2. **To take a photo, tap the round button at the bottom of the screen. To take a video, press and hold down on the button for up to 10 seconds.**
3. **(Optional) Add comments to your snap or video before publishing:**
   - *To type text:* Click the T icon.
   - *To draw or write text:* Click the pencil icon.
   - *To add a sticker:* Click the square sticky note icon or click the scissor icon to create your own sticker.
4. **Tap Send To.**
5. **Decide what to do with the snap or video:**
   - Send it to an individual.
   - Add it to your story, so everyone can see it for up to 24 hours.
   - Add it to My Memories to permanently save your snap.
6. **Tap the Send button, at the bottom right of the screen.**

TIP

Have fun with Snapchat! Inject some personality into your snaps. Take advantage of the tools, filters, and embellishments to put a fun spin on your images. (See the later section "Using lenses, filters, and geofilters" for details.)

Congratulations! You're now snapping!

Telling Your Snapchat Story

Now that your brand is on Snapchat, how will you tell your story? As a brand, you'll probably want to use Snapchat differently than an individual does. For example, if you share only selfies and personal messages, your Snapchat community will be bored. Snaps should be representative of your brand, while still appealing to the people who prefer to use Snapchat over other social networks.

The following list shares some of the ways brands are using Snapchat to reach their customers and online community:

- **Product launch:** Snapchat is the perfect platform for a product launch. Think about doing a series of quick reveals before the product launch date to pique interest.
- **Behind-the-scenes update:** Go backstage at the theater, a concert, or a sports or keynote-speaking event. Or give a tour of the parts of your business that people don't usually get to see.
- **Home tour:** Realtors can share photos of available homes in their areas.
- **Product demo:** Show how your products work or offer life hacks using your products.
- **Live update from an event:** Report live from parades, rock concerts, football games, high school sports, and more.
- **Exclusive content for the Snapchat community:** Share images and video your customers don't see on Facebook, Twitter, and Instagram. Give them a reason to follow you.
- **Target specific followers:** If you think that a member of your Snapchat community would benefit from your product or service, reach out privately with an offer. For example, if you're promoting a spa brand and you notice a harried mother among your Snapchat followers, you could privately reach out and say "You could probably use a break! Here's a 50 percent discount at our spas."
- **Call to action:** Create snaps that encourage users to sign up for your newsletter, read an article, or shop at your website.
- **Announcement:** Announce new hires, new products, new fashion colors, events, or other noteworthy items.
- **Job opportunities:** GrubHub recently announced a job opportunity for someone with Snapchat skills. People could apply by sharing innovative Snapchat doodles — a creative way to find applicants with a particular set of skills.
- **Guest introduction:** Will you be interviewing a guest on your podcast or YouTube show? Use Snapchat to reveal your latest guest.

- **Recipe or tantalizing food item:** Use food items to direct snappers to your restaurant or food blog. Taco Bell is a good example of a Snapchat account that uses snaps to introduce new menu items.
- **Photo, video, or other contest:** Encourage your Snapchat community to get creative and send you fun video, photos, doodles, or other snaps. Provide a prize and choose a winner.
- **Animations and a series of video:** Use a series of photos to create an animation or show movement beyond a regular snap by adding several photos, one after another, to your Snapchat story. Or make several 10-second videos and share to your story one after another, to tell a longer story.
- **Your own geofilters:** Create and use your own geofilters and share them with your Snapchat community. See the "Using lenses, filters, and geofilters" section, later in the chapter.
- **Coupons:** Use the Doodle feature to create coupons and share codes and discounts.
- **Directions to your website, blog, or sales page:** Share a URL to drive traffic back home.

REMEMBER

Don't share content for the sake of sharing content. Like all platforms that your brand uses, add Snapchat to your marketing strategy so you can plan thoughtful content that your Snapchat community will enjoy. Quality is better than quantity.

Knowing who is viewing your stories

You can see who is viewing your stories. This capability gives you a good indication of how well people are responding to your content, and whether certain types of content receive more views than others. You can also see which time of day gets you the most or least amount of views.

Knowing who is viewing your stories (and how many are doing so) helps you create a better content strategy and target your community. Moreover, it enables you to reward the people who view your snaps the most.

Take these steps to see who is viewing your stories:

1. **Go to your story.**

   Under each image or video under your story, you'll see an eye icon.

2. **Tap the eye icon for a list of everyone who viewed your story.**

TIP

When you share several snaps to your story, you might notice that certain people stop viewing your snaps after a while. Knowing where viewership drops off can help you determine when people get bored or when you're sharing too much. For example, if your story features ten snaps, people don't have to view them all. Then can swipe away at any time.

The beauty of Snapchat is that users don't have to commit a lot of time for snaps. If your story is too long, people begin swiping away. If you're planning a call to action, make sure you place it where your viewers are least likely to swipe away.

Engaging with Snapchat

Sharing on Snapchat is fine, but it's not a one-sided platform. Snapchat is set up for engagement so you can have conversations with individual members of your Snapchat community.

When you swipe up at the bottom of someone's snap, you see Send a Chat, where you can type your comments. These comments are viewed only by the original snapper. Say you share a snap that shows the office cat sleeping under a desk. People might ask about the cat's owner and the cat's name, whether anyone in the office is allergic to cats, who takes care of the cat on weekends, or who vacuums the cat hair from the office furniture.

A picture of a cat probably doesn't have anything to do with your product or service, but showing an office pet does add a human side to your company. Moreover, people appreciate it when you take time to answer questions and snap back. You didn't make a direct sale, but now you're on the radar, word will spread about your engagement, and more people will follow your snaps. People will begin feel like they know the people behind the brand, which makes them trust you. When it's time to buy, they'll come to you.

Here are a few best practices for engaging with your Snapchat community:

- **Share content that prompts a response.** Poll your co-workers. What kind of content makes them want to respond? See how other brands are sharing and the type of content that gets the biggest response. Don't just share content because you can. Share content because you want to talk to people.
- **Ask open-ended questions.** Ask questions that go beyond a simple yes-or-no answer and require a thoughtful response.
- **Encourage your community to snap responses.** When you share a snap, encourage your community to respond. Sometimes you have to put the idea in their head so they'll do more than just view.

- **Encourage different types of responses.** Ask a question and encourage your community to respond with a sticker, a doodle, or a special filter. Make engagement fun!
- **Respond to every comment and snap.** Why encourage conversation when only one person is taking time to talk? If someone cares enough to respond to your snap, show her it means something to you and respond in kind.
- **Use humor when possible.** People aren't on Snapchat for deep, meaningful conversation. Keep it light and fun.
- **Reward those who reach out with snaps.** When people comment with a thoughtful response or clever snap, reward them with a freebie or a discount code.

TIP

What type of content provokes the most engagement? Keep a spreadsheet and log the types of content you post, the amount of views the content receives, and the amount of and types of engagement you receive. Knowing how your community reacts and responds can help you plan future content.

Using lenses, filters, and geofilters

Snapchat allows snappers to use different lenses and filters to add whimsy and personality to snaps. Lenses can illustrate a mood, show holiday spirit, or add life and color to an image. Filters can display causes, show attendance at events, and promote a business.

Lenses

A lens adds special effects to your face, such as cat ears or a Santa hat. You set the lens in place before taking your selfie snap:

1. **In the main Snap screen, just before taking your selfie snap, press the middle of the screen (not the camera button).**

   You'll see a series of bubbles containing pictures. Each bubble contains a lens.
2. **Select the lens you'd like to use.**
3. **You may have to drag the image around to position the filter to fit a face or head.**

   For example, you might need to raise your eyebrows — or in the case of the vomiting rainbow, open your mouth. Follow instructions and adjust your position as needed.
4. **Take your snap and share as you normally would.**

Filters

Unlike lenses, filters are added after you take your snap. For example, you can add the temperature, or a holiday garland to frame your snaps, or use a special geofilter to add your location.

REMEMBER

Many filters are available for a limited amount of time. If you love a certain filter, make sure to snap a screenshot or save it to your Memories. You might not be able to find it again later!

To use a filter, do the following:

1. **Make sure location services is enabled on your smartphone.**

   You can't use filters without it.

2. **Take your snap as usual.**
3. **Swipe right or left to see the different filters.**
4. **Select the filter you'd like to use.**
5. **Tap Send To to share as usual.**

TIP

To jazz up your snaps, try using both a lens and a filter. But be careful about over embellishing. You don't want your snap to look so busy that it loses its essence.

Geofilters

In the past, people could create on demand geofilters for special events, such as weddings and milestone parties, with the caveat that no business-related logos or branding could be used. However, Snapchat now offers brands the capability to create their own branded on-demand geofilters. Unlike the geofilters used for weddings and parties, businesses must disclose that they are behind the on-demand geofilter they created.

The benefit of an on-demand geofilter is that everyone in your community can use them to commemorate an event. For example, if 1,000 people use your geofilter during your event, your branding might be seen by tens of thousands of people, if not more. Geofilters are a form of advertising that will reach Snapchat's demographic.

Businesses must follow Terms of Use when creating geofilters. For example, brands can use logos or other branded content but can't use emails, phone numbers, personal information, or images of people. Also, it should go without saying that brands can't use illegal drugs or illegal activities in geofilters.

TIP

Take some time to familiarize yourself with Snapchat's rules regarding on-demand geofilters at its Submissions Guidelines page: `https://geofilters.snapchat.com/submission-guidelines`.

To create an on-demand geofilter for your brand, you have to use Snapchat's website — not the app — at `www.snapchat.com/on-demand`.

You have to pay to create an on-demand geofilter. Filters start at $5 but prices can go much, much higher (think $400+), depending on how much space your geofilter will encompass and how much time you want it to be available.

Take these steps to upload an on-demand geofilter:

1. **Go to `www.snapchat.com/on-demand` and click Create Now, as shown in Figure 2-6.**
2. **Log into your Snapchat account.**
3. **Download a template.**

   Your design team much create the geofilter according to Snapchat's specifications. Images should be 1080 px by 1920 px and saved as a PNG file.
4. **To upload your geofilter to Snapchat, click Choose File.**
5. **Select the date range in which people can use your on-demand geofilter.**

   For example, if you are marketing for a convention, you want to select dates coinciding with that event.
6. **Select the location in which your geofilter will be used.**
7. **Confirm your geofilter, and select whether it's for personal or business use.**
8. **Add payment information.**

Snapchat will review your on-demand geofilter to ensure that it follows their submission guidelines. You can check on orders at the Snapchat website's My Orders page. Snapchat will also send you an email confirmation.

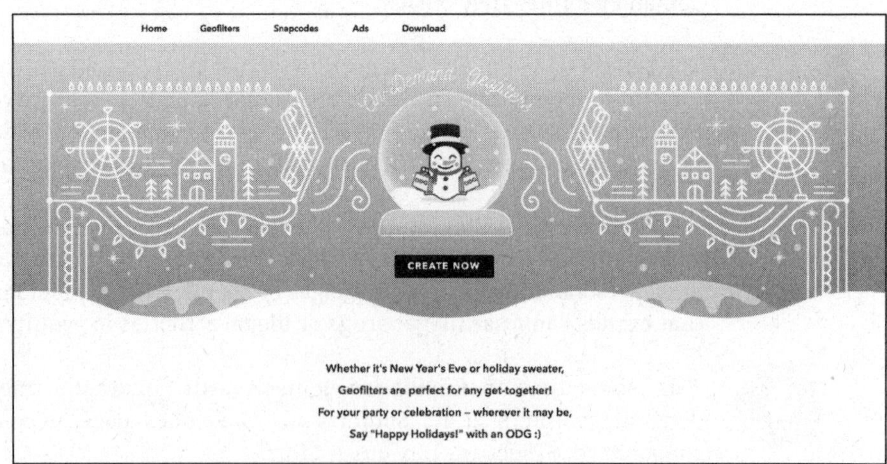

FIGURE 2-6: Click Create Now to get started creating your on-demand geofilter.

IN THIS CHAPTER

» Using Instagram for branding

» Getting set up with Instagram

» Choosing photos to share

» Making your photos searchable with hashtags

» Creating a community on Instagram

Chapter 3 Getting Started with Instagram

Have you ever noticed how people tend to react more to imagery than text on the social networks? That's because they see photos before they read text. So it's always in a brand's best interest to accompany great text with a great photo. Many times, though, the photo speaks for itself, and few words are needed. In fact, brands can find their community is receptive to hanging out with them on a more visual platform, and that's where Instagram comes in.

Instagram is a social network based on photos, not words. Although Instagram allows hashtags, likes, and comments, you won't see many text-heavy updates or link sharing. Instead, both individuals and brands alike let their photographs do the talking. In fact, many people prefer Instagram to other social platforms because there's less chatter.

Instagram gives you an opportunity to show your brand's creative side and think outside the box. Instead of attracting people with written stories, you're presenting a more visual experience.

In this chapter, we talk about how to set up an Instagram account and share photos and video with your community.

Promoting Your Brand on Instagram

Like Snapchat (see Chapter 2 in this minibook), Instagram is a mobile platform. Although you can view Instagram photos online with your regular web browser, you're limited in what you can do. The majority of people using Instagram to view photos and interact are doing so with smartphones and tablets.

WARNING

You can't set up an Instagram account or upload photos to your Instagram account from your computer; you can only view and like photos from your computer. If you want to sign up for an Instagram account or share photos with your community on Instagram, you must use a mobile device.

Here are a few examples of how brands use Instagram in creative ways, while still staying in their comfort zones:

- The Starbucks account shares images of its customers, its baristas, and even members of the executive team trying new flavors and blends.
- Red Bull Energy Drink uses its Instagram account to appeal to adrenaline junkies by posting photos of skydivers or skateboards high in the air.
- Nike shares photos of athletes doing what they do best.
- King Arthur Flour shares recipes with mouthwatering photos.
- Jimmy Choo shares stunning images of its shoes.
- Home Goods shares home-decorating options and tips.
- The Paris Opera Ballet shares behind-the-scenes images and scenes from performances.

Be creative with your Instagram photos. The best Instagram strategy is to keep it simple. You don't need to take a trip to Europe to take photos to share with your community, because your brand has enough interesting things going on in your own backyard.

Almost every brand can present a more visual side to its community by using Instagram, although you might not immediately see what your brand should highlight. In the section "Determining What Is Photo-Worthy for Your Brand," later in this chapter, we throw out some suggestions for photogenic moments.

Creating and Using Your Instagram Account

Is your mobile device in hand? Good. In the following sections, we discuss how to set up an Instagram account, upload photos, and control notifications.

Setting up your account

Follow these steps to set up an Instagram account:

1. **Locate the Instagram app on iTunes or Google Play and download it to your mobile device.**
2. **Choose to register with your Facebook account or with your phone or email account, as shown in Figure 3-1.**

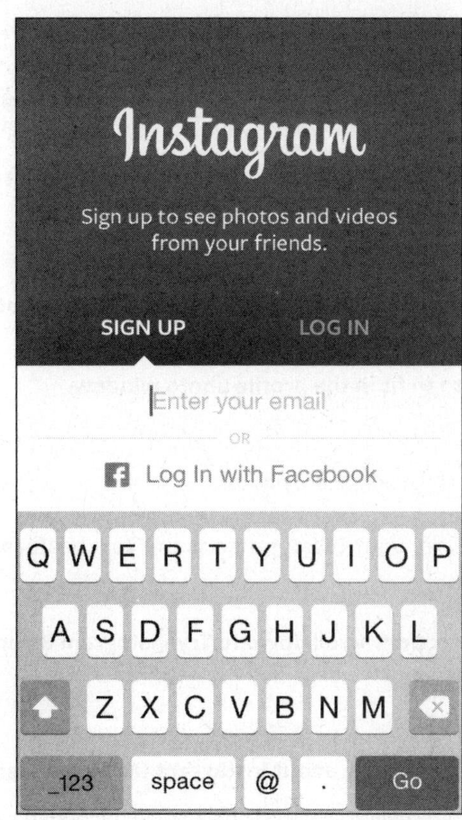

FIGURE 3-1: Use Facebook or your email address to create an Instagram account.

3. **Do one of the following:**
   - *Facebook account:* Enter your Facebook login information.
   - *Email account:* Enter your email address and the password you want to use for the site and select Next.
4. **Upload your profile photo and fill in your name and password information.**
5. **Create your username.**
6. **(Optional) Connect to Facebook to choose friends to follow.**
7. **(Optional) Search your email contacts for friends on Instagram.**
8. **Tap the Done link to get started using Instagram, or follow some of Instagram's suggestions for users to follow.**

Before getting started, you'll want to upload your profile photo. After all, Instagram is a visual platform and you'll attract more followers with a catching profile image.

Take these steps to upload your profile photo, if you haven't already done so:

1. **Click Settings (gear icon), at the top right of your screen. Then scroll down and tap Edit Profile.**

   You can change your profile photo also by tapping Edit Profile at the top center of the screen.
2. **Tap Change Profile Photo.**
3. **Import the photo from Facebook or Twitter, take a new photo, or select a photo from your mobile device's image library.**
4. **Position your photo to fit in the profile photo window.**
5. **Tap Done.**

   Now you're ready to take and share photos.

If you would like to change your Instagram account to a business account, do the following.

1. **In the Edit Profile section, scroll down to Try Instagram Business Tools and tap this option.**

   A Welcome screen appears.
2. **Click Continue to learn more about Instagram for businesses.**

   You are taken through several screens showing you the benefits of Instagram's business tools.

3. **Tap Continue at the bottom of each page until you land on the page asking you to connect to Facebook.**

   You create a business profile via your Facebook brand pages, so you must access your Facebook brand page to set up your business account.

4. **Tap Continue as *your Facebook account name.***
5. **Select the Facebook page you'd like to connect to and then tap Next.**
6. **Enter your businesses contact information and tap Done.**

   You must enter in least one contact method.

7. **Follow the instructions to set up your Instagram business profile and upload a profile photo.**

   You're now ready to get started on Instagram.

Sharing photos

You can share photos on Instagram by following these steps:

1. **Open the Instagram app on your mobile device and select the Photo Upload button (square with a plus sign).**
2. **Do one of the following**
   - *Select a photo from your smartphone's library.*
   - *Tap the photo or video option, and then snap your photo or record video using the round button at the bottom of the screen.*
3. **(Optional) Select a filter to enhance the photo.**

   You see the photo you want to display, along with various filters, as shown in Figure 3-2. The filters are fun ways to highlight your photo with different borders and tones or even black and white. If you like the photo as-is, don't worry about a filter.

TIP

   Take the time to familiarize yourself with Instagram's different filter options because you might find some that make your photos look awesome.

4. **Tap Next.**
5. **Write a caption and add hashtags, if needed.**

   For more on hashtags, see the later section "Using Hashtags in Your Instagram Posts."

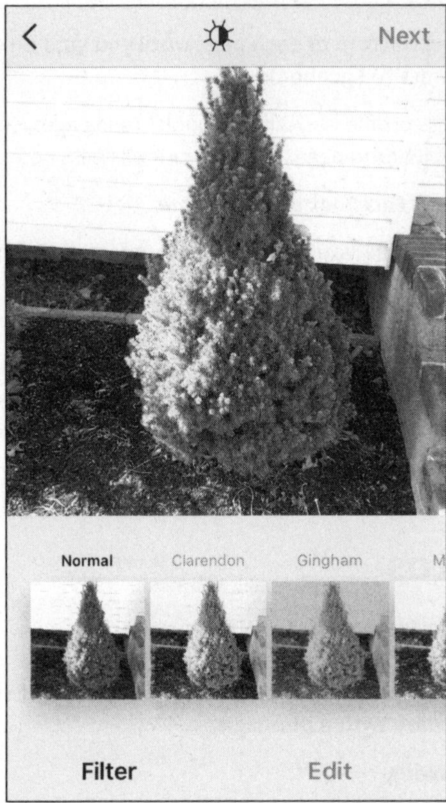

FIGURE 3-2: Instagram comes with a variety of filters you can use to enhance your photos.

6. **(Optional) Tag people, check into a location, and select other social networks on which you'd like to share your photo, as shown in Figure 3-3.**

   You can upload your Instagram photos to both Facebook and Twitter at the same time you're Instagramming. Your photo gets increased visibility when you share it on multiple channels, which means more opportunities for others to like, share, comment, and recognize your brand.

   WARNING

   When you post the same content on every platform, people may not feel the need to follow you on every platform. You may gain more Instagram followers if you don't share the same images on Facebook, Twitter, and other platforms.

   If you're not logged into these social networks, you may be taken to a screen at those social networks so you can log in.

7. **Tap Share, located at the top right of the screen.**

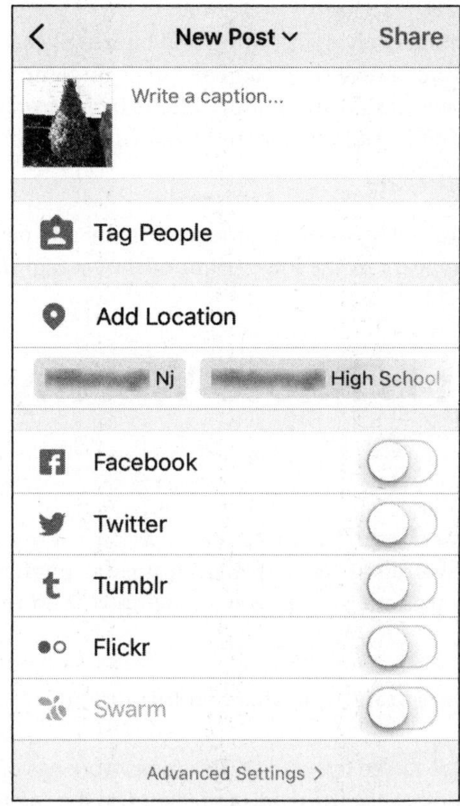

FIGURE 3-3: You can upload photos to Facebook and Twitter from Instagram.

Controlling notifications

You can set up your account so that you can receive Instagram notifications on your mobile device, even when you're not using the app. To do so, follow these steps:

1. **Click your profile (person icon) in the lower-right corner of the Instagram screen, and select Options.**
2. **At the top right of the profile screen that appears, tap Settings (gear icon) to open a drop-down list.**
3. **Scroll down to Push Notification.**
4. **Select whom you want to receive notifications from.**

   For example, you might want to receive notifications only from people you follow.

TIP

If you find that your phone is always beeping and buzzing because you're receiving Instagram notifications every time someone likes or comments on a photo or sends a friend request, you can turn off notifications in your smartphone's notification center. Look for the Instagram app in the notification center and select your desired notification settings.

TIP

If you receive a like, you're tagged in an image, or someone new followed you, a red heart notification appears in the lower right of the Instagram app screen.

Determining What Is Photo-Worthy for Your Brand

You may be thinking your brand isn't as visual as an energy drink or a coffee brand. The truth is, few brands can tell their stories in photos. Most, however, can find some ways to present photos while staying true to their brand's focus and mission.

Here are some of the ways brands can share on Instagram:

- **Teamwork:** Fans love to see the behind-the-scenes workings of a brand. Don't shy away from showing the team at meetings, in the cafeteria, or chatting it up in the hallway.
- **Test kitchens and factories:** Who doesn't love to see how products are made or served to the public? Unveiling the mystery (without giving away company secrets) will endear you to fans.
- **Products and ingredients:** Show what goes into a product. For example, if yours is an organic food brand using only wholesome ingredients, share photos of some of your suppliers, such as farms and farmers markets. Showing what goes into a product is also a great tool for selling.
- **Outings:** Share photos of the team picnic or conference.
- **Ideas for using the product or service:** What are some of the things people make with your products? Share how others use what you sell.
- **Sightings in the wild:** If you spot people using your products on the street, share photos on Instagram, but get permission first.

With Instagram, the possibilities are endless. You don't need expensive equipment or a degree in photography. You need only the ability to understand what your community responds to.

TIP

Before taking photos, do a search and see how other brands and individuals are using Instagram. If you tap Explore (magnifying glass icon), shown in Figure 3-4, random images from Instagram users appear in a grid on your screen. A search bar also appears, which you can use to search other brands on Instagram. You might get some inspiration, and you'll see how the brands are interacting.

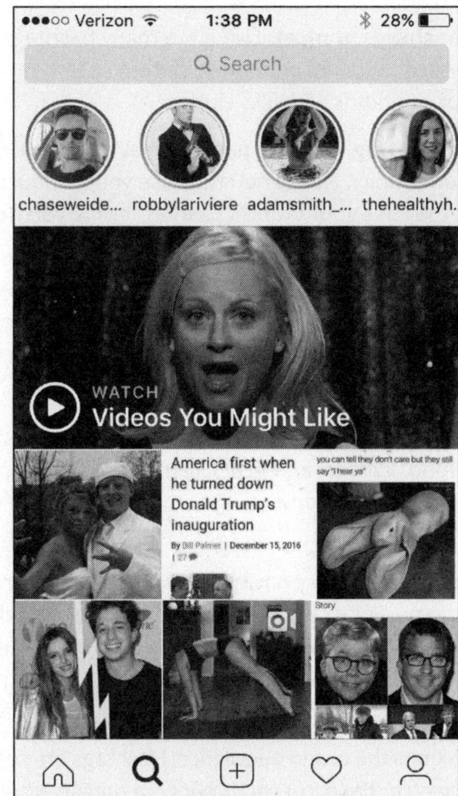

FIGURE 3-4: Use the magnifying glass icon to view random photos or search for other Instagram accounts.

Using Hashtags in Your Instagram Posts

Hashtags help to make a photo searchable. For example, if you post a photo of shoes on Instagram and use the hashtag #shoes, #style, or #fashion (or a combination), that photo will show up in the streams of others who are looking for items by using the same hashtag. When someone clicks the hashtag, public images labeled with that hashtag will appear.

REMEMBER

Hashtagged content has a limited shelf life, especially content with a popular hashtag. If the topic is trending or popular, your content may be visible at the top of the search for only a few minutes or hours. Play around with both popular and less trendy hashtags to see where you receive the most engagement.

Here are some hashtag best practices:

- **Use two or three hashtags at most.** Using too many hashtags makes a post too busy. Sure, your post appears on many different searches now, but most people prefer to look at photos with less clutter.
- **Make up your own hashtag.** Create a hashtag that suits your brand and share it with your community. Now when they use your product or take part in a related activity, they use your brand's hashtag, giving you more visibility and prompting others to try the same.
- **Keep an eye out for trending hashtags.** Hashtags don't have to be brand related. Plenty of hashtags relate to holidays, current events, and television shows. Don't spam a hashtag with irrelevant content, but if you have an image appropriate for trending hashtags, don't be afraid to use it.
- **Think of popular things people like to do or buy.** Some popular hashtags on Instagram are #food, #shoes, and #cats. Familiarize yourself with popular hashtags but keep in mind that content with a popular hashtag won't stay at the top for long.
- **Take part in hashtag memes.** Try having fun with your Instagram account by taking part in a meme. For example, you can use #ThrowbackThursday or #TBT to share photos of your business in its early stages or #outfitoftheday to show what your staff is wearing.
- **Hashtags work best with public accounts.** Brands shouldn't have private accounts because it limits the brand's audience: Hashtags are seen only by people who have access to the account. If yours is a private account with 50 followers, it has the potential to be seen by only 50 people. If your account is public, your image has the potential to be seen by hundreds, if not thousands.

If you want to make your account private so only people you choose to be friends with can see your photos, follow these steps:

1. **On your profile screen, select Edit Profile.**
2. **Click the gear icon at the top right and then select Private Account.**
3. **Scroll down to the bottom of the page to the area where it says Posts Are Private.**
4. **Flip the little toggle switch to the right.**

Keep in mind that with a private account, you have to manually approve any friend request. With a public account, anyone can follow and view your photos.

WARNING

People come to Instagram for the visuals. Although you should give the photo a brief caption or description, you'll lose people if you write an essay.

Finding Friends and Fans on Instagram

What good is having an Instagram account if you have no friends to share your photos with?

To search for people or brands to follow, follow these steps:

1. **Tap the magnifying glass icon.**
2. **In the search box, type the name or Instagram handle of the person or brand.**

   TIP

   You can also search hashtags for topics related to your business. For example, if you restore classic cars, you might use the #classiccars, #classiccarspotting, and #classiccarsdaily hashtags, which are the most popular hashtags in that topic. Now you can see some of the classic car enthusiasts are on Instagram. Follow them, and they may follow you in return to see photos of your restorations.

3. **When you find an account you're interested in, click the Follow button to follow that account.**

   The account's photos automatically appear in your feed, unless you're following a person or brand with a private account. You must request permission to follow someone who has a private account. Many of the people you follow will follow you in return.

TIP

Online communities are made up of like-minded people. It's a waste of time to follow people who have no interest in what you do. Find people with whom you have a common interest for a mutually beneficial relationship.

Make sure to tell your Facebook, Twitter, and blog communities that you're now on Instagram. If people follow you on one social media site, they'll likely follow you on another.

Using Instagram Stories

Instagram has a stories feature that enables users to share rapid-fire images and video. Similar to Snapchat stories (see Chapter 2 in this minibook), Instagram stories give a place to add a sequence of photos or a video to illustrate a story. In this way, prolific Instagram posters can share a group of photos without hogging their friends' feeds.

Take these steps to use Instagram stories:

1. **On your home screen, tap the Your Story button, at the top right below the camera icon.**
2. **Take a photo by tapping the round button at the bottom, or take a video by holding down the button for up to 10 seconds.**
3. **(Optional) Enhance your photo or video:**
   - *Add a sticker:* Tap the square button with the smiley face.
   - *Add a doodle:* Tap the paintbrush.
   - *Add text:* Tap the Aa button.

   For more on enhancements, see Instagram's Help Center at `https://help.instagram.com/`.
4. **Save the photo, add it to your story, or click the arrow button to share to your story or with specific users.**
5. **Tap Send, at the bottom of the screen.**

Instagram and Snapchat stories share many of the same features. For example, video and photos uploaded to Instagram stories are temporary, unlike photos posted to Instagram on your regular feed. You can also see who viewed your Instagram stories. If you're using Instagram to share stunning one-off images rather than a story, don't feel you need to use the additional features. Use Instagram in a manner that best suits you and your community.

8 Other Social Media Marketing Sites

Contents at a Glance

CHAPTER 1: **Weighing the Business Benefits of Minor Social Sites** 491

Reviewing Your Goals 492
Researching Minor Social Networks 493
Assessing the Involvement of Your Target Audience 496
Choosing Social Sites Strategically 498

CHAPTER 2: **Maximizing Stratified Social Communities** 503

Making a Bigger Splash on a Smaller Site 504
Taking Networking to the Next Level 504
Selecting Social Networks by Vertical Industry Sector 506
Selecting Social Networks by Demographics 510
Selecting Social Networks by Activity Type 512
Finding Yourself in the Real World with Geomarketing 515
Spacing Out with Twitter 517
Finding Your Business on Facebook 518
Making Real Connections in Virtual Spaces 521
Making Deals on Social Media 523
Setting Terms for Your Coupon Campaign 526
Comparing LivingSocial and Groupon 531
Diversifying Your Daily Deals 533

CHAPTER 3: **Profiting from Mid-Size Social Media Channels** 535

Deciding Whether to Invest Your Time 535
Spotting Your Audience with Spotify 536
Turning Up New Prospects with Tumblr 538
Promoting Video with Vimeo 540
Live Streaming with Periscope 542

CHAPTER 4: **Integrating Social Media** 545

Thinking Strategically about Social Media Integration 546
Integrating Social Media with E-Newsletters 547
Integrating Social Media with Press Releases 551
Integrating Social Media with Your Website 557

CHAPTER 5: **Advertising on Social Media** 561

Integrating Social Media with Paid Advertising 561
Advertising on Facebook and Instagram 564
Advertising on Twitter 568
Advertising on LinkedIn 573
Advertising on Pinterest 576

IN THIS CHAPTER

» Reviewing goals for social media marketing

» Conducting social media marketing research

» Assessing audience involvement

» Choosing minor social communities strategically

Chapter 1

Weighing the Business Benefits of Minor Social Sites

Without a doubt, Facebook, Twitter, LinkedIn, and Google+ are the elephants in the social marketing zoo, at least in terms of the largest number of visits per month. But this is one big zoo, as shown in Figure 1-1, which displays only 35 of more than 300 significant social sites. Among these sites, you'll find lions and tigers and bears, and more than a few turtles, trout, squirrels, and seagulls.

You have to assess your business needs, research the options, and select which (if any) of these minor social marketing sites belongs in your personal petting zoo. In this chapter, we look at methods for doing just that.

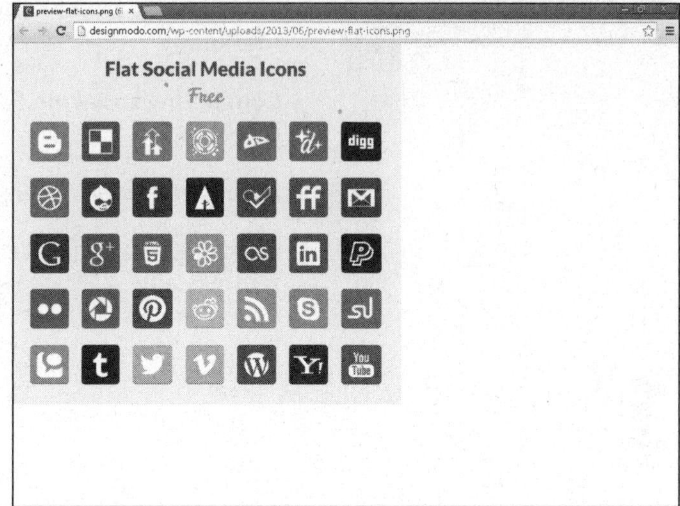

FIGURE 1-1: The zoo of social media sites is vast. Your time, however, is limited.

Reproduced with permission of Designmodo, Inc.

REMEMBER

With the exception of blogs (which can become your primary web presence if you use your own domain name), these smaller sites are best used to supplement your other social marketing efforts.

Reviewing Your Goals

In Book 1, we suggest that you develop a strategic marketing plan. If you haven't done so yet, there's no time like the present. Otherwise, managing your social networks can quickly spin out of control, especially when you start to add multiple smaller sites for generating or distributing content.

REMEMBER

Marketing is marketing, whether offline or online, whether for search engine ranking or social networking. Obviously, your primary business goal is to make a profit, but your goals for a particular marketing campaign or social media technique may vary.

As we discuss in Book 1, social media marketing can serve multiple goals. It can help you

- Cast a wide net to catch your target market.
- Brand.

- Build relationships.
- Improve business processes.
- Improve search engine rankings.
- Sell when opportunity arises.
- Save money on advertising.

Your challenge is to decide which goal(s) apply to your business and then to quantify objectives for each one. Be sure that you can measure your achievements. You can find additional measurement information in Book 9.

Researching Minor Social Networks

Doing all the necessary research to choose the right mix of social networks may seem overwhelming, but, hey, this is the web — help is at your fingertips. Table 1-1 lists many resource websites that have directories of social networking sites, usage statistics, demographic profiles, and valuable tips on how to use different sites. The selection process is straightforward, and the steps are quite similar to constructing an online marketing plan, as described in Book 1, Chapter 3.

Follow these general steps to get your research under way:

1. **Review the strategy, goals, and target markets for your social marketing campaign, as described in Book 1.**

   If your B2B business needs to target particular individuals during the sales cycle, such as a CFO, buyer, or project engineer, be specific in your plan.

2. **Decide how much of your, your staff's, or a third party's time, and possibly budget, you want to commit to minor social networking sites.**

   WARNING

   Don't underestimate how much time social media marketing can take. After you're comfortable with Facebook and (if they fit) Twitter or LinkedIn, it's okay to start with just one or two minor sites and slowly add services over time.

3. **Skim the directories and lists of social media in (refer to Table 1-1) to select possibilities that fit your goals.**

   For more ideas, simply search using terms for your business area plus the words *social network* or *social media* (for example, *fashion social network*).

TABLE 1-1 **Social Network Research URLs**

Site Name	URL	What It Does
Alexa	www.alexa.com/siteinfo	Ranks traffic and demographic data by site
DisplayPlanner by Google	https://adwords.google.com/da/DisplayPlanner/Home	Compiles traffic data, demographics, and device use by site; requires a Google account
Experian Marketing Services	www.experian.com/marketing-services/online-trends-social-media.html	Presents the top ten social sites by visits per week
Google Toolbar	www.google.com/toolbar	Installs Google Toolbar with Google PageRank (not available for all browsers)
HubSpot	http://blog.hubspot.com/blog/tabid/6307/bid/33663/7-Targeted-Social-Networks-Niche-Marketers-Should-Try.aspx	Describes seven attractive niche social media sites
Mashable	http://mashable.com	Presents social media news and web tips
	http://mashable.com/category/social-media	Lists stories and resources about social media
	http://mashable.com/category/social-network-lists	Lists of older social media sites by topic
Moz	http://moz.com/beginners-guide-to-social-media	Provides the "Beginners Guide to Social Media"
Quantcast	www.quantcast.com	Compiles traffic and demographic data by site
SitePoint	www.sitepoint.com/social-networking-sites-for-business	Lists 20 social networking sites for business professionals
Wikipedia	http://en.wikipedia.org/wiki/List_of_social_networking_websites	Directory of more than 200 social networking sites

4. **Review the demographics and traffic for each possibility by using a site such as Alexa and Quantcast (as discussed in Book 1, Chapter 3), and then cull your list to keep only those that fit your target market and marketing objectives.**

   Figure 1-2 displays the relative market share, according to StatCounter Global Stats (http://gs.statcounter.com/social-media-stats/all/worldwide/ - monthly-201606-201701-bar), for the seven top-ranked social media services in the United States from June 2016 to January 2017.

Market share is ranked not by traffic to the sites themselves, but rather by the amount of traffic they refer to other sites. This approach may be valuable for business analysis because it discounts personal users who stay on social media sites to communicate with their friends. The Other category in this figure encompasses LinkedIn, Delicious, Digg, Google+, and many more sites.

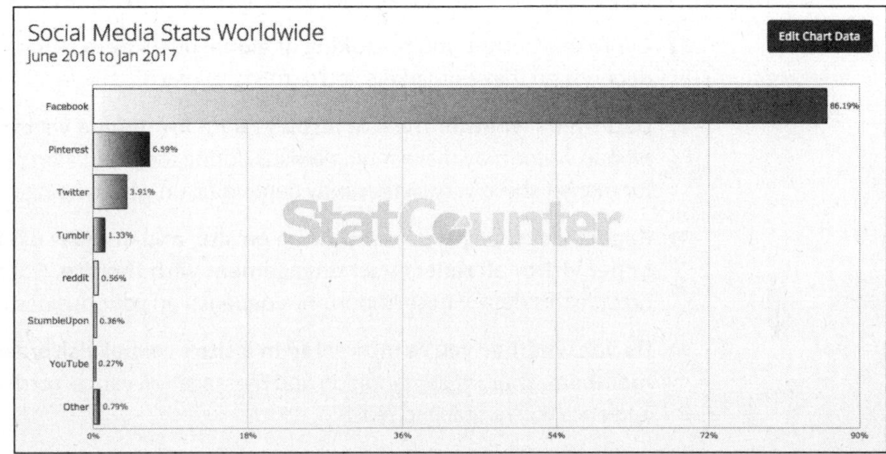

FIGURE 1-2: Factor in relative market share, using data such as that from StatCounter Global Stats.

Source: StatCounter Global Stats, `http://gs.statcounter.com`

5. **Review each network (see suggestions in the following bullet list) to make sure you feel comfortable with its web presence, user interaction, Google PageRank, features, ease of use, and ability to provide key reports. Prioritize your sites accordingly.**
6. **Enter your final selection in your Social Media Marketing Plan (described in Book 1, Chapter 3), and set up a schedule for implementation and monitoring on your Social Media Activity Calendar (see Book 1, Chapter 4).**
7. **Implement your plan. Modify it as needed after results come in.**

   Wait at least a month before you make changes; gaining visibility in some social network sites can take time.

TIP

For leads to other social networks that appeal to your audience, look for a section named Other Sites Visited (or similar wording) on one of the statistical sites.

Keep in mind these words of caution as you review statistics for various minor social networks in Steps 3 and 4 of the preceding list:

- **Not all directories or reports on market share define the universe of social media or social networks the same way.** Some sources include blogs, social bookmarking sites such as Delicious, or news aggregators. Small social networks may come and go so quickly that the universe is different even a few months later.
- **Confirm whether you're looking at global or US data.** What you need depends on the submarkets you're trying to reach.
- **Determine whether the site displays data for unique visitors or visits.** A unique visitor may make multiple visits during the evaluation period. Results for market share vary significantly depending on what's being measured.
- **Repeat visits, pages per view, time on site, and number of visits per day or per visitor all reflect user engagement with the site.** Not all services provide this data, whose importance depends on your business goals.
- **Decide whether you're interested in a site's casual visitors or registered members.** Your implementation and message will vary according to the audience you're trying to reach.
- **Check the window of measurement (day, week, month, or longer) and the effective dates for the results.** These numbers are volatile, so be sure you're looking at current data.

TIP

Regarding social media or everything else, consider online statistics for relative value and trends, not for absolute numbers. Because every statistical service defines its terms and measurements differently, stick with one source to make the results comparable across all your possibilities.

Assessing the Involvement of Your Target Audience

After you finish the research process, you should have a good theoretical model of which minor social networks might be a good fit for your business. But there's nothing like being involved. Our advice in the preceding section recommends visiting every site to assess a number of criteria, including user interaction. If you plan to engage your audience in comments, reviews, forums, or other user-generated content, you *must* understand how active participants on the network now interact.

Start by signing up and creating a personal profile of some sort so that you can access all member-related activities. The actual activities, of course, depend on the particular network.

Lurking

Spend time watching and reading what transpires in every interactive venue on the site, without participating. In the olden days of Internet forums and chat rooms, you were *lurking.* You can make a number of qualitative assessments that can help you determine whether this site is a good fit for you:

- **Quality of dialog:** Do statements of any sort float in the ether, or does interaction take place? Does a moderator respond? The site owners? Other registered members? Is there one response or continual back and forth? If you intend to establish an ongoing business relationship with other participants on the network, you want to select a site where ongoing dialog is already standard practice.
- **Quality of posts:** Are posts respectful or hostile? Do posts appear automatically, or is someone reviewing them before publication? Do they appear authentic? Because you're conducting business online, your standards may need to be higher than they would be for casual, personal interaction. Anger and profanity that might be acceptable from respondents on a political news site would be totally unacceptable on a site that engages biologists in discussion of an experiment.
- **Quantity of posts compared to the number of registered users:** On some sites, you may find that the same 20 people post or respond to everything, even though the site boasts 10,000 registered members. This situation signals a site that isn't successful as a social network, however successful it might be in other ways.

Responding

After you have a sense of the ethos of a site, try responding to a blog post, participating in a forum, or establishing yourself as an expert on a product review or e-zine listing. Assess what happens. Do others respond on the network? Email you off-site? Call the office?

Use this side of the lurk-and-response routine to gain a better understanding of what you, as a member and prospective customer, would expect. Will you or your staff be able to deliver?

TIP

If a site requires more care and feeding than you have the staff to support, consider dropping it from your list.

Quantifying market presence

In addition to assessing the number of unique visitors, visits, and registered members, you may want to assess additional components of audience engagement. Sites that provide quantitative information, such as Quantcast, help you better understand your audience's behavior, learn more about their lifestyles and brand preferences, and target your message. You can learn about these concepts:

- **Affinity:** A statistical correlation that shows the strength of a particular user behavior, such as visiting another site, relative to that of the US Internet population as a whole — for instance, whether an Instagram user is more or less likely than the general Internet population to visit YouTube
- **Index:** The delivery of a specific audience segment, such as women or seniors, compared with their share of the overall Internet population
- **Composition:** The relative distribution of the audience for a site by audience segment, such as gender, age, or ethnicity
- **Addict:** The most loyal component of a site's audience, with 30 or more visits per month
- **Passer-by:** Casual visitor who visits a site only once per month
- **Regular:** A user partway between Addict and Passer-by; someone who visits more than once but fewer than 30 times per month

Choosing Social Sites Strategically

It may seem ridiculously time-consuming to select which minor social marketing sites are best for your business. Why not just throw a virtual dart at a list or choose randomly from social sites that your staff likes to visit? Ultimately, you save more time by planning and making strategic choices than by investing time in a social media site that doesn't pay off.

TIP

If you're short of time, select sites that meet your demographics requirement but on which you can easily reuse and syndicate content, as described in Book 2, Chapter 1. You can replicate blog postings, for instance, almost instantly on multiple sites.

If you truly have no time to select one of these sleek minor critters, stick to one of the elephants and add others later.

Somebody's Mother's Chocolate Sauce, shown in Figure 1-3 and described in the nearby sidebar, uses multiple social media channels to achieve its marketing goals.

FIGURE 1-3: Somebody's Mother's Chocolate Sauce generates traffic to its website from a variety of social media, as shown by the chiclets in the lower-right corner.

Reproduced with permission of Somebody's Mother's Chocolate Sauce

REMEMBER

Even the smallest social network sites can be valuable if they have your target market. All the averages mean nothing. It's about *your* business and *your* audience. Niche marketing is always an effective use of your time. Fish where *your* fish are!

SOMEBODY'S MOTHER'S SAYS, "TRY SOCIAL MEDIA!"

Owner Lynn Lasher started Somebody's Mother's in April 2005 to teach her three children how to start a business, to assume responsibility for their own financial well-being, and to take matters into their own hands. One weekend when she was out of work, she asked someone who was demonstrating salsa in a neighborhood grocery store how he got his product on the shelves. Thus inspired, she decided to sell her mother's chocolate sauce. Within two days, her company was born. Within ten years, she had created a profitable business without incurring debt, made (and learned from) her inevitable mistakes on a smaller stage, improved product quality, and earned a loyal customer following. (Plus two of her children have become entrepreneurs themselves.)

For Lasher, both homemade foods and mothers are special. Her product, her website, and her social media presence reflect that. Because mothers "are almost never validated or recognized, much less compensated," Lasher says, she began using quotes about mothering or parenting on the jar lids of her products, as seen in the nearby screenshot.

Reproduced with permission of Somebody's Mother's Chocolate Sauce

Audrey Marshall, the VP of Online Marketing and PR for Somebody's Mother's, explains that the company started with a website immediately and began utilizing social media in 2008 with the channels available at that time: Facebook, Twitter, and Myspace. Seeing social media as an opportunity to reach new online audiences for the brand, Marshall has since adopted additional platforms, including YouTube, Pinterest, Tumblr, and Flickr.

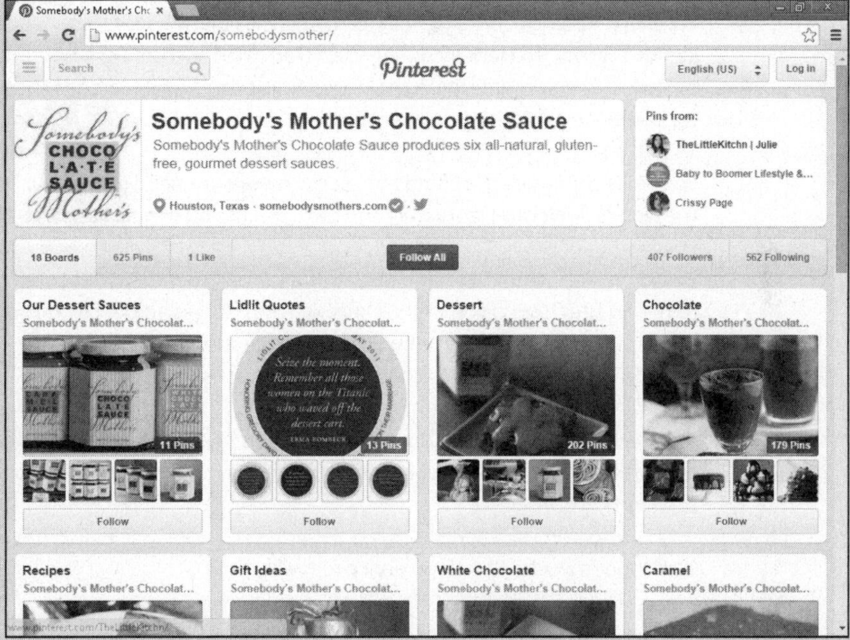

Reproduced with permission of Somebody's Mother's Chocolate Sauce

"It was never our goal to sign up for all the social media platforms available," she explains. "Rather, it's about knowing our target audience, where they exist online, and how best to engage with them." The company's posts primarily target mothers and *foodies* (people who are interested in cooking or baking, and trying out new recipes).

For Marshall, each social media platform requires a slightly different focus, even when she's posting the same content. "For example, on Tumblr and Pinterest, visual media is incredibly important, whereas on Twitter and Facebook, you can have more of a dialogue with your community. It's important for us to have a consistent brand identity in all of our posts, with the opportunity for sales conversions as appropriate."

(continued)

(continued)

Somebody's Mother's posts to each social media platform at least several times per week. Rather than adhering to a rigid schedule, she takes her cues from her audience, based on tent-pole events (such as holiday seasons), specialty food news, trending topics, and so on. In total, she spends one to two hours a week on social media: prepping posts, responding to comments, and engaging with the audience.

Currently, she uses a tool called Buffer to schedule posts, and Google Analytics, Facebook Insights, and other platform analytics to track visits, user engagement, and similar metrics. To track incoming visits from sites such as TasteSpotting, StumbleUpon, or Reddit, she primarily looks at Google Analytics. Finally, Marshall checks Alexa to monitor Somebody's Mother's site ranking.

She cross-promotes the company's social media profiles, linking to all its profiles from the website (refer to Figure 1-3), and between the others, as appropriate.

Based on her experience, Marshall adds a note of caution about submitting products to review sites. She recommends knowing your target audience and your community before asking for a review. When the audience match is right, product submissions are more likely to result in sales conversions and click-throughs.

Marshall offers one more important reminder: "You can never stop learning about social media. Rather, you have to learn to grow with it and update your strategies as the platforms evolve."

Somebody's Mother's web presence follows:

- `www.somebodysmothers.com`
- `www.facebook.com/somebodysmothers`
- `www.twitter.com/somebodysmother`
- `www.pinterest.com/somebodysmother/`
- `http://plus.google.com/+somebodysmothers`
- `www.youtube.com/somebodysmothers`
- `www.flickr.com/photos/somebodysmothers`
- `http://instagram.com/somebodysmothers`

IN THIS CHAPTER

» Valuing stratified social communities

» Making business connections online

» Searching for networks by industry, demographics, and activity type

» Examining geolocation services for Foursquare, Twitter, and Facebook

» Organizing meet-ups and tweet-ups

» Starting a social coupon campaign

Chapter 2
Maximizing Stratified Social Communities

Social-networking communities, like other marketing outlets, can be sliced and diced many ways. They can be sorted vertically by industry or horizontally by demographics, such as age, gender, ethnicity, education, or income. By doing a little research, you can *stratify* (classify) them according to other commonly used marketing segmentation parameters, such as life stage (student, young married, family with kids, empty nester, retired) or *psychographics* (beliefs or behaviors).

If you want to delve even further into niche sites, you can find social media channels that are driven by type of activity, geographical location, or by types of social offers. In this chapter, we discuss how you can find these smaller niche sites and how you can get value from them.

Making a Bigger Splash on a Smaller Site

Stratified sites may have much smaller audiences than sites such as Pinterest or Twitter. If you choose correctly, however, the users of these sites will closely resemble the profile of your typical client or customer, making them better prospects. Compare it to the difference between advertising at the Super Bowl versus distributing a flyer at a local high school football game. It all depends on where your audience is.

Your business can also make a much bigger splash on smaller sites. Frankly, it's so difficult to gain visibility and traction on a large social-networking site that you almost need a marketing campaign just for that purpose (for instance, to acquire 2,000 likes on Facebook).

On a smaller site, your business becomes a big fish in a small pond, quickly establishing itself as an expert resource or a source of great products or services.

Taking Networking to the Next Level

From your own experience, you know the importance of offline networking to find vendors, employees, and customers. Social media marketing is, first and foremost, a method of networking online.

Business connection sites have proliferated in the past several years. These sites are generally appropriate for soft selling, not for hard-core marketing. Although referrals are used primarily for making business-to-business (B2B) connections, especially when targeting those with a specific job title, you never know when a referral will bring you a customer.

TIP

Make a habit of including a link to your primary website on every profile, and using some of your preferred search terms in your profile title and text. These techniques increase your inbound links and may help with search engine ranking, as described in Book 2, Chapter 2.

Table 2-1 lists cross-industry directories. Visit the ones that seem appropriate, using the tactics described in Chapter 1 of this minibook to make your selections.

TABLE 2-1 Business Networks

Website	URL	What It Is
Chief Financial Officer Network	www.linkedin.com/groups?gid=51826	Network of high-level CFOs, financial executives, and accounting leaders (requires LinkedIn account)
Data. com Connect	https://connect.data.com	Business directory of B2B professionals
Doostang	www.doostang.com	Career community for professionals seeking new jobs
Medium	http://www.medium.com/	Community for publishing articles and commenting on and sharing published articles
MeetTheBoss TV	www.meettheboss.tv	Video network and roundtables for high-level business leaders
Naymz	www.naymz.com	Networking platform for professionals that has tools to measure and manage your reputation
PartnerUp	https://plus.google.com/communities/105088976956808519330	Google+ community for small-business owners
Spoke	www.spoke.com	Company and business informational database, curated by members
StartupNation	www.startupnation.com	Entrepreneurial article based business advice and networking platform
Talkbiznow	www.talkbiznow.com	Business services and collaboration network
TheFunded.com	http://thefunded.com	Community of entrepreneurs who rate and compare investors and funding sources
XING	www.xing.com	Global networking for professionals
Yammer	www.yammer.com	Free networking tool for networking within a company

TIP

Be selective. Participating in multiple sites productively is time-consuming. Keep clear records of all sites that have your business profile. If your situation changes, you probably have to update your profiles individually.

Figure 2-1 shows a networking profile for PatentPlaques.com, a company that makes patent award and recognition products on Spoke. In this case, the company takes advantage of a professional networking audience to showcase its products at www.spoke.com/companies/patentplaques-com-3e122f809e597c1003388881. This Spoke page offers a full profile, which links to PatentPlaques.com's website, and it's loaded with keywords.

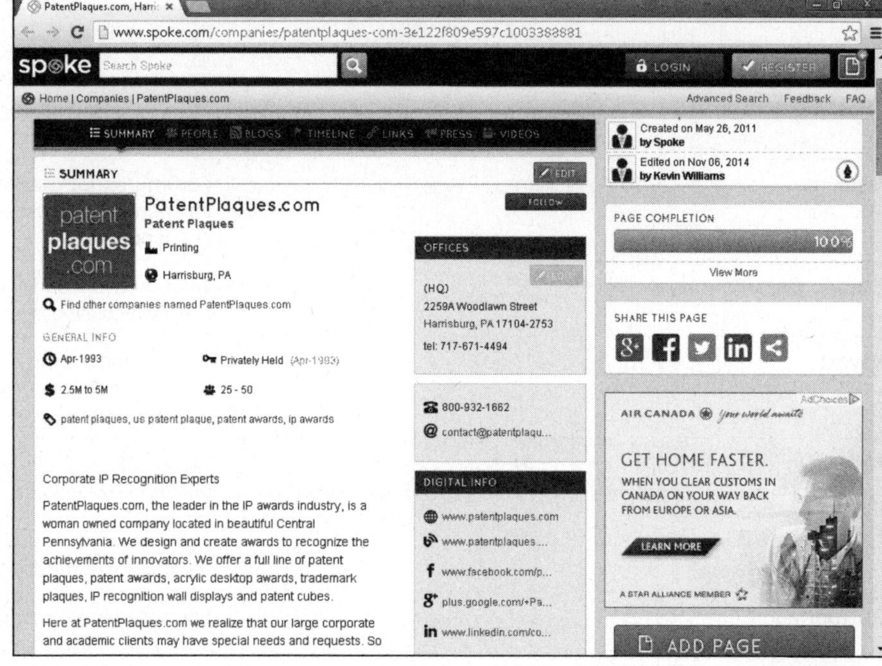

FIGURE 2-1: PatentPlaques.com uses the business directory on Spoke to promote its patent recognition and award products.

Reproduced with permission of PatentPlaques.com

REMEMBER

You can syndicate content postings (see Book 2, Chapter 1), but you usually can't syndicate profile entries.

TIP

You may want to submit your profile to several likely sites on a one-time basis, but commit to only several in terms of community participation. Otherwise, you may go into overload!

Selecting Social Networks by Vertical Industry Sector

Whether you're marketing B2B (business-to-business) or B2C (business-to-consumer), you can find dozens of industry- or interest-specific social networks. Search online for communities in your industry, using the strategies described in

Chapter 1 in this minibook. As long as the social network is large enough to support your time investment and continues to attract new users, you should enjoy enough of payback to make your effort worthwhile.

Vertical industry sites, other than shopping, are particularly appealing for B2B marketers. If you use some adroit maneuvering, you can intersect with the sales cycle, reaching the appropriate decision-maker with the right message.

For the retail community, the growth of social shopping sites is a new avenue to reach consumers who want to spend after they see what everyone else is buying. Users flock to these sites for the latest product reviews, real-time deals, and news about the hottest items.

Track results so that you can decide which sites work best for you. If a site doesn't produce leads or sales after a few months, find another.

REMEMBER

If you want to promote your products or services to more than one online community, customize your profiles and messages accordingly. For instance, a sporting goods store might promote camping gear on a social network for backpackers and running gear on one for joggers.

The list of vertical market social networks seems endless and ever changing. You'll find more at `http://blog.hubspot.com/blog/tabid/6307/bid/33663/7-Targeted-Social-Networks-Niche-Marketers-Should-Try.aspx`. Table 2-2 provides a sample of some of these networks just to give you an idea of the range. This list does not include blogs, bookmarking sites, or news aggregators.

TABLE 2-2 **Vertical Market Social Networks**

Website	URL	Description
Art		
ArtSlant	`www.artslant.com`	Contemporary art network with profiles for artists, art professionals, art organizations, and art lovers
DeviantArt	`www.deviantart.com`	Post and share original artwork
Auto		
CarGurus	`www.cargurus.com`	Automobile community with reviews, photos, and opinions
Motortopia	`www.motortopia.com`	Community for lovers of cars, motorbikes, planes, and boats

(continued)

TABLE 2-2 ***(continued)***

Website	URL	Description
Books		
Goodreads	www.goodreads.com	Book recommendations to share
LibraryThing	www.librarything.com	Book recommendations and online catalog
Design		
Design Float	www.designfloat.com	Web design-related content sharing, advertising, digital art, and branding
Environment		
Care2	www.care2.com	Eco-friendly lifestyle site
Make Me Sustainable	www.makemesustainable.com	Environmental community
TreeHugger	www.treehugger.com	Environmental topics at interactive community
Entertainment, Film, and Music		
CreateSpace	www.createspace.com	Creation, collaboration, and distribution for writers, musicians, and filmmakers
Fanpop	www.fanpop.com	Network of fan clubs for television, movies, music, and more
Flixster	www.flixster.com	Movie lovers community
Last.fm	www.last.fm	Music community
Mediabistro	www.mediabistro.com	Careers and community for media professionals
Myspace	www.myspace.com	Social networking site for music entertainment
Pandora	www.pandora.com	Music community
Spotify	www.spotify.com	Music community
Medical		
PatientsLikeMe	www.patientslikeme.com	Patients, healthcare professionals, and industry organizations making connections
Sermo	www.sermo.com	Physician community
Legal		
Lawyrs.net	www.lawyrs.net	International social networking community for lawyers and law students

Website	URL	Description
Philanthropy and Nonprofits		
Care2	www.care2.com	Online community for people passionate about making a difference
ChangingThePresent	www.changingthepresent.org	Nonprofit giving community
Pets		
Uniteddogs	www.uniteddogs.com	Social networking for dogs and their owners
WellPaw	www.wellpaw.com	Social pet community
Shopping, Fashion, and Collecting		
Curiobot	www.curiobot.net	Collection of the most interesting items for sale on the Internet
Gilt	www.gilt.com	Flash sales on women's apparel
Polyvore	www.polyvore.com	Product mixing and matching from any online store
Rue La La	www.ruelala.com	Flash sales
Stylehive	www.stylehive.com	Stylish people connecting
ThisNext	www.thisnext.com	Product discovery, recommendations, and sharing
Wanelo	www.wanelo.com	Discover and bookmark products
Sports		
Athlinks	www.athlinks.com	Database with all types of sports race results and athlete community
BeRecruited	https://new.berecruited.com	Connecting high school athletes and college coaches
Science and Technology		
ResearchGate	www.researchgate.net	Social network for scientists to connect and make their work more visible

REMEMBER

As always, include a link to your primary website and use some of your preferred search terms in your postings and profiles. If these sites have blogs or accept photos, video, or music, you can syndicate that type of content to many sites simultaneously.

Selecting Social Networks by Demographics

No one ever has enough staff and time to do everything. You already know that the more tightly you focus your marketing efforts, the better the payoff from your investment. If you created a strategic plan in Book 1, Chapter 1, return to it to analyze and segment your markets demographically into smaller, niche markets that you can reach with a coordinated campaign.

TIP

Think online guerrilla marketing. Go after one niche market online at a time. After you conquer one, go after the next. If you scatter your efforts across too many target markets at one time, your business won't have enough visibility in any of them to drive meaningful traffic your way.

Table 2-3 describes some sites that are primarily demographically and geographically stratified. You can find many, many more. As usual, qualify the sites for your business by following the concepts described in Chapter 1 of this minibook.

TABLE 2-3 Demographically and Geographically Stratified Sites

Website	URL	Description
Ethnic		
Black Business Women Online	`www.mybbwo.com`	A social network for black women in business, women entrepreneurs, and bloggers
BlackPlanet.com	`www.blackplanet.com`	African American network that includes a job section by way of Monster.com
MiGente.com	`www.migente.com`	Largest Latin American community; includes a job section by way of Monster.com
High School and College		
Classmates	`www.classmates.com`	Networking with members of your graduating class at all levels
MeetMe	`www.meetme.com`	Networking site for high school and college students and grads
Generational		
Club Penguin	`www.clubpenguin.com`	Disney site for children under 12
More	`www.more.com`	Community for women over 40
ThirdAge	`www.thirdage.com`	Community for Baby Boomer women

Website	URL	Description
Local		
Citysearch	www.citysearch.com	Localized directory with reviews and comments
Kudzu	www.kudzu.com	Local business directory with reviews and daily deals
Local.com	www.local.com	Local business directory with deals, events, and activities listings
Manta	www.manta.com	Local business directory for small businesses
MerchantCircle	www.merchantcircle.com	Find, review, and comment on local businesses
Nextdoor	https://nextdoor.com	Private social network for neighborhoods
Tribe	www.tribe.net	Local-resident connections for advice and sharing about local resources
TripAdvisor	www.tripadvisor.com	Reviews of flights, hotels, vacation rentals, restaurants, and things to do
Zomato	https://www.zomato.com	Restaurant listings and reviews from critics, food bloggers, and friends
Yelp	www.yelp.com	Local business reviews and comments
International		
Badoo	http://badoo.com	Popular international social networking and dating site
Nexopia	www.nexopia.com	Canada's largest social networking site for young people
Sonico	www.sonico.com	Latin American social networking site
Zorpia	http://en.zorpia.com	International friendship network
Moms		
CafeMom	www.cafemom.com	Largest social-networking, blogging, and community site for moms and parenting
MommySavers	www.mommysavers.com	Money-saving community and tips for moms
Seniors		
Grandparents.com	http://community.grandparents.com	Social networking and news site for grandparents
Wealthy		
ASMALLWORLD	www.asmallworld.com	Private international community of culturally influential people

As usual, customize your message and profile for the audience you're trying to reach. Be sure to include a link to your primary website and some of your key search terms in any profile or posting.

Figure 2-2 shows how businesses can take advantage of demographically targeted sites. The advertisement to work from home that appears at the top of a page on MommySavers clearly targets stay-at-home moms.

FIGURE 2-2: MommySavers is an example of a demographically targeted social network.

Reproduced with permission of Kimberly Danger, Founder of Mommysavers.com

Selecting Social Networks by Activity Type

We can imagine what you're thinking. Why in the world would you want more than one service of a particular type, such as video sharing or blogging? The answer is simple: to improve search engine rankings and inbound links from high-ranking sites. When your content appears on multiple sites, such as those listed by activity in Table 2-4, you're simply casting a wider net and hoping to catch more fish.

TABLE 2-4 **Social Networks by Activity Type**

Website	URL	Description
Networking and Profiles		
hi5	`www.hi5.com`	Social entertainment for the youth market over 18 worldwide with personal profiles
MocoSpace	`www.mocospace.com`	Smartphone-compatible online community
Image Sharing		
Flickr	`www.flickr.com`	Well-known photo-sharing site
Gentlemint	`http://gentlemint.com`	A site "to find and share manly things"; similar to Pinterest but with a male demographic
HoverSpot	`http://hoverspot.com`	Free social network with good photo-sharing capabilities
Instagram	`http://instagram.com`	An image-sharing and photo-manipulation site, especially for images taken on smartphones
Photobucket	`http://photobucket.com`	Free image hosting, and photo and video sharing
Pinterest	`www.pinterest.com`	Visual bookmarking site
SlideShare	`www.slideshare.net`	Presentation sharing site
TasteSpotting	`www.tastespotting.com`	Food and recipe image-sharing site; a visual potluck
Video Sharing (YouTube Alternatives)		
Dailymotion	`www.dailymotion.com`	Video-hosting and -sharing community
Jing	`www.techsmith.com/jing.html`	Video-hosting and -sharing tool
Livestream	`http://new.livestream.com`	Platform for live, interactive broadcast video
Ustream	`www.ustream.tv`	Platform for live, interactive broadcast video
Vimeo	`http://vimeo.com`	Video-hosting and -sharing community
Vine	`https://vine.co`	Six-second looping video platform
Unique Services		
eHow	`www.ehow.com`	Content submissions on how to do things
HubPages	`http://hubpages.com`	Publish content on thousands of topics on which you happen to be an expert
Mahalo	`www.mahalo.com`	Content submissions on how to do things
Meetup	`www.meetup.com`	Local-group organizing for face-to-face meetings
Quora	`www.quora.com`	Group-sourced answers to questions

TIP

The secret to keeping this situation manageable is syndication, via a dashboard such as Hootsuite or Netvibes, or by using Really Simple Syndication (RSS), as discussed in Book 2, Chapter 1. You post an image, a video, or a blog entry to your primary site, and your distribution service automatically updates other services with the same content.

Even with syndication, use some common sense. It doesn't help to drive the wrong fish to your website and dilute your conversion rate. Of course, if you've monetized your site by showing ads by the impressions, then the more eyeballs, the merrier.

Because setting up multiple accounts can be time-consuming, you may want to stagger the process. By now, you automatically include in any profile or posting a link to your primary website and some of your key search terms.

For example, The Karen Martin Group (`www.ksmartin.com`) takes advantage of SlideShare (see Figure 2-3) to establish credibility and provide evidence of its expertise. By viewing any of her 79 presentations or 60 videos, prospective clients can get a very good sense of the skills and services her company provides. The company profile on the left links to her website and displays a number of relevant tags (keywords) for search.

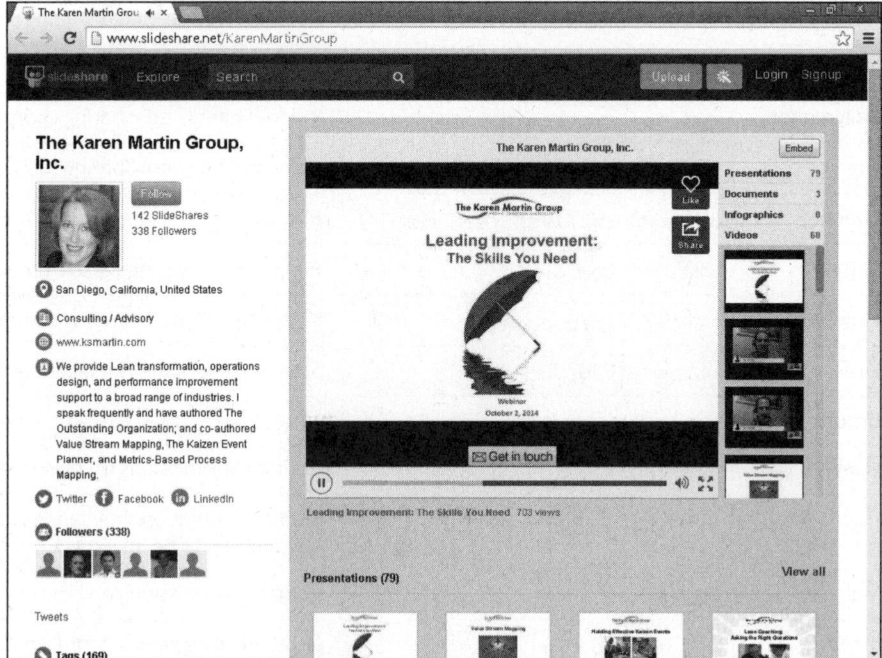

FIGURE 2-3: The Karen Martin Group uses SlideShare to establish credibility, experience, and expertise.

Reproduced with permission of Karen S. Martin

Finding Yourself in the Real World with Geomarketing

Location, location, location: It's the mantra of real estate and yet another feature of successful social media marketing. The convergence of mobile devices (smartphones and tablets) with GPS and social media offers a great opportunity for marketers. You can inform potential customers that you offer exactly what they're looking for, when they're looking for it, and provide directions to get them there from their current location.

In this book, we use the term *geomarketing tools* to refer to social media services that incorporate knowledge of users' locations or that bring people together in a specific, real-world space.

Several location-based services, including *social mapping* (identifying where people are) and location-based marketing games, are available for geomarketing, though the number of independent vendors has diminished in favor of check-in and location-tagging options on Facebook, Twitter, and Instagram.

REMEMBER

Before you undertake geomarketing, follow the directions for local optimization in Book 2, Chapter 2 to improve your success rate.

Going geo for good reason

The techniques we describe in this section apply to businesses that exist in the physical world with their own storefront or that offer events that bring people together face-to-face. Pure cyber-businesses may not find these ideas as useful, but you never know what creative idea will hit you. Although geolocation services are particularly appropriate for business-to-consumer (B2C) operations, we also offer some intriguing business-to-business (B2B) applications in this chapter.

For most businesses, geomarketing involves a teaser deal that attracts residents or out-of-town visitors who check in online or with a mobile device when they arrive at the establishment. This concept is particularly attractive for events, tourist sites, restaurants, and entertainment venues. Almost all these services notify their subscribers by email or text message, or on their mobile apps, whenever an offer is available nearby.

Deciding whether geomarketing is right for you

Geomarketing isn't for every business. Whether you should use a geomarketing service depends on the nature of your business, whether your customer base is already using it, and which location-based activities consume your prospective customers' time. Mull over these factors before you take the leap:

- **Don't reinvent the wheel.** Many smartphone apps already offer a location-specific tool — for example, a weather report, road conditions, a list of gas prices at stations around town — and then add a sponsor. If all you're trying to do is reach the on-the-go consumer who is ready to buy, do you need more than that? Maybe a pay per click (PPC) ad on a mobile search engine solves your needs.
- **Numbers matter.** Enough people living near or planning to visit your location have to use a particular geomarketing application to make it worth the effort. This issue is nontrivial because most services don't publicize this data. Try to research the number of users in your area with both the service provider and a third-party source, such as Alexa. The numbers can fluctuate widely and are difficult to find.

  After you estimate the size of the potential audience (the *reach*), remember that only a small percentage of the audience is likely to become customers. Your best bet: Ask existing customers whether they use Foursquare, Facebook check-ins, or other services.

  TIP

  To get an idea of the number of members, try creating a user account. Then scan the list of places in your area (sometimes called places, locations, or venues) for the inclusion of neighbors and competitors, and look at the maximum number of check-ins at those locations. For instance, even if you don't ordinarily serve Foursquare fanatics, a high-tech conference that draws a huge number of users may be a one-time opportunity worth taking advantage of.
- **Prospective customers must be willing to participate.** You must take privacy issues into account. Although about 30 percent of all users include location tagging on their posts (so their friends know where they are), the percentage declines with age.
- **Local is not always enough.** No matter the size of the total user base for your neighborhood, you may draw a large audience of Foursquare users only if you happen to own the pizza place across the street from the computer science building at the local college, not if you offer a deal to seniors at a local retirement community who show up for early-bird specials.

- **Demographics are fluid.** Be cautious: The demographics and statistics of users may fluctuate.
- **The temptation is great to "go geo."** Don't jump into geomarketing just because it's cool or trendy.

For a summary of geolocation services, see Table 2-5.

TABLE 2-5 Geolocation Services

Geolocation	Site URL for Businesses	Number of User Accounts & Notes
Everplaces	`https://everplaces.com`	A mash-up of Pinterest and Foursquare
Facebook Location	`https://www.facebook.com/about/location`	More than 1.86 billion worldwide monthly active users (undetermined number who use check-in or tag location)
Findery	`https://findery.com/`	A place-sharing site and travel community
Instagram	`https://help.instagram.com/236245819849257`	600 million active users, many of whom share locations from Instagram to Facebook, and Twitter; location is not automatically tagged
Twitter Geolocation	`https://support.twitter.com/articles/78525-about-the-tweetlocation-feature`	313 million monthly active users; geotags available on all tweets but turned off by default
Yelp	`https://biz.yelp.com/support/what_is_yelp`	24 million monthly unique visitors

Spacing Out with Twitter

The importance of integrating social media with location hasn't been lost on Twitter.

Checking in on Twitter

Like many other social networks, Twitter offers users the ability to check in to specific locations when they tweet. To use this feature, click the location icon. When asked to turn on Locations, tap the Turn On Location Now option. (Unless you turn off Locations later, you won't have to turn it on again.)

Searching real space with Twitter

The search function can help you estimate the number of local Twitter users in a city or within a certain radius. Go to `https://twitter.com/search-advanced`. In the Places section, enter a neighborhood, city, or latitude and longitude; then click search. By default, Twitter searches within a 15-mile radius. To enter a place in Advanced Search, you must enable the location capability on your mobile device.

TECHNICAL STUFF

To change the search radius, use the search operators in the Near This Place text box, such as *Coliseum near: Los Angeles within: 5 miles.*

Finding Your Business on Facebook

Facebook offers its users four ways to relate to the real world: geotagging, places nearby, check-ins, and offers.

Geotagging on Facebook

On both its desktop and mobile app versions, Facebook allows users to add a location to any post, whether text, image, or video. If someone else tries to tag a post that names another Facebook user who isn't a friend, the second person must approve the geotag before it appears. For more information, see `www.facebook.com/about/location`.

Getting close with places nearby

Places Nearby appears as an option only when you use the Facebook app on mobile devices with location turned on. Users find places by tapping Nearby Places on the app menu. Facebook, being Facebook, doesn't just list everyone within 100 feet. Instead, it displays places nearby based on check-ins, likes, and friends' recommendations. The places that a Facebook user sees vary based on how many engagement actions she and her friends have taken.

Checking in on Facebook

To enable check-ins at your business, you must choose Local Business as the category for your Facebook page and add your business address. If you already have a page, you can change its category. (Log in as the page administrator, and click the About tab on the left side of the page. On the page that appears, click the Edit link in the Category row and select Local Businesses from the drop-down choices.)

You can also set up Facebook ads to generate check-ins, which is available only to people using the Facebook app on mobile devices with location turned on. From their news feeds, users must tap the Check-in icon and select their location. They can add a description of what they're doing and then tap Post to share their location with their friends.

TIP

Post a counter card at your business to remind people to check-in. For more information on check-ins, see `www.facebook.com/help/343548832389235`.

Results for check-ins are visible on your Facebook Insights page (see Book 5, Chapter 2) but only after 30 people have checked in at your business. To understand any of these Facebook geomarketing options in more detail, see Book 5 or read *Facebook Marketing All-in-One For Dummies*, 3rd Edition, by Andrea Vahl, John Haydon, and Jan Zimmerman (Wiley).

REMEMBER

The local review site Yelp (`www.yelp.com`) has a location-based check-in feature on its Android and iOS devices. Instagram and Snapchat also offer optional geotags. Users must always turn on geotags; geotags default to Off on all social media for security and privacy reasons.

Making a Facebook offer they can't refuse

If you want to improve traffic from Facebook users when they are close by, use Facebook offers to entice folks with a discount or other special offer on your Facebook timeline or in a mobile ad. Although there's no charge to write an offer as a simple post, Facebook will charge if you decide to boost your post or advertise your offer. For more about Facebook advertising and boosted posts, see Book 5, Chapter 3.

WARNING

All offers must comply with Facebook's Terms and Conditions. For more about creating offers, see Facebook's help center at `www.facebook.com/business/help/1446432849003728`.

First, you must create an offer either directly from your Facebook page or from the Ads Create tool. To do this from your page, follow these steps:

1. **On your page's timeline, click the Create an Offer button, below the Write Something area.**
2. **On the pop-up that appears, click the blue Get Started button.**
3. **Fill out the various options for your offer.**

   For example, select whether your offer is online, in stores, or both.

4. **On the same page, fill in your link, the offer type, and descriptive information.**

   You can also choose to boost your post. We cover this in detail in Book 5, Chapter 3.

5. **Click the Create Offer button.**

   You return to your page, and the offer now appears at the top of your timeline.

6. **Choose one of two ways to inform Facebook users know about your offer:**

   - *Boost the post.* If you didn't boost your offer when you created it, you can still go back and do so. This is optional, but it's a way to get more eyeballs on your offer.
   - *Advertise the offer.* For advertising directions, skip to the following numbered list.

   For more detailed directions and suggested tactics for both boosting posts and advertising on Facebook, see Book 5, Chapter 3.

TIP

For more information on creating an offer from your business page, go to `www.facebook.com/help/410451192330456`.

Alternatively, you can advertise the offer using the Ads Create tool by following these steps:

1. **Log in as the page administrator.**
2. **Click the down arrow at the far right of the top navigation to open a drop-down list. Then select Create Ads.**
3. **On the Objectives screen that appears, choose Get People to Claim Your Offer from the list.**

   The screen expands to the right.

4. **Choose the offer from the list in the right panel.**

   If you don't already have an eligible offer to advertise, you're prompted to create one by clicking the + icon to the right of the prompt. This takes you to the pop-up screen described in the preceding list. Follow the directions to fill out all the required fields. After you preview and edit your offer to perfection, click Create Offer.

5. **Click Continue.**

   The screen expands below the Objectives section.

6. **Keep scrolling down to view the options for targeting your market, setting your budget, and selecting text and links.**

7. **Now go through the standard steps of the Ads Create tool to promote your offer with an ad.**

   See Book 5, Chapter 3 for more information about creating an ad, defining a target audience, and setting a budget.

TIP

   For location-based offers that people will redeem in your store, be sure that the Mobile News Feed option is selected in the Text and Links section.

For more information on creating an offer by using the Ads Create tool, go to www.facebook.com/help/102534329872055.

Making Real Connections in Virtual Spaces

Meet-ups and tweet-ups bridge the gap between the cyberworld and the one we live in. These services make it easy for people who have similar interests to organize meetings for fun, advocacy, learning, or simply to meet one another.

Meeting through Meetup

Meetup (www.meetup.com), which has been around since 2002, bills itself as "the world's largest network of local groups," claiming that more than 29 million members attend nearly 585,000 meetings per month held by more than 268,000 local groups located in 180 countries.

Meetup charges organizers a fee ranging from $10 to $15 per month for using its platform Meetup pages (as shown in Figure 2-4) to help people find or start a group located near them. The system includes an easy-to-use interface to identify either groups or meet-ups (via calendar view) within a certain distance.

Click a group or a meet-up to find directions to future meet-ups and check out the history of a Meetup group. Meetup lets you easily invite your Facebook friends to join you at a meet-up or see whether you have friends participating in other Meetup groups.

In an inevitable mash-up, Meetup now allows Groupon fans (described in the section "Comparing LivingSocial and Groupon," later in this chapter) to hook up at official and self-organized events through http://groupon.meetup.com. What an easy way to find your target market in a location close to you!

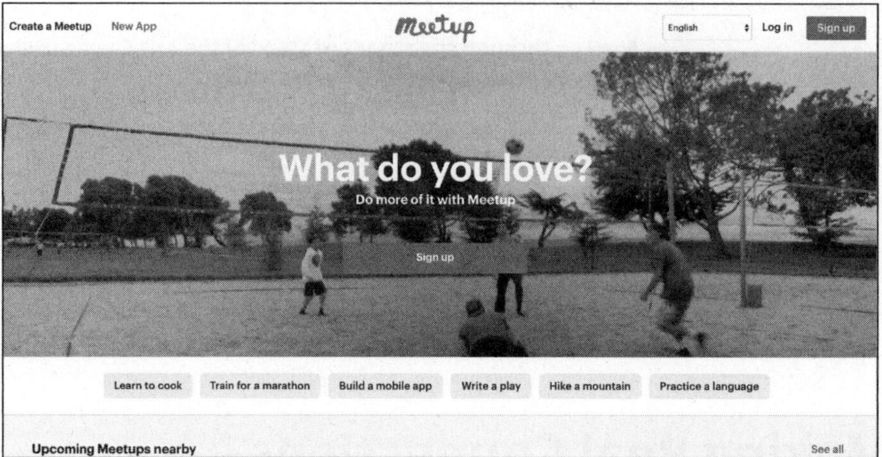

FIGURE 2-4: A Meetup search for small-business activities near Denver produces several results.

Tweeting for meeting in real space

The term *tweet-up* has been part of the Twitter lexicon for a long time; it describes a live meeting of Twitter users or, more generally, any face-to-face event organized by way of social media.

Twitter is already influencing traditional gatherings, such as large conferences and seminars. Small groups with a particular interest or agenda can now more easily meet with each other socially or in a *rump session* (the "meeting" after the meeting). And many attendees have started tweeting questions and commentary during presentations, using the hashtag (#) to mark tweets related to a particular session. This technique can either unnerve or energize presenters. Some tech-savvy people read the tweet stream as the session goes on and respond to questions on the fly.

In either case, a tweet-up is definitely another way to take networking to the next level.

Marketing with meet-ups and tweet-ups

Meet-ups and tweet-ups offer you an exquisite opportunity to reach out to new customers, even if they're only complementary to your primary business. Contact meeting organizers to see whether you can

- Host an event at your restaurant or another event location. For example, a company selling kitchen countertops could offer to hold cooking classes in its showroom.
- Offer a discount to members or for the event.

- Give a presentation or teach a class at a future meeting, which is an excellent way for a B2B or service provider to establish expertise in an area.
- Provide information to members.

Attending a meeting first is helpful (but not required) to make sure that the makeup of the group fits your target audience and to meet the leaders.

You can gauge interest by using Meetup to estimate the number of members in similar groups in your location(s).

Making Deals on Social Media

A group of friends hitting the mall is the offline definition of *social shopping.* Online, though, social shopping means something quite different: A group of folks (sometimes, strangers) saves money by volume buying with a group coupon. The group coupon emerged several years ago as a way to aggregate new buyers, usually in specific cities, by offering a half-off, one-day promotion online or by email. The underlying assumption was that by attracting a high volume of customers, a business could still make money on a highly discounted deal, buy goodwill and exposure, or fill their businesses during off-times or off-season.

The best-known and oldest of these coupon services are Groupon (`www.groupon.com`), which went public in fall 2011, and LivingSocial (`www.livingsocial.com`). (Groupon and LivingSocial are described in the section "Comparing LivingSocial and Groupon," later in this chapter.) Both companies have expanded to offer specific tourism-related deals, as well as deals on goods, tickets, and national brands.

Seeing an opportunity for profit, dozens of other companies — some national, some regional or local — have entered the group-coupon frenzy. The competition has had several consequences:

- With more coupon vendors to choose from, merchants have more leverage negotiating deals on favorable terms.
- Familiarity has taken the bloom off the discount rose.
- Some customers, who have come to expect major discounts as a matter of course, pressure merchants to bend the rules in their favor by threatening bad online reviews.

Using high-discount coupons can indeed bring new and repeat customers. On the downside, businesses may be exposed to significant financial risk and bad publicity. Many companies are now rethinking the shared coupon experiment or taking advantage of less costly local sites, offering daily deals.

In the following sections, which primarily address the needs of business-to-consumer (B2C) companies, you can assess the risks and benefits of high-discount group deals. With this information, you can decide whether a deal strategy makes sense for your particular business.

Offering savings, gaining customers

Offering a discount to attract customers is an obvious B2C technique used for ages by service and product companies: bars and restaurants, tourist destinations, health and beauty salons, events, recreation, personal services, and more.

Generally, customers who sign up for a deal service receive a daily email offering some product or service for an average 57 percent off, though deals may range from 30 to 90 percent off.

In the past, a minimum number of deals had to be purchased during a specific time period. If the minimum wasn't reached, the deal didn't go through. Most of the deal sites have now eliminated the minimum requirement, finding that they were able to sell enough deals without any problem.

Most, but not all, daily deal sites are set up geographically, with users signing up to see deals near their homes or watching for deals they can use on their next vacation. For an example of a typical deal like this, DailyDealOmaha (`www.dailydealomaha.com/deal/omaha`) offers high-discount deals weekly.

So that's how it works for users. To see how online coupons affect your end of the rope as a business, see the section "Making an attractive offer," later in this chapter.

Consider these points before you decide whether to pursue a high-discount deal strategy:

- **Ultimately, the coupon companies select which businesses participate at which time and set the schedule for featuring offers.** You may not get the time frame that you want.
- **A link to your site will appear in the offer.** In preparation, you should be willing to create a separate landing page on your website for the offer.

- **Some sites offer national deals, particularly for large, web-based retailers, online shopping, and travel.** For a national reach, you might target multiple individual cities within your national audience with separate offers. This approach works for participating franchises or branches in several cities.
- **Confirm that the deal service you select reaches your city.** Because tourists and local residents are your primary audience, a service must have enough email subscribers interested in a specific geographic area to make your deal workable.

You can make online couponing work for a business-to-business (B2B) audience, but it's a little more complicated. A successful B2B deal depends on the size and quality of the email list that the coupon service maintains, an attractive offer on a product or service of wide interest (payroll services or office supplies, perhaps), and recommendations from employees to employers. For example, Rewardli (`www.rewardli.com/offers`) focuses on the B2B deal market.

Making an attractive offer

Sometimes, you just want people in your door, virtual or otherwise. If you offer a *loss leader* (a sale below cost), try not to sell too far below cost. Selling hundreds of $4 ice-cream cones for half-price is one thing as long as you cover your cost of goods and service; discounting hundreds of $40 haircuts at half-price may leave you short on the rent.

If you're in a position to handle a potential loss, there are some viable reasons to consider online deals as a tool in your marketing arsenal:

- **There are no upfront payments.** That's a good thing for your cash flow (if you get paid promptly by the coupon service).
- **There are backloaded payments.** The coupon company gets paid from revenues only if the minimum number of offers is purchased — and usually you can set the minimum and maximum number of coupons sold (more on that in a bit).
- **Coupon deals often provide a stream of new customers in a relatively short length of time.** Compare the result to how long it takes other forms of advertising to produce new business. If you just opened a new business, coupons may be a good technique.
- **Word-of-mouth works.** Buyers might bring their friends to share the experience.
- **Factor estimated add-on purchases, as well as lifetime-customer value, into your calculation.** The lifetime-customer value is the value of estimated

repeat purchases from the same customer. Obviously, new customers who make multiple, repeat purchases are more valuable than customers who buy only once — for example, tourists. Try to make your offer something worth a repeat buy or set the offer low enough that you can generate an up-sale from most buyers.

Setting Terms for Your Coupon Campaign

You have many ways to refine and tailor your coupon campaign, within limits. You do want customers, but you don't want to lose your shirt, either. To limit your discount exposure, you may be able to tweak the coupon vendor's share of revenue, the time frame during which the offer will be honored, the maximum number of deals, and more.

WARNING

Be sure to read the fine print before you sign with a coupon service. Each company has different rules.

The depth of the discount

Typically, the buyer receives 30 to 50 percent (or more) off the standard price. Then the coupon service gets its slice: sometimes as high as an additional half of how much the buyer pays. So, as the merchant, you receive only 25 percent of your list price. For example:

30-minute parasailing adventure	$100
Customer coupon discount (50% off)	$50
Coupon service's cut	$25
Merchant's final take	$25

The percentages vary by company and by the nature of the offer, but thanks to the competition for deals, you may sometimes be able to negotiate better terms on the coupon service's cut, especially with some of the smaller deal companies (or if you're a huge multinational corporation).

The scope of the deal

Consider how you will establish the parameters of an offer to best meet your goals and objectives:

- **Assess your net return.** The coupon company takes its cut off the revenue first. The coupon firm collects payments from customers by credit card and sends you a check for your share afterward. The schedule of payments varies by coupon company.

WARNING

  Watch the schedule of payments carefully. Delayed payments from the coupon service can create an unnecessary cash flow crisis for your company.

- **Set the maximum number of deals you will offer.** Set a maximum number of deals to limit both your financial and service exposure. A cap makes sense, especially for event organizers and service providers. For example, your small theater company may have a fixed number of seats, you may have room for only a certain number of people in a dance class, or you may have enough stylists to handle only a certain number of haircuts per day.
- **Determine how long the offer will last.** You specify the time frame over which buyers can exercise a deal, usually several months to a year. Keep in mind how much product, space, and staff you'll need to fulfill your end of the deal.

WARNING

  Some deal companies require you to honor a group deal forever.

- **Timing is everything.** Schedule the term of your offer so you don't have buyers showing up on your doorstep all at one time — unless the offer is for a scheduled event or you intentionally set a short period for redemption. Most merchants see a peak in redemptions the first 30 days after an offer and the last 30 days before expiration.

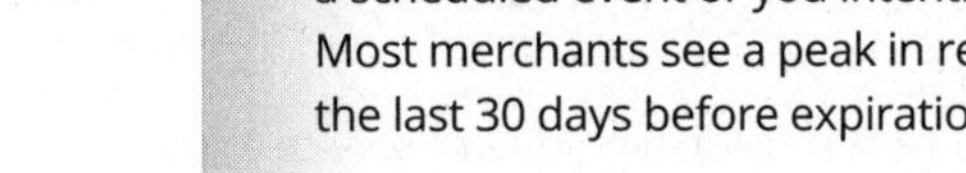

Grappling with the gotchas

Watch for landmines like these before signing up for a deal:

- **Late customers:** The fine print on some deals (and the law in some states) allows buyers to receive a discount equal to the amount they paid for their coupon — even if the deal itself has expired. For instance, suppose someone saved $6 on a pound of coffee costing $14 with a deal that expired on 12/31/16. Even if he comes into your store a year later, you may have to give him $6 off a pound of coffee, whose price has now increased to $16. However, you don't have to honor the original discounted net price on the product that he buys. In the previous example, you wouldn't have to sell the $16 pound of coffee for $8 (its price with the original deal), but you would have to sell it for $10.

WARNING

  Be cautious when making offers that include a percentage discount; a fixed-dollar discount is better.

- **Special package deals:** Many companies create a unique package or service just for their deal offer. You are usually not required to continue to offer that product or service beyond the term of the deal. For instance, say your company usually offers only hour-long dance lessons for couples and prices them at $40 per hour. For the deal only, you offer a half-hour dance lesson for couples valued at $20 but sold at $10. After the offer has expired, coupon buyers may be able to get $10 off the $40 price, but you aren't required to offer the half-hour lesson anymore.
- **Bookkeeping nightmares:** These deals can leave you with a record-keeping headache, from tracking outstanding and redeemed offers at the register to holding potential entries on your books, even for expired coupons. Talk to your accountant about the impact on your financial statements for these ongoing liabilities.
- **Waiting for payment:** Payment isn't swift, either. Some coupon services divide your payments into three installments paid over 60 days, which could create cash flow problems for you if large numbers of buyers redeem their coupons quickly.
- **Price-gouging customers:** Nasty deal-seekers may threaten to write bad reviews if you don't meet their demands to provide more than the deal offered. They may demand a higher-priced product or service at the same discount, a greater quantity than you offered, or a deeper discount.
- **Being unprepared:** If you can't provide high-quality service to meet the demand with the staff or space you have, you may lose not only the customer but also your reputation, if poor reviews appear online. Depending on the deal you're offering, protect yourself from unhappy customers by requiring appointments, stating "subject to availability" (say, for a massage or a haircut), and allowing adequate time to redeem the offer.

Measuring success

Good coupon sites offer detailed analytics, similar to newsletters, stating the number of offers emailed, number and percent of offers opened, number and percent of viewers who clicked for details, and the number and percent of viewers who purchased the deal. Additionally, they can provide how many viewers purchased more than one deal, total number of deals sold, and total dollar value received.

Copy this information to a spreadsheet so that you can do the following:

- Assess whether the offer was financially successful for your business.
- Obtain clues about what factors might have affected an offer that didn't draw buyers.

» Compare the success and parameters of offers that you have sent out through the same company to see which offers are the most successful.

» Compare what happens with the same offer distributed through different companies.

If you can't figure out how to analyze results from your coupon site, ask your bookkeeper or accountant. They eat numbers for lunch.

REMEMBER

Do the math. What percentage of customers might convert or upgrade their purchase? What's a reasonable lifetime-customer value for each one? How does it compare to the cost of acquisition? Get help from your accountant, if needed.

WARNING

Seller beware! Small businesses with shallow pockets sometimes can't handle the pressure of serving so many customers. Many companies, especially restaurants, now report a loss in revenue whenever existing customers snap up their coupon deals. Receiving less than half the full price for a meal or service can turn coupon deals into an expensive loyalty program for existing clientele.

Further leveraging your deal

Many companies offer extra options to their coupon buyers in the hope that deals will go viral:

» **Opportunities to share opinions and photos:** Coupon buyers, for example, may have the opportunity to share on Facebook or Twitter, entering comments about a company that's offering a deal. Other sites encourage participation in a social activity, such as ranking a service or posting photos. These actions are often perceived as testimonials by other prospective buyers and encourage them to purchase coupons. Almost all deal sites provide share buttons that facilitate users sharing deals with others on their own social media pages.

» **Easy-to-share links to send deals to friends:** If three or more friends share a deal, the referrer receives a freebie. Include this element as an allowance in your revenue calculations. If someone organizes a share campaign, total revenues may decline.

  This share-this-deal functionality encourages people who receive a daily coupon email, or people who visit your site, to tell their friends about the deal on Facebook and Twitter, and by email.

» **Affiliate options:** Recommending a deal to others or signing up to promote offers on a commission basis usually generates internal *deal bucks* (additional discounts, not cash). Groupon, for instance, offers bucks to first-time buyers who make referrals, and a 10 percent commission for members of Groupon's

Affiliate programs. LivingSocial lets users earn deal bucks if they make purchases with its branded Visa card.

- **Easy integration with Facebook, Twitter, and email to share deals:** Most services offer mobile apps for iPhone, iPad, and Android devices.

TIP

After the offer appears, you can promote the deal in your newsletter, on your social media outlets, and elsewhere, although you may not have much notice.

More upsides and downsides

As a merchant, you gain brand awareness, a direct appeal to locally targeted markets, word-of-mouth advertising, and high visibility to a new customer stream. The low-cost offer supposedly reduces customers' perceived risk of trying something new. It's your job to turn these one-time experimenters into loyal repeat customers.

In theory, compared with how long it takes other forms of advertising to produce new business, your business benefits from this approach by obtaining a stream of new customers in a relatively short length of time. The concept assumes (but this assumption doesn't always prove to be true) that when an offer brings prospects in the door, satisfied customers will proceed to spend more money through these avenues:

- **Impulse buys and add-ons:** Hey, you got them in the door, right? Time to exploit customers' good moods for your deal. See whether you can get them to cough up a little more cash. Say your buyers get 50 percent off a specialty burrito. You can then entice them to spend their savings on drinks, sides, or a take-home purchase: "This cupcake from the offer was so good that I'm buying a dozen to take home."
- **Repeat customers:** This is worth repeating (pun intended). Deliver quality on your discount deal, and you'll likely build a solid client base. One great massage, and that client may be yours every two or three weeks for years.
- **Word-of-mouth:** Worth repeating, too. Buyers might bring friends.

REMEMBER

Human nature being what it is, customers cashing in your deal don't always generate gold:

- **One-hit wonders:** Many people who use these deals are there only for the discount and have no intention of returning. That's life — and why you have to remember to price your deal with a profit margin/loss you can live with.
- **Cannibalizing existing customers:** Loyal patrons who would have paid full price or happily taken a 5 or 10 percent discount are now receiving a product or service at half-off, causing a loss in regular revenue.

- **Customer service versus aggressive customers:** An ugly side of human nature is that some deal redeemers, regardless of the deal's conditions, can be unreasonable and sometimes unpleasant. They demand to use more than one coupon per purchase, want to buy an item that's not on the offer, or otherwise take advantage of merchants who don't want to have anyone making a scene in their business.
- **Succumbing to greediness:** An overwhelmed business that can't meet the demand of a deal's sales is toast. When a business is pressured into selling more deals than it can manage, everyone — staff, customers, and business owners — has a bad experience. Unhappy customers threaten to post negative reviews on sites such as Yelp, and some actually do.

To be fair, Groupon is aware of the criticisms and has tried to address them by offering less price-driven deals and additional, pro-business tools. It also launched Groupon Pages, a listing directory for local businesses. It hopes that Pages will offer merchants an additional online presence to increase reach and sales.

Comparing LivingSocial and Groupon

LivingSocial and Groupon reach fairly similar US audiences demographically, and both have expanded into the international market. For a more detailed comparison, see Table 2-6.

TABLE 2-6 Comparing Groupon and Living Social

Groupon	LivingSocial
74% are female.	66% are female.
61% have a college education; 14% have a graduate degree.	76% have a college degree.
68% are 18 to 34 years old.	77% are between ages 25 and 54.
73% say Groupon is the reason they visited a particular merchant.	87% bought something online in the last six months.
79% of customers have referred someone to the business.	51% are loyal to brands they love.

Sources: *file:///Users/deborahng/Downloads/LivingSocial_Media_Kit_Online.pdf*
http://files.shareholder.com/downloads/AMDA-E2NTR/0x0x893166/FC1FA47E-435C-44AA-9AC3-69A82725F351/Groupon_Q2_2016_Public_Fact_Sheet.pdf

In the following sections, we discuss these two services in more detail.

Digging into Groupon

Like Don Vito Corleone in *The Godfather*, Groupon makes "an offer you can't refuse" to 133 million daily app users. Groupon is far and away the largest of the group coupon sites, claiming that more than 50 million unique customers purchased at least one Groupon offer in 2016. By comparison, LivingSocial, its closest competitor, claims 14.5 million members worldwide.

In addition to its featured deals in seven topical categories, Groupon classifies deals in sections called Goods for products and Getaways for travel. In its "Best of Groupon" section, you'll find a collection of Kids & Family deals. Groupon also offers an affiliate program and in-house credits for referring deals to friends.

TIP

After your offer appears, you can promote the deal in your own newsletter, blog, social media outlets, and elsewhere, although you may not have much notice. The share-this-deal functionality encourages people who receive your daily Groupon email, or those who visit your site, to tell their friends about the deal on Facebook, Pinterest, and Twitter, and by email.

Merchant satisfaction

Groupon contends (`www.groupon.com/merchant`) that its merchants are more than satisfied, with more than 79 percent of merchants saying they had increased brand perception and awareness among consumers. According to Groupon, 84 percent of businesses reported getting new customers and 65 percent claimed customers spent more than the face value of their coupon.

WARNING

Independent studies, which are hard to find, don't always concur with this rosy assessment.

REMEMBER

Speak with your accountant about how to handle revenue from Groupon and similar deals. Prepaid income is usually treated as a liability on your balance sheet until you fulfill the obligation or until the time expires to exercise the offer. (Think gift cards.) You may also encounter state-by-state issues regarding sales tax.

LivingSocial

Although a competitor, LivingSocial (`www.livingsocial.com`) is now owned by Groupon. It offers enticing coupon deals, with a focus on local travel and events. Launched in August 2009, LivingSocial says it now reaches more than 14.5 million subscribers around the world.

The benefits are the same as with other deal sites: brand awareness, direct appeal to locally targeted markets, word-of-mouth advertising, high visibility to a new customer stream, and easy results tracking. LivingSocial, which has long offered travel deals under LivingSocial Escapes, also has categories for family deals, nationwide deals, at-home deals, online shopping, coupons, and gifts.

Like Groupon, LivingSocial is trying to get out of the daily deal grind. Instead of relying on random deals delivered by email, it's trying to shift to a website and mobile app that allow shoppers to browse for offers from local businesses.

LivingSocial integrates with Facebook, Twitter, and email, and has apps for both the iPhone and Android. Like Groupon, it offers an affiliate program and in-house rewards for referrals.

Diversifying Your Daily Deals

Many businesses have discovered smaller daily deal sites that are far less risky for the merchant. Some of these are local sites; some are national online opportunities targeting a particular product or market. Table 2-7 provides several examples. For sites in your area, try searching for your city or your product, plus the words *daily deals* or *group coupons.*

TIP

Ask other local merchants about their experiences before you sign up with any deal sites.

TABLE 2-7 **Group Coupon and Daily Deal Sites**

Name	URL for Media Kit and Advertising Information	Description
Facebook Offers	`www.facebook.com/business/help/1446432849003728`	Create an offer users can claim and share with their friends
Gilt City	`https://vendornet.giltcity.com`	Local deals in selected cities to reach an affluent market
HauteLook	`www.hautelook.com/about`	Daily discounts on top fashion and lifestyle brands
Rue La La	`www.ruelala.com`	High-style, short-lived, online flash sale boutiques; runs nationwide to members
Yelp for Business Owners	`https://biz.yelp.com/support/deals`	Deals promoted on Yelp, a consumer-rating site
Yipit	`www.yipit.com`	Compiled deals and coupons from multiple, partnered sources offered by location, interest, and brand
Zulily	`www.zulily.com/index.php/vendor`	Daily deals targeting moms, babies, and kids

IN THIS CHAPTER

» Building business with music on Spotify

» Topping off a rich-media blog with Tumblr

» Vying for video with Vimeo and Periscope

Chapter 3
Profiting from Mid-Size Social Media Channels

New social media channels and apps seem to spring up faster than weeds. Minor channels may burst on the scene and die quickly, or grow up to become the next blockbuster innovation in social marketing. In this chapter, we look at some of the mid-size social media channels.

These channels aren't quite large enough to justify their own chapters yet, but their user bases qualify them as reaching more than niche markets, discussed in Chapter 1 of this minibook. You may have heard of some of them; others may elicit the reaction, "I don't have a clue."

Take a look to see whether any of them make sense for your business. With adroit marketing, you can gain an edge in brand visibility and reach, long before the channel becomes crowded with marketing copycats. In particular, if you're looking for younger audiences, you can establish your social credibility by being there first.

Deciding Whether to Invest Your Time

Consider each of these minor-league social media channels through the lens of your business. Can you piggyback on their moment of fame — bringing some glory to your business — before they become so bloated with competing businesses that your company becomes just another ant in the anthill? The criteria are simple:

- Is there enough online buzz about the new channel for you to leverage publicity for your own benefit as a pioneer?
- Does the channel reach your desired audience?
- Is the social space (whether music, images, blogs, or communities) a good fit for your company and its marketing goals?
- Do you have an innovative spirit and the ability to act quickly?
- Can you think of a clever way to use the technology to get attention, grow your brand, or gather leads while you're still a big fish in a small pond?
- Can you experiment for a reasonable price or level of effort?
- Can you extricate yourself quickly if something doesn't work without damping your enthusiasm for trying something else new another time?

If the answers are yes, go for it! See if you can become the equivalent of the first company to accept a tweeted takeout order or the first company to reply to a disappearing photo with a disappearing coupon.

Spotting Your Audience with Spotify

A commercial music-streaming service, Spotify accesses more than 20 million songs and allows users to create their own customized playlists. Because Spotify playlists are easy to share with other social media channels, its influence extends beyond the site itself.

Founded in 2008 in Sweden and available in the US since 2011, Spotify has more than 100 million active users per month, of which 25 million are paid subscriptions. Demographically speaking, Spotify appeals to younger users — 40 percent are 18 to 24 years old — and its mobile user base is growing rapidly.

If you're in a creative business or trying to reach users who enjoy certain types of music, Spotify may be a valuable social media channel for you. Consider running contests or starting a collaborative playlist to interact with prospective customers.

REMEMBER

A recent comScore study found that people who stream music are more likely to be strong brand advocates than those who don't. According to the study, Spotify users are especially likely to recommend something to friends and pay more for brands they value.

Spotify offers a broad menu of advertising options, as shown in Figure 3-1,which are detailed on www.spotify.com/us/brands/formats:

- **Sponsored session:** Sponsor a 30-minute, ad-free session in exchange for users viewing your short video.
- **Video takeover:** An advertising break dedicated to your brand, including video and display ads.
- **Audio:** A cross-platform ad that includes an audio spot, cover art, and a link.
- **Display:** Run-of-site (ROS) leaderboard ads (the large banners at the top of a page) seen when users interact with Spotify.
- **Home page takeover:** A full day of dedicated advertising on the Spotify home page.
- **Branded playlist:** Customized user-generated playlists with your logo, text, and a link to your campaign.
- **Advertiser page:** A complete, multimedia, microsite that appears between screens of the Spotify player.
- **Overlay:** Spotify's Welcome Back screen. Returning members are greeted with a menu of options, including your ad.
- **Branded Moments:** Advertisers have a variety of options, including sponsoring commercial free music and sharing a video.

To get started with advertising, fill out the contact form at the bottom of www.spotify.com/us/brands.

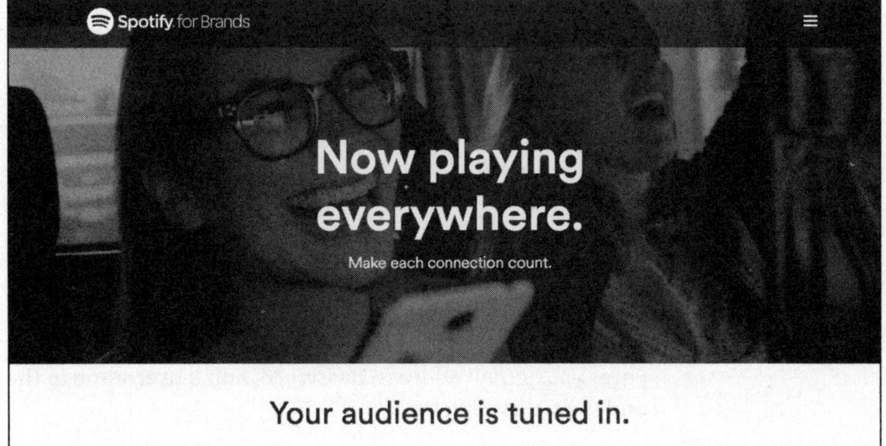

FIGURE 3-1: Spotify offers a variety of advertising options for brands.

Profiting from Mid-Size Social Media Channels

Turning Up New Prospects with Tumblr

Tumblr is a microblogging platform and social-networking website that allows users to post multimedia and other content to a short-form blog from a desktop or a mobile app. Many users take advantage of the Tumblr dashboard to reblog content they find there. Brands are also finding Tumblr to be a great source for finding leads and meeting new people (see Figure 3-2).

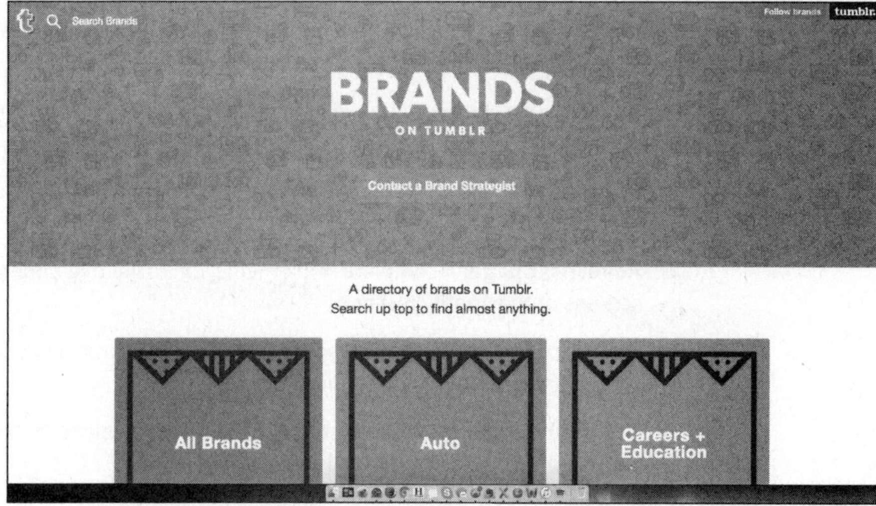

FIGURE 3-2: An easy-to-use blogging platform, Tumblr offers another route for branding and lead generation.

Founded in 2007 and acquired by Yahoo! in June 2013, Tumblr boasted more than 200 million blogs and more than 130 billion posts by Fall 2016. Like with many of the channels in this chapter, Tumblr has great appeal to a younger audience (46 percent of users are 16 to 24 years old), fairly evenly divided by gender.

With 550 million active users per month, the site may well be worthwhile for branding, mining for prospects, and increasing customer loyalty with content and customers.

Setting up an account

Getting started as a contributor is easy. At Tumblr.com, follow these steps:

1. **Enter your email address, password, and a username in the text boxes, and then click Sign Up.**
2. **In the How Old Are You text box that appears, enter your age, and then select the Terms of Service check box. Click Next.**

3. **Enter the letters and numbers that appear in the CAPTCHA box.**

4. **In the text box, enter what you see in the picture, and then click Almost Done.**

   The Welcome to Tumblr page appears.

5. **Select five blogs that you want to follow.**

   (If you can't be bothered, click Skip in the bottom right of the page.)

   Your Tumblr dashboard appears, where you're invited to create your own Tumblr blog.

6. **Verify your email address by clicking the link in the message that Tumblr sends you.**

7. **When you're offered a choice in Settings, select a name for your Tumblr, which can be a subdomain of your existing website.**

   That's it.

Advertising on Tumblr

Tumblr offers a wide variety of advertising options, all native to the channel. (Scroll down to the advertising options on `www.tumblr.com/business/`). According to one study, "Tumblr is ranked #1 in social sentiment toward brands," with users highly likely to recommend brands they follow to others. Options include the following:

- **Sponsored posts:** Promoted on a cost per engagement (CPE) basis (*engagement* means when a viewer likes or shares the post); targeting offered by interest, location, or gender.
- **Sponsored video posts:** Charged on a cost-per-view (CPV) basis. These posts auto-play with muted audio on user dashboards; you can reuse videos from other sources, such as Instagram and Periscope.
- **Sponsored day:** Enables a brand to pin its logo to the top of the dashboard for an entire day, which links to a branded tab on Tumblr's popular Explore page. Content is selected by you, so you can highlight blog posts, images, and more.

For more advertising information, go to `www.tumblr.com/business`.

TIP

Tumblr offers case studies so you can see some real-world examples of how Tumblr advertising works for and benefits different brands. To access case studies at Tumblr, go to `http://marketr.tumblr.com/tagged/case-study`.

Analyzing Tumblr results

Tumblr offers access to content and advertising analytics only to advertisers. Their analytics package breaks down results into paid and organic engagement numbers. To reach these results, click Analytics in the right column of the dashboard.

As an alternative, you can connect your blog to Google Analytics.

If you don't plan to advertise, be sure to select a blog theme that will allow you to paste a Google Analytics ID number into the Appearance section of the Customize Theme page. (See Book 9, Chapter 1 for more on Google Analytics.) You'll need to set up your Google Analytics account first to get the ID number. If your blog is already set up, try connecting it to Google Analytics by clicking Settings (gear icon) at the top of your dashboard. Next, click your chosen blog on the left side of the page, and then click customize in the Theme section.

Promoting Video with Vimeo

Vimeo, shown in Figure 3-3, is a social media community geared toward visual artists, filmmakers, and videographers. It was created in 2004 as an outlet for creative work, compared to the more popular, trending, and commercial use of YouTube. Users can upload, view, share, and comment on videos.

The demographics are attractive: 170 million registered users as of Fall 2016. The audience skews to a college-educated, high-income population with a 2:1 ratio of men to women.

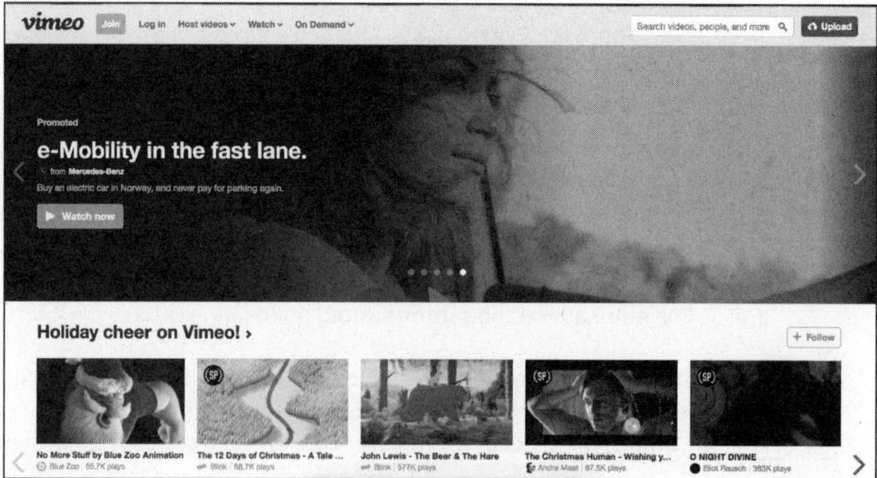

FIGURE 3-3: Showcase your brand's talent and creative side with Vimeo.

If you're in a creative profession (graphic arts, advertising, music, dance, theater, comedy, or other performance arts), Vimeo is an excellent and cost-effective showcase for promoting the quality of your work to an appreciative audience and maybe picking up a few gigs!

Signing up for a Vimeo business account

With the creation of business accounts — at $50 per month or $599 per year — Vimeo recognized that it needed financial support from business subscribers to avoid having to run banner advertisements on uploaded videos. (Vimeo offers both free accounts and Plus accounts for $60 a year to individuals.)

According to Vimeo, the business account gets businesses the following:

- Up to 5TB of video storage
- Team collaboration
- Marketing and analytics tools
- A customizable player, including your company colors and logo above your videos
- Mobile compatibility
- Capability to embed videos on your own site

Vimeo Business has some downsides. Vimeo obviously has less traffic than YouTube, and it may be at risk of being eliminated from Google search results pages. (Nothing keeps you from posting your videos in both locations, however.)

TIP

Go for community and relationship building on Vimeo by interacting with the people who leave comments. This interaction may encourage your fans to return to view future work. Good relationships are like planting seeds. You never know when they may sprout into qualified leads, or even a collaborative effort.

Advertising on Vimeo

Most businesses advertise on Vimeo simply by creating a PRO account and uploading their work. You're not permitted to upload commercial videos any other way. To create an account, go to `http://vimeo.com/business` and click Join Now. In the Create Your Vimeo Account window that appears, enter your email address, username, and password; then click Continue. In the Checkout page that opens, supply your credit card information, and then click Place Order. For information about more elaborate brand channels, see `http://vimeo.com/about/advertisers`.

All business accounts come with an Advanced Statistics package that goes beyond what you see above your videos. You can find more information on `http://vimeo.com/stats`. For videos embedded on your site, you can also integrate with Google Analytics by using a plug-in.

Live Streaming with Periscope

Periscope is a live streaming app that enables the user to broadcast from anywhere. Like Instagram and Snapchat, Periscope is only available as a mobile app. Thus, you live stream directly from your smartphone.

Your customers don't have to be members of Periscope to watch a live stream, so you can link to your Periscopes from your Twitter and Facebook accounts so anyone can watch. However, live Periscope videos aren't permanent. After 24 hours, the video expires and is removed from your account. You still have the option to save the video to your mobile device, after which you can upload it to YouTube or another platform for viewing forever.

Periscope also offers live viewers the ability to interact with the person doing the livestream. They can comment, ask questions, and share feedback and reactions.

Currently, Periscope has more than 100 million active users.

Some of the benefits of Periscope follow:

- **Share an event as it happens.** You can livestream a keynote address, a musical performance, or the office holiday party. Make sure you have permission, though, because copyright laws are still in effect.
- **Use different methods to take video.** Use a drone, a digital camera, or GoPro to livestream video. Take your audience to new heights, and don't rely solely on your smartphone.
- **Draw on the screen.** Periscope Sketch enables the user to draw onscreen as the livestream is taking place to better highlight an area or illustrate a point. Sketches are a temporary part of the video, lasting only a few seconds.
- **Save and upload your video to another platform.** Although video lasts for only 24 hours on Periscope, you can save the video to upload it to a more permanent platform, such as YouTube.
- **Engage with your customers and community.** You can see community reactions as they happen and respond in kind.

- **Enjoy an unlimited video length.** Livestream for as little or as long as you like. The only thing that's stopping you is your smartphone's battery life.
- **Reach a new demographic on a new platform.** Attract new customers from the Periscope community.

Intrigued? Here's how to get started with Periscope:

1. **Download the Periscope app from the App or Google Play store.**
2. **Sign in to Periscope using your Twitter account or phone number, as shown in Figure 3-4.**
3. **(Optional) Choose up to 14 people to follow. Tap Next.**

   If you don't want to follow anyone at this time, tap Skip.
4. **(Optional) Set up notifications. Toggle the buttons to determine which notifications to keep on or turn off.**

   Or tap the Skip button.

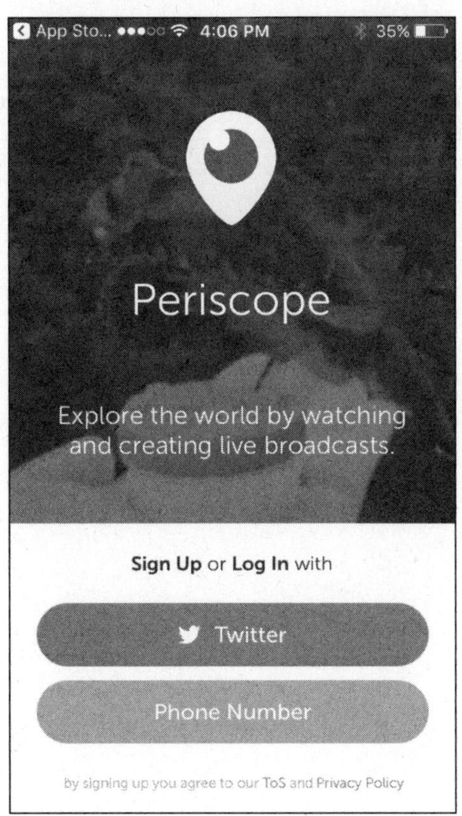

FIGURE 3-4: Signing in to Periscope is as easy as using your Twitter account or entering your phone number.

Profiting from Mid-Size Social Media Channels

You're ready to go live!

Take these steps to livestream your first video:

1. **Tap the camera icon, at the bottom of your screen.**
2. **Tap the screen where it says Enable the Camera, Microphone, and Location.**

   You have to do all three to take your first video. Periscope must know your broadcasting location, but that location won't appear on your livestream.
3. **Enter a title for your livestream.**
4. **Select your privacy options, and then tap the check icon.**

   For example, you'll be asked if you want to tweet your location, set limits for chat, set privacy options for livestreams, and add your location to your stream. You can also choose Leave as Public or tap the drop-down to create a group of followers to show the video to.
5. **Tap Go Live.**

You're now live!

TIP

When you swipe right during your broadcast, you can turn your camera angle between front facing and rear facing.

IN THIS CHAPTER

» Integrating social media with e-newsletters

» Incorporating social media into press releases and public relations

» Leveraging social media with website features

Chapter 4
Integrating Social Media

A volatile debate rages in marketing circles: Has social media become so prohibitively popular — and social media companies so desperate to monetize their sites and satisfy their investors — that it's no longer possible to be successful with only free posts and content?

Statistical analysis by Wordstream.com (www.wordstream.com/blog/ws/2016/01/25/does-facebook-advertising-work) shows a steady decline in organic reach for brands. Instead, promoted posts, ads, and posts from friends squeeze out your attempts to communicate for free.

You can address this problem in two ways: Beat 'em or join 'em. In this chapter, we talk first about beating 'em by combining social media with email, press releases, or websites to increase reach.

If those methods don't work, you can always join 'em by paying to promote your posts, tweets, and pins to reach the audience you want. We discuss a range of advertising possibilities on four primary social media channels: Facebook, Twitter, LinkedIn, and Pinterest.

Thinking Strategically about Social Media Integration

For many businesses, social media marketing adds to the richness of the company's marketing mix with a purpose of its own. Others see it as a low-cost boost to standard press release distribution, email newsletter subscribers, loyalty programs, or other forms of marketing.

These more traditional marketing efforts can go viral when you take advantage of social media integration to do the following:

- Increase newsletter subscriptions.
- Broaden the audience for event announcements.
- Maximize the distribution of press releases and other news.
- Drive traffic to your hub website to encourage users to take advantage of special features.
- Cross-post content in all these venues to increase reach.

In Book 2, Chapter 4, we discuss simple integration techniques, such as displaying chiclets to invite people to follow your company on social media outlets and implementing share buttons to encourage viewers to share your pages with others.

WARNING

Keep in mind that a social media campaign may take six months to a year to reach maturity. Don't stop using other tactics that now reach your target markets successfully. Wait for results from metrics showing that social media perform at least as well before you abandon a current technique. And you can't know what to measure unless you first set goals for your integration efforts, which we discuss in Book 1, Chapter 1. Sometimes you're after sales, sometimes leads, sometimes brand recognition, or sometimes just your 15 minutes of fame.

Whatever you're planning, take advantage of the measurement tools we discuss in Book 9 to establish baselines for traffic, click-through rate (CTR), conversion rates, and return on investment (ROI) for existing marketing methods so that you can detect any lift (or drop) that integration brings.

In its "2016 Social Media Marketing Industry Report," Social Media Examiner asked businesses whether they integrated their social media with other marketing techniques. An amazing 81 percent of respondents replied affirmatively. Consider their experiences while you move forward with your own plans for social media integration.

TIP

Access the "2016 Social Media Marketing Industry Report" at www.socialmediaexaminer.com/wp-content/uploads/2016/05/SocialMediaMarketingIndustryReport2016.pdf. The report will give you a good idea of how fellow marketers are integrating social media into their marketing strategies, and where they're headed in the future.

REMEMBER

Include your integrated marketing tactics on your Social Media Marketing Plan (see Book 1, Chapter 3) and schedule activities on your Social Media Activity Calendar (see Book 1, Chapter 4).

TIP

To define the specific form your integration methods will take, who will execute them and when, and how you will measure the results, create a block diagram showing how content will flow as part of your integration plans (see Book 1, Chapter 3).

Integrating Social Media with E-Newsletters

Marketers spend a good portion of their time on different social networking platforms to best reach their customers. However, there are still good reasons for maintaining and cross-posting between social media and your e-newsletter campaigns.

With so many people using social media to consume content, why are marketers even using newsletters? Many marketers have found targeted email campaigns to be more effective than social media when it comes to sales and messaging. Popular newsletter services include MailChimp (see Figure 4-1), Constant Contact, AWeber, and Infusionsoft.

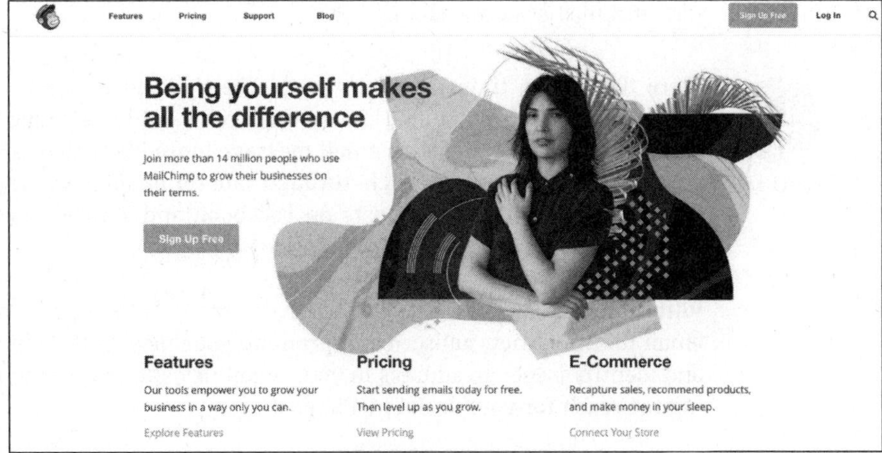

FIGURE 4-1: A newsletter service such as MailChimp gives you the tools you need to integrate social media.

What follows is a look at some of the reasons to take advantage of email newsletter campaigns:

- **Target customers.** With email, you can send campaigns to everyone on your list or to specific groups of people. You can target people by age, location, income range, and other demographic information.
- **Reach more people.** With social media campaigns, you're reaching the people who are online at the moment. Emails, however, can be opened at any time.
- **Share different forms of content at once.** Rather than strategically timed, one-at-a-time post drips, emails enable you to outline and link to a variety of content at once.
- **Update your customers.** Your customers can learn what's new with your company, including new hires, product launches, and other milestones.
- **Share discounts, coupons, and sales messages.** If people know you're sharing coupons, discounts, and other perks, they're more likely to sign up for and open your emails in the future.
- **Direct traffic to your website.** Email newsletters are another way to drive people to targeted pages on your website.
- **Personalize your messages.** Emails are more personal than a social media post in that you can use names and other information to appeal to every individual on your list.
- **See how content performs.** Newsletter platforms provide analytics so you can see how many people opened your emails, which links were clicked, and how your emails convert to sales.
- **Everyone checks email.** With social media, not everyone will see your content. However, email is delivered to every mailbox. (Whether or not people open that mail is another story.)

REMEMBER

More than three times as many people have email accounts than Twitter and Facebook accounts combined. Email open rates, which average in the 20 percent to 25 percent range, make an email message more likely to be seen than the same post in Facebook. And the click-through rate for email is about 50 percent higher than that for social media posts on Facebook and Twitter (`www.mailmunch.co/blog/email-marketing-vs-social-media/`).

With numbers like these, you have every reason to integrate social media with email to attract new subscribers, promote your newsletter, obtain content ideas, and identify issues to address in your email newsletters, not to mention increasing the reach for your social media posts.

Gaining more subscribers

Wherever and whenever prospects discover your presence on social media, try to provide them with other opportunities to find out how you might be able to solve their problems. Your online newsletter is certainly one of those opportunities. Follow these guidelines to gain more newsletter subscribers:

- **Include a link for newsletter subscription on your blog, in all your other social media pages, and in your email signature block.** Constant Contact (`https://marketplace.constantcontact.com/Listing/applications/constant-contact-labs-facebook/PML-0239`) and MailChimp (`https://us6.admin.mailchimp.com/facebook`), among others, have apps you can add to your Facebook page to allow individuals to sign up for your newsletter. You never know — you might reach dozens, hundreds, maybe thousands of new prospects.
- **Treat your newsletter as an event on social media networks.** Add a preview of topics or tweet an announcement of your newsletter a day or so in advance. Include a linkable call to action to subscribe in both cases.
- **Post a teaser line in your social media outlets with a linkable call to action.** You might say, for example, "To learn more about healthcare reform for small businesses, sign up for our newsletter."
- **Post newsworthy findings.** Use material from your newsletter on social news services such as Digg and Reddit (see Book 2, Chapter 4) to attract more readers.
- **Include edited versions of social media posts in your newsletters.** This tactic increases reach for important items.
- **Link to a sample newsletter or newsletter archive from your blog, your website, or the About section or a tab on your Facebook page.** Prospective subscribers can see your newsletter's usefulness. Of course, also indicate the frequency with which you email newsletters.

Finding more followers and connections

Email integration with social media works both ways: You can drive people from your newsletter to social media services or use social media services to gain subscribers. Here are some guidelines for finding more followers and connections:

- Include share buttons in every issue of your newsletter.
- Add options for signing up for social media on the email registration page on your website (if possible).
- Use your e-newsletter to make an offer or run a contest for social media participants.

REMEMBER

Cross-promote your email newsletter on all your social media channels. Remember to post all your social venues, not just your hub website, in your email signature block.

Finding and sharing content

Writing content continuously for newsletters and social media is always a challenge. However, you can exploit the easy interaction between the two to lighten your writing burden:

- **Take advantage of social-marketing capabilities from your email service provider.** Many companies now let you easily send your email directly to Facebook and other social-networking pages (`https://us6.admin.mailchimp.com/facebook`).
- **Mine social media for content.** Read related information on social news sites, listen to hot topics that come up in LinkedIn and Facebook groups, and watch for trending topics. Pay attention to comments on your own and other people's forums, message boards, and social communities. Those comments may clue you in to concerns, trends, or industry news.
- **Use Google Alerts, Social Mention, Twitter Search, and other search functions for mentions of your company.** You can turn positive comments into testimonial content on your newsletter, social media outlet, or website (with permission), or respond to many people at a time who may have read a negative comment.
- **Create a Q&A section in your regular newsletter.** Respond to questions that are common across social media venues.
- **Use keywords and tags to identify social news and content related to your industry.** In turn, be sure to include keywords in any newsletters or newsletter announcements that may be reposted on the web.
- **Pursue market intelligence even further by using the advanced Twitter Search features.** Sort tweets geographically through an advanced search to see which topics are of interest locally, in locations where you have offices, or wherever large clusters of your customers or prospects live or work. Then segment your mailing list accordingly, if appropriate. Follow these steps:

  1. *Go to* `https://twitter.com/search-home` *and click the Advanced Search link located under the Search box.*
  2. *Under Places, enter location information in the Near This Place text box.*

     If you enter a zip code or city, the search results will automatically be set to a 15-mile radius.

3. *Click the blue Search button to see the geographic subset of search results.*

   Because trending topics may vary by region, this approach lets you discover topics that are of interest to prospects or customers in different locations.

TIP

Use Google Trends (`www.google.com/trends`) to figure out the day of week and time of year when users are most likely to use specific search terms, such as *Christmas tree ornaments* in November or December. Use that information to schedule your topical email blasts. There's nothing like having information show up in someone's inbox just when he's looking for it!

Integrating Social Media with Press Releases

The reasons for dealing with public relations and press release distribution haven't changed since the explosion of social media — just the methodology and relative prominence. Where once you worried only about the care and feeding of a small covey of journalists, now you must nourish a veritable horde of bloggers, individual influencers, authors of e-zine articles, editors of online publications, and individuals who will recommend your article on a social news service.

TIP

In companies that view social media primarily as a public relations vehicle, the public or community relations person (or contractor) may be the one who coordinates the social media marketing strategy.

All these venues, not just standard media, open a door to public attention. Take advantage of them all as a cost-effective way to achieve these goals:

- **Broadcast announcements of products, appearances, and events.** Alerting target markets to new products and services is one of the most traditional uses of publicity.
- **Build brand recognition.** Whether it's acknowledgment of your participation in community events, awareness of your position in your industry, or simply the frequent repetition of your name in front of your audience, press coverage brings you publicity at a relatively low cost.
- **Ask journalists, authors, or bloggers to write about your company.** Stories about your firm — at least, the positive ones — boost your credibility, extend your reach, and provide you with bragging destinations for links from your site. Trade press is especially critical for business-to-business (B2B) companies.

- **Drive traffic to your website.** Online press releases almost always have at least one link to your central web presence, and often more. Social media offers a mechanism for distributing linkable press content around the web that others may embed. The accumulation of long-lasting inbound links obviously has a greater effect than a one-time release.
- **Improve search engine ranking.** You can gain many inbound links to your site when your release posts on multiple press outlets. Press sites generally transfer their high page rankings to your site; Google, in particular, weighs mentions in blogs and press sites (and other rich content) highly. Your visibility on preferred search terms may also rise, especially if you optimize your press releases and subheads for keywords (within reasonable constraints).

Setting up an online newsroom

If you haven't already done so, set up an online newsroom (media page) for the press on your primary website. Use this newsroom to present any press releases you create, provide writers with downloadable logos and images, link to articles and posts written about your company, and let writers sign up for Really Simple Syndication (RSS) feeds for future release.

Also consider setting up this newsroom as a separate section in blog format (another way to integrate social media!) to aggregate queries, moderated posts, and trackbacks from individual releases. Give each release a unique URL, and place your headline on the page title.

Cultivating influencers

Identifying influencers is one key way to get into a conversation. Influencers are people whose blogs, tweets, or Facebook pages drive much of the conversation in a particular topic area. They often have a loyal following of readers who engage in dialog, and repeat and amplify discussions the influencer began. In the olden days, press folks would cultivate public relations and press contacts the same way you now cultivate influencers.

Here's a quick checklist for finding these key figures to approach with a request for coverage:

- **Find conversations on blogs, Twitter, Facebook, forums, message boards, communities, and industry-specific social media.** To do so, use keywords relevant to your company, brand, product, industry, and competitors. You can find such searches on Meltwater's IceRocket (`www.icerocket.com`) or LittleBird (`www.getlittlebird.com`).

- **Use search tools on particular networks and aggregator searches, such as Social Mention or Mention.** Those who post most often, or who have a lot of connections or followers, may be the experts or influencers you seek. Monitor the conversations for a while to be sure that you identified the right folks.
- **Use standard search techniques to locate trade publications or related newsletters.** Publication sites may include links to their own social media sites. Or you can identify specific writers and editors whose interests sync with yours and search for their individual blogs and social networking accounts.
- **Become a contributor who answers questions on related subjects in various social media venues.** You can (and should) identify yourself, without promoting your company or products in your comments. Before you ask for anything, engage in the conversation and offer links to related posts and articles. Because links are the currency of social media, link from your site to influencers' sites, blogs, and tweets, and become a connection or follower.

TIP

To track your contacts, bookmark the conversations you find, organizing them in subfolders by the name of the influencer.

Distributing your news

Frankly, the more sites, the merrier. Although you'll pay a penalty for duplicate website content in search engines, press releases don't seem to suffer.

REMEMBER

Place identifying tags on links in different press releases so that you can tell which releases generate click-throughs to your site. If you create only one release a month, this isn't essential; however, if you have an active campaign with numerous press mentions or other types of postings on the same source sites, these identifying tags are absolutely critical.

Table 4-1 shows a partial list of press and PR online resources.

Posting on your own sites

Post your release, at minimum, on your own website and blog. You can, however, easily add releases to your other social-networking profiles, if it's appropriate. For instance, an author might post a release for each book she writes but wouldn't necessarily post a press release for everyone hired at her company.

TIP

To simplify your life, use syndication tools such as Hootsuite, TweetDeck, Netvibes, or Sprout Social (see Book 2, Chapter 1) to post press releases and newsletter content on your blog, Facebook page, and elsewhere. Of course, then the content will be identical.

TABLE 4-1 **Publicity and PR Resources**

Name	URL	Description
24-7 Press Release	www.24-7pressrelease.com	Disseminates news to online media, print media, journalists, bloggers, and search engines.
Business Wire	www.businesswire.com/files/whitepapers/press-release-optimization-guide.pdf	"A Guide to Press Release Optimization."
BuzzStream	www.buzzstream.com/social-media	Fee-based social CRM and monitoring service.
ClickPress	www.clickpress.com	Free and premium press-release posting on-site.
Help a Reporter Out (HARO)	http://helpareporter.com	Matching reporters to sources.
iNewsWire	www.i-newswire.com	Submits press releases and other content to news, social media, and media outlets. Premium starting at $99/month.
PitchEngine	www.pitchengine.com	Social PR platform, social media release creation and distribution; paid versions starting at $39/month.
Press About	www.pressabout.com	Paid press release distribution in the form of a blog.
PRLog	www.prlog.org	Free basic distribution for press releases; paid versions with wider distribution for $49 or $349 per release.
PRWeb	http://service.prweb.com/learning/article/press-release-grader	Free press-release grader service.
Reddit	www.reddit.com	Social news site that accepts links to releases.
The Open Press	www.theopenpress.com	Paid on-site press-release posting.
Tiny Pitch	http://tiny.pr	Free service; turns a press release into a web app that can be shared on social networks and with your contacts.

Using standard press distribution sources

Many paid online press-release distribution sources exist. Among the most well-known are Business Wire, VocusPR, PR Newswire, PRWeb, and Marketwired. Sometimes, distribution services offer levels of service at different prices depending on the quantity and type of distribution, geographical distribution, and whether distribution includes social media, multimedia, offline publications, or other criteria.

Table 4-1, presented in the preceding section, includes several options for free distribution. Many free services don't distribute your releases — except perhaps to search engines — but, rather, simply post them on their sites for finite periods. Whether they're free or paid, be sure to read carefully what you're getting. Perhaps the most straightforward example of integrating press releases with social media is the distribution of a release announcing your social media activities.

REMEMBER

Post linkable event announcements on calendars all over the web, as well as event pages on Facebook and other social media. Calendars may be an old-fashioned, pre–social media technique, but many high-ranking calendar pages feed page rank value until your event occurs and the listing expires.

Using bloggers as a distribution channel

You've laid the groundwork by identifying appropriate bloggers and other influencers and participated on their publications. The next step is to get them to post your news. The most discrete way is to email it (or a link to it) with a cover note to see whether the recipient wants to share the article with readers or comment on its content.

Because you're pitching the bloggers, include in your cover note why you think readers of the blog would be interested and also a descriptive paragraph about your company. It's considered bad form to submit your press release as a post on most blogs — bad enough that a moderator probably would exclude it.

Using social news services and other social networks

You can send similar emails to individuals and influencers you have identified as participating in key discussions about related products or issues, including a short notice about a press release on Twitter and a mention to groups and professionals on sites such as Facebook and LinkedIn.

You can submit your release to the few social news services that permit you to submit your own link to your press release, such as Reddit. In other cases, you may need to submit to social news and bookmark services from another identity, or wait until the story appears on a blog and submit the blog post instead.

Emphasizing content

As always, content, tone, and interest level are the keys to catching people's attention. Keep your release to about 400 words or fewer if you're including multimedia, but don't go below 100 words lest your release is viewed by search engines as spam.

TECHNICAL STUFF

Keep your headline to about 80 characters and use an <h1> HTML header tag.

Combine anchor text (see Book 2, Chapter 2) with the URL in parentheses right next to it (to cover all bases), but don't use the same anchor text twice. On some press distribution services — and, of course, on social media — you have a chance to submit keywords or tags, which is an essential process for leveraging your press release for search engine optimization (SEO) purposes.

Be sure that some or all the keywords or tags that you identified are also included in the headline or first paragraph of the release. Try to use at least some of your primary set of search terms, as described in Book 2, Chapter 2. For instance, good keywords or tags appearing in a headline, subhead, or lead paragraph might be *food technology, social media week, cooking app,* or *sidechef.*

Pressing for attention

One possible way around the mash-up between social media and publicity is to create a socially friendly press announcement that you can post easily on multiple social media and encourage engagement. PitchEngine has a free app called Tiny Pitch that will convert content you create on any device into just such a format, complete with a logo, images, likes, a message feature, and a share button.

Measuring results

The same social-monitoring tools that you use to find influencers can be applied to track key performance indicators for your press efforts, such as Google Alerts, Social Mention, and Twitter Search. Assessing results from your publicity is a good place to use all that qualitative data, as well as advertising measurements, for online brand awareness and equity.

REMEMBER

Measure baselines before you begin your press campaigns, and be sure that before-and-after results span comparable time frames. Here are a few key performance indicators that you might find relevant:

- Number of online mentions of company, brand, product or service line, or individual products or services anywhere online, including social media, during a specific time frame.

- Number and location of media placements; where and when mentions occurred, a press release was published, or an article about your company or product appeared on a recognized media outlet — whether online or offline.
- Site traffic generated from press releases and other linkable press-related mentions; see referrer logs in your web stats software for number of inbound links from each source. Include comparative click-through rates (CTRs) and conversion rates, if available. To make this process easier, tag links with the identifiers related to the topic or date of the press release.
- Social media campaign participation and sentiment using monitoring tools; see Book 2, Chapter 1.
- Average frequency of the product, company, or brand conversations related to the release compared to the frequency of conversations before the release.
- Estimated costs (hard dollars and labor) that were spent. Be sure to include costs for paid distribution, if used. To compare ROI for publicity to other methods, you compare costs to the value of sales that can be traced back to the release (if any). If you can't trace back sales, you might be able to compare brand engagement.

Integrating Social Media with Your Website

Any website can incorporate a myriad of features that integrate with social media, going well beyond the obvious and oft-repeated reminders to include Follow Us On and share buttons everywhere, including product pages in stores. You can get clever: Include links to your help forum or YouTube video tutorials as part of the automated purchase confirmation email you send to buyers.

And, of course, this integration can work the other way: integrating your social media with your website.

In some cases, old-fashioned versions of social media — on-site forums, chat rooms, product reviews, and wikis — effectively draw repeat visitors to the hub site, avoiding any integration with third-party social media sites.

More advanced sites have already implemented social media techniques on-site, including blogs, communities, and calls for user-generated content — photos and videos of people using your product or suggesting creative new designs and applications, as well as ratings.

Several strategic factors may affect your decision whether to implement such techniques on-site or off:

- The cost of development, storage, support, and ongoing maintenance versus costs off-site
- SEO and link strategies
- Plus-and-minus points of managing a more centralized and simplified web presence

A few on-site techniques, such as loyalty programs, work just as well on social media (for example, special offers for those who like you on Facebook). Three other popular methods practically cry out for integration: coupons, discounts, and freebies; games and contests; and microsites (more about these methods in the following sections). For more information about on-site and other forms of online marketing, see *Web Marketing For Dummies*, 3rd Edition, by Jan Zimmerman (Wiley).

TIP

Brainstorm ways that an integrated website and social media campaign might succeed for you. Diagram it and figure out what you'll measure to assess your accomplishments.

Coupons, discounts, and freebies

It doesn't take much monitoring of Facebook, LinkedIn, and Twitter, as well as social news, bookmarking, and shopping streams, to see how frequently they're used to offer time-limited deals, coupons, special promotions, discounts, and free samples.

The sense of urgency in certain social media environments catches viewers' interest. Just like the competitive energy of an auction may cause bidders to offer more than they intend, the ephemeral nature of real-time offers may inspire viewers to grab for a coupon they might otherwise have passed up.

The upside and downside of real-time social media is precisely the immediacy of these offers and how quickly a chain of other posts extinguishes them from awareness. You have a chance to move overstock quickly, bring in business on a slow day, or gain new prospects from a group you might not otherwise reach without making a long-term, and perhaps too-expensive, commitment.

Here are some points to keep in mind when offering coupons, discounts, and freebies:

- Pin your offer and contest posts to the top of your Facebook timeline to make sure they continue to be seen. Consider paying to boost these posts to promote your specials.
- Preplan and schedule your posts, repeating them frequently enough throughout the day to appear in real-time search results and near the top of chronologically organized posts on any social media site that doesn't permit pinning them to the top.
- Always link back to your primary website or blog, not only to explain the details of the offer but also to enjoy the inbound link value, offer additional goods and services, and capture prospect information.
- Be sure to use a unique promotion code for each offer and tag your links with identifiers to track the source of click-throughs and conversions.

Most of the hundreds of online coupon sites already have a presence on Twitter, Facebook, Digg, and elsewhere. You can use their services or simply create a coupon of your own.

REMEMBER

Whether you offer a discount through your website, social media, or any other form of advertising, be sure to include the impact of the discount in your cost analysis. Giving away a free soda may cost a business only 10¢ (mostly for the cup!), but if it gives away 1,000 drinks, the discount costs $100.

In Chapter 3 of this minibook, we discuss the group-purchasing model for coupons, which is dependent on volume use reaching a critical mass.

Contests and games

Your imagination is the only limit to contests and games that you can post on your site and cross-promote via social media. As usual, make sure that viewers link back and forth among your sites, ensuring that an inbound link to your primary web presence exists. The goals of your contest may vary:

- Branding and name recognition
- Building relationships through entertainment
- Obtaining feedback and building community through customer-generated content
- Locating hard-to-find resources, clients, or vendors
- Cross-promoting

» Acquiring testimonials

» Getting input into your own brainstorming process about where your product or service should go

TIP

Like with special offers, be sure to include the cost of prizes and the labor involved in running the contest in your analysis of ROI. Depending on the goal of the contest, you may be looking for new visitors, repeat visitors, leads, or sales.

You can find ideas for creating more effective contests and games at www.socialmediaexaminer.com/six-ways-supercharge-contests-social-media.

Microsites

Microsites are branded environments specific to a particular product, line, or brand. Created like any other free-standing websites with their own domain names and only a few pages, microsites are usually dedicated to a specific product or service. Often used with a new product introduction or special promotion, microsites may facilitate social media–style activities specific to that project. Often, user conversations or user-generated content contributions are incorporated into the site.

Many microsites incorporate highly focused presentations to launch a new product, turn a sale into an event, provide how-to instruction, or target specific demographic groups.

A microsite is an excellent way to branch out from the design of your main site and show off your style and skills. It might portray your brand in a new light — one that connects more closely to users and makes a creative impact on them. And beyond the aesthetic design, an easy and engaging interaction will make the experience more enjoyable and beneficial for your users.

Private membership sites

Private membership sites are subscription-based sites whose content is visible only to subscribers. Private membership sites can be free or paid, but they're a way to offer something of value to your online community. Private membership sites can be forums where online communities interact and share ideas, places to receive exclusive content, or learning and teaching experiences such as online courses.

Because people sign up to join private membership sites (especially if they're paying for the experience), they're more invested in the content and in participation.

IN THIS CHAPTER

- » Using paid advertising on social media
- » Promoting your content with advertising
- » Engaging through ads

Chapter 5
Advertising on Social Media

Many social media sites offer the capability to advertise. You might be wondering why you should pay for advertising on social media sites when you can just publish a post and send it off to the masses. Well, posting to social media doesn't necessarily mean you're getting as many views as you should. Some sites, for example Facebook, don't make it easy for consumers to see posts from brands — even if those people liked the brand's page. When you pay for advertising on social media sites, you're paying for the ability to reach more people.

Integrating Social Media with Paid Advertising

Social media has the advertising world in ferment. As applications from social media companies mature, audiences grow, and technology improves, the companies expand their advertising opportunities to make money for their investors — everyone is just trying to make a buck, especially through mobile advertising.

Advertising on social media sites

Many social media sites, especially blogs, have long accepted advertising that you can incorporate into your plans for paid advertising (if any). Some large channels (such as Google+, Blogger, and YouTube) and many smaller social media venues display standard PPC, banner, and multimedia ads from Google AdWords or Yahoo! Advertising. Other social media channels offer their own advertising programs.

Later in this chapter, we discuss four of the major ones: Facebook, Twitter, LinkedIn, and Pinterest. Table 5-1 lists additional popular social media sites offering paid advertising; we encourage you to explore these on your own.

TABLE 5-1 Social Media Sites Offering Paid Advertising

Name	URL for Media Kit or Advertising Information	Resources
Facebook	www.facebook.com/advertising	www.facebook.com/business/products/ads www.facebook.com/help/458369380926902
Instagram	http://instagram.com/about-ads	
LinkedIn	www.linkedin.com/advertising	
Pinterest	https://ads.pinterest.com	https://business.pinterest.com/promoted-pins
Reddit	www.reddit.com/advertising	www.reddit.com/wiki/selfserve
Snapchat	www.snapchat.com/ads	https://storage.googleapis.com/snapchat-web/success-stories/pdf/overview/pdf_snap_ads_overview_en.pdf
Spotify	www.spotify.com/us/brands	www.spotify.com/us/brands/formats
Twitter	https://ads.twitter.com	https://business.twitter.com/ad-products
		https://support.twitter.com/groups/58-advertising
Vimeo	http://vimeo.com/about/advertisers	http://vimeo.com/help/faq/vimeo-membership/vimeo-pro#can-i-use-vimeo-pro-to-upload-videos-that-contain-ads
YouTube	www.youtube.com/yt/advertise	

TIP

Plan. All the major social media advertising channels review and approve ads before allowing them to post. Allow 24 hours for turnaround, although sometimes it takes much less time, and occasionally it takes much longer.

Exploring the growth in social advertising

The increased advertising offerings on social media channels could be interpreted as attempts to overcome consumers' acquired *banner blindness* to ads appearing in predictable online locations — and a deep desire to cut into Google's share of total online advertising revenue.

eMarketer (`www.emarketer.com/Article/US-Digital-Ad-Spending-Surpass-TV-this-Year/1014469`) showed Google garnering almost a 32 percent share of the US mobile digital advertising market at the end of 2016, compared to Facebook's 22 percent.

But there's more than Google envy at play. The growth in social advertising is also driven by the greater reach, better analytics, higher click-through rates, and higher degree of engagement with mobile ads. Mobile ads not only catch people who seek something specific, but they catch them at the very moment they're on the move and interested in a purchase.

WARNING

Demand for mobile advertising will likely drive up costs while performance and targeting improve. If mobile ad space becomes scarce, competition for it will increase. Don't expect social media channels to increase the number of ads they show to a particular user. They can simply raise their prices, in effect slamming shut the advertising window for small businesses that have limited budgets.

For more information on online advertising, check out `www.adopsinsider.com/`, which features tips and information for anyone who wishes to learn more about digital ads.

Maximizing your advertising dollars

You can and should take advantage of targeting your audience as closely as the tools allow, selecting by geography, demographics, education, and interest area whenever possible. Some folks object to the targeting: Older women seem to receive a disproportionate number of ads for skin creams and diets; those who change their status to Engaged are quickly deluged with ads from wedding service providers.

You can evaluate advertising placements on these sites just as you would evaluate advertising placed anywhere else. Using the advertising metrics discussed in Book 9, Chapter 6, consider cost per click (CPC), cost per 1,000 (CPM) impressions, click-through rate (CTR), and the resulting conversions to decide whether any of these ads pay off for you.

WARNING

Sometimes, social media advertising is less expensive than traditional pay-per-click (PPC), banner, or retargeting ads through search engines, but not always.

CPC refers to the measure of how one will pay for an ad; PPC is more about the system of buying the ads.

Results so far indicate that display ads appearing on social media pages generally perform about the same as display ads on other sites. The average CTR in 2016 was 0.17 percent, according to Smart Insights (`www.smartinsights.com/internet-advertising/internet-advertising-analytics/display-advertising-clickthrough-rates/?new=1`).

REMEMBER

So many variables affect CTR — ad size, placement, quality of the ad, match to audience, and value of the offer — that it's hard to predict exactly how your ad will perform. Compare your CTR to the numbers in the preceding paragraph.

REMEMBER

Averages are averages. The range at both ends may be extreme. Like so much material on the web, the only metrics that matter are your own.

Although you can test the same ad in several places at the same time to see which publishers yield the most bang for your advertising buck, also take into consideration whether the audiences on different social channels respond to a different message.

Advertising on Facebook and Instagram

Facebook offers several forms of advertising, each of which can appear in three places: in the right-hand column of a desktop Facebook page, in a user's desktop news feed, or with Facebook's mobile news feed.

Instagram ads appear for those who are viewing the app on mobile devices but aren't visible for desktop users.

TIP

News feed ads are much more visible to viewers because they appear in the middle of posts from their friends and others, and because they almost always involve large, eye-catching graphics. Right-column ads are often ignored, so you might want to save those for branding.

Like Google AdWords, pricing is on a bid basis, where you can set your daily maximum and campaign duration.

Getting started

To start developing a Facebook ad campaign, access your Facebook account and then follow these steps:

1. **To start advertising, go to** `www.facebook.com/ads/create`.

   Alternatively, select Create Ads from the drop-down list that appears when you click the down-pointing arrow in the top-right corner of the blue toolbar at the top of your page.

2. **On the screen that appears, establish an objective for your ad by selecting an option from the Choose Your Objective page, under the What's Your Marketing Objective menu.**

   Choose the objective that comes closest to your needs. Don't worry — you can always change your mind later! Facebook distinguishes the following objectives:

   - *Send people to your website:* Drive traffic to your website (away from Facebook).
   - *Increase brand awareness:* Increase awareness of your company by promoting to people who are most likely to be interested in it.
   - *Increase local awareness:* Promote to people who live in the area.
   - *Reach:* Target your ad to reach the maximum amount of people.
   - *Increase conversions on your website:* Promote specific actions (conversions) on your website, such as a newsletter sign-up, white paper download, or purchase.
   - *Drive people to a brick-and-mortar location:* Promote to the people who live in the area with the types of content that will encourage them to visit a specific location.
   - *Product catalog sales:* Drive sales by displaying enticing pictures from an online catalog.
   - *Boost your posts:* Promote a specific post on your timeline to increase reach; this is an internal Facebook objective.
   - *Promote your Page:* Increase traffic or likes to grow your brand or audience; this is an internal Facebook objective.
   - *Get installs of your app:* Encourage downloads of your apps.
   - *Increase engagement in your app:* Encourage people to use your desktop app.
   - *Raise attendance at your event:* Get more people to attend your events.

- *Get people to claim your offer:* Offer discounts, promo codes, or coupons for buyers to use on your site, in your storefront, or when purchasing a service.
- *Get video views:* Get more people to view your videos.

After you select an objective, you are sent to an explanation panel at the bottom of the page.

3. **Enter a name for your campaign in the Campaign Name box and then click the blue Continue button to start your campaign.**
4. **Define your audience.**

   You can choose to Create New for a new target audience, or use a Saved Audience from a previous campaign. For our purposes, we'll create a new target audience.

   Select options to target audiences based on specific demographics, including location, age, gender, language, and interests.

   Next, select how you want to reach this target audience, such as through an app, an event, or a Facebook page. You can also choose whether to limit and add to friends only, or friends of friends.
5. **Choose the page you want to promote.**

   Enter the page's URL, or select it from the drop-down list that appears when you place your cursor in the Choose Page field.
6. **Click Save This Audience.**
7. **Choose your placements:**
   - *Instant articles*: This new Facebook tool allows media publishers to deliver interactive articles to readers via Messenger or the mobile app.
   - *Automatic placements:* Your ad will automatically target your audience based on where they're likely to have the best performance.
   - *Edit placements:* Gives you the option of removing placements, which can reduce the amount of people who see your ad.
8. **Determine your budget.**

   Use the drop-down menu to decide how much you'd like to spend and for how long. For example, you can choose to spend $5 per day for 30 days.
9. **(Optional) Choose advanced settings.**

   If you select this option, you can choose how you want ads delivered based on goals. However, Facebook sets the bid amount based on how effectively they can optimize delivery. In this scenario, you're charged for impressions. You can also schedule ad delivery — all the time or per a schedule — and the type of delivery.

TIP

If you've never worked with Facebook ads before, it's better to go with the basic options. When you get the hang of Facebook advertising, you can play around with advanced options.

10. **Give your ad set a name, and then click the blue Continue button.**

    You can name the ad what you like, but most people name it to describe the type of campaign.

11. **Choose your ad's format.**

    For example, you can have a carousel of images, a single image, a slide show, a video, or a story canvas.

12. **Choose the page you're promoting and the text to go with your ad.**
13. **Enter a URL if the ad is to direct traffic, and choose a call of action if necessary.**
14. **Preview your ad to make sure it's exactly as you'd like it.**
15. **Review and place your order.**

Boosting or promoting a post

You can boost a post directly from your Facebook page. By boosting a post, you get more views on a specific, targeted post. Follow these steps:

1. **Go to any recent post.**
2. **Click the Boost Post button at the bottom of the post.**
3. **In the pop-up window that appears, choose your audience, budget, and how you want the Boost Post campaign to run.**
4. **Click Boost.**

A boosted post has two special characteristics:

- It appears higher in viewers' news feeds, so it attracts more attention.
- It gets a much broader distribution than an ordinary post. You can boost any post, including status updates, photos, offers, or videos.

  Only 6 to 8 percent of your followers or likes may actually see a specific, un-boosted post in their news feeds. There's simply too much material for Facebook to show everyone everything. By boosting a post, you ensure wider distribution to your likes and to followers who may not yet have liked your page, thus dramatically increasing the reach for that post.

WARNING

In January 2015, Facebook implemented a new policy to reduce the number of free, organic posts in news feeds that Facebook deems to be too promotional. These include posts that only push a product purchase or app installation; only ask viewers to enter a promotion or sweepstakes; and duplicate the content of a paid ad. You have to pay for a boosted post or an obvious advertisement in a news feed to distribute this type of information.

Paying for your Facebook ads

Facebook offers a bid-based ad auction. You specify the amount you're willing to pay, but the winning bid may vary constantly based on the number of competing ads and the quality of your ad performance.

As with online advertising elsewhere, Facebook generally offers several options for pricing ads:

- **Cost per click (CPC):** You pay for the ad only when someone clicks on an ad that takes him or her to either an external link or another internal Facebook page. The minimum bid for a click is one cent. You might also pay per type of engagement, such as a like or a comment.
- **Cost per thousand (CPM) impressions:** Your cost is based on how many thousands of people see your ad, whether they click or not. This type of pricing makes more sense for branding ads.
- **Flat fee (available only for boosted posts):** You set a flat fee to boost a post that will last for the length of time you set for your boost campaign. Charges, which are calculated by impression, are deducted from that budget.

REMEMBER

No matter what option you select, Facebook will never charge more per click than you enter, or charge more than the lifetime or daily budget you specify when you set up your ad campaign.

For more information on Facebook advertising, see *Facebook Marketing All-in-One For Dummies*, 3rd Edition, by Andrea Vahl, John Haydon, and Jan Zimmerman (Wiley), or visit `www.facebook.com/advertising`. (For more about Facebook, in general, see Book 5.)

Advertising on Twitter

Like Facebook, Twitter offers you the ability to reach more people through advertisements. By using Twitter ads, you can create campaigns to meet specific goals, gain followers, and drive engagement.

In this section, you explore how to get started with Twitter ads and how to use them to achieve your goals.

Promoting your tweets

Promoted tweets, like organic tweets, may include hashtags, rich media, and links to your website, and they offer the same forms of engagement: replies, favorites, and retweets.

Unlike organic tweets, however, you can target non-followers by demographics, interests, keywords, geography, device, similarity to current followers, and more. You pay only when someone engages with your tweet. Whether you promote an existing organic tweet or create a new one, you can reach a new audience to grow your Twitter presence.

Promoted tweets may appear other places besides viewers' timelines, including in search results for terms or trends, on Twitter's mobile products, and syndicated to some third-party clients, such as Hootsuite.

Pretest your content or look at results of existing organic tweets to select one for promotion that already performs well. According to BI Intelligence, a good engagement rate for a promoted tweet would be about 3 percent.

For more information on the different campaign types, see `https://business.twitter.com/en/advertising/campaign-types.html`.

Promoting your account

Like a promoted tweet, a promoted account can be targeted to your desired audience. However, it differs from a tweet in content and format. A promoted account ad includes a short, vivid description of the benefits of following your business on Twitter, plus your company logo and a call to action.

For this type of promotion, you might want to target users who are similar to your existing followers, are similar to influential figures in your industry, or share an interest in the products, services, issues, or concepts relevant to your business.

Promoted accounts appear in somewhat different places than promoted tweets. In addition to the timeline, they appear in the Who to Follow widget, which appears on multiple pages. This advertising choice is priced on a cost-per-follow (CPF) basis. You pay only when new visitors choose to follow your account.

Promoting a trend

Trending topics, which appear on the left side of a viewer's home page, show topics of interest in different countries during a 24-hour window. Promoted trends, if any, are labeled in this module. Although trends are updated every 24 hours, you can promote a trend for several weeks if you want.

TIP

Promoted trends are fairly subtle. They make sense for large corporate branding campaigns, when you need to reach a mass (relatively untargeted) audience, or if you want to launch a new product line — say to promote the next Apple iPhone introduction.

A promoted trend generally boosts tweets about your brand for about two weeks. Think of it as a top-of-funnel feeder, getting a large number of people to at least hear about you. (To learn more about conversion funnels, see Book 1, Chapter 1.)

Remarketing with Twitter

Like remarketing products on other platforms, Twitter remarketing lets you target only Twitter users who have already visited your website. Twitter visitors who see one of your promoted tweets or Twitter cards will then see a reminder ad to help keep your company top of mind.

For more information, see `https://blog.twitter.com/2016/website-conversion-tracking-and-remarketing-made-easier-and-more-flexible`.

Engaging your Twitter audience

It does sometimes seem that social media platforms are spending more time watching their competitors than developing new ideas of their own. Fortunately, Twitter, like Facebook, enables you to place ads that help you to achieve your goals and provide an engaging, interactive experience for your audience.

While your audience reacts to your content, you can achieve the following objectives:

- **Increase traffic or conversions on your website.** Follow Twitter's targeting options for keywords, location, or interest to drive a more qualified audience to your website.
- **Increase the number of installations of your app or engagement with it.** Create campaigns designed so that Twitter users can download and open your app from a tweet.

» **Increase your Twitter followers.** Target Twitter users who are most like your current followers or who match the profile of those you seek as followers.

» **Improve lead generation.** Add a special lead generation card to your tweet. This allows prospects to share their contact information with two simple clicks instead of leaving Twitter or filling out a form. Then, all you have to do is follow up.

For more information, see `https://business.twitter.com/solutions/grow-followers` or `https://business.twitter.com/solutions/tweet-engagements`. (For more about Twitter, in general, see Book 4.)

Pricing and bidding on Twitter

Twitter's ad prices are based on actions other than clicks. You bid a price for a specific action based on the type of advertising you choose. You're charged a flat price only when a viewer takes that action, whether it's submitting information through your campaign, following you, or retweeting.

REMEMBER

Twitter doesn't charge for organic tweets.

Follow these steps to bid:

1. **Go to** `https://biz.twitter.com/start-advertising` **to set up your account.**
2. **Using the drop-down menus, indicate the country where your business is located and whether your monthly budget will be less than or more than $5,000.**
3. **Click the Let's Go button at the bottom of the screen.**
4. **Click the down arrow on the Create Campaign button in the top-right corner of the screen.**

   A drop-down menu with advertising objectives appears.
5. **Select your objective from the six choices on the list.**

   The choices are Followers, Website Clicks or Conversions, Tweet Engagements, App Installs or Re-engagements, Leads on Twitter, and Custom. A new screen appears for the objective you selected.

   - *Followers:* Helps you to grow a Twitter follower base.
   - *Website Clicks or Conversions:* Directs people to your website or specific sales pages.

- *Tweet Engagements:* Geared toward encouraging retweets, likes, and conversation.
- *App Installs or Re-engagements:* Promotes your apps to new users or encourages previous users of that app to revisit. You can choose options based on your objective.
- *Leads on Twitter:* Encourages lead generation to drive potential customers to perform a specific action.
- *Custom:* Allows you to customize your advertising experience.

6. **Name your campaign.**

   Choose a name that describes your goal or target audience.

7. **Determine tracking options so you can see specific metrics such as site visits, purchases, and other options.**
8. **Select your audience.**

   You can target specific ages and demographics, including location, language, gender, mobile users and more.

9. **In the budget section, set a daily spending maximum.**

   No matter where you set your maximum bid, Twitter won't charge more than a penny above the next highest bid until you reach your maximum price. You'll receive information about what other advertisers are bidding so you can optimize your spending.

   Set a total budget (optional) for the duration of your campaign. Your ads will stop showing as soon as your budget has been met.

10. **Under Creative Options, create a new tweet or promote an existing tweet.**
11. **Click the Launch button at the top right.**

Dealing with Twitter cards

Twitter cards allow you to attach photos, videos, and other rich media to tweets. And guess what? Twitter cards are free. However, you'll have to set up a payment account to create them.

TECHNICAL STUFF

Although it's possible to create some Twitter cards on your own, you'll probably need the person who handles coding for your website to deal with some of the less intuitive options.

Twitter offers the following types of cards:

- **Summary card (default):** Includes title, description, thumbnail, and Twitter account information
- **Summary card with large image:** Same as the default summary card, plus a large photo
- **Photo card:** One photo only
- **Gallery card:** Four photos
- **App card:** Info about a mobile app, including a download link
- **Player card:** Offers video, audio, or other rich media as part of a tweet
- **Product card:** Displays optimized product information

Because most Twitter cards interact with your website, your web developer will need to add a few lines of HTML code to your site. When users tweet a link to your content, their tweet will include a card that their followers can see. For more information, send your developer to `https://dev.twitter.com/cards/overview` or `https://dev.twitter.com/cards/getting-started`.

Advertising on LinkedIn

Without a doubt, LinkedIn is the best social media channel for reaching professionals and business-to-business prospects. Although its user population is smaller than many of the other, broader B2C social media channels, LinkedIn still offers opportunities for advertising to reach targeted populations.

Be cautious about creating too narrow a target market for your advertising in LinkedIn. You can quickly exhaust the potential reach for your ad if the base is too small.

Like Facebook, LinkedIn offers a combination of externally focused ads that appear in the right column of various pages and promoted posts that appear in viewers' news feeds to drive people to a specific post you've created.

Ads may appear on the profile pages of other LinkedIn members, on a user's own home page, in a user's message inbox, on a search results page, or on LinkedIn group pages.

Follow these steps to set up an ad account on LinkedIn:

1. **Go to** `https://business.linkedin.com/marketing-solutions/ads#` **and click the Create Ad button located at top right. Log in using your LinkedIn password.**
2. **From the Campaign Manager dashboard, choose the type of ad you want to place:**
   - *Sponsored Content:* Attracts new people to your LinkedIn page, and drives engagement with branded content.
   - *Text Ads:* Targeted campaigns appearing in LinkedIn's right sidebar. You can tailor them to meet budgetary needs.
   - *Sponsored Inmail:* Send targeted direct messages.
3. **Add your LinkedIn business page.**
4. **Name your campaign.**

   Most people include details such as date, demographic information, or campaign type.
5. **Add information about your brand.**

   Include the target URL, the title of your ad, and the ad copy.
6. **Save your ad to put it in LinkedIn's queue to review.**
7. **Select your target audience, choose your price, and enter payment info.**

After your ad is approved, it will run as requested.

Targeting your LinkedIn ads

Not surprisingly, the categories available for targeting an audience on LinkedIn are different from the categories you see on Facebook or Twitter. LinkedIn collects many strictly business-oriented items that other social media simply don't ask about for their profiles.

Because members supply most of the information in their own profiles, business pages, and showcase pages that LinkedIn uses for targeting, you have to accept that self-revealed information may not always be accurate. LinkedIn generally allows you to select multiple items in a category or offers you the chance to drill down so that you can narrow a field. Categories include the following:

- **Job title:** Choose C-suite executives, purchasing agents, members of technical staff, and more.

- **Job function:** Select from engineers, human resources, or marketing, for example.
- **Company or industry:** Select from dozens of drill-down categories.
- **Member schools:** Choose different schools and types of schools.
- **Fields of study:** Target academic experience.
- **Degrees:** Reach members by levels of education.
- **Years of experience:** Choose targeted audience based on how long they've been working and doing business.
- **Member skills:** Target specific levels and areas of expertise.
- **Company size:** Based on the number of employees.
- **Company name:** Great for targeting everyone on LinkedIn who works for a large multinational corporation — for example, everyone who might need your travel services.
- **Job seniority:** Position in firm, such as owner.
- **Member age:** Standard demographic choices.
- **Member gender:** Standard demographic choices.

Pricing and bidding

LinkedIn's pricing and bidding structure works much like Facebook and Twitter. You specify a daily budget and a bid price based on either cost per click (CPC) or cost per thousand (CPM) impressions. Like with other advertising options, LinkedIn must approve your ads. You can start and stop your ads whenever you want.

TIP

LinkedIn requires a $10-per-day minimum budget. LinkedIn will suggest a bid range based on the competition, but the choice is up to you. It also charges a one-time $5 activation fee.

Generally, clicks on LinkedIn are more costly than on Facebook and other social media advertising channels because it delivers such a coveted and detailed target audience.

For more information, see `www.linkedin.com/ads/start` or `http://partner.linkedin.com/ads/info/Ads_faqs_updated_en_US.html`. (For more about LinkedIn, in general, see Book 6.)

Advertising on Pinterest

As we discuss in Book 7, Pinterest has now accumulated 100 million active users. In 2016, Pinterest released an advertising option called Promoted Pins, which allows you to target non-followers with pins of interest and drive those users directly to your website.

TECHNICAL STUFF

Pinterest allows advertisers to place conversion pixels on their website to track from click-through to purchase. Your programmer will need to place a tiny piece of code on your site, probably on the thank-you page following a purchase.

Based on information provided by its users, Pinterest lets you target your audience by geography, demographics, devices, and search-term use. It also allows advertisers to supply coded identifiers that can be matched to Pinterest users to define a target audience. For example, the email addresses of your newsletter subscribers can be cross-matched to the database of Pinterest users.

Pinterest has established some specific rules for what constitutes an acceptable Promoted Pin and reviews all Promoted Pins. In particular, Pinterest specifies, "There can be no promotional information, calls to action, service claims, price listing, or deceptive content in the pin image. Ads must be accurate, and lead to a relevant landing page with no sign-up requests."

Pricing and bidding

Charges for Promoted Pins are based on a cost per click (CPC). As usual, you specify a daily budget, duration, and a CPC bid. You're charged only when someone clicks from your Promoted Pin to your website.

WARNING

Pinterest is still rolling out Promoted Pins to selected advertisers while it works out any kinks. To apply for inclusion, go to `https://business.pinterest.com/promoted-pins`.

For more information, see `https://help.pinterest.com/articles/advertiser-sharing` or `www.socialmediaexaminer.com/use-pinterest-promoted-pins`. (For more about Pinterest, in general, see Book 7, Chapter 1.)

Engagement ads

Users have obviously started to tune out banner ads online, even when the ads spill all over content and refuse to close, irritate eyeballs with annoying animation, or interrupt concentration with surprising bursts of unwanted sound. New forms of advertising that incorporate user information from social media are beginning to populate pages all over the Internet.

The fuse was lit for this form of innovation, and social media technologies ignited it, for good or ill. The marriage of advertising message with individual user information — with the potential of turning every viewer into a shill — has serious implications for privacy. Although the Interactive Advertising Bureau (IAB) has published best practices for user opt-in and privacy protection (`www.iab.net/socialads` and `www.iab.net/sm_buyers_guide`), it isn't clear how well they will be followed. The IAB defines these engagement ads, sometimes called *social banners*, as

> *a type of banner that incorporates social or conversational functionality within it. . . . The key to success is for social banner ads to enable consumers to have a real interactive experience within the unit, as opposed to just passively viewing the content within the ad.*

TIP

Comment-style ads seem to work well for entertainment, new products, cars, and clothes, although virtual gift ads seem to attract consumer product and entertainment advertisers. Clicking the like button on an ad now turns viewers into connections for that brand. This call-to-action ad works well for any established brand, luxury products, and products or entertainers that have a passionate following.

More complex engagement ads draw content from a social network: the photo image and name from a profile (presuming an emotionally effective brand endorsement) or user-generated phrases from tweets, blogs, or RSS feeds. Users review the modified ads; if they agree to allow it, the ads are then distributed to their personal networks. For these complex ads to operate, the user must already be connected to her social network. (One could imagine using these ads to play an interesting game of rumor.)

TECHNICAL STUFF

Interactive engagement ads probably require involvement from tech support or your web developer.

Marketers currently hypothesize that engagement ads, like promoted tweets, have an enhanced value based on factors other than click-through rates (CTRs), such as how long consumers spend interacting with an ad or how often consumers share the ad with their friends. If the sharing results in a cascading effect of recommended impressions to presumably qualified prospects, who just so happen to be friends, all the better for you.

PROMOTING ENGAGEMENT WITH PROMOTED TWEETS

Chegg (www.chegg.com) is a one-stop shop for high school and college students. Whether they need a tutor, homework help, assistance with SATs, or information about colleges, career choices, or scholarships, students can find time- and money-saving services on the site or on the Chegg blog (see nearby art). Chegg also acts as a huge textbook online swap meet, allowing students to rent, buy, or sell textbooks at great prices

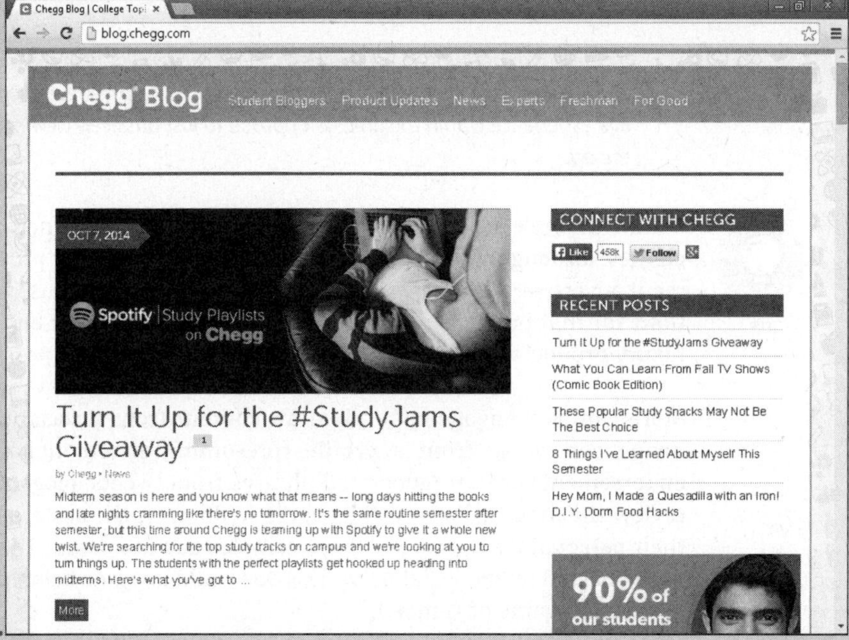

Reproduced with permission of Chegg, Inc.

Founded in 2005, Chegg has moved fast to build a successful community; it reported annual revenue of more than $300 million in 2015.

According to Usher Lieberman, VP of Corporate Communication, Twitter just happened to be the first social channel Chegg used, simply because that was where Chegg's student customers could be found. Chegg's first tweet in 2008 — *We rent textbooks for really cheap* — was a serendipitous success. "Today, there is very much a master plan for how we leverage social channels . . . . We utilize a lot of sophisticated tools and we listen to our students and are engaged in an ongoing dialogue with them. Our customer support team monitors these channels closely and responds, usually within minutes, to customers who reach out," Lieberman notes. "We do track sales against social media performance, but our primary metric is brand engagement."

To meet the needs of a company its size, Chegg uses two full-time staff leaders devoted to social media and a customer support team for added resources, especially during busy seasons. "We operate off of an editorial calendar and generally plan our posts several weeks in advance. That said," he indicates, "we have the flexibility to respond in real-time and engage our audience via all of our social channels."

Chegg took advantage of promoted tweets on Twitter (see the nearby figure) and promoted posts on Facebook to run a two-week seasonal campaign during one of its busiest sales seasons — the textbook rush in Winter 2014. "Promoting the posts (Facebook and Twitter) was critical as it allowed our message to rise above the noise in organic messaging," says Lieberman. The promoted tweets ran concurrently with other messages and didn't affect the frequency with which Chegg handled its myriad other social activities.

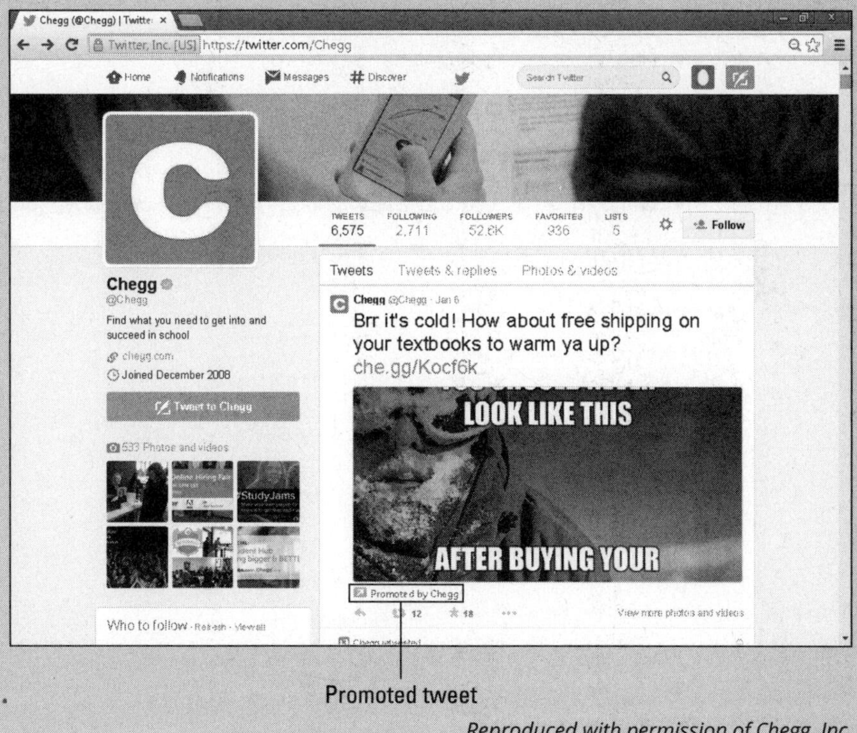

Reproduced with permission of Chegg, Inc.

(continued)

(continued)

Lieberman stresses that he utilizes promoted options strategically and sparingly. "We use promoted tweets and posts when we feel a message really needs to be seen by a maximum audience. This isn't something we do all the time. In fact, it is the exception. We also advertise on Facebook, but generally do not have spends on other networks."

He offers succinct advice to businesses seeking cost-effective advertising. "Test, test, test, and know your audience. It doesn't matter how much you spend promoting your message; if it doesn't resonate with your audience, you are not going to get the results you want or need . . . . [You need to know] what are their challenges, what problems are you trying to solve for them right now, what can you possibly say that will get them talking . . . . Don't start a campaign thinking how much you can spend; think about what you have to say, then figure out how much it will cost to get your audience talking about your message."

Chegg's web presence follows:

- `www.chegg.com`
- `https://twitter.com/chegg`
- `www.facebook.com/chegg`
- `http://instagram.com/chegg`
- `http://blog.chegg.com`
- `www.linkedin.com/company/chegg-inc.?trk=company_logo`
- `www.youtube.com/user/cheggchannel`

9 Measuring Results and Building on Success

Contents at a Glance

CHAPTER 1: **Delving into Data** 583

Planning a Measurement Strategy 584
Selecting Analytics Packages 589
Getting Started with Google Analytics 594
Integrating Google's Social Media Analytics 596

CHAPTER 2: **Analyzing Content-Sharing Metrics** 599

Measuring the Effectiveness of Content Sharing with Standard Analytics 599
Evaluating Blog-Specific Metrics 603
Visualizing Video Success 605
Understanding Podcast Metrics 606
Measuring Your Results from Pinterest 609
Comparing Hard and Soft Costs versus Income 614

CHAPTER 3: **Analyzing Twitter Metrics** 617

Tracking Website Referrals with Google Analytics 618
Tracking Shortened Links 618
Using Twitter Analytics 619
Using TweetDeck 622
Using Third-Party Twitter Analytics Applications 622
Tracking Account Activity with the Notifications Tab 623
Using the Hashtag as a Measurement Mechanism 625
Calculating the Twitter Follower-to-Following Ratio 626

CHAPTER 4: **Analyzing Facebook Metrics** 627

Monitoring Facebook Interaction with Insights 627
Using Page Insights 628
Exploring the Insights Overview and Detail Pages 630

CHAPTER 5: **Measuring Other Social Media Networks** 635

Plugging into Social Media 635
Measuring LinkedIn Success 636
Monitoring Social Mobile Impact 640

CHAPTER 6: **Comparing Metrics from Different Marketing Techniques** 643

Establishing Key Performance Indicators 644
Comparing Metrics across Social Media 646
Integrating Social Media with Web Metrics 653
Using Advertising Metrics to Compare Social Media with Other Types of Marketing 655
Juxtaposing Social Media Metrics with Other Online Marketing 658
Contrasting Word-of-Web with Word-of-Mouth 660

CHAPTER 7: **Making Decisions by the Numbers** 663

Using Metrics to Make Decisions 663
Knowing When to Hold and When to Fold 664
Diagnosing Problems with Social Media Campaigns 669
Fixing Problems 670
Adjusting to Reality 675

IN THIS CHAPTER

» Understanding the difference between monitoring and measuring

» Setting up your measurement plan

» Selecting analytics packages that meet your marketing objectives

» Learning to use Google Analytics

» Discovering Google Social Analytics

Chapter 1 Delving into Data

Web analytics is the practice of analyzing performance and business statistics for a website, social media marketing, and other online marketing efforts to better understand user behavior and improve results. Some might call web analytics more art than science; to others, it's black magic.

The amount of data that can be acquired from online marketing efforts vastly exceeds the amount available using traditional offline methods. That statement alone makes online marketing, including social media, an attractive form of public relations and advertising.

In the best of all possible worlds, the results of your marketing efforts should appear as increased profits — in other words, as an improved bottom line with a nice return on investment (ROI). You're more likely to achieve this goal if you make analytics part of a process of continuous quality improvement.

TIP

Before getting mired in the swamp of online marketing data, assess the performance of your hub website. If you aren't making a profit from that core investment, it doesn't matter whether you fill the conversion funnel (see Book 1, Chapter 1) with fantastic traffic from social media, exhibit a soaring click-through rate, or tally revenues through the roof. If you aren't sure how your hub site is performing, use the tools in this chapter and ask your web developer and bookkeeper for help.

Planning a Measurement Strategy

The basic principle "You can't manage what you don't measure" applies doubly to the online universe. Do you know whether Facebook or LinkedIn drives more traffic to your site? Whether more people buy after reading a blog post about pets than after reading a blog post about plants? If not, you're simply guessing at how to expend your precious marketing dollars and time.

To make the most of your effort, return to the goals and objectives you established on your Social Media Marketing Goals statement (see Book 1, Chapter 1 or download it from (www.dummies.com/go/socialmediamarketingaio4e).

Ask yourself what you need to measure to determine your accomplishments. Would interim measurements help you decide whether a particular aspect of a social media campaign is working?

For instance, if one of your goals is to substitute social media marketing for paid advertising, compare performance between the two. If you initiated social media activities to improve a ranking on search engine results pages (SERPs), you must measure your standing by keywords at different times. In either case, of course, you might want to track visitors to the site who arrive from either a social media referral or from natural search to see whether they continue to a purchase.

Fortunately, computers do one thing extremely well: count. Chances are good that if you have a question, you can find an answer.

WARNING

Because computers count just about everything, you can quickly drown in so much data that you find it impossible to gather meaningful information, let alone make a decision. The last thing you need is a dozen reports that you don't have time to read.

Unless you have a very large site, monitoring statistics monthly or quarterly is usually sufficient. You might check more often when you first initiate a specific social media campaign or another online marketing activity, if you invest significant amounts of money or effort into a new campaign, or if you support your site by way of advertising (in which case, monitoring traffic is the sine qua non of your existence).

REMEMBER

In your Social Media Marketing Plan (see Book 1, Chapter 3, or download it from www.dummies.com/go/socialmediamarketingaio4e, add your choice of measurement parameters and analytical tools, as well as the names of the people who will be responsible for creating reports. Schedule the frequency of analytical review on your Social Media Activity Calendar (see Book 1, Chapter 4).

Monitoring versus measuring

For the purposes of this book, we discuss only quantitative data as part of the measurement process. Use monitoring tools to review such qualitative data from social media as

- The degree of customer engagement
- The nature of customer dialog, sometimes called sentiment
- Your brand reputation on a social network
- The quality of relationships with your target market
- The extent of participation in online conversations
- Positioning in your industry versus your competitors

If you have no monitoring tools in place yet, turn to Book 2, Chapter 1.

REMEMBER

"Real people" usually review subjective monitoring data to assess such ineffable qualities as the positive or negative characteristics of consumer posts, conversational tone, and brand acknowledgment. Notwithstanding Hal in the movie *2001: A Space Odyssey*, we don't yet have analytical software with the supple linguistic sophistication of the human brain.

Setting aside the squishy qualitative data, you still have two types of quantitative data to measure:

- **Internal performance measurements:** Measure the effectiveness of your social media, other marketing efforts, and website in achieving your objectives. Performance measurements include such parameters as traffic to your social pages or website, the number of people who click-through to your hub presence, which products sell best, and *conversion rate,* or the percentage of visitors who buy or become qualified leads.
- **Business measurements:** Primarily dollar-based parameters — costs, revenues, profits — that go directly to your business operations. Such financial items as the cost of customer or lead acquisition, average dollar value per sale, the value assigned to leads, the break-even point, and ROI fall into this category. For more about measuring ROI, see Book 1, Chapter 2.

Deciding what to measure

Most of the key performance indicators (KPIs) and business criteria you measure fall into one of the following categories:

- **Traffic:** You must know the number and nature of visitors to any of the sites that are part of your web presence.
- **Leads:** Business-to-business (B2B) companies, service professionals, and companies that sell expensive, complex products often close their sales offline. Online efforts yield prospects, many of whom — you hope — will become qualified leads as they move down the conversion funnel.
- **Financials:** Costs, sales, revenue, and profits are the essential components of business success. Analytics let you track which sales arrive from which sources and how much revenue they generate.
- **Search marketing:** As discussed in Book 2, Chapter 3, optimizing social media can improve visibility in search engine results. Not only do many social media sites appear in search results, but your hub site also gains valuable inbound links from direct and indirect referrals.
- **Other business objectives:** You may need customized analytics to track goals and objectives that don't fall into the other categories.

Chapter 6 in this minibook discusses KPIs in depth.

Don't plan on flying to the moon based on the accuracy of any statistical web data. Definitions of parameters differ by tool. Does a new visitor session start after someone has logged off for 24 minutes or 24 hours? In addition, results in real-time tools sometimes oscillate unpredictably.

TIP

If a value differs from what you expected, try running your analytics again later or run them over a longer period to smooth out irregularities.

Relative numbers are more meaningful than absolute ones. Is your traffic growing or shrinking? Is your conversion rate increasing or decreasing? Focus on ratios or percentages to make the data more meaningful. Suppose that 10 percent of a small number of viewers to your site converted to buyers before you started a blog, compared to only 5 percent of a larger number of viewers afterward. What does that tell you?

Figure 1-1 shows what most businesses are measuring online. You can find a lot of research about typical performance on different statistical parameters. Though it's nice to know industry averages for benchmarking purposes, the only statistics that matter are your own.

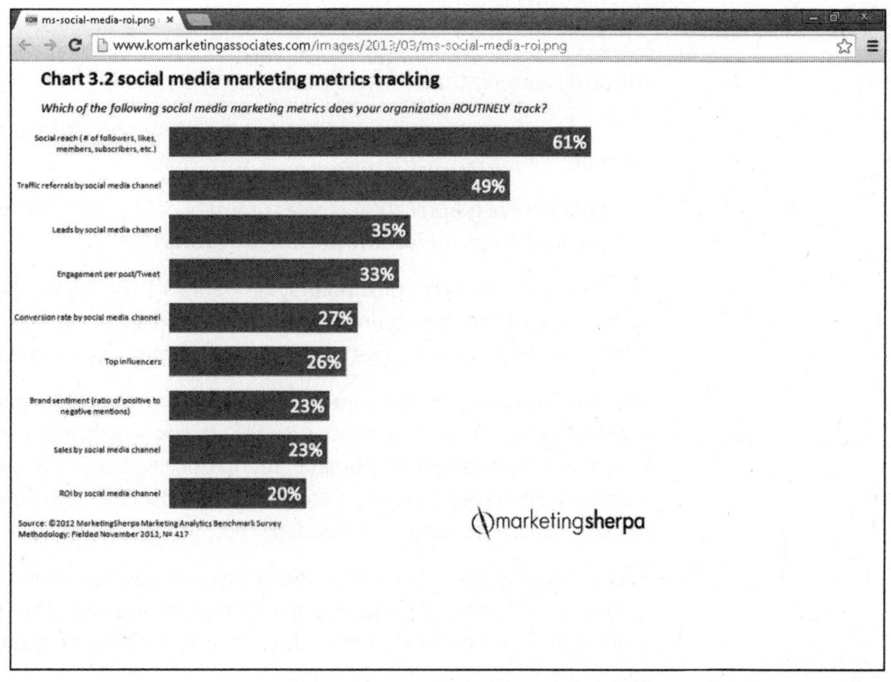

FIGURE 1-1: Social media marketing metrics routinely tracked by businesses.

Reproduced with permission of Marketing Sherpa

TIP

Regardless of how you go about the measurement process, you must define success before you begin. Without some sort of target value, you can't know whether you've succeeded. Keep your handy, dandy Social Media Marketing Goals statement (see Book 1, Chapter 1) accessible while you review this chapter.

A good measurement strategy determines how much data to leave out, as well as how much to measure. Unless you have a huge site or quite a complex marketing campaign, you can focus on just a few parameters.

Establishing responsibility for analytics

Chances are good that your business isn't large enough to field an entire team whose sole responsibility is statistical analysis. Even if you aren't running an employment agency for statisticians, you can still take a few concrete steps to ensure that the right data is collected, analyzed, and acted on:

1. Ask your marketing person (is that you?) to take responsibility for defining what needs to be measured based on business objectives.

   Consult with your financial advisor, if necessary.

2. Have your programmer, web developer, or go-to IT person select and install the analytics tools that will provide the data you need.

   Make ease of use, flexibility, and customizability important factors in the decision.

3. If a *dashboard* (a graphical executive summary of key data) isn't part of the analytical package, ask your IT person to set one up.

   Try the Google Analytics dashboard (see Figure 1-2) or the HubSpot dashboard for multiple media (see Figure 1-3). Dashboards display essential results quickly, preferably over easy-to-change time frames of your choice.

4. Let your marketing, IT, and content management folks work together to finalize the highest priority pages (usually landing pages and pages within your conversion funnels). When possible, set up tracking codes for links coming from social marketing pages. IT should test to ensure that the data collection system works and adjust it as needed.

5. Your marketing person can be responsible for regularly monitoring the results, adjusting marketing campaigns, and reporting to you and other stakeholders. Have your IT person validate the data and audit tracking tags at least twice a year — they can easily get out of sync.

6. Always integrate the results of your social media and online marketing efforts with offline marketing and financial results for a complete picture of what's happening with your business. Compare against your business goals and objectives and modify as needed.

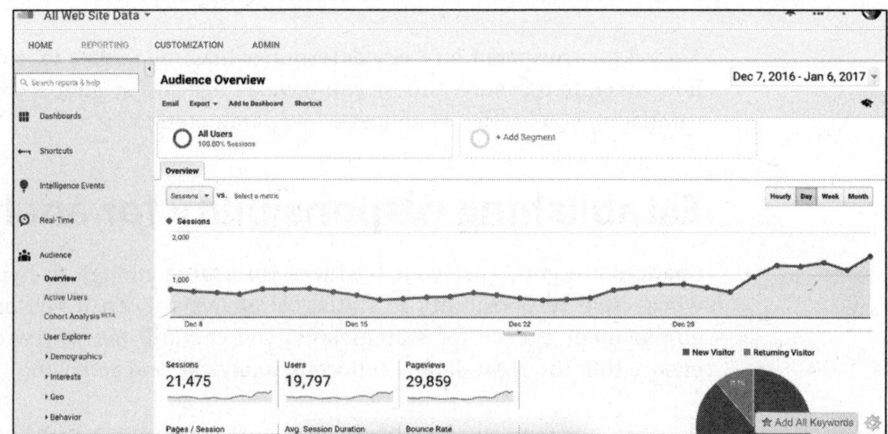

FIGURE 1-2: A typical Google Analytics dashboard displays key web statistics.

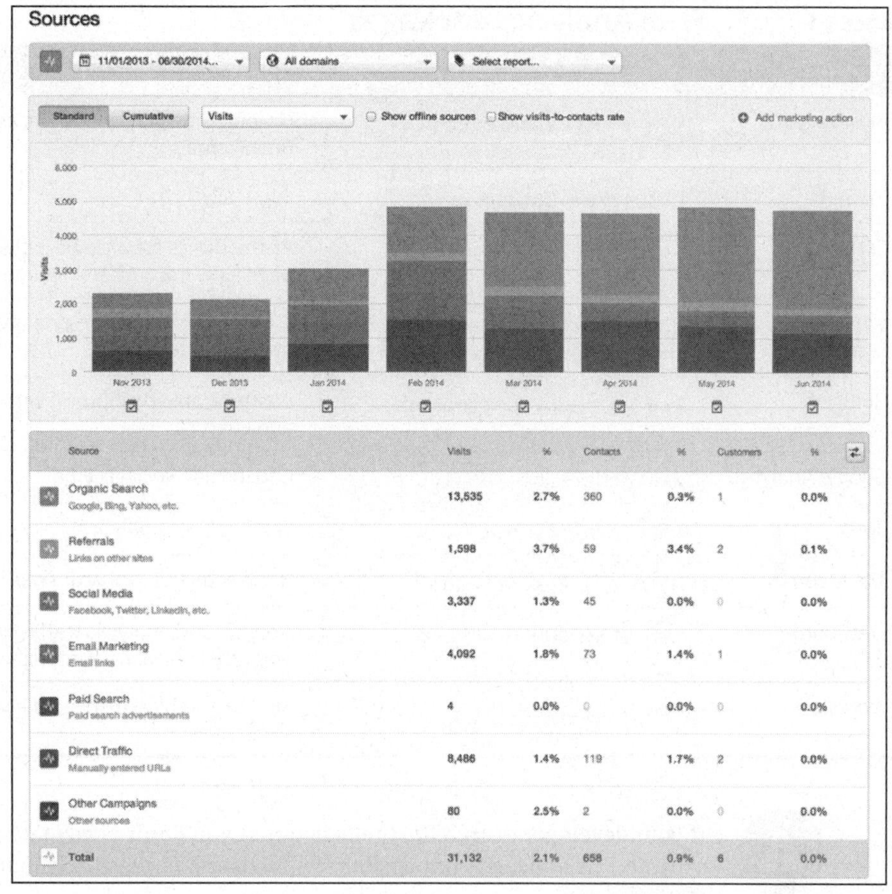

Source	Visits	%	Contacts	%	Customers	%
Organic Search Google, Bing, Yahoo, etc.	13,535	2.7%	360	0.3%	1	0.0%
Referrals Links on other sites	1,598	3.7%	59	3.4%	2	0.1%
Social Media Facebook, Twitter, LinkedIn, etc.	3,337	1.3%	45	0.0%	0	0.0%
Email Marketing Email links	4,092	1.8%	73	1.4%	1	0.0%
Paid Search Paid search advertisements	4	0.0%	0	0.0%	0	0.0%
Direct Traffic Manually entered URLs	8,486	1.4%	119	1.7%	2	0.0%
Other Campaigns Other sources	80	2.5%	2	0.0%	0	0.0%
Total	31,132	2.1%	658	0.9%	6	0.0%

FIGURE 1-3: A HubSpot page showing the distribution of visits by source.

Reproduced with permission of HubSpot, Inc.

TECHNICAL STUFF

Aggregate all analytics in one place. You're unlikely to find a premade dashboard that includes everything you need to measure for your specific campaigns. Your programmer may have to export data into Excel, PDF, or email format; save it all in one place; and then build a custom spreadsheet to generate combined reports for your review.

Selecting Analytics Packages

Ask your developer or web host which statistical packages are available for your site. Unless you have a fairly large site or need real-time data, one of the free packages in Table 1-1 should work well. Review your choices to select the best fit for your needs. In many cases, Google Analytics is the best answer.

TABLE 1-1 Free Analytics Packages

Name	URL	Notes
AFS Analytics	`www.addfreestats.com`	Graphical display; real-time, adjustable time frame
AWStats	`http://awstats.org`	Log analysis tool
Clicky	`http://clicky.com`	All the basics for a single website; 3,000 daily page view max; offers paid options
eXTReMe Tracking	`http://extremetracking.com/?free`	Free version limited to one tracker on one page per site
GoingUp!	`www.goingup.com/features`	Customizable dashboard with graphs and charts
Google Analytics	`www.google.com/analytics`	Can include social media
Piwik	`http://piwik.org`	Open source analytics
Site Meter	`http://sitemeter.com`	Basic analytics tool with graphs and charts
StatCounter	`www.statcounter.com`	Accepts and analyzes traffic from many blogs and other social networking websites
Webalizer	`www.webalizer.org`	Simple graphical display that works well with small sites

WARNING

If your developer or web host tells you that you don't need statistics, find another provider. It's nearly impossible to measure success without easy access to statistics.

The specific suite of statistical results that a package offers may influence your choice of tools. Unfortunately, you can't count on getting comparable results when you mix and match different tools. Each one defines parameters differently (for example, what constitutes a repeat visitor). Consequently, you need to watch trends, not absolute numbers.

If you have a large site with heavy traffic or extensive reporting requirements, free packages — even Google Analytics — might not be enough. You can find dozens of paid statistical programs in an online search; Table 1-2 lists 13 of them. Several are fairly inexpensive, but the ones marked *enterprise-level solution* in the Cost column of Table 1-2 can escalate into real money.

REMEMBER

Not all marketing channels use the same yardstick — nor should they. Your business objectives drive your choice of channels and therefore your choice of yardsticks.

TABLE 1-2 Paid Statistical Packages

Name	URL	Cost
Adobe Analytics	www.adobe.com/solutions/digital-analytics.html	Enterprise-level solution; includes social media.
Chartbeat	http://chartbeat.com	Starting at $9.95 for standard real-time web analytics for five sites.
Clicky	http://clicky.com/compare	Paid options start at $9.99/month for 1 million page views/month.
eXTReMe Tracking	http://extremetracking.com	$4.50 per month.
Hootsuite	https://hootsuite.com/products/insights	Pricing is based on number of items monitored; contact for custom quote.
IBM Enterprise Marketing Management	www-03.ibm.com/software/products/en/category/enterprise-marketing-management	Enterprise-level solution; includes social media.
Sawmill LITE	www.sawmill.net/lite.html	Lite version $99 for 1 profile; $199 for 5 profiles. Professional level starts at $199; Enterprise level starts at $599 based on the number of profiles.
Site Meter	http://sitemeter.com	Premium starts at $6.95 per month.
Site Stats Lite	www.sitestats.com	Cost varies by page views and features; Lite version starts at $15 per month; Professional at $20 per month; Enterprise at $30 per month.
Upsight	www.upsight.com	Analytics for mobile and social apps. Free for up to 50K active monthly users; enterprise level priced on custom basis.
VisitorVille	www.visitorville.com	Real-time 3-D statistics; from $19.95 per month.
Webtrends Social Measurement	http://webtrends.com/solutions/digital-measurement/social-measurement	Enterprise-level solution; includes social media.
Woopra	www.woopra.com	Starts at $79.95 per month. Also has a free version.

Some paid statistical packages are hosted on a third-party server. Others are designed for installation on your own server. Generally, higher-end paid statistical solutions offer several benefits:

- Real-time analytics (no waiting for results)
- Sophisticated reporting tools by domain or across multiple domains, departments, or enterprises
- Customizable data-mining filters
- Path-through-site analysis, tracking an individual user from entry to exit
- Integrated traffic and store statistics
- Integrated qualitative and quantitative analytics for multiple social media services
- Analysis of downloaded PDF, video, audio, or another file type
- Mapping host addresses to company names and details
- Clickstream analysis to show which sites visitors arrive from and go to

Don't collect information for information's sake. Stop when you have enough data to make essential business decisions.

Reviewing analytical options for social media

Depending on what you're trying to measure, you may need data from some of the analytical tools available internally from a particular social media channel or statistics from social bookmarking sites such as AddToAny (`www.addtoany.com`) or from URL shorteners, which we discuss the following section.

Table 1-3 summarizes which social media services integrate with Google Analytics for traffic monitoring and which also offer their own internal performance statistics. See Chapters 2 through 5 in this minibook for a detailed discussion of analytics on specific social media services.

Register for free optional statistics whenever you can.

TABLE 1-3 **Analytics for Specific Social Networks**

Website	URL	Integrates with Google Analytics?	Own Analytics Package?
Facebook Page Insights	`www.facebook.com/help/336893449723054`	Yes	Yes
Google+ Platform Insights	`https://developers.google.com/+/features/analytics`	Yes	Yes
LinkedIn Analytics Tab	`http://help.linkedin.com/app/answers/detail/a_id/26032/~/analytics-tab-for-company-pages`	Yes	Yes
Meetup Group Stats	`http://help.meetup.com/customer/portal/articles/868781-meetup-group-stats`	Yes	Yes
Twitter Analytics	`https://analytics.twitter.com`	Yes	Yes
YouTube Analytics	`www.youtube.com/analytics`	Yes	Yes (must have an account with a channel)

Selecting a URL-shortening tool for statistics

One type of free optional statistics is particularly handy: traffic generated by shortened URLs, as described in Book 2, Chapter 1. Be sure to select a free shortener that offers analytics, such as the following:

- **Bitly (**`http://bitly.com`**):** A free account (registration required) to track statistics from shortened links
- **Google URL Shortener (**`http://goo.gl`**):** Google's free URL shortener
- **Ow.ly (**`http://ow.ly`**):** Hootsuite's free URL shortener
- **Snipurl (**`http://snipurl.com`**):** Stores, manages, and tracks traffic on short URLs

TIP

To access a shortcut to results for links shortened with Bitly, paste the short URL into a browser, followed by the plus sign (for example, `https://bitly.com/Xv1TDI+`). A page appears showing how many clicks the short URL received. After you sign into your Bitly account, you can see additional metrics, such as those shown in Figure 1-4.

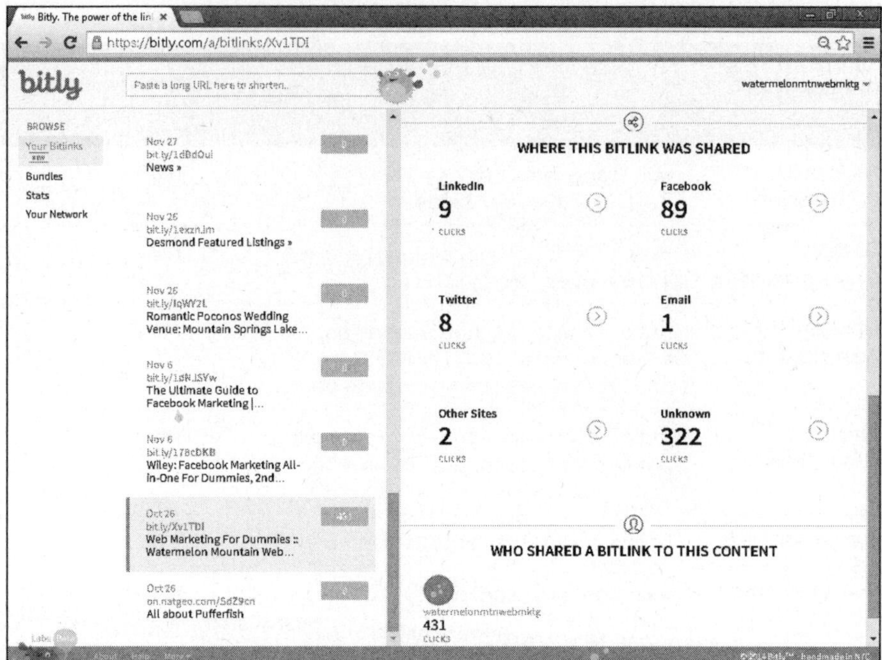

FIGURE 1-4: Bitly offers several displays for traffic statistics.

Reproduced with permission of Watermelon Mountain Web Marketing, www.`watermelonweb.com`

TIP

You can use a dashboard tool such as Netvibes to see all your stats in one convenient place. See Book 1, Chapter 4 for more details about dashboards.

Getting Started with Google Analytics

Google Analytics is so popular that it justifies some additional discussion. This free, high-quality analytics tool works well for most website owners. It now incorporates many social media services as part of its analysis and scales well from tiny sites to extremely large ones.

TIP

Start with the free Google Analytics and switch to an enterprise-level solution when and if your web effort demands it.

Among its many advantages, Google Analytics offers

- More in-depth analysis than most other free statistical packages
- Plenty of support, as shown in Table 1-4
- Easy-to-set specific time frames to compare results to other years

- Many of the more sophisticated features of expensive software, such as path-through-site information
- Customization of the dashboard display
- Conversion funnel visualization, shown in Figure 1-5
- Analysis by *referrer* (where traffic to your site has linked from) or search term
- Tracking of such key performance indicators as returning visitors and *bounce rate* (percentage of visitors who leave without visiting a second page)
- Customizable reports to meet your needs that you can have emailed automatically to you
- Social analytics capabilities
- Seamless integration with AdWords, the Google pay-per-click program

TABLE 1-4 **Helpful Google Analytics Resource URLs**

Name	URL	Description
"15 Google Analytics Tricks to Maximize Your Marketing Campaign"	`www.forbes.com/sites/jaysondemers/2014/08/20/15-google-analytics-tricks-to-maximize-your-marketing-campaign`	Useful Google Analytics tips and tricks
About Social Analytics	`https://support.google.com/analytics/answer/1683971?hl=en&ref_topic=1316551`	Guide to the features of Google's social media tools
Analytics Academy	`https://analyticsacademy.withgoogle.com/explorer`	Google Analytics Academy courses
Analytics Help Center	`https://support.google.com/analytics/?hl=en#topic=3544906`	Google Analytics support
Google Analytics Solutions	`http://analytics.blogspot.com`	Google blog for all things analytics
"How to Prepare for Google Analytics IQ"	`https://support.google.com/analytics/answer/3424288?hl=en`	Online Google Analytics training
"How to Set Up Goals in Google Analytics"	`http://blog.gumroad.com/post/87921227603/how-to-set-up-goals-in-google-analytics`	Setting up goals
KISSmetrics 50+ Google Analytics Resources	`https://blog.kissmetrics.com/google-analytics-resources-2015/`	Collection of Google Analytics guides

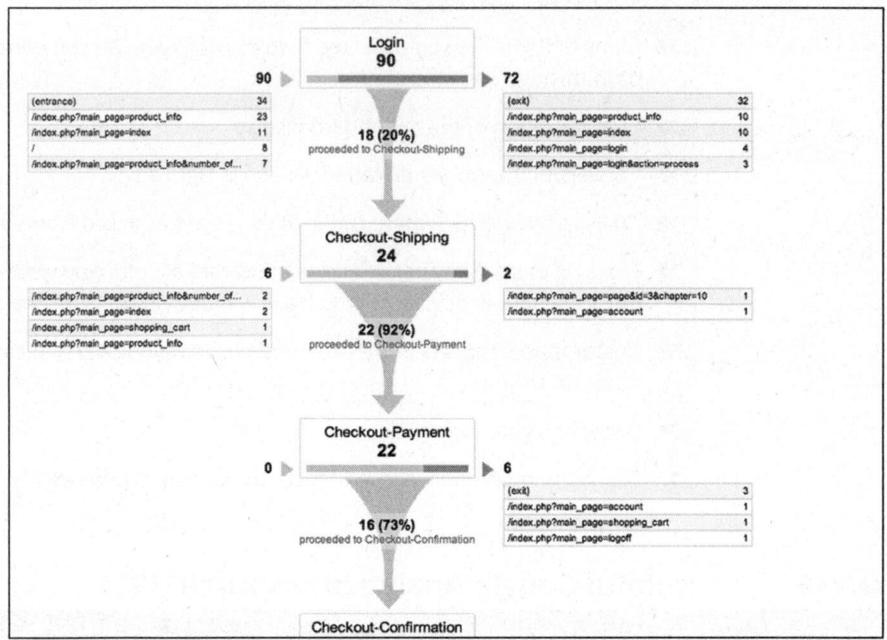

FIGURE 1-5: A sample conversion funnel for Google Analytics.

Reproduced with permission of WebReach Ireland Ltd.; `www.webreach.ie`

TECHNICAL STUFF

Google provides steps for installing Analytics at `www.google.com/analytics`. This task definitely isn't for anyone who is faint-of-programming-heart. Get help from your developer. For detailed information on installing Google Analytics, refer to the help sites listed in Table 1-4 or go to `https://support.google.com/analytics/?hl=en#topic=3544906`.

TECHNICAL STUFF

You must tag each page of your website with a short piece of JavaScript. The tagging task isn't difficult. If your site uses a template or a common server-side include (for example, for a footer), you place the Analytics code once, and it appears on all pages. You should start seeing results within 24 hours.

Integrating Google's Social Media Analytics

You can still identify traffic arriving at your site from social media services simply by looking at All Referrers under Acquisition in your Google Analytics account. However, Google's Social Media Analytics makes it much easier to integrate statistical results from social media services into your reports and to assess the business value of social media. Take advantage of the Social option to pre-filter for social-site referrers only.

Start by clicking Acquisition in the left navigation, as usual. Then click again to expand the Social option, as shown in Figure 1-6, and select Network Referrals. As shown in Figure 1-6, Google Social Analytics compares sessions from social media to all sessions in the graphs and lists traffic from individual social media sources below the graphs.

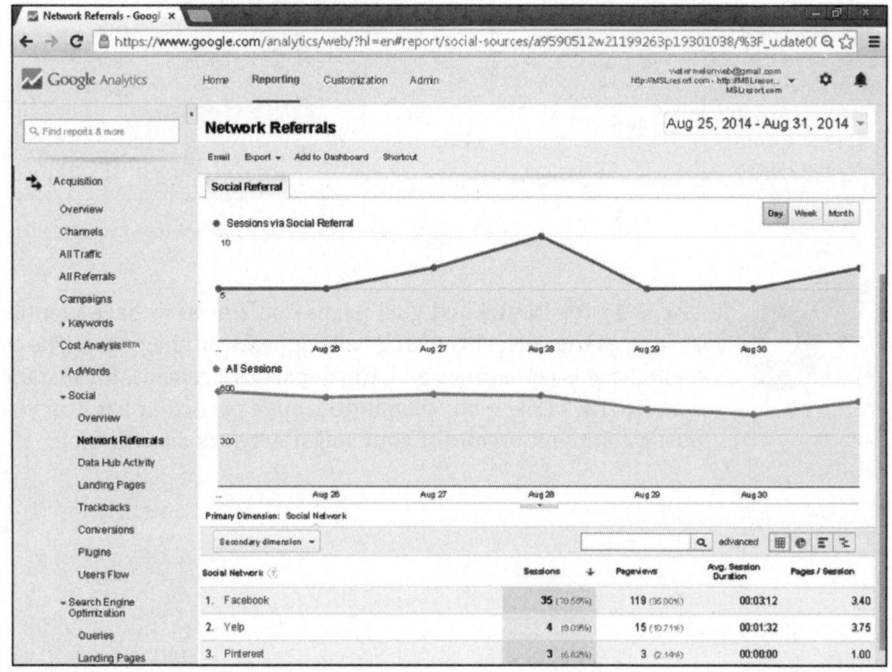

FIGURE 1-6: The Social section of Google Analytics makes it easy to collect and compare referrals from social networks.

Alternatively, below the Social options in the left navigation, click Users Flow. In the Select Segment drop-down list (at the top of the Social Users Flow page), select Referral Traffic. The resulting display, shown in Figure 1-7, appears.

Some social media services, such as Facebook and Meetup, make it easy to integrate their data with Google Analytics by enabling you to place Google Analytics tracking code on your social media pages. Of course, Google-owned Blogger, Google+, and YouTube, as well as the RSS service FeedBurner, are already compatible with Analytics.

REMEMBER

Web analytics, from Google or anywhere else, are valuable only if you use them to improve users' experience on your site and your bottom line.

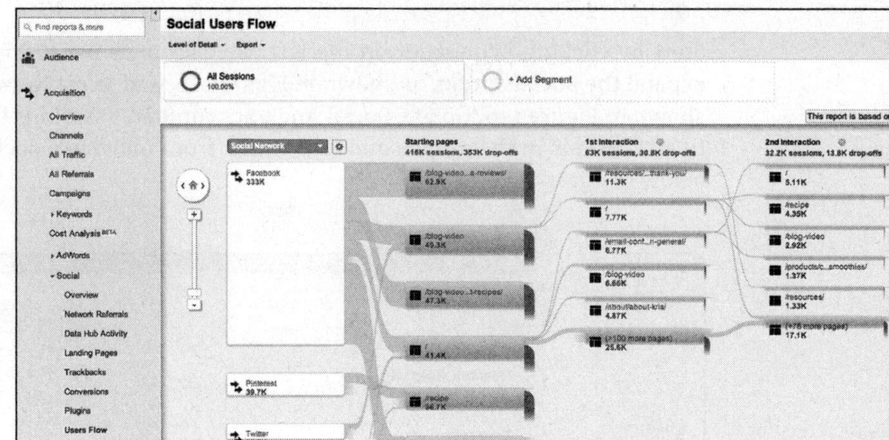

FIGURE 1-7: The Social Users Flow page displays the path taken by visitors who arrive at your site from various social media.

Source: `https://megalytic.com/blog/social-insights-from-google-analytics`

TIP

The URLs for funnel and goal pages don't need to have identical domain names, as long as the correct tracking code appears on the pages. The thank-you page for a purchase is sometimes on a third-party storefront, for instance. Or perhaps you want to track how many people go from a particular page on your main website to post a comment on one of your social network sites or blog.

IN THIS CHAPTER

- Using standard analytics to evaluate content-sharing success
- Evaluating internal metrics for blogs, videos, podcasts, and photos
- Estimating ROI for content sharing

Chapter 2

Analyzing Content-Sharing Metrics

You've built a blog, updated hundreds of photos, created a podcast, or shot a series of videos. You've nurtured and fed your effort with multiple posts and episodes. You've promoted your creative endeavor, and now you want to know how many people have visited, how engaged they were, and most of all, whether they shared your content with others, giving your efforts maximum exposure.

Developing good content is hard work. Like with any of your other marketing efforts, you need to understand your return on investment (ROI). In this chapter, we show you how to figure out your ROI and evaluate the effectiveness of your content-sharing social channels.

Measuring the Effectiveness of Content Sharing with Standard Analytics

If you use content as a marketing tool, how do you know whether your message is getting out there? How do you measure your results? How viral is your content? Are viewers or readers recommending your content to people other than those you reached directly through your own efforts? Your website stats reveal the most information, but you can also glean effective information from specific statistics for each type of content sharing.

Maximizing website stats

You can find an amazing amount of information about the effectiveness of your content simply by using the program that tracks your website statistics, whether that's Google Analytics or any other program we mention in Chapter 1 of this minibook. Table 2-1 summarizes which of the primary content-sharing sites integrate with Google Analytics or offer their own.

TIP

Perhaps the easiest solution is to install Google Analytics on every content-sharing platform for which it's offered.

Review your general statistics to find the following types of information:

- **The number of visitors who land on the home page of your blog or other content site:** Watch for variations in the number and timing of visits, as well.
- **The number of visitors seeking specific posts, videos, or podcasts:** This information tells you that visitors found the post through an external link or perhaps a specific set of keywords in a search engine. Most analytics enable you to search content results to the page level.
- **How visitors arrived at your content-sharing site:** Someone might have used a search engine, entered the URL for your social-sharing presence, or linked from another website.
- **How long visitors remain on a specific post page:** If the duration of a visit is shorter than the potential length of time spent reading the post and pondering its contents, the post wasn't effective. You can infer the effectiveness of a post from the bounce rate.

REMEMBER

Capitalize on effective posts by creating similar posts. When you analyze your web statistics, you'll know which posts are effective.

- **The number of unique visitors to your content-sharing site compared to the number of visitors to your website:** For instance, content posts can consist of unique information about your products or services. The more unique visitors you have to specific content posts — or to your content, in general — the better your information is received. If your blog attracts more unique visitors than your site does, consider creating links in your blog posts to related information on your website. If your site receives more hits than your blog, add some links from the specific products or services you offer to blog posts about these specific items.

TABLE 2-1 **Analytics Availability on Content-Sharing Sites**

Website	URL	Description	Google Analytics Integration?	Own Analytics Package?
Image Sharing				
Flickr	`www.flickr.com`	Well-known photo-sharing site	No	No
Instagram	`http://instagram.com`	Popular app used to share photos and videos from mobile device on social media sites	Yes	No
Pinterest	`www.pinterest.com`	Share and collect photos on visual scrapbooks	Yes	Yes
Video/Audio Sharing				
Medium	`http://medium.com`	Write and share blog posts	No	Yes
Spotify	`www.spotify.com`	A digital music service where you can listen to millions of songs	No	Yes
Ustream	`www.ustream.tv`	Platform for live, interactive broadcast video	No	Yes
Vimeo	`https://vimeo.com` `https://vimeo.com/upgrade?v=c`	Created by filmmakers and videographers to share creative work; commercial accounts available on Pro version	Yes	Yes
YouTube	`www.youtube.com`	Well-known video sharing site	Yes	Yes
Blogs				
Blogger	`www.blogger.com`	Google's blog platform	Yes	Yes
Tumblr	`www.tumblr.com`	Share text, photos, links, music, videos, and more	No	Yes
Typepad	`www.typepad.com`	Inexpensive blog platform	Yes	Yes
WordPress.com	`https://wordpress.com`	Blog/website platform with hosting	No	Yes
WordPress.org	`https://wordpress.org`	Blog/website platform without hosting	Yes (with plug-ins)	Yes

- **The number of people who linked to your website from one of your content-sharing pages.** The more people link from a content-sharing site, the more effective that channel is for your marketing.
- **The geographical location of your content visitors:** If the majority of visitors are from a country or an area other than your target market, change your message.
- **The direction of traffic:** After you have an established content-sharing presence, your traffic rate and number of incoming links to your website should increase. If they aren't increasing, consider shaking things up a bit by offering different content. Look at which posts have been popular in the past. Expand on those topics or put a new spin on them, and carefully monitor the results.
- **Which pages are most frequently used to enter or leave the site:** If visitors are entering and exiting the home page and spending only a short length of time on your site, they're skimming only one or two posts before getting out of Dodge. If you're facing this situation, it's time to rethink your message. Visitors entering your site on a specific page, however, have honed in on a specific post from either a search engine result or an incoming link. If you have a lot of these kinds of visitors and they're spending a fair amount of time on your site and exiting from a different page, you have an effective content-sharing site.

Tracking comments

Beyond statistics, one of the most valuable ways to assess the success of your content-sharing sites is by tracking how many and what type of comments people leave. Look for the following information in the Comments section on blogs, YouTube, podcasts, and any other content-sharing sites that permit comments, reviews, rankings, or likes and unlikes.

TIP

Third-party social alert and monitoring sites may help you analyze comments for sentiment (an assessment of the positive or negative feelings found in comments). See Book 2, Chapter 3 for helpful tools to use when the number of comments becomes overwhelming.

Here are some metrics to watch when assessing comments:

- **Number of comments on each blog post:** This information is important if your goal is to stimulate interaction with potential customers. If certain blog posts are drawing more comments than others, the information in those posts is more relevant to your subscribers.

- **Comment length:** If you've written a lengthy post and you receive lengthy comments, you've struck a chord with subscribers and presented useful information. If comments are sparse, however, which indicates that you haven't given your user-base food for thought, consider changing the nature of your posts or the type of information you post.
- **The tone of comments on your posts:** If comments on the majority of your posts sound positive and you receive a lot of comments, you're sending the right message. You can be somewhat controversial at times and stir up provocative comments, but unless you're a shock jock, make it the exception and not the rule. If, on the other hand, the comments aren't flattering, you know what you need to do.

TIP

If the number of comments for new posts is decreasing, you're losing your audience — and you probably need to review your messages. Be sure that you're inviting responses with an open question like, "What do you think?" You may need to provide explicit directions about where to click to make a comment.

If you're receiving comments on individual podcast episodes, people are downloading the podcast from your website rather than using a subscription. Analyze which episodes reward you with the most comments — and then include that type of information in future podcasts.

- **Number of visitors versus the number of comments:** If you have a fairly high ratio of comments to visitors, you're creating interesting material that gets visitors thinking.

Evaluating Blog-Specific Metrics

Each of the primary blogging sites provides analytics information such as that seen in Figure 2-1. Blogger, WordPress, Tumblr, and Typepad all integrate with Google Analytics. However, Blogger (which is owned by Google) and Typepad (`http://help.typepad.com/overview_and_stats.html`) offer their own proprietary tools, in addition or as an alternative to Analytics. WordPress.com, the hosted version of this popular blog software, does offer its own statistical package at `http://support.wordpress.com/stats`.

TIP

If your blog is your only online effort, internal statistics may be enough. However, if you want to be able to compare and contrast multiple components of your web presence, you need Google Analytics or another package.

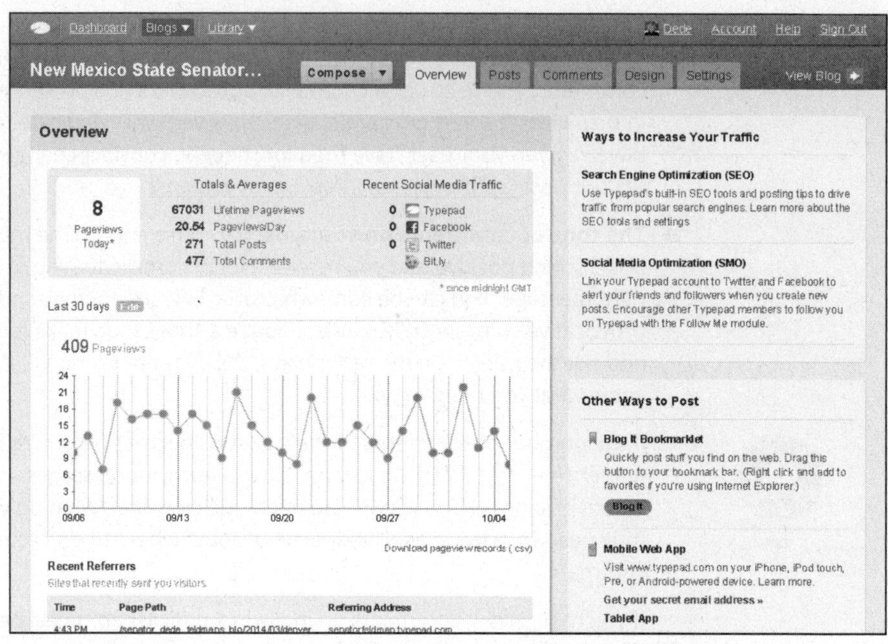

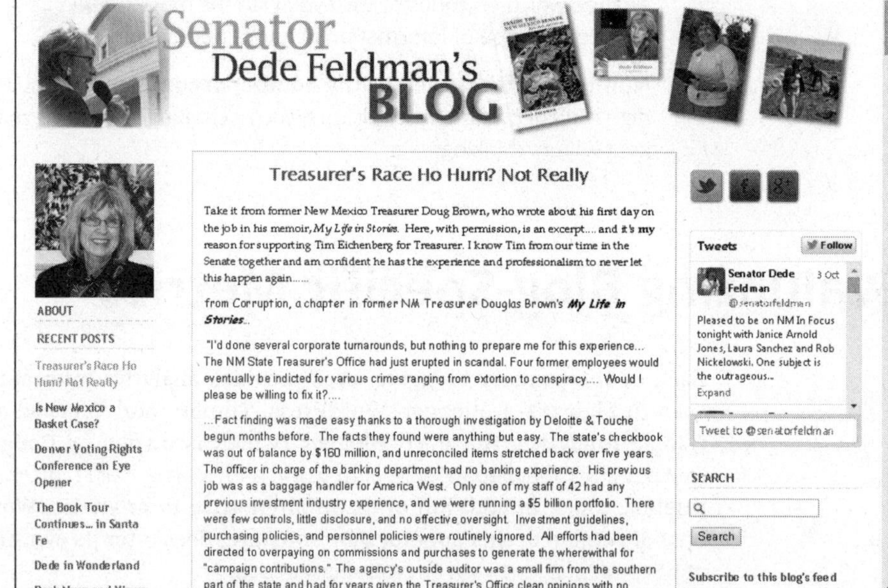

FIGURE 2-1: Typepad stats (top) for the blog run by former New Mexico State Senator Dede Feldman (bottom).

Reproduced with permission of Dede Feldman Co., Melody Mock, designer; Suzanne Prescott, manager

Of course, you'll watch for the number of incoming visitors in your blog dashboard. You also want to look at the number of people who have decided to *follow* you — by subscribing through the service, getting email notifications, or using RSS.

Visualizing Video Success

After you post a video to a third-party site (such as YouTube or Vimeo), you can look there for some stats about views, click-throughs, and more.

After logging into YouTube, type `www.youtube.com/analytics` into the address bar to get to the screen shown in Figure 2-2. The Overview display shows how many subscribers you have and the total number of views for your channel.

The left navigation column of this dashboard offers a Views Reports option, which deals with traffic metrics in greater deal, and an Engagement Reports option, which deals with comments, subscribers, and shares. (See Figure 2-2.)

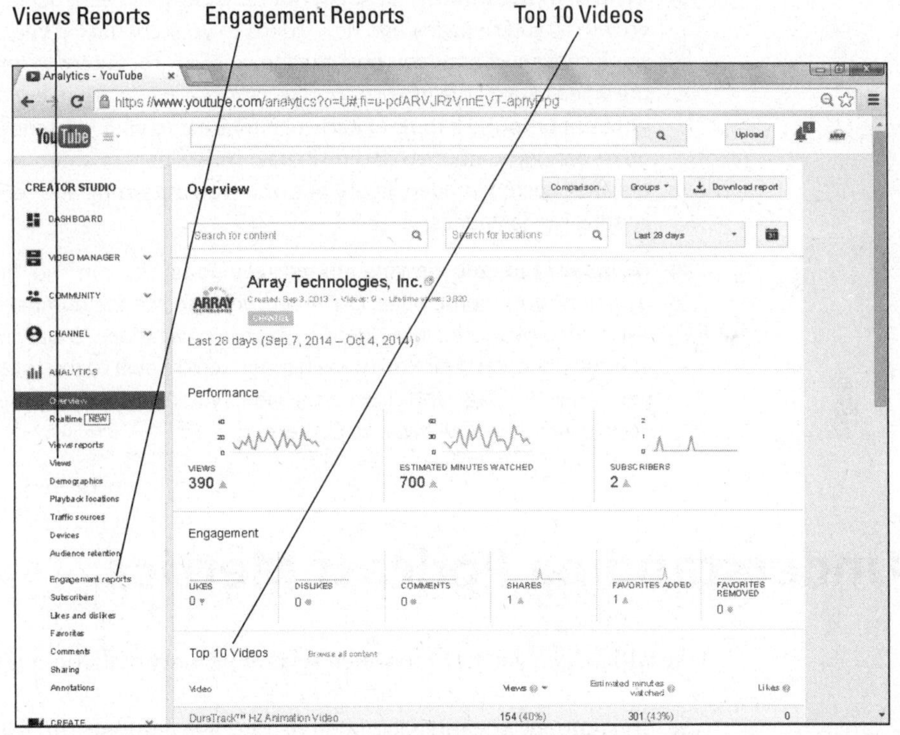

FIGURE 2-2: Viewing statistics for YouTube videos.

Reproduced with permission of Array Technologies, Inc.

TIP

As an alternate path to Analytics, start by clicking My Channel in the left navigation after you log in. If the left navigation is not visible on your screen, click the three-bar icon next to the YouTube logo in the top-left corner to extend the navigation. Then click Video Manager below the top search box (above the center graphic), followed by a click on Analytics in the left navigation.

On Vimeo, you need to subscribe to the PRO option (the paid version for commercial customers) to see statistics. Log in and hover your cursor over the My Videos icon in the top navigation bar. When you click My Stats in the drop-down list that appears, a graph appears, displaying comment quantity, likes, total downloads, and total plays by date, as well as statistics for embedded videos.

To assess the performance of your video content, watch the following important metrics:

- **Number of subscribers:** At YouTube, you find this information in the left sidebar of your YouTube channel page. If you're creating relevant videos, you should notice a steady increase in subscribers with each new video you upload.
- **Growth in the number of subscribers:** You should experience steady growth as you regularly add new videos to your channel. If you notice a significant spurt after you post a video, analyze its content to determine why the video caused the growth spurt. Chances are good that you did something different or found a topic of particular interest to your subscribers. If, on the other hand, you notice a decline in new subscribers or a decrease in subscribers after posting a video, figure out what you did wrong and refrain from posting similar videos.
- **Number of people viewing individual videos:** You can find this information by visiting your home page. On Vimeo, you can see the number of plays for each video by clicking My Videos in the top navigation. To view metrics on a specific video, on your YouTube channel, scroll down to the list of videos on your Analytics page and click on the video you want. You can toggle between Top 10 Videos and Browse All Content.

Understanding Podcast Metrics

Like with blogs, you need to watch several primary statistics on your podcasts:

- **The number of people listening to your live podcast:** This tells you the effectiveness of your marketing efforts. When you have a lot of visitors, you've created informative media that's in demand.
- **The number of unique page views for your podcast:** You can figure out which posts are being received well. Use this information for planning future episodes of your podcast.

» **The number of people who subscribe to follow your podcast:** This measure of engagement indicates whether your content is helping you develop a loyal following of listeners.

» **The number of people who rate your podcast highly or refer it to others or both:** High ratings and referrals indicate that others are helping share your message.

TIP

Include a social media share button (see Book 2, Chapter 4) whenever possible to encourage your readers, viewers, and listeners to post the link to your material on their own social media pages.

When you make your podcast available from the iTunes store (whether for free or for a fee), you're out there with the heavy hitters — and have access to additional analytical information. You have no way, at least for now, to find out how many iTunes users subscribe to your podcast, but you can find out the popularity of your podcast by following these steps:

1. **In the address bar, enter** `www.apple.com/itunes/podcasts/` **to launch your iTunes desktop, or launch the iTunes desktop app directly.**
2. **Click the link for the iTunes Store, and scroll to the bottom of the page.**
3. **Click Podcasts.**
4. **Enter a keyword that's associated with your podcast in the Search text box in the top-right corner of your iTunes window, and then click Search (magnifying glass icon).**

   Because this function searches the entire iTunes Store, add the word *podcast* to your keyword. For example, if you've created a photography podcast, *photography* might be the keyword, and the complete search term would be *photography podcast.*

   The most popular podcasts appear in a table, which includes a Popularity column. The small, individual bar graphs in this column show the relative popularity for each podcast.
5. **Analyze the resulting list to see where your podcast appears.**

   If your podcast doesn't appear in the list, click the See All button at the top right of the table. When you find your podcast on the resulting screen, click it.

TIP

You can also sort podcast episodes by podcast name, episode name, time duration, popularity, or price by clicking on the desired column title to re-sort the table. You're looking for popularity: When you see bars extending all the way across the Popularity column, you know that the episode is quite a popular one.

Take advantage of iTunes to rank the relative popularity of multiple podcast episodes. This information is useful in planning future episodes. To rank podcasts by popularity, follow these steps after you enter the iTunes Store and select Podcasts from the More pop-up menu:

1. **In the Search text box in the top-right corner of the iTunes window, enter the name of your podcast.**

   Your podcast thumbnail appears.

2. **Click your podcast thumbnail.**

   A new page appears, displaying information about your show. The Details tab displays a table listing all your episodes, as shown in Figure 2-3.

3. **Click the tab for Ratings and Reviews in the top navigation.**

   You can see your star rating and read reviews left by listeners for individual episodes. You can also see your overall star rating in the left pane of your podcast page. (Refer to Figure 2-3.)

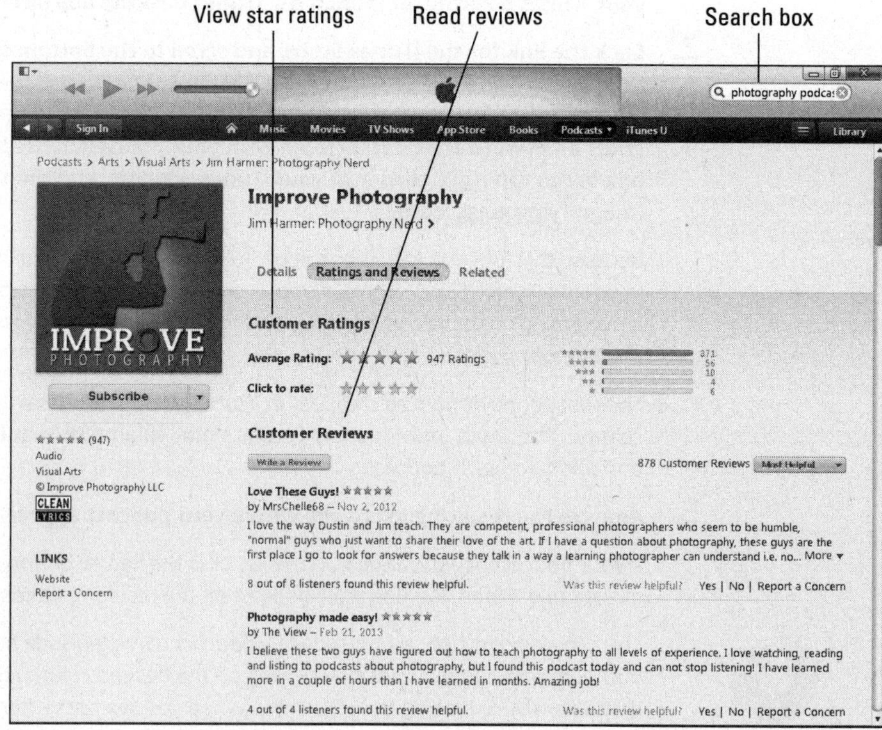

FIGURE 2-3: Podcast statistics from iTunes display the ratings and reviews for podcast episodes.

Measuring Your Results from Pinterest

When it first launched, Pinterest offered only the briefest of statistics on the number of boards, pins, likes, followers, and following, running across the page horizontally below your header image, as shown in Figure 2-4.

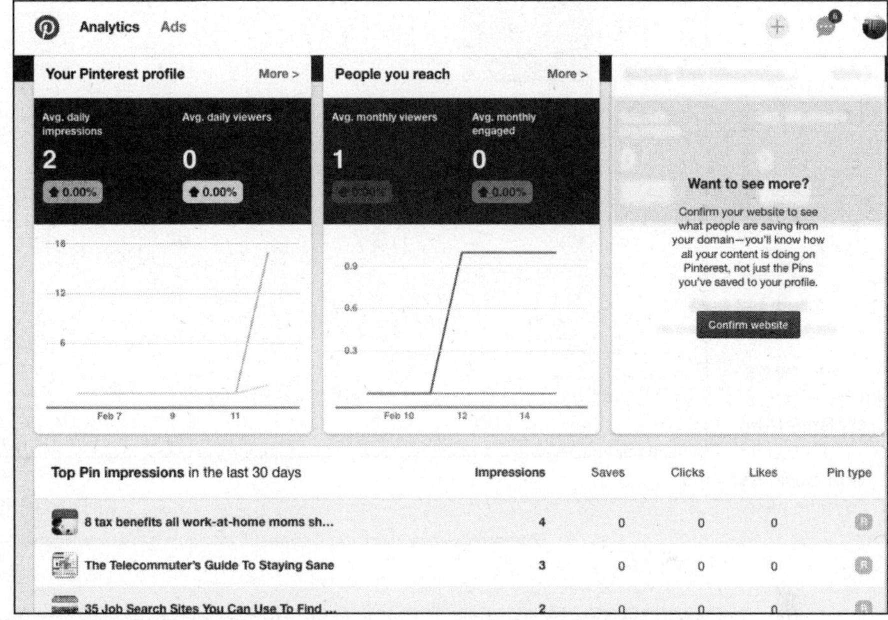

FIGURE 2-4: Basic statistics on pins and followers are visible to everyone who visits your Pinterest site.

TIP

All viewers, including your competitors, can see these statistics. Of course, you can see the basic statistics showing how your competitors perform on Pinterest, too.

Now Pinterest offers useful, private analytics that show how users interact with your pins, your profile, and your website. You can also use Pinterest Analytics to find out more about the demographics of your audience.

To access Pinterest Analytics, you must first create a business account, as described in Book 7. From your business account, go to your Profile page, click Settings (gear icon), and then select Analytics from the pop-up menu that appears, as shown in Figure 2-5.

REMEMBER

You can easily convert a personal account that you've been using for your business into a business account, as described in Book 7.

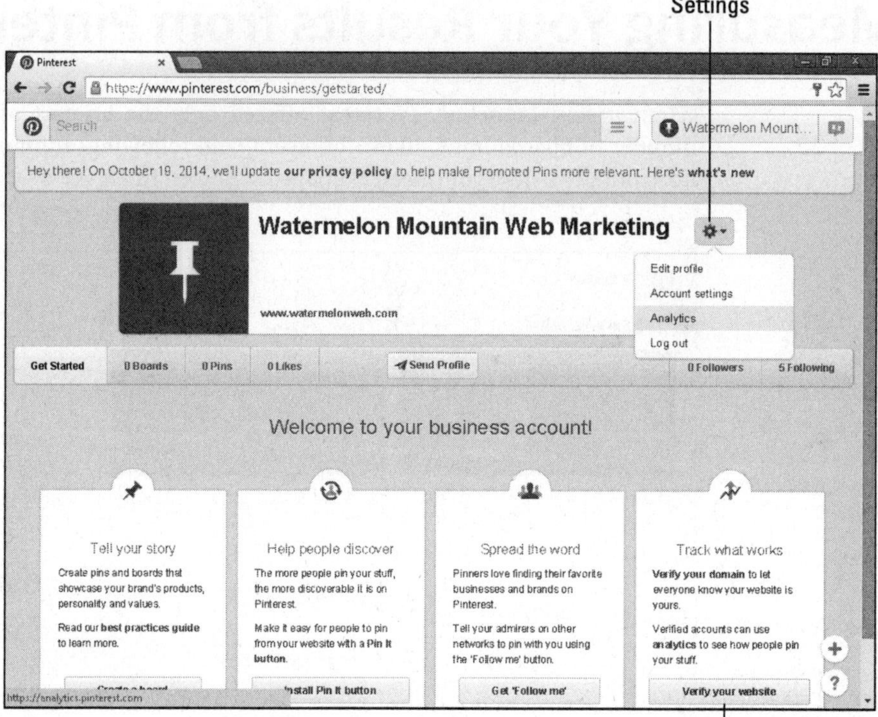

FIGURE 2-5: Access Pinterest Analytics from the menu bar on your business Profile page.

Reproduced with permission of Watermelon Mountain Web Marketing, `www.watermelonweb.com`

After you're in Analytics, the screen shown in Figure 2-6 appears, displaying a running summary of activity for the past 30 days, including impressions, clicks, repins, likes, and pin type (this data appears below the graphs).

For additional detail in each category, select a tab from the top navigation for Your Pinterest Profile, Your Audience, or Activity from *Your Website.*

For more information, see `https://business.pinterest.com/blog/how-use-pinterest-analytics-change-way-you-pin` and `https://help.pinterest.com/articles/pinterest-analytics`.

Discovering details about your Pinterest profile

After you log in and reach the Analytics page of your Pinterest profile (`https://analytics.pinterest.com`), select the Your Pinterest Profile tab at the top of the page. Profile information is divided into four sections: Impressions, Saves, Clicks, and Likes.

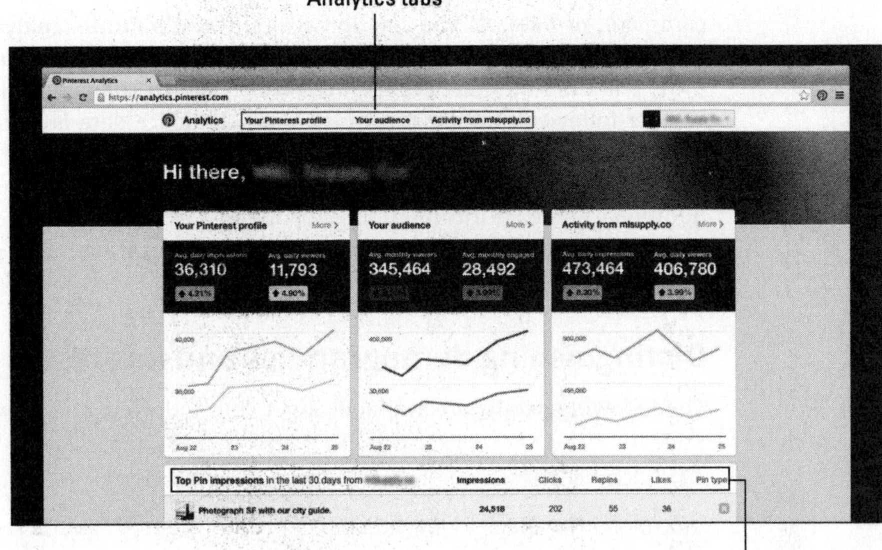

FIGURE 2-6: Pinterest's analytics provide valuable information about users and how they interact with your pins and profile.

Source: `https://help.pinterest.com/sites/help/files/help-center-analytics-1dashboard.jpg`

You can filter data by time frame using the date range settings. Or you can choose to filter by device (for example, mobile versus website) with the All Apps option. If you want to conduct further analysis offline, export these average daily metrics to a CSV file with the Export Data button.

REMEMBER

Perhaps the most important measure is the number of repins, because that shows which images are shared by others — their viral quality. The more others share your pins, the greater your reach. The top repinned pins are available in the detail section.

For more information about profile analytics, visit `https://help.pinterest.com/en/articles/your-pinterest-profile-analytics`.

Finding out about your Pinterest audience

As with all marketing, it's helpful to understand the demographics of your audience and to compare the demographics of Pinterest users to those of your desired target market and also to users on your other social media channels. After you log in and reach the Analytics page (`https://analytics.pinterest.com`), select the People You Reach tab at the top of the page.

The People You Reach tab offers self-provided details about your followers and viewers, and those who interacted with your content (for example, with a repin, comment, or like). As you can do with Pinterest's Profile analytics (see the preceding section), you can filter data by device or by date range to view trends over time. Use the All Audiences menu to filter data to show only the characteristics of your followers. Unlike the Profile data, audience data is aggregated monthly, not daily.

Additional audience information is further divided into two sections: Demographics and Interests. You can take advantage of this information to guide your selection and organization of future pins and boards.

Distinguishing demographics and interests

The following details are available about your followers and viewers:

- Monthly average number of the unique impressions for your pins
- Monthly average for the number of people who repinned, clicked, liked, or otherwise engaged with your pins
- Demographic information about country, language, metropolitan area, and gender is compiled based on information entered by Pinterest users in their own settings

Interpreting interests

The Interests view provides insight into three aspects of followers' activity:

- **Interests:** What subject areas your followers are exploring
- **Boards:** A visual collection of boards that contain your pins; shows how your audience organizes your material and assesses your brand
- **Businesses:** Other business accounts that your audience follows

For additional information on audience analytics, visit `https://help.pinterest.com/en/articles/your-audience-analytics`.

Analyzing interactions between your website and Pinterest

You can use the Activity from *Your Website* tab to discover which content receives a like and which content people click to visit your primary website. In this section, you can find daily averages for the number of impressions, repins, and clicks for those pins that link to your site, and track how people have used any Pin It buttons you placed on your website. To see this option, you must first verify your site, as we describe in this section.

Verifying your site

To get Pinterest analytics for website interactions, you must first confirm your domain ownership by following these steps:

1. **Click Analytics at the top right of the page.**

   On the analytics page, you'll see a box to the left asking you to confirm the website.

2. **Click the Confirm Your Website button.**

   The Confirm Your Website pop-up window appears (as shown in Figure 2-7).

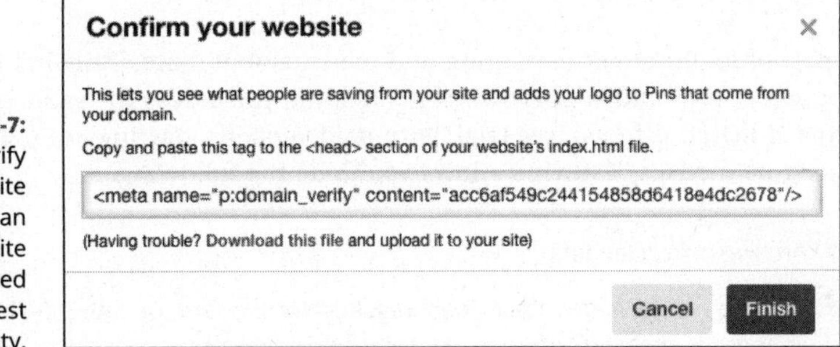

FIGURE 2-7: You need to verify your website before you can view website analytics related to Pinterest activity.

3. **Copy and then paste the tag into the <head> tag on the index page of your site.**

   You may need to ask your programmer to assist.

4. **Click the Complete Verification button in the pop-up window to finish the process.**

   The Activity from *Your Website* graph should now appear on your Analytics Summary page. If it doesn't appear, click the Refresh button on your browser.

Analyzing website interaction

After you've verified your site, it's easy to view the data for website interaction. Log in, access the Pinterest Analytics page (`https://analytics.pinterest.com`), and select the Activity from *Your Website* tab at the top of the page.

As with other Pinterest analytics, you can select the desired time frame for analysis by using date range setting.

For more information, see `https://help.pinterest.com/en/articles/activity-your-website`.

REMEMBER

Look at referrers to your primary website in Google Analytics to compare how much traffic to your site comes from Pinterest or other image-sharing sites versus traffic that arrives from websites, other social media, advertising, or search engines.

Third-party Pinterest analytics

In addition to the comparative data you find in the Social section of Google Analytics, you can obtain Pinterest information from Tailwind (`www.tailwindapp.com/features`), a third-party provider of Pinterest tools.

As part of its Pinterest marketing and management suite, Tailwind measures the progress of pins and boards over time, helping you assess the value of Pinterest in terms of ROI. It offers a free trial, with paid versions starting at $9.99 per month. Among its metrics, Tailwind allows you to do the following:

- Archive historical data.
- Analyze pin performance by hashtag, keyword, board, or category, including changes in the performance of specific pins over time.
- Compare the viral value and engagement levels of your Pinterest content against that of your competition.
- Integrate with Google Analytics.
- Analyze revenue and site traffic generated from Pinterest.

Comparing Hard and Soft Costs versus Income

Smart business people don't spin their wheels. If something doesn't gain traction, they do something else. After analyzing the number of visitors that your content-sharing effort receives, consider your ROI to see whether the effort is really worthwhile. (For more on ROI, see Book 1, Chapter 2.)

Unless you're selling your content, this is a subtle number to figure out. You need to derive sales results indirectly.

Remember to consider two types of costs in your evaluation:

- **Hard:** The number of man-hours needed to create content for your podcast, blog, photos, or videos. Also, the cost to host any media online, which would be web hosting fees and any fees you pay to a designer to get your media online. If you're paying for premium video hosting such as Vimeo Plus, factor in this cost, as well.
- **Soft:** The amount of time you personally spend creating content. Did that time take you away from any other profitable activities, such as hobnobbing with the rich and famous, or other potential clients?

TIP

Include a question at your online checkout that asks buyers which forms of social media they use. If you aren't using a social media network that attracts your customers, you may want to modify your social media efforts to see whether you can increase your business.

IN THIS CHAPTER

- » Checking inbound website referrers and followers
- » Using Twitter's own analytics programs
- » Following your Twitter metrics with third-party options
- » Keeping tabs on your Twitter presence
- » Getting the right follower-to-following numbers

Chapter 3
Analyzing Twitter Metrics

After your Twitter marketing campaign has been rolling for a while, you need to check out both your performance metrics and the return on your time investment. You can do this in many ways:

- » By using an analytics program such as Google Analytics
- » By using Twitter Analytics (https://analytics.twitter.com/about)
- » By using a Twitter analytics tool such as Hootsuite or TweetDeck
- » By looking at the information on your Twitter page

We discuss all these methods in this chapter.

Tracking Website Referrals with Google Analytics

If you already utilize Google Analytics (as discussed in Chapter 1 of this minibook), you can easily track the number of referrals from Twitter to your website or blog. This information is useful if one of your marketing goals is to drive more traffic to your website by way of Twitter.

TECHNICAL STUFF

If you use Twitter's Web Intents JavaScript Events (`https://dev.twitter.com/web/javascript/events`) to measure user interaction, you can track far more than referrals, including the number of tweets and follows generated from your website. For more information on tracking and integration with Google Analytics, see `https://developers.google.com/analytics/devguides/collection/gajs/gaTrackingSocial#twitter` and `www.optimizesmart.com/social-interactions-tracking-through-google-analytics`.

To most easily see how much traffic comes to your website from Twitter, use Google Social Analytics (see Chapter 1 of this minibook). Simply log in to your Analytics account and click Acquisition in the left navigation. Choose Social ⇨ Network Referrals. Your Twitter numbers appear as part of Social Referrals, as shown in Figure 3-1.

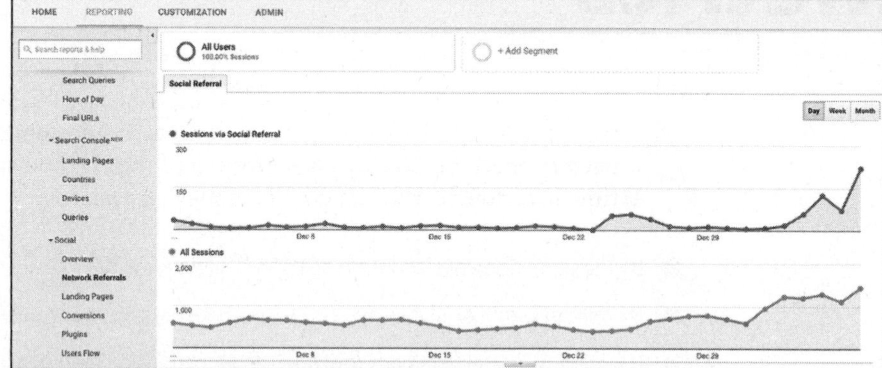

FIGURE 3-1: Referrers from social media are accessible through Google Analytics' Social feature.

Tracking Shortened Links

You can easily track shortened links from Twitter back to your website if you use Bitly or bit.do to shorten your URLs (as we discuss in Chapter 1 of this minibook and Book 2, Chapter 1). With Bitly, simply add a plus sign (+) to the end of the URL to track the source of links to your site. With bit.do, add a minus sign (–) to the URL to obtain free statistics in real-time.

WARNING

Twitter's own link-shortening service, found at `http://t.co` for logged-in users, works only on links posted on Twitter.com. Because it was set up primarily to avoid spamming, it doesn't work as a general shortening service for other sites or apps.

Using Twitter Analytics

Twitter now offers its own analytics program with three distinct dashboards (`https://analytics.twitter.com/about`). Twitter Analytics offers more than merely statistics on tweet activity, engagement, and followers. By paying attention to these statistics, you can learn how to make your tweets more successful, while discovering essential marketing information about your followers, such as demographics, geographic location, and interest areas. Take advantage of each of these dashboards:

- **Twitter Activity dashboard:** This overview dashboard displays how your tweets perform in real-time, as shown in Figure 3-2. You can compare month-over-month results for impressions, retweets, and engagement levels. Clicking an individual tweet displays a details page with additional information about engagement for that tweet: retweets, replies, favorites, follows, link clicks, and embedded media clicks. For additional information, see `https://support.twitter.com/articles/320043-tweet-activity-dashboard`.
- **Audience dashboard:** Discover more about your followers' gender, location, interests, age, and other details. You can choose to display your growth in followers over time, as shown in Figure 3-3.
- **Twitter Cards dashboard:** Unlike the other dashboards, this one is also a management tool. It allows you to incorporate rich media into your tweets, and then provides information about how the media has been shared. By paying attention to your results, you can learn how to improve such metrics as app installs, clicks, and retweets. Figures 3-4 and 3-5 show examples of Twitter Cards dashboard displays.

TECHNICAL STUFF

Implementing Twitter Cards is a multistep process. Ask your programmer to follow the directions at `https://dev.twitter.com/cards` and then request approval at `https://cards-dev.twitter.com/validator`. Alternatively, your programmer could add the following metatag to your web pages:

```
<meta name="twitter:site" content="@yourusername">
```

In both cases, Twitter Cards analytics will become available 24 hours after you tweet links to your content.

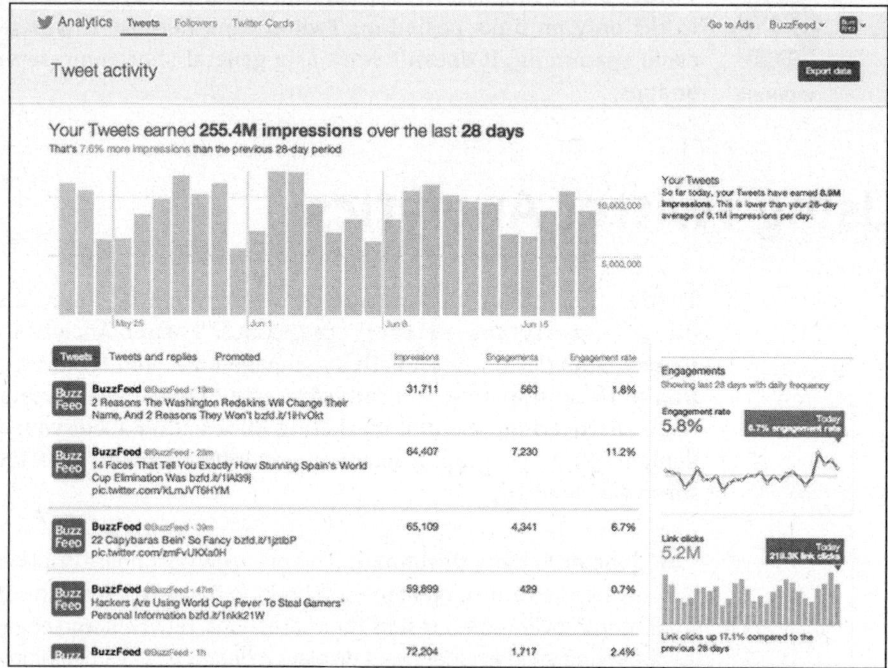

FIGURE 3-2: The basic Twitter Analytics Content dashboard displays tweet activity.

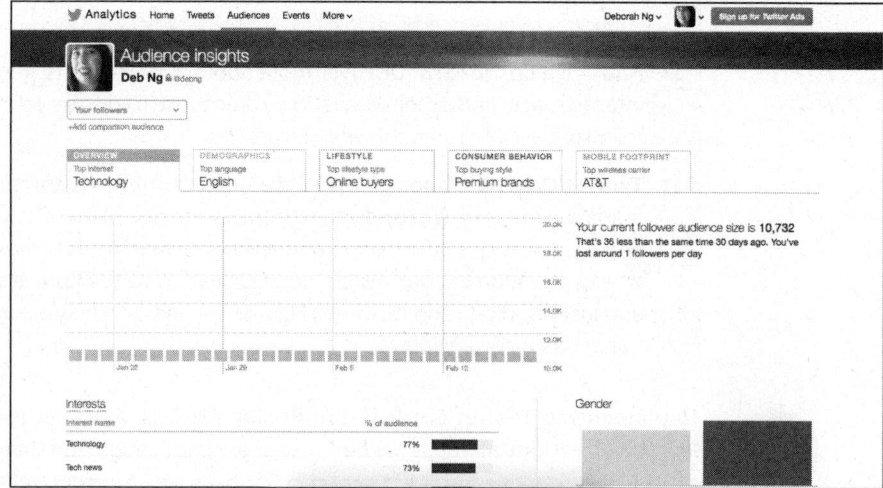

FIGURE 3-3: The Twitter Followers dashboard tracks the growth of followers over time.

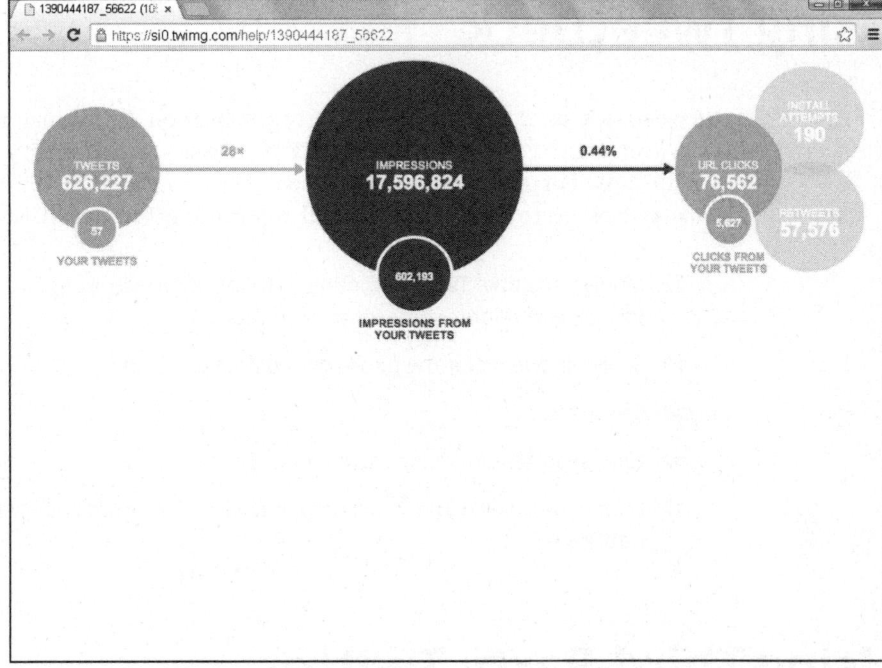

FIGURE 3-4: The Snapshot portion of the Twitter Cards dashboard is a graphic display of how your Twitter content is performing.

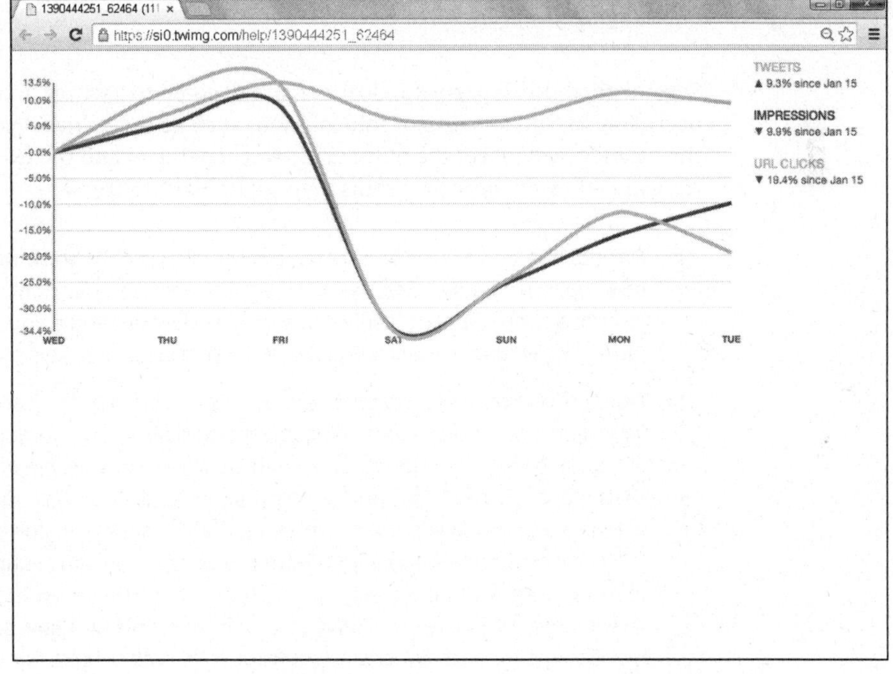

FIGURE 3-5: The Time portion of the Twitter Cards dashboard displays how tweets, impressions, and URL clicks vary over time.

Using TweetDeck

TweetDeck used to be a third-party application for managing and analyzing Twitter activity. Twitter modified TweetDeck's functionality after purchasing it in 2011. For more information, see `https://about.twitter.com/products/tweetdeck`. Here are the most useful applications for TweetDeck:

- » Monitor multiple Twitter accounts with one interface, including tweeting and following from one, some, or all accounts.
- » Schedule tweets for the future on multiple accounts.
- » Set up alerts.
- » Filter searches on multiple accounts.
- » Create multiple custom timelines from various accounts to insert on your website(s).

Using Third-Party Twitter Analytics Applications

Several good third-party applications are devoted to Twitter analytics. Enter your username to find all sorts of information, such as the subjects you tweeted about, the hashtags you used, the number of tweets per day, and the extent of your reach. Here are a few analytic programs you might want to try:

- » **TweetStats** (`http://tweetstats.com`) creates graphs showing what you've been up to on Twitter. See the number of tweets sent per hour, day, or month; a tweet timeline; reply statistics; a review of people you retweet; and more. TweetStats, a free tool, provides helpful visual displays by time frame.
- » **TwitterCounter** (`http://twittercounter.com`) claims to track more than 94 million Twitter users, providing information about the number of followers of your account, the number of accounts you're following, tweets, top 100 Twitter users, worldwide rank of your Twitter feed, and much more. As shown in Figure 3-6, it's excellent for comparing metrics such as followers versus following, which don't appear in Twitter Analytics. You can set up your account to receive regular updates and notifications or use their new browser-based Tweet Stats plug-in, which allows you to receive stats, grading, and recommendations for each tweet straight from your Twitter feed. For more information on the Tweet Stats plug-in, see `http://twittercounter.com/pages/plugin`.

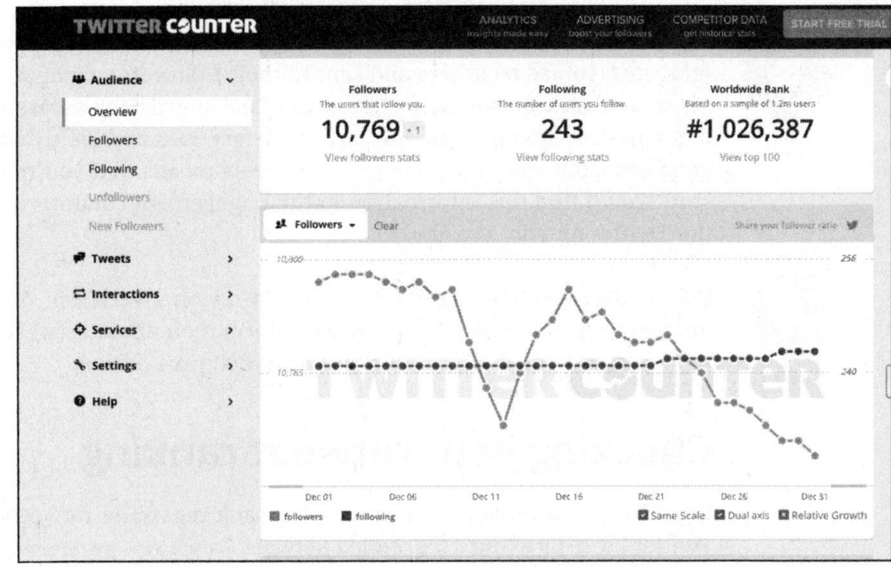

FIGURE 3-6: Analytic programs such as TwitterCounter can help you understand the value of Twitter.

TIP

You can find more Twitter tools at www.razorsocial.com/free-twitter-analytics/.

Tracking Account Activity with the Notifications Tab

Your Twitter account's Notifications tab provides a running review of retweets and favorites. To view this tab, log in to your Twitter account. Notifications and Mentions both appear at the top of the left column, as shown in Figure 3-7. Clicking Notifications displays that information in the right column.

FIGURE 3-7: You can monitor retweets, favorites, mentions, and replies from the Notifications tab.

TIP

One of the most important things to track is the number of messages that are *retweeted* (copied by others and sent to their followers), compared to all the messages you've sent yourself. That's the best metric for assessing whether your messages are going viral. No hard-and-fast rule applies to what constitutes a good ratio, but a high percentage of retweets means that you're sending the right stuff. You'll find this information in the Engagement columns on the right side of the Twitter Activity Dashboard.

TIP

Use Twitter Analytics (refer to Figure 3-2) or TweetDeck or another Twitter management tool to find aggregated information about retweets, mentions, and replies in statistical format during a specified time period.

Checking your retweet ranking

If you're adventurous, you can see your rank regarding retweets compared to all Twitter users by using a tool called Retweet Rank (`www.retweetrank.com`). Knowing how many people retweet shows the popularity of your tweets, as well as your reach and influence. The more retweets, the better.

Enter your username in the Twitter Username text box and click Go to see the results. If you log in with your Twitter handle, you can also see a variety of recent Twitter stats on a weekly dashboard. For longer-term records, you need the paid version of Retweet Rank. The paid version also helps you see exactly which tweets strike a chord with your followers and which followers retweet most often.

Monitoring the Mentions tab

The Mentions tab filters out the stream to display only replies and mentions. You access the Mentions tab just as you do the Notifications tab described previously. Any tweet that's created as an @reply to one of your posts will appear in the Mentions stream with @username at the beginning of the tweet.

REMEMBER

When you start a tweet with *@username,* that tweet's reach is limited to only your own and the addressee's followers. To reach a broader audience, use something other than the at symbol (@) as the first character. This can be as simple as the word Hi, a single character of punctuation, or any other short character string that you want.

By comparison, a *mention* is defined as a tweet that includes *@username* anywhere in the body of the tweet (refer to Figure 3-7).

TIP

To see other users' mentions (perhaps a competitor's), search for all tweets mentioning their *@username* in the Search text box.

Gleaning meaning from direct messages

Hmmm. We know what you're thinking: Why would you want to analyze your direct messages? After all, you know to whom you send direct messages — but which of your followers sent direct messages to you, and what was the subject matter of those messages? The answer to this two-part question tells you which followers are engaging you as a source of information and tells you the type of information they're requesting. If the same topic shows up in several direct messages, you can tweet about it and write blog posts about it.

To review your direct messages, click the envelope icon to the left of the search bar in the top navigation (refer to Figure 3-7). Note which subjects prompted direct messages and expand on those subjects in future tweets. Whenever you receive a direct message regarding one of your tweets, it's a good sign that the topic is worthy of further embellishment.

Using the Hashtag as a Measurement Mechanism

As we discuss in Book 4, when people want to make sure the word they're searching for is the main subject of the post and not just randomly added, they use the hashtag symbol (#).

The use of hashtags with your Twitter username is another way to measure your popularity on Twitter. If a lot of people, including those who don't follow you, take the time to precede your username with a hashtag, you're being directly referenced in a Twitter post. You can easily find out whether your username or brand is hashtagged.

Go to `https://twitter.com/search-home` and enter #*yourusername* (where *yourusername* is your actual username) in the Search field. The Twitter search engine returns a list of tweets with your username preceded by the hashtag. In the results, you'll probably see some other usernames you recognize and some you don't for people who have hashtagged you in their tweets. You may also see some bad press. Monitoring hashtags is a wonderful way of finding out who's talking about you and what they're saying. You may also find some people you want to follow.

TIP

FollowFriday, or #FF, is a Twitter hashtag tradition. Users incorporate this hashtag in their Friday tweets to give someone a shout-out by recommending a company or an individual that others might want to follow. Fridays are a good day to check the use of your name or brand as a hashtag.

Calculating the Twitter Follower-to-Following Ratio

The Twitter follower-to-following (TFF) ratio is calculated by dividing the number of followers of your username by the number of people you follow. This valuable information is public for any Twitter user who stops by your piece of the Twitterverse. If you're following a lot of people and not many people are following you, it may look like you're simply trying to sell something, especially if almost all your tweets are about your own company, brand, or products.

There's no official number for TFF, but as a rule of thumb, your marketing goal is to have at least one and a half times the number of followers as the number of people you follow. Strive for a ratio of two or three! This ratio should provide a good balance for generating, receiving, and sharing content.

REMEMBER

Include linkable calls-to-action on your website and other social media to remind visitors to follow you on Twitter.

IN THIS CHAPTER

» Keeping tabs on users with Facebook Insights

» Using Facebook Insights to improve content

» Downloading Insights data

» Understanding the Insights Overview dashboard

» Diving into Insights detail pages

Chapter 4 Analyzing Facebook Metrics

You've created a spiffy Facebook page, added a couple of bells and whistles, posted regularly to your timeline, responded to comments, and recruited likes. One of your goals was probably to drive more traffic to your website. But how do you calculate the fruits of your efforts?

In this chapter, we show you some ways to measure the effectiveness of your Facebook presence using Facebook's own analytics package, called Insights. For more information on Facebook for marketing, see Book 5.

Monitoring Facebook Interaction with Insights

Facebook offers the following forms of analytics, which it calls Insights:

- **Page insights:** Shows performance of your Facebook page, including engagement, reach, and demographics

» **App insights:** Displays performance for your web and mobile applications

» **App events:** Shows actions taken by app users; also profiles those app users so that you can improve the targeting of your custom audiences and increase reach.

In this chapter, we discuss only page insights because those analytics are critical to all Facebook marketers.

For additional analytical information, see `www.facebook.com/insights` or *Facebook Marketing All-in-One For Dummies*, 3rd Edition, by Andrea Vahl, John Haydon, and Jan Zimmerman (Wiley).

Using Page Insights

If you're looking for standard measurements for regular timeline posts, the recently expanded page insights feature provides valuable, free, content-focused metrics.

WARNING

Your Facebook page must have 30 likes before you can access page insights.

By analyzing user growth, demographics, and engagement with content, you can better focus on content that helps you hold onto people in your audience, and encourage them to share your material with their friends.

REMEMBER

Gathering data for data's sake doesn't make sense. You need to take advantage of the data to modify your content stream. The principle is the same as with all marketing: If it works, keep doing it; if it doesn't work, stop.

Accessing Insights

As usual, Facebook provides multiple — and sometimes confusing — ways to accomplish a task.

First, log in as administrator; then follow one of these three methods to access Insights for a particular page (see Figure 4-1 for the Insights Dashboard Overview page that appears):

» In the left navigation, select the page you want to review (in the Pages section). When that page opens, click Insights in the row of navigation above the cover photo.

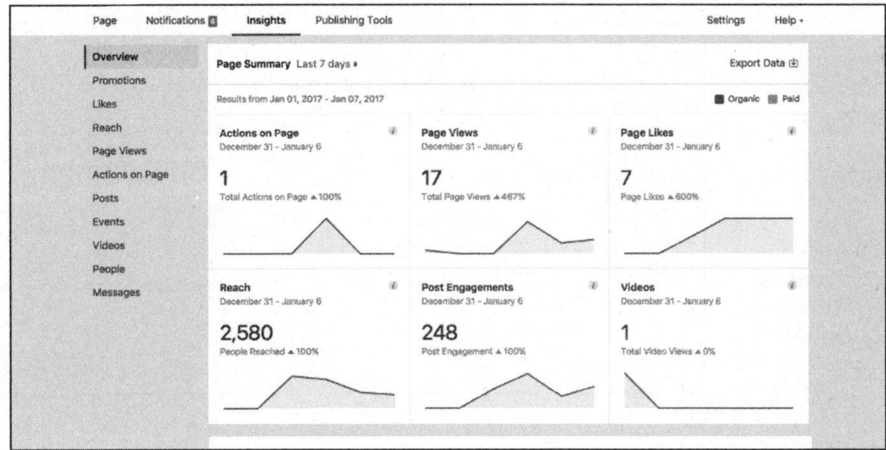

FIGURE 4-1: The Insights Dashboard Overview page provides basic traffic and user information.

- Type `www.facebook.com/insights` in the address bar of your browser. In the Page Insights section, click the thumbnail for the page that has the insights you want to see.
- Click the ellipsis button (. . .) below your page's cover photo and choose View Insights from the pop-up menu that appears.

REMEMBER

Facebook sometimes uses the word *fans* in page insights and elsewhere as a synonym for people who like your page.

Exporting Insights

To download the data in Insights, click the Export tab in the top-right corner of the dashboard, as shown in Figure 4-2. (This may not work with all browsers.) You can specify the following:

- The date range for which you want to get data
- Whether you want data in Excel or CSV (comma-separated values) format
- Whether you want to see data at the page level or for each post or video

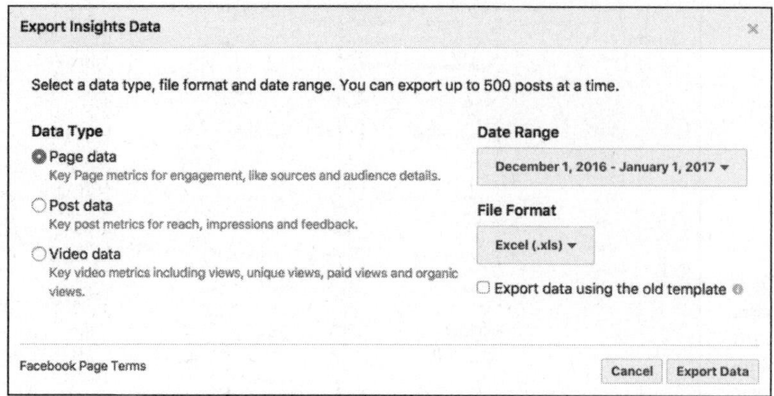

FIGURE 4-2: The pop-up window for exporting Insights.

Exploring the Insights Overview and Detail Pages

You can find the following insights on the Insights Overview dashboard at the Page level (refer to Figure 4-1):

- **Page likes:** Shows both the total number of different people who have liked your page over all time and the number of new likes for the past week.
- **Post reach:** Displays the total number of different people who have viewed any of your content (including ads) during the past week and the week before, as well as the subtotal of just those who have viewed your page posts.
- **Engagement:** Indicates how many different people have taken some social action on your posts, broken down by likes, comments, shares, and post clicks during the past week.
- **Your five most recent posts:** Below the graphs, a table offers details for your five most-recent posts. The columns show the published date and time, the post, and the post's type, targeting, reach, and engagement.

TIP

Take advantage of competitor research! If you continue scrolling past the table of Your 5 Most Recent Posts, you see the Pages to Watch section (see Figure 4-3). This section compares your page and posts to other Pages on Facebook so that you can see how you match up against your competition. Click the Add Pages button to select other companies' Facebook pages to monitor. In the ensuing pop-up, enter the name of the company in the search field, labeled Search for a Page to Watch. From the list that appears, select the pages you want by clicking the button labeled +Watch page. Repeat the process until you finish adding Pages. Then click the Done button or close the window.

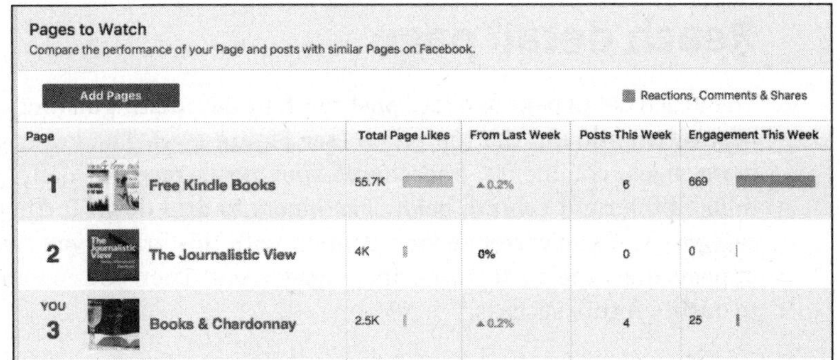

FIGURE 4-3: Take advantage of the Pages to Watch feature to keep tabs on your competitors' performance.

If you click the title of the graph (refer to Figure 4-1), additional information for each of these categories appears in a detail page. On each detail page, click the tabs in the second row of navigation to view the other detail pages, described in the following sections.

Likes detail page

The Likes detail page allows you to view likes by the day, instead of by the week, as well as net likes (likes minus unlikes), as shown in the lower graph in Figure 4-4. It also distinguishes paid likes from organic likes.

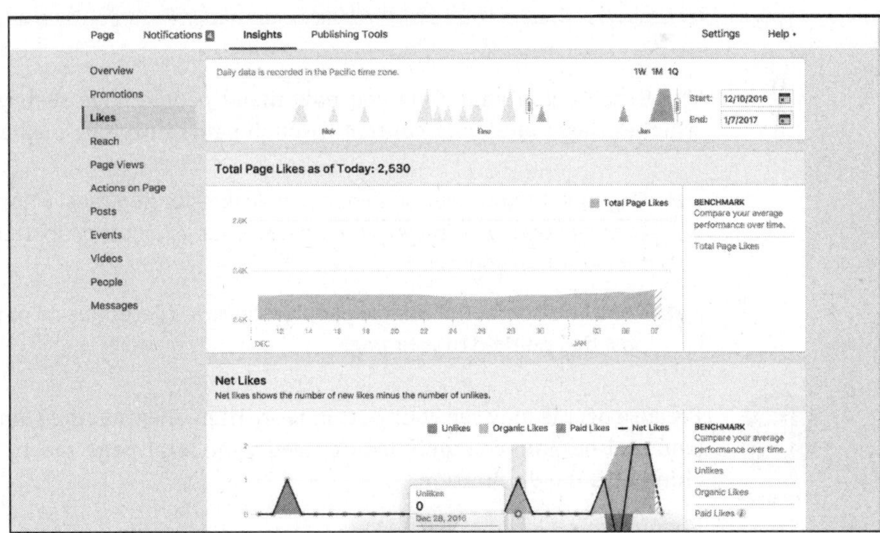

FIGURE 4-4: The detail page for likes.

TIP

For additional information about unlikes and how they decrease your reach, click the Unlikes link below the word *Benchmark* to the right of the graph.

Reach detail page

The Reach detail page displays post reach by day, distinguishing paid from organic post distribution in the top graph (see Figure 4-5). The lower graph shows how many likes, comments, and shares your posts received daily. Click the labeled links in the right column below *Benchmark* to drill down further in each of these categories. If you correlate your content with this graph, you can tell which types of posts draw the most traffic and engagement. Then you can create similar posts to ensure future success.

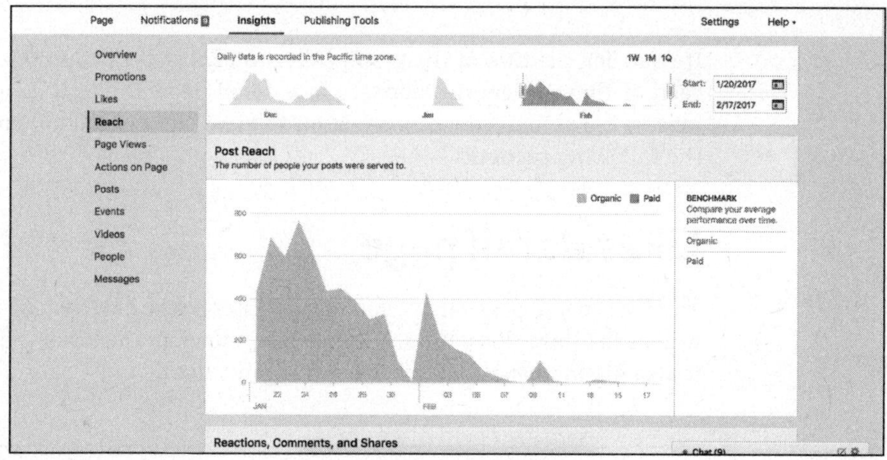

FIGURE 4-5: The Reach detail page.

The Reach detail page tells you how many people have seen your content, and whether they found your content through paid or organic means:

- **Organic:** The number of unique people (fans or non-fans) who saw any content about your page in their news feeds as a post or shared by their friends, or on your page.
- **Paid:** The number of unique people who saw a Facebook ad or promoted post that pointed to your page.

REMEMBER

Because people may see your post in more than one way, the sum of reach through paid and organic channels may exceed your total page reach. Total page reach eliminates the duplication.

TIP

Recent studies show that shorter posts (40 to 80 characters) increase engagement on Facebook. So, to keep your fans coming back for more, break a popular subject into several small tidbits, and use a URL shortener that also offers analytics, such as Bitly. For more on shortener analytics, see Chapter 1 of this minibook.

Page Views detail page

In the Page Views detail page, the graphs break down how many people view your page, as shown in Figure 4-6, and include demographic information.

For more information about how to take advantage of the Insight details pages, see `www.facebook.com/help/336893449723054`.

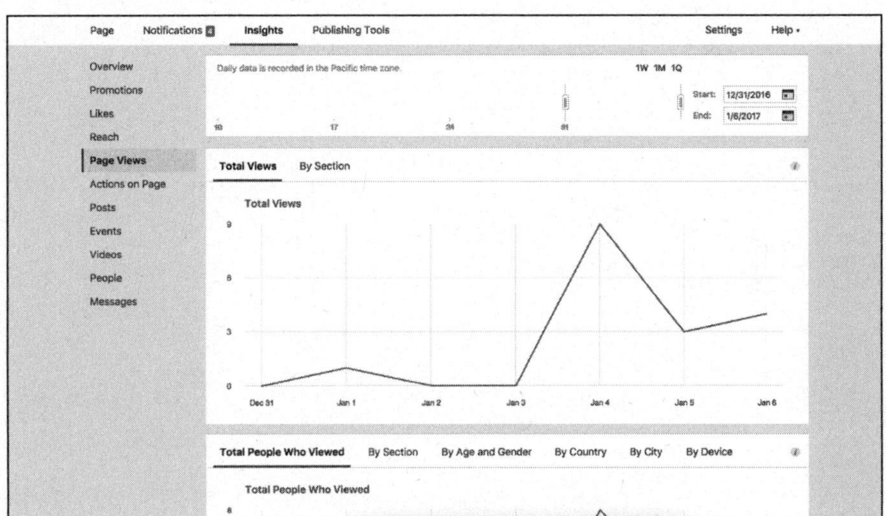

FIGURE 4-6: The Page View detail page.

Analyzing Facebook Metrics

IN THIS CHAPTER

- » Tracking social plug-in results
- » Measuring LinkedIn success
- » Mixing it all up with social mobile metrics

Chapter 5 Measuring Other Social Media Networks

At this point, social media performance metrics are probably dancing in your head, having replaced sugar plums as your objects of desire. The newer and less popular sites have fewer metric options, but they are important if you've selected any of them as part of your social marketing mix. Therefore, in this chapter, we look at performance measurements for social plug-ins such as share buttons and chiclets and the mobile versions of your social media pages.

Plugging into Social Media

The term *social plug-ins* refers to social media share buttons and other tools that allow your social media services to interact with your website and each other. In Google Analytics, you can find reports on the performance of plug-ins by going to Acquisition⇨Social⇨Plugins in the left navigation (see Figure 5-1).

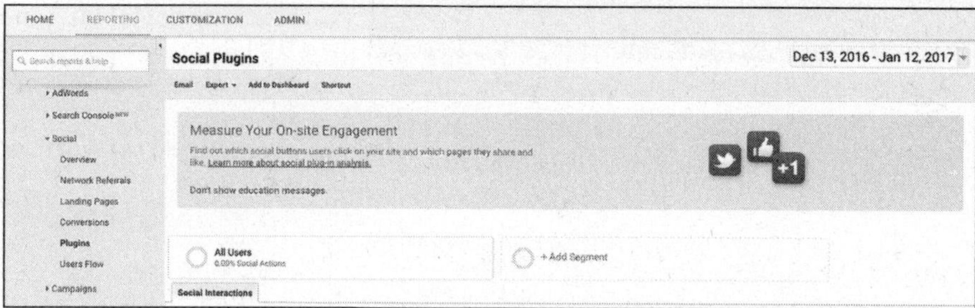

FIGURE 5-1: Social Plugins statistics show how your share buttons perform.

Select a Primary Dimension option below the graph to determine which statistical sorting method will be applied first to the analysis of your social media plug-ins. In the row below that, you can select one of the two remaining sorting methods as an optional secondary dimension from the drop-down list. The definitions for these choices follow:

- **Social Entity:** The default setting; the page URL that was shared
- **Social Network:** The social media channel on which the social action occurred (for example, Facebook or Pinterest)
- **Social Network and Action:** The social media channel and the action that occurred (for example, Facebook with a like, share, or comment)

In Figure 5-1, the primary dimension is Social Entity (the default choice), and the secondary dimension is Social Source and Action.

TIP

You can change the appearance of data in the report simply by clicking one of the four buttons to the right of the Secondary Dimension drop-down list (refer to Figure 5-1). For each primary dimension, you may select Table (grid icon), Percentage (pie chart icon), Performance (bar graph icon), or Comparison view (positive and negative bar graph icon).

Measuring LinkedIn Success

LinkedIn is a helpful place to meet professionals and extend your network. However, if you aren't getting referrals or if people aren't viewing your profile or asking you to connect to their networks, do some analysis to see what is happening.

One of your LinkedIn marketing goals is probably to drive more traffic to your website. As always, you can see how many people are coming to your site from LinkedIn by using Google's Social Analytics (see Chapter 1 of this minibook).

To see how the results for your B2B business translate into conversions, look at the Social Value report in Google Analytics (see Chapter 6 of this minibook), which you can find by scrolling down the Overview page. (Choose Acquisition⇨Social⇨Overview.)

To see LinkedIn performance metrics, log in to LinkedIn as an administrator. When you click the profile icon at the far right of the top navigation, a drop-down menu appears for Account & Settings. Click the row for your Company Page/Manage. On the next screen that appears, check out the following:

- **Home:** This tab shows the number of followers in the top right, along with directions for sharing an update and performance details on recent updates.
- **Analytics:** On this tab, you can see key performance metrics for updates, reach, visitors, and followers, described in the following sections. You can obtain additional detailed information in these categories, as shown in the three graphs described in the following sections.

Updates

The Updates section, shown in Figure 5-2, contains a table with your most recent updates. Each update displays the following:

- **Preview:** The first few words of each post.
- **Date:** The date each update was posted.
- **Audience:** Whether the post was sent to all followers or a targeted subset of followers.
- **Sponsored:** Whether an update was promoted.
- **Impressions:** The number of times each update was shown to LinkedIn members.
- **Clicks:** The total number of clicks on content, company name, or logo within the post (doesn't include engagement numbers, as described later in this list).
- **Interactions:** The number of times people liked, commented on, or shared an update.
- **Followers Acquired:** The number of followers gained from a specific sponsored update.
- **Engagement:** A measure uniquely defined by LinkedIn, this percentage is calculated by adding the number of interactions to the number of clicks and the number of followers acquired, and then dividing the result by the number of impressions.

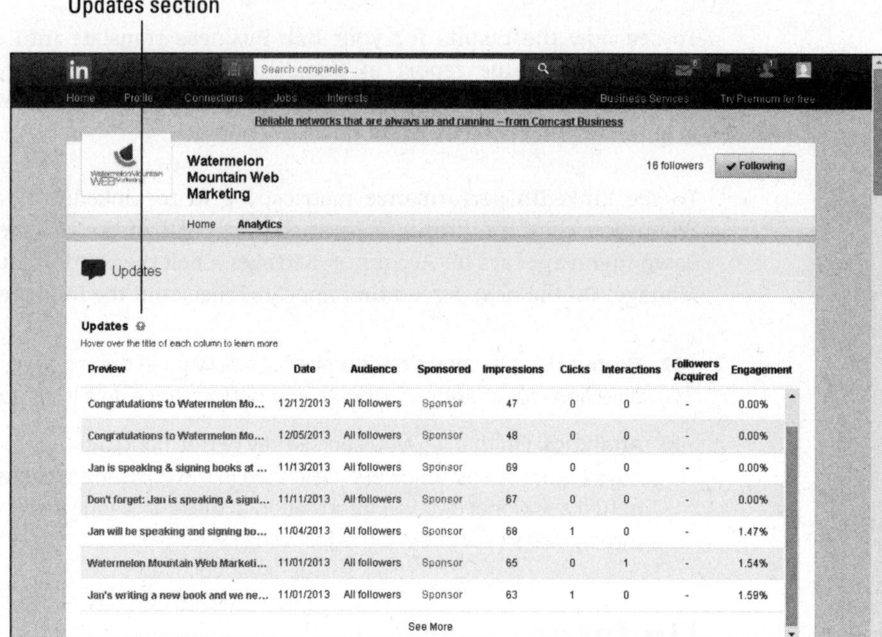

FIGURE 5-2: LinkedIn offers analytical detail for Updates.

Reach & Engagement

Reach & Engagement graphs, which appear below the Updates section of the Insights dashboard, display trends for Impressions and Engagement over time. In the top right of this section, select from nine time intervals, ranging from Today to Last 6 Months, as shown in Figure 5-3.

On the Reach graph on the left, you can toggle between Impressions (total number of times any update was viewed) for that time period, or Unique (number of unique LinkedIn viewers) for your updates. Numbers for both organic (unpaid) and sponsored (paid) updates are available.

On the Engagement graph on the right, you can rotate the display for the selected time frame to show Clicks, Likes, Comments, Shares, Followers Acquired, or Engagement Percent.

Followers

The Followers section, shown in Figure 5-4, is divided into four areas. It offers data on follower demographics, acquisition trends over time, and competitive comparison:

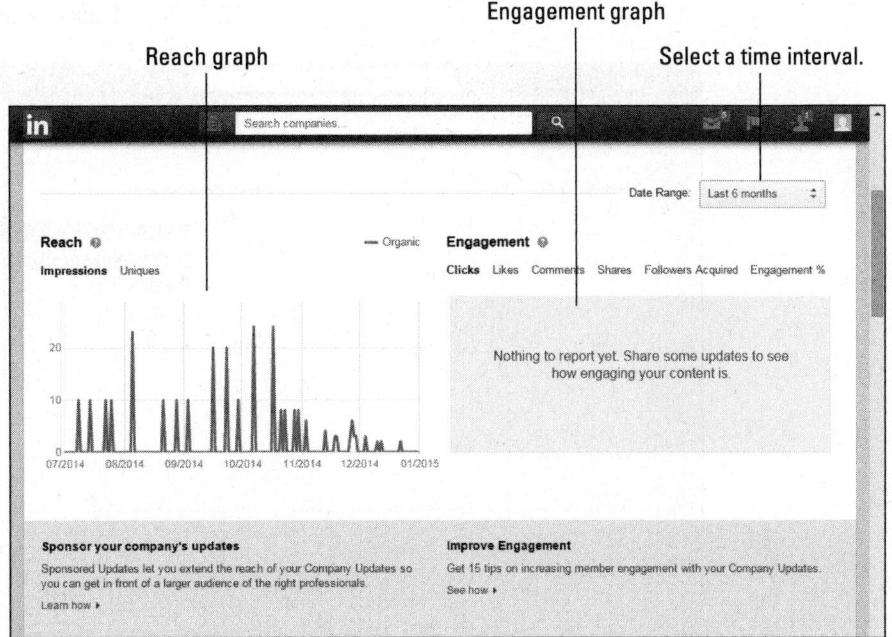

FIGURE 5-3: LinkedIn offers analytical detail for Reach & Engagement.

- **Total:** The number of LinkedIn members following your company page.

REMEMBER

  The number displayed here is updated only once a day, so it may differ from the number on the Home tab, which updates in real-time.

- **Follower Demographics:** A breakdown of your followers by seniority, industry, company size, job function, and employee/non-employee status. Select which detail appears by using the drop-down list in the upper-right corner of the graph.
- **Follower Trends:** Changes in your number of followers over time. Select the desired date range for this trend from the Date Range drop-down list.
- **How You Compare:** This list, not shown in Figure 5-4, compares your number of followers to the number of followers for similar businesses' company pages.

TIP

If you aren't attracting a lot of company page views, look at the first two sentences of your company page. Because people initially see only those lines, try to make them more compelling. You may find that the page description metatag you wrote for your website is just the ticket. (See Book 2, Chapter 2 for more on metatags.)

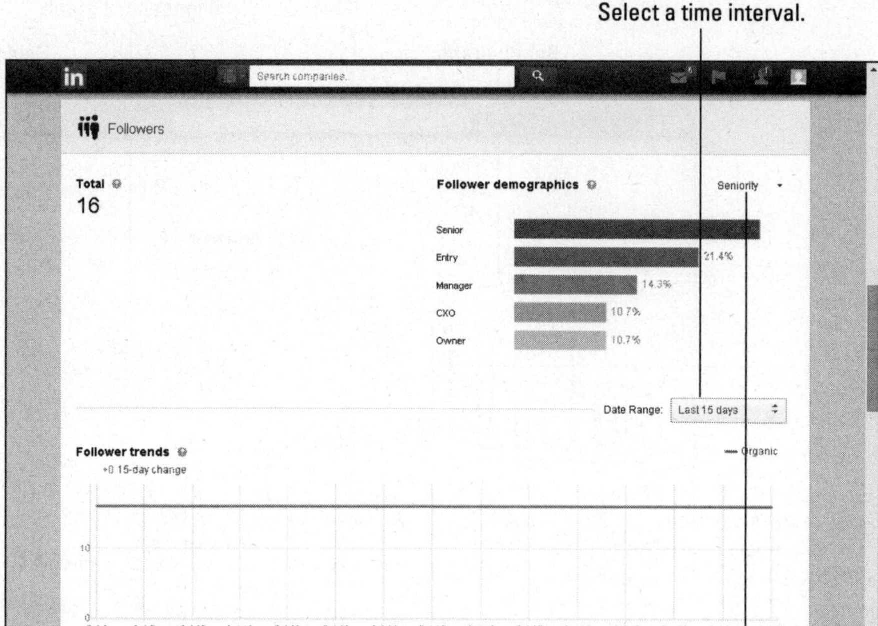

FIGURE 5-4: LinkedIn offers analytical detail for Followers.

Reproduced with permission of Watermelon Mountain Web Marketing, watermelonweb.com

Monitoring Social Mobile Impact

Mobile analytics is a bit different than web-based analytics. Because almost every social media service has a mobile application, as we discuss in Book 8, Chapter 5, it's helpful to compare the effectiveness of social media in mobile versus web-based environments.

You can most easily compare these platforms by segmenting social visitors. In Google Analytics, follow these steps:

1. **Choose Acquisition⇨Social⇨Network Referrals.**
2. **Select Source from the Secondary Dimension drop-down list below the line graph.**

   A list appears, like the one in Figure 5-5, displaying social source referral URLs that may or may not include an m. to identify it as a mobile address.

TIP

You might want to set up a separate conversion funnel for social mobile users so you can track mobile results independently.

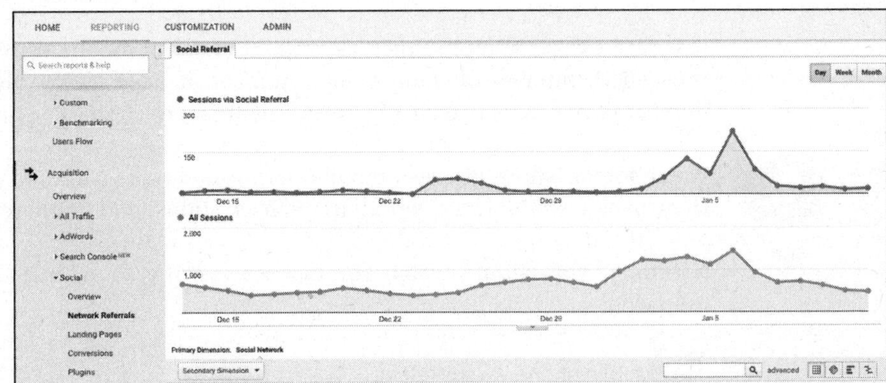

FIGURE 5-5: You can see which social mobile referrals came from mobile (m.) sites in Google Analytics.

TECHNICAL STUFF

Facebook uses the internal redirects l.facebook.com and lm.facebook.com to distinguish access via http versus https protocol. Subdomain identifier l.facebook corresponds to web-based Facebook access, and lm.facebook corresponds to mobile-based access.

Like with all analytics, which elements you decide to measure and compare depend on your goals and objectives. Are you measuring the success of your own mobile site, the use of your social media pages on mobile devices, the number of visitors from social mobile pages to your primary website, or the level of foot traffic to a brick-and-mortar store? You can see some of these statistics in Figure 5-6, in a report provided by Apsalar, a vendor of mobile analytics services.

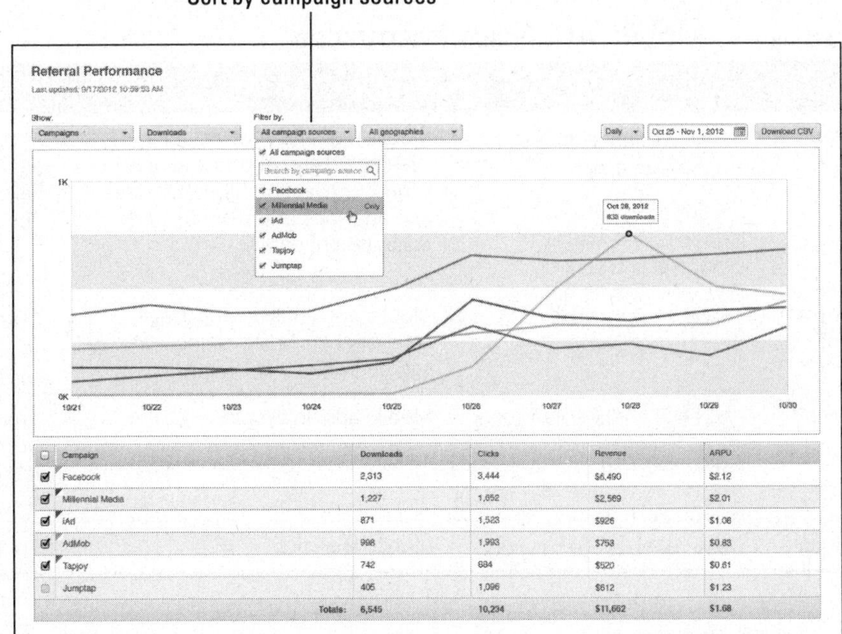

FIGURE 5-6: Apsalar provides helpful mobile-only statistics to assess performance of your mobile social pages and mobile ad campaigns.

Standard site parameters, such as amount of social mobile traffic, click-through rate (CTR), number of impressions, number of page views, visit duration, and number of new versus repeat visitors still apply, of course.

TIP

Watch for variations between mobile visitors and web visitors to your social media sites on conversion rates, newsletter subscriptions, and brand recall.

Naturally, you should watch for metrics specific to mobile use, such as the following:

- Mobile phone versus tablet.
- Use by operating system (iOS versus Android, primarily). You can see these details in Google Analytics by choosing Audience ⇨ Mobile ⇨ Devices. (This approach doesn't necessarily distinguish mobile social networks from other mobile users.)
- Mobile payment methods, codes, and coupons.
- Click-throughs from a social mobile site to your regular, tablet, or mobile site.
- Click-to-call rate versus clicks to your primary, mobile, or tablet-specific site.
- Behavioral differences between users of your social media pages on the web versus on a mobile platform.

Table 5-1 provides some third-party resources for mobile analytics.

TABLE 5-1 **Mobile Analytics Resources**

Name	URL	What You Can Find	Cost
Apsalar	Free version at `https://apsalar.com` Paid version at `https://apsalar.com/pricing-2`	Mobile app analytics including real-time daily cohorts and user-centric conversion funnels, cross-app analytics, and revenue and engagement data	Free for in-app versions; business levels start at $999/month
Flurry from Yahoo!	`www.flurry.com`	Mobile app analytics for usage, category benchmarks, and audience segmentation	Free
Mixpanel	`https://mixpanel.com`	Mobile app analytics	Free for small data sets; see `https://mixpanel.com/pricing`
Netbiscuits	`www.netbiscuits.com`	Mobile analytics	Free

IN THIS CHAPTER

- » Comparing metrics among social media
- » Integrating social media metrics with web metrics
- » Analyzing social media with advertising metrics
- » Comparing social media with other online marketing

Chapter 6
Comparing Metrics from Different Marketing Techniques

By now, you may be asking yourself whether web *metrics* (the science of measurement) are worth the trouble. They certainly matter if you have a business with a finite amount of time, money, or staff — which covers just about every business.

Metrics aren't about determining whether your company is the best in any particular marketing or advertising channel. They're about deciding which channels offer your company the best value for achieving your business objectives. Not to denigrate your instinct, but metrics are simply the most objective way to optimize your marketing effort.

REMEMBER

Marketing isn't rocket science. If your metrics show that a particular tactic is working, keep doing it. If they show it isn't working, try something else. Don't be afraid to experiment with different methods.

Establishing Key Performance Indicators

The most important items to measure — the ones that reflect your business goals and objectives — are *key performance indicators* (KPIs). They may vary by type of business, but after they're established, they should remain consistent over time.

An e-retailer, for instance, may be more interested in sales by product category or at different price points, though a business-to-business (B2B) service company might want to look at which sources produce the most qualified prospects. The trick is to select five to ten relevant metrics for your business.

REMEMBER

If something isn't measured, it can't be evaluated. If it can't be evaluated, it isn't considered important.

While you read this chapter, you can establish your own KPIs. Then you can combine them with other information about how your various marketing efforts contribute to sales and leads, your bottom line, and your return on investment (ROI). Armed with this information, you'll be in a position to make strategic business decisions about your marketing mix, no matter what size your company.

TIP

Enter at least one KPI for each business goal on your Social Media Marketing Plan (see Book 1, Chapter 3). Some business goals share the same KPI. Schedule a review of the comparative metrics on your Social Media Activity Calendar (discussed in Book 1, Chapter 4) at least once per month or more often if you're starting a new endeavor, running a brief, time-constrained effort, or handling a large volume of traffic.

Overcoming measurement challenges

Measuring success among forms of social media, let alone between social media and any other forms of marketing, is a challenge. You're likely to find yourself comparing apples to not only oranges but also mangoes, pineapples, kiwis, pears, and bananas. In the end, you have to settle for a fruit salad or smoothie.

TIP

Install the same statistical software, whether it's Google Analytics or another package, on all your sites. Your sites may not have identical goals (for instance, users may not be able to purchase from your LinkedIn profile or request a quote from your wiki), but using the same software will ensure that metrics are consistently defined. In fact, the availability of compatible analytics packages may influence your selection of a host, development platform, or even web developer.

Using A/B testing

You may want to apply *A/B testing* (comparing a control sample against other samples in which only one element has changed) to your forays into social media.

Just as you might use A/B testing to evaluate landing pages or emails, you can also compare results between two versions of a blog post or compare performance of two different headlines for an update on a social media service, while keeping all other content identical.

If you're comparing performance (click-throughs to your site) of content placed in different locations — for example, on several different social bookmarking sites or social news services — use identical content for greater accuracy.

REMEMBER

Don't rely on absolute measurements from any online source. Take marketing metrics with a shaker full of salt; look more at the trends than at the exact numbers. Be forewarned, though, that the temptation to treat numbers as sacrosanct is hard to resist.

To no one's surprise, an entire business has grown up around web metrics. If you have a statistical bent, join or follow the discussions on the resource sites listed in Table 6-1.

TABLE 6-1 **Online Metrics Resources**

Site Name	URL	What It Offers
eMetrics	`www.emetrics.org`	Events and conferences on marketing optimization
HubSpot	`http://blog.hubspot.com/marketing/how-to-run-an-ab-test-ht`	A/B testing how-to FAQs article
Huge	`www.hugeinc.com/ideas/report/social-roi`	Guide to tracking social media ROI
HubSpot	`https://blog.hubspot.com/marketing/a-b-test-checklist#sm.0001ug35mv1a9ndw8smyebn51fukf`	A/B testing checklist
VWO	`https://vwo.com/ab-testing/`	A/B testing guide
Web Analytics Demystified Blog	`http://blog.webanalyticsdemystified.com`	Digital measurement techniques
Web Analytics World Blog	`www.webanalyticsworld.net`	Current news on the web analytics and digital marketing front
WebProNews	`www.webpronews.com`	Breaking news blog for web professionals, including analytics topics
Webtrends	`http://webtrends.com/resources/overview`	Resources for analytics and other marketing topics

Comparing Metrics across Social Media

We talk throughout this book about various genres of social media services. Each genre has its own arcane measurements, from hashtags to comments, from posts to ratings, from membership numbers to sentiment.

TIP

Use medium-specific metrics to gauge the efficacy of different campaigns within that medium or to compare results from one site within a genre to another.

However, to assess the overall effectiveness of social media efforts and your total marketing mix, common metrics cross boundaries. Surprise! These common metrics look a lot like the statistics discussed in Chapter 1 of this minibook. By using the right tools, or by downloading analytics to a spreadsheet and creating your own graphs, you can compare data for various social media.

REMEMBER

Online traffic patterns may vary for all sorts of reasons and for different businesses. Watch for cyclical patterns across a week or compare the same time frames a year apart. Merchants often do this for same-store sales to compare how a store is performing compared to past years.

Carefully aggregate measurements over exactly the same time frame and dates. You obviously don't compare weekly data from a blog to monthly data for a website. But neither should you compare Tuesday traffic on one source to Saturday traffic on another, or compare November and December clicks for an e-commerce site that sells gift items (which is probably quite high) to January and February clicks (which are probably low). Compare, instead, to the same time frames from the preceding year.

In most cases, these metrics become some of the KPIs on your list:

- **Traffic (visits):** The overall measure of the number of visits (not visitors) made to your site or to a particular social media presence over a set period. Facebook (see Figure 6-1) offers page administrators traffic data in its free analytics at `www.facebook.com/insights` (you must be logged in). Google Social Analytics enables you to compare traffic from different social media sources, as we discuss in Chapter 1 of this minibook.
- **Unique users:** The number of different users (or, more specifically, IP addresses) who visited. Depending on your business model, you may want to know whether you have ten visits apiece from 100 ardent fans (multiple repeat users) or 1,000 users, each of whom drops in once. This type of detail is available for some, but not all, social media services.
- **Keywords:** The list of search terms or tags used to find a particular web posting. Phrases are often more useful than individual words.

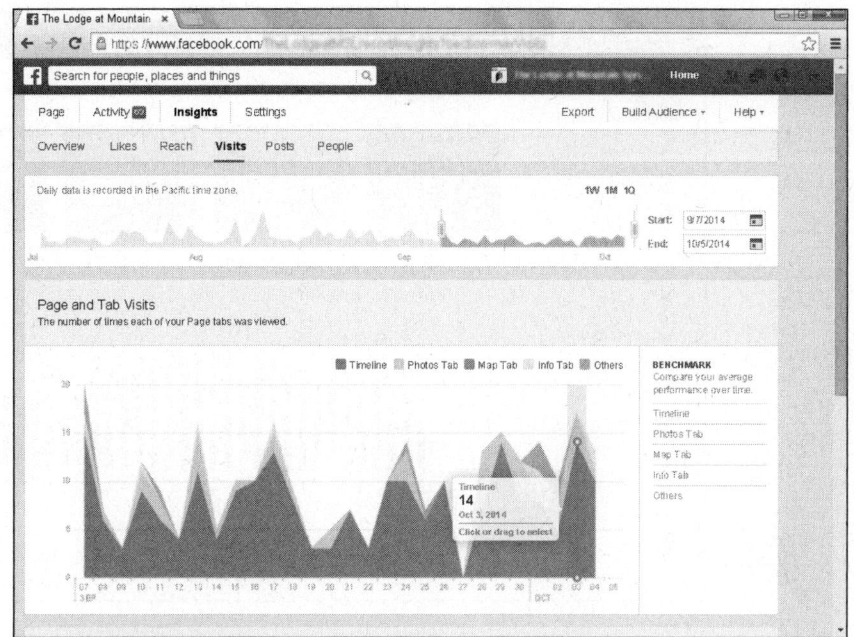

FIGURE 6-1: Facebook's Insights analytics tool displays Facebook traffic over a customized report time frame.

- **Referrers:** A list of traffic sources that tells you how many visitors arrive at your web entities from such sources as search engines, other websites, paid searches, and many, but not all, other social media services. Some even identify referrers from web-enabled cellphones.

  You can find a section like this in most analytics programs. Those traffic sources may be aggregated and displayed graphically for easy review, as shown in Shoutlet's Social Analytics feature (see Figure 6-2). This feature compares the performance of social posts across networks for a holistic view of campaign metrics.

  Keeping track of users' paths among many components of a complicated web presence isn't easy, but it's worth it. You may find that your marketing strategy takes B2B prospects from LinkedIn to your blog and then to a microsite. Or you may watch business-to-consumer (B2C) clients follow your offers from a social news service to a store widget on Facebook before they conclude with a purchase on your site. We talk more about tracking your links in the following section.

- **Click-through rate (CTR):** The number of click-throughs to your site from a particular source divided by the number of visitors (traffic) that arrived at that source. If 40 people view your Facebook stream in one day, for instance, and 4 of them click-through to your primary site, the CTR is 10 percent (4 ÷ 40). You may need to derive this data by combining traffic measurements from particular social media services with information from the Referrers or Entry Pages sections of your analytics program. In some cases, the CTR becomes the conversion measure for a particular social media service.

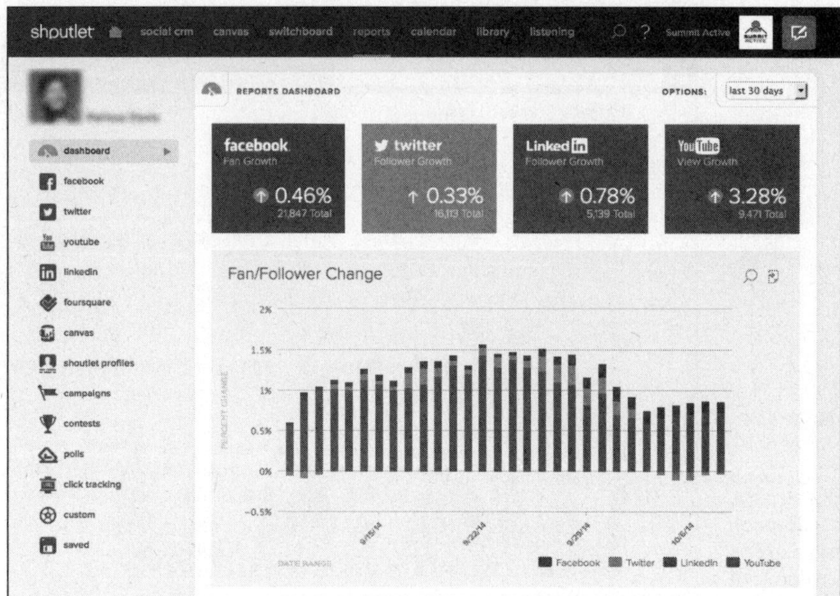

FIGURE 6-2: The Shoutlet analytics report provides the total number of referrals by source in the top boxes, and a graph depicting the relative growth of traffic by source at the bottom.

Reproduced with permission of Shoutlet, Inc.

Table 6-2 suggests some useful KPIs that can track by genre and social media platform.

TABLE 6-2 **Social Media by Genre and KPI**

Social Genre	Site Examples	Useful KPIs to Check
Bookmarking	Delicious, StumbleUpon	Traffic, keywords, CTR
Community	Facebook Groups, forums, Yahoo! Groups	Traffic, users, time, keywords, CTR
Information	Blogs, webinars, wikis	Traffic, users, time, keywords, referrers, CTR
Media sharing	Podcasts, Instagram, Pinterest, YouTube	Traffic, users, time, keywords, CTR, number of views, Likes, Followers
Network	Facebook, LinkedIn, Twitter	Traffic, users, time, keywords, CTR
News	Digg, Reddit	Traffic, keywords, CTR
Review	Angie's List, Epinions, TripAdvisor, Urbanspoon, Yelp	Traffic, CTR, user ratings, leads
Shopping	Fab, ThisNext	Traffic, keywords, CTR

Tagging links

Tagging your links with identifying code is especially helpful for tracking clicks that arrive from e-newsletters, email, widgets, banner ads, and links from a mobile phone because they otherwise aren't distinguishable in the referrer list.

TECHNICAL STUFF

Tagging links offers one other advantage: the ability to track the effect of dark social media traffic. *Dark traffic* arrives at your site via an intermediate stop on some site other than the social media page on which you posted your original link. (For instance, someone shares the link you placed on Facebook with one of his friends via email or text message.) Unless you tag your links, Google can't identify traffic from these sources, so it gets reported as direct traffic.

An unidentified referrer is usually displayed on a row with only a / (slash) in its name. This unspecified / category includes people who type your URL on the address bar of their browsers because they remembered it, were told about it, or have bookmarked your site.

Tagging links manually

If you have only a few such unspecified sources, simply tag the inbound link with additional, identifying information. Add ?src= and the landing page URL. Follow that, in any order, with the source (where the link appeared, such as Merchant-Circle), the medium (pay-per-click, banner, email, and so forth), and campaign name (date, slogan, promo code, product name, and so on). Separate each variable with an ampersand (&). The tagged link will look something like `www.`*`yoursite`*`.com/`*`landingpage`*`?src=yahoo&banner&july14`.

REMEMBER

Google AdWords does this tracking for you automatically. Be sure that you have linked your Analytics and AdWords accounts together and enabled auto-tagging. You can still use either the manual method described in this section or the Google tag builder described in the following section for all non–AdWords campaigns.

Using Google's URL builder to tag links

Google's automated tool for creating tagged links can be used for any advertising campaign or medium, not just Google AdWords. Follow these steps:

1. **Go to** `https://ga-dev-tools.appspot.com/campaign-url-builder/`.
2. **In the Website URL text box, enter your website's address.**
3. **In the Campaign Source text box, enter the referrer, such as Facebook, newsletter, or Google Ads.**

4. **In the Campaign Medium text box, enter the type of ad.**

   For example, the ad type may be promoted post, banner, retargeting, or print.

5. **(Optional) Enter keywords or target audience demographics in the Campaign Term text box.**

6. **(Optional) Include text from the body or headline of each ad in the Campaign Content text box to differentiate ads.**

   This step is often helpful for A/B testing when you're trying to decide which headline or offer works better in an ad.

7. **In the Campaign Name text box, enter an easily identifiable product name, slogan, promo code, holiday, or theme.**

8. **Click the Submit button.**

   Your custom URL, which appears below the button, looks something like `http://www.watermelonweb.com/?utm_campaign=holidayparties2014&utm_medium=banner&utm_source=chambernewsletter`.

As far as the user is concerned, the link automatically redirects to the correct landing page. However, you can count each distinctive URL in a list of referrers or, in the case of Google Analytics, by choosing Acquisition⇨Campaigns, as shown in Figure 6-3.

TIP

You can use tagged links to identify traffic coming from offline sources. Create an obvious, easy-to-remember URL for print, radio, or TV ads that looks something like `http://dell.com/tv`. Then ask your programmer to create a redirect from the obvious URL to your tagged link. Because the tagged link will show up as the referrer in Google Analytics, you can determine how successfully your offline advertising drives traffic to your site. The redirect link will look something like this one from Dell: `http://accessories.us.dell.com/sna/category.aspx?c=us&category_id=5914&cs=19&l=en&s=dhs`. Redirects are a great way to distinguish how often your video ads are seen on YouTube versus television, for example.

The process of tagging links may be time-consuming, but being able to monitor a particular campaign more accurately is worth your trouble.

REMEMBER

Generate a separate, unique, shortened link for tweets, LinkedIn updates, and mobile sites, if needed. *Always* test to ensure that the modified link works correctly.

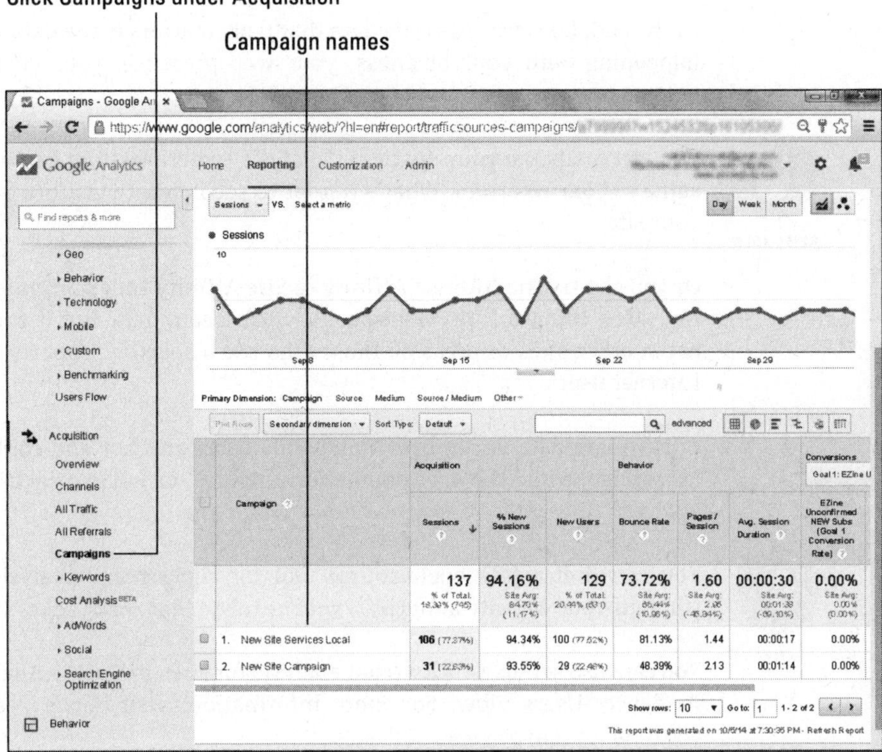

FIGURE 6-3: You can easily track results for non-AdWords campaigns in Google Analytics.

Reproduced with permission of Brad Cavanaugh, Air One, Inc.

Analyzing the clickstream

Clickstream analysis is a fancy name for tracking users' successive mouse clicks (the *clickstream*) to see how they surf the web. Clickstream analytics are usually monitored on an aggregate basis.

Server-based clickstream analysis provides valuable insight into visitor behavior. For instance, by learning which paths users most frequently take on a site and which routes lead to sales, you can make changes in content and calls to action, as well as identify ways to simplify navigation and paths to check out.

On a broader level, clickstream analysis gives you a good idea where your visitors were before they arrived at your website or social media service, and where they went afterward.

REMEMBER

Aggregated data about user behavior or industry usage is useful while you design your social media marketing strategy. This analysis may also help explain why a campaign is or isn't working.

In the end, however, the only data that truly matters is the data that shows what's happening with your business, your web presence, your customers, and your bottom line.

You can easily see your upstream analysis (where visitors came from). That's the same as your referrers. What's harder to see is where visitors go when they leave your site.

Or you can try the Interest Affinity or Site Affinity Index on Quantcast for quantified sites. It doesn't provide specific clickstream data, but it compares the interest in other sites or areas by those who use a specific property to that of average Internet users.

Clickstream data varies over time while users run hot and cold about a particular service, while the user population changes, or while a social media technique evolves.

You can find a free open-source tool for clickstream analysis of users' paths through your website at `http://sourceforge.net/projects/statviz`.

You can also set up a clickstream analysis for sites in Google Analytics by choosing Audience⇨Users Flow. For more information, visit `https://support.google.com/analytics/answer/2519989`.

Tracking your own outbound links

Google Analytics lets you track outbound downstream clicks from your own pages. Your programmer must tag all outbound links you want to track, which involves some JavaScript customization. Send your programmer to `https://support.google.com/analytics/answer/1136920`.

For additional help, have your programmer visit Google's Universal Analytics Upgrade Center at `https://developers.google.com/analytics/devguides/collection/upgrade`. If you haven't already upgraded to Google's Universal Analytics, you'll find that upgrading makes the entire tracking process easier.

If you need to tag many external links, try the automated tagging solution we discuss in the section "Using Google's URL builder to tag links," earlier in this chapter.

To see the number of clicks to each external link in Google Analytics, choose Behavior⇨Events⇨Overview, and look under whatever category name your programmer set up to track these external links.

Integrating Social Media with Web Metrics

In addition to creating your hub website, you may have developed sites either as subdomains within your primary domain name or with auxiliary domain names. These sites may take several forms:

- **Microsites:** These small, dedicated sites that have their own domain names are usually developed for a specific event, product, product line, service, or another promotion, or as specialized landing pages for an advertising campaign. Whether the microsite is permanent or temporary, you must make a strategic choice to create one, judging cost, branding needs, search engine optimization (SEO), and other marketing efforts against potential benefits.
- **Blogs:** All blogs and other information-sharing sites, such as webinars and wikis, can be fully tracked with analytical software. Some sites, such as Blogger (`https://support.google.com/blogger/answer/7039627?hl=en`), offer Google Analytics integration, but not all hosted solutions do so. Although you can obtain statistics from certain hosted communities or third parties, you may not be able to customize them or integrate them with your other statistics.
- **Communities:** All online communities, for example forums, social network groups, chat rooms, and message boards, fall into this category. Although they may have their own internal statistics, also investigate whether you can customize those statistics to meet your needs before you select software or a hosted platform. For instance, Yahoo! Groups (`https://groups.yahoo.com`), LinkedIn Groups (`https://www.linkedin.com/directory/groups/`), Facebook Groups (`https://www.facebook.com/groups`), and Google Groups (`https://groups.google.com/`) are inexpensive community alternatives, but they provide only limited statistics.

For statistical purposes, as well as SEO, own the domain names of microsites, blogs, and communities pages, rather than host them on another server (`http://`*`myblog`*`.wordpress.com`). Sites can almost always be tracked with your preferred analytics package if they're separately registered domains (`www.`*`mymicrosite`*`.com`), were created as subdomains (`http://blog.`*`yourdomain`*`.com`), or live within a directory (`www.`*`yourdomain`*`.com/blog/blog-title`).

The use of KPIs at these additional sites makes it easier to integrate user activity on your social media channels with what happens after users arrive at your primary website. To complete the analysis, add a few more comparative indicators, each of which you can analyze independently:

- **Conversion rate:** You're already computing the percentage of visitors who complete tangible goals on your primary website, whether they purchase a product or complete a request form. Now compare the conversion rate (for the same available goal) by traffic source to the average conversion rate across all sources for that goal. Figure 6-4 displays the Social Value option in Google Analytics, which analyzes conversion rate to assess the relative value of links from various social media. (Go to Acquisition⇨Social⇨Overview and scroll down.)

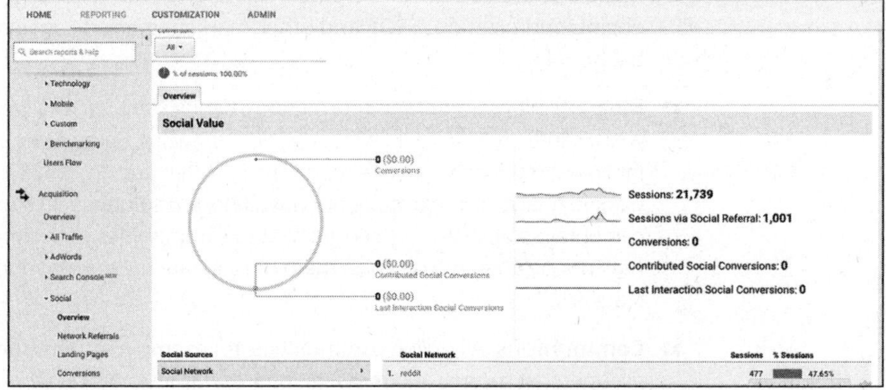

FIGURE 6-4: Google Analytics displays Social Value in chart and linear forms as part of the Social Overview page.

Reproduced with permission of Hutton Broadcasting, LLC

- **Sales and lead generation:** These numbers may come from your storefront package or be based on measurements tracked offline.
- **Downloads:** Track the number of times users download video or audio files, slide-show PDF files, white papers, or application forms from your sites.

TECHNICAL STUFF

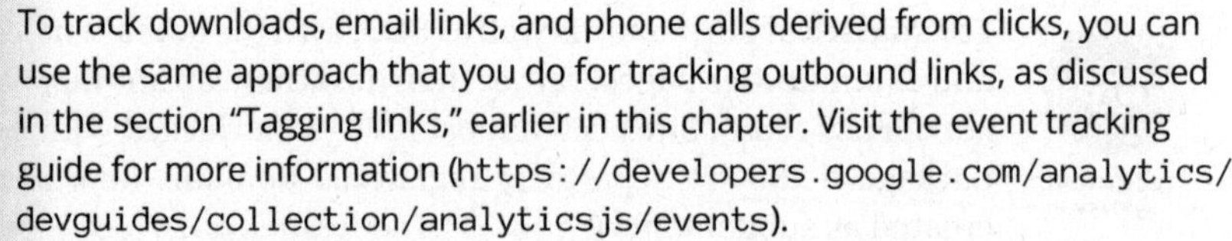

To track downloads, email links, and phone calls derived from clicks, you can use the same approach that you do for tracking outbound links, as discussed in the section "Tagging links," earlier in this chapter. Visit the event tracking guide for more information (`https://developers.google.com/analytics/devguides/collection/analyticsjs/events`).

- **Pages per view, pages viewed:** Microsites, communities, and blogs usually offer enough content to make these parameters reasonable to measure. Tracking this information by social source, however, as shown in Figure 6-4, can be valuable. Page views are available for most blogs but not necessarily for all other services.

- **Time per visit:** The average length of time spent viewing material is a good, but not exact, proxy for the number of pages per view. Naturally, users spend less time reading a single tweet than they might spend on your blog or website, but fractions of a second are indications of trouble everywhere.
- **Bounce rate:** For another indication of interest in your content, determine the percentage of visitors who leave without visiting a second page (related to time per visit). Like with pages per view or time per visit, the bounce rate may be a bit misleading. If many people have bookmarked a page so that they can immediately find the information they want, your bounce rate may be higher than expected, although pages per view or time per visit may be low. You may want to sort bounces by upstream source.

Using Advertising Metrics to Compare Social Media with Other Types of Marketing

Because you generally don't pay social media services, social media marketing is incredibly appealing as a cost-effective substitute for paid ads. You can convert the advertising metrics in the following sections to compare the cost effectiveness of your various social media efforts or to analyze social media outlets versus other forms of promotion, online and off.

Obtaining metrics for paid advertising

With the exception of pay-per-click advertising, which exists only online, the metrics used for paid advertising are the same whether you advertise online or offline. Most publishers offer advertisers a *media kit* that includes demographics, ad requirements, and ad rates based on one or more pricing models.

Advertising costs vary over time based on demand and availability, as well as the overall economy. Ad prices are generally based on what the market will bear — that is, the most that an advertiser is willing to bid. New, real-time bidding schemes for online advertising may make prices even more volatile. Life is negotiable in many advertising marketplaces, except for those that operate as self-service networks. It never hurts to ask for what you want.

Many social media sites don't charge for posting content because their true goal is to sell either premium services or advertising. Your content generates what they sell: an audience. The more user eyeballs a social media service can deliver to its advertisers, the greater its own advertising revenue. In essence, you manufacture their product in exchange for getting some of that traffic for yourself.

CPM

Cost per thousand (CPM) impressions, one of the most consistently used metrics in advertising, work across all forms of media. CPM is based on the number of times an ad is viewed, whether it's calculated for ads on TV, billboards, or in print magazines; received as dedicated emails; or viewed on web pages.

CPM is simple to calculate: Divide the cost by (.001) of the number of impressions (views). The more narrowly defined the audience, the higher the CPM. You can find a handy CPM calculator at `www.clickz.com/static/cpm-calculator`.

For instance, the CPM for a 30-second broadcast Super Bowl ad in 2017 averaged almost $45, but the actual dollar cost — $5 million — was high because the audience was 111.3 million TV viewers. By contrast, CPM for a small, highly targeted audience of CEOs in high-tech companies may run $100 or more.

Because you may have difficulty tracking from impression to action in some channels, CPM models are often used to measure branding campaigns.

Compare CPM with a *cost-per-action* (CPA) advertising model and its subset, *cost-per-click* (CPC) ads. CPA advertising triggers payment only when a user takes a specific action, such as downloading a white paper; signing up for a newsletter; registering for a conference; or becoming a fan, friend, or follower. At the far end of the CPA spectrum, when CPA is based on a user purchase, it approaches a sales commission model.

In the classic definitions of CPA, CPC, and CPM, rates don't include the cost of producing an ad, the commission paid to an agency, or your own labor to research and review ad options. From a budget point of view, you need to include all these factors in your cost estimates.

A web-only metric, CPC (or sometimes *PPC*, for pay-per-click) falls within the CPA model because advertisers are charged only when a viewer clicks a link to a specified landing page. The CPC model is often used for ads in the rightmost columns of search engines and also for clicks obtained from banner, video, and online classified ads, and from shopping comparison sites and paid directory listings. For additional resources for paid online advertising, consult Table 6-3.

TABLE 6-3 **Online Advertising Resources**

Name	URL	What You Can Find
DoubleClick by Google	www.google.com/doubleclick	Ad management and solutions
Internet Advertising Competition	www.iacaward.org/iac	Annual Internet ad competition produced by the Web Marketing Association
Small Business Association	www.sba.gov/content/online-advertising	Resources for online advertising
The Webby Awards	www.webbyawards.com	Interactive advertising competition
Word of Mouth Marketing Association	http://womma.org	Membership group, resources, events

REMEMBER

Always ask which statistics a publisher provides to verify the results of your ads. Some confirm impressions, as well as clicks or other actions (check against your own analytics program); some provide only impressions; and some publishers can't — or won't — provide either one.

Even if you pay a flat fee, such as for an annual directory listing, you can compute CPC and CPM after the fact, as long as the publisher provides you with the number of impressions and you can identify click-throughs.

Reach

Reach is the estimated number of potential customers (qualified prospects) you can target in a specific advertising medium or campaign. You can apply the concept of reach, by extension, to specific social media channels, anticipated traffic on your website, or other populations, such as the addresses on your email list. Reach is sometimes expressed as a fraction of the total audience for an advertising campaign (for example, potential customers divided by total audience).

The number of potential customers may be the total number of viewers in a highly targeted campaign, or only a segment of them. In the case of the Super Bowl example in the earlier section "CPM," for instance, a beer ad may be targeted at males ages 25 to 64; only that demographic percentage of the audience should be calculated in reach.

TIP

For the best results, identify advertising venues where the number of potential customers (reach) represents a large share of potential viewers (impressions). Return to your early market research for viewer demographics from Quantcast or review media kits to estimate the reach of each publication or social media site you're considering.

Applying advertising metrics to social media

Because publishers receive no payments for most social media appearances, comparing free social media marketing to paid advertising requires a little adjustment. How can you compare the CPM or CPC for something that's free versus something you pay for? Although you can acquire information about page views *(impressions)*, clicks, and other actions (conversion goals) from your analytics program, cost requires a little thought.

One possibility is to modify the cost of advertising to include labor and hard costs for production, management, and commission, and any fees for services, such as press release distribution. Then estimate the hard costs and the amount of work in labor dollars required to create and maintain various elements of your social media presence. If you outsource the creation of ads or social media content to contractors such as copywriters, videographers, photographers, or graphic designers, include those expenses.

Don't go crazy trying to calculate exact dollar amounts. You simply estimate the relative costs of each medium or campaign to compare the cost-effectiveness of one form of promotion to another. Social media marketing may be relatively inexpensive, but if you see only one action or impression after 20 hours of labor, you need to decide whether it's worth it.

Juxtaposing Social Media Metrics with Other Online Marketing

Regardless of any other online techniques you use, you can combine links with source tags, analytics program results, and advertising metrics to compare social media results to results from other online techniques.

Refine your list of KPIs for these elements:

» **Email newsletters:** Whether you use your own mailing list or rent one, you measure

- *Bounces:* Bad email addresses
- *Open rate:* The percentage of good addressees that open your newsletter, roughly equivalent to reach as a percentage of impressions

- *Click-through rate (CTR):* The percentage of people who click through to a web page after opening a newsletter
- *Landing pages:* Where newsletter recipients "go" when they click a link in a newsletter

Well-segmented, targeted lists result in better reach. If you rent lists, be sure to include the acquisition cost per thousand names, as well as the transmission cost, in your total cost for CPM (cost per thousand) comparison. Most newsletter services and list-rental houses provide all these metrics.

» **Coupons, promotion codes:** Online coupons can be tracked similarly to regular banner ads. However, for both promotion codes and coupons, track which offers produce the best results, which are almost always sales or registrations.

» **Press releases:** Sometimes press releases are hard to track online because many free press distribution services don't provide information on page views or click-throughs. By contrast, most paid distribution services tell you the click-through rate and the number of impressions (or number of times someone viewed your release) on their servers. Although these services can tell you where the release was distributed, they don't know what happened afterward. A press release is a good place to include an identifier in the links, as described earlier in the "Tagging links" section. The tag enables you to track entry pages. You may also see a spike in daily or hourly traffic to your site shortly after the distribution time.

» **Product placement in games and other programs:** Advertisers can now place the equivalent of banner ads or product images within online video games. If the ads are linkable, you can find the CTR and impressions to calculate CPM and CPC (cost per click). Offline games with product placement must be treated as offline marketing elements.

» **Online events:** Track live concerts, chats, speeches, and webinars with KPIs for registration — request an email address, at minimum — even if the event is free. Though not everyone who registers attends, this approach also provides a helpful set of leads and a built-in audience to notify of future events. Of course, you can also check referrers and entry pages.

» **Disaggregated components, such as third-party blogs, chat rooms, RSS feeds, regular email, or text messaging:** Tagged links that pass through from these forms of communication are probably your best bet.

You can incorporate a special tag for links forwarded by others, although you might not be able to tell how they completed the forwarding (for example, from a ShareThis feature versus email) unless you have implemented social media plug-ins. It all depends on what you're trying to measure.

Be sure to register for optional analytics when you install a Share function from sites such as AddThis or ShareThis, which integrate with Google Analytics. Then you can see where and how often users forward your link through these services.

Contrasting Word-of-Web with Word-of-Mouth

Word-of-mouth is, without a doubt, the most cost-effective form of advertising. Ultimately, that force powers all social media, with its peer-to-peer recommendations and referrals.

Try to keep your expectations in check. According to Microsoft research in 2012, less than 1 percent of social media content goes viral. In this case, *viral* is defined as reaching a much larger audience via peer-to-peer sharing compared to the audience reached by the original post.

Recent research on the effect of social media as a form of word-of-mouth is both intriguing and contradictory:

- Mention (www.mention.com) found that 76 percent of more than 1 billion brand mentions on the web and social media were basically "meh" — neither positive nor negative. The remaining mentions are more likely to stand out.
- According to eMarketer, about 68 percent of social media users 18 to 34 years old, and 53 percent ages 33 to 35 are at least somewhat likely to be influenced to make a purchase based on a friend's social media posting.
- Lithium Technologies found that 70 percent of consumers read online reviews when considering a brand.

Keep these points in mind while you consider the positive and negative effects of participation in social media. Review sites can have a significant effect on your marketing, but the effect of individual recommendations may be overrated except in special cases.

You can monitor mentions of your company online and the tone of those responses, as discussed in Book 2.

Your analytical task here is to compare the efficacy of "word-of-web" by way of social media to its more traditional forms. Tracking visitors who arrive from offline is the trickiest part. These visitors type your URL in the address bar of their browsers either because they've heard of your company from someone else (word-of-mouth) or as a result of offline marketing.

Offline marketing may involve print, billboards, radio, television, loyalty-program key-chain tags, promotional items, packaging, events, or any other great ideas you dream up.

By borrowing the following techniques from direct marketing, you can find ways, albeit imperfect, to identify referrals from offline sources or other individuals:

- **Use a slightly different URL to identify the offline source.** Make the URL simple and easy to remember, such as `http://`*`yourdomain`*`.com/tv`; `http://`*`yourdomain`*`.com/wrapper`; `http://`*`yourdomain`*`.com/nyt`; or `http://`*`yourdomain`*`.com/radio4`. These short URLs can show viewers a special landing page — perhaps one that details an offer or a contest encouraged by an offline teaser — or redirect them to an existing page on your site. Long, tagged URLs that are terrific for online sourcing and hard-to-remember shortened URLs are not helpful offline.
- **Identify referrals from various offline sources.** Use different response email addresses, telephone numbers, extensions, or people's names.
- **Provide an incentive to the referring party.** "Tell a friend about us. Both of you will receive $10 off your next visit." This technique can be as simple as a business card for someone to bring in with the referring friend's name on the back. Of course, the card carries its own unique referral URL for tracking purposes.
- **Stick to the tried-and-true method.** Always ask, "May I ask how you heard about us?" Then tally the results.

You can then plug these numbers into a spreadsheet with your online referral statistics to compare offline methods with online social media.

IN THIS CHAPTER

» Making decisions based on metrics

» Diagnosing and fixing problem campaigns

» Keeping your online marketing grounded

Chapter 7

Making Decisions by the Numbers

The 2016 *Social Media Marketing Industry Report* from Social Media Examiner showed that 86 percent of professionals whose companies use social media said want to be able to measure their return on investment (ROI). By using the tools for assessing qualitative and quantitative results, including ROI, they can certainly count themselves among those who do!

However, there's no point in collecting metrics just to save them in a virtual curio cabinet. The challenge is to figure out how to use the numbers to adjust your online marketing campaigns, whether they need fine-tuning or a major overhaul. In this chapter, we show you how to analyze problems, see what your data reveal, and then use the results to modify your marketing approach.

Using Metrics to Make Decisions

In spite of the hype, social media is, at its core, a form of strategic marketing communications. As a business owner, you must balance the subjective aspects of branding, sentiment, goodwill, and quality of leads with the objective performance metrics of traffic and click-through rate (CTR) and the business metrics of customer acquisition costs, conversion rate, sales value, and ROI. The balance point is unique to each business at a specific time. Alas, no fixed rules exist.

As part of your balancing act, you'll undoubtedly also tap your instincts, incorporating casual feedback from customers, the ever-changing evolution of your market, your budget, and your assessment of your own and your staff's available time and skills.

Even after you feel confident about your marketing program, keep watching your metrics as a reality check. Data has a funny way of surprising you.

TIP

Don't become complacent. Continue to check your performance and business metrics at least monthly. How do they compare to what your instinct is telling you?

Knowing When to Hold and When to Fold

Watch for a few things in your metrics. As always, you evaluate comparative results, not absolute numbers. Keep an eye on these characteristics:

- Negative and positive trends that last for several months
- Abrupt or unexpected changes
- No change in key performance indicators (KPIs), in spite of social media marketing activities
- Correlations between a peak in traffic or sales with a specific social marketing activity

Layering activity timelines with metrics, as shown in Figure 7-1, is a simple, graphical way to spot this type of correlation. Establishing baseline metrics for your hub presence first truly helps in this process. It also helps if you add social media techniques one at a time — preferably with tracking codes.

TIP

Don't make *irreversible* decisions based on one event or from an analytical time frame that's too short for the marketing channel you're trying to implement. There are no rules for a time frame that is too short or too long. Your overall campaign may be designed to take off like a rocket in less than a week, or it may be set up to take 6 to 12 months to bear fruit. Be patient. Monitor your social media campaigns and rely on your business instincts.

You may find a time delay between the initiation of an effort and its effect on metrics, for these reasons:

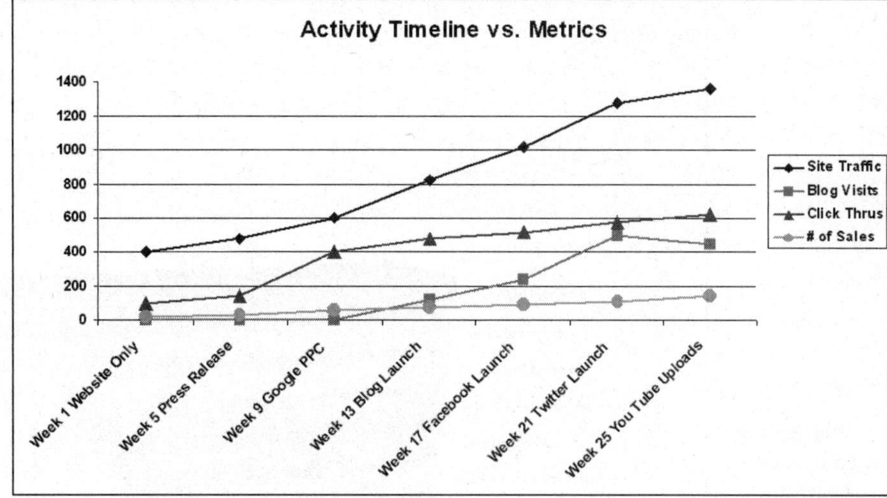

FIGURE 7-1: Correlating an activity timeline with key performance indicators provides useful information.

Reproduced with permission of Watermelon Mountain Web Marketing, watermelonweb.com

- Viewers may wait to see a history of posts before engaging, let alone clicking through to your main hub.
- By definition, establishing a relationship with viewers or prospects takes time, just as it does in real life.
- Our brains haven't changed in spite of the Internet: As every brand marketer knows, most people still need to see something seven times to remember it.
- Many types of social media display a greater cumulative effect over time as viral marketing takes hold.
- Your mastery of a new medium usually improves as you climb the learning curve.

With positive results, the answer is simple: Keep doing what you're doing, and even more so. After you identify the elements responsible for your success, repeat them, amplify them, multiply them, and repurpose them.

Neutral or negative results force you to evaluate whether you should drop the activity or invest the effort needed to identify the problem and try to fix it. Ultimately, only you can decide whether you want to continue sinking time and effort into a social marketing method that doesn't produce the results you want.

Make a chart for yourself like the one from Social Media Examiner shown in Figure 7-2. It shows how 2,800 marketers rank their accomplishments from using social media. How do your efforts stack up?

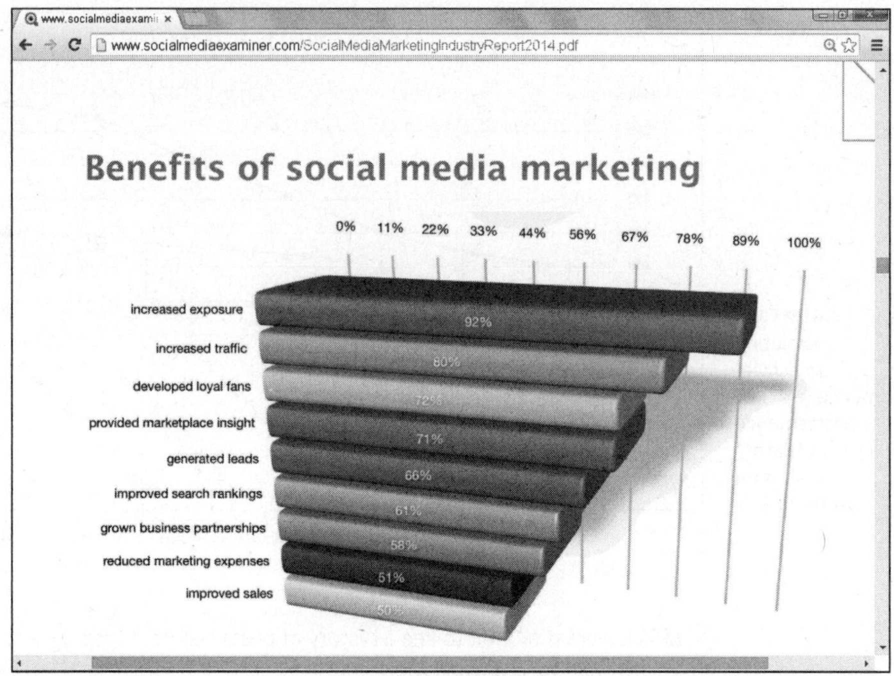

FIGURE 7-2: Compare the benefits you receive from social media with the benefits identified by marketers in other businesses.

Reproduced with permission of Social Media Examiner

TREKKING THROUGH SOCIAL MEDIA

Inspired by a love of the outdoors, KEEN, Inc., manufactures hybrid outdoor and casual footwear with an innovative design that supports the lifestyles and outdoor adventures of active people around the world. Founded in 2003, KEEN is one of the fastest-growing brands in the outdoor industry and has quickly become a well-respected brand, with a loyal following. Through its Hybrid.Care giving program, KEEN has partnered with nonprofit organizations around the world that are working toward building stronger communities and a healthier planet, and stands behind those partners that are actively working to inspire responsible outdoor participation and land and water conservation.

According to Eric King, KEEN's social media manager, the company's social media presence has evolved to "meet our fans wherever they are." KEEN started with Facebook in 2008 as part of a sustainability campaign targeting college students, and has added other channels incrementally since then. "Since social marketing is constantly evolving, it can be tricky to know exactly what to plan for, but we try to do everything possible to stay on top of the latest tools and trends and be nimble enough to take advantage of the right opportunities that come along," King says.

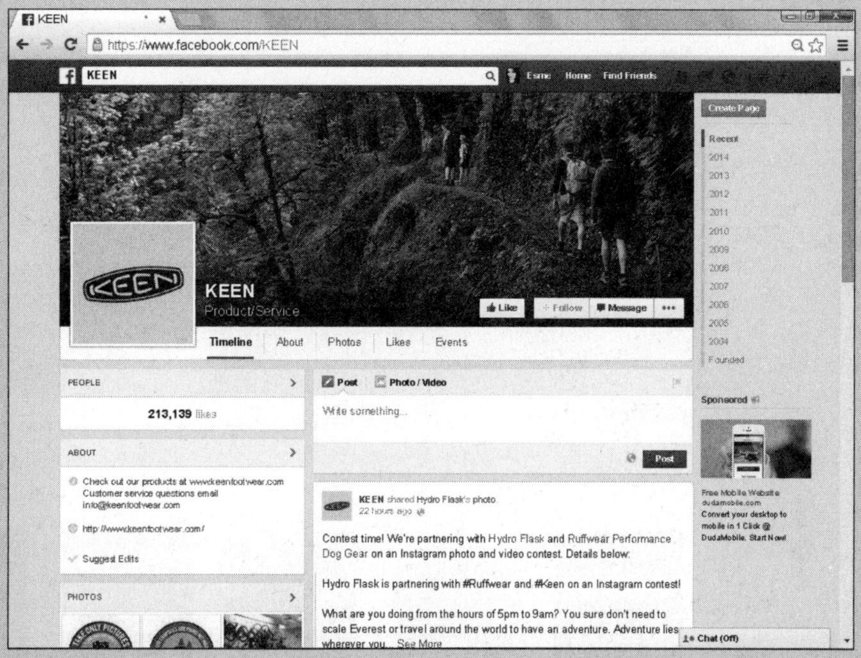

Reproduced with permission from KEEN FOOTWEAR

King's approach is driven by content. "We decide which content we need first, create that content, and then determine the most appropriate posting dates and times by looking at our analytics. We do schedule most of our content in advance, but also leave some slots open for opportunities that come up in real-time."

KEEN aims for a broad range of content, including product photography, brand storytelling, Ambassador and Hybrid Care partner updates, sneak peeks, and fan photos. The effort is managed by one dedicated person in-house, plus employee contributors and some outside content creators.

King tries to tailor content for each social media channel separately, considering everything from age demographics to topic affinities. He then researches which themes or content mediums will work best for each channel. "For example," he finds, "Instagram and Tumblr are ideal for posting lookbook-style inspirational images, while Facebook and Twitter are better suited for asking our community questions and then responding to their suggestions."

(continued)

(continued)

Reproduced with permission from KEEN FOOTWEAR

To keep track of all this social media traffic, KEEN uses a sophisticated analytics program called Crimson Hexagon for "social listening." KEEN manages the analysis in-house, going beyond just the numbers to understand the why. As King explains, "We study what's being said about KEEN online, how much of the conversation is positive or negative, how it compares to what's being said about our competitors, and then how we can use all this information to inform future strategy."

King's advice to other marketers is straightforward: "Know exactly what your goals are and how you plan on tracking them at the start of every year and every campaign. Be consistent with your tracking and set clear KPIs [key performance indicators] that can be tied back to definitive numbers. Finally, make sure that everyone who is involved is on the same page and working toward one common goal."

He follows his own advice. KEEN's goals, which are to increase brand awareness and engagement, have evolved over time as KEEN has "placed more priority in listening to what our fans have to say . . . so we can be more intentional with how we're communicating with them. . . . We want to make it clear that we're listening and that we care about what the community has to say."

KEEN's web presence follows:

- www.keenfootwear.com
- http://www.facebook.com/KEEN
- http://twitter.com/keen
- http://pinterest.com/keenfootwear
- http://instagram.com/keen
- www.youtube.com/user/keenoutdoor
- www.keenfootwear.com/blog

Diagnosing Problems with Social Media Campaigns

Put on your business hat when you detect a problem. Some techniques may be worth modifying and trying again, but others should be dropped. Ultimately, the decision is a business one, not a technological one.

Be patient when assessing cost of customer acquisition and ROI, although a few trend lines in your metrics might give you pause:

- Traffic to a social media service never picks up, or falls and remains low after an initial burst.
- Traffic to the social media site holds steady, but the click-through rate (CTR) to your master hub or other sites is low.
- Follow-through on intermediate calls to action is low in performance metrics.
- Traffic and click-throughs increase, but the leads aren't well qualified.
- Traffic and engagement, which had been increasing for quite a while, fall and continue to fall; small dips and rises are natural.
- A conversion rate tracked back to a social media service is unintentionally lower than from other sources, and average sales value is lower. (Good strategic reasons for these results might exist, of course. You might deliberately target the younger student audience on Foursquare with less expensive options than those offered to an older, more affluent audience on Facebook.)

- The cost of customer or lead acquisition is much higher than for other channels, making the ROI unattractive. For example, a high-maintenance blog might generate a few leads but be relatively expensive compared to prescheduled tweets that drive more traffic successfully.

Fixing Problems

Underlying problems with low traffic on social media usually can be slotted into a few categories:

- Problems locating your social media presence
- Mismatch between channel and audience
- Poor content
- No audience engagement
- Problems with the four Ps of marketing: product, price, placement or position (distribution), and promotion

After these problems are diagnosed, they can be handled in roughly the same way, regardless of the social media venue used.

Before you panic, make sure that you've set reasonable expectations for performance and business metrics. Research the range of responses for similar companies or view your competitors' social media sites to see how many responses, comments, and followers they have. Although you can't foretell their ROI, you can assess their traffic and inbound links. Your results from social media may be just fine!

TIP

Use the social monitoring tools described in Book 2, Chapter 3 to discover how your competitors are doing on social media compared to your business. Many of these tools enable you to check any domain name.

Be careful with interpretation, however; if your competitors began working on their social media campaigns long before you did, they are likely to have very different results.

Remember that the social media audience is fickle. A constant demand exists for changes in content, approach, tools, and tone to keep up.

Your social presence can't be found

Driving traffic to your social media presence is as challenging as driving people to your site. If traffic is still low after about four weeks, ensure that all your social media sites are optimized for external search engines such as Google and internal (on-site) search tools used by different social media services. Turn to Book 2, Chapter 2 for optimization techniques.

The source of the problem may be poorly selected search terms or tags, a headline or description that contains no keywords, or content that hasn't been optimized. Unless your hub presence, whether it's a blog or website, is well optimized itself, your social media presence may suffer, too.

Be sure that posts occur often enough for your social media page to appear in real-time search results.

Inappropriate match between channel and audience

The symptoms for a mismatch usually show up quickly: People take little or no interest in your social media postings, you suffer from low CTR, and your bounce rate is high whenever visitors do click through.

To start with, you may have chosen an inappropriate social media service or the wrong group within a network. For example, young tech males like Reddit, but if you want a social site about weddings and interior decor, try Pinterest instead.

The solution: Return to your Social Media Marketing Plan (see Book 1, Chapter 3). Review the demographics and behavioral characteristics for the social media service you're using. They may have changed over time; for example, Facebook is still enormously popular with 18- to 29-year-olds, in spite of recent growth in older users, but that may not last. The youngest of social media users are already migrating toward Snapchat! Find a social venue that's a better fit, revise your plan, and try again.

Use Quantcast or Alexa to check demographics on social media sites if you aren't sure.

Poor content

Content problems are a little harder to diagnose than visibility problems, especially if the problem appears with your first posts. In that case, the problem may also look like a channel mismatch, with content that simply doesn't appeal to your target market or is inappropriate for the channel.

However, if you experience a persistent dip in traffic, comments, or CTR from your blog, Facebook stream, Pinterest, podcast, YouTube, or any other social media account, you have other difficulties. Perhaps the content isn't timely, or isn't updated frequently enough.

Or perhaps content quality itself has degraded. Content creators are commonly enthusiastic at the beginning of a project but may lose interest after a period of time. Or they may have a backlog of media and ideas that can be repurposed and posted initially; after that's depleted, they may run out of ideas. As a result, later content may not be as valuable to your market, lack appropriate production values, or simply become boring.

Watch for burnout. After the backlog of media is used up, the insistent demands for new content can easily become a burden. Creators often lose interest, or they focus on quantity rather than on quality.

Compare the individual posts that produced an increase in traffic, responses, or CTR to ones that are failing. Tally posts by the names of their creators and what the posts were about. Start by asking previously successful creators to develop new material along the lines of older, successful content. If that doesn't work, watch the most popular tags to see what interests visitors and try to tie new content into those topics, if appropriate.

Finally, try assigning fresh staff members, recruiting guest writers and producers, or hiring professionals for a while. If this change produces better results, you have indicators for a long-term solution.

Lack of audience engagement

If you see traffic to the social media service holding steady but lack follow-throughs from calls to action, or you have an unusually low CTR to your hub site, you may not be engaging your audience. Watch especially for engagement parameters that never take off or that dip persistently.

Review user comments, retweets, and other interactions on each service. You can use the internal performance metrics for Twitter, Facebook, and your blog to assess numerical results of engagement. Then review the chain for interaction between social media visitors and your staff. Are visitor responses being acknowledged? Is there follow-up? One of the biggest challenges in social media is establishing a relationship with your visitors and maintaining a back-and-forth conversation.

A lack of engagement may presage a lack of brand recognition, loss of customer loyalty, and reduced referrals from visitors to their friends or colleagues.

The four Ps of marketing

Perhaps you're getting traffic and click-throughs to your hub site and generating plenty of leads but still not closing or converting to sales. It might be time to go back to the basics.

TIP

Review a web analytics report generated before you started your social media marketing efforts. Make sure your website is well optimized for search, your online store (if you have one) is working well, and your conversion rate is solid. Fix any problems with your website before you try to adjust your social media campaign.

Product, price, placement or position (distribution), and promotion — the four Ps — are considered the basic elements of traditional marketing. These terms apply to social media and other forms of online marketing, as well.

Product

Your *product* is whatever good or service you sell, regardless of whether the transaction takes place online or off. Product also includes such elements as performance, warranties, support, variety, and size. Review your competition to see which features, benefits, or services they offer, and which products they're featuring in social media. If you have an online store, look at your entire product mix and merchandising, not just at individual products. Ask yourself these questions:

- Are you selling products that the people you're targeting with social media want to buy?
- Do you have enough products or services to compete successfully in this environment?
- Are you updating your offerings regularly and promoting new items often?

Price

Price comparison sites such as Shopping and discount stores online already put price pressure on small businesses. Now mobile social media shopping sites, with the rapid viral spread of news about special offers and price breaks, have put cost-conscious shoppers firmly in the driver's seat.

No longer can you check only competitors' websites and comparison-shopping sites for prices. Now you must check to see what they offer visitors to their Facebook, Twitter, or LinkedIn pages; their blog readers; those who receive their e-newsletter; and social shopping page customers to gain new customers and hold onto them as loyal, repeat buyers. Any single product or service may now have multiple prices, depending on who's buying.

TIP

Use social shopping and other sites to assess your prices against your online competition. Are yours significantly higher or lower, or are they price competitive?

Your small business can have difficulty competing in the market for standard manufactured goods such as baby clothes or DVDs unless you have excellent wholesale deals from manufacturers or distributors. But you can compete on price on customized goods or services or by offering unique benefits for buying from your company.

If you must charge higher prices than your social media competitors, review your value proposition so that people perceive an extra benefit. It might be a $5 promotional code for a discount on another purchase, a no-questions-asked return policy, exclusivity, or very accessible tech support.

WARNING

Be careful not to trap yourself into matching prices against large companies with deep pockets. Make tactical financial decisions about loss leaders and discounts for users of particular social media. Consider a less-than-full-featured product or service package for social media users if needed (sometimes called the *freemium* business model).

Placement or position

Placement or position refers to how products and services are delivered to consumers (distribution channels). Where and how are your products and services available? Your website needs to serve as a 24/7 hub for customer research, support, and sales online, but social media offers new opportunities to serve your clients. Best Buy, for example, has already become famous for its *twelpforce*, in which employees use Twitter to field customer support questions and make product recommendations.

TIP

With multiple social marketing outlets, you must be alert for the effects of *channel cannibalization* (the use of multiple distribution channels that pull sales from each other). Products or services sold directly from social media outlets may depress the sales numbers on your website.

Promotion

Your online and social media marketing plans fall into the *promotion* category, which includes all the different ways you communicate with customers and prospects, both online and offline. This also includes making people aware of your multiple points of visibility online, almost as though you're marketing another product. Careful cross-promotion among all your online venues is now as critical as integrating online and offline advertising. Are people aware of all your social media pages? Are you using the right calls to action on those pages to get people to buy?

Don't continue investing in a social media technique just because everyone else is doing it.

Adjusting to Reality

Many times, expectations determine whether a marketing technique is seen as a success, a waste of time, or something in between. It isn't possible for a particular social media service to produce extraordinary changes in traffic or conversions. In most cases, though, your victories will be hard-won, while you cobble together traffic from multiple social media sources to build enough of a critical mass to gain measurable sales.

Achieving that goal usually involves many people, each of whom may become a committed champion of the method she or he has been using. When you decide to pull the plug on one of your social media techniques — or just decide to leave it in a static state — try to still keep your employees engaged.

Unless social media participants have proved themselves to be nonperformers, try to shift them into another channel so that they can retain a direct relationship with customers.

Avoid the temptation to recentralize your social media marketing in one place, whether it's PR, marketing communications, management, or customer support. Instead, try to maintain the involvement of someone from each of those functional areas, as well as subject area experts from such diverse departments as manufacturing, sales, and research and development (R&D).

Marketing is only part of a company, but all of a company is marketing.

As wild a ride as social media may seem, it's more of a marathon than a sprint. Given that it may take months to see the return on your marketing efforts, you may need to nourish your social media sites for quite a while.

Feeding the hungry maw of the content monster week in and week out isn't easy. You need to not only keep your staff engaged and positive, but also keep your content fresh. Take advantage of brainstorming techniques that involve your entire team to generate some new ideas each month. Here are a few suggestions to get you started:

- Create unique, themed campaigns that last one to three months. Find an interesting hook to recruit guest posts or writers, perhaps letting a few people try your product or service and write about it.
- Distribute short-term deals using some of social media channels described in Book 8, such as providing location-based coupons on cellphones or distributing offers to Meetup attendees.
- Write a Wikipedia entry about your product or business from a consumer's point of view.
- Make friends on Facebook by incorporating an interactive application, such as a poll or sweepstakes entry.
- Reach one or more of your discrete niche markets by using some of the smaller alternative social media services listed in Book 8, Chapter 3, or in Book 2, Chapter 3.
- If you aren't gaining traction with groups on LinkedIn or Facebook, post on someone else's old-fashioned forum, message board, or chat room on a relevant topic.
- Tell a story about your product or service in pictures or video and upload it to Instagram, Snapchat, Periscope, Pinterest, YouTube, or another image service.

REMEMBER

Every marketing problem has an infinite number of solutions. You have to find only one of them!

Index

Symbols and Numerics

(hashtags)
  defined, 139
  in Facebook posts, 364
  Instagram, 485–487
  search terms in, 160–161, 310
  searching for on Twitter, 303
  trending, on Twitter, 303–304
  in tweets, 168, 304–305
  in Twitter campaigns, 308
  Twitter chat, finding, 328–329
  as Twitter measurement mechanism, 625
#FF (FollowFriday) hashtag, 625
@reply, Twitter, 301, 302, 305, 306
+ (plus sign) button, Pinterest, 442
"15 Google Analytics Tricks to Maximize Your Marketing Campaign", 595
24-7 Press Release, 554
123RF, 252
140-character limit, Twitter, 290–291, 304
2016 Social Media Marketing Industry Report, 546–547, 663
2020AVE, 110

A

A/B testing, 644–645
About page
  Facebook, 343, 349–350, 360
  using Pinterest boards as, 446
accountant, getting help from, 33
achievements, in LinkedIn profile, 397
acquiring customers. *See* cost of customer acquisition
activity timelines, layering with metrics, 664, 665
activity type, social networks by, 512–514
Add Friends feature, Snapchat, 468, 469
Added Me icon, Snapchat, 468
addict, defined, 498
addictiveness of social media, 20
Addictomatic, 120
add-ons, 530
AddThis, 204
AddToAny, 204, 592
Admin panel, Facebook, 343–344
administrative features, Facebook, 348–349
administrators, LinkedIn company pages, 412–413
Adobe Analytics, 591
AdPreview tool, Google, 154
Ads Create tool, Facebook, 520–521
Ads Manager, Facebook, 377–378, 379
advertiser pages, Spotify, 537
advertising
  alternative opportunities for, 19
  Chegg use of, 578–580
  cost-per-action, 656
  cost-per-click, 656, 657
  Door to Door Organics use of, 30
  engagement ads, 576–577
  on Facebook, 222–223, 562, 564–568
  free, 19
  HCSS use of, 51
  on Instagram, 564
  integrating social media with paid, 561–563
  on LinkedIn, 562, 573–575
  maximizing advertising dollars, 563–564
  metrics for, comparing marketing types with, 655–658
  on mobile social media, 222–223
  in overall marketing effort, 20
  paid, 19, 561–563, 655–657
  pay-per-click, 153, 564, 656
  on Pinterest, 576
  on Spotify, 537
  on Tumblr, 539

advertising *(continued)*
on Twitter, 222–223, 562, 568–573
on Vimeo, 541–542
word-of-mouth, 530, 660–661
word-of-web, 660–661
advertising, Facebook
ad types, 375–377
Ads Manager, 377–378, 379
boosted posts, 567–568
cost of, 374, 376, 568
creating ads, 377–378
general discussion, 564–568
geographic segmentation, 58–59
guidelines for, 377
Insights section, 349, 379
mobile social media, 222–223
offers, 519–521
overview, 366, 373, 562
reasons to invest in, 375
ROI, measuring, 379–380
targeting fans, 378–379
AdWords, Google, 134, 135, 163, 649
affinity, defined, 498
affinity groups, 55, 62–63
AFS Analytics, 590
Albuquerque Economic Development, 10, 11
Alexa
affinity groups, segmenting by, 62, 63
Certified Site Metrics, 63
demographic information, 56, 57
levels of paid plans, 56
overview, 15
researching minor sites on, 494
algorithms, search engine, 131, 132, 142
All in One SEO Pack, WordPress, 164
All Rights Reserved images, 250
Alltop, 190
<alt> tags
multimedia, 166
search terms in, 146, 147
alternative advertising opportunities, 19
Amazon aStore, 117
American Bar Association, 94
American Express, 89
analytics. *See also* Facebook Insights; Google Analytics; performance metrics; Twitter performance metrics
blogs, 603–604
in content-marketing strategy, 270
of content-sharing services, overview, 599–603
coupon services, 528–529
Facebook Insights, 370–372
Facebook Live, 387
KEEN use of, 666–669
LinkedIn, 636–640
measurement strategy, 584–589
mobile, 220–221, 640–642
overview, 583
packages, 589–594
Pinterest, 609–614
podcasts, 606–608
press releases, 556–557
responsibility for, establishing, 587–589
return on investment, 614–615
social media options, 592–593
social plug-ins, 635–636
Somebody's Mother's use of, 502
URL-shortening tools for, 593–594
video, 605–606
Vimeo, 542
Analytics Academy, 595
Analytics Help Center, 595
analytics programs, 281–283, 589–594, 644. *See also specific programs*
Analytics tab, LinkedIn, 637–640
anchor text, 145, 167
announcements
to LinkedIn groups, 418, 427–428
on Snapchat, 471
anonymous browsing, LinkedIn, 396–397
Apache Mod_Rewrite module, 149
apps. *See also specific apps*
defined, 13
Facebook, 348, 365–366, 367
Facebook Insights, 628

mobile social media, 212–215
social e-commerce, 117–118
Twitter, 318–320
Apsalar, 641, 642
Arcadia Ales, 197–200
Archibeque Law Firm, 143–144
Array Technologies, 10, 12
art social networks, 507
ArtSlant, 507
Ask to Be Recommended feature, LinkedIn, 403
ASMALLWORLD, 511
Athlinks, 509
Attentio, 97, 125
auctions
Facebook advertising, 568
LinkedIn advertising, 575
Twitter advertising, 571–572
audience. *See also* target audience
mismatch between channel and, 671
Pinterest analytics, 611–612
social media, 14
Audience dashboard, Twitter Analytics, 619, 620
audio ads, Spotify, 537
audio sharing sites, 9, 601. *See also* content-sharing services; *specific sites*
auto join, LinkedIn groups, 423
auto messages, on Twitter, 294
auto social networks, 507
auto-follow programs, 292, 315
avatar, Twitter profile page, 314, 316–317
average variable costs, 44
awards, in LinkedIn profile, 397
AWStats, 590

B

B2B (business to business) companies
defined, 34
group coupons, 525
HCSS social media marketing example, 48–52
market research, 64–65
mobile social marketing, 217
revenue drivers, 27
selling directly on social media, 110
B2C (business to consumer) companies. *See also* social shopping services
defined, 34
market segmentation, 54–63
revenue drivers, 27
selling directly on social media, 110
background photo, LinkedIn, 400, 411
backlinks, 259
badges, e-commerce, 108, 110
Badoo, 511
Basecamp, 79, 274
Batchbook, 43
Beetailer, 115
behavioral segmentation, 61
BeRecruited, 509
Best Buy, 674
BI Intelligence, 569
bid-based ad auction
Facebook, 568
LinkedIn, 575
Twitter, 571–572
Big Cartel, 117
BigCommerce, 117
BIgMarketing for Small Business, 103
Bigstock, 252
Bing
real-time search, 175
SEO for, 131–132
Bing Places for Business Portal, 153
Bing Toolbar, 183
Bing Webmaster Tools, 152
bio, Twitter profile page, 314
bit.do, 618–619
Bitly, 107, 155, 593–594, 618–619
Blab.im, 102
Black, Rachel, 74, 75
Black Business Women Online, 510
black hat techniques, 146
BlackPlanet.com, 510
blocking people, on Twitter, 307–308

blog directories, 163
blog posts, 242–243
blog rolls, 162, 163
Blogger
analytics, 601, 603
optimizing blogs, 164–165
permalinks, 166
bloggers, as press release distribution channel, 555
BloggyEsq, 94
blogs. *See also specific blogging sites*
analytics, 601, 603–604
benefits of, 238–241
bookmarks for, 194
comments, tracking, 602–603
content marketing, 231
as content platforms, 237, 238–243
deciding to use, 241
establishing expertise through, 268
Facebook Live for, 382
guest blogging, 258–262, 265, 268
hub sites, 21
LinkedIn, 413, 430–433
monitoring tools for, 125
optimization of, 161–166
performance metrics, 653–655
permalinks, assigning, 165–166
press releases, posting on, 553
setting up, 241–243
as social content-sharing services, 9
Tumblr, 538–540
Twitter chats, promoting on, 332
BlogSearchEngine, 125
Blue Rain Gallery, 9, 10
Bluehost, 242
boards, Pinterest
collaborative, 447–448, 459–460
creating first, 447–448
defined, 438
driving traffic with, 455–458
group, 459–460
keywords in, 458
overview, 445–446
pinning to, 448–449
planning initial, 446–447
on profile page, 443
searching for, 440
secret, 447
body text, search terms in, 146
book social networks, 508. *See also specific networks*
bookkeeper, getting help from, 33
bookmarking services. *See* social bookmarking services; *specific services*
books
establishing expertise through, 268
in Pinterest boards, 446
boosted posts, Facebook, 376, 378–379, 520, 567–568
bots (robots), 131
bottom line. *See* business metrics
bounce rate, 282, 595, 655
bounces, newsletters, 658
Brand 24, 120
brand advocates, finding on Twitter, 323
brand pages, Pinterest, 441–442. *See also* Pinterest
Branded Moments, Spotify, 537
branded playlists, Spotify, 537
branding
blogs, influence on, 240–241
content-marketing strategy goals, 264
CPM models, 656
with Facebook, 341–342, 359
growing community through, 269
matching social media services to goals, 25
overview, 15–16
with press releases, 551
from social-bookmarking and social news services, 186–187
through content marketing, 229, 230, 233
through Twitter, 289, 295, 323
through Twitter chats, 331–332
brandjacking, 95
brand-monitoring tool, 120

brands
Facebook, appeal on, 340–341
Facebook, liking other on, 353–354
Facebook, sharing story on, 359–361
Instagram, promoting on, 478, 484–485
Pinterest, researching on, 439–440
Pinterest boards, showcasing on, 446
reputation, protecting, 95–97
Snapchat, geofilter use by, 475–476
Snapchat, telling story on, 471–473
Twitter, researching on, 296
Twitter, searching for on, 303
Twitter chat guests, finding, 331
BrandsEye, 97, 125
Brandwatch, 66
breadcrumb trails, 150–151
break-even point, 44–45
bricks-and-clicks method, 34, 40
Briscoe, Jack, 50, 51
Brooklyn Kitchen, 156
Bruce Clay, Inc., 174
budget
content marketing, 231
Facebook advertising, 566
social media platform choice, relation to, 256
Twitter advertising, 572
Buffer, 105, 319
business accounts
Instagram, 480–481
Vimeo, 541
business case for social media marketing. *See also* business metrics; online market research
alternative advertising opportunities, 19
benefits, understanding, 13–19
branding, 15–16
business processes, improving, 16–17
cons, 19–20
defining social media marketing, 9–13
effectiveness, 14
example of, 28–31
human resources needed, 20
integrating into overall marketing effort, 20–22
overview, 7–8
relationships, building, 16
search engine rankings, improving, 17
selling opportunities, 17–19
small businesses, 8, 18
strategic plan, developing, 22–28
target market, reaching, 14–15
business metrics. *See also* analytics; performance metrics
break-even point, 44–45
cost of customer acquisition, 35–39
example of, 48–52
KPIs for sales, establishing, 39–42
leads, tracking, 43
lifetime customer value, 37
measuring, 585–586
net profit margin, 45
overview, 33–34
reasonable expectations for, 670
resources for, 35
revenue versus profit, 45
ROI, determining, 45–48
ROI, preparing to calculate, 34–35
business networks, 504–506. *See also specific networks*
business planning resources, 22
business processes, improving, 16–17
business to business (B2B) companies
defined, 34
group coupons, 525
HCSS social media marketing example, 48–52
market research, 64–65
mobile social marketing, 217
revenue drivers, 27
selling directly on social media, 110
business to consumer (B2C) companies. *See also* social shopping services
defined, 34
market segmentation, 54–63
revenue drivers, 27
selling directly on social media, 110

Business Wire, 554
Buy Now app, Twitter, 111
Buyable Pins, Pinterest, 111, 112, 439
BuzzFeed, 190
BuzzStream, 554

C

CafeMom, 511
Calendar and Time Management Software for Windows Reviews, 80
calendar software, 79, 80
call to action (CTA)
 in content-marketing strategy, 273
 driving traffic through, 266
 engagement ads, 577
 Facebook Live, 384
 sales, making through, 267
 on Snapchat, 471
cannibalization, channel, 674
cards, Twitter, 572–573, 619–620
Care2, 508, 509
career page, LinkedIn company pages, 411
career summary, LinkedIn, 396
CarGurus, 507
category pages, 137
CCA (cost of customer acquisition)
 comparing, 36–38
 diagnosing problems, 669–670
 overview, 35–36
 retaining customers, 38–39
Certified Site Metrics, Alexa, 63
ChangingThePresent, 509
channel cannibalization, 674
channels, social media. *See* social media services; *specific channels*
charitable endeavors, in LinkedIn profile, 397
Chartbeat, 591
Chat button, Snapchat, 467
chats, Snapchat, 467
chats, Twitter
 benefits of, 327–328
 guests for, finding, 331–332
 hashtag for, finding, 328–329
 hosting, 333–335
 management programs, 329–330
 overview, 289, 327
 promoting, 311, 332–333
cheat sheet, 4
check stand provider, 108
checking in
 on Facebook, 518–519
 on Twitter, 517
CheckMoz, 179
Chegg, 578–580
chiclets, 202–203, 635–636
Chief Financial Officer Network, 505
Choi, Solomon, 218, 220
Citysearch, 511
Claritas My Best Segments tool, 59, 60
Classmates, 510
click bait, 235, 367
Click to website ads, Facebook, 376
ClickPress, 554
clickstream analysis, 62, 651–652
click-through rate (CTR)
 as KPI, 647
 newsletters, 659
 social media advertising, 564
Clicky, 590, 591
Clickz interactive ROI calculator, 46
clients, searching for on Twitter, 303
closed groups, Facebook, 368–369
Club Penguin, 510
Clutch, 8
collaborative boards, Pinterest, 447–448, 459–460
collecting, social networks focused on, 509
college social networks, 510
colleges, finding Twitter chat guests at, 331
comments
 on blogs, 243
 on content-sharing services, tracking, 602–603
 on LinkedIn, 432

on Pinterest pins, 438, 461
search terms in, 161
on Snapchat, 473–474
on Vimeo, 541
comment-style ads, 577
communication
growing community through, 268
through content marketing, 233
community
blogs, influence on, 239
content-marketing strategy goals, 268–269
Facebook, inviting people to, 351–353
Facebook, involving, 365–368
in Facebook content strategy, 358, 359
Facebook Live, engaging with via, 388–389
importance of, 258
Instagram, 487
LinkedIn, 395, 418–421
Pinterest, building, 452–453, 456, 459–462
Snapchat, engaging with, 473–474
social listening, growing with, 322
Twitter, 288, 309
Twitter chats, promoting through, 333
when guest blogging, 260
community-building services. *See also specific services*
KPIs for, 648
overview, 13
performance metrics, 653–655
companion website, 4
company news, sharing on LinkedIn, 413
company pages, LinkedIn, 173
administrators, 412–413
benefits of, 410
creating, 410–413
overview, 409
sharing content, 413
showcase pages, 414–416
comparison shopping, 217
competitors
comparing social media use, 670
LinkedIn company pages of, 411
monitoring on Twitter, 323
search terms for, 134
social media use, 255
complaints, responding to on Twitter, 306, 322, 324–326
composition, defined, 498
comScore, 128, 132, 173, 208, 536
Connect Daily, 80
connections, LinkedIn, 395, 422–423
Constant Contact, 549
contact info, Facebook About page, 343, 360
content creators, 274
content inventory, 271–272
content marketing. *See also* content platforms; content strategy, Facebook
balancing evergreen and timely content, 278
benefits of, 228–230
core message, 270
defined, 228
editorial calendar, 276–277
executing strategy, 279
expertise, establishing, 268
getting content seen, 275
goals, determining, 263–269
issues with, 671–672
by KEEN, 667
lead generation, 269
on LinkedIn company pages, 410, 413
making content stand out, 233–235
measuring success, 281–283
newsletters, 550–551
online community, growing, 268–269
overview, 227–228, 263
press releases, 555–556
putting strategy on paper, 270–274
sales, making, 232–233, 266–267
sharing content with public, 280–281
through Twitter, 289, 308
traffic, driving, 265–266
Content Marketing Institute, 64

content platforms. *See also* content marketing
blogs, 238–243
choosing, 231–232
in content-marketing strategy, 270
guest blogging, 258–262
images, 249–254
LinkedIn as, 429–434
overview, 237–238
podcasts, 243–246
social media, 254–258
video interviews, 248–249
viral videos, 246–247
content strategy, Facebook
closed or secret groups, 368–369
community, involving, 365–368
contests, 367
creating, 358–359
discounts, 367–368
groups, creating, 369–370
hashtags, using in posts, 364
Insights panel, 370–372
overview, 357
polls, 366
quizzes, 366–367
shareable content, 362–364
sharing brand story, 359–361
tips for good content, 361–362
content-distribution tools, 104–106. *See also specific tools*
content-sharing services. *See also specific services*
analytics, 599–603
blogs, 603–604
comments, tracking, 602–603
overview, 9–10, 599
podcasts, 606–608
return on investment, 614–615
video, 605–606
contests
Facebook, 367
on Snapchat, 472
in social media integration, 559–560
controversy, 332, 362
conversational marketing, 288. *See also* Twitter
conversion funnel, 15, 40, 596
conversion rate, 585, 654, 669
copyright, 91, 92, 250–251
correspondent, in content-marketing strategy, 274
cost of customer acquisition (CCA)
comparing, 36–38
diagnosing problems, 669–670
overview, 35–36
retaining customers, 38–39
cost of goods, 44
cost per engagement (CPE) ads, 539
cost per thousand (CPM) impressions, 568, 656–657
cost-per-action (CPA) advertising, 656
cost-per-click (CPC) advertising
Facebook advertising, 568
overview, 656, 657
Pinterest Promoted Pins, 576
social media advertising, 564
cost-per-follow (CPF) ads, 569
cost-per-view (CPV) ads, 539
costs
advertising, 655–657
break-even point, calculating, 44
content marketing, 273
Facebook advertising, 374, 376, 568
hard, 615, 658
LinkedIn advertising, 575
Pinterest advertising, 576
return on investment, determining, 45
social media marketing, 26, 658
soft, 615
Twitter advertising, 571–572
coupons, 558–559, 659. *See also* group coupons; social shopping services
cover photo, Facebook, 343, 346–347, 360
CPA (cost-per-action) advertising, 656
CPC (cost-per-click) advertising
Facebook advertising, 568
overview, 656, 657
Pinterest Promoted Pins, 576
social media advertising, 564

CPE (cost per engagement) ads, 539
CPF (cost-per-follow) ads, 569
CPM (cost per thousand) impressions, 568, 656–657
CPV (cost-per-view) ads, 539
crawlers, 131
Crazy Egg, 51
Create Bigmoji icon, Snapchat, 468
CreateSpace, 508
Creative Commons license, 91, 250–251, 252
credit, giving on Pinterest, 461
CRM (customer relationship management), 43
cross-industry directories, 504–506
cross-linking, 155, 158
cross-postings, automating, 104
CTA (call to action)
  in content-marketing strategy, 273
  driving traffic through, 266
  engagement ads, 577
  Facebook Live, 384
  sales, making through, 267
  on Snapchat, 471
CTR (click-through rate)
  as KPI, 647
  newsletters, 659
  social media advertising, 564
Curiobot, 509
cursing, on Twitter, 311
custom URL, for Facebook, 350–351
customer relationship management (CRM), 43
customer service
  in mobile social marketing, 217
  Twitter, using for, 322, 323, 324–326
customer support, offering on Twitter, 289
customers. *See also* online market research; target audience
  versus community, 258
  content-marketing strategy goals, 264
  conversion funnel, 15
  cost of customer acquisition, 35–39, 669–670
  as driving selection of social media alternatives, 53
  finding on Twitter, 288, 300
  gaining new, on Twitter, 326
  group coupon issues, 528, 530–531
  group coupons, attracting with, 524
  lead generation, 269
  listening to with Twitter, 321–326
  matching social media services to goals, 25
  needs of, focusing on, 267
  retaining, 38–39
  social media use, 255
  targeting with newsletters, 548

D

Daily, Andrea, 28, 29, 30, 31
daily deals, 533
DailyDealOmaha, 524
Dailymotion, 513
dark traffic, 649
dashboards
  analytics, 588, 589, 594
  blog, 242
  social media, creating, 81–84
  Twitter Analytics, 619
Data.com Connect, 505
deal bucks, 529–530
deals, offering special. *See* coupons; group coupons; promotional codes
Delicious, 183, 190, 191
demographic segmentation, 55, 56–57
demographically stratified sites, 510–512
demographics
  LinkedIn analytics, 639
  mismatch between channel and audience, 671
  Nielsen PRIZM data, 59
  Pinterest audience analytics, 612
  of social media users, 60
description metatags, 141–142
descriptions, Pinterest pins, 455, 456–458, 462
Design Float, 508
design social networks, 508
desktop applications, Twitter, 318–319

DeviantArt, 507
Digg, 185, 186, 202, 213
DiggDigg, 455
digital advertising. *See* advertising; social media advertising
digital marketing. *See* social media marketing
direct messages (DMs), Twitter, 294, 306, 325, 326, 625
direct sales, 17–19, 39, 110–112
disclosure statements, 93, 95
DisclosurePolicy, 94, 95
discounts. *See also* group coupons
  in Facebook content strategy, 367–368
  growing community through, 269
  role in brand likes on Facebook, 340
  as shareable Facebook content, 363
  in social media integration, 558–559
  in Twitter campaigns, 309
display ads, Spotify, 537
displaying products on social media, 108, 110
DisplayPlanner by Google, 494
distribution services, press, 554–555
DMs (direct messages), Twitter, 294, 306, 325, 326, 625
domain name
  for analytics, 653
  blog, 162
  email addresses with, 161
  hub sites, 21
Door to Door Organics, 28–31
Doostang, 505
DoubleClick by Google, 657
*Dough*Nation promotion, i Fratelli, 73–75
download time, minimizing, 152
downloads, as KPI, 654
Downloads tab, companion website, 4, 101
downstream clicks, tracking, 652
Dreamstime, 252
duplicate content
  editorial calendar, benefits for, 276
  in SEO, 147–148
  WordPress, 164

E

eBay, 117
e-books, establishing expertise through, 268
eCairn, 125
e-commerce badges, 108, 110
e-commerce software, 40–41
e-commerce tools
  displaying products on social media, 108, 110
  example of, 113–115
  overview, 108
  selling directly on social media, 110–112
  selling through links, 108, 109
  third-party products for selling, 115–118
Ecwid, 115
editorial calendar
  in content-marketing strategy, 270, 273
  Facebook Live, 389
  role in getting content seen, 276–277
editors, in content-marketing strategy, 274
education, in LinkedIn profile, 401
eHow, 513
E-junkie, 117
Electronic Frontier Foundation, 94
Elegant Themes, 205
Elyash, Michael, 113, 114
email, to LinkedIn groups, 418, 427–428
email addresses, 161
email newsletters
  content, finding and sharing, 550–551
  in Facebook content strategy, 359
  followers and connections, finding more, 549–550
  integrating social media with, 547–551
  KPIs for, 658–659
  lead generation, 269
  overview, 18
  reasons to use, 548
  sales, making through, 232–233, 267
  sharing content through, 281
  subscribers, gaining more, 549
emailmonday, 175

eMarketer, 563, 660
emergency information, in mobile social marketing, 216
eMetrics, 645
employees, involving in social media campaign, 86–87, 88
endorsement, product, 93, 95
endorsements, LinkedIn
  asking for, 405–406
  opting out of, 406–407
  overview, 394, 402
  removing from profile, 406
  reordering, 406
e-newsletters
  content, finding and sharing, 550–551
  in Facebook content strategy, 359
  followers and connections, finding more, 549–550
  integrating social media with, 547–551
  KPIs for, 658–659
  lead generation, 269
  overview, 18
  reasons to use, 548
  sales, making through, 232–233, 267
  sharing content through, 281
  subscribers, gaining more, 549
engagement
  content-marketing strategy goals, 264
  defined, 16, 96
  in Facebook Insights, 630
  Facebook Live, 384, 388–389
  issues with, 672–673
  LinkedIn analytics, 637, 638, 639
  LinkedIn showcase pages, 415
  on minor social marketing sites, 496–498
  on Snapchat, 473–474
  through content marketing, 283
  Tumblr sponsored posts, 539
  Twitter advertising, 570–571
engagement ads, 576–577
enterprise-level monitoring tools, 125–126
enterprise-level statistical programs, 590–591
entertainment social networks, 508
environment social networks, 508
ethnic social networks, 510
etiquette
  Pinterest, 461–462
  Twitter, 310–311
Etsy, 117
event tracking, Google Analytics, 654
events
  Facebook, 354–355, 360, 376, 383, 384
  KPIs for, 659
  publicity, in mobile social marketing, 217
  tickets, selling, 18
EventsLink Network Website Calendar, 80
evergreen content, 230, 278
Everplaces, 517
Experian Marketing Services, 494
experience, in LinkedIn profile, 401
expertise
  blogging, benefits of, 239
  content marketing benefits, 229–230
  content platform choice, 231
  content-marketing strategy goals, 264, 268
  Facebook, establishing on, 354
  in Facebook content strategy, 359
  guest blogging to grow, 258–262
  LinkedIn, establishing with, 395, 418
experts, involving in social media campaign, 87
Explore button
  Instagram, 485, 487
  Pinterest, 442, 443
Export tab, Facebook Insights, 629–630
external search optimization. *See* search engine optimization
eXTReMe Tracking, 590, 591

F

Facebook. *See also* Facebook advertising; Facebook content strategy; Facebook Insights; Facebook Live
  About page, 343, 349–350
  acquisitions by, 102
  administrative features, 348–349

Facebook *(continued)*
apps, 348, 365–366, 367
Arcadia Ales use of, 199
audience for, 14
boosted posts, 567–568
branding with, 341–342
brands, appeal of on, 340–341
checking in on, 518–519
Chegg use of, 578–579
creating content, 257
custom URL for, 350–351
direct sales on, 111
Door to Door Organics use of, 29, 30
events, creating, 354–355
as full network, 10, 11
geomarketing on, 518-521
geotagging, 518
groups, 369–370, 653
HCSS use of, 49, 51
Instagram account, creating with, 479–480, 481
inviting people to community, 351–353
keeping current with news and updates, 341
liking other brands, 353–354
Living Royal use of, 113
location search function, 58–59
matching to goals, 25
mobile analytics, 641
mobile app, 212, 213
offers, 519–521, 533
optimizing, 169–170
overview, 339
page components, 342–344
Places Nearby, 518
real-time search, 176
rules of, 161
selling on, 365–366
sharing content on, 280
signing into Pinterest with, 441
16 Handles use of, 218
sticky content, 345, 347–348
Terms of Use, 365, 367
timeline, 345–348
timing posts for news sites, 196
tracking options for sales, 42
Twitter chats, promoting on, 332
usage statistics, 128
Facebook advertising
ad types, 375–377
Ads Manager, 377–378, 379
boosted posts, 567–568
cost of, 374, 376, 568
creating ads, 377–378
general discussion, 564–568
geographic segmentation, 58–59
guidelines for, 377
Insights section, 349, 379
mobile social media, 222–223
offers, 519–521
overview, 366, 373, 562
reasons to invest in, 375
ROI, measuring, 379–380
targeting fans, 378–379
Facebook Connect, 93
Facebook content strategy
closed or secret groups, 368–369
community, involving, 365–368
contests, 367
creating, 358–359
discounts, 367–368
groups, creating, 369–370
hashtags, using in posts, 364
Insights panel, 370–372
overview, 357
polls, 366
quizzes, 366–367
shareable content, 362–364
sharing brand story, 359–361
tips for good content, 361–362
Facebook Insights
accessing, 628–629
advertising, 349, 379
content strategy, 370–372
Export tab, 629–630
Likes detail page, 631

overview, 593, 627–628
Overview dashboard, 628, 629, 630–631
Page Views detail page, 633
Reach detail page, 632
traffic data, 646, 647
Facebook Live
benefits of, 382–384
brainstorming ideas for, 389–390
businesses using, 382
engaging with community via, 388–389
overview, 381
setting up live stream, 384–387
shareable Facebook content, 363
Facebook Location, 517
Facebook Marketplace, 365
Facebook Offer function, 368, 376
Facebook Store, 365
family life cycle, 60, 61
fan pages. *See* Facebook; pages, Facebook
Fanpop, 508
fans, Facebook, 629
Fark, 186
fashion social networks, 509
Feature option, LinkedIn groups, 426
Federal Trade Commission (FTC), 93, 94
fee-based monitoring tools, 125–126
feedback
in Facebook content strategy, 359
growing community through, 269
on LinkedIn showcase pages, 415
role in brand likes on Facebook, 341
feedback widgets, 118
"15 Google Analytics Tricks to Maximize Your Marketing Campaign", 595
filenames, search terms in, 166
film social networks, 508
filters
Instagram, 481–482
Snapchat, 464, 467, 475
financials, in measurement strategy, 586
Findery, 517
FindLaw, 94
fixed costs, 44
fixed-dollar discounts, group coupons, 527
Flash animation, 147
flat fee ads, Facebook, 568
Flickr
analytics availability on, 601
mobile app, 213
overview, 252, 513
sharing images on, 253
Flixster, 508
Fluid IT Services, 21
Flurry from Yahoo!, 642
FolkD, 183
Follow Us buttons (chiclets), 202–203, 635–636
followers
on Pinterest profile page, 443
Snapchat, tips for adding, 469–470
Twitter, 297, 300, 308, 311, 626
Followers section, LinkedIn Analytics tab, 638–640
FollowFriday (#FF) hashtag, 625
following
on Instagram, 487
on Pinterest, 443, 452–453
Twitter follower-to-following ratio, 626
foodies, 501
Forrester Research Inc., 37, 39
forums, monitoring tools for, 125
four Ps of marketing, 673–675
Foursixty program, Living Royal, 114
Foursquare, 213
free advertising, 19
free analytics packages, 590
freebies, in social media integration, 558–559
FreeImages, 91, 252
freemium tools, 97, 674
friends
following on Pinterest, 452
inviting to like Facebook page, 351–352
FTC (Federal Trade Commission), 93, 94
full networks, 10. *See also specific services*

G

games
  product placement in, 659
  in social media integration, 559–560
GanttProject, 79
generational social networks, 510
Gentlemint, 513
geofilters, Snapchat, 467, 472, 475–476
geographic segmentation, 55, 58–60
geographically stratified sites, 510–512
geomarketing tools. *See also specific services*
  deciding to use, 516–517
  Facebook, 518–521
  overview, 12–13, 515
  reasons to use, 515
  summary of services, 517
  Twitter, 517–518
geotagging, Facebook, 518
gift ideas, in Pinterest boards, 446
Gilt, 509
Gilt City, 533
goals
  content marketing, 231, 263–269, 270
  establishing, 25
  Facebook advertising, 565–566
  Facebook content strategy, 358, 359
  KPIs for, 644
  in measurement strategy, 584
  reviewing, 492–493
GoingUp!, 590
Goodreads, 62, 508
goo.gl (Google URL Shortener), 155, 593
Google
  AdPreview tool, 154
  advertising market share, 563
  advertising on, 223
  algorithm changes, 142
  B2B mobile use, 217
  DisplayPlanner by, 494
  DoubleClick by, 657
  duplicate content, 147–148
  free or low-cost images, 91
  metatag length, 141
  personalized search, 154, 155
  real-time search, 175, 177–178
  researching successful Twitter brands, 296
  search terms, researching with, 134
  SEO for, 129, 131–132, 177–178
  Social Media Analytics, 596–598, 618, 646
  tagging links, 649–651
  Universal Analytics Upgrade Center, 652
  URL configuration, 149
Google +1 buttons, 178
Google AdWords, 134, 135, 163, 649
Google Alerts, 50, 119, 120
Google Analytics
  clickstream analysis, 652
  content marketing, 281
  content-sharing sites, availability on, 601
  conversion rate, 654
  dashboard, 588
  Door to Door Organics use of, 30
  e-commerce tracking, 41
  event tracking, 654
  HCSS use of, 51
  lead-monitoring and CRM, 43
  mobile analytics, 640–642
  outbound links, tracking, 652
  overview, 590, 594–596
  referrers to primary website, 614
  resources, 595
  Social Media Analytics, 596–598
  social media services integrating with, 592–593
  social plug-ins, 635–636
  Social Value option, 637, 654
  tagging links, 649–651
  Tumblr analytics, 540
  Twitter performance metrics, 618
  website statistics, 600

Google Analytics Solutions, 595
Google Bookmarks, 183
Google Calendar, 79, 80, 81, 277
Google Groups, 653
Google Index Status page, 152
Google My Business, 153
Google News, 125, 341
Google Search Console, 134, 143
Google Sites, 14
Google Toolbar, 494
Google Trends, 63, 120–121, 135, 175, 551
Google URL Shortener (goo.gl), 155, 593
Google+
  analytics, 593
  matching to goals, 25
  mobile app, 213
  optimizing, 170–171
  promoting Twitter chats on, 333
  real-time search, 176, 178
grammar, in tweets, 290
Grandparents.com, 511
group boards, Pinterest, 459–460
group coupons
  attractive offers, making, 525–526
  benefits of, 530
  comparing LivingSocial and Groupon, 531–533
  daily deals, 533
  deciding to use, 524–525
  depth of discount, 526
  extra options, 529–530
  measuring success, 528–529
  overview, 523–524
  possible issues, 527–528, 530–531
  scope of deal, 526–527
  setting terms for campaign, 526–528
Groupon
  addressing issues with coupons, 531
  comparing to LivingSocial, 531–533
  deal bucks, 529–530
  Meetup integration with, 521
  merchant satisfaction, 532
  overview, 523, 532
  Pages, 531
groups, Facebook
  closed or secret, 368–369
  creating, 369–370
  Facebook Live, 383
groups, LinkedIn
  approving or preapproving members, 423–424
  benefits of, 417–418
  community, growing with, 418–421
  featuring posts from community members, 426
  growing, 422–424
  guidelines for, 421
  importance of, 396
  inviting people to, 422–423
  Jobs tab, adding, 426–427
  managing moderation queue, 425–426
  moderating, 424–428
  overview, 394, 417
  performance metrics, 653
  sending weekly email to, 427–428
  setting up, 419
  standard or unlisted, 420–421
GrubHub, 471
guest blogging
  driving traffic through, 265
  establishing expertise through, 268
  finding relevant blogs, 260–261
  overview, 258–259
  pitching content, 260–261
  promoting posts, 261–262
  understanding, 259–260

H

hard costs, 615, 658
HARO (Help a Reporter Out), 554
Harvard Business School, 35, 37, 45
hashtag jacking, 305, 364
Hashtagify.me, 125

hashtags (#)
defined, 139
in Facebook posts, 364
Instagram, 485–487
search terms in, 160–161, 310
searching for on Twitter, 303
trending, on Twitter, 303–304
in tweets, 168, 304–305
in Twitter campaigns, 308
Twitter chat, finding, 328–329
as Twitter measurement mechanism, 625
Hashtracking, 305, 330
Hassell, Karmene, 197, 198–199
HauteLook, 533
HCSS, 48–52
header photo, Twitter profile page, 314, 315–316
headlines
LinkedIn blogs, 433
search terms in, 146, 161
social news stories, 193
headshots, in LinkedIn profile, 398
heat maps, 51, 282
Help a Reporter Out (HARO), 554
hero image, LinkedIn showcase pages, 415–416
hi5, 513
high school social networks, 510
high-discount coupons. *See* group coupons
Highwire, 117
hiring, LinkedIn use for, 394, 395
history boards, Pinterest, 446
Home Goods, 478
home page
LinkedIn, 431
Pinterest, 442
home page takeover, Spotify, 537
Home tab, LinkedIn, 637
Hootsuite
Arcadia Ales use of, 199
business metrics, 35
HCSS use of, 50
overview, 105, 591
social media dashboard, 83, 84
social media policy resources, 90
as Twitter app, 319
HoverSpot, 513
"How to Prepare for Google Analytics IQ", 595
"How to Set Up Goals in Google Analytics", 595
HowSociable, 121
how-to content, 265, 413, 446
hub site. *See also* search engine optimization; websites
defined, 21
performance of, 583
social media integration with, 557–560
HubPages, 513
HubSpot
B2B market research tools, 64
dashboard, 588, 589
HCSS use of, 50, 51
lead monitoring, 43
overview, 103
researching minor sites on, 494
sources for social share buttons, 204
timing posts for social media, 196
web metrics, 645
Huge, 645
human resources, 20
humor, 290, 363, 456, 474
Hybrid.Care giving program, KEEN, 666

I

I Build America site, 49
i Fratelli Pizza, 73–76
IAB (Interactive Advertising Bureau), 577
IBM Enterprise Marketing Management, 591
IceRocket, 121, 125, 176, 552
Iconosquare, 50
icons, explained, 3
iFrame-based solutions, 169
IFTTT (If This Then That), 122
image sharing sites. *See* content-sharing services; photo-sharing sites; *specific sites*

images. *See also* Instagram; Pinterest; Snapchat
as content platform, 237, 249–254
download time, minimizing, 152
Facebook, 342–343, 346–347
finding online, 251–253
header, for Twitter profile, 314, 315–316
legal issues, 91, 93, 250–251
LinkedIn blogs, 433
LinkedIn company pages, 411, 413
LinkedIn profile, 398–400
LinkedIn showcase pages, 415–416
optimizing, 164, 166–167, 249, 266
pinning on Pinterest, 448–451
Pinterest profile, 443
search terms in, 146, 147
sharing on Facebook, 360, 363
sharing on photo-sharing sites, 253–254
social content-sharing services, 9
WordPress blogs, 164
Image/Video button, Snapchat, 467
impulse buys, 530
inbound links
blogs, 162, 163
in SEO, 129, 155–157
from social-bookmarking and social news services, 186
index, defined, 498
Index Explore tool, Bing, 152
Index Status page, Google, 152
indexing sites, 150–152
industry news, sharing, 413
industry-specific social networks, 506–509
iNewsWire, 554
influencers
as distribution channel for press releases, 555
identifying, 66, 552–553
infographics, 267
information services, KPIs for, 648. *See also* blogs
InjuryLawyerNM.com, 143–144
Insights, Facebook
accessing, 628–629
advertising, 349, 379
content strategy, 370–372
Export tab, 629–630
Likes detail page, 631
overview, 593, 627–628
Overview dashboard, 628, 629, 630–631
Page Views detail page, 633
Reach detail page, 632
traffic data, 646, 647
Instagram
advertising on, 562, 564
analytics availability on, 601
Arcadia Ales use of, 199
brand, promoting on, 478, 484–485
creating content, 256
Door to Door Organics use of, 30
filters, 481–482
finding friends and fans on, 487
as geolocation service, 517, 519
hashtags, 485–487
HCSS use of, 49
Living Royal use of, 113–114
matching to goals, 25
notifications, 483–484
overview, 477, 513
private accounts, 486–487
public accounts, 486
setting up account, 479–481
sharing photos, 481–483
16 Handles use of, 218
as social content-sharing services, 9, 10
stories, 488
timing posts for news sites, 196
as Twitter app, 319
integrating social media. *See* social media integration
intellectual property law, 90, 91, 92, 461
Interactive Advertising Bureau (IAB), 577
interactive engagement ads, 576–577
interactive ROI calculator, 46
interest groups, segmentation based on, 55, 62–63
interests, in Pinterest audience analytics, 612
internal performance measurements, 585–586

internal search optimization. *See* search engine optimization
international social networks, 511
International Technology Law Association, 94
Internet Advertising Competition, 657
Internet Legal Research Group, 94
Internet marketing. *See* online marketing; social media marketing
interviews, video, 248–249
invitations, LinkedIn groups, 422–423
ISAPI Rewrite for Microsoft, 149
iStockphoto, 252
IT team, in analytics, 589
ITBusinessEdge, 89
iTunes
  getting podcasts on, 246
  podcast popularity, analyzing, 607–608

J

Jackson, David, 245
Jimmy Choo, 478
Jing, 513
job openings
  on LinkedIn, 394, 410
  searching for on Twitter, 303
  on Snapchat, 471
Jobs tab, LinkedIn groups, 426–427

K

Karen Martin Group, 514
KEEN, Inc., 666–669
Keotag, 203
key performance indicators (KPI)
  across social media, 646–648
  measurement strategy, 586
  for microsites, blogs, and communities, 653–655
  for other online marketing, 658–659
  performance metrics, 644–645
  press release integration, 556–557
  for sales, 39–42
  storefront statistics, 40
Keyword Planner, Google AdWords, 134, 135, 163
keyword stuffing, 146
keywords (search terms)
  analytics programs, discovering from, 282
  in blogs, 162
  choosing, 133–136
  in content-marketing strategy, 270
  defined, 228, 239
  in first paragraph, 143–145
  importance of, 132–133
  as KPI, 646
  in LinkedIn profile, 396
  local search optimization, 153
  in metatags, 139–142
  Pinterest, using on, 439–440, 456, 457, 458
  placement on site, 136–137, 145–146, 148
  placing on social media, 160–161, 167–168, 172–173
  in press release, 556
  resources, 135
  searching for on Twitter, 303, 323
  in social bookmark service submissions, 191
  tags and tag clouds, 137–138
  in tweets, 310
KGen, 135
King, Eric, 666–668
King Arthur Flour, 478
KISSmetrics 50+ Google Analytics Resources, 595
KPI (key performance indicators)
  across social media, 646–648
  measurement strategy, 586
  for microsites, blogs, and communities, 653–655
  for other online marketing, 658–659
  performance metrics, 644–645
  press release integration, 556–557
  for sales, 39–42
  storefront statistics, 40
Kudzu, 511

L

landing pages, newsletters, 659
Lasher, Lynn, 500

Last.fm, 508
Lawyrs.net, 508
leads
as comparative indicator, 654
content-marketing strategy goals, 265, 269
in measurement strategy, 586
tracking, 43
LEADSExplorer, 43
lede, writing good, 193
legal issues, 90–95, 250–251
legal social networks, 508
lenses, Snapchat, 467, 474
LibraryThing, 508
Lieberman, Usher, 578–579
life stage analysis, 55, 60–61
lifestyle, segmentation based on, 55, 61–62
lifetime customer value, 37, 525–526
like bait, Facebook, 367
LikeableMedia Blog, 89
Likes, Facebook, 349, 351–354, 370–371, 372, 380
Likes detail page, Facebook Insights, 631
liking pins, Pinterest, 438, 460
link juice, 155, 157, 162, 183, 186
link shorteners, 155, 619
Link Sleuth, Xenu, 152
LinkedIn. *See also* LinkedIn groups
advertising on, 562, 573–575
analytics, 593, 636–640
Ask to Be Recommended feature, 403
benefits of using, 394–395
blogging on, 430–433
company pages, 173, 409–413
connections, 395
as content platform, 429–434
creating content, 257
endorsements, 402, 405–407
HCSS use of, 49, 51
home page, 431
Home tab, 637
location search function, 58
matching to goals, 25
mobile app, 213
optimizing, 172–173
overview, 10, 12, 393, 409
photos for, 398–400
privacy settings, 396–397
private messages, 407
professional image, projecting, 396–397
profiles, managing, 395–401
promoting Twitter chats on, 333
real-time search, 176
recommendations, 402–404
sharing content with other social media, 433–434
showcase pages, 410, 414–416
16 Handles use of, 219
social media policy resources, 89
timing posts for news sites, 196
LinkedIn groups
approving or preapproving members, 423–424
benefits of, 417–418
community, growing with, 418–421
featuring posts from community members, 426
growing, 422–424
guidelines for, 421
importance of, 396
inviting people to, 422–423
Jobs tab, adding, 426–427
managing moderation queue, 425–426
moderating, 424–428
overview, 417
performance metrics, 653
sending weekly email to, 427–428
setting up, 419
standard or unlisted, 420–421
Linkroll, 183
links
content marketing, 232, 264–265
on Facebook, 360
to group coupons, 529
inbound, 129, 155–157
including on social media sites, 18
from LinkedIn, 173
on LinkedIn posts, 432
to newsletter subscription, 549

links *(continued)*
outbound, tracking, 652
from Pinterest, 171
search terms in, 145
selling through, 108, 109
in SEO, 155–158
sharing through Twitter, 293–294, 298
tagging, 649–651, 659
from Twitter, 168–169
when guest blogging, 260
lists, driving traffic through, 266
Lithium, 126, 660
LittleBird, 552
live streaming, with Periscope, 542–544
live video, on Facebook. *See* Facebook Live
Livestream, 513
Living Royal, 113–115
LivingSocial
comparing to Groupon, 531–533
deal bucks, 530
overview, 523
local business announcements, 217
local Reddits, 200
Local Search Association, 128
local search, SEO for, 153–155
local social networks, 511
Local.com, 511
location, segmentation based on, 55, 58–60
location-based services. *See* geomarketing tools
logos
brand, on Facebook, 360
legal issues, 92
in LinkedIn profile, 399
LinkedIn showcase pages, 416
long description metatags, search terms in, 166
long-tail keywords, 133
loss leaders, 525
loyalty
content-marketing strategy goals, 264
growing community through, 269
role in brand likes on Facebook, 340
lurking, 497

M

Mahalo, 513
MailChimp, 547, 549
Make Me Sustainable, 508
manager, LinkedIn groups, 424–425
Manta, 511
maps
heat, 51, 282
search, posting business on, 153
market, target. *See* target audience
market research. *See* online market research
market segmentation
affinity groups, 62–63
defined, 54
demographic, 56–57
geographic, 58–60
life stage analysis, 60–61
overview, 54–56
psychographics or lifestyle, 61–62
marketing. *See also* content marketing; performance metrics; social media integration; social media marketing
advertising metrics, comparing types with, 655–658
comparing social media to other online, 658–660
conversational, 288
cost of, 38
four Ps of, 673–675
integrating social media into overall effort, 20–22
offline, 661
Marketing Land, 103, 208
marketing team
in content-marketing strategy, 274
editorial calendar, benefits for, 276
responsibility for analytics, 588–589
social media, building, 85–87
MarketingProfs, 83, 103
MarketingSherpa, 103
Marleylilly, 108, 109
Marshall, Audrey, 501–502
Mashable, 89, 90, 103, 494

measurable objectives, setting, 26
measurement strategy. *See also* analytics; performance metrics
  challenges, 644
  establishing responsibility for analytics, 587–589
  monitoring versus measuring, 585
  overview, 584
  social media measurement, 118
  what to measure, 586–587
media. *See also* images; video
  in LinkedIn blogs, 433
  in LinkedIn profile, 397
media kit, 655
media sharing services, 648. *See also* content-sharing services; photo-sharing sites; *specific services*
Mediabistro, 508
medical social networks, 508
Medium, 505, 601
MeetEdgar, 50, 83
meeting services, 12–13. *See also specific services*
MeetMe, 510
MeetTheBoss TV, 505
Meetup, 513, 521–523, 593
Meltwater IceRocket, 552
members, LinkedIn groups, 419, 422–424, 425, 426
memes, 256, 486
memories, Snapchat, 467
Mention, 119, 122, 660
Mentions tab, Twitter, 624
Mercantec, 41, 117
merchant satisfaction, Groupon, 532
MerchantCircle, 511
metadata, 138
MetaFilter, 186
metatags
  overview, 138–139
  page description, 141–142
  page title, 139, 141
  search terms in, 161, 166
  viewing, 139, 140
metrics. *See also* analytics; measurement strategy; Twitter performance metrics
  A/B testing, 644–645
  activity timelines, layering with, 664, 665
  adjustments to campaign, making, 675–676
  advertising metrics, comparing marketing types with, 655–658
  break-even point, 44–45
  calculating ROI based on, 47, 48
  clickstream analysis, 651–652
  comparing across social media, 646–652
  comparing social media to other online marketing, 658–660
  cost of customer acquisition, 35–39
  decision-making based on, 663–666
  diagnosing problems, 669–670
  example of, 48–52
  fixing problems, 670–675
  integrating social media with, 653–655
  KEEN use of, 666–669
  KPIs, establishing, 644–645
  KPIs for sales, establishing, 39–42
  leads, tracking, 43
  lifetime customer value, 37
  measurement challenges, 644
  measurement strategy, 585–586
  measuring, 585–586
  net profit margin, 45
  outbound links, tracking, 652
  overview, 33–34, 643
  reasonable expectations for, 670
  resources, 645
  resources for, 35
  revenue versus profit, 45
  ROI, determining, 45–48
  ROI, preparing to calculate, 34–35
  social plug-ins, 635–636
  tagging links, 649–651
  word-of-web versus word-of-mouth, 660–661
microblogging. *See* Tumblr; Twitter
microsites, 560, 653–655
Microsoft, 660

mid-size social media channels. *See also specific sites*
  deciding to use, 535–536
  overview, 535
  Periscope, 542–544
  Spotify, 536–537
  Tumblr, 538–540
  Vimeo, 540–542
MiGente.com, 510
minor social marketing sites. *See also specific sites*
  choosing strategically, 498–499
  goals, reviewing, 492–493
  involvement on, assessing, 496–498
  overview, 491–492
  researching, 493–496
  Somebody's Mother's use of, 499, 500–502
Mixpanel, 642
mobile advertising. *See* advertising; social media advertising
mobile analytics, 220–221, 640–642
mobile apps. *See also* Instagram; Snapchat
  Periscope, 542–544
  for social media, 212–215
  Twitter, 319–320
mobile devices
  activities on, 211–212
  demographics of mobile users, 210–211
  search optimization for, 148, 173–175
  social media use on, 208–210
  tablet use, 221–222
  usage statistics, 208
mobile social marketing
  advertising, 222–223
  harvesting leads and sales, 216–217
  measuring success, 220–221
  mobile apps, 212–215
  mobile social media use, 208–210
  overview, 207
  16 Handles use of, 218–220
  tablet use, 221–222
mobile websites, 211–212
MocoSpace, 513
moderating LinkedIn groups, 424–428
moderator, LinkedIn group, 424–425
MommySavers, 511, 512
moms, social networks for, 511
monitoring, versus measuring, 585
monitoring tools, 124–126, 670. *See also* social media monitoring tools; *specific tools*
MOOVIA, 79
More, 510
Morguefile, 252
Moss, Skyler, 49, 50, 51
Motortopia, 507
Moz, 143, 494
MozBar, 143
Mozilla Lightning Calendar, 80
mozRank Pro Checker, 179
multimedia, optimizing, 166–167. *See also* media; *specific media*
Multi-product carousel ads, Facebook, 376
music, selling, 18
music social networks, 508, 536–537
Musical.ly, 102
My Best Segments tool, Claritas, 59, 60
My Contests, 367
My Friends icon, Snapchat, 468
My Yahoo!, 83
Myspace, 508

N

name recognition. *See* branding
National Retail Federation, 35
natural search, 131
navigational items, search terms in, 146
Naymz, 97, 505
Nearby Places, Facebook, 518
negativity, 302, 325, 362, 458
net profit margin, 45
Netbiscuits, 642
NetSphere Strategies, 89
Netvibes, 82–83, 594
networking services, 10–12, 648. *See also specific services*
networking tool, Twitter as, 299. *See also* Twitter

news
Facebook Live for, 382
on LinkedIn, 395, 410, 413
in mobile social marketing, 216
press releases, 551–557
role in brand likes on Facebook, 340
searching for on Twitter, 303
news services. *See* social news services; *specific services*
newsletters
content, finding and sharing, 550–551
in Facebook content strategy, 359
followers and connections, finding more, 549–550
integrating social media with, 547–551
KPIs for, 658–659
lead generation, 269
overview, 18
reasons to use, 548
sales, making through, 232–233, 267
sharing content through, 281
subscribers, gaining more, 549
newsrooms, online, 552
Newsvine, 186
Nexopia, 511
Nextdoor, 511
niche markets, 54, 510. *See also* market segmentation
niche sites. *See* stratified social-networking communities
Nielsen Online, 126
Nielsen PRIZM system, Tetrad, 59
Nike, 478
No Derivative Works images, 250
<nofollow> tag, 183
Nolo, 94
nonprofits, 509
notifications
Facebook, 345, 349
Instagram, 483–484
LinkedIn groups, 425
Snapchat, 470
Twitter mobile app, 320
Notifications button, Pinterest, 443, 444
Notifications tab, Twitter, 623–625

O

objectives, quantifiable, 26
Offer function, Facebook, 368, 376
offers, Facebook, 519–521, 533
offline content, placing share information in, 353
offline marketing, 661
Olivier Blanchard Basics of Social Media ROI, 35
on demand geofilters, Snapchat, 475–476
123RF, 252
140-character limit, Twitter, 290–291, 304
one-percent rule, 267
online advertising. *See* advertising; social media advertising
online cheat sheet, 4
online community
content-marketing strategy goals, 268–269
growing with social listening, 322
importance of, 258
online market research
B2B markets, 64–65
B2C market segmentation, 54–63
influencers, identifying, 66
motivation to use social media, 66
other types of, 65–67
overview, 53
target market, locating, 54
online marketing. *See also specific forms of online marketing*
comparing social media results to, 658–659
integrating social media into, 20–22
ROI for different types of, 36, 37
online newsrooms, 552
online resumes, LinkedIn, 395–401
online stores, 18, 108, 110
OnlyWire, 105
on-site marketing, 557–560
open rate, newsletters, 658
optimization. *See* search engine optimization
Oracle Social Cloud, 97

organic post distribution, 632
organic search, 131
outbound links, tracking, 652
overlays, Spotify, 537
Overview dashboard, Facebook Insights, 628, 629, 630–631
Ow.ly, 107, 155, 593
owner, LinkedIn groups, 424

P

package deals, 528
page content, search terms in, 161
page description metatags, 139, 141–142
page insights, Facebook, 627, 628. *See also* Facebook Insights
Page like ads, Facebook, 376
Page likes, in Facebook Insights, 630
Page post engagement ads, Facebook, 376
page title metatags, 139, 141
page views, 282, 654–655
Page Views detail page, Facebook Insights, 633
pages, Facebook. *See also* Facebook; Facebook content strategy
  branding with, 341–342
  components of, 342–344
Pages, Groupon, 531
Pages to Watch section, Facebook Insights, 630–631
paid advertising, 19, 561–563, 655–657. *See also* advertising
paid post distribution, 632
paid search results, 131
paid statistical programs, 590–592
Panalysis, 35, 37, 38, 42
Pandora, 508
parallax design, 147
Paris Opera Ballet, 478
PartnerUp, 505
passer-by, defined, 498
PatentPlaques.com, 505–506
PatientsLikeMe, 508
payments, from coupon services, 527, 528
PayPal, 117
pay-per-click (PPC) advertising, 153, 564, 656
Payvment, 41
People You Reach tab, Pinterest Analytics, 611–612
percentage discounts, group coupons, 527
performance metrics. *See also* analytics; business metrics; Facebook Insights; Google Analytics; performance metrics, Twitter
  A/B testing, 644–645
  adjustments to campaign, making, 675–676
  advertising metrics, comparing marketing types with, 655–658
  calculating ROI based on, 47, 48
  clickstream analysis, 651–652
  comparing across social media, 646–652
  comparing social media to other online marketing, 658–660
  decision-making based on, 663–666
  diagnosing problems, 669–670
  fixing problems, 670–675
  integrating social media with, 653–655
  KEEN use of, 666–669
  KPIs, establishing, 644–645
  measurement challenges, 644
  measurement strategy, 585–586
  outbound links, tracking, 652
  overview, 643
  reasonable expectations for, 670
  resources, 645
  social plug-ins, 635–636
  tagging links, 649–651
  word-of-web versus word-of-mouth, 660–661
performance metrics, Twitter
  direct messages, 625
  Google Analytics, tracking with, 618
  hashtags, 625
  Mentions tab, 624
  Notifications tab, 623–625
  overview, 617
  Retweet Rank, 624
  shortened links, 618–619

TFF ratio, 626
third-party analytics applications, 622–623
TweetDeck, 622
Twitter Analytics, 619–621
Periscope, 25, 102, 542–544
permalinks, blog, 163, 165–166
permissions, images, 250–251
personal social media accounts, 85
personalized search, 154, 155
personas, in social media marketing, 51
personnel, in social media campaign, 86–87, 88
pets, social networks focused on, 509
Pew Research Center
demographics of Internet users, 60
demographics of mobile users, 210
mobile search, 173–174
Pinterest use, 184
social media use, 61, 102
tablet use, 221
philanthropy social networks, 509
Photobucket, 513
photographs. *See* images
photo-sharing sites. *See also* content-sharing services; *specific sites*
analytics, 601
finding images on, 251–253
overview, 513
sharing images on, 253–254
Pin It button, 178, 454
pinned posts, Facebook, 344, 348
pinned tweets, 317–318
pinner, defined, 438
pinning
on Facebook, 345, 347–348
on Pinterest, 448–452
pins, Pinterest
Buyable Pins, 111, 112, 439
commenting on, 438, 461
defined, 438
descriptions for, 455, 456–458, 462
driving traffic with, 455–458
keywords in, 458
liking, 438, 460
pinning process, 448–452
plus sign button options, 442
on profile page, 443
Promoted Pins, 576
repinning, 438, 449, 453–454, 611
rich, 172
searching for, 439
tagging people on, 451–452, 455–456
tips for, 449–451
Pinterest. *See also* pins, Pinterest
advertising on, 562, 576
analytics, 601, 609–614
audience analytics, 611–612
boards, 445–448
community, building, 459–462
creating content, 256
direct sales on, 111, 112
driving traffic with, 455–458
following on, 452–453
getting started, 439–440
Google real-time search, 178
group boards, 459–460
joining, 441–442
Living Royal use of, 113
matching to goals, 25
mobile app, 214
navigating, 442
optimizing, 171–172
overview, 252, 437, 513
profile, setting up, 442–445
profile analytics, 610–611
rules of etiquette, 461–462
searching, 439–440
sharing on, 453–455
social bookmarking, 183–184
tagging on, 451–452
third-party analytics, 614
timing posts for news sites, 196
tracking options for sales, 42
understanding, 438–439
website interaction analytics, 612–614

Pinterest Follow button, 454
Piqqus, 202
PitchEngine, 554, 556
Piwik, 590
Pizza *Dough*Nation promotion, i Fratelli, 73–75
placement, in four Ps of marketing, 674
Places Nearby, Facebook, 518
plug-ins. *See also specific plug-ins*
  blog, 243
  social, performance metrics, 635–636
  WordPress, 164
plus sign (+) button, Pinterest, 442
podcasts
  analytics, 606–608
  comments, tracking, 603
  as content platforms, 237, 243–246
  deciding to use, 244–245
  driving traffic and landing sales with, 246
  optimizing, 166–167
policy, social media marketing, 87–90
PolicyTool for Social Media, 89
polls, Facebook, 366
Polyvore, 509
popularity, value of, 201
Popurls, 188, 190
position, in four Ps of marketing, 674
Post reach, in Facebook Insights, 630
posts, blog, 242–243
PPC (pay-per-click) advertising, 153, 564, 656
Practical eCommerce, 117
preapproving members, LinkedIn groups, 419, 423–424
presence. *See* branding
Press About, 554
press releases
  content, emphasizing, 555–556
  distributing news, 553–555
  influencers, cultivating, 552–553
  integrating social media with, 551–557
  KPIs for, 659
  measuring results, 556–557
  online newsrooms, setting up, 552
  socially friendly, 556
price, in four Ps of marketing, 673–674. *See also* costs
privacy
  LinkedIn settings for, 396–397
  respecting, 93
private accounts, Instagram, 486–487
private conversations, on Twitter, 294, 306, 325
private groups, LinkedIn, 420–421, 423–424
private membership sites, 560
private messaging
  Facebook, 345, 348
  LinkedIn, 407
PRLog, 554
processes, improving, 16–17
product endorsement relationships, 93, 95
product placement, KPIs for, 659
product tree, 40
ProductCart, 41
product-oriented brands, blogging by, 240–241
products
  content marketing, 232
  displaying on social media, 108, 110
  displaying value of, 20
  four Ps of marketing, 673
  improving with social listening, 323
  on LinkedIn showcase pages, 414–415
  in Pinterest boards, 446
  Snapchat, featuring on, 471
profanity, on Twitter, 311
professional image, on LinkedIn, 396–397
professional networks, 10, 64. *See also specific networks*
professionals, involving in social media campaign, 87
profile photo
  Facebook, 342–343, 346
  Instagram, 480
  Snapchat, 466
Profile screen, Snapchat, 468–469
profiles
  LinkedIn, 395–401, 430
  Pinterest, 442–445, 610–611

social media, 161, 167
Twitter, 167–168, 313–318
profit
break-even point, 44–45
versus revenue, 45
profit margin, 45
project management software, 274, 279
project manager, in content-marketing strategy, 274
ProjectLibre, 79
projects, in LinkedIn profile, 401
promoted accounts, Twitter, 569
Promoted Pins, Pinterest, 576
promoted trends, Twitter, 570
promoted tweets, 569, 578–579
promotion
in four Ps of marketing, 675
on Instagram, 478, 484–485
on LinkedIn showcase pages, 414–416
through Twitter chats, 331–332
on Twitter, 291–295
promotional codes
growing community through, 269
KPIs for, 659
offering, 18
PRWeb, 554
psychographics, 55, 61–62, 503
public accounts, Instagram, 486
publications, in LinkedIn profile, 401
PublicLegal from the Internet Legal Research Group, 94
public-speaking networks, 331
publishing companies, 331
punctuation, in tweets, 290
pure-play enterprises, 34

Q

QR codes, 217
Quantcast
affinity groups, segmenting by, 62, 63
clickstream analysis, 652
demographic information, 56, 57
overview, 15
researching minor sites on, 494
quantifiable objectives, setting, 26
quantified sites, 62
quantitative information. *See also* analytics
measuring, 585–587
on minor social marketing sites, 498
QuizMaker, 367
quizzes, Facebook, 366–367
Quora, 513

R

Radian6, 305
Ragan, 66
Rank Tracker, 179
ranking, search engine. *See* search engine optimization; search engine ranking
Rapport Online, 36, 37
rate of return, ROI as, 46
reach, 657
Reach & Engagement section, LinkedIn Analytics tab, 638, 639
Reach detail page, Facebook Insights, 632
Really Simple Syndication (RSS), 104, 125, 167
real-time search
Google, 177–178
optimizing for, 175–176
recommendation services, 12. *See also specific services*
recommendations, LinkedIn
for company pages, 411
giving, 403–404
overview, 394, 402
receiving, 396, 402–403
recruiters, LinkedIn use by, 394, 395
Red Bull Energy Drink, 478
Reddit
advertising on, 562
Arcadia Ales use of, 197–198
local, 200
overview, 186
press releases, 554
subreddits, 192

redirects, 650
referrers
  analysis by, 595, 614
  as KPI, 647
registrations, in content-marketing strategy, 264
regular, defined, 498
relationship selling, defined, 9
relationships
  building, 16
  driving traffic through, 266
  Vimeo, cultivating on, 541
remarketing, Twitter, 570
Remember icon, explained, 3
repeat customers, 530
repinning, on Pinterest, 438, 449, 453–454, 611
reputation
  blogs in management of, 239
  when guest blogging, 261
Requests to Join function, LinkedIn groups, 426
research. *See* online market research
ResearchGate, 509
responding
  on minor social marketing sites, assessing, 497–498
  to tweets, 302
responsive design, 212
resumes, LinkedIn, 395–401
retaining customers, 38–39
return on investment (ROI)
  content-sharing services, 614–615
  determining, 45–48
  diagnosing problems, 669–670
  Facebook advertising, 379–380
  interactive ROI calculator, 46
  of online-marketing tactics, 36, 37
  overview, 33
  preparing to calculate, 34–35
  from social media marketing, 27–28
Retweet Rank, 624
retweets, 168, 290, 294, 306–307, 624
revenue. *See also* return on investment
  break-even point, calculating, 44
  net profit margin, 45
  versus profit, 45
  from social media marketing, 27
ReverbNation, 18
review sites, 13, 502, 648, 660. *See also specific sites*
reviews, bookmarks for, 194
Rewardli, 525
rich pins, Pinterest, 172
Ridiculously Responsive Social Sharing Buttons, 204
rights, to images, 250–251
robots (bots), 131
Rocket Lawyer, 89
ROI (return on investment)
  content-sharing services, 614–615
  determining, 45–48
  diagnosing problems, 669–670
  Facebook advertising, 379–380
  interactive ROI calculator, 46
  of online-marketing tactics, 36, 37
  overview, 33
  preparing to calculate, 34–35
  from social media marketing, 27–28
rolling averages, 36
ROS (run-of-site) leaderboard ads, 537
RSS (Really Simple Syndication), 104, 125, 167
Rue La La, 509, 533
rules of etiquette
  Pinterest, 461–462
  Twitter, 310–311
rump session, 522
run-of-site (ROS) leaderboard ads, 537

S

sales. *See also* e-commerce tools; return on investment; social shopping services
  as comparative indicator, 654
  content-marketing strategy goals, 264, 266–267
  Facebook advertising ROI, 380

in Facebook content strategy, 358, 359, 365–366
KPIs for, establishing, 39–42
landing with podcasts, 246
LinkedIn showcase pages, 414–416
opportunities for, 17–19
through content marketing, 232–233, 282, 283
on Twitter, 309, 311
sales calculator, 42
sales cycle, 34
Salesforce Marketing Cloud, 126
Save It button, Pinterest, 438
Sawmill LITE, 591
schedule, social media marketing campaign, 78–81
schedule of payments, coupon services, 527, 528
scheduled tweets, 293
School of Podcasting, 245
science social networks, 509
score, Snapchat, 467
SDL SM2, 97
search
on blogs, 243
on Instagram, 485, 487
on Pinterest, 439–440, 442
Twitter, advanced features, 518, 550–551
Twitter, as monitoring tool, 124, 125, 323–324
Twitter, finding followers with, 300
Twitter, overview, 303–304
Twitter, real-time search with, 176
Search Engine Guide, 143
Search Engine Journal, 143
Search Engine Land, 83, 143, 155
search engine marketing (SEM), 131
search engine optimization (SEO)
blogs, 161–166
content to avoid, 147–148
defined, 131
download time, minimizing, 152
driving traffic through, 266
Facebook, 169–170
first paragraph, writing, 143–145
focusing on top search engines, 131–132
Google real-time search, 177–178
Google+, 170–171
images, 166–167, 249
inbound links, 129, 155–158
indexing site, 150–152
issues with, 671
LinkedIn, 172–173, 411
for local search, 153–155
matching social media services to goals, 25
in measurement strategy, 586
metatags, 138–142
for mobile, 173–175
monitoring ranking, 178–179
overview, 17, 127–128, 142, 159–160
for personalized search, 154
Pinterest, 171–172, 457
podcasts, 166–167
real-time search, 175–178
resources, 143
search terms, importance of, 132–138
search terms, placing, 145–146, 160–161
social bookmarking, 182
social media links, 157–158
statistical case for, 128–130
tactics for social media, 130
terminology related to, 131
Twitter, 167–169
updating often, 145
URLs, 148–149
value of, 200
video, 166–167
search engine ranking
blogs, influence on, 239
content marketing, 228, 264
improving, 17
monitoring, 178–179
press releases, improving with, 552
social bookmarks and news services, effect on, 186
when guest blogging, 260
Search Engine Rankings, 179
Search Engine Watch, 35, 143

search maps, posting business on, 153
search terms (keywords)
analytics programs, discovering from, 282
in blogs, 162
choosing, 133–136
in content-marketing strategy, 270
defined, 228, 239
in first paragraph, 143–145
importance of, 132–133
as KPI, 646
in LinkedIn profile, 396
local search optimization, 153
in metatags, 139–142
Pinterest, using on, 439–440, 456, 457, 458
placement on site, 136–137, 145–146, 148
placing on social media, 160–161, 167–168, 172–173
in press release, 556
resources, 135
searching for on Twitter, 303, 323
in social bookmark service submissions, 191
tags and tag clouds, 137–138
in tweets, 310
SearchCRM, 35
seasonal content, planning, 276
Secondary Dimension drop-down list, Google Analytics, 636
secret boards, Pinterest, 447
secret groups, Facebook, 368–369
segmentation, market
affinity groups, 62–63
defined, 54
demographic, 56–57
geographic, 58–60
life stage analysis, 60–61
overview, 54–56
psychographics or lifestyle, 61–62
self-hosted blogs, 241–242
selfies, in LinkedIn profile, 399
selling opportunities. *See* e-commerce tools; sales; social shopping services
SEM (search engine marketing), 131
SEMrush keyword tool, 134, 135, 136
Send Invitations page, LinkedIn, 419
senior social networks, 511
sentiment
analyzing comments for, 602
brand, 96–97
Sentiment 140, 97
SEO (search engine optimization)
blogs, 161–166
content to avoid, 147–148
defined, 131
download time, minimizing, 152
driving traffic through, 266
Facebook, 169–170
first paragraph, writing, 143–145
focusing on top search engines, 131–132
Google real-time search, 177–178
Google+, 170–171
images, 166–167, 249
inbound links, 129, 155–158
indexing site, 150–152
issues with, 671
LinkedIn, 172–173, 411
for local search, 153–155
matching social media services to goals, 25
in measurement strategy, 586
metatags, 138–142
for mobile, 173–175
monitoring ranking, 178–179
overview, 17, 127–128, 142, 159–160
for personalized search, 154
Pinterest, 171–172, 457
podcasts, 166–167
real-time search, 175–178
resources, 143
search terms, importance of, 132–138
search terms, placing, 145–146, 160–161
social bookmarking, 182
social media links, 157–158
statistical case for, 128–130
tactics for social media, 130
terminology related to, 131
Twitter, 167–169

updating often, 145
URLs, 148–149
value of, 200
video, 166–167
SEO Hacker, 170
SERank, 179
Sermo, 508
services. *See also specific services*
content marketing, 232
displaying value of, 20
improving with social listening, 323
on LinkedIn showcase pages, 414–415
social media, types of, 9–13
Settings button
Pinterest profile, 443
Snapchat, 468
Settings page, Facebook, 343–344
share buttons
on blogs, 243
driving traffic through, 266
Facebook, 352–353
on LinkedIn, 433–434
overview, 202, 203–206
performance metrics, 635–636
on Pinterest, 454–455, 456
sharing content, 257
on social shopping services, 529
Share icon, Snapchat, 468
shareable content, 235
Shareaholic, 204
ShareThis, 204, 454–455
share-this-deal functionality, 529
Shopial, 116
Shopify, 41, 116
Shop.org, 37, 39
shopping, bookmarks for, 195
shopping services. *See* social shopping services; *specific services*
short message networks, 10. *See also specific services*
short message service (SMS), 217
short URLs, 106–107, 593–594, 618–619, 661
Shoutlet Social Analytics feature, 647, 648
showcase pages, LinkedIn, 410, 414–416
Shutterstock, 252
sidebars, on blogs, 243
sign-ups, through content marketing, 283
SimilarSites, 65
Site Meter, 590, 591
Site Stats Lite, 591
sitemap (XML) feeds, 151–152
SitePoint, 494
SiteProNews, 103
16 Handles, 218–220
skills, in LinkedIn profile, 397, 401, 402, 405–407
SKUs, multiple, 42
Slashdot, 186
SlideShare, 513, 514
Small Business Association, 657
small businesses, social media marketing by, 8, 18, 77
Smart Insights, 564
SmartAddon, 204
SmartInsights, 39
smartphones, 208, 209, 210. *See also* mobile devices; mobile social marketing; Snapchat
Smartsheet, 79
SMO (social media optimization), 127, 131. *See also* search engine optimization
SMS (short message service), 217
Snap button, Snapchat, 468
Snap code, 469
Snap screen, Snapchat, 467, 468
Snapchat
advertising on, 562
benefits of, 463–464
brand story, telling, 471–473
chats, 467
creating content, 256
engaging with, 473–474
filters, 464, 467, 475
followers, tips for adding, 469–470
geofilters, 467, 472, 475–476
as geolocation service, 519
knowing who is viewing stories, 472–473
lenses, 467, 474

Snapchat *(continued)*
matching to goals, 25
memories, 467
overview, 463
score, 467
screens, touring, 467–469
setting up account, 464–466
16 Handles use of, 219–220
taking snaps, 470
terminology related to, 467
snapcode, 467
snaps, Snapchat
defined, 467
taking, 470
Snipurl, 107, 593
Social Analytics feature, Shoutlet, 647, 648
social banners, 576–577
social bookmarking services. *See also specific services*
application-specific bookmarks, 194–195
benefiting from, 186–187
bookmark swapping, 202
choosing service, 187–189
encouraging others to bookmark or rate site, 201–202
general discussion, 182–184
getting inbound links from, 155–156
KPIs for, 648
monitoring results, 189–190
overview, 12, 181
researching, 188
submitting to, 190–191
timing submissions, 195–196, 200
social commerce, 39
social content-sharing services. *See* content-sharing services; *specific services*
Social Drift, 184
Social Fresh, 97
social geolocation and meeting services, 12–13. *See also specific services*
social listening, with Twitter, 321–326
social mapping, 515
Social Marker, 189
social media. *See also* social media advertising; social media integration; social media services; *specific platforms*; *specific social media marketing entries*
analytical options for, 592–593
changes in use of, 102
choosing between platforms, 255–256
community, importance of, 258
as content platform, 237, 254–258
creating and sharing content, 256–257
driving traffic through, 266
finding Twitter chat guests on, 331
mobile apps for, 212–215
mobile use of, 208–210
press releases, posting on, 553, 555
searching on, 128, 129
sharing content on, 280, 433–434
sharing to from Instagram, 482–483
Social Media Activity Calendar
business metrics, reviewing, 34
comparative metrics, 644
measurement strategy, 584
minor social marketing sites, 495
overview, 81
real-time search efforts, 178
scheduling on, 101
social monitoring tools, 120
time commitment, controlling, 78
updating content, scheduling, 145
social media advertising. *See also* Facebook advertising
Chegg use of, 578–580
engagement ads, 576–577
growth in, 563
Instagram, 564
LinkedIn, 562, 573–575
maximizing advertising dollars, 563–564
overview, 561–563
Pinterest, 576
Spotify, 537
Tumblr, 539
Twitter, 222–223, 562, 568–573
Vimeo, 541–542

Social Media Analytics, Google, 596–598, 618, 646
social media buttons, 202–206
social media director, 85–86
Social Media Examiner
benefits of social media use, 663, 665–666
legal resources, 94
social media integration, 546–547
social media marketing resources, 103
social media resources, 89
Social Media for Firefox, 190
Social Media Governance, 89
social media integration
newsletters, 547–551
overview, 545
press releases, 551–557
thinking strategically about, 546–547
website, 557–560
social media marketing. *See also* mobile social marketing; *specific marketing aspects*; *specific social media platforms*; strategic social media marketing plan
addictiveness of social media, 20
alternative advertising opportunities, 19
benefits of, understanding, 13–19
brand reputation, protecting, 95–97
branding, 15–16
business processes, improving, 16–17
cons of, 19–20
dashboard, creating, 81–84
defining, 9–13
effectiveness of, 14
example of, 28–31
general discussion, 1–4
human resources needed for, 20
integrating into overall marketing effort, 20–22
legal issues, 90–95
as long-term commitment, 16
overview, 7–8, 77
policy, creating, 87–90
relationships, building, 16
resources for keeping current with, 102–103
schedule, 78–81
search engine rankings, improving, 17
selling opportunities, 17–19
by small businesses, 8, 18
strategic plan for, developing, 22–28
target market, reaching, 14–15
team, building, 85–87
Social Media Marketing Goals statement, 4, 22, 23–25, 587
Social Media Marketing Group on LinkedIn, 103
Social Media Marketing Plan
business metrics, including on, 34
entering tools on, 101
example of, 68–71
form for, 4
measurement strategy, 584
minor social marketing sites, 495
mismatch between channel and audience, 671
overview, 67
setting up, 72
Social Media Marketing Policy, 87–90
social media marketing team, 85–87
social media monitoring tools
deciding on tool to use, 119
deciding what and why to monitor, 118–119
free or inexpensive, 120–124
overview, 118, 670
social media optimization (SMO), 127, 131. *See also* search engine optimization
social media services. *See also* mid-size social media channels; minor social marketing sites; *specific services*; stratified social-networking communities
comparing metrics across, 646–652
mismatch between audience and, 671
terms of service regarding selling on, 108
top ranked, 494, 495
tracking options for sales, 42
types of, 9–13
social media site, defined, 9. *See also* social media services; *specific sites*
Social Media Today, 103
Social Mention, 122, 123
social networks, 10–12. *See also* social media; social media services; *specific networks*; stratified social-networking communities

social news services. *See also specific services*
Arcadia Ales use of, 197–200
benefiting from, 186–187
choosing service, 187–189
as distribution channel for press releases, 555
encouraging others to bookmark or rate site, 201–202
general discussion, 185–186
getting inbound links from, 155–156
KPIs for, 648
monitoring results, 189–190
monitoring tools for, 125
overview, 12, 181
preparing stories for success, 193–194
researching, 188
selecting content for, 192–193
submitting to, 192–194
timing submissions, 195–196, 200
social plug-ins, 635–636
social share buttons. *See* share buttons
social sharing services, 155–156. *See also* content-sharing services; *specific services*
social shopping services. *See also specific services*
attractive offers, making, 525–526
benefits of, 530
comparing LivingSocial and Groupon, 531–533
daily deals, 533
deciding to use, 524–525
defined, 523
depth of discount, 526
extra options, 529–530
KPIs for, 648
measuring success, 528–529
overview, 12, 507, 523–524
possible issues, 527–528, 530–531
resources, 509
scope of deal, 526–527
setting terms for campaign, 526–528
Social Users Flow page, Google Analytics, 597, 598
Social Value option, Google Analytics, 637, 654
SocialAdr, 189
SocialFlow, 106
SocialOomph, 125
SocialSearch, 175, 176
soft costs, 615
software
analytics packages, 589–594
e-commerce, 40–41
lead-monitoring and CRM, 43
for scheduling, 79, 80
Soldsie, 117
Some Rights Reserved images, 250
Somebody's Mother's, 499, 500–502
Sonico, 511
SoundCloud, 18
Sovrn, 125
spamming
on Facebook, 354, 355, 368
on Pinterest, 449, 462
on Twitter, 292, 310
special deals. *See* coupons; group coupons; promotional codes
specialty networks, 10. *See also specific networks*
specialty search engines for social media, 175, 176
spiders, 131
splash pages, 148
SplendidCRM, 43
Spoke, 505–506
sponsored days, Tumblr, 539
sponsored posts, Tumblr, 539
sponsored sessions, Spotify, 537
sponsored video posts, Tumblr, 539
sports social networks, 509
Spotify
advertising on, 562
analytics availability on, 601
general discussion, 536–537
overview, 508
Spreesy, 41, 118
Sprout Social, 122, 319
standard group, LinkedIn, 420–421, 423–424
Starbucks, 478
StartupNation, 505
StatCounter, 494–495, 590
State of Retailing Online study, 37, 39
static page, blogs, 243

Statista, 208, 222
statistical analysis. *See* analytics
status updates, search terms in, 161
sticky content, Facebook, 345, 347–348
stock images, 91
Storefront Social, 116, 118
storefront solutions, 40–41, 117–118
StoreYa, 116
stories
  Google+, 170
  Instagram, 488
  Snapchat, 463, 467, 471–473
Strategic Business Insights, 61, 62
strategic social media marketing plan. *See also* online market research
  estimating costs, 26
  example of, 28–31
  goals, establishing, 25
  goals, reviewing, 492–493
  overview, 22
  quantifiable objectives, setting, 26
  researching minor sites for, 493–496
  ROI, valuing, 27–28
  social media integration, 546–547
  Social Media Marketing Goals form, 22, 23–25
  target markets, identifying, 26
strategy, content marketing
  content inventory, 271–272
  delegating tasks, 273–274
  elements of, 270
  executing, 279
  goals, determining, 263–269
  overview, 263
  putting on paper, 270–274
stratified social-networking communities. *See also* social shopping services
  by activity type, 512–514
  business networks, 504–506
  demographic and geographic stratification, 510–512
  geomarketing tools, 515–521
  making splash on, 504
  for meeting offline, 521–523
  overview, 503
  vertical industry sites, 506–509
streaming
  live, with Periscope, 542–544
  music, on Spotify, 536–537
  video, on Facebook. *See* Facebook Live
StumbleUpon, 178, 182, 183, 202
Stylehive, 18, 509
subgroups, LinkedIn, 418
subreddits, 192
subscribers
  analyzing, 606, 607
  newsletter, 549
subscription-based sites, 560
subscriptions, in content marketing, 264, 283
Sulia, 102
summary, LinkedIn profile, 401
Sumo.me Image Sharer, 454
SVN/Walt Arnold Commercial Brokerage, Inc., 10, 11
swearing, on Twitter, 311
syndicated submission sites, 163
syndicating content, 104, 157, 514, 553
Sysomos Heartbeat, 126

T

tablets, 221–222. *See also* mobile devices; mobile social marketing
tabs, Facebook, 344, 361
tag clouds, 134–135, 137–138, 191
TagCrowd, 137, 138
tagging
  links, 649–651, 659
  on Pinterest, 451–452, 455–456
tags
  defined, 137
  Google Analytics, 596
  versus metatags, 139
  multimedia, 166
  in press release, 556
  search terms in, 160
  WordPress, 164

Tailwind, 614
Talkbiznow, 505
Talkwalker Alerts, 123
target audience. *See also* online market research
  in content-marketing strategy, 270
  Facebook advertising, 566
  identifying in strategic plan, 26
  LinkedIn showcase pages, 415
  locating online, 54
  reaching, 14–15
targeting fans, in Facebook advertising, 378–379
task delegation, in content-marketing strategy, 270, 273–274
TasteSpotting, 513
Teamwork, 274
TechCrunch, 90, 103
TechHive, 103
Techmeme, 103
Technical Stuff icon, explained, 3
technology social networks, 509
TechRepublic, 89
Tetrad Nielsen PRIZM system, 59
text links, 145
text speak, 304
TFF (Twitter follower-to-following) ratio, 626
The Karen Martin Group, 514
The Open Press, 554
The Review Stew, 93, 95
TheFunded.com, 505
ThirdAge, 510
third-party e-commerce products, 115–118
third-party Pinterest analytics, 614
third-party Twitter analytics applications, 622–623
ThisNext, 509
time commitment, controlling, 78–79
time per visit, as KPI, 655
timelines
  Facebook, 344, 345–348, 359
  layering with metrics, 664, 665
timely content
  balancing with evergreen content, 278
  planning, 276
Tiny Pitch, 554, 556
TinyURL, 107, 155
Tip icon, explained, 3
title metatags, 139, 141
titles
  in content marketing, 235
  LinkedIn profile, 396
  Pinterest board, 458
  in Pinterest pin descriptions, 457
  search terms in, 161, 166
tools. *See also specific tools*
  content-distribution, 104–106
  e-commerce, 108–118
  freemium, 97
  monitoring, 124–126
  overview, 101–102
  social media marketing resources, 102–103
  social media monitoring, 118–124
  URL-snipping services, 106–107
top-of-mind awareness. *See* branding
TopRank Online Marketing Blog, 103
trackbacks, 163
Trackur, 96, 97, 123
trademarks, 92
traffic
  assessing, 15
  content-marketing strategy goals, 264, 265–266
  dark, 649
  diagnosing problems, 669–670
  Facebook advertising ROI, 380
  in Facebook content strategy, 359
  as KPI, 646
  LinkedIn groups, driving with, 418
  matching social media services to goals, 25
  in measurement strategy, 586
  newsletters, driving with, 548
  patterns of, 646
  Pinterest, driving with, 455–458
  podcasts, driving with, 246
  press releases, driving with, 552
  referrers, discovering from analytics programs, 282

social media presence, bettering, 671
from social-bookmarking and social news services, 186–187
website statistics, 602
when guest blogging, 260
transcriptions, 167
TreeHugger, 508
trending hashtags, Twitter, 303–304
trends, promoted, on Twitter, 570
Tribe, 511
TribePro, 189
TripAdvisor, 511
trophies, Snapchat, 468
Trumba, 80
Tumblr
advertising on, 539
analytics, 540, 601, 603
overview, 538
setting up account, 538–539
tutorials, on LinkedIn company pages, 413
Tweet Stats plug-in, TwitterCounter, 622
TweetCaster, 319
TweetChat, 318, 329–330
TweetDeck, 106, 125, 319, 622
tweets. *See also* Twitter
analytics, 619, 620
daily number of, 14
defined, 14
hashtags in, 168, 304–305
ideal number of, 297
keywords, using in, 310
140-character limit, 290–291, 304
optimizing, 168
pinned, 317–318
promoted, 569, 578–579
questions and complaints, responding to, 324–325
real-time search efforts, 178
responding to, 302
retweets, 168, 290, 294, 306–307, 624
scheduled, 293
tips for, 304–305
TweetStats, 622
tweet-ups, 13, 97, 311–312, 522–523
twelpforce, Best Buy, 674
2020AVE, 110
24-7 Press Release, 554
Twitaholic, 66, 67
Twitter. *See also* tweets; Twitter chats; Twitter performance metrics
advertising on, 222–223, 562, 568–573
apps, 318–320
audience for, 14
avatar, 314, 316–317
blocking people, 307–308
campaign for, creating, 308–309
checking in on, 517
Chegg use of, 578–580
content, creating, 256
customers, gaining on, 326
deciding to use, 288–289
direct messages, 294, 306, 325, 326, 625
direct sales on, 111
enhancing experience on, 313
finding followers, 300
geomarketing on, 517–518
handle, 167
header photo, 314, 315–316
influencers, identifying, 66, 67
keywords, using on, 310
link-shortening service, 107, 619
location search function, 58
matching to goals, 25
Mentions tab, 624
mobile app, 214
monitoring tools for, 125
networking on, overview, 299
Notifications tab, 623–625
observing conversations on, 301
140-character limit, 290–291, 304
optimizing, 167–169
overview, 10, 11, 287
profile page, 313–318
promoted accounts, 569

Twitter *(continued)*
promoted trends, 570
promoting on, 291–295
quality, focusing on, 297–298
questions and complaints, responding to, 324–326
remarketing, 570
researching other brands on, 296
rules of etiquette, 310–311
sales, tracking options for, 42
search function, advanced features, 518, 550–551
search function, as monitoring tool, 124, 125, 323–324
search function, finding followers with, 300
search function, overview, 303–304
search function, real-time search with, 176
sharing on, 280, 305–310
16 Handles use of, 218
social listening, 321–326
timing posts for news sites, 196
trending hashtags, 303–304
tweet-ups, 13, 97, 311–312, 522–523
Twitter chats, promoting on, 332
Web Intents JavaScript Events, 618
Twitter Activity dashboard, Twitter Analytics, 619, 620
Twitter Analytics, 593, 619–621
Twitter Cards, 572–573, 619–620
Twitter Cards dashboard, Twitter Analytics, 619, 621
Twitter chats
benefits of, 327–328
guests for, finding, 331–332
hashtag for, finding, 328–329
hosting, 333–335
management programs, 329–330
overview, 289, 327
promoting, 311, 332–333
Twitter follower-to-following (TFF) ratio, 626
Twitter Geolocation, 517
Twitter Marketing, 103
Twitter performance metrics
direct messages, 625
Google Analytics, tracking with, 618
hashtags, 625
Mentions tab, 624
Notifications tab, 623–625
overview, 617
Retweet Rank, 624
shortened links, 618–619
TFF ratio, 626
third-party analytics applications, 622–623
TweetDeck, 622
Twitter Analytics, 619–621
TwitterCounter, 622–623
2 Create a Website, 107
Typepad, 601, 603, 604

U

UberSocial, 106
Ubersuggest, 135
unique users, as KPI, 646
unique visitors, 600
Uniteddogs, 509
Universal Analytics Upgrade Center, Google, 652
unlisted group, LinkedIn, 420–421, 423–424
updates
LinkedIn company pages, 413
in mobile social marketing, 216
in newsletters, 548
role in brand likes on Facebook, 340
search terms in, 161
in SEO, 145–146
Updates section, LinkedIn Analytics tab, 637–638
Upsight, 591
upstream analysis, 652
URLs
custom, for Facebook, 350–351
identifying offline sources, 661
search terms in, 146, 148
in SEO, 148–149

shortened, 106–107, 593–594, 618–619, 661
Twitter profile page, 314
UrlTrends, 143
US Copyright Office, 94
US Patent and Trademark Office, 94
user feedback, 118
Ustream, 513, 601

V

VALS (Values and Life Styles) survey, 62
vanity retweets, 307
variable costs, 44
verifying website, for Pinterest Analytics, 613
vertical industry sites, 506–509
video. *See also* Facebook Live
analytics, 605–606
bookmarks for, 195
as content platform, 237, 246–249
driving traffic through, 265
establishing expertise through, 268
in LinkedIn blogs, 433
on LinkedIn company pages, 411, 413
in mobile social marketing, 217
optimizing, 166–167
Periscope, live streaming with, 542–544
sharing on Facebook, 360, 363
snaps, 470
social content-sharing services, 9
viral, 246–247, 265, 363
video interviews, content marketing through, 248–249
video sharing sites, 513, 601. *See also* content-sharing services; *specific sites*
video takeover, Spotify, 537
Vimeo
advertising on, 541–542, 562
analytics, 601, 606
business accounts, 541
overview, 513, 540–541
Vine, 102, 513
viral, defined, 660
viral videos
content marketing through, 246–247
driving traffic through, 265
as shareable Facebook content, 363
visibility. *See* branding
visitor posts, Facebook, 343
visitors, in website statistics, 600
VisitorVille, 591
visits, as KPI, 646
volunteer work, in LinkedIn profile, 397
VWO, 645

W

Walt Arnold Commercial Brokerage, 10, 11
Wanelo, 509
Warning icon, explained, 3
wealthy, social networks for, 511
web analytics. *See* analytics
Web Analytics Demystified Blog, 645
Web Analytics World Blog, 645
Web Intents JavaScript Events, Twitter, 618
web metrics. *See* performance metrics
Webalizer, 590
Webby Awards, 657
WebProNews, 645
websites. *See also specific sites*
companion to book, 4
contests and games, 559–560
coupons, discounts, and freebies on, 558–559
hub sites, 21
indexing, 150–152
integrating social media with, 557–560
legal resource, 94
marketing-effective, 20
microsites, 560, 653–655
mobile, 211–212
Pinterest interaction analytics, 612–614
press releases, posting on, 553
private membership, 560
referrals from Twitter to, tracking, 618
referrers to primary, 614
social media policy resource, 89
statistics for, 600, 602

Webtrends, 591, 645
weekly email, to LinkedIn groups, 418, 427–428
WellPaw, 509
WhatIs, 35
Whole Foods Market, 439
WhosTalkin, 123–124, 190
widgets
  defined, 13
  Elegant Themes, 205
  feedback, 118
  social media dashboard, 84
  Social Mention, 122
Wikimedia Commons, 252
Wikipedia, researching minor sites on, 494
wikis, 13
Wishpond, 118
Woopra, 591
Word of Mouth Marketing Association, 94, 657
Wordle, 137
word-of-mouth advertising, 530, 660–661
word-of-web advertising, 660–661
WordPress
  analytics, 601, 603
  optimizing blogs, 164
  permalinks, 166
  setting up blogs, 241–242
WordStream, 135, 545
Wordtracker, 135, 163
writing for LinkedIn, 431–433
Wylio, 252

X

Xenu Link Sleuth, 152
XING, 505
XML (sitemap) feeds, 151–152

Y

Yahoo!
  Flurry, 642
  real-time search, 175, 176
  SEO for, 131–132
Yahoo! Calendar, 79, 80, 81
Yahoo! Groups, 653
Yahoo! Localworks, 153
Yahoo! News, 125
Yahoo! Toolbar, 183
Yammer, 505
Yelp, 511, 517, 519
Yelp for Business Owners, 533
Yext.com, 153
Yikyak.com, 102
Yipit, 533
Yoast SEO plug-in, 164
YouTube
  advertising on, 562
  analytics, 593, 601, 605, 606
  matching to goals, 25
  16 Handles use of, 219

Z

Zomato, 511
ZoomRank, 179
Zorpia, 511
Zulily, 533

About the Authors

Jan Zimmerman has found marketing to be the most creative challenge of owning a business for the more than 35 years she has spent as an entrepreneur. Since 1994, she has owned Sandia Consulting Group and Watermelon Mountain Web Marketing (`www.watermelonweb.com`) in Albuquerque, New Mexico. (*Sandia* is Spanish for *watermelon.*) Jan's web marketing clients at Watermelon Mountain are a living laboratory for experimenting with the best social media, search engine optimization, and other online marketing techniques for bottom-line success.

Her consulting practice, which keeps Jan aware of the real-world issues facing business owners and marketers, provides the basis for her pragmatic marketing advice. Ranging from hospitality and tourism to retail stores, B2B suppliers, trade associations, colleges, and service companies, her clients have unique marketing needs but share similar business concerns and online challenges.

Throughout her business career, Jan has been a prolific writer. She has written three editions of *Web Marketing For Dummies,* four editions of another book about marketing on the Internet, as well as the books *Doing Business with Government Using EDI* (Van Nostrand Reinhold) and *Mainstreaming Sustainable Architecture* (High Desert Press). She has also co-authored three previous editions of *Social Media Marketing All-in-One For Dummies* and co-authored the third edition of *Facebook Marketing All-in-One For Dummies.* Her concern about the effect of technological development on women's needs led to her book *Once Upon the Future* (Pandora Press Focus) and the anthology *The Technological Woman* (Praeger).

The writer of numerous articles and a frequent speaker on web marketing and social media, Jan has long been fascinated by the intersection of business, technology, and human communication. In her spare time, she crews for the hot air balloon named *Levity* to get her feet off the ground and her head in the clouds.

Jan can be reached at books@watermelonweb.com or 505-259-2528. Your comments, corrections, and suggestions are welcome.

Deborah Ng is a freelance writer, published author, and social media consultant specializing in online community development. She blogs about books at `www.BooksandChardonnay.com` and shares tips for people who telecommute at `www.telecommunity.net`.

When Deb's not writing or boosting Facebook posts, her favorite things are nagging her family, vacuuming dog hair tumbleweeds from her tile floor, and climbing mountains of laundry.

Just kidding! She loves none of those things!

Deb is always up for a good binge-watch, passionate about books, and her famous sangria brings all the boys to the yard.

Dedication

Jan Zimmerman: In memory of my beloved brother, Howard Zimmerman. Because you always had my back.

Deborah Ng: To my husband Bert and son Timothy — my light and my life. And coffee. Lots and lots of coffee.

Authors' Acknowledgments

Jan Zimmerman: No nonfiction writer works alone, and this book is no exception. The more books I write, the more I realize how much I depend on others. In particular, this edition couldn't have been written without the wonderful help of web marketing assistant, researcher, and copyright hound, Sandra Flowers, whose dedication to the task made this book possible, and Shawna Araiza, a highly experienced, senior web marketing associate at Watermelon Mountain Web Marketing.

Together, they conducted background research, compiled sites for the numerous tables in this book, created graphics, and rooted out arcane online facts. Between them, they checked hundreds of links and reviewed dozens and dozens of sites for screen shots. (Not many people are asked to search for a good marketing post on Facebook!) Finding exemplary companies for case studies — and clearing more than one hundred copyrights — required endless calls and emails, for which Sandra deserves all the credit.

I owe my staff a great debt for handling the research on this book at a very complicated time of my life, and working doubly-hard to try to keep the book close to schedule — not to mention their patience and computer support. I am especially grateful to Shawna for taking over much of our client workload so I had time to write.

As always, my family, friends, and cats earn extra hugs for their constant encouragement. I'm lucky to have friends who accept that I cannot be there for them as much as they are there for me. The garden, the house, the car, and the cats, alas, are not so forgiving. Special thanks to my clients, who teach me so much and give me the opportunity to practice what I preach.

I'd especially like to thank Susan Pink, project editor and copy editor for Wiley, for her flexibility, skills, and fine eye for detail — not to mention her patience, and technical editor Michelle Krasniak, for her knowledgeable assistance. Together, they made this book much better than it started out. My thanks to all the other staff at Wiley — from the art department to legal — who have provided support. If errors remain, they are indubitably mine.

My appreciation goes out also to my agent, Margot Hutchison of Waterside Productions. Margot and her extraordinary family continue to teach us, at `http://teamsam.com`, lessons about what's truly important in life.

Deborah Ng: A special thank-you to Amy Fandrei, for her continued faith in me, and to my patient editors, Susan Pink and Michelle Krasniak, for their guidance and direction.

Publisher's Acknowledgments

Acquisitions Editor: Amy Fandrei

Project and Copy Editor: Susan Pink

Technical Editor: Michelle Krasniak

Editorial Assistant: Serena Novosel

Production Editor: Siddique Shaik

Cover Image: © Bet_Noire / iStockphoto

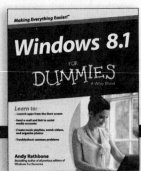